FDR Country 214
Columbus. 220
Along I-16: Statesboro to
   Swainsboro 228

▶ **Savannah** **232**
Sights 238
Entertainment and Events 277
Shopping 284
Sports and Recreation 288
Accommodations 293
Food 297
Information and Services. 305
Getting There and Around 307
Outside Savannah. 308

▶ **South Georgia** **316**
Jimmy Carter Country 320
Southwest Georgia 329
Thomasville and Vicinity 335
The Okefenokee Swamp. 342

▶ **The Golden Isles**. **349**
Brunswick and Glynn County 353
Jekyll Island. 361

St. Simons Island. 369
Darien and McIntosh County 378
Cumberland Island and St. Marys . . 386

▶ **Background**. **392**
The Land 392
Flora and Fauna. 398
History 402
Government and Economy. 412
People and Culture 414

▶ **Essentials** **416**
Getting There and Around 416
Recreation. 418
Tips for Travelers 420
Health and Safety 421
Information and Services. 423

▶ **Resources** **425**
Suggested Reading. 425
Internet Resources 426

▶ **Index**. **429**

▶ **List of Maps** **449**

Discover Georgia

Coca-Cola. *Gone with the Wind.* Martin Luther King Jr. Jimmy Carter. James Brown. Ted Turner. Jackie Robinson. The Allman Brothers. Ray Charles. Uncle Remus. Hank Aaron. R.E.M. How many states have offered as many iconic names to the world as Georgia?

The influence of Georgia goes far beyond its region. Its effect on the American experience, and indeed the world's, has been profound but also difficult to qualify. A Deep South state with one of the nation's most cosmopolitan cities, a physically immense place with a tight-knit, small-town feel, Georgia defies easy labels.

Georgia, it seems, is comfortable doing double duty as both the prototypical Southern state of Sherman-scarred legend and Scarlett O'Hara-derived myth, as well as one of America's engines of lasting change and innovation.

For example, you could make the case that the state's history of racial intolerance is more than balanced out by its role as epicenter of the American civil rights movement and birthplace of its key leader, Dr. King. One person might laugh at the derisive portrayal of North Georgia bumpkins in James Dickey's *Deliverance*, both in print and on film, but another could just as easily point to the long list of truly world-changing global initiatives spawned in Georgia, such as Habitat for Humanity, the Ted Turner Foundation, or the Centers for Disease Control.

However, Georgia's main export to the world is its culture, specifically its folk culture, born from hard knocks and a deeply felt historical perspective. There are few corners of the planet that haven't been touched by the rhythms and melodies of the Peach State's musical titans, who often came from poverty and suffered from outright discrimination. There are few university students who haven't studied the works of Georgia's great writers and poets, most of whom struggled, successfully or not, with a host of personal demons and with the often-contradictory demands of regional and national identity. The common theme of Georgia arts, music, and letters is the conflict between the urge to transcend one's surroundings and the desire to celebrate one's roots.

It's still hard to say why so many big names have come out of this place. But they've no doubt left their mark, and no matter where they might travel to, Georgia has left its mark on them... as it likely will on you.

Planning Your Trip

▶ WHERE TO GO

Atlanta

There's always something to do in one of America's most dynamic and progressive cities, a burgeoning multi-ethnic melting pot that also has a friendly flavor of the old South just beneath the surface. For every snarled intersection, a delightfully bucolic neighborhood tantalizes with cafés, shops, and green space. Adventurous restaurants and quirky nightlife venues are particular specialties here.

North Georgia

The Blue Ridge Mountains are the backdrop for this inspiring, scenic area full of waterfalls, state parks, and outdoor adventures for the whole family. While not the best place to visit in winter, North Georgia in spring and summer provides a welcome respite from the state's scorching temperatures. Its accessibility to Atlanta is a convenient advantage.

Piedmont

Green, rolling countryside and classic antebellum architecture are the calling cards here, where old meets new on a daily basis in what was once a center of Georgia's old Confederate power structure. The University of Georgia's influence around Athens and the culture of the Savannah River valley in the Augusta area reign supreme.

Middle Georgia

From Macon to Columbus, the rhythmic heart of Georgia is the soulful cradle of the state's incredibly rich musical tradition... and where its best barbecue is located! Its therapeutic value isn't only found in the legendary Warm Springs that gave solace to FDR. Middle Georgia is a place to take stock mentally and spiritually as well, by getting in touch with some of the South's most cherished roots.

Savannah

Georgia's grand old city isn't just full of history, though that's certainly very much

The live oak is an iconic image of the region.

TENNESSEE
NORTH CAROLINA
North Georgia
SOUTH CAROLINA
Piedmont
Atlanta
A L A B A M A
Middle Georgia
Savannah
South Georgia
Golden Isles
FLORIDA
0 50 mi
0 50 km
© AVALON TRAVEL

destination, with as many or more things to do on any given day than cities two or three times its size. Come prepared for high tea or a rowdy party; either way Savannah's got you covered.

South Georgia

The state's agricultural cornucopia and home of former President Jimmy Carter offers quite a few surprises among the peanuts and pecans, including the mighty, mysterious Okefenokee Swamp. The state's most sparsely populated area is also its largest, so be prepared to do some driving. You'll be sure to come across some pleasant, unexpected discoveries.

The Golden Isles

History and salt-kissed air meet in the marshes of Georgia's chains of relatively undeveloped barrier islands. The feeling is timeless and tranquil. The Golden Isles comprise one of America's hidden vacation gems, and one of the most unique ecosystems in North America.

worth exploring. It has found new life as an arts and culture mecca and world-class

▶ WHEN TO GO

First things first: Georgia gets very hot in the summer. For most parts of the state, August is the month you don't want to be here. An exception, however, would be North Georgia, where the mountain air keeps things a bit cooler.

Conversely, winters are mild throughout the state except in North Georgia, where many attractions, trails, and even some roads are closed due to ice and snow. Always check ahead.

Autumn leaf-watching season in North Georgia is extremely popular. While there are plenty of great state parks, they fill up well in advance. Because of the general dearth of lodging in the area, you should try to book well in advance for a fall trip to the mountains.

The hurricane threat on the coast is highest in August and September. Obviously there's no way to plan your trip in advance to avoid a hurricane, but that would be the time when trips, especially by plane, are most likely to be disrupted.

Savannah hotel rooms are difficult to get in the spring and fall, but especially difficult around St. Patrick's Day in the middle of March.

The Masters golf tournament in Augusta in April fills hotels, vacation rentals, and bed-and-breakfasts for many miles around throughout northeast Georgia and well into South Carolina.

Athens is much slower in the summer since most classes are not in session at the University of Georgia. However, during home football weekends in the fall, hotel rooms may be booked many months in advance.

great egret perched on a limb in Savannah

creekside trail

▶ BEFORE YOU GO

Georgia is a very laidback state. Aside from some areas of Atlanta, such as Buckhead, dress is generally casual or casual-to-hip. Dress is more conservative in rural areas both north and south, but because of the often hot and sticky weather, even in those areas there's a lot of leeway.

Atlanta's public transit system, MARTA, is extensive and very reasonably priced. For anywhere outside of Atlanta a car is absolutely necessary.

Most people flying into Georgia do so through Hartsfield-Jackson International Airport in Atlanta, the busiest airport in the world. When there is a delay there, there's a delay pretty much everywhere. If you end up missing a flight, there are dozens of hotels in the vicinity with shuttle service to and from the airport.

a horse-drawn carriage at Old City Market in downtown Savannah

Explore Georgia

▶ BEST OF GEORGIA

The Peach State is physically immense, the largest east of the Mississippi River, so understandably it will take more than a few days to cover the highlights. A vehicle is required for this grand tour of Georgia, beginning in Atlanta and ending in Savannah on the coast.

Day 1

Your first day in Atlanta brings you up to Buckhead to visit the Atlanta History Center, with a tour of the ornate and unique Swan House. Do some shopping at Lenox Square and Phipps Plaza. For the afternoon head Downtown to the Martin Luther King Jr. National Historic Site and pay your respects to this great Georgian. Tonight if the Braves are in town go see a game at Turner Field.

Day 2

This morning head to Centennial Olympic Park and enjoy the Georgia Aquarium or perhaps some cheesy fun at the World of Coca-Cola. Head back to Midtown for lunch at Empire State South before visiting the High Museum of Art for the afternoon. After dinner and cocktails at Einstein's, take in a show at the historic Fox Theatre.

Day 3

Drive the short distance north of Atlanta to Amicalola Falls State Park and stay at the lodge there. Spend the early afternoon hiking in the area, especially around Springer Mountain, southern terminus of the Appalachian Trail (you'll have to come back to hike that when you have a few months!). If that's too strenuous, shoot over on Highway 52 to Dahlonega and learn about America's first gold rush at the Dahlonega Gold Museum on the square. Either way, tonight

the Swan House in Buckhead, Atlanta

Georgia Aquarium in Atlanta

have brats and brews in the nearby Alpine village of Helen.

Day 4

Today head east and enjoy the view from the top of Black Rock Mountain State Park before stopping for a bite in charming Clayton. Spend the afternoon at nearby Tallulah Gorge State Park. Later head back to the lodge at Amicalola Falls.

Day 5

Take I-85 South through Atlanta to Highway 27 and down to little Warm Springs to visit President Roosevelt's Little White House and the nearby therapeutic pools where he swam. After lunch in cute Pine Mountain, head down to the wild folk-art compound of Pasaquan in Buena Vista before hitting Americus for the night, staying at the historic high-Victorian Windsor Hotel.

Day 6

Today you visit nearby Plains, birthplace and still home to President Jimmy Carter. Visit his old high school, now a museum, and his boyhood farm. From there continue west on Highway 27 to Providence Canyon, a stunning and unique state natural area, before heading back to the Windsor Hotel.

Day 7

This morning head 12 miles northeast of Americus to Andersonville and the National Prisoner of War Museum, a stirring and affecting site encompassing Civil War history and beyond. From here you take back roads to I-75 again, this time north to Macon, hitting the ancient Indian mounds at Ocmulgee National Monument before getting to the best B&B in town, the 1842 Inn. (If you want to rough it, stay a bit north of town at historic Indian Springs State Park, the first state park in the nation.)

Day 8

Enjoy your luxurious breakfast at 1842 Inn before touring the incredible Hay House

historic Windsor Hotel in Americus

nearby, one of the South's great house museums. For a change of pace after lunch, stop at the new Allman Brothers Band Museum at the Big House. At night, take the Lights on Macon free walking tour of the historic Intown neighborhood near the 1842 Inn.

Day 9

This morning head east on I-16 to Savannah, where you'll spend the day walking the moss-draped squares and perhaps touring the Owens-Thomas House before checking into a boutique hotel like The Bohemian Hotel or a classic B&B like the Eliza Thompson House. Tonight, dine in style at Elizabeth on 37th and end with a nightcap at Rocks on the Roof at the Bohemian Hotel while watching the ships go up and down the river. Or, take one of the many ghost tours in town, if that's your thing.

Day 10

Get up early for the drive down to the Jekyll Island Historic District and the beachcombing on the nearby strand. After a late lunch

at the Jekyll Island Club, drive a short ways down to St. Simons Island and spend the afternoon at historic Fort Frederica National Monument before dinner in the old Village and the drive back to Savannah.

Day 11

Have a morning stroll in green Forsyth Park in Savannah's Victorian district and lunch at world-famous Mrs. Wilkes' Dining Room (get in line early!) before heading back to downtown proper and the Telfair Museums on Telfair Square. Save time to visit the nearby Ellis Square and City Market area and do some shopping on bustling Broughton Street.

Day 12

This morning drive east to beautiful Bonaventure Cemetery on your way out to Fort Pulaski National Monument and the Tybee Lighthouse on Tybee Island for a day of beach-oriented fun. On the way back to downtown Savannah, grab fresh shrimp and oysters at Desposito's.

► # MOUNTAINS AND MARSH: HIKE, CLIMB, OR KAYAK

For campers and green-minded adventurers, this hiking, rafting, and kayaking trip covers the most authentically unspoiled and scenic recreational offerings of the Peach State.

Cloudland Canyon State Park at the northwest tip of Georgia. Then head out for a day of canyon floor hiking and a guided cave tour. Consider joining the Canyon Climbers Club.

Day 1

Begin by setting up camp at amazing

Day 2

This morning drive east to set up camp for

CIVIL WAR SITES

Georgia wasn't the huge battleground that Virginia was in the Civil War. But it has more than its share of key sites.

ATLANTA

- **Atlanta Cyclorama:** This unique attraction combines art with action to portray the siege of Atlanta.

- **Atlanta History Center:** This Buckhead site has an outstanding permanent Civil War exhibit.

- **Gainesville:** The home and final resting place of Robert E. Lee's second-in-command, James Longstreet, contains monuments to his life and times.

- **Kennesaw Mountain National Battlefield Park:** The opening stages of the Battle of Atlanta are documented outside of Marietta.

- **Stone Mountain:** The world's largest relief sculpture portrays Robert E. Lee, Jefferson Davis, and Stonewall Jackson.

NORTH GEORGIA

- **Chickamauga & Chattanooga National Military Park:** The last major Confederate victory is marked in this sprawling site and museum.

- **Tunnel Hill:** This entertaining site played a role in the "Great Locomotive Chase" intrigue.

PIEDMONT

- **Athens:** Its double-barrelled cannon

was never used in combat but is now an entertaining photo opportunity.

- **Augusta:** A huge chimney marks the site of the old Confederate Powderworks, the largest gunpowder facility in the South.

- **Crawfordville:** A.H. Stephens Historic Park marks the home of Confederate Vice President Alexander H. Stephens.

- **Madison:** General William T. Sherman didn't burn this charming little town in part because of his friendship with a local Unionist senator.

- **Washington:** The nostalgic home of Confederate Secretary of State Robert Toombs is located in the first city named after George Washington.

MIDDLE GEORGIA

- **Columbus:** At the National Civil War Naval Museum, find out everything you ever wanted to know about the Confederate Navy.

- **Magnolia Springs State Park:** This is the site of Camp Lawton, a POW camp even bigger than Andersonville.

- **Milledgeville:** Union troops ransacked Georgia's statehouse, but it stands today as the Old Capitol Museum.

SAVANNAH

- **Fort McAllister:** The surrender of this earthwork installation removed a three-night stay at Vogel State Park, one of the first two state parks in Georgia. You'll hike just south of here today throughout the Raven Cliffs Wilderness Area and will cross portions of the great Appalachian Trail. Don't miss the falls!

Day 3

Drive up to Brasstown Bald to hike up to the tallest point in the state. If it's a clear day you can see the Atlanta skyline from the summit. This evening treat yourself to a fun, touristy night out in the recreated Alpine village of Helen before heading back to Vogel State Park.

Day 4

Get up early for a long day of whitewater rafting on the Chattooga River where Georgia meets the Carolinas and where the movie *Deliverance* was filmed. Tonight head into downtown Clayton for the flatbread

the last barrier to General William T. Sherman's entry into Savannah.

· **Fort Pulaski:** It was considered impregnable but fell to the first use of rifled cannon. Well-preserved and interpreted, the grounds are beautiful.

· **Green-Meldrim House:** Sherman's headquarters after his March to the Sea is now a grand church rectory open to public tours.

SOUTH GEORGIA

· **Andersonville:** Explore the notorious POW camp and visit the adjacent National Prisoner of War Museum.

· **Fitzgerald:** A former Union soldier founded this picturesque town after the war.

· **Irwinville:** The Jefferson Davis Memorial Historical Site marks the location where the Confederate president was arrested.

Chickamauga battlefield

Tallulah Gorge walking bridge

camping in North Georgia

pizza and craft beer at Zeppelin's before heading back to Vogel State Park.

Day 5

Break camp and head to Tallulah Gorge State Park, another Canyon Climbers Club location, where you'll get your free permit to hike across the bottom of the gorge floor. Tonight, head south to the college town of Athens, splurge on a hotel room, and enjoy some nightlife and live music.

Day 6

Today is a long drive to the coast. Break it up in an interesting fashion with a stop near Swainsboro at the unique Ohoopee Dunes Natural Area, a remnant of the ancient seafloor. Tonight you camp at the Hostel in the Forest near Brunswick to prepare for your paddle down the Altamaha River tomorrow.

Day 7

Today you meet with the folks at Altamaha Coastal Tours for your pre-arranged custom guided kayak trip through the amazing Altamaha River, including old-growth cypress stands and maybe even a picnic on a sandbar.

Day 8

Break camp and head to the great Okefenokee Swamp for a day of canoeing. You'll set up at Stephen Foster State Park at the west entrance, where you'll rent a canoe for your blackwater fun. Tonight, head into the nearby "big city" of Waycross for a great sit-down dinner at Pond View Fine Dining.

Days 9-10

Early this morning take the ferry to Cumberland Island National Seashore for an overnight camping stay. Spend today and part of tomorrow morning hiking through the maritime forest, beachcombing, checking out the Dungeness ruins, and looking for those famous wild horses before the ferry takes you back to shore.

▶ GEORGIA'S MUSICAL LEGACY

Get some insight into the backgrounds and experiences of the people who made Georgia a musical powerhouse.

Atlanta

Eat at the Flying Biscuit Cafe, first opened by Emily Saliers of the Indigo Girls. Then it's over to Little Five Points and a rockabilly show at The Star Community Bar. Don't forget to pay your respects to the King at their shrine to Elvis! Hip-hop fans might prefer Compound in Downtown. Will you see Young Jeezy or Big Boi? Head over to Decatur for the legendary Monday open mic night at Eddie's Attic in Decatur, breeding ground of acts like John Mayer, the Indigo Girls, and yes, Justin Bieber.

Athens

Take the local music walking tour downtown, with side trips to the rail trestle on the R.E.M. album "Murmur" and the remains of the church where they first rehearsed. Browse the vinyl at legendary Wuxtry Records. Have a sublime vegetarian lunch at The Grit, on a block restored in part by singer Michael Stipe. Carnivores can have a burger at The Grill, downstairs from the original location of the legendary 40 Watt Club. Do a downtown bar crawl and take in a late show at the current location of the 40 Watt Club or the historic, restored Georgia Theatre around the corner.

Augusta

Visit the Augusta Museum of History and its great exhibit on native son James Brown, the "Godfather of Soul." Get your picture taken with the James Brown statue on Broad Street. Enjoy a show at The Soul Bar on Broad Street, a longtime musician's hangout across the street from the Imperial Theatre where Brown often rehearsed his bands.

Macon

Tour the Allman Brothers Band Museum at the Big House, the band's former home and practice space. For lunch go for meat 'n' three at H&H Restaurant, where the band often dined. Pay your respects at the gravesites of Duane Allman and Berry Oakley at picturesque Rose Hill Cemetery, where you can also see the memorial to "Little Martha." Honor two of Macon's favorite native sons at the Otis Redding Statue at Gateway Park on the Ocmulgee River, and Little Richard's boyhood home in the Pleasant Hill Historic District.

Allman Brothers Band Museum at the Big House

RED CLAY WRITERS

Uncle Remus Museum, Eatonton

Erskine Caldwell: Visit the Augusta Museum of History to learn more about the region chronicled in the novel *Tobacco Road*.

James Dickey: Raft the Chattooga River, where the film adaptation of his novel *Deliverance* was filmed.

Joel Chandler Harris: Visit the Uncle Remus author's home in Atlanta: the Wrens Nest. See his birthplace at the Uncle Remus Museum in Eatonton.

Carson McCullers: Visit the Carson McCullers Center for Writers and Musicians, her childhood home administered by Columbus State University.

Margaret Mitchell: In Atlanta, go to the Margaret Mitchell House and Museum to see where *Gone with the Wind* was written. The typewriter she used is at the Atlanta-Fulton Public Library.

Flannery O'Connor: See where she grew up at the Flannery O'Connor Childhood Home in Savannah. Visit Andalusia in Milledgeville, where she wrote most of her novels, and the nearby Flannery O'Connor Room at Georgia College and State University.

Eugenia Price: Visit her church, Christ Church, on St. Simons Island.

Alice Walker: Take the Alice Walker Driving Trail in her hometown of Eatonton.

Georgia has an extremely rich and varied literary history, with stories of sin, redemption, human resilience, and folly as distinctive and gritty as the red Georgia soil itself. No matter how famous they got, most Georgia writers rarely strayed far from their roots. Here are some major sights associated with Georgia's writers.

▶ WHAT'S COOKIN'?

Georgia is a big state with a big appetite. Here are some of the Southern culinary highlights to liven up your trip with the best it has to offer, from fried okra to fried catfish.

Atlanta

Midtown Atlanta's favorite old-school Mary Mac's Tea Room brings Southern class to the traditional meat 'n' three. Don't forget the "pot likker" to dip your cornbread in (page 72)!

Bacchanalia, Atlanta's premiere fine dining spot features a five-course prix fixe that rivals that of any other restaurant in the country, courtesy of the farm-to-table vision of owners Anne Quatrano and Clifford Harrison (page 77).

North Georgia

It's easy to remember where to find the nearly century-old, family-style Dillard House; it's in the town of Dillard in far North Georgia. Great for breakfast and brunch or dinner, they serve up all the old-time Southern favorites (page 98).

Piedmont

Thank the building's owner, R.E.M.'s Michael Stipe, in part for the existence of Athens's go-to spot, The Grit, for unbelievably delicious, all-vegetarian cuisine in a friendly hipster/hippie atmosphere. It's an easy walk from the main downtown area (page 153).

Blue Willow Inn, the main claim to fame of tiny Social Circle serves classic Southern comfort food, buffet-style, in a historic building (page 163).

Middle Georgia

Considered by many to be Georgia's best barbecue joint, Fresh Air Barbecue is also one of its oldest, with roots going back to pre-Depression days. The original location is in Jackson, Ga., and they feature a tangy sauce unlike most Peach State 'cue spots (page 204).

Savannah

Savannahians in the know will tell you that it's Mrs. Wilkes's, not the Lady & Sons, that delivers by far the best down-home cookin' in Georgia's first city. Mrs. Wilkes' Dining Room serves family-style dining and mouth-watering fried chicken are the draws (page 300).

For the absolute freshest local seafood, hit Desposito's, a humble cinder-block spot underneath a bridge in the fishing village of Thunderbolt, adjacent to Savannah (page 303).

The Golden Isles

The Shellman Bluff area near Darien, Ga., features several totally authentic fresh-catch waterfront seafood spots, but Speed's Kitchen is generally considered the best (page 382).

Set within an Italian Villa-style cottage on the grounds of the historic, swank Jekyll Island Club, Courtyard at Crane features Mediterranean-meets-the South takes on crab cakes, lobster, and shrimp (page 368).

The Grit, an Athens favorite for decades

AFRICAN AMERICAN HISTORY

First African Baptist Church

Georgia has played a critical role not only in the American civil rights movement but also in the history of African Americans since before the nation's inception.

ALBANY

- **Albany Civil Rights Institute:** Explores the Albany Movement of the early 1960s, a critical early phase of civil rights and of Martin Luther King Jr.'s legacy.

ATLANTA

- **Atlanta University Center:** This influential collection of historically black colleges and universities–Spelman College, Morehouse College, and Clark Atlanta University–occupies a contiguous space near Downtown.

- **Martin Luther King Jr. National Historic Site:** The centerpiece of study of the civil rights movement's greatest hero, this site comprises his birth home, the King Center for Nonviolent Social Change, the tomb of Dr. King and his wife Coretta Scott King, the central Visitors Center, and Historic Ebenezer Baptist Church.

- **Sweet Auburn:** The MLK Jr. National Historic Site is within this district, marking the most influential traditionally black neighborhood in Atlanta.

AUGUSTA

- **Augusta Museum of History:** The city museum has a permanent exhibit honoring native son James Brown, the "Godfather of Soul."

- **Lucy Craft Laney Museum of**

Black History: The museum is set in a historically black neighborhood and is devoted to chronicling the black experience in Augusta.

MACON

- **Douglass Theatre:** This was a key stop on the old "Chitlin' Circuit" and is still in operation as a showcase of black culture.

- **Tubman African American Museum:** This museum is particularly focused on black arts and culture.

PLAINS

- **Jimmy Carter National Historic Site:** The president's early political career was largely based on fighting for social justice and equal rights. The museum at Plains High School, the 1976 campaign headquarters at the train depot, and his boyhood farm all examine aspects of this important facet of Carter's life and times.

SAPELO ISLAND

- This Sea Island retains ancestral African American communities with direct links to General Sherman's "40 Acres and a Mule" order.

SAVANNAH

- **First African Baptist Church:** The oldest black congregation in America worships in a historic building in downtown Savannah built by enslaved people.

- **Pin Point Heritage Museum:** This museum chronicles the oystering community where Supreme Court Justice Clarence Thomas grew up.

- **Ralph Mark Gilbert Civil Rights Museum:** Formerly a black-owned bank, this museum interprets Savannah's key role in civil rights in Georgia.

THOMASVILLE

- **Jack Hadley Black History Museum:** This museum chronicles the legacy of African Americans in Thomasville, including the first black West Point graduate, Lt. Henry O. Flipper, whose grave is also downtown.

ATLANTA

Atlanta defies easy description even for those who live here. It's a sprawling metropolis made up of friendly, bucolic neighborhoods. It's a concrete jungle sprinkled with lush green space. It's a center of dyed-in-the-wool Southern arts and culture filled to the brim with transplants from elsewhere. It's in the middle of the Bible Belt but is legendary, even notorious, for its nightlife.

All these things are true in their own ways, and there's no use trying to sort them out. Indeed, the only constant in Atlanta life is change.

To the rest of Georgia, Atlanta is often an object of derision, both for its role as state capital as well as for its traffic and rampant growth. Atlanta is far and away the most commercially important city in the Southeast. Love it or hate it, everyone knows the city is a vast and vigorous economic engine that has almost single-handedly catapulted Georgia into the top nine most populous states.

Befitting a city that literally rose from the ashes of the Civil War, you can be anything you want here without worrying too much about who or what came before. Unlike some of the more rigidly stratified cities in the South, with historic social and economic divides, "the city too busy to hate" just wants to know what you're doing right now. This isn't always good—as Atlantans themselves will frankly admit, they've done a horrible job preserving their history—but sometimes it can be almost as refreshing as an ice-cold Coke-Cola on a summer day.

ATLANTA

HIGHLIGHTS

of this major tourist attraction (page 28).

(**Martin Luther King Jr. National Historic Site:** This stirring and expansive tribute to the civil rights leader contains many historically significant buildings such as his birth home (page 30).

(**Zoo Atlanta:** A world-class gorilla habitat and two charming pandas are among the highlights (page 33).

(**High Museum of Art:** The multi-story modern building contains a plethora of American arts and crafts, from folk art to high art, with some Old Masters mixed in as well (page 36).

(**Fox Theatre:** This wildly ornate, Moorish-themed historic venue remains in constant use. It's Midtown's most cherished locale (page 39).

(**Michael C. Carlos Museum:** This small but significant museum hosts intriguing Egyptian and Greek artifacts in an intimate setting (page 41).

(**Atlanta History Center and Swan House:** View the excellent Civil War exhibit and tour the magnificent, one-of-a-kind Swan House (page 42).

(**Decatur:** This small city adjacent to Atlanta has one of the nation's most happening foodie and café scenes, all within a couple of blocks (page 81).

LOOK FOR (TO FIND RECOMMENDED SIGHTS, ACTIVITIES, DINING, AND LODGING.

(**Georgia Aquarium:** The largest single aquarium tank in the world is the centerpiece

HISTORY

The words "Atlanta" and "history" rarely seem to occupy the same sentence, but the truth is that Atlanta's history is more interesting than it's generally given credit. While Georgia's first city, Savannah, was founded over a century before Atlanta, in typical spirit once Atlanta got going, it moved fast.

It's a city built quite literally by the railroads. In 1837, after the cruel mass removal of Creek and Cherokee tribes and the subsequent influx of white settlers, the Western &

Atlantic Railroad chose a spot just east of the Chattahoochee River as the southern end of a track into Tennessee. The little town that emerged around the zero milepost was simply called Terminus. Soon two other tracks met up with the Western & Atlantic, and it became clear that Terminus wouldn't remain the end of the line for much longer and possibly that a more attractive name would be needed. In 1843 its name was changed to Marthasville, in honor of the daughter of former Governor Wilson Lumpkin, a major railroad booster.

A scant two years later the name was

changed again to its modern version. There are conflicting stories about the origin: One theory says Atlanta is a feminine version of "Atlantic" and a nod to its first railroad line. Another much more romantic version says it was renamed in honor of Martha Lumpkin's middle name, Atalanta, itself an homage to a Greek goddess.

Despite its modern association with the Confederacy, largely due to *Gone with the Wind,* Atlanta and in particular its growing business community was far less enamored of the idea of secession than most of the deep South. In the pivotal 1860 presidential election, a majority of Atlanta's votes went to Unionist candidates Stephen A. Douglas and John Bell. The Civil War initially provided an enormous economic boost to Atlanta, which rapidly became one of the Confederacy's largest industrial centers. The population exploded from about 9,000 to over 20,000 by the time General William Sherman's army approached the city's outskirts in the summer of 1864.

After a lengthy bombardment and Sherman's outmaneuvering of Confederate General Albert Hood, Atlanta fell to Union troops on September 2. The 4,000 remaining citizens who hadn't already fled the siege were ordered to evacuate, and thus the stage was set for the beginning of the notoriety of General Sherman. On November 15, a massive fire swept the city: It originated in the planned destruction of industrial and manufacturing areas, but through the carelessness of Union troops quickly spread to residential areas. Most of the city was burned to the ground and all its rail lines were destroyed. The fall of Atlanta mortally crippled the Confederate war effort, secured the reelection of Abraham Lincoln (which had been very much in doubt), and kicked off Sherman's "March to the Sea," which would conclude in Savannah that Christmas.

But the railroad again came to Atlanta's rescue. Only a few months after war's end, all five of its main lines were up and running, kept busy transporting material and people to rebuild the city. The new spirit of rebirth was so contagious, in fact, that in 1868, while you could still smell the ashes of the wartime conflagration, Georgia politicos decided to move the state capital from Milledgeville—so symbolic of the old South—to Atlanta, its new commercial powerhouse.

Influential local newspaper editor Henry W. Grady popularized both the phrase "New South" as well as the attitude behind it. By 1900, about 150 trains a day called on Atlanta, and the population had swollen to nearly 100,000, 40 percent of them African Americans drawn here by the promise of a new start. Though segregation was very much in effect, Atlanta quickly became not only the birthplace of a large black middle class, but the home of four institutions of higher learning for African Americans: Morris Brown College, Clark College, Morehouse College, and Spelman College, all of which joined existing white institutions such as Georgia Tech, Oglethorpe University, Agnes Scott College, and Emory University.

However, there were severe growing pains. A race riot in 1906 claimed 12 lives. In 1913 came the notorious Leo Frank case, in which a Jewish businessman wrongfully convicted of the murder of a non-Jewish woman named Mary Phagan was subsequently pulled from his jail cell in Milledgeville and lynched. In 1915 the resurgent Ku Klux Klan made its national headquarters at Stone Mountain.

In the 1920s, progressive, business-minded community leaders such as Mayor Ivan Allen Sr. helped bring the community back together and diversify the local economy, with General Motors and Sears-Roebuck bringing a major presence to town. Simultaneously, Auburn Avenue became the city's center of African American culture and commerce, with "Daddy King," Martin Luther King Sr., in the pulpit at Ebenezer Baptist Church. The "roar" in the Roaring Twenties in Atlanta came from its burgeoning airfield, soon to be named for its chief advocate, city councilman and mayor William Hartsfield.

Also in the 1920s, a humble, local newspaper reporter named Margaret Mitchell, sidelined by an ankle injury, wrote *Gone with the*

ATLANTA

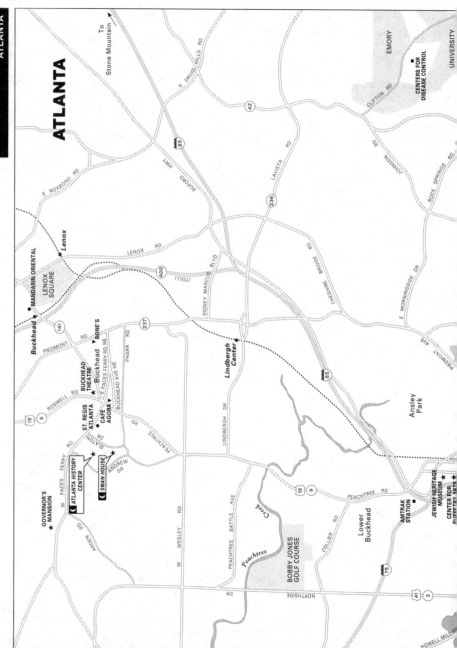

ATLANTA

To Stone Mountain

EMORY

CENTERS FOR
DISEASE CONTROL

UNIVERSITY

CLIFTON RD

N DRUID HILLS RD

42

JOHNSON RD

LAVISTA RD

BUFORD HWY

E ROXBORO RD

85

236

ROCK SPRINGS RD

Lenox

LENOX RD

400
(TOLL)

CHESHIRE BRIDGE RD

E MORNINGSIDE DR

MANDARIN ORIENTAL

LENOX
SQUARE

Buckhead

SIDNEY MARCUS BLVD

PIEDMONT AVE

141

PIEDMONT RD

BONE'S

237

PHARR RD

Lindbergh
Center

85

Ansley
Park

BUCKHEAD
THEATRE

Buckhead

E PACES FERRY RD NE

BUCKHEAD AVE NE

ROSWELL RD

9
19

ST. REGIS
ATLANTA

CAFE
AGORA

PHARR RD

PEACHTREE RD

LINDBERGH DR

SLATON DR

ATLANTA HISTORY
CENTER

SWAN HOUSE

ANDREW
DR

9
19

PEACHTREE RD

JEWISH HERITAGE
MUSEUM

AMTRAK
STATION

CENTER FOR
PUPPETRY ARTS

GOVERNOR'S
MANSION

W PACES FERRY RD

ARDEN RD

W WESLEY RD

PEACHTREE BATTLE AVE

COLLIER RD

Lower
Buckhead

Peachtree Creek

BOBBY JONES
GOLF COURSE

75

NORTHSIDE DR

41
3

HOWELL MILL RD

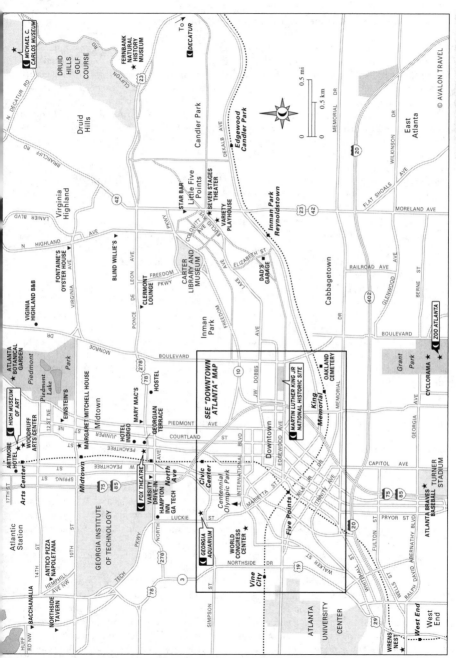

© AVALON TRAVEL

Wind, another of Atlanta's great exports. The premiere of the film came in 1939 with a star-studded gala; in a precursor to Atlanta's reputation as a racially enlightened Southern city, co-star Hattie McDaniel became the first-ever African American Oscar winner.

As with many cities in the South, World War II brought an enormous economic boost as well as social change when women and African Americans entered the workforce in large numbers for the first time. The largest local operation was the Bell bomber plant, which by war's end employed about 30,000. The post-war era in Atlanta was a perfect microcosm of larger national urban trends: a rapidly-growing middle class, an increasing in corporate presence, and white flight to the suburbs.

The 1960s, in particular, gave proof of Atlanta's new nickname, "the city too busy to hate," actually coined by Hartsfield as mayor. His successor, Ivan Allen Jr., himself the son of an Atlanta mayor, formed a close partnership with local black civil rights leaders, chief among them Martin Luther King Jr., in order to promote fair housing and equal opportunity in the workplace as well as send a signal to the private sector at large that Atlanta was a great place to do business. By the end of the decade all three of Atlanta's major sports teams—the Braves, the Falcons, and the Hawks—would be in place. In 1969, with the election of the city's first African American mayor, Maynard Jackson, Atlanta proper had become a majority-black city. Three years later, Atlantan Andrew Young was elected Georgia's first black congressman since Reconstruction.

The 1970s signaled Atlanta's arrival as a top-tier convention and business hub. In 1971 the airport was renamed Hartsfield Atlanta International Airport and within a decade was the world's busiest (Maynard Jackson's name was added in 2003). By the middle of the decade Atlanta was America's third-busiest convention center. Those trends continued through the go-go 1980s and well into the 1990s.

In something of an unanticipated development Atlanta was awarded the 1996 Summer Olympics (it was the centennial of the games and Athens, Greece, was considered the frontrunner). Though unfortunately remembered by most for the terrorist bombing that took place, it was actually a successful staging overall and resulted in several important infrastructure improvements, chiefly Turner Field, athlete dorms which became housing for Georgia Tech and Georgia State University, and of course Centennial Olympic Park, site of the bombing and currently the hub of several major tourist attractions.

PLANNING YOUR TIME

Atlanta is fun for a day or for several days, and there's always something to do any day of the week. Shoppers, be sure to carve out time to enjoy the city's many shopping opportunities, whether they be in the Lenox and Phipps malls in Buckhead or the little shops in Virginia-Highland and Decatur.

If you're driving a car, at some point you will be faced with Atlanta's heavy traffic. Weekday morning and afternoon rush hours are ridiculous; try to make plans to be as near your destination as possible before getting caught up in them. That said, for the most part traveling around Atlanta is a pleasure and not unusually time-consuming.

Afternoons in July and August are uncomfortably hot, so plan accordingly, especially if visiting an outdoor site like Stone Mountain. Zoo Atlanta is well worth a visit but if the weather's hot, go right when it opens before the animals seek refuge from the heat.

NEIGHBORHOODS

Despite its ever-growing size, Atlanta remains a city of neighborhoods, and neighborhoods within neighborhoods, each with a separate character and feel. The specific geography is an inexact and debatable science, but here's an overview:

Downtown: This is the beating commercial and political heart of Atlanta as well as its most socioeconomically challenged area. It includes the state capitol, Turner Field, Centennial Olympic Park, and the Martin Luther King Jr. National Historic Site as well as skyscraping office buildings and hotels galore. Neighborhoods within Downtown include **Sweet Auburn, Fairlie-Poplar,** up-and-coming **Old Fourth Ward,** and **So-No** (South of North Avenue).

Five Points: Not to be confused with Little Five Points, this downtown area adjacent to Underground Atlanta is literally the city center. During the first days of settlement, the intersection of Peachtree, Decatur, and Marietta Streets with Edgewood Avenue was chosen as the central point around which all development would radiate, and indeed that white marker still exists to this day, Atlanta's oldest single historic artifact.

Grant Park: This verdant Victorian area southeast of Downtown hosts Zoo Atlanta, the Cyclorama, and Oakland Cemetery. Up-and-coming **Cabbagetown** is adjacent.

Midtown: Where Atlanta's cultural community is best represented, the area between Downtown and Buckhead includes the Georgia Tech campus as well as the last vestiges of Atlanta's Victorian heyday, like the Margaret Mitchell House and the Fox Theatre.

Piedmont Park: East of Midtown is Piedmont Park, not only a friendly and recently expanded green space but a thriving neighborhood and café scene. It was previously known mostly as the center of Atlanta's gay community but is now increasingly all things to all people.

Inman Park: This rejuvenated, gentrified Queen Anne garden suburb was Atlanta's first planned neighborhood, Buckhead before there was a Buckhead.

Little Five Points: The gateway to East Atlanta at the intersection of Moreland and Euclid Streets is also the center of Atlanta bohemian culture, thrift shopping, and raucous nightlife.

Atlantic Station: This planned development opened in 2005 and lies west of Midtown on the other side of I-75/85. Named for the historic Atlantic Steel mill, which was once the

key feature here, it has an assortment of LEED-certified restaurants and upper-end shops, all in a New Urbanist atmosphere.

Westside: This increasingly trendy light industrial area just west of Downtown offers little in the way of tourist attractions, but some of the best up-and-coming restaurants in the city are here.

West End: Not to be confused with the Westside, the West End is Atlanta's oldest historic district and has a wonderful collection of mostly Victorian architecture, best represented by the Wren's Nest, home of Joel Chandler Harris.

Buckhead: The traditional home of Atlanta's "old money" was not long ago also the center of Atlanta nightlife. Things have changed, and it's returning to its roots as a shopping and residential center. Buckhead occupies the entire northern fifth of Atlanta and its burgeoning population would technically make it Georgia's third-largest city.

Virginia-Highland: Atlanta's first streetcar suburb boasts charming Craftsman bungalows and remains one of its liveliest and most livable neighborhoods, with a high quality of life and an impressive restaurant and nightlife component. Note "Highland" is always singular.

Poncey-Highland: This subset of Virginia-Highland contains the Jimmy Carter Library and includes a large stretch of bustling Ponce De Leon Avenue, with a number of the city's older taverns and restaurants.

Druid Hills: This residential area adjacent to Virginia-Highland is primarily known as the home of Emory University and the Fernbank Natural History Museum. Most of it is in DeKalb County.

Decatur: Not an Atlanta neighborhood but an entirely separate city and the DeKalb County seat, fun, foodie-oriented Decatur is, however, directly connected to Atlanta by its own MARTA station. Driving east on Ponce De Leon Avenue gets you here eventually.

ATLANTA

Sights

DOWNTOWN
Centennial Olympic Park

For some reason the world seems to have forgotten that Atlanta hosted an actual summer Olympics in 1996. Perhaps the memory of the domestic terrorist attack that happened during the games has overshadowed the competition itself. In any case, after a 1998 rehab to accommodate regular daily use, Centennial Olympic Park (265 Park Ave., 404/222-7275, www.centennialpark.com, daily 7am-11pm, free) remains a well-maintained 21 acres of friendly green space adjoining the Pemberton Place attractions of the Georgia Aquarium and the World of Coca-Cola, amid a sea of downtown skyscrapers. Indeed, Centennial is the largest urban green space in the country developed in the last quarter-century. You can take a walk through the middle and enjoy the verdant expanse. Kids can splash and cool off in the colorful Fountain of Rings, which boasts over 250 water jets and

Gateway of Dreams monument by sculptor Raymond Kaskey, in Centennial Olympic Park

provides numerous special light shows, with the streams going as high as 30 feet.

As for the bombing near the north end of the park committed by Eric Rudolph (for which the late Richard Jewell was unjustly tried and convicted by the media), it's commemorated by the Quilt of Remembrance, in honor of the 111 people injured and the lone fatality, Alice Hawthorne.

◖ Georgia Aquarium

If you compare the Georgia Aquarium (225 Baker St. NW, 404/581-4000, www.georgiaaquarium.org, Sun.-Fri. 10am-5pm, Sat. 9am-6pm, tickets vary) with premier research-educational aquariums around the country, you might be disappointed. The main purpose of this aquarium is to entertain, and it's quite good at that. Completed in 2005 and largely funded by Home Depot mogul Bernie Marcus, the Georgia Aquarium anchors one corner of Centennial Olympic Park and is already one of the state's primary tourist destinations (so don't expect a relaxing jaunt).

The focal point is the huge Ocean Voyager exhibit, the largest single aquarium tank in the world (6.3 million gallons). You observe the hundreds of species inside during a walk through a 100-foot viewing tunnel around which the tank is formed. Kids and adults alike thrill to the sight of enormous and often scary-looking creatures, such as hammerhead sharks and manta rays floating just a few feet over their heads. For an even more up-close experience, the Georgia Explorer area has touchpools with horseshoe crabs, stingrays, and other coastal creatures.

The newest development is Dolphin Tales, billed as a "Broadway style" show featuring a cast of dolphins. That's certainly fun, but a more authentic nod to marine mammals can be found with the delightful beluga whales of the Cold Water Quest exhibit.

While the Georgia Aquarium is worth visiting, your experience will be enhanced by

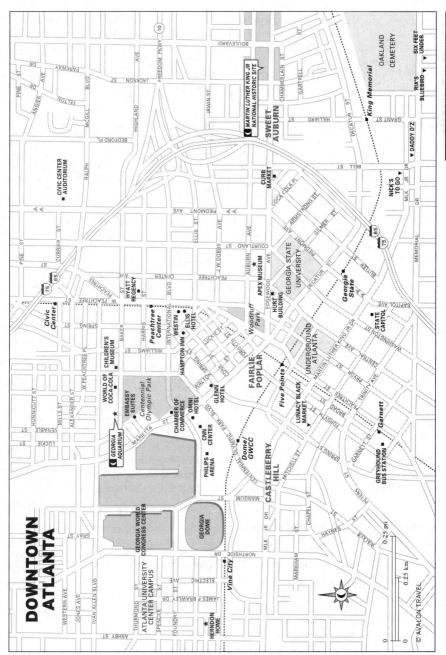

DOWNTOWN ATLANTA

SIX FEET UNDER ▶

RIA'S BLUEBIRD ▶

OAKLAND CEMETERY

DADDY DZ ▶

NICK'S TO GO ▶

◀ MARTIN LUTHER KING JR NATIONAL HISTORIC SITE

SWEET AUBURN

King Memorial

CURB MARKET

CIVIC CENTER AUDITORIUM

Civic Center

HYATT REGENCY

APEX MUSEUM

GEORGIA STATE UNIVERSITY

Georgia State

STATE CAPITOL

Peachtree Center

CHILDREN'S MUSEUM

WESTIN

ELLIS HOTEL

HURT BUILDING

Woodruff Park

HAMPTON INN

WORLD OF COCA-COLA

EMBASSY SUITES

Centennial Olympic Park

GLENN HOTEL

FAIRLIE POPLAR

Five Points

UNDERGROUND ATLANTA

GEORGIA AQUARIUM

CHAMBER OF COMMERCE

CNN CENTER

LUNACY BLACK MARKET

PHILIPS ARENA

Dome/ GWCC

CASTLEBERRY HILL

Garnett

GREYHOUND BUS STATION

GEORGIA DOME

GEORGIA WORLD CONGRESS CENTER

ATLANTA UNIVERSITY CENTER CAMPUS

Vine City

HERNDON HOME

0   0.25 mi

0   0.25 km

© AVALON TRAVEL

arriving as early in the day as you can to avoid peak crowds and the attendant onslaught of large baby strollers. (Also keep in mind that your tickets are for a specific time of entry.) Two MARTA rapid transit stations are near the Aquarium: the CNN-Georgia World Congress Center station and Peachtree Center station.

World of Coca-Cola

If you want to immerse yourself in Atlanta's number-one export, or if you really just love the taste, don't miss the over-the-top World of Coca-Cola (121 Baker St. NW, 404/676-5151, www.worldofcoca-cola.com, daily, hours vary, $16 adults, $12 children). Essentially one long, cheerful commercial for the iconic Georgia creation (including a mandatory six-minute video prior to entering the exhibits), World of Coca-Cola is a quick, fun experience that is perhaps Atlanta's number-one guilty pleasure. Think Disney with syrup. After the video, you get free rein to examine Coca-Cola memorabilia and pop art (some of it extremely valuable), watch endless loops of historic Coca-Cola commercials, and—the unquestionable highlight: Taste dozens of samples of Coca-Cola products from six continents to your heart's content. Every guest leaves with their own little bottle of Coke, bottled on the premises in a cool overhead bottling plant that runs visibly through the interior of the building. Then, of course, there's a gift shop featuring every imaginable Coke-themed product you can imagine. Cheesy? Commercial? Yes and yes. But also good clean fun that the whole family will enjoy and a refreshing break from the Georgia heat. Daily hours change frequently, so check the website.

Imagine It! The Children's Museum of Atlanta

The now-prime territory across the street from Centennial Olympic Park is where the city chose to build its entry into the burgeoning kids museum category. Imagine It! The Children's Museum of Atlanta (275 Centennial Olympic Park Dr., 404/659-5437, www.childrensmuseumatlanta.org, Mon.-Fri. 10am-4pm, Sat.-Sun. 10am-5pm, $12.75) opened in

2003 and is a pioneer in the "museum without walls" concept. Unlike many other children's museums, which seem to have one eye on what parents expect, the focus here is on the power of play. There's a splash space, a farm space, a crawl space, and even a place where they just get to paint the walls.

◖ Martin Luther King Jr. National Historic Site

Easily one of the most expansive urban National Park Service-administered sites, the Martin Luther King Jr. National Historic Site (450 Auburn Ave., 404/331-5190, www.nps. gov, Memorial Day-Labor Day daily 9am-6pm, Labor Day-Memorial Day daily 9am-5pm, free) isn't only a moving elegy to the great Atlantan, but an overview of the most crucial epoch of the civil rights movement itself. The facility, itself part of an even larger National Preservation District, comprises several wide-ranging features, all within a single block of historic (and historically African American) Auburn Avenue: The **Visitors Center** (450 Auburn Ave.); the restored original sanctuary of **Historic Ebenezer Baptist Church** (corner of Auburn Ave. and Jackson St., www.historicebenezer.org); the **King Center for Nonviolent Social Change** (449 Auburn Ave.) directly across the street, and where King and his wife are buried; the heavily-visited **King Birth Home** (501 Auburn Ave.); and the nearby **Fire Station Number 6,** which played a key role in the desegregation of Atlanta's fire department.

Most visitors save time to pay their respects at the tomb of Dr. King and his wife Coretta Scott King at the King Center, situated at the end of a beautiful reflective pool and marked by an eternal flame (Dr. King was originally interred at Southview Cemetery). The King Center's other publicly accessible component is the Freedom Hall and its associated exhibits. But obviously there is much more to the entire site and you should reserve a fair amount of time to take it all in, especially if you're going on one of the guided tours, such as the popular Birth Home tour (make sure to arrive early to book space).

A "COKE-COLA" AND A SMILE

In the years after the Civil War, Atlanta was a boomtown, with its forward-looking business community using the city's destruction as a reason to rebuild bigger and better. By 1868, Atlanta was the new capital of Georgia, and a year later a former Confederate officer and druggist from Columbus, Georgia, moved here seeking opportunity.

John Pemberton was interested in the growing market for health tonics and hit upon a recipe using kola nut and coca leaf extracts. The first version was "French Wine Cola," but one of Pemberton's partners came up with "Coca-Cola," and the world's premier brand name was born.

Twenty years later Asa Griggs Candler bought Pemberton's company and had two great ideas. First was the idea of selling the product—the ingredients of which were secret, as they are to this day—in syrup form, to be carbonated right at the soda fountain. The second was franchising bottling rights nationwide, which catapulted Coca-Cola to prominence and created a number of family fortunes.

When the Woodruff family acquired Coca-Cola in 1919, president Robert Woodruff set his sights on global expansion. During World War II, in a brilliant blend of patriotism and business savvy, he promised a five-cent bottle to every U.S. serviceman no matter where they were stationed. It was not only a step towards expanding into 200 countries: By gaining the label of "wartime production" Coca-Cola could circumvent the rationing of sugar, its syrup's main ingredient!

There've been missteps along the way, chiefly the "New Coke" debacle, humorously chronicled at the **World of Coca-Cola** (121 Baker St. NW, 404/676-5151, www.worldofcoca-cola.com, daily, hours vary, $16 adults, $12 children), where you can sample a room full of Coke products. The company got in trouble when it was revealed that its Dasani bottled water was just purified City of Atlanta tap water. While the company maintains the product never contained actual cocaine (the drug wasn't made illegal until 1906), many analysts say it likely contained very minimal traces through the 1920s.

While the company is called Coca-Cola, Atlantans often ask to drink a "Coke-Cola."

Coca-Cola's philanthropic legacy is felt in Atlanta today at the Robert Woodruff Memorial Arts Center, Emory University, and the Centers for Disease Control and Prevention, among many others. Individually, the late Robert Woodruff's acts of philanthropy changed the face of the state, but exactly how much we may never know; most of his gifts are reckoned to be anonymous.

A good bit more emotional in content than the typical education-heavy federally preserved site, the Visitors Center focuses a great deal on the sacrifice of King and his family, with an entire room devoted to a display of the humble wagon which served as his hearse following his assassination in 1969. An accompanying exhibit of photojournalism from that fateful time brings home just what a disturbing paradigm shift actually took place across America on his death. The Visitors Center also contains an extensive array of interactive video displays chronicling key moments in King's public career.

Even more moving than King's tomb is the experience within the church where he preached, Ebenezer Baptist, now called the "Historic Sanctuary" to differentiate itself from the mega-church across the street (the "Horizon Sanctuary"). This is a particularly exciting aspect in that it was only fully restored and open to the public as recently as 2001, with more restoration pending. (The historic sanctuary was the site of a lesser-known tragic incident in 1974, when King's mother "Mama King" was shot and killed while playing the organ right before a church service by a man with no known motive. Three other people were shot.)

Little "M.L.," as he was known as a child, was baptized in the church while his father

© JIM MOREKIS

Historic Ebenezer Baptist Church in "Sweet Auburn"

"Daddy King" acted as pastor. Of course, Martin Luther King Jr. would go on to become a pastor at Ebenezer himself, first as co-pastor along with his father in 1960 and then as full pastor when his father died in 1968. Thankfully, Daddy King wouldn't live to see his church host the funeral of his son only a year later. The sanctuary is kept as it would have looked during that time, with a continuous loop of King speeches and sermons.

A visit to the King birth home is also quite touching in that you really get a taste of life on Auburn Avenue in the 1930s, which while segregated was at that time lacking the more modern type of urban blight that unfortunately is endemic along most of the street today. Indeed, Dr. King and his two siblings were all born in the same room in this 1895 house.

The King family was far from poverty-stricken; Daddy King was one of Atlanta's leading black citizens and all of the King children attended college. But the house is far from ostentatious. Within, the family rooms

are preserved in a slice-of-life manner, with games and clothes strewn around the children's rooms, for example, instead of the more typical bare-bones aspect of many house museums. While most pieces are period and not actually King family items, the dishes in the kitchen are indeed relics of their time here. (Photography in the house is prohibited by request of the King family.)

As I mentioned, the free tour of the Birth Home is quite popular, but there are no advance reservations. To secure a spot you need to show up early the same day of the tour and book your space, preferably right at 9am when they open. If you arrive later in the day, you'll almost certainly be out of luck. However, as park rangers are quick to point out, there's a well-done video in the Visitors Center that gives you an extensive virtual tour.

A nice plus of visiting the MLK Jr. National Historic Site is the very large quantity of free parking. While I do encourage you to lock your car and keep valuables out of sight, you'll be happy not to be subject to downtown Atlanta's otherwise draconian parking enforcement.

CNN Studio Tour

Cable news may not be the ground-breaking novelty it once was, but the CNN Studio Tour (One CNN Center, 404/827-2300, www.cnn.com, daily 9am-5pm, $15 adults, $12 children) offers an opportunity to see how the world's first 24-hour cable news channel operates, as well as to get a glimpse further inside two other landmark Ted Turner enterprises, Turner Network Television (TNT) and Turner Broadcasting Systems (TBS). The 14-story CNN Building itself is pretty impressive, despite industry layoffs having taken a certain toll on the number of employees you'll see (not to mention CNN's increasing reliance on its New York studio). If you'd like, you can take a crack at anchoring your own "show" with the option to buy the demo tape! The walking tours, departing every 10 minutes, are 55 minutes long and sell out very quickly, so book ahead. There are daily elevator-assisted tours at 10:30am, 1:30pm, and 3:30pm. The CNN

Tour is one of the featured attractions in the Atlanta CityPASS (www.citypass.com, five attractions for $69).

State Capitol

Known colloquially as "the Gold Dome" for its shiny gilded top (among other less charitable, more descriptive names), the circa-1889 Georgia State Capitol (206 Washington St. SW, 404/330-6150, Mon.-Fri. 8am-5pm) is where the Peach State's often-ugly sausage-making of laws happens. The state legislature, officially called the General Assembly, only meets for about 40 days each winter. But despite that brief annual meeting (or because of it?), Georgia has gained a reputation as one of the most corrupt states in the union. Until very recently, rural legislators routinely ate so many roasted peanuts during extended sessions that the floors would be covered with shells.

To learn more about the history of the General Assembly and see various historical and political artifacts, you can get a brochure and take a self-guided tour of the **Capitol Museum** (www.libs.uga.edu, free). A free iPhone app is also available at the website. The grounds, while not the equal of the gorgeous State House grounds one state over in Columbia, South Carolina, are attractively maintained and feature various statuary, including a tribute to a group of African American legislators who were briefly kicked out of the Capitol during Reconstruction.

APEX Museum

Another place to learn about Georgia black history is at the APEX Museum (135 Auburn Ave., 404/523-2739, www.apexmuseum.org, Tues.-Sat. 10am-5pm, $6 adults, $5 children), short for African American Panoramic Experience. APEX centers on three permanent exhibits: "Africa: The Untold Story," which chronicles humanity's rise in the African continent on to the trans-Atlantic slave trade; "Sweet Auburn: Street of Pride," a recreation of the historic center of Atlanta's black middle class and the neighborhood in which APEX sits; and "The Georgia Negro," based on W.E.B. Dubois's historic exhibit from the 1900 Paris Expo documenting black middle class life in Georgia.

Atlanta-Fulton Public Library

The "Central Library" (One Margaret Mitchell Sq., 404/730-1700, www.afplweb.com, Mon.-Thurs. 9am-8pm, Fri.-Sat. 9am-6pm, Sun. 2pm-6pm, free), by far the largest public library branch in the city, was designed and completed in 1980 by Marcel Breuer, noted German Expressionist of the Bauhaus School. While the first four floors contain just about everything you'd ever want in the way of library offerings, the fifth floor has the most visitor appeal, containing the small but interesting Margaret Mitchell exhibit (including the typewriter on which she wrote *Gone with the Wind*), a genealogy collection, and a history collection on Atlanta and Georgia.

GRANT PARK
◖ Zoo Atlanta

There are larger zoos and there are more significant zoos. But few combine size with educational enjoyment as well as Zoo Atlanta (800 Cherokee Ave. SE, 404/624-9453, www.zooatlanta.org, daily 9:30am-5:30pm, $20.99 adults, children 3-11 $15.99), the pride of Grant Park. Primates are the prime specialty of Zoo Atlanta, and their expansive, open gorilla habitat isn't only very enjoyable, it's a center of global gorilla research (Diane Fossey was a key collaborator). Venerable old Willie B., a silverback gorilla, lived at the zoo from 1961 until his death in 2000, but his garrulous image remains a symbol of Zoo Atlanta, especially since the zoo's significant upgrade and renovation in the late 1980s. Atlantans have responded, and Zoo Atlanta's not just for tourists; it's not unusual to overhear visitors talking about animals they've seen several times before.

While there's a strong emphasis on crowd favorites from the African plains, like gorillas, elephants, giraffes, zebras, and a lion who sleeps 23 hours a day, the other key attraction at Zoo Atlanta is its pair of delightful giant pandas, Lun Lun and Yang Yang. Despite the sumptuous, specially built pagoda in which they cavort

© JIM MOREKIS

Zoo Atlanta

for your enjoyment, the pandas are actually the property of China (a return date is pending).

A hallmark of any visit to Zoo Atlanta is the winding, very viewable layout of the habitats, often enabling several different views of the same animals. This experience is enhanced by a clear devotion to educational aspects, such as habitat destruction and food sources.

As with any zoo in the South, you'll want to get here as early in the day as possible to catch the animals before the heat drives them into shade and sleep (not to mention avoiding the crush of deluxe, double-wide baby strollers when the crowd starts hitting at about 11am). Getting to Grant Park early will also help you get a parking space in the smallish zoo lot.

Atlanta Cyclorama

Back in the days before TV or even movies, a main form of popular entertainment was the "cyclorama," or circular painting wrapping 360 degrees around the viewer. Commonplace in the Victorian era, there are only three left intact in the country. The grandest by far is

the Atlanta Cyclorama (800 Cherokee Ave., 404/658-7625, www.atlantacyclorama.org, Tues.-Sat. 9:15am-4:30pm, adults $10, children $8), an old-school, over-the-top depiction of the Battle of Atlanta and the circumstances surrounding it.

Comprising a massive oil painting supplemented in the foreground by meticulously detailed figures of Civil War soldiers and functionaries, the Cyclorama is an immersive experience with some things in common with modern 3D film screenings. The difference here, other than the no electricity part, is that you sit on a rotating platform in the center of the Cyclorama building while narration describes the various events you're witnessing of the 1864 engagement that ushered in Sherman's "March to the Sea." Guided tours happen every hour on the half-hour (except for 12:30pm).

As you might expect from such a venerable institution, the Cyclorama and the accompanying small Civil War Museum have seen better days. Funding is a continual challenge, and a

© JIM MOREKIS

Atlanta Cyclorama in Grant Park

new generation of demanding tourists and their tech-savvy progeny might find it a little rough around the edges. That said, for those with an appreciation for nostalgia, the Cyclorama is a delightfully charming and quirky piece of Atlanta history, in its own right as well as in its depiction of the battle, and an irreplaceable slice of Americana. And the location, directly adjacent to the entrance to Zoo Atlanta, couldn't be more convenient.

Oakland Cemetery

While not as ornately Victorian in its embellishments as say Savannah's Bonaventure Cemetery, Atlanta's Oakland Cemetery (248 Oakland Ave., www.oaklandcemetery.com, daily 8am-8pm, free) is nonetheless a visually compelling and strangely relaxing location filled with history. The three most famous perpetual denizens are legendary golfer Bobby Jones, Atlanta's first African American mayor Maynard Jackson, and of course iconic writer Margaret Mitchell. (There are lots of Mitchells buried in Oakland Cemetery, but technically

the author of *Gone with the Wind* is not one of them; she was married to John Marsh when she died and her tombstone bears that surname.)

There is also an extensive Jewish section as well as a separate African American section, a legacy of segregation. Significantly, given his key role in the city's history, Mayor Jackson isn't interred in the latter section; his humble tomb instead occupies a quiet corner of a verdant picnic area.

Oakland is the beneficiary of a very effective nonprofit organization, which helps fund upkeep, and it shows. The landscaping, in particular, is excellently maintained and creatively designed and adds much to your enjoyment. The visitors center onsite offers tour information, and, perhaps oddly, cemetery-themed souvenirs.

Cemetery-sponsored guided tours are available Saturdays and Sundays at 10am, 2pm, and 4pm, no reservations required and all leaving from the visitors center. Weekday tours are available by appointment. There are also Saturday evening "Twilight Tours" leaving at

6:30pm. Those might seemingly be intended to cash in on the ghost story-paranormal craze, but actually they tend to focus on interesting areas of (real life) local history.

If you don't want to take a tour, that's fine too. Signage clearly points you to the key gravesites.

MIDTOWN
◖ High Museum of Art

It bills itself as the most important art museum in the Southeast, and while that may be somewhat arguable, there's no doubt that the High Museum of Art (1280 Peachtree St. NE, 404/733-4400, www.high.org, $19.50 adults, $12 children 6-17) is a crucial element of Atlanta cultural life and represents a significant collection of American art in its own right. The building itself, a gleaming white modernist structure not dissimilar in look and feel to New York's Guggenheim (here you also take a winding staircase up through the exhibits), seems strangely at home in posh Midtown, despite its architecture having absolutely nothing to do with any other building in the area. A large reason for the High's physical harmony with its neighborhood has to do with being setback within a well-maintained urban green space.

Once inside the cavernous interior, you'd be excused for briefly thinking that no amount of art could ever fill the space adequately. Indeed, you should take a few minutes to study the somewhat confusing layout of the three separate buildings (all linked by a skybridge) that comprise the High.

The vast bulk of the museum's noteworthy permanent collection occupies three floors in the Stent wing, expertly arranged in viewing areas which help split up the huge square footage into manageable chunks. One very enjoyable curatorial aspect of the High is the way furniture, crafts, and sculpture are intermingled with oils and watercolors, rather than sequestered into separate genres.

There is a smallish collection of European art, including works by Manet, Durer, and Bellini, but the High's claim to fame is its gathering of work by American artists and

High Museum of Art

MARGARET MITCHELL'S LEGACY

She was less than five feet tall, but she changed the world. Her novel *Gone with the Wind* would become one of the world's most-printed books and inspire one of cinema's most popular films.

Margaret Mitchell was a reporter for the *Atlanta Journal-Constitution* when she had to quit due to a nagging ankle injury. Her husband John, anxious to give her something to do while confined to the ramshackle apartment on Peachtree Street they called "the Dump," urged her to write a book.

It took nearly 10 years to write, but once published in 1936 *Gone with the Wind* took the world by storm. A scant three years later the blockbuster film premiered at Atlanta's now-demolished Loew's Grand Theatre, with a crowd of a million gathered to see the greatest stars of the day. Generally shy, Mitchell spoke briefly at the premiere.

Coming from a long line of Atlantans, she was well equipped to write the ultimate tale of the old South. Her grandfather told her stories about serving in the Confederate army. Like her heroine Scarlett O'Hara, Mitchell was rebellious: During the Roaring Twenties, "Peggy," as she styled herself, adopted the Flapper look and lifestyle, at one point calling herself an "unscrupulous flirt."

At age 22 she married an abusive alcoholic. The best man, John Marsh, would become her second husband. They were together when she was killed at age 48, hit by a speeding car just a few blocks from her house.

The best place to experience her legacy is at "The Dump" itself, the **Margaret Mitchell House and Museum** (990 Peachtree St., 404/249-7015, www.margaretmitchellhouse.com, Mon.-Sat. 10am-5:30pm, Sun. noon-5:30pm, $13 adults, $8.50 children). The typewriter she used to write *Gone with the Wind,* however, is at a special Mitchell exhibit on the fifth floor of the **Atlanta-Fulton Public Library** (One Margaret Mitchell Sq., 404/730-1700, www.afplweb.com, Mon.-Thurs. 9am-8pm, Fri.-Sat. 9am-6pm, Sun. 2pm-6pm, free).

Down Peachtree Street, you can visit the Georgian Terrace Hotel, where Clark Gable and Vivien Leigh stayed during the premiere. Up in Marietta you can visit the Gone with the Wind Museum: Scarlett on the Square.

For a kitschy look at the Battle of Atlanta in *Gone with the Wind,* visit the **Cyclorama** (800 Cherokee Ave., 404/658-7625, www.atlantacyclorama.org, Tues.-Sat. 9:15am-4:30pm, adults $10, children $8) in Grant Park. The author is buried in nearby **Oakland Cemetery** (248 Oakland Ave., www.oaklandcemetery.com, daily 8am-8pm, free). But don't look for the name "Mitchell," she lies next to her husband John Marsh and bears his name.

craftspeople (not all of them Southern by any means). Don't miss the Folk Art collection upstairs, with a significant representation of work by noted Georgia outsider artist Howard Finster.

Margaret Mitchell House and Museum

Perhaps more accurately called Margaret Mitchell's apartment, this charmingly restored "Dump," as the great author and her husband John Marsh affectionately referred to it, takes you back in time to that 10-year span in the 1920s and 1930s when Mitchell wrote *Gone*

with the Wind while recovering from a nasty ankle injury.

The furnishings at the Margaret Mitchell House and Museum (990 Peachtree St., 404/249-7015, www.margaretmitchellhouse.com, Mon.-Sat. 10am-5:30pm, Sun. noon-5:30pm, $13 adults, $8.50 children) aren't even close to original, since the three-story 1899 building, converted to an apartment in 1919, was severely blighted in the late 1970s, vandalized and essentially open to the elements. Indeed, it was slated for demolition until a cadre of local residents and donors teamed up to save the house in the late 1980s. Mayor

© JIM MOREKIS

Margaret Mitchell House and Museum

Andrew Young was instrumental in making sure the building suffered no further abuse.

However, the Dump's tribulations still weren't over. After renovations had begun, not one but *two* separate fires struck, one in 1994 and another in 1996, only 40 days before the home's scheduled reopening. Finally, in May 1997, the house was open to the public and is now not only a literary shrine of global renown, but also a delightful sliver of old Atlanta nostalgia amidst the silver skyscrapers and the massive Federal Reserve bank across the street.

Using Mitchell's own journal notes, restorationists furnished the tiny one-bedroom second-story flat as closely as they could to what they thought was authentic when the building housed the Crescent Apartments, with the Marshes in Apartment Number One. Your experience is by guided tour, leaving every half-hour and meeting in the cute and well-stocked gift shop. While the house opens at 10am, the first tour of the day doesn't begin until 10:30am. A charming tour guide will walk you through a small set of displays about Mitchell's

young life and burgeoning journalism career before escorting you into the actual apartment.

Be sure to check out the small but interesting exhibit on the filming of *Gone with the Wind* in the restored building across the courtyard. With a particular emphasis on the cast and crew's interaction with the city of Atlanta, the exhibit also features the original, huge portrait of Vivien Leigh as Scarlett O'Hara that is seen in the film.

A combo ticket ($22 adults, $12 children) with admission to the Mitchell House and the Atlanta History Center is available at either location or online.

The Fed Museum

Directly across the street from the Margaret Mitchell House, though utterly different in look and purpose, is the Atlanta Monetary Museum, more commonly called The Fed Museum (1000 Peachtree St., www.frbatlanta.org, Mon.-Fri. 9am-4pm, free). Within the hulking Federal Reserve Bank of Atlanta building, the Fed Museum offers not only some surprisingly interesting exhibits on the history of money, from barter to modern times, but some amazing behind the scenes looks at enormous amounts of cash being counted, sorted, and bundled in various ways. There's a real $100,000 bill on display. You can take home some shredded money as a souvenir. As you'd expect, security is extremely tight (you even have to store your cell phone), but the Fed Museum routinely hosts local school tours and conducts the security procedures in a friendly fashion. It doesn't take long to visit, but in all this is one of the best free, fun, and informative hours you'll spend in Atlanta.

Atlanta Botanical Garden

If you love orchids, you'll go nuts for the Atlanta Botanical Garden (1345 Piedmont Ave., 404/876-5859, www.atlantabotanical-garden.org, Nov.-Mar. Tues.-Sun. 9am-5pm, Apr.-Oct. Tues.-Sun. 9am-7pm, Thurs. until 10pm, $18.95 adults, $12.95 children, parking $2 per hour). The centerpiece of this gorgeous 30-acre gem right beside Piedmont Park is the **Dorothy Chapman Fuqua Conservatory,** which specializes in rain forest habitat. Within the Conservatory you'll find the *piece de resistance,* the **Fuqua Orchid Center,** which bills itself as the largest collection of orchid species in the United States. It features a special section devoted purely to mountain-habitat orchids as well as a massive display of tropical-rain forest species.

The sprawling grounds comprise a collection of themed gardens, including a Japanese garden, a rose garden, a working organic herb garden, and a children's garden with sculptures and exhibits. A good way to enjoy it, albeit in the dark, is during one of the frequent Concert in the Garden series. Past performers have included Merle Haggard, Aaron Neville, and Neko Case.

◖ Fox Theatre

Truly one of the all-time classic vintage venues, The Fox Theatre (660 Peachtree St. NE, 404/881-2100, www.foxtheatre.org) is without question Atlanta's most beloved landmark

and a priceless piece of Americana. Its Rococo Moorish-Egyptian theme, complete with faux minaret and stylized hieroglyphics, is a nod to its original incarnation, never realized, of being a Shriners temple. When completed in 1929 it was as a movie theater in a popular chain developed by William Fox. The 4,600-seat "Arabian courtyard" auditorium, including nearly 100 crystal stars, did not actually host the world premiere of *Gone with the Wind* in 1939. But the Fox Theatre was the only theater in Atlanta at the time that allowed both white and black patrons. The "Colored" box office window is still here, at the back entrance.

Over 300 performances a year are held at the Fox these days, from traveling Broadway shows to musical performances to, yes, movies. Today, movies are still shown at "the Fabulous Fox," generally on a state-of-the-art new digital projector. However, the audience sing-alongs that occasionally precede the features are shown on the original 1929 projector.

The grand Egyptian Ballroom, designed after a temple for Pharaoh Ramses II (the mezzanine ladies' lounge has a replica of King Tut's

the Fox Theatre

© JIM MOREKIS

throne), continues to host large gala events and dances. The Fox also features its original pipe organ, nicknamed "Mighty Mo," occasionally played during special performances such as Atlanta Ballet's annual *Nutcracker.*

In a distressingly familiar Atlanta story, but in this case one with a happy ending, the Fox was nearly demolished. Southern Bell made an offer on the property in 1974 with the intention of building a new headquarters on the site. This galvanized a community effort that resulted in the Fox's entry on the National Register of Historic Places, and National Landmark status in 1976. There's an entire Fox Theatre Historic District now, including the Fox, the Georgian Terrace hotel across the street, the Ponce De Leon Apartments, and the Cox-Carlton hotel, now Hotel Indigo.

Jimmy Carter Library and Museum

First, to clear up any confusion: the Jimmy Carter Library and Museum (441 Freedom Pkwy., 404/865-7100, www.jimmycarter-library.gov, Mon.-Sat. 9am-4:45pm, Sun. noon-4:45pm, library hours Mon.-Fri. 8:30am-4:30pm, $8 adults, 16 and under free) are on the grounds of the globally renowned **Carter Center,** but they're not one and the same entity.

The Carter Center nonprofit pursues the former president's goals of international cooperation, free and fair elections, and human rights, and isn't usually open to the public. Since 1986 the public component has belonged to the Museum and Library, which houses not only about 27 million of the president's papers and records but exhibits of his life and work both in the White House and after. Highlights include a life-size Oval Office replica, furnished as if it were still 1974, and Carter's Nobel Peace Prize. A 10 million-dollar renovation was completed in 2009. (If you're looking for political memorabilia from Carter's campaigns, you might be disappointed; most of that is in various buildings in the Jimmy Carter National Historic District in his hometown of Plains, Georgia, a couple of hours south.)

You'll note that the spacious boulevard called

Freedom Parkway links the Carter Center to the Martin Luther King Jr. National Historic Site, and indeed the two sites are only about five minutes away by car. There was a certain amount of controversy over this, however, with a revealing lesson in Atlanta politics, which always seems to center on roads.

When he was Governor of Georgia, Carter had already stopped a highway project that was set to go through the area. The land lay fallow until after his presidency, when a plan emerged to build the Parkway, which was originally going to be called the Jimmy Carter Parkway and only serve the Center, which perhaps fittingly occupies the hill on which General Sherman encamped during the Battle of Atlanta. Neighborhood groups fought the project, and it was stalemated until Atlanta's victorious bid for the 1996 Olympics, when city leaders decided the whole thing needed to be in place.

In any case, the president and his wife Rosalyn both maintain offices at the Carter Center and can occasionally be seen coming to and fro. The grounds are particularly nice and are free and open to the public whether or not you enter the museum building.

William Breman Jewish Heritage Museum

The William Breman Jewish Heritage Museum (1440 Spring St., 678/222-3700, www.thebreman.org, Mon.-Thurs. 10am-5pm, Fri. 10am-3pm, Sun. 1pm-5pm, $12 adults, $6 children), often just called the Breman, aspires to chronicle and honor the whole of the Jewish experience in Atlanta since antebellum years, but with a nod to greater events such as the Holocaust and aspects of social justice. The Breman is also the caretaker of a significant archive and library of letters and documents detailing Jewish history and regional genealogy. The Cuba Archives and Genealogy Center catalogs Jewish life in Georgia and Alabama.

Museum of Design Atlanta

It bills itself as the only museum in the South devoted purely to design. In any event,

Museum of Design Atlanta (MODA, 1315 Peachtree St. NE, 404/979-6455, www.museumofdesign.org, Tues.-Sat. 10am-5pm, Sun. noon-5pm, $10 adults, $5 children and students) is 5,000 square feet of display space devoted to a constantly shifting array of exhibits, focusing on some aspect of modern design; there are no permanent displays. Past exhibits have included a look at cutting-edge chair design and the evolution of skateboard art. It's a fun visit in a hip environment. On the last Thursday night of the month the museum stays open until 8pm and admission includes a cocktail. MODA is near the Woodruff Arts Center, and the nearby Arts Center MARTA transit station is very convenient. However, they have no parking lot; you're urged to pay to park at the LAZ lot at 1337 Peachtree Street.

DRUID HILLS
Fernbank Museum of Natural History

Since opening in the early 1990s, the Fernbank Museum of Natural History (767 Clifton Rd. NE, 404/929-6300, www.fernbankmuseum.org, Mon.-Sat. 10am-5pm, Sun. noon-5pm, $17.50 adults, $15.50 children) in Druid Hills has become a staple of the Atlanta cultural scene as well as a regular stop for local schoolchildren. While now a separate entity, the Museum is an offshoot of the nearby Fernbank Science Center, a project of the DeKalb County Public Schools.

The main permanent exhibit at Fernbank and by far the most attention demanding is the "Giants of the Mesozoic" display of massive, life-size dinosaur sculptures, including a 120-foot Argentinosaurus, the largest dinosaur known to science. Another permanent exhibit is "A Walk Through Time in Georgia," which tells the story of the Peach State in geological and biological terms. For many visitors, though, the highlight is the 300-seat IMAX theater, which hosts a steady schedule of beautifully-shot nature films. Every Friday night sees another edition of "Martinis and IMAX," featuring a movie, finger food, and access to a cash bar for one low admission price.

The **Fernbank Science Center** (156 Heaton Park Dr., 678/874-7102, http://fsc.fernbank.edu, Mon.-Wed. 9am-5pm, Thurs.-Fri. 9am-9pm, Sat. 10am-5pm, free), though a separate facility, has a cool observatory with frequent planetarium shows (Thurs.-Fri. 9am-10:30pm).

Adjacent to the Museum and the Center is huge Fernbank Forest, one of the last remaining old-growth urban tree canopies in the United States. The 65-acre stand recently changed hands from the Science Center to the Museum, and as of this writing is off-limits to self-guided tours until a management-preservation plan can be decided upon. However, the Museum allows access to the two parks it runs, Dellwood and Deepdene, in the beautiful **Olmstead Linear Park** (near intersection of Moreland and Ponce de Leon Aves., 404/377-5361, www.atlantaolmstedpark.org), running along adjacent Ponce de Leon Avenue.

◀ Michael C. Carlos Museum

One of the most enriching small museums I've found anywhere, the Michael C. Carlos Museum (571 S. Kilgo Circle NE, 404/727-4282, www.carlos.emory.edu, Tues.-Fri. 10am-4pm, Sat. 10am-5pm, Sun. noon-5pm, $8 adults, $6 children) on the Emory University quadrangle is one of Atlanta's hidden gems. The comparatively young age of the museum building itself, built in 1985 and majorly upgraded in 1993, is matched by its dynamic, intimate approach to its subject matter, primarily Greco-Roman, pre-Columbian, and Egyptian antiquities.

The collections, some of which date from an early collegiate collection in the Victorian era, are small, but their presentation is extremely well-curated and annotated, as befitting a university-affiliated institution. You can get up-close and personal with just about everything, including the priceless sculptures.

These days the centerpiece of the Carlos is its extremely well preserved collection of Egyptian funerary artifacts (interestingly, many were acquired from a curiosity museum in upstate New York). You enter the Egyptian section on a dramatically lighted, gradual ramp bearing a

© JIM MOREKIS

Michael C. Carlos Museum

you might expect, the emphasis being on vibrant multimedia. Ongoing exhibits include a "Global Symphony," a 100-foot-long chronicle of the fight against diseases like polio and HIV-AIDS; "The Story of CDC," a history of the Centers and the evolution of their role; and the massive sculpture "Messengers." Indeed, you're just as likely to see cutting-edge art, dealing with socio-political topics at the Museum's rotating exhibits, as you are anything of an overtly medical nature.

BUCKHEAD
◖ Atlanta History Center and Swan House

The Atlanta History Center (130 W. Paces Ferry Rd., 404/814-4000, www.atlantahistorycenter.com, Mon.-Sat. 10am-5:30pm, Sun. 1pm-4pm, $16.50 adults, $11 children) is a well-run, sharp city museum with a huge added bonus: the historic and beautifully restored Swan House (tours Mon.-Sat. 11am-4pm, Sun. 1pm-4pm), one of the finest house museums in the South.

The History Center itself offers a multitude of well-curated exhibits, including the obligatory city history section (try to catch one of the free guided docent tours for much more information than the exhibits show). You'll learn about Atlanta's Dr. Jekyll and Mr. Hyde personality as a city that looks back with nostalgia but also ruthlessly tears down the old in favor of the new.

The Center's big draw is the excellent Civil War exhibit, "Turning Point," containing one of the most impressive collections of Union and Confederate arms, uniforms, equipment, and household items I've seen in any comparable museum. Other exhibits include an excellent collection of Southern folk pottery, a quick look at the area's Native American past, and a room devoted to Atlanta's hosting of the summer Olympics in 1996.

The History Center has also been busy in other ways. They purchased the nearby historic Swan House directly from Mrs. Inman, heir to the Inman fortune (and whose son is the namesake for nearby Inman Park), exactly

huge stylized map of the Nile River. Inside the hall are several mummies, most bearing incredibly vivid, un-restored, and un-retouched paint from thousands of years ago. If mummies aren't your thing, the topmost floor has an impressive collection of African folk masks and crafts and the museum has a vibrant collection of pre-Columbian native American antiquities.

The museum is near the main entrance to the Emory campus off the traffic circle at Oxford and Decatur. Parking is available in a nearby parking garage.

Centers for Disease Control Museum

Possibly Atlanta's most offbeat museum and perhaps its most interesting is the David J. Sence Centers for Disease Control Museum (1600 Clifton Rd. NE, 404/639-0830, www.cdc.gov, Mon.-Fri. 9am-5pm, free), located on the world-famous campus of the crucial public health research institution. Until recently called "Global Odyssey of Health," the CDC Museum is a bit less clinical in nature than

© JIM MOREKIS

historic Swan House in Buckhead

as she left it. What this means to visitors is they have an opportunity to tour this magnificent, 14,000-square-foot, elegantly and charmingly appointed mansion stocked almost completely with *original* furnishings. This is almost unheard of in the house museum world, which generally depends on approximating furnishings by period and almost never has the luxury of featuring original items.

Designed by Philip Trammell Shutze, the multi-story Swan House dates from "only" 1928, but looks and feels significantly older thanks to the taste level of the owners, Edward and Emily Inman. Edward made his fortune as a cotton middleman. You'll get a distinct *Downton Abbey* vibe as you take your guided tour from room to room and note how marvelously clubby and cozy the house feels despite its swank opulence.

The History Center has expanded its grounds by several acres, and the most visible proof is the presence of the **Tully Family Farm,** a replica of a working farm circa 1800, about

when the first white settlers put down roots in the Atlanta area.

There are a couple of dining options at the History Center: The Coca-Cola Cafe on the upper level, a throwback soda fountain snack shop featuring Georgia's best-known export; and the Swan Coach House, a restored building that now houses a sit-down restaurant (reservations recommended).

The Atlanta History Center also operates the Margaret Mitchell House, and you can purchase a combo ticket ($22 adults, $12 children) from either place. The Center is also one of several attractions featured in the Atlanta CityPASS package ticket (www.citypass.com, $69).

Governor's Mansion

The official residence of the chief executive of the Peach State, the Governor's **Mansion** (391 W. Paces Ferry Rd. NW, http://mansion.georgia.gov, tours Tues.-Thurs. 10am-11:30am, free) is not to be confused with the much larger and more ornate State Capitol or "Gold Dome" downtown. This handsomely appointed, 30-room Greek Revival home in Buckhead is open for free tours for a short window each week. Keep in mind it's not exactly historic, given that it was only built in 1967.

WEST END
The Wren's Nest

Generations of Americans have enjoyed the folk tales of Uncle Remus and Brer Rabbit, the brainchildren of the great Joel Chandler Harris, the South's answer to Mark Twain (and nearly as popular in his day). The memory of the author and his creations is preserved at Harris's West End home, The Wren's Nest (1050 Ralph David Abernathy Blvd., 404/753-7735, www. wrensnestonline.com, Tues.-Sat. 10:30am-2:30pm, $8 adults, $5 children), including many original furnishings. The estate's name comes from a family of wrens who made a nest in the mailbox. Atlanta's oldest house museum, the Wren's Nest's preservation was encouraged in the early 20th century by Andrew Carnegie and President Theodore Roosevelt himself.

Harris, also known as a vigorous and progressive editor at the *Atlanta Journal-Constitution,* lived in this Queen Anne house from 1881-1908, during which time he wrote many of his most famous tales gathered in the global best-seller *Uncle Remus: His Songs and His Sayings.* Though white, Harris's pioneering work in oral folk history enabled priceless aspects of Southern African American culture to be preserved for future generations. A particular highlight is storytelling time each Saturday at 1pm, courtesy of the "Wren's Nest Ramblers," the resident group of African American storytellers who bring Harris's tales to life. (Those who want to further their Brer Rabbit experience can drive a couple hours south to Eatonton, Georgia, and visit Harris's birthplace at the Uncle Remus Museum.)

Six Flags Over Georgia

A favorite day trip destination of generations of Georgians, Six Flags Over Georgia (275 Riverside Pkwy. SW, 770/739-3400, www. sixflags.com, $57, children under 48 inches

tall $40, children under 2 free, parking $20) is known to thrill seekers the world over for its vast assortment of roller coasters. Many are authentically wooden and structured for maximum speed in the old school way, while the newer variety emphasize the modern focus on heavy G-force and twists and turns. The 100-acre park features no less than 37 "thrill rides" ranging from the mild kiddie ride Tweetie's Tree House (Six Flags has an extensive licensing agreement with Warner Bros. movie and cartoon characters; Batman and Superman feature prominently here) to the monster world-class "hypercoaster," Goliath, opened in 2006. Of course you can still ride that vintage classic, The Great American Scream Machine, which back when it opened in 1973 was the world's tallest and fastest rollercoaster.

The Atlanta park is the second of the two original parks in the Six Flags franchise. In Georgia's case the sextet of banners supposedly represents the six controlling powers of the state throughout its history, with a separate section in the park: Spain, France, Great Britain, the United States, and the Confederacy (though the French connection seems tenuous at best).

It's not cheap, and it can get pretty crowded. Your best bet for a slightly thinner crowd is to come weekdays during summer and April, May, September, and October.

UNIVERSITIES AND COLLEGES
Georgia Tech

Anchoring a large portion of downtown and midtown Atlanta, the Georgia Institute of Technology (North Ave., 404/894-2000, www. gatech.edu), always simply called "Georgia Tech" or even just "Tech," is one of the nation's oldest, largest, and best engineering schools. Founded in 1885 specifically as an effort to reboot the South's industrial efforts in the wake of the Civil War, Georgia Tech has charted a parallel track of success with its host city, also completely remade after the war. It is also one of the few premier engineering-research schools in America that is a fully public institution.

By far the most interesting portion of campus

for visitors is the nine-acre "Old Campus" or Hill District, the original Tech campus and site of a dozen of its oldest and most picturesque buildings. A highlight is Tech Tower, named for its large, lighted "Tech" signage on each of its four sides. For decades students competed to "steal the T" as part of a traditional prank; however, the practice is much frowned upon today. Tech Tower is the oldest surviving building on campus and the main administrative headquarters. Other important sights on "the Hill" include the YMCA building, funded by tycoon John D. Rockefeller and now the alumni offices; the old Andrew Carnegie school library, now the president's office; and Lyman Hall, first of many Tech chemistry buildings. Most other parts of Tech's campus are much younger and have a generic, suburban feel quite unlike the concrete jungle surrounding it. An exception is on East Campus, home of most Tech freshmen, who often eat at the ornate, circa-1928 Brittain Dining Hall.

The Georgia Tech Yellow Jackets play football at Bobby Dodd Stadium at Historic Grant Field. While improved since its early days, Grant Field is the oldest major university gridiron in the United States, built in 1905. As skyscrapers have sprung up around it, the view from a typical Jacket home game is quite different from the bucolic setting of the typical college football stadium.

Georgia Tech's other mascot is the "Ramblin' Wreck," a 1930 Ford Coupe in the school colors of gold and white and supposedly a reference to the makeshift vehicles used by Tech engineers serving in faraway locales. Students from Tech's main rival, the University of Georgia, have stolen the Wreck at least twice.

Georgia Tech provided much of the athlete housing for the 1996 Summer Olympics held in Atlanta; after the games the housing was converted into student dormitories. The enormous investment had the ancillary effect of substantially upgrading the entire area, formerly quite seedy, well into the future. Another major investment came in 2003 with the completion of Technology or Tech Square, a mixed-use, public space containing administrative buildings, shops, cafés, the Barnes & Noble that is the official Tech bookstore, and even a hotel. Constructed on previously vacant lots of urban blight, Tech Square has significantly upgraded the entire area between the Downtown Connector and Spring Street.

Don't be surprised to hear an old-fashioned steam whistle while walking around the Tech campus. An old school tradition, the whistle blows five minutes before the top of each hour during regular class time.

Emory University

A private university occupying 630 acres in the verdant, quiet Druid Hills residential area in northeast Atlanta, Emory University (1615 Pierce Dr. NE, 404/727-6123, www.emory.edu) hasn't been in town the entire time; it was founded in 1836 in Oxford, Georgia. However, in 1915 a land grant by Asa Candler, then-president of Coca-Cola, enabled the school to move to the state capital, beginning a long association with the locally-based soft drink giant. In 1979, another Coca-Cola president, Robert Woodruff, donated over $100 million in Coke stock to Emory, the largest-ever gift to a university up to that time. The infusion of capital ensured Emory's success far into the future and dramatically expanded its ability and reach. In 1994, the Emory business school was renamed for Robert Goizueta, yet another Coca-Cola president and college benefactor.

However, you'll find very little commercial nods to Coca-Cola on Emory's understated, wooded campus. Despite Emory's old-fashioned roots as a Methodist institution, it is on the leading edge of design, with over two million square feet of building space LEED-certified to state-of-the-art sustainability and conservation standards. By far the main attraction for visitors is the Michael C. Carlos Museum (571 S. Kilgo Circle, 404/727-4282, www.carlos.emory.edu, Tues.-Fri. 10am-4pm, Sat. 10am-5pm, Sun. noon-5pm, $8 adults, $6 children), an excellently designed and curated museum devoted to Egyptian, Greco-Roman, and ancient American artifacts.

Intriguingly, despite Emory's religious

affiliation, its mascot is the vaguely demonic Lord Dooley, a skeleton dressed all in black and nicknamed the "Lord of Misrule." Each spring the university marks "Dooley Week," when the mascot roams the campus making impromptu classroom stops, dismissing the entire class unless the professor can correctly answer a question about Emory history.

Historically Black Colleges and Universities

Perhaps nowhere else is Atlanta's importance to African American history so clear as in the presence of several of the country's oldest and most influential historically black colleges and universities (HBCUs), all nearby to each other in southwest Atlanta and since 1929 gathered in a consortium called the Atlanta University Center.

All member institutions share the **Robert W. Woodruff Library** (111 James P. Brawley Dr. SW, 404/978-2067, www.auctr.edu), whose main claim to fame these days is as the new home of an expansive collection of papers from Martin Luther King Jr., purchased from the King estate in 2006 and deeded to King's alma mater, Morehouse College. The papers are available for public research use.

The first higher education institution in the United States established especially for African Americans to attain graduate degrees was Atlanta College, founded in conjunction with the Freedmens Bureau in the months immediately following the Civil War. A few years later, Clark College was founded to grant undergraduate degrees. In 1929 both merged to form **Clark Atlanta University** (223 James P. Brawley Dr., 404/880-8000, www.cau.edu), which today has about 4,000 students and maintains its Methodist affiliation. It's one of only four HBCUs with full research institution status. Famed author and civil rights activist W.E.B. DuBois was a longtime sociology professor here.

Easily the most well known of Atlanta's HBCUs, however, are **Morehouse College** (830 Westview Dr., 404/681-2800, www. morehouse.edu) and **Spelman College** (350 Spelman Lane, 404/681-3643, www.spelman. edu). While technically unaffiliated, they're often mentioned in the same breath not only because of their academic excellence but because of their unique nature; Morehouse is an all-men's school, while Spelman is all female. Between them they account for an amazing variety of high-profile alumni, including Martin Luther King Jr. and his daughters, filmmaker Spike Lee, actor Samuel L. Jackson, authors Alice Walker and Tina McElroy Ansa, and Atlanta's first black mayor, Maynard Jackson.

Morehouse College was founded in 1867 as the Augusta Institute, later the Atlanta Baptist Seminary. In the 1890s came a land grant by industrialist John D. Rockefeller and the move to its present location, as well as another name change, this time to Atlanta Baptist College. By 1913 it was given its current name. Early on, the concept of the "Morehouse Man" became a byword for strict standards of personal and academic excellence, centering on "The Five Wells": well-read, well-spoken, well-traveled, well-dressed, and well-balanced. In 2009, Morehouse somewhat controversially banned certain indicators of hip-hop culture from college events, including grills on the teeth, bandannas or do-rags on the head, and low-riding pants. Parts of the campus, including Archer Hall and Graves Hall, were sets in alumnus Spike Lee's movie *School Daze*. Morehouse's most famous ambassadors are the Morehouse Glee Club, an internationally-renowned organization which has performed at presidential inaugurations and Super Bowls and has even recorded with the Atlanta Symphony Orchestra. The affiliated Morehouse School of Medicine is one of the South's premier med schools.

America's oldest institution for African American women, Spelman College was founded in 1881 as the Atlanta Baptist Female Seminary by two abolitionists from Massachusetts. The school's current name is an homage to industrialist (and noted Baptist) John D. Rockefeller's wife Laura Spelman Rockefeller, an early benefactor and supporter. The oldest building on campus, Rockefeller

Hall, dates from 1886. Many Spelman students were active in the early days of the civil rights movement, often mentored by longtime professor and noted counter-culture author and historian Howard Zinn (he was dismissed because of his activism in 1963). The Cosby Academic Center on campus is a result of the enormous philanthropy toward the college on the part of Bill Cosby and his wife Camille in the 1980s and 1990s; their daughter was a graduate. The **Spelman College Museum of Fine Art** (350 Spelman Lane, 404/681-3643, www.spelman. edu, Tues.-Fri. 10am-4pm, Sat. noon-4pm, $3 suggested donation) is in the Cosby Center and is devoted purely to artwork by female artists covering the African Diaspora.

Morris Brown College (643 MLK Jr. Dr., 404/739-1010, www.morrisbrown.edu) has the distinction of being the first African American college self-funded entirely by African Americans, almost all of them former slaves. However, Morris Brown lost accreditation in 2002 after a financial scandal and things only went downhill from there. An unpaid bill led to water service being briefly cut off in 2008, and in 2012 the college filed for bankruptcy and underwent foreclosure. However, the school did enjoy a brief spate of popularity after being featured in the popular film *Drumline*. No longer technically a member of the Atlanta University Center organization, Morris Brown currently has fewer than 100 students and faces a very uncertain future.

Georgia State University

Despite its heavily urban, occasionally sketchy setting downtown and its notoriously unattractive "concrete campus," Georgia State University (30 Courtland St., 404/413-2000, www.gsu.edu) is actually not as young as you'd think, with roots dating back to 1913. It's not as small as you'd think either; its enrollment is second largest in the state, behind only the enormous University of Georgia in Athens.

Though long thought of as a commuter school, a label which is more of a comment on its lack of a cohesive campus identity than its actual student body, Georgia State has in recent years become an important community force in downtown revitalization as it continues to expand its facilities. A billion-dollar expansion in 2006 is a chief example, as is the establishment in 2010 of a football program. Of prime interest to visitors is the school-run **Rialto Center for the Arts** (80 Forsyth St., 404/413-9849, www.rialtocenter.org) in the Fairlie-Poplar district, hosting most performances of Georgia State's esteemed music department.

Entertainment and Events

NIGHTLIFE
Live Music

"Died and gone to heaven" takes on new meaning at the downtown club **Masquerade** (695 North Ave. NE, 404/577-8178, www.masqueradeatlanta.com), certainly one of the South's most venerable live music venues, bringing in name acts (Matisyahu, Grouplove, GWAR) as well as on-fire metal-indie bands (Lazer/Wulf, Bad Books) and the occasional MMA fight to its rambling, castle-like space, a former mill. Most touring bands play upstairs on the third level, named "Heaven." The grungier and more local acts tend to play, you guessed it, in "Hell." (And yes, there's a Purgatory as well). Outside is its **Music Park,** basically a huge open space where the occasional rowdy outdoor show will be held (Alabama Shakes, North Mississippi Allstars). A rite of passage for generations of Atlantans and Southern music fans, the Masquerade is loud, dark, divey, and can get very crowded. But two possible bonuses are that, unlike most Atlanta clubs, Masquerade does host all-ages shows and no smoking is ever allowed in the building.

The main rock 'n' roll bar in happening Little Five Points is **The Star Community Bar** (437 Moreland Ave., www.starbaratlanta.com, Thu.-Sun. 4pm-3am), more colloquially just called "Star Bar" and known far and wide as a

Southern hipster mecca and live music joint. It also boasts one of the coolest Elvis shrines outside of Memphis, upstairs in a special "vault." You might have never heard of the bands that play here on a nightly basis, but, hey, it's a hipster bar, that's the point. They feature "celebrity bartenders" each weekend afternoon; again, no one you've likely ever heard of but fun nonetheless. Mondays feature some occasionally quite good standup comedy, and every second Thursday of the month is "Free for Y'all Night," that is, see a band for no cover charge.

The premier bigger-name live music venue in Little Five Points is **Variety Playhouse** (1099 Euclid Ave. NE, 404/524-7354, www.variety-playhouse.com), a former movie theater converted into a concert space, with a mix of assigned seating and a dance floor up front near the stage. Their calendar of touring acts runs the gamut from well-established names (David Byrne, John Hyatt) to acts which are perhaps one step away from cutting-edge (Grace Potter, Carolina Chocolate Drops, Feist). This being Little Five Points, jam-bands like Dark Star Orchestra play here often. (Helpful hint: Buy tickets directly through the venue to avoid Ticketmaster surcharges.) They do have beer and wine, but the best way to enjoy a night out at Variety Playhouse is to sample food and drink elsewhere in this lively entertainment district before (and after!) the show. Parking is notoriously horrendous in Little Five Points; if there's no spot left in the Variety's free lot out back, I'd suggest going ahead and paying to park in one of the many private lots all around and be done with it, the nearest MARTA station being quite a hike. Unlike most nightspots in Atlanta, no smoking is allowed here.

The best blues joint in Atlanta proper and easily one of the more authentic dive bars in town as well, **Northside Tavern** (1058 Howell Mill Rd., 404/874-8745, www.northsidetavern.com, daily noon-3am) features live blues and jazz seven nights a week and has a beat-up interior to match that crushing schedule. This now 40-year-old hole-in-the-wall isn't much to look at inside or out, the restrooms are legendarily bad, but the dark smoky vibe,

the surprisingly diverse and vibrant clientele, the cheap beer (nothing on tap, sorry!), and of course the music all combine for one of the more unique Southern nightlife experiences in Atlanta or beyond.

One of Atlanta's most iconic live music hubs, **Blind Willie's** (828 N. Highland Ave., 404/873-2583, www.blindwilliesblues.com) brings the blues (and some jazz) six nights a week, generally for a pretty low cover charge. Situated in Atlanta's hip Virginia-Highland neighborhood, Blind Willie's gets a crowd that is occasionally a bit upscale for most blues joints, with the music starting a good hour earlier than at most music spots around town. But everyone has a good time, and there's usually plenty of dancing.

Renowned as a late-night party place and metal club for the last 20 years, **The Highlander** (931 Monroe Circle, 404/872-0060, www.the-highlanderatlanta.com, Mon.-Sat. 11am-3am, Sun. 12:30pm-midnight) in Midtown has experienced a renewed popularity in the wake of an episode of "Diners, Drive-ins, and Dives" on The Food Channel. The focus food-wise is on the delectable burgers, which some call the best in Atlanta. The "Pasta-rella" sticks are also worth the trip. It's important to keep in mind this is primarily a bar, so you have be 21 or over to get in. And also, in keeping with the Atlanta bar scene, it can get smoky.

One of Atlanta's premier live music clubs, East Atlanta's **The Earl** (488 Flat Shoals Ave., 404/522-3950, www.badearl.com) also boasts some of its best burgers (the Guacamole Burger is a fave rave, and don't forget the sweet potato fries). The acts tend toward the indie or heavy side, and are generally bands on their way up to better things, in short, a great place to catch great bands in an intimate venue while you still can.

Like great, loud music? Love unicorns? Then **The Drunken Unicorn** (736 Ponce de Leon Ave., no phone, www.thedrunkenunicorn.net) in Poncey-Highland is for you. In classic rock bar style, it's basically a dark dungeon with a smallish stage and a really good sound system. The focus is on the bands, metal, punk, indie, basically anything non-mainstream, and the beer is cheap and flowing. They're directly underneath **Friends on Ponce** (736 Ponce de Leon Ave., 404/817-3820, www.friendson-ponce-atl.com), a neighborhood gay bar.

No ATL pub crawl is complete without a visit to **Smith's Olde Bar** (1578 Piedmont Ave., 404/875-1522, www.smithsoldebar.com, Mon.-Sat. noon-3am, Sun. noon-midnight)—or "S.O.B.," get it?—in the Piedmont Park-Morningside area just northeast of Midtown. Combine an Irish pub with a blues-rock club with a pool hall with a sports bar, but with a more open-minded attitude in this gay-friendly area of town, and you have a fairly complete nightlife experience. Through the years Smith's stage has hosted a virtual Who's Who of big names-before-they-were-big, from Maroon 5 to Kings of Leon, all in an intimate, wood-and-whiskey-soaked atmosphere. Indeed, a brass plaque here famously boasts "The Best Musicians and the Greatest Music Fans Walk Through These Doors."

The **Apache Café** (63 3rd St. NW, 404/876-5436, www.apachecafe.info, Mon.-Sat. 9pm-3am, Sun. 7pm-midnight), a humble dive near the Varsity downtown has long been known as a friendly venue for up-and-coming local soul-folk singer-songwriters and spoken word artists, with a long-running open mic night on Sundays that remains extremely popular.

Dive Bars

In a city that already has its share of quirky, one-of-a-kind bars and clubs, the **Clermont Lounge** (789 Ponce de Leon Ave., 404/874-4783, www.clermontlounge.net, Mon.-Sat. 1pm-3am) in Virginia-Highland is perhaps the quirkiest and most unique. Originally a 1960s hotel bar in a hotel that has since shut down, the Clermont is a combination strip club-hipster dive with kitsch cachet to burn (movie stars in town often can be seen slumming here). The vibe isn't so much classic gentleman's club as it is sheer spectacle, with the generally over-the-hill but spirited topless dancers being an assortment of ages and body types. The booze is plentiful and cheap, the ubiquitous PBR running a buck apiece most nights, the company

interesting and varied, and the burlesque entertainment...well, it is what it is.

No look at Atlanta nightlife is complete without a look at **Sister Louisa's Church of the Living Room & Ping Pong Emporium** (466 Edgewood Ave., 404/522-8275, www.sister-louisaschurch.com, Mon.-Sat. 5pm-3am, Sun. 5pm-midnight), which, amazingly, is exactly what the name implies. Except "Sister Louisa" is actually a guy, specifically Grant Henry, a former priest who turned in his robes for, well, different robes and now serves libations and has painted some interesting quasi-religious themed artwork for the walls as well. There's even an "organ karaoke" night on Wednesdays, which is exactly what it sounds like. As for the ping-pong, yes there's one table upstairs. The main show at "Church," as everyone calls it, is the clientele itself, a mix of uber-hipsters, freaks, those of vague gender, and of course lookie-loos in search of the wild side of Atlanta life, if only for one night. It gets quite packed on weekends after 11pm, but can be surprisingly relaxed before then. Sister Louisa's has fully embraced the hipster sangria trend, and they do mix a mean batch.

You'll find **El Bar** (939 Ponce de Leon Ave., 404/881-6040, Wed.-Sat. 10pm-3am) right behind and sort of underneath the El Azteca restaurant in Virginia-Highland, and if you like crazy nights, a combination of hip-hop and club music, and excellent and creative drink specials (the house specialty is a shot of tequila with a Miller High Life), you will have lots of *amor* for El Bar. It's cozy and crowded late on weekend nights, but that's how they roll.

Taverns and Pubs

The very personification of the neighborhood bar and grill, **Manuel's Tavern** (602 N. Highland Ave., 404/525-3447, www.manuelstavern.com, Tue.-Sat. 11am-2am, Sun.-Mon. 11am-midnight) is nearly as well known for its food as its spirits and convivial atmosphere. Older generations knew "Mannie's" as where Atlanta's old-school Democratic power structure let their hair down and exchanged scuttlebutt. I suspect that perception has dwindled along with the actual amount of Democrats in Georgia. In any case, Manuel's remains a Poncey-Highland must-visit for the beer connoisseur and comfort-food maven alike. The burgers, huge and juicy, are a big draw, as are the omelets and steaks. You can't beat the location, close to Virginia-Highland proper and Little Five Points. And did I mention the big, free parking lot, a comparative rarity in Atlanta?

Virginia-Highland's favorite bar is **The Righteous Room** (1051 Ponce de Leon Ave., 404/874-0939, Mon.-Thu. 11:30am-2am, Fri. 11:30am-3am, Sat. noon-3am, Sun. noon-2am), which also gets most everyone's vote for best bar food in Atlanta. The burgers in particular deserve the raves they get, but the menu is surprisingly extensive, with good veggie selections and even a salmon quesadilla. Caveat: Remember that as of this writing smoking is still allowed in Atlanta bars, so you might get a snoot full of second-hand nicotine with your delicious grub.

Yes, the name's a joke: **Euclid Avenue Yacht Club** (1136 Euclid Ave. NE, 404/688-2582, www.theeayc.com, Mon.-Thurs. 3pm-2am, Fri.-Sat. noon-3am, Sun. noon-midnight) has nothing to do with yachts, or indeed boats of any kind. But this staple of the Little Five Points (L5P) bar scene does have something of a clubby atmosphere in the sense that it's really more of an old-school neighborhood blue-collar bar than some of the more hipster-oriented dives which have sprung up in L5P over the past few years. It's also not a place for those with a need for a hugely diverse beer or cocktail menu. This is no-frills, good time Atlanta in one of its liveliest neighborhoods.

If a fun and clean sports bar environment is what you want, head to Druid Hills to **Famous Pub & Sports Palace** (2947 N. Druid Hills Rd, 404/633-3555, www.famouspubsports. com, Mon.-Fri. 11am-3am, Sat. 11:30am-3am, Sun. 11am-3am). They will have all the games on huge high-def flat screens, and while the rest of Atlanta's nightlife scene still allows smoking, Famous is strictly smoke-free by choice. They have a full menu of typical but tasty pub food,

from burgers to wings. It's roomy and friendly inside and out, with extensive patio seating, but still gets packed on college football Saturdays.

If Atlanta's great lineup of dive bars isn't your cup of PBR, maybe the **Tin Roof Cantina** (2591 Briarcliff Rd., 404/329-4700, www.tinroofcantina.com, Mon.-Fri. 4pm-4am, Sat.-Sun. noon-3am) in Brookhaven is more your speed. This later incarnation of a once-legendary Buckhead dive has plenty of patio space, plenty of channels with plenty of games, plenty of parking (not a given for Atlanta bars), and plenty of live music Wednesday-Monday nights starting at about 10pm. The menu is strong on tacos, burritos, and the like, all served in very large portions, with a pared-down late-night menu focusing more on burgers and wings.

Nightclubs and Dancing

For a cover in the $5-10 range you can go underground, literally, and dance all night to the DJs spinning old-school hip-hop and dance-pop at the epicenter of the ATL serious club scene, **MJQ** (736 Ponce de Leon Ave., 404/870-0575, Mon.-Wed. 10pm-4am, Thu.-Fri. 11pm-4am, Sat. 11pm-3am), situated in the same complex as the also-popular Drunken Unicorn. While weekends are packed, it's Wednesday nights when MJQ is really bangin'. Like many of Atlanta's better clubs, there's no sense coming before midnight or so.

Probably Atlanta's premier gay dance club, **The Jungle Club** (215 Faulkner Rd. NE, 404/844-8800, www.jungleclubatlanta.com, daily 5pm-3am) is also one of the more serious purveyors of straight-up house music and its sub-variants, often bringing in world-class DJs for a long night of partying until dawn. The drag shows are also a big draw, particularly for the regular Wednesday night "Fantasy Girls" extravaganza.

Atlanta's go-to spot for authentic Latin-salsa dancing—actually the DJs spin everything from reggaeton to merengue—**La Rumba II** (4300 Buford Hwy., 678/789-2888, www.larumba2.com, Thu.-Sun. 10pm-4am) is the latest incarnation of a local Latino favorite (it was originally La Rumba, then La Pachanga, and now back to La Rumba). La Rumba II is also known for its great food, served late into the night.

If you're looking for the classic multi-level high-dollar hip-hop club-dance-Red Bull and vodka scene with all that implies, go straight to **Compound** (1008 Brady Ave., 404/898-1702, www.compoundatl.com, Thu.-Sat. 9pm-3am) and hope you look good enough to make it in. This is often where the hottest after-parties happen in the VIP rooms (you know who you are), and the prices, both to get in as well as to park, match.

PERFORMING ARTS

Because of its size, wealth, and population of affluent transplants from all areas of the country and world, Atlanta offers a huge variety of fine arts performance and takes its place among America's leading cultural centers.

Venues

Without question Atlanta's leading overall cultural venue is the **Robert W. Woodruff Memorial Arts Center** (1280 Peachtree St. NE, 404/733-4200, www.woodruffcenter. org). You'd be forgiven for thinking the "memorial" in the name refers to legendary philanthropist Mr. Woodruff, who provided much of the funding for its construction. The memorializing in question refers to the tragic airplane crash in Paris that claimed the lives of eight movers and shakers in the Atlanta art community in 1962, leading to the establishment of the Arts Center in 1968. This attractive 12-acre campus, around which Midtown has built a reputation as a leading arts center, includes five basic components: 1800-seat Symphony Hall, home of the Atlanta Symphony Orchestra; the High Museum of Art (itself comprising several buildings); the 765-seat Alliance Theatre, home of the theatre company of the same name; Young Audiences, a youth outreach and arts education center; and the 400-seat 14th Street Playhouse.

One of America's great historic venues, the 4600-seat **Fox Theatre** (660 Peachtree St. NE, 404/881-2100, box office 855/285-8499, www.

foxtheatre.org) continues to host a full slate of productions, generally touring road shows and benefit performances. Its architecture and charmingly over-the-top Moorish-Egyptian design make it worth seeing even if you're not attending a show here.

For many years it was known to Atlanta music fans as The Roxy, anchor of the Buckhead nightlife scene and host to some of the greatest names in rock 'n' roll. Today the fully restored and renamed, circa-1930 **Buckhead Theatre** (3110 Roswell Rd., 404/843-2825, www.thebuckheadtheatre.com) continues to host some of the biggest names in indie music as well as the occasional theatrical production.

The fairly new **Verizon Wireless Amphitheatre** (2200 Encore Pkwy., 404/733-5010, www.vzwamp.com), one of many bearing that name throughout the United States, is in the northern suburb of Alpharetta. In addition to hosting frequent concerts by the Atlanta Symphony Orchestra, it hosts some of the biggest names in music in its 12,000-seat setting, such as Maroon 5, John Mayer, Zac Brown, and My Morning Jacket. Seating close to the stage is reserved and under a roof. There's a non-roofed general admission lawn area farther away, to which many folks bring picnics.

Verdant **Piedmont Park** (1320 Monroe Dr., 404/875-7275, www.piedmontpark.org) in Midtown hosts some of Atlanta's most popular live shows, often free ones, such as Music Midtown and the Pride Fest. Nearby **Atlanta Botanical Garden** (1345 Piedmont Ave. NE, 404/876-5859, www.atlantabotanicalgarden. org) also hosts a well-received concert series during the summer. Buckhead's answer to Piedmont Park, the amphitheatre at **Chastain Park** (4469 Stella Dr., 404/233-2227, http://chastainseries.com) is also a popular place to see a live show during the summer.

For years, The Omni was a premier local sports and entertainment venue. In 1999 that decaying cavern was demolished, and on that site now sits the 18,000-seat **Philips Arena** (1 Philips Dr., 404/878-3000, www.philipsarena. com) adjoining the CNN Center. (Local resident Elton John played its inaugural show.)

"The Phil" is home of the Atlanta Hawks basketball team, it's the first LEED-certified NBA arena, and it hosts such a full schedule of concerts that it's considered the third-busiest concert facility in the United States.

The 4600-seat **Boisfeuillet Jones Civic Center** (395 Piedmont Ave., 404/658-7159, www.atlantaciviccenter.com), usually just called "Civic Center," hosts large concerts and trade shows. It was once Atlanta's premier convention center but that baton was long since passed to the Georgia World Congress Center adjoining the CNN Center and Philips Arena.

Atlanta's newest large-scale venue, **Cobb Energy Performing Arts Centre** (2800 Cobb Galleria Pkwy., 770/916-2800, www.cobbenergycentre.com), is situated right at the intersection of I-75 and the I-285 Perimeter just northwest of town. The Centre has a very full calendar of traveling road shows and concerts and hosts the Atlanta Opera's regular season performances.

Music and Dance

Long considered the leading orchestra of the Southeast and one of the best in the country, the nearly 70-year-old **Atlanta Symphony Orchestra** (1280 Peachtree St. NE, 403/733-5000, www.atlantasymphony.org) performs under the baton of conductor and music director Robert Spano, whose vision includes championing new works by up-and-coming conductors. The affiliated **Atlanta Symphony Chorus** is an award-winning entity in its own right and is one of the world's leading groups of its kind. The Atlanta Symphony Orchestra (ASO) performs at least 200 concerts a year, most at the Atlanta Symphony Center in the Woodruff Memorial Arts Center on Peachtree Street. But they frequently can be seen at huge outdoor shows as well, at places like Verizon Wireless Amphitheatre and Chastain Park.

Since their inception in the 1970s the **Atlanta Chamber Players** (www.atlantachamberplayers.com) have relied on a core group from the ASO to perform small-scale, intimate concerts from the chamber repertoire. They play a wide variety of venues, from the High Museum of Art to college campuses to local churches.

The first dedicated baroque ensemble in the Southeast, the **Atlanta Baroque Orchestra** (770/557-7582, www.atlantabaroque.org) is under the direction of Julie Andrijeski and makes its home base well outside the Perimeter in the northern suburb of Roswell, playing mostly at the Roswell Presbyterian Church.

Once the Marietta Symphony, then the Cobb Symphony, and now the **Georgia Symphony Orchestra** (770/429-7016, www.georgiasymphony.org), this all-professional group performs at various venues just north of Atlanta, with its main base being the Bailey Center at Kennesaw State University. Recent concerts included Mahler's Symphony No. 1 and a pops program featuring the music of Radiohead.

The **Georgia State University Symphony Orchestra** (404/413-5900, www.music.gsu.edu) is entirely affiliated with Georgia State University, which has a sprawling campus downtown. Its music department is excellent, and audiences at their performances are the beneficiaries. They typically play at the Rialto Center for the Arts in Fairlie-Poplar.

The highly regarded **Atlanta Opera** (404/881-8801,www.atlantaopera.org) has had to move locations a lot over the years to accommodate growing crowds, from the Woodruff Center to the Fox Theatre to the Civic Center, and now to the huge, plush new Cobb Energy Performing Arts Centre (2800 Cobb Galleria Pkwy.) in northwest Atlanta at I-75 and I-285. The 2012 season included *Carmen, La Traviata,* and *The Italian Girl in Algiers.*

The smaller **Capitol City Opera** (678/301-8013, www.ccityopera.org) concentrates more on light opera, such as *Cosi Fan Tutte,* and operates in close affiliation with Oglethorpe University. They generally perform at the university's Conant Performing Arts Center.

Closing in on the century mark, the **Atlanta Ballet** (404/873-5811, www.atlantaballet.com) has a long and storied history, but it's not hidebound by any means. These days it's as known for its innovation as for its tradition, regularly performing work by new choreographers. As with just about every other ballet company, the annual holiday *Nutcracker* performance is its most anticipated and successful show of the year, but by no means the only noteworthy performance. Highlights from the 2012 season include *Cinderella, Michael Pink's Dracula,* and David *Bintley's Carmina Burana.* The Atlanta Ballet juggles three main performance venues, the massive new Cobb Energy Performing Arts Centre (2800 Cobb Galleria Pkwy.), the Fox Theatre (660 Peachtree St. NE), and the Gwinnett Performing Arts Center (6500 Sugarloaf Pkwy.) east of town.

Billing itself as the nation's only fully-integrated dance company, **Full Radius Dance** (404/724-9663, www.fullradiusdance.org) incorporates dancers with disabilities into its calendar of original choreography, wheelchairs and dancers moving together in rhythm. Most of their shows are at 7 Stages (1105 Euclid Ave. NE) in Little Five Points. They also offer a wide variety of outreach and education to the local population with disabilities.

Theater

The "establishment" company in Atlanta is **Alliance Theatre** (404/733-4650, www.alliancetheatre.org), performing primarily at the Woodruff Memorial Arts Center (1280 Peachtree St. NE) in Midtown. Since its founding in 1968, Alliance has served not only as the city's premier theater company but also as a developing ground for theatrical acting and directing talent from all over the Southeast. Even the "mainstream" works performed on the main Alliance Stage represent the cutting-edge of New York and London drama, such as *Zorro* and *Next to Normal,* while performances at the smaller Hertz Theatre concentrate on underground works and new writers.

The 30-year-old **Horizon Theatre** (1083 Austin Ave., 404/584-7450, www.horizontheatre.com) performs in an intimate space in Little Five Points, but don't let the small size of the room fool you: This is a fully professional theater presenting important work through the course of its five-show main season, and

it's probably Atlanta's favorite theater company. They host and sponsor the annual New South Play Festival, focusing on new work from, for, or about the South.

Since 1988 **Actor's Express** (887 W. Marietta St., 404/607-7469, www.actors-express.com) has provided Atlanta audiences with an enriching alternative to the usual chestnut offerings, with just enough familiarity to keep a high profile. A recent season included performances of *Equus* as well as *Bloody Bloody Andrew Jackson.* While Actor's Express has had various homes during their history, they currently perform in the historic restored space of the King Plow Art Center just west of Downtown proper.

Atlanta's most politically vibrant theater, **7 Stages** (1105 Euclid Ave. NE, 404/523-7647, www.7stages.org) operates in its own space in the heart of Little Five Points, and appropriate to its bohemian location provides a steady season of compelling, often controversial performances. Anytime a play comes under fire for receiving National Endowment for the Arts funding, you can bet that 7 Stages will go out

the 7 Stages theater in Little Five Points

© JIM MOREKIS

of their way to perform it. 7 Stages has a vibrant youth and international outreach program, frequently collaborating with guest artists from Europe and Asia.

The professional **Theatrical Outfit** (84 Luckie St., 678/528-1500, www.theatricaloutfit.org), Atlanta's third oldest theater group, now operates out of the first LEED-certified theater building in the United States: the new Balzer Theatre at Herren's in Midtown. It's actually on the site of the old Herren's, the first restaurant in Atlanta to voluntarily desegregate. Theatrical Outfit focuses heavily on developing Atlanta-area writers, directors, and actors.

The **Center for Puppetry Arts** (1404 Spring St. NW, 404/873-3089, www.puppet.org) is America's largest group dedicated to the art form. It not only hosts a regular season of performances at its space in Midtown, but there is a puppetry museum onsite, which includes a Jim Henson Wing, memorializing the Muppets founder (and ribbon-cutter of the Center itself back in 1978).

The improv gurus at **Dad's Garage** (280 Elizabeth St. NE, 404/523-3141, www.dadsgarage.com) near Inman Park specialize in staging bawdy original scripts and also feature a heavy weekly schedule of improv, some of it themed and quite long-running. The audience gets to drink beer and wine throughout the shows; this is not for kids.

The **New American Shakespeare Tavern** (499 Peachtree St. NE, 404/874-5299, www.shakespearetavern.com) is intended in both look and feel to closely replicate the Elizabethan play-going experience, right down to the Globe Theatre-inspired facade of the building itself in the SoNo district on Peachtree Street. This beloved project of the Atlanta Shakespeare Company seeks to break down the barriers that sometimes make the enjoyment of The Bard's work a rather stuffy experience. Here, you can purchase food and drink, right up to showtime, bring it back to your table to enjoy during the show. And even though you have advance tickets, just as in Shakespeare's time, the key is to get here when the doors open to snag a good

spot. Many folks do just that, and enjoy adult beverages for a while before showtime.

The **Georgia Shakespeare** company (4484 Peachtree Rd. NE, 404/504-1473, www.gashakespeare.org) puts on a full season of The Bard within the confines of host institution Oglethorpe University. While the shows are within a theater venue, many people opt for a pre-show picnic on the scenic grounds just outside.

CINEMA

In addition to a plethora of the usual generic multiplexes, Atlanta offers several unique movie-going experiences. The oldest operating movie theatre in Atlanta is the **Plaza Theatre** (1049 Ponce De Leon Ave., 404/873-1939, www.plazaatlanta.com) in Midtown. It delivers a steady diet of kitschy classics and pulp fiction-style movies, with frequent midnight screenings of the Rocky Horror Picture Show.

For a flavor of high-quality Los Angeles-style cinema, head to Landmark Theatres' **Midtown Art Cinema** (931 Monroe Dr., 404/879-0160, www.landmarktheatres.com), generally considered the best new-release theatre in the city with the best atmosphere.

There are two IMAX theatres in Atlanta: the Fernbank Museum of Natural History's **Rankin M. Smith IMAX Theatre** (767 Clifton Rd., 404/929-6400, www.fernbankmuseum.org), which shows science and nature-related films; and **Regal Atlantic Station Stadium 16 & IMAX** (261 19th St., 404/347-9894, www.imax.com), which offers various IMAX-formatted films in addition to a wide variety of non-IMAX new releases.

FESTIVALS
January

Understandably, a huge focus in his hometown is the **Martin Luther King Jr. Birthday Celebration** (404/526-8900, www.thekingcenter.org). The civil rights leader's birthday and national holiday is marked with a variety of events, most centering in or around the MLK Jr. National Historic Site (www.nps.gov) in Downtown. The keynote event is

WHAT HAPPENED TO BUCKHEAD?

Back in the 1980s and 1990s, Buckhead was a nationally renowned Party Central: specifically in the several-block entertainment area known as Buckhead Village. It was jammed with bars and live music venues that stayed hopping until 4am every night and attracted everybody from college students to yuppies to visiting CEOs. Here's how it happened, and how it all went away:

A gradual downturn through the 1970s convinced city officials to lift minimum parking requirements for nightclubs in order to encourage development. That it did, and soon the Village was chock-a-block with popular watering holes and hordes of partiers pub-crawling between them, an atmosphere that was likened to "Mardi Gras every night."

The 1980s were the glory days, with the Roxy Theatre (now the restored Buckhead Theatre) hosting some of the hottest bands on a weekly basis. By the mid-1990s, however, the Village had over 100 liquor licenses, gangsta rap was more popular than rock 'n' roll, and the crowds and cruising became more unruly.

Everything came to a head one January Sunday in 2000 when the Super Bowl was being played in Atlanta. Two people were shot and killed at a club called Cobalt in a high-profile case involving NFL player Ray Lewis, who was implicated in the killings. Though Lewis was later acquitted, the PR damage was done. Another multiple shooting a couple of years later involving the rapper P. Diddy's entourage sealed Buckhead Village's fate. Residents persuaded the city to make last call at 2:30am and to tighten up on liquor licenses.

Partying gradually followed the path of least resistance to other areas of town. Developer Ben Carter began buying up the Village's nine acres to make way for his massive and ambitious Buckhead Atlanta multi-use planned development. In 2007, acknowledging the imminent demise of the Village's old character, a "Bye Bye Buckhead" party was held that attracted thousands. Soon nearly all the clubs were bulldozed, just in time for the market collapse. The last of the old bars to close was Fado's Irish Pub.

In 2011 the OliverMcMillan company took over the stalled development. As of this writing, their cranes work slowly over the desolate urban stretch.

---

the annual March (www.mlkmarchaaar.org) down Auburn Avenue from Peachtree Street to Jackson Street. Ebenezer Baptist Church typically hosts an annual memorial service, and the MLK Jr. Birth Home often holds an open house. While the Atlanta Symphony Orchestra has generally played a memorial concert at King's alma mater, Morehouse College, in recent years they've begun playing the concert at Atlanta Symphony Hall on Peachtree Street.

March

Since 1976 the **Atlanta Film Festival** (678/929-8103, www.atlantafilmfestival.com) has brought Academy-Award qualifying indie and first-run films to town. Its main venue these days is the Landmark Midtown Art Cinema (931 Monroe Dr. NE, 404/879-0408, www.landmarktheatres.com).

April

For 75 years Atlantans have gathered in Piedmont Park for the annual **Dogwood Festival** (Piedmont Park, 404/817-6642, www.dogwood.org). While the focus is obviously on the blooming dogwoods, the Festival itself is largely an open-air arts-and-crafts market featuring vendors from all over the Southeast, plus of course lots of food and music.

It's not often that a neighborhood festival is recommended for out-of-town visitors, but that's the case with the always fun and festive **Inman Park Festival** (www.inmanparkfestival. org), which happens the last weekend in April. Set in Atlanta's first planned neighborhood and now one of its most vibrant and up-and-coming, the festival features music, an eccentric and fun Saturday parade, and a popular tour of homes on Friday, and of course the area's many awesome new restaurants are open, often with extended hours. It's a festival of a neighborhood artfully reclaimed from blight, and the overall sense of optimism pervades.

May

The city's premier foodie event is the **Atlanta Food & Wine Festival** (404/474-7330, www.atlfoodandwinefestival.com). Perhaps strangely, given Atlanta's long association with high-profile chefs, it's a comparatively young event, having only started in 2006. Eateries and eaters, both highfalutin and lowbrow, come together for this popular Midtown event. The typical host venue is the Loews Atlanta Hotel at 11th and Peachtree Streets, with booths including the popular Tasting Tents radiating out a couple of blocks. Extensive evening events happen at various establishments around town, and there are frequent classes, seminars, and demonstrations as well. Tiered ticketing provides various levels of access, from the basic one-event ticket at $65 to an all-inclusive weekend pass for $500.

The **Atlanta Jazz Festival** (404/546-6820, www.atlantafestivals.com) is one of America's largest free jazz fests. Location and timing of the festival have bounced around over the years, but the current incarnation in Piedmont Park over the Memorial Day Weekend seems to be a real crowd-pleaser.

June

If you're in Atlanta in June it seems a shame to miss the **Virginia-Highland Summer Fest** (http://vahi.org), which offers the chance to enjoy the full measure of fun in one of the city's most popular and vibrant neighborhoods.

July

Stone Mountain Fourth of July (1000 Robert E. Lee Blvd., Stone Mountain, 770/498-5690, www.stonemountainpark.com, $10 parking) celebrations are always hugely well attended and feature a variety of events, culminating of course in a big fireworks display launched from areas at the top and bottom of Stone Mountain itself. Immediately prior to the fireworks,

which are actually put on two consecutive nights, is a special laser show. I strongly advise getting here early as parking places and good spots on the lawn from which to observe the fireworks fill up fast.

A large section of Midtown shuts down for the annual **Peachtree Road Race** (404/231-9064, www.peachtreeroadrace.org), happening each Fourth of July rain or shine. Even MARTA adjusts its schedule, starting trains at 5am that day to accommodate the lack of automotive traffic and the rush of runners and observers. The six-mile course starts in Buckhead and winds down Peachtree to take 10th Street to the finish in Piedmont Park, where an assortment of food, drink, and fun awaits. The foot race starts at 7:30am, with a wheelchair race beginning at 6:45am.

The **Chattahoochee River Summer Splash** (678/538-1200, www.nps.gov) in late July offers a festive opportunity for a six-mile float down the Chattahoochee River National Recreation Area.

The **National Black Arts Festival** (404/730-7315, http://nbaf.org) focuses on the African American cultural experience, including music, theater, literature, and film. The main weekend event centers on activities in Centennial Olympic Park, but satellite events happen at venues all around, including a gallery crawl and multiple jazz concerts.

September

Definitely not to be confused with Underground Atlanta, the **Atlanta Underground Film Festival** (1200 Foster St., www.auff.org) hosts edgy short films curated from national submissions. The venue, the Goat Farm Arts Center, is a restored warehouse and multi-use performing arts hub for Atlanta's more cutting-edge arts community.

Easily Atlanta's most highly regarded single music event, **Music Midtown** (www.musicmidtown.com) in Piedmont Park still offers a stunning variety of top-name artists despite the economy having taken a toll on its attendance in recent years. What used to be a three-day event is now down to two, but the 2012 edition featured Foo Fighters, Pearl Jam, the Avett Brothers, and local hero Ludacris. Not too shabby.

October

The South's largest such event and one of the oldest Pride Festivals in the United States, the over-40-year-old **Atlanta Pride** (404/382-7588, www.atlantapride.org) attracts huge crowds to Piedmont Park and satellite venues over the course of an October weekend, timed to mark the Stonewall riots and National Coming Out Day. Entertainment is top notch, with past performers including Nicki Minaj and Indigo Girls. And of course the main event is the Pride Parade down Peachtree Street to Piedmont Park on Saturday and its spinoff parades, the Dyke March and the Trans March.

Technically separate from Atlanta Pride but happening concurrently, **Out on Film** (404/296-3807, www.outonfilm.org) has been screening gay- and lesbian-oriented fare for a quarter century now. Currently based at the Landmark Midtown Art Cinema (931 Monroe Dr. NE, 404/879-0408, www.landmarktheatres.com), the festival also offers extensive Q&As with filmmakers and a host of special events.

The **Little Five Points Halloween** (404/230-2884, www.l5phalloween.com) celebration is everything you'd expect from this hipster-bohemian area. Let's just say it's probably not for small children.

The most vibrant, homegrown musical genre is celebrated at the **A3C Hip Hop Festival** (www.a3cfestival.com), which calls itself the nation's largest hip-hop festival. It happens over a long weekend and features concerts, workshops, and merchandise. Performances and events come fast, furious, and in dizzying numbers, with a focus on up-and-coming artists rather than huge names. Past lineups have included Raekwon, Yelawolf, and Twista.

Atlanta has a large and influential Greek-American community, and the annual **Atlanta Greek Festival** (404/633-5870, www.atlantagreekfestival.org) packs in the crowds for a taste of souvlaki, baklava, and other goodies. There is of course music and dancing as well. It happens at the grounds of the Greek Orthodox Cathedral of the Annunciation (2500 Clairmont Rd. NE) in North Druid Hills.

The most important annual cycling-blading-skating event is **Atlanta Streets Alive** (404/881-1112, www.atlantastreetsalive.com) every October, with several miles of North Highland Avenue being shut off to car traffic and restricted to bikes and skaters only. Businesses and restaurants stay open along with lots of activities.

ATLANTA

Shopping

Atlanta is the Southeastern mecca of shopping. Every possible chain and boutique brand is represented along with a vibrant independent retail community. Mall shoppers won't be disappointed either; Atlanta has some of the nation's oldest. Though, the malls have all been substantially renovated since then, of course.

Atlanta's key shopping districts are the Buckhead-Perimeter area north of Downtown; Midtown (including Virginia-Highland, Little Five Points, and Atlantic Station); and Downtown itself.

ANTIQUES

Easily Atlanta's most beloved antiques-vintage store, **Paris on Ponce** (716 Ponce de Leon Ave., 404/249-9965, www.parisonponce.com, Mon.-Sat. 11am-6pm, Sun. noon-6pm) in Virginia-Highland, is as the name implies redolent of old Europe and full of unique furniture and assorted decorative items, all with a certain whimsical and quirky allure that treads the line between classic and kitsch.

The **Miami Circle Design District** (www.miamicircleshops.com) in Buckhead is commonly considered the headquarters of the hardcore Atlanta antiquing community, and indeed of the entire Southeast. Located in a large cul-de-sac, it comprises about 80 antique shops, home goods stores, and art galleries; the enormity of its offerings is obviously beyond our scope here. But a few highlights are the ornate home goods of **Burroughs Wellington** (631 Miami Circle, 404/264-1616, www.burroughswellington.com, Mon.-Sat. 10am-5pm); the fabrics and furniture of **Curran Designers** (737 Miami Circle, 404/237-4246, www.curran-aat.com, Mon.-Sat. 10am-5:30pm); the classic Euro stylings at **Foxglove Antiques** (699 Miami Circle, 404/233-0222, www.foxgloveantiques.com, Mon.-Sat. 10am-5pm); and the unique Chinese offerings at **Mandarin Antiques** (700 Miami Circle, 404/467-1727, www.mandarinantiquesinc.com, Mon.-Fri. 10am-5:30pm, Sat. 10am-5pm).

Another antiques center in Buckhead is the **West Village** (www.westvillagega.com), a loose collection of quaint and quirky antiques and home goods merchants within the triangle formed by East Andrews Drive, Roswell Road, and West Paces Ferry Road.

Up near the Perimeter, in the town of Chamblee, is the perennially popular **Chamblee Antique Row** (3519 Broad St., 770/458-6316, www.antiquerow.com), a retail district comprising nearly two dozen antique and clothing stores, plus a few restaurants. Charming and pedestrian-friendly, it's a quick three blocks from the Chamblee MARTA station.

ART GALLERIES

While you're taking in the more traditional exhibits at the High Museum, you might want to extend your Midtown art crawl to **Atlanta Contemporary Art Center** (535 Means St., 404/688-1970, www.thecontemporary.org, Tues.-Sat. 11am-5pm, Sun. noon-5pm), a nonprofit cooperative established in 1973 and in its current space since 1989, dedicated to the work of new Atlanta artists.

A massive converted warehouse hosting about 300 individual studios and performing arts spaces, **Goat Farm Arts Center** (1200 Foster St.) on the west edge of Midtown is one of Atlanta's most unique cultural spaces. It has two indoor performance spaces and three outdoor stages, all hosting experimental or indie-style work. The Goat Farm is performance- and exhibition-based, and doesn't really have regular hours. You can visit anytime, and the on-site coffee shop is open daily 10:30am-7pm.

An important part of the burgeoning art scene in the Atlantic Station area, **Sandler Hudson Gallery** (1009 Marietta St., 404/817-3300, www.sandlerhudson.com, Tues.-Fri. 10am-5pm, Sat. noon-5pm) focuses on contemporary Southern artists. In addition to its display space there's a sculpture area on the roof.

A key arts anchor in the up-and-coming Castleberry Hill area, **Besharat Gallery** (175

Peters St., 404/524-4781, www.besharatgallery.com, Fri.-Sat. 11am-6pm) and its companion space **Besharat Contemporary** (163 Peters St., 404/577-3660, www.besharatcontemporary.com, Tues.-Sat. 10am-5pm) together comprise one of the most-balanced visual arts experiences in the city, blending a respect for craft and tradition with a real commitment to showcasing more modern sensibilities. Nearby is **Zucot Gallery** (100 Centennial Olympic Park Dr., 404/380-1040, www.zucotgallery.com, Tues.-Fri. 3pm-9pm, Sat. noon-10pm), which keeps things fresh in its compellingly minimalist space by completely changing out the entire exhibit every two months or so.

Since 1997, **Young Blood Gallery and Boutique** (636 N. Highland Ave., 404/254-4127, www.youngbloodgallery.com, Tues.-Sat. noon-8pm, Sun. noon-6pm) has been a key part of the renaissance of the Virginia-Highland area as well as a leading exponent of the Atlanta underground arts and music scene. Their offerings tend toward the bold, modern, and vibrant, with a strong nod toward sequential art.

BOOKS

Atlanta has several unique and independent bookstores, though sadly the most notable of which, the gay- and lesbian-oriented Outwrite Books, closed in 2012.

It's not affiliated with Georgia Tech, but it is near campus and those of a math and science bent will enjoy the quirky, over half century-old **Engineer's Bookstore** (748 Marietta St., 404/221-1669, www.engrbookstore.com, Mon-Fri. 9am-5:30pm, Sat.10am-2pm), which is exactly what the name indicates: a haven for technically-oriented tomes.

Since 1989, Inman Park has been home to **A Cappella Books** (208 Haralson Ave., 404/681-5128, www.acappellabooks.com, Mon.-Sat. 11am-7pm, Sun. noon-6pm), which deals in new, used, and rare volumes and features a remarkably well-informed, engaged staff.

Bound To Be Read Books (481 Flat Shoals Ave., 404/522-0877, www.boundtoberead-books.com, Tues.-Thurs. 11am-9pm, Fri.-Sat.

11am-10pm, Sun. 1pm-6pm), an East Atlanta staple, has a very wide assortment, from fiction to technical books to gay and lesbian studies and literature.

The Green Room Actors Lounge (25 Bennett St., 404/351-4736, www.thegreen-roomatl.com, Wed. noon-9pm, Thu. noon-6pm, Fri. noon-11pm, Sat. 1pm-midnight) combines racks of books on acting, directing, and other aspects of show business with a stocked bar in a tony atmosphere. This is a favorite hangout of Atlanta's sizable theater community.

CLOTHES AND FASHION

The funky **Little Five Points** (L5P) neighborhood is a major thrift-vintage-counterculture shopping destination. The closest thing to an anchor store is **Junkman's Daughter** (464 Moreland Ave., 404/577-3188, www.thejunkmansdaughter.com, Mon.-Fri. 11am-7pm, Sat. 11am-8pm, Sun. noon-7pm), a combination vintage-novelty-tchotchke store and quasi-tourist trap. My favorite vintage shop in L5P is **Stefan's Vintage** (1160 Euclid Ave., 404/688-4929, www.stefansvintageclothing.com, Mon.-Sat. 11am-7pm, Sun. noon-6pm), the oldest store of its kind in Atlanta and where you can score some remarkable, wearable finds.

In the **Peachtree Battle** (2341 Peachtree Rd., www.branchprop.com) shopping center in Buckhead, a sort of deluxe strip mall setting, you'll find fun locally-owned stores such as the **Frolic Boutique** (2385 Peachtree Rd., 404/846-8002, www.frolicboutique.com, Mon.-Sat. 11am-6pm) and **Mint Julep** (2353 Peachtree Rd., 404/814-9155, www.mintjulepga.com, Mon.-Sat. 10am-6pm, Sun. 1pm-5pm), Atlanta's Lilly Pulitzer outlet.

The vibrant and friendly Virginia-Highland neighborhood offers a charming array of largely independent, locally-owned stores, often with a twist, such as the vintage store **Mooncake** (1019 Virginia Ave., 404/892-8043, Mon.-Sat. 11am-7pm), which hosts frequent trunk shows, and the original location of **Bill Hallman** (792 N. Highland Ave., 404/876-6055, www.bill-hallman.com, Mon.-Sat. 11am-8pm, Sun.

noon-7pm), which features a sleek take on both men's and women's up-to-the-moment fashions.

GROCERIES AND MARKETS

In addition to an endless variety of typical chain grocery stores, Atlanta has three locations of **Whole Foods** (www.wholefoodsmarket.com): in Buckhead (77 W. Paces Ferry Rd., 404/324-4100, Mon.-Sat. 7:30am-10pm, Sun. 9am-9pm); in Midtown (650 Ponce de Leon Ave., 404/853-1681, daily 8am-10pm); and in the suburb of Sandy Springs (5930 Roswell Rd., 404/236-0810, Mon.-Sat. 7am-10pm, Sun. 8:30am-9pm).

But the best overall health foods market in Atlanta is in Little Five Points, **Sevananda Natural Foods Market** (467 Moreland Ave., 404/681-2831, www.sevanandacoop.com, daily 8am-10pm). This member-owned organic foods cooperative has been around since the dawn of the health food movement in the early 1970s and offers not only tons of fresh produce and a deli, but every vitamin and health supplement you might want.

Specialty retailer **Trader Joe's** (www.traderjoes.com) has several Atlanta locations, chief among them the Midtown location (931 Monroe Dr., 404/815-9210, daily 8am-10pm) and the Buckhead location (3183 Peachtree Rd., 404/842-0907, daily 8am-9pm).

The metro Atlanta area is blessed with a wide variety of farmers markets. Each Saturday from April through mid-December in Midtown you'll find the **Peachtree Road Farmers Market** (2744 Peachtree Rd., www.peachtreeroadfarmersmarket.com, Apr.-mid-Dec. Sat. 9am-noon), on the grounds of the Cathedral of St. Philip. It is one of the largest in the metro area.

The most diverse farmers market is up in Doraville at the **Buford Highway Farmers Market** (5600 Buford Hwy., 770/455-0770, www.aofwc.com, daily 8am-10pm), which takes full advantage of the many cultures present in the area to provide a stunning array of produce and goods you're unlikely to find elsewhere.

Downtown near the Martin Luther King Jr. Historic Site you'll find the indoor **Sweet Auburn Curb Market** (corner of Edgewood Ave. and Jessie Hill Pkwy., 404/659-1665, www.sweetauburncurbmarket.com, Mon.-Sat. 8am-6pm), whose roots go back to the 1920s when it was called the Municipal Market and was a center of the local black community.

The **Grant Park Farmers Market** (600 Cherokee Ave., www.grantparkmarket.org, Apr.-Dec. Sun. 9:30am-1:30pm) is open April through December.

HOME GOODS

Chief among Atlanta's home goods offerings is one of the few **IKEA** (441 16th St., 404/745-4532, www.ikea.com, daily 10am-9pm) locations in the Deep South. You'll find it and its signature Swedish meatballs on the west side of town.

Virginia-Highland is definitely the main neighborhood for fun home goods shopping. Don't miss the quirky attraction of **Richards Variety** (931 Monroe Dr., 404/879-9877, www.richardsvarietystore.com, Mon.-Sat. 10am-8pm, Sun. noon-6pm), a half century-old staple featuring unusual novelties, toys, costumes, and other assorted party supplies.

Into recycling and sustainable living? Hit the **Re-Inspiration Store** (591 N. Highland Ave., 404/352-1971, www.reinspirationstore.com, Mon.-Thurs. 11am-6pm, Fri.-Sat. 10am-6pm, Sun. noon-5pm), right across from the iconic Manuel's Tavern. You'll find funky items and gifts made from repurposed things like spark plugs, pop tops, and shell casings.

Also in Virginia-Highland you'll find the charming and unique **The Indie-pendent** (1052 St. Charles Ave., 404/313-0004, www.theindie-pendent.com, Thurs.-Sat. 11am-5pm, Sun. 1pm-5pm), a hip and happening collection of DIY-style, regionally-handcrafted kitchen, home, and garden goods and jewelry and art.

MALLS

Atlanta's premier mall and one of the nation's oldest, having opened in 1959, is **Lenox Square** (3393 Peachtree Rd. NE, 404/233-6767, www.

simon.com, Mon-Sat. 10am-9pm, Sun. noon-6pm) in Buckhead, with about 250 stores on its four levels. Of course the current incarnation bears no resemblance whatsoever to the Eisenhower administration version; many costly renovations over the years have kept it at the cutting edge of retail, and unlike many suburban malls, Lenox is right in the middle of busy urban action. Anchor stores are Macy's, Bloomingdale's, and Neiman Marcus, and there's a *massive* Forever 21 as well as an Apple retail location. This being Buckhead, there are also many high-dollar boutique outlets of note: Faconnable, Nicole Miller, Bulgari, Fendi, Cartier, Burberry, and Prada, to name but a few. There's a convenient MARTA stop.

Close to Lenox Square and owned by the same investment group is **Phipps Plaza** (3500 Peachtree Rd. NE, 404/262-0992, www.simon.com, Mon-Sat. 10am-9pm, Sun. noon-5:30pm), an even more upscale Buckhead mall. Its anchors are Saks Fifth Avenue, Nordstrom, and Belk, with an impressive list of boutiques including Armani, Valentino, Jimmy Choo, Versace, and Tiffany. Also like Lenox Square, Phipps Plaza actually has fairly old roots by mall standards, having been built in 1969. Needless to say it has upgraded many times since then and is a veritable gleaming cathedral of upscale commercialism.

The simply and aptly named **Perimeter Mall** (4400 Ashford Dunwoody Rd., 770/394-4270, www.perimetermall.com, Mon-Sat. 10am-9pm, Sun. noon-7pm) was the first such project along the I-285 corridor north of Atlanta proper in the satellite city of Dunwoody (it's served by the Dunwoody MARTA station). Current anchors are Von Maur, Dillard's, Macy's, and Nordstrom, and there's an Apple retail store.

Way outside the Perimeter in Buford, Georgia, about 30 miles from Downtown Atlanta, is the massive **Mall of Georgia** (3333 Buford Dr., Buford, 678/482-8788, www.mallofgeorgia.com, Mon-Sat. 10am-9pm, Sun. noon-6pm). It has over 200 stores on three levels, including anchors Belk, Dillard's, JCPenney, Macy's, Nordstrom, Dick's Sporting Goods, and Haverty's, plus an Apple retail store.

A totally reclaimed light industrial area turned mixed-use, **Atlantic Station** (1380 Atlantic Dr., 404/733-1221, www.atlanticstation.com, Mon-Sat. 10am-9pm, Sun. noon-7pm) offers an outdoor pedestrian-style mall featuring H&M, Z Gallerie, and more familiar chain stores such as Banana Republic, American Eagle, and Nine West. Atlantic Station occasionally hosts traveling exhibits, such as a recent stop by a show of artifacts from the Titanic.

About halfway between Atlanta and Macon off I-75 you'll find the sprawling **Tanger Outlet Center** (1000 Tanger Dr., Locust Grove, 770-957-5310, www.tangeroutlet.com, Mon.-Sat. 9am-9pm, Sun. 11am-7pm), which has bargain outlets ranging from J. Crew to Lucky Brand to Skechers.

If you're staying Downtown in the cluster of high-rise hotels, the most convenient shopping center is **The Mall at Peachtree Center** (231 Peachtree St. NE, 404/654-1296, www.peachtreecenter.com, Mon.-Sat. 10am-6pm, Sun. hours vary) at the corner of Peachtree Street and International Boulevard and directly connected to the Hyatt Regency and the Marriott Marquis. It features about 60 stores of varying quality, but these days the food court is more active than the retail sector, with 30 food outlets to choose from.

As the name implies, **Underground Atlanta** (50 Upper Alabama St., 404/523-2311, www.underground-atlanta.com, Mon.-Thurs. 10am-8pm, Fri.-Sat. 10am-9pm, Sun. noon-6pm) is an underground mall, legacy of an urban layer built up in the 1920s over previously existing rail lines. It has gone through several incarnations over the last half century, as the city tries to keep it afloat as a viable entertainment and shopping destination (a recent effort involved extending bar closing times to 4am). Sketchy and long removed from its heyday in the 1980s, Underground Atlanta today is an idea that sounds cooler than it really is; even the shops are mostly downscale here in an area of town which frankly is not Atlanta's safest or most welcoming. There will be many signs and ads urging you to go here, but I advise against it.

MUSIC AND RECORDS

In Little Five Points you'll find a couple of neat indie record stores. **Criminal Records** (1154 Euclid Ave., 404/215-9511, www.criminalatl. com, Mon.-Sat. 11am-9pm, Sun. noon-7pm) not only has an outstanding selection of happening music, they often host record release parties with live entertainment by the hottest regional bands.

Wax 'n' Facts (432 Moreland Ave., 404/525-2275, www.waxnfacts.com, Mon.-Sat. 11am-8pm, Sun. noon-6pm), in business since 1976, has an awesome vinyl collection and also hosts performances.

OUTDOOR OUTFITTERS

Huge outdoor retailer **REI** (www.rei.com) has two locations in the metro area: one near Druid

Hills (1800 Northeast Expressway, 404/633-6508, Mon.-Sat. 10am-9pm, Sun. 11am-6pm) and the other on the Perimeter (1165 Perimeter Center, 770/901-9200, Mon.-Sat. 10am-9pm, Sun. 11am-6pm).

Regional chain **Half Moon Outfitters** (1034 Highland Ave., 404/249-7921, www.half-moonoutfitters.com, Mon-Fri. 10am-7pm, Sat. 10am-8pm, Sun. 11am-6pm) has a friendly location in Virginia-Highland, selling clothing in addition to gear.

In Buckhead, go to **High Country Outfitters** (3906 Roswell Rd., 404/814-0999, www.high-countryoutfitters.com, Mon.-Fri. 10am-8pm, Sat. 10am-6pm, Sun. noon-6pm), serving Atlanta since 1975.

For those wanting trendy adventurous outerwear, head to the **North Face retail store** (35A W. Paces Ferry Rd., 404/467-0119, www. thenorthface.com, Mon.-Sat. 10am-8pm, Sun. 11am-6pm) in Buckhead.

Sports and Recreation

Atlanta's generally moderate weather and fairly mild winters mean residents spend a lot of time outdoors, a nice break from the city's legendary congestion. Generally considered an awful spectator sports town, Atlanta is better oriented to those of the more active persuasion, and it has plenty of parks and facilities to accommodate them.

PARKS

For a city known for its well-used superhighways, Atlanta has a surprisingly large amount of green space, and it is heavily used and admired by residents.

First landscaped in 1904, **Piedmont Park** (1320 Monroe Dr., 404/875-7275, www.pied-montpark.org, daily 6am-11pm) in Midtown is the most popular public park, not to mention the most conveniently located. Two major expansions, one in 2008 and one in 2011, brought its area to 190 acres and added a bathhouse-pool area. In addition to miles of jogging and biking paths, there's a bocce court

and a leash-free dog park. A legacy of Atlanta's Victorian era expansion, Piedmont Park includes some areas of the old Civil War battlefield. It has hosted much sports history as well, being the home of the Atlanta Crackers pro baseball team and, during the leather helmet era, the home of the great University of Georgia and Georgia Tech football rivalry.

Chastain Park (Lake Forest Drive and Powers Ferry Rd., www.chastainpark.org, daily dawn-dusk) in Buckhead is actually Atlanta's largest park at nearly 300 acres. It includes a popular amphitheater, a pool, a golf course, a new tennis center, and lots of jogging and biking opportunities.

Atlanta's oldest park is **Grant Park** (bordered by Boulevard SE, Atlanta Ave., Cherokee Ave., Sydney St., Park Ave., and Berne St.), where you'll find Zoo Atlanta and the Cyclorama. It befell neglect until the 1990s, and is sort of playing catch-up with the other city parks. It is currently under the stewardship of the Grant Park Conservancy (404/521-0938, www.gpconservancy.org), which offers walking tours exploring the rich Victorian history of the park and surrounding neighborhood of the same name.

Downtown has the 200-acre, six-mile-long **Freedom Park** (North Ave. and Moreland Ave., www.freedompark.org, daily dawn-dusk) linear green space between the Martin Luther King Jr. National Historic Site and the Jimmy Carter Library. It is best known in local lore as being the former civic battleground of the "Freeway Revolt," a successful grassroots effort in the 1970s to stop the massive proposed Stone Mountain Freeway from paving over the entire area. (You may have noticed by now that most Atlanta politics revolve around roads of some type.)

An ambitious, evolving, ongoing project, the **Atlanta BeltLine** (http://beltline.org) seeks to connect virtually nearly 50 neighborhoods throughout the entire metro area to a nearly 40-mile network of multi-use trails loosely based on old rail lines, with at least five MARTA public transit stops along the way. The first phase of the Beltline opened to the public: The Eastside Trail connects Piedmont Park, Inman Park, and the Old Fourth Ward and is probably the most germane to visitors.

RUNNING, WALKING, AND BIKING

Piedmont Park (1320 Monroe Dr., 404/875-7275, www.piedmontpark.org, daily 6am-11pm) has three basic footpaths (no bicycles allowed): the Active Oval, the Lake Loop, and the Park Loop, and they interlock for a customized experience. Cycling is only allowed on the main roadway through the park and the meadow paths at 10th Street. **Chastain Park** (www.chastainpark.org) has two freshly renovated 5K loops and a 3K loop. Park at Powers Ferry Road near the amphitheater.

Atlanta has a robust running community, with a roster of marathons, triathlons, 5Ks, and 10Ks. Though it's a fairly short race, the city's marquee runner's event is the **Peachtree Road Race** (404/231-9064, www.peachtreeroadrace.org), a very popular six-mile course down the

city's main street each Fourth of July morning, ending in Piedmont Park. Other key events on the running calendar include the **ATL 20K Relay and 10K** on Labor Day weekend, the **Allstate Half-Marathon** in October, and the **Atlanta-Chattanooga-Atlanta Relay** in October. Go to http://rungeorgia.com for more info.

The moderately hilly terrain of the Georgia Piedmont makes it good bicycling territory. There's a bike path from Piedmont Avenue downtown all the way to Stone Mountain. Within **Stone Mountain Park** (1000 Robert E. Lee Blvd., 770/498-5690, www.stonemountainpark.com, daily 10am-10pm, $10 entrance fee) are a lot of opportunities as well. The **Atlanta BeltLine** (http://beltline.org) offers multi-use trails all around metro Atlanta, with a completed course connecting Piedmont Park, Inman Park, and the Old Fourth Ward. See www.atlantabike.org for more info.

There's an actual velodrome in the Atlanta area, **Dick Lane Velodrome** (1889 Lexington Ave., 404/769-0012, www.dicklanevelodrome.com) in East Point, one of only a couple dozen such facilities in the United States. Races are every Saturday night.

RAFTING AND BOATING

Whitewater rafting in the ATL? Most definitely. **"Shootin' the Hootch,"** or rafting down the Chattahoochee, has been a rite of passage for environmentalists and partying college students alike for decades. A 50-mile stretch of the river is managed by the National Park Service as the **Chattahoochee River National Recreation Area** (www.nps.gov). Several private companies are authorized to offer tube and raft rental; the two recommended options are **Chattahoochee Outfitters** (203 Azalea Dr., 770/650-1008, daily Apr.-Nov., Fri.-Sun. Dec.-Mar.), who leave from the northern suburb of Roswell, and **High Country Outfitters** (3906B Roswell Rd., 404/814-0999, www.highcountryoutfitters.com, Mon.-Fri. 10am-8pm, Sat. 10am-6pm, Sun. noon-6pm) who put in at two locations (Johnson Ferry and Powers Island). Keep in mind that generally speaking children under five aren't allowed to "shoot the hootch" at all for safety reasons. Of course you can opt to put your own vessel into the Hootch.

SWIMMING

Piedmont Park sports a new **Aquatic Center** (404/875-7275, www.piedmontpark.org, summer Mon.-Fri. 10am-5pm, Sat.-Sun. noon-5pm, $4 adults, $2 children). **The Grant Park Pool** ($4 adults, $2 children) has weekend hours during the summer. The **Candler Park Pool** ($4 adults, $2 children) is operated by the City of Atlanta.

GOLF

Two public courses of note are in Buckhead. The 18-hole, public **Bobby Jones Golf Course** (384 Woodward Way, 404/355-1009, www.bobbyjonesgc.com, $30-45) has been around since 1932 and sits atop part of the old Battle of Peachtree Creek site. The suitably named Peachtree Battle Creek winds amidst five holes. **North Fulton Municipal Golf Course** (216 W. Wieuca Rd. NW, 404/255-0723, www.americangolf.com/north-fulton-golf-course, $40) is in Chastain Park and gets very crowded.

TENNIS

The **Sharon J. Lester Tennis Center** (400 Park Dr., 404/853-3461, www.utatennis.com, Mon.-Thurs. 9am-10pm, Fri. 9am-9pm, Sat.-Sun. 9am-6pm) at Piedmont Park offers 12 lighted hard courts. The **Chastain Park Tennis Center** (110 W. Wieuca Rd. NW, 404/255-3210, www.utatennis.com, Mon.-Thurs. 9am-9pm, Fri. 9am-1pm and 3pm-7pm, Sat. 9am-7pm, Sun. 11am-7pm) is a brand new, Earthcraft building with nine lighted hard courts.

SPECTATOR SPORTS

The term "fair weather fan" may have been coined with Atlantans in mind. Atlanta sports fans are among the most lukewarm in the United States, at least with regards to professional sports. College football, on the other hand....

The major league baseball **Atlanta Braves** (Turner Field, 755 Hank Aaron Dr. SE, www.

atlanta.braves.mlb.com) play at Turner Field, aka "The Ted," and are quite popular by Atlanta standards. But you can usually score tickets ($30-80) since the games rarely sell out, with average attendance hovering around 30,000. A day at The Ted is an iconic Atlanta experience, both because of the ballpark's own charms (including above-average food) as well as the fact that Braves fans tend to be very well behaved. Unlike many metro area ballparks, there are plenty of pay-parking areas within a quick walk, about $10 per car. The closest MARTA stop is Five Points Station, which isn't close to the stadium at all, but every game day special Braves shuttles run from Underground Atlanta right across from Five Points directly to Turner Field and back again. The Braves shuttle is free with a MARTA transfer ticket; alternatively you can buy a Breeze card ($5.50) at Underground Atlanta. Shuttles begin 90 minutes before game time.

The NFL **Atlanta Falcons** (1 Georgia Dome Dr., 404/223-8444, www.atlantafalcons.com) play at the Georgia Dome just down the road from Turner Field. There is a Georgia Dome MARTA stop, but the Vine City Station is about as close. Tickets run anywhere from $60-180. The Falcons have an interactive site at http://vsv.falcons.com, which is specially designed to help with seating and parking issues.

The NBA **Atlanta Hawks** (1 Philips Dr., 404/878-3000, www.nba.com, www.philipsarena.com) play in the newish Philips Arena next to the CNN Center Downtown. While the team is much better these days than in some eras past, the games almost never sell out and single game tickets are quite affordable considering the upscale experience in "The Phil" (even the restrooms are nice). There's a Philips Arena MARTA Station that drops you off right here, so transportation and parking are no excuses not to go.

The **Atlanta Silverbacks** (3200 Silverbacks Way, 404/969-4900, www.atlantasilverbacks.com) play professional soccer at the second-tier level in the North American Soccer League. Their home pitch is the soccer-specific Silverbacks Park in Chamblee, just outside

Turner Field, home of the Atlanta Braves

town, which once hosted an Adidas commercial featuring David Beckham.

Atlanta has had two professional hockey teams in the past, the Atlanta Flames (which departed for Calgary in 1980) and the Atlanta Thrashers (who moved to Winnipeg in 2011). Currently the only pro action on the ice is from the **Gwinnett Gladiators** (Arena at Gwinnett Center, 6400 Sugarloaf Pkwy., 770/497-5100, www.gwinnettgladiators.com), who play in Duluth.

Autumn in the South means college football. Like most Georgians, Atlanta mostly roots for the Georgia Bulldogs in Athens, but in-town the hottest ticket is for **Georgia Tech** (www.

ramblinwreck.com) home football games. The Yellow Jackets play Downtown at Bobby Dodd Stadium at Historic Grant Field at North Avenue and Techwood Drive on the corner of campus (the Yellow Jackets' chief rivals, the Georgia Bulldogs, jokingly refer to Tech as the "North Avenue Trade School").

For years Georgia State University was primarily known as an urban commuter school, but the addition of a high-level football program in 2010 immediately made the **Georgia State Panthers** (1 Georgia Dome Dr., www.georgiastatesports.com) a high-profile enterprise. They play in the Georgia Dome.

ATLANTA

Accommodations

As a major commercial center, convention location, and home to the world's busiest airport, Atlanta understandably offers a truly mind-boggling number of hotel rooms. As you might expect, there is a huge range in quality, from world-class to miserable. One local plus, however, is that because of the massive volume of lodging, prices are often surprisingly reasonable; though always be sure to inquire beforehand about common and typically poorly-publicized surcharges such as parking and high-speed Internet.

Hartsfield-Jackson International Airport is virtually a city of its own, with an extensive lodging infrastructure to match (at least 60 hotels in the immediate area). Prices are a bit lower than in more desirable areas of town, but the service is typically much lower as well, not to mention the high stress level of most guests either rushing to catch a plane or dead-tired from flying all day.

Because of Atlanta's size and the fact that there's not a huge price variation throughout the city, these accommodations are organized by area first and then by price.

DOWNTOWN
$150-300
Fresh off a $65 million renovation, one of downtown's oldest premier properties is now one of the most posh. Built in the late 1960s and virtually the harbinger of Atlanta's boom period, the ◖ **Hyatt Regency** (265 Peachtree St. NE, 404/577-1234, www.atlantaregency. hyatt.com, $190-230) offers all the crisp professionalism of that chain with a modernist minimalism. The renovated rooms are geared to the tourist as well as the business traveler and conventioneer, with all the in-room amenities everyone demands these days along with the usual crisp professionalism of the Hyatt chain. Designed by noted Atlanta architect John Portman (a nearby street is named after him), the Hyatt's atrium is something of an architectural legend in its own right: The ultra-fast

glass elevators were the first of their kind in Atlanta and still offer a thrill for guests of all ages. When first built, the 24-story Hyatt was considered very tall and featured a revolving restaurant at the top, which subsequently closed as much taller skyscrapers rose all around it. The Hyatt now offers two good dining options on the ground floor. The attractions of Centennial Olympic Park, such as the Georgia Aquarium and the World of Coca-Cola, are a short walk away.

It's no longer the tallest hotel in the world, as it briefly was when first built in 1976, but the 73-story **Westin Peachtree Plaza** (210 Peachtree St. NE, 404/659-1400, www.starwood.com, over $250) still offers stunning views, not the least of which can be found at its famous revolving rooftop restaurant, the Sun Dial (daily lunch and dinner, $20). Each of the nearly 1,100 rooms in this John Portman-designed edifice (he also designed the Hyatt

the Hyatt Regency, downtown

© JIM MOREKIS

Regency and the nearby Marriott Marquis) feature floor-to-ceiling windows. While taller than Portman's Hyatt, the Westin looks very similar and is often mistaken for it. The rooms aren't large, but they are well equipped and tastefully furnished.

One of the better Downtown stays and probably the best stay for any Georgia Tech-oriented visit is the **Hampton Inn Atlanta-Georgia Tech** (244 North Ave. NW, 404/881-0881, www.hamptoninn.com, $160). Situated literally on the edge of Tech's sprawling urban campus, the Hampton Inn is also quite convenient to the Centennial Olympic Park attractions like the Georgia Aquarium and the World of Coca-Cola. Be aware, however, that as with many Downtown hotels, parking is valet-only and not cheap.

If it's access to the Centennial Olympic Park area you're looking for, look no further than the **Embassy Suites Hotel** (267 Marietta St., 404/223-2300, www.embassysuites.com, $180-300), literally adjacent and within a stone's throw of the Georgia Aquarium (ask about package deals). The pool area actually overlooks the well-maintained park, which is a nice touch.

Over $300

Now run by the Marriott chain, Atlanta's first entry into the boutique hotel market was **Glenn Hotel** (110 Marietta St., 404/521-2250, www.glennhotel.com, over $300). The main attraction of this property in the renovated Fairlie-Poplar district is the use of "personal hosts," that is, butlers, who are on call for you 24 hours a day. There's a popular rooftop bar, the SkyLounge, which is definitely worth a visit for the scintillating views as well as the signature cocktails. The in-house restaurant, Glenn's Kitchen, is a cut above most hotel offering and specializes in New Southern cuisine.

MIDTOWN
$150-300

Perhaps surprisingly, Atlanta is actually behind the curve in the boutique hotel trend. One of the newest and most charming is the

◀ **Artmore** (1302 W. Peachtree St., 404/876-6100, www.artmorehotel.com, around $150), an independently-owned delight in Midtown. This restored 1925 Spanish Mediterranean, with an art deco look inside and out, offers a little taste of Beverly Hills in this older area of Atlanta, but without the exorbitant price. Unlike most boutique hotels, the rooms are quite, well, roomy. While the breakfast is called continental, it's likely one of the most extensive and well-prepared continental breakfasts you'll enjoy. While not particularly suitable for business travelers, this is a fantastic and, for Atlanta, inexpensive choice for a romantic getaway or a fun-loving family stay.

While occasionally overlooked because of its location across the street from the Fox Theatre and right next to the equally historic (and huge) Georgian Terrace Hotel, **Hotel Indigo** (683 Peachtree St., 404/874-9200, www.hotelindigo.com, $175) offers one of Atlanta's few real boutique hotel experiences. Like most boutique hotels, the emphasis is on quality rather than size, and the Indigo's bedrooms and bathrooms are pretty small. Pet-friendly and personable, the Indigo is a nice break from the occasionally impersonal level of service at Atlanta's bigger chain hotels.

Atlanta doesn't have much history left, but the **Georgian Terrace Hotel** (659 Peachtree St. NE, 866/845-7551, www.thegeorgianterrace.com, $175-350) is still here. This grand 1911 Beaux Arts masterpiece hosted Clark Gable, Vivien Leigh, and other *Gone with the Wind* cast members for the film's premiere, and the Georgian Terrace still retains that old Hollywood appeal. Contrary to popular opinion, the film's premiere didn't take place across the street at the Fox Theatre, nonetheless it's thrilling to have that ornate historic venue to gaze on, and of course to visit for a show. Other famous guests at the Georgian Terrace have included F. Scott Fitzgerald, Walt Disney, President Calvin Coolidge, and Arthur Murray, who literally began his dance instruction career in the hotel's ballroom. While the rooms have of course been renovated since then, most recently in 2009 (there's actually an entire new

Georgian Terrace Hotel

© JIM MOREKIS

section built in 1991 originally as condos), keep in mind this is a historic property with the usual eccentricities, including slow elevators and rooms which often vary widely in size and orientation. A bustling restaurant of fair-to-middling quality, Livingston's, spills out onto the roomy patio area along Peachtree Street. And, two words: Rooftop pool!

BUCKHEAD
Over $300

Atlanta's premier luxury-spa hotel, the **(Mandarin Oriental** (3376 Peachtree St. NE, 404/995-7500, www.mandarinoriental.com) is an oasis of calm in busy Buckhead, but with every bit of the swank expected in that tony area. The emphasis at the Mandarin is on pampering guests to the nth degree, from the plush and spacious bedrooms to the luxurious bathrooms to the state-of-the-art high-def plasma TVs artfully arranged throughout. There are several tiers of rooms, from the "budget" two-person King ($325) up to the incredible Mandarin Suite ($7,000). The level of relaxed attentiveness and confident professionalism of the staff is something of a local legend.

Buckhead's other premier luxury-spa lodging, the Starwood property **(St. Regis Atlanta** (88 W. Paces Ferry Rd., 404/563-7900, www.stregis.com, $450-700), is particularly recommended for those for whom a swank, old-school hotel pool experience is a must (it's open 24 hours a day!). The rooms are world-class as well, with a level of taste and furnishing which seem almost too good to be true. The extremely high level of customer service is vectored through butlers, who seemingly exist to serve your every whim at any hour of the day, providing everything from ice (no loud vending machines) to wakeup calls. As at the Mandarin, there's an ultra-exclusive penthouse suite, the Empire.

PERIMETER
Under $150

For a stay up near "the Perimeter," aka I-285 north of Buckhead, you'll do no better than **(Holiday Inn Perimeter/Dunwoody** (4386

Chamblee-Dunwoody Rd., 770/457-6363, www.holidayinn.com, under $150), one of the more well-appointed and professionally staffed examples of that hotel chain, at incredibly low prices for Atlanta. They have state-of-the-art room renovations (including the trendy Keurig one-cup coffeemakers) and a hotel bar that's clearly a step above the usual.

$150-300

Another good stay in the clean and safe (if overly commercial) Perimeter area is the **Sheraton Atlanta Perimeter** (800 Hammond Dr., 404/564-3000, www.sheratonperimeter. com, under $200). While it's clearly designed more for the business traveler in mind, the hotel boasts an attentive staff and rooms, which are well appointed and cleanly maintained.

BED-AND-BREAKFASTS AND HOSTELS
Under $150

For a quiet experience more typical of Southern B&Bs, try **Sugar Magnolia Bed and Breakfast** (804 Edgewood Ave., 404/222-0226, www. sugarmagnoliabb.com, $150 and under) in peaceful Inman Park, which still manages to be plenty close to a lot of key attractions. There are four rooms, all at quite reasonable rates, in this historic property, including the extravagant Royal Suite, which features a king bed in a curtained alcove and a whirlpool tub.

Atlanta doesn't offer much in the way of hostels. In fact, as of this writing there's only one, the 85-room Atlanta **International Hostel** (223 Ponce de Leon Ave., 404/875-9449, www.atlantainternationalhostel.com, under

$30), offering stable, safe accommodations in a restored Victorian. There's free continental breakfast every day, free parking, a pool table, and an assortment of cute pets. Wi-Fi, however, is an added daily cost. The Midtown location on bustling, fun Ponce de Leon Avenue near the Fox Theatre and locally renowned Mary Mac's Tea Room is not the world's safest locale, but is primed for access to dining and nightlife as well as for public transportation (only four blocks from the North Avenue MARTA station).

$150-300

Atlanta has precious few true B&Bs, but a good one is **Virginia Highland Bed & Breakfast** (630 Orme Circle, 404/892-2735, www.virginia-highlandbb.com, $119-219), which capitalizes on the obvious charms of its namesake neighborhood with sumptuous beds and a much more private, intimate setting than you'll get at one of the many hundreds of hotels in the rest of the city. There are four rooms; the largest is the garden apartment, which sleeps four with two bedrooms and two baths.

The five-suite, eco-friendly **Stonehurst Place** (923 Piedmont Ave., 404/881-0722, www.stonehurstplace.com, $160-400) offers a top-of-the-line B&B experience in Midtown. The rooms, including the art on the walls, are impeccably furnished with a good mix of old-school traditional taste and cutting-edge amenities like iPod-iPhone docking stations. It's even pet-friendly. The breakfasts are to die for, with unique but still comfort-oriented dishes such as a green chili egg puff and goat cheese phyllo bites.

Food

Atlanta isn't known as one of America's great food towns, but it's getting there. A remarkable resurgence of foodie culture with a typically Atlantan overlay of Southern charm is happening across town, particularly in Midtown, on the Westside, in Virginia-Highland, and in the Cabbagetown-Grant Park area.

DOWNTOWN
American

No other restaurant qualifies for the title of "Atlanta institution" more than **The Varsity** (61 North Ave. NW, 404/881-1706, www.the-varsity.com, Sun.-Thurs. 10am-11:30pm, Fri.-Sat. 10am-12:30am, $5), which since 1928 has fed generations of budget-conscious Georgia Tech students and is one of the last surviving quirky Southern fast-food diners. The cavernous space, largest drive-in restaurant in the world, they say, is daunting enough, but the counter experience is really what amps up your adrenaline. In decidedly non-Southern fashion,

© JIM MOREKIS

The Varsity drive-in

the grimly determined counter staff, like something out of a "Seinfeld" episode, demand to know "What'll you have?!". You'll quickly stammer something off the greasy-spoon style menu, probably a chili-cheese dog and onion rings washed down with their signature orange drink. (And don't forget Coca-Cola. The downtown Varsity is allegedly the world's largest single sales point of the iconic Georgia drink.) There are several satellite Varsities throughout Georgia now, as far afield as Athens and Dawsonville, but this original location on North Avenue astride I-75 is the one and only in this author's opinion.

If you're as hooked on bison burgers as I am, you'll take comfort in the presence of **Ted's Montana Grill** (133 Luckie St., 404/521-9796, www.tedsmontanagrill.com, Sun.-Thurs. 11am-10pm, Fri.-Sat. 11am-11pm, $15) in Fairlie-Poplar. Atlanta icon Ted Turner opened the now-national chain in 2002 with restaurateur George McKerrow Jr. This is the original, flagship location and it still serves as a reminder of Turner's pioneering, hugely important work in bringing back the American buffalo population of the West. The payoff, of course, is delicious bison meat served up in a variety of dishes at the restaurant. If buffalo is a little too adventurous for you, there's also a good selection of classic seafood, beef, and poultry dishes. Ted's work doesn't stop with ranching, however; his place is 99 percent plastic free. Even the straws are recyclable paper. There are now several other locations in the metro area, including a Midtown edition (1874 Peachtree St., 404/355-3897).

If you're staying in one of the large, swank hotels in or near Peachtree Center close to Centennial Olympic Park and you don't particularly feel like eating in the hotel but you also don't want to go far take a stroll to **Max Lager's** (320 Peachtree St., 404/525-4400, www.maxlagers.com, Mon.-Sat. 11:30am-11pm, Sun. 4pm-11pm, $15). At the oldest brewpub in the city you can enjoy a pint of one of their very good handcrafted beers and a tasty dinner cooked in their signature wood-fired grill (my favorite is the bison burger, but any of the salmon dishes are also recommended).

New Southern

Surely one of the most unique dining experiences in Atlanta, **C Lunacy Black Market** (231 Mitchell St. SW, 404/736-6164, www. lunacyblackmarket.com, Wed.-Sat. 6pm-10pm, $20) combines haute cuisine with the comfort of a living room, at almost unbelievably low prices. This small-plate restaurant does most everything differently, down to the menus, which are written in marker on cardboard. You're seated in one of a variety of homey areas of the lengthy dining room, whether at a big comfy sofa or at a cleared-off corner of the wine table. Once there, you order to your heart's content from the cardboard menu. Perhaps the al dente Asian-themed collards, the perfect tomato-mozzarella plate, or the mouth-watering braised beef? All those fresh, dynamic, but perfectly married flavors would be satisfying enough, but when you take a gander at the prices, generally under $4 per plate, you'll think you've died and gone to foodie heaven. To be fair, these small plates are *small.* But I've gotten away with a great dinner for two with wine for under $40. The food is so good I almost felt guilty about paying so little.

GRANT PARK
Brunch

Though it comes across as a venerable institution, **Ria's Bluebird** (421 Memorial Dr., 404/521-3737, daily 8am-3pm, $15) near Grant Park is actually a fairly new place. Hipsters and preppies alike pack the place for their large, delicious breakfasts and brunches, served by a cadre of inked servers who are nicer than they actually look. All of the omelets are great, and they're very good about offering a range of veggie options (two words: tempeh reuben). There's almost always a line to get in.

Coffee and Sweets

Known all over town for their dark arts with a French press, making espresso, and raising latte foam pulling to a fine art, the folks at **Octane Coffee** (437 Memorial Dr., 404/815-9886, http://octanecoffee.com, Mon. 7am-6pm, Tues.-Fri. 7am-midnight, Sat. 8am-midnight, Sun. 8am-10pm) take coffee seriously. They take painting seriously too, and the main Grant Park location (there's another on the Westside) features local artists all over the walls on steady rotation. The vibe is crisp and ultra-modern rather than cozy and quirky, with hipsters and mover-shaker types alike enjoying the range of java, chai, and yes, craft brews.

Greek

If you gotta get your gyro on, go no farther than **C Nick's Food To Go** (240 Martin Luther King Jr. Blvd., 404/521-2220, Mon.-Fri. 11am-7:30pm, Sat. noon-7pm, $7), a local food icon and one of the best little Greek joints I've found stateside. It's not much to look at: a nearly windowless cinderblock building with faded blue paint in a less-than-upscale part of town, catty-corner to the popular Daddy D'z BBQ Joynt. Sometimes you'll order from Nick

© JIM MOREKIS

Nick's Food To Go serves Greek food.

himself, who's well known to many local politicos who come here from the nearby state capitol for a quick lunch. But the food, authentic, perfectly spiced, and made to order with fresh ingredients, is more than worth the eyesore. This is one of the few places left where you can get an honest-to-Athena lamb gyro (other meats are available). The souvlaki is also a specialty. Even if all you want is a hearty Greek salad, you're assured of crisp lettuce and juicy tomatoes. While as the name implies the food is all technically to-go (you pick up at a window facing the parking lot), there are a couple of picnic tables onsite.

Seafood

Yep, it's called **Six Feet Under Pub and Fish House** (437 Memorial Dr., 404/525-6664, www.sixfeetunderatlanta.com, Mon.-Thurs. 11am-1am, Fri.-Sat. 11am-2am, Sun. 11am-midnight, $15) because it's right across the street from historic Oakland Cemetery. In fact, from a perch on the third floor deck you can count the headstones. The menu at this multi-level, wood-paneled gastropub leans heavily to the seafood side, with some great raw bar stuff and fried oysters and shrimp and the like. It's not a microbrewery, but craft-artisanal beers are a big part of the experience, with frequent brew-related events and contests. There's a second location on the Westside (interestingly, the first restaurant in town to use wind power), but the cemetery location is the original.

Look for the full parking lot at the corner of Memorial Drive and Martin Luther King Jr. Drive and you've found **Daddy D'z BBQ Joynt** (264 Memorial Dr., 404/222-0206, www.daddydz.com, Sun.-Thurs. 11am-10:30pm, Fri.-Sat. 11am-midnight, Sun. noon-9:30pm, $12), generally considered one of the city's best barbecue restaurants. Atlanta isn't considered a 'cue capital—too many Northern transplants, you see—but Daddy's is certainly the real thing, especially when it comes to their signature ribs ($25 for a full slab). Portions are enormous and generally come with Texas toast. The sides, such as Brunswick stew and cornbread, are nearly as well regarded as the meats. They also offer an interesting appetizer, the "Que Wrap," consisting of pulled pork wrapped in fried dough.

MIDTOWN
Classic Southern

The closest thing Atlanta has to Paula Deen's Lady & Sons in Savannah in both menu and media hype if not sheer volume of butter, **◖ Mary Mac's Tea Room** (224 Ponce de Leon Ave., 404/876-1800, www.marymacs.com, daily 11am-9pm, $20) on Ponce just down from the Georgian Terrace Hotel has packed in tourists and locals alike for 60 years with its range of Deep South specialties, some served "family style," like baked chicken, meatloaf, and grilled liver and onions. They have seafood as well, mostly of the tried-and-true fried variety. And yes, there's a fried green tomato appetizer.

At the other end of the price scale and with status as the best inexpensive joint in Atlanta, **Eats** (600 Ponce de Leon Ave., 404/888-9149, www.eatsonponce.com, daily 11am-10pm, $5) lives up (or down?) to its name in gloriously humble fashion. The specialty is the excellent jerk chicken, served in heaping portions (not on Friday, though, then you get jerk tilapia). BBQ and lemon pepper flavors are available for the spice-averse. How inexpensive? The meat and three-veggie combo plate and we're talking very large servings here runs a paltry $4.75. Because of the inclusive hours you see a large slice of Atlanta life come in and out of these doors on one of Atlanta's most interesting thoroughfares.

While the name implies a trendy celeb-centered focus (please say I don't have to tell you who Gladys Knight is), the truth is that **Gladys Knight and Ron Winan's Chicken and Waffles** (529 Peachtree St., 404/874-9393, Mon.-Thurs. 11am-11pm, Fri.-Sat. 11am-4am, Sun. 11am-8pm, $10-15) represents an old Harlem tradition come South: A late-night hybrid dinner-breakfast to close out your evening of partying. So on weekends the kitchen stays open 'til 4am serving up their eponymous chicken 'n' waffles as well as other staple Southern comfort foods such as fried green tomatoes, fried catfish, chicken wings, and... collard green spring rolls? Yep.

New Southern

If you're looking for a cool place for drinks or a meal near Piedmont, perhaps before a concert, look no further than **Einstein's** (1077 Juniper St., 404/876-7925, www.metrocafes. com, Mon.-Thurs. 11am-11pm, Fri. 11am-midnight, Sat. 9am-midnight, Sun. 9am-11pm, $15). With plenty of indoor and outdoor seating, a large and very friendly staff, great signature drinks, excellent burgers, and a solid small plates menu, they've pretty much got all your social needs covered. Their location, a block off Peachtree Street and another block or so to the park, cannot be topped and is one of Atlanta's favorite see-and-be-seen locales, especially at Sunday brunch. This restaurant should not be confused with Einstein's Bagels.

What's that you say? You want a great taqueria with Korean flair and flavor? That would be **Takorea** (818 Juniper St., 404/532-1944, www.mytakorea.com, Mon.-Thurs. 11:30am-10pm, Fri.-Sat. 11:30am-11pm, Sun. noon-10pm, $10), a concept restaurant that has actually managed to make their concept work. Chef Tomas Lee combined both of his culinary loves into this unique Midtown spot, which has a surprisingly sleek and sexy interior for a self-described "street food" joint. They also have a very interesting cocktail list, including a specialty martini made with a distinctive Korean liquor called soju.

Chef Ryan Smith has worked in some of Atlanta's finest restaurants, and now he's running his own kitchen at **C Empire State South** (999 Peachtree St. NE, 404/541-1105, www.empirestatesouth.com, Mon.-Thurs. 7am-10pm, Fri. 7am-11pm, Sat.-Sun. 10:30am-11pm, $25-35) in Midtown right on Peachtree Street, across the street from Margaret Mitchell's house. Empire State is somewhat unusual among the city's better restaurants

© JIM MOREKIS

bocce ball courtyard at Empire State South

in two ways: 1) The menu is extremely pared down; and 2) they offer breakfast on weekdays in addition to lunch and dinner. Did I mention the bocce ball courtyard? The morning meal is a simple yet versatile menu of Southern biscuits and New York bagels (get it? Empire State?), while the lunch menu focuses on high-quality sandwiches and one or two more savory dishes, such as a great pork belly. Dinner is a more heavy-hitting affair, with a full range of delicious, quirky appetizers like the farm egg and the octopus sausage (!) and entrées like the Georgia trout and the rib eye for two.

INMAN PARK AND LITTLE FIVE POINTS
Breakfast and Brunch

A beloved metro chain with nine Atlanta franchises to choose from, **Flying Biscuit Cafe** (1655 McLendon Ave., 404/687-8888, www.flyingbiscuit.com, daily 7am-10pm, $10) began in Candler Park near Little Five Points as an organic-friendly culinary project funded by Indigo Girls member and native Atlantan Emily Saliers. While not every location offers a dinner menu, all are best known for their delicious and cost-effective brunches served all day, which emphasize various specialty omelets such as the Piedmont with tasty chicken sausage. Even their namesake biscuits 'n' gravy feature an egg on top. That said, Flying Biscuit is also a big hit with the vegan crowd, offering a range of items. Cozy and often crowded, expect a wait at peak periods at all locations.

Coffee and Sweets

Atlanta has its share of good-to-great coffeehouses, but my favorite is **Inman Perk** (240 N. Highland Ave., 404/678/705-4545, www.inmanperkcoffee.com, Mon.-Thurs. 6am-11pm, Fri. 6am-10pm, Sat. 7am-10pm, Sun. 8am-11pm) in, yes, Inman Park. In keeping with some of the New Urbanist vibe you often see throughout Atlanta's up-and-coming neighborhoods, Inman Perk's exterior is resolutely modernist, even Bauhaus. Inside it's a little more like a typical coffeehouse, with a large amount of seating and good Wi-Fi. Not only is

the coffee several cuts above a Starbucks or even the usual locally-owned java joint, they boast a wide selection of teas as well. And if you prefer alcohol to caffeine, they have a good menu of craft beers and interesting wines as well.

Italian

Upscale Italian is the name of the game at Inman Park, with the one-two combination of **Sotto Sotto** (313 N. Highland Ave., 404/523-6678, www.urestaurants.net, Mon.-Thurs. 5:30pm-11pm, Fri.-Sat. 5:30pm-midnight, Sun. 5:30pm-10pm, $18-40) and its adjacent sibling **Fritti** (309 N. Highland Ave., 404/880-9559, www.urestaurants.net, Mon.-Thurs. 11:30am-11pm, Fri.-Sat. 11:30am-midnight, Sun. 12:30pm-10pm, $10-20). Sotto Sotto specializes in Tuscan cuisine, which is quite a bit different from the tomato-dominated stereotype of Italian food (though they do have a killer lasagna). Here you'll find succulent shellfish, delicate risotto, homemade pasta from scratch, and a very extensive wine list, all presented with top-notch service. Fritti is where you go for wood-fired pizza in the trendy thin-crust genre from farther south in Italy's boot. Typical offerings are the gorgonzola, pineapple, and balsamic vinegar pizza and the Funghi di Bosco with white truffle oil and portobello mushrooms.

Steaks and Burgers

Small plates, big plates, cold plates, "second mortgage plates," **Rathbun's** (112 Krog St., 404/524-8280, www.rathbunsrestaurant.com, Mon.-Thurs. 5:30pm-10pm, Fri.-Sat. 5:30pm-11pm, $18-40) has it all. The new toast of the ATL foodie scene—exec chefs Kevin and Kent Rathbun beat Bobby Flay in an episode of *Iron Chef America*—this aspirational enterprise in Inman Park seeks to inject an almost ridiculous amount of innovation and flavor explosion across a wide-ranging menu. Where else can you find a hot smoked salmon tostada, a 22-oz. bone-in rib eye, char-grilled octopus, roasted bone marrow, elk, duck breast with Thai risotto, and eggplant steak fries all in one place? And that's just a sampling of the rotating offerings. This is not to be confused with Rathbun's Steakhouse, owned by the same restaurant group.

As much tourist attraction as awesome burger spot, **Vortex** (438 Moreland Ave., 404/688-1828, www.thevortexbarandgrill. com, Sun.-Thurs. 11am-midnight, Fri.-Sat. 11am-2am, $10) dominates one approach to Little Five Points with its iconic zombie monster entrance. After walking through the skull's demonic open mouth, you sit down in a rather boisterous atmosphere and enjoy some of the larger, better burgers in town, with attitude to spare. The catch: Because this is specifically a "smoking allowed inside" restaurant, by law no one under 18 is permitted inside. There's a second version in Midtown.

BUCKHEAD
Classic Southern

A "diner" pretty much in name only—it's not cheap and it offers valet parking—**Buckhead Diner** (3075 Piedmont Rd. NE, 404/262-3336, www.buckheadrestaurants.com, Mon.-Sat. 11am-midnight, Sun. 10am-10pm, $15-25) is primarily known as a place where celebrities can get a bite to eat in an atmosphere that is neither problematic for them nor exclusive to the rest of us. What this means in practice is you will get a mighty fine yet simply envisioned comfort-food meal, perhaps the signature roast beef sandwich with an opener of pimento cheese fritters, and maybe spot someone like Jane Fonda a few tables over. Overall, Buckhead Diner is one of those true Atlanta experiences, from the signed photos of movie stars on the wall to the long-serving staff decked out in old-school white coats.

Mediterranean

The crispiest, tastiest, fluffiest, most melt-in-your-mouth falafel I've had anywhere is at **Cafe Agora** (262 E. Paces Ferry Rd., 404/949-0900, www.cafeagora.com, Mon.-Thurs. 11am-10pm, Fri.-Sat. 11am-4am, Sun. 11am-9pm, $7-12), a Buckhead ethnic-food staple that specializes in freshly cooked, authentic Greek-Turkish cuisine made by the owners themselves using Old World recipes. They also deal a mean gyro, and have a full range of homemade hummus, tabbouleh, dolmades, and baba ghanoush. You can't go wrong with anything on the menu. And it's all served 'til 4am on weekends! A new storefront location, smaller but just as good, has opened in Midtown (92 Peachtree Pl. NE, 404/253-2997, Mon.-Sat. 10am-10pm), literally just around the corner from the Margaret Mitchell House.

Steaks

Widely considered one of the best steakhouses in the United States, **C Bone's** (3130 Piedmont Rd. NE, 404/237-2663, www.bonesrestaurant.com, Mon.-Fri. 11:30am-2:30pm and 5:30pm-10pm, Sat.-Sun. 5:30pm-10pm, $30-50) is a throwback to the time when corporate movers-and-shakers gathered for three-martini lunches and enormous slabs of expertly seared beef. Some of that still goes on, of course, but in a changing world Bone's has gained slightly more feminine appeal over the years, while still retaining that flavor of clubby nostalgia. Even waiting for your table at the bar is an old-school experience in and of itself. There are actually some great seafood dishes on the menu, such as the crab-stuffed trout and their signature lobster bisque, but obviously the steaks are the draw here. All are amazing, but I call your attention to the two dry-aged items on the beef menu: a bone-in rib eye and a porterhouse for two. Needless to say, this isn't a particularly vegetarian-friendly restaurant.

Vietnamese

The best Vietnamese food in Buckhead is at **C Chateau de Saigon** (4300 Buford Hwy. NE, 404/929-0034, www.chateaudesaigon. com, Sun.-Mon. and Wed.-Thurs. 11am-10pm, Fri.-Sat. 11am-11pm, $10-25). The menu is quite extensive, and you'll find all the usual fare, from pho to bun to fried rice entrées to spring rolls. But don't stop there. There are some real gems here, including "shaken beef" filet mignon, "hot pots" where raw ingredients are cooked tableside, "sizzling fish" also cooked while you watch, and an entire page of clay pot offerings. There's even an entire sub-menu of tofu dishes.

VIRGINIA-HIGHLAND
Breakfast and Brunch

A Virginia-Highland brunch staple, **Murphy's** (997 Virginia Ave., 404/872-0904, www. murphys-atlanta-restaurant.com, Mon.-Thurs. 11am-10pm, Fri. 11am-11pm, Sat. 8am-11pm, Sun. 8am-10pm, $20) nearly always has a wait on Sundays but most will say it's worth it. Crab cake Benedict and shrimp and grits are particular faves, and the smoked salmon is highly recommended for fans of that delicacy. Every table gets a basket of delicious muffins and biscuits with jam.

While they did indeed start out chiefly as purveyors of sweet treats, **Highland Bakery** (655 Highland Ave. NE, 404/586-0772, www.highlandbakery.com, Mon.-Fri. 7am-4pm, Sat.-Sun. 8am-4pm, $4-12) in nearby Old Fourth Ward has expanded its menu far beyond muffins and the like. Nowadays it's better known for its delectable breakfast and brunch offerings, from ricotta pancakes to fried chicken Benedict. The combination of down-home comfort food and the assortment of hipster servers has attracted a devoted following that has spread out to Highland Bakery's two subsequent locations, one in Midtown and one in Buckhead.

Italian

The Virginia-Highland neighborhood is picture-perfect for a relaxing lunch or dinner, and a great place to get just that is at one of the area's most beloved restaurants, **C La Tavola** (992 Virginia Ave., 404/873-5430, www.latavola-trattoria.com, Mon.-Thurs. 5:30pm-10pm, Fri.-Sat. 5:30pm-11pm, Sun. 11am-3pm and 5:30pm-10pm, $15-25). As the name implies, this is essentially an old-school trattoria with just enough bistro-style, open-kitchen atmosphere to keep a trendy edge. Northern Italian specialties such as risotto and mussels are the order of the day here, along with delights such as delicious prosciutto and perfect crusty bread. There's a full antipasti menu and a delightful

assortment of Italian desserts such as tiramisu, panna cotta, and crostata. In all, it's a great place for a low-key romantic experience.

Seafood

A raw bar may not be the first thing that comes to mind when you think of Atlanta, but **C Fontaine's Oyster House** (1026 N. Highland Ave., 404/872-0869, www.nnnw-corp.com, Mon. 11:30am-1am, Tues. 4pm-2:30am, Wed.-Sat. 11:30am-2:30am, Sun. noon-midnight) is easily the best shellfish joint in town, as well as just a fun place to hang out into the wee hours, with the bar staying open past the usual kitchen closing time of midnight on weekends (11pm during the week). You can sit at a booth or at the bar to enjoy the range of fresh seafood. Gulf oysters, raw or steamed, will run you about $10 a dozen, and "specialty" oysters about twice that. They offer several roasted oyster options as well. A lot of folks just split one of the combination platters, running around $40, which provide a sampling of boiled shrimp, snow crab legs, oysters, and mussels. In keeping with the vaguely New Orleans-Cajun approach to the menu, their po-boys are amazing: You get your choice of oyster, shrimp, scallops, catfish, or crawfish.

DRUID HILLS
Ethiopian

Did someone say Ethiopian cuisine? Yes, Atlanta has it, along with a fairly large Ethiopian population, and the best place for it is **Desta Ethiopian Kitchen** (3086 Briarcliff Rd. NE, 404/929-0011, www.destaethiopiankitchen.com, Mon.-Thurs. 9am-midnight, Fri.-Sun. 9am-1am, $10-15). You eat Ethiopian food with thin, tasty bread rather than utensils, and your friendly server will provide plenty of it. The cuisine ranges from tasty stews to split pea soup and expertly prepared tilapia.

PERIMETER
Chinese

North of Buckhead just outside the Perimeter is the closest thing to a classic Chinatown spot, **Canton Cooks** (5984 Roswell Rd. NE,

404/250-0515, Thurs.-Tues. 11am-2:30am, $10-15), offering delicacies such as fried fish maw, Peking spare ribs, fried squid, and of course General Tso's chicken. Possibly the best Chinese restaurant in the city, this humble spot is in a strip mall near a Whole Foods in the northern Atlanta suburb of Sandy Springs and is a favorite of that area's burgeoning Chinese population.

WESTSIDE
Italian

One of Atlanta's more full-immersion dining experiences is at **C Antico Pizza Napoletana** (1093 Hemphill Ave. NW, 404/724-2333, www.anticoatl.com, Mon.-Sat. 11:30am "until they run out of dough," about 11pm or midnight, pizza $20), where you'll find Old World authentic Naples-via-Brooklyn pizza in a hot, loud environment seemingly tailor-made for enjoying a big tasty pie. It's not all a bed of roses: The wait is usually quite long, they're closed on Sundays, and you can only add one topping to the pie of your choice. That's right: only one ingredient, no exceptions. But the thing is, all the major ingredients (prosciutto, pecorino, sopressata, etc.) come directly from Italy and the pies are exactly as you would find them in Naples. Each pizza feeds a lot of people.

You'll never set foot in an Olive Garden again after a visit to **Osteria del Figo** (1210 Howell Mill Rd., 404/351-3700, www.figo-pasta.com, Mon.-Thurs. 11:30am-9:30pm, Fri. 11:30am-10pm, Sat. noon-10pm, Sun. noon-9:30pm, $12), a unique pasta restaurant which matches flavor with value. Though overshadowed in the local culinary scene by the five-star Bacchanalia across the parking lot, Figo (part of a citywide chain of similar pasta places) is no slouch, offering a wide-ranging menu of pastas, regional Italian sauces (tomato-based and cream-based), and specialty melt-in-your-mouth meatballs. You place your order and pay for it first, then sit down in the well-appointed dining room, where you're served by the waitstaff. There's a bit of a learning curve involved because of the menu's sheer size and frankly daunting plethora of custom combinations, but the counter staff is knowledgeable and can help match the sauce with the pasta.

New Southern

The most sought-after table in Atlanta is within the hallowed confines of **C Bacchanalia** (1198 Howell Mill Rd., 404/365-0410, www.starprovisions.com, Mon.-Sat. from 6pm, $25-35, five-course prix fixe $85), a southeastern mecca of so-called New American cuisine that continues to top most of the foodie lists for the city. Through their Star Provisions cooperative-conglomerate (you actually enter the restaurant through the retail arm), chef-owners Anne Quatrano and Clifford Harrison concentrate on sourcing all foods organically, locally, and regionally, many from their own Summerland Farm and associated abattoir. The menu centers on a five-course prix fixe that includes a cold appetizer, fish, entrée, cheese course, and dessert (*amuse-bouche* generally comes around as well). Typical dishes include a delectable slow roast porchetta, a perfect red snapper, the signature crab fritter, and yes, foie gras. You can order à la carte from the bar area. Don't expect to walk in and get a table; reservations fill up months in advance. Directly next door, Chef David Carson runs the kitchen at **Quinones at Bacchanalia** (1198 Howell Mill Rd., 404/365-0410, www.starprovisions.com, Mon.-Sat. from 6pm), a smaller, more Southern-tinged dining room that also relies on the tried-and-true five-course prix fixe.

ATLANTA

Information and Services

HOSPITALS

The main trauma center in Atlanta and in the entire Southeast is **Grady Memorial Hospital** (80 Jesse Hill Jr. Dr., 404/616-1000, www.gradyhealth.org). If you're in a serious accident while near Atlanta this is definitely the place to go.

Other important facilities include **Piedmont** **Atlanta Hospital** (1968 Peachtree Rd., 404/605-5000, www.piedmonthospital.org) north of Downtown, part of a metro-wide hospital chain; and **St. Joseph's Hospital** (5665 Peachtree Dunwoody Rd., 678/843-7001, www.stjosephsatlanta.org) even farther north at the Perimeter.

ATL LINGO

- AJC: Nickname for the city's daily newspaper of record, the *Atlanta Journal-Constitution*.

- The ATL: Hip-hop slang for Atlanta.

- Brookwood Split: The spot south of Buckhead where I-75 and I-85 separate north of The Connector.

- The Connector: That portion of I-75 and I-85 that passes directly through the center of Downtown.

- Dirty South: Subgenre of hip-hop produced in the ATL.

- Grady: Shorthand for the hulking Downtown presence of Grady Memorial Hospital, the South's premier trauma center. The Connector goes around it at the "Grady Curve."

- The Hootch: The Chattahoochee River. One "shoots the Hootch," that is, rides a whitewater raft or tubes downstream. The Chattahoochee is also a key source of drinking water for Atlanta.

- Hotlanta: Using this nickname for Atlanta will mark you as a tourist or a generally lame person. Avoid it at all costs.

- L5P: Acronym for Little Five Points.

- Peachtree: Generally refers to Peachtree Street, the historic north-south main avenue through the heart of Atlanta. Do not confuse it with the 70 other roads in Atlanta bearing some variant of "Peachtree." Movers and shakers all wanted a prestigious address on Peachtree Street. If they couldn't have that, nearby streets were named to feature the word, for example, Peachtree Circle, Peachtree Lane, and so on. Adding to the confusion is the fact that Peachtree Street becomes Peachtree Road in Buckhead. While Georgia is the Peach State, local folklore says Peachtree is probably a corruption of "pitch tree," a pine tree used for sap.

- The Perimeter: The vast swath of I-285 encircling the city and the demarcation between Atlanta proper and its fast-growing suburbs. Rush-hour traffic jams are the stuff of nightmares, with the northern portion, or "Top End," the most congested.

- Ponce: What locals call Ponce de Leon Avenue. The most posh area during Atlanta's Victorian heyday, this sinuous and now occasionally seamy street is a center of dining and nightlife. If you insist on the full name, avoid Spanish inflection and say "LEE-on."

- Spaghetti Junction: The sprawling 14-bridge cloverleaf that includes the intersection of "The Perimeter" (I-285) and I-85 and handles over a quarter million vehicles a day.

- The Ted: Nickname for Turner Field, home of the Atlanta Braves major league baseball team. This is not to be confused with the nearby Georgia Dome, home of the Atlanta Falcons.

MEDIA
Newspapers

The newspaper of record in Atlanta is the venerable *Atlanta Journal-Constitution* (www.ajc.com). Famous alumni include Margaret Mitchell and Henry Grady.

But for complete arts and entertainment listings, in addition to a good amount of counterculture politics, you'll want to check out *Creative Loafing* (www.clatl.com), the city's longtime alt-weekly, which by some reckonings actually has the higher circulation of the two.

While the iconic gay paper *The Southern Voice* is sadly no more, Atlanta's sizeable LGBT community is served by *Project Q Atlanta* (www.projectqatlanta.com) and by *Edge* (www.edgeatlanta.com).

Radio

Traffic reports are very important in Atlanta, and many locals tune to **WSB** 750AM and 95.5FM. **SiriusXM** also has Atlanta traffic at Channel 134.

The Atlanta radio dial is full of options, but one of the more unique is the Georgia Tech student-run station, **WREK** 91.1FM. The local Georgia Public Broadcasting public radio station is **WABE** 90.1FM.

LIBRARIES

The main branch of the **Atlanta-Fulton Public Library System** (One Margaret Mitchell Sq., 404/730-1700, www.afplweb.com, Mon.-Thurs. 9am-8pm, Fri.-Sat. 9am-6pm, Sun. 2pm-6pm) frequently hosts exhibits, and its most notable standing exhibit is the Margaret Mitchell room on the fifth floor.

The major universities also have worthy libraries: the vast **Georgia Tech Library** (704 Cherry St., 404/894-4500, www.library.gatech.edu, Mon.-Thurs. 7:30am-10pm, Fri. 7:30am-6pm, Sat. 9am-6pm, Sun. noon-10pm) and the **Georgia State University Library** (100 Decatur St., 404/413-2820, www.library.gsu.edu, Mon.-Fri. 8:30am-5:15pm), which is open to non-students.

Getting There and Around

BY CAR

Often to the chagrin of residents, Atlanta is a major nexus of Interstate highways and that's how most drivers enter and leave. Major thoroughfares are north-south arteries **I-75** and **I-85,** which actually combine into a single road through Downtown, separating a little south of Buckhead (from there I-75 heads into Chattanooga, Tennessee, and I-85 into Greenville, South Caarolina). Northeast on I-85 is the infamous **"Spaghetti Junction,"** a vast collection of interchanges and one portion of highway with an incredible 18 lanes.

I-285, called **"the Perimeter"** by locals, and in portions labeled the "Atlanta Bypass," forms a vast circle around the metro area and serves primarily as a commuter avenue. It carries a quarter million vehicles a day at speeds ranging from blindingly fast to a barely perceptible crawl. Traffic is much worse at the **"Top End"** of the Perimeter, north of Atlanta

near the city's most populous suburbs. New variable speed limit signs have been installed in portions of the Top End to adjust the speed limit from a max of 65 mph to lower limits to account for congestion and delays. Nonetheless try to avoid it during rush hour if at all possible.

I-20 runs east-west along the bottom of the Atlanta metro area, its eastern end passing through Augusta and its western end going into Alabama. It's called Ralph David Abernathy Parkway near Downtown.

A key non-Interstate route is **Highway 78,** called Stone Mountain Parkway east of the city and Ponce de Leon Avenue in town.

With Atlanta's heavy traffic and frequent accident and road construction delays, monitoring traffic conditions is a full-time job that's never dull. Local radio station **WSB** at 95.5FM and 750AM generally has the most frequent and up-to-date reports. **SiriusXM** also has a good satellite station covering DC-Baltimore-Atlanta traffic at Channel 134.

On-street metered parking is available in increments of a half-hour and 1-4 hours. Parking enforcement in Atlanta is extremely aggressive. While meter enforcement times vary depending on zone, most in the tourist-frequented areas are enforced Monday-Saturday 7am-10pm. As of this writing there's talk of 24-hour meter enforcement. There are many dozens of parking garages and public and private parking lots at various costs; an excellent resource with interactive mapping is www.atlantadowntown.com.

BY AIR

Hartsfield-Jackson Atlanta International Airport (6000 North Terminal Pkwy., 404/530-6600, www.atlanta-airport.com, airport code ATL) is the world's busiest, serving nearly 100 million passengers a year. Situated seven miles south of Atlanta proper astride Fulton and Clayton counties, Hartsfield-Jackson is Georgia's largest employer and is in many ways a city unto itself. In one spot, I-75/85 actually goes *under* one of the runways.

Its flagship airline is Delta, whose hub here is the largest in the world, comprising 60 percent of the airport's traffic. In all, about two dozen airlines fly in and out; domestic highlights include Southwest, AirTran, American, United, and US Airways, with international highlights including Air France, British Airways, KLM, Korean Air, and Lufthansa.

The massive **Hartsfield-Jackson Rental Car Center** opened in 2009 and houses 10 airport rental agencies, with room for more. Though freestanding, it is fully integrated with the airport by a people-moving transportation system, the ATL Skytrain, as well as its own access highway. The airport's transit system is the Plane Train, which provides full transport from terminal to terminal, including the brand-new Maynard Jackson International Terminal, which opened in 2012.

Parking at the domestic terminal is in two tiers. The four-level Daily Parking area ($3/

hour, $16/day) is closest to the terminal and provides a large amount of covered spots. The uncovered Economy lots ($3/hour, $12/day) are the cheapest, and have a free shuttle that runs daily 8am-midnight.

There is an international shuttle connector (daily, 24 hours, free) to link up international passengers with both the rental car center and the domestic terminal, where the MARTA station is located.

The airport MARTA rapid transit station is on the north side of the airport near the baggage claim area. Unlike some metro transit systems that use a rotating fare system, all rides on MARTA regardless of distance are $2.50 one-way, including to and from Hartsfield-Jackson.

Various taxi services operate out of Hartsfield-Jackson, and the fare from the airport to Downtown will run you about $40.

MARTA PUBLIC TRANSIT

Atlanta's main public transit entity is MARTA (Metropolitan Atlanta Rapid Transit Authority, www.itsmarta.com, $2.50 one-way). While often the butt of jokes locally and certainly not on par with more expansive transit systems such as New York's or San Francisco's, MARTA is a very handy and extremely cost effective way to avoid the snarling traffic jams prevalent throughout Atlanta. There are two main components: the rapid transit trains and the extended bus system.

The train system layout is very simple: The two north-south lines, Gold and Red, go from Hartsfield-Jackson International Airport in the south and split in Buckhead, the Red line going to Sandy Springs and the Gold to Doraville. The main east-west route is the Blue line spanning the diameter of the I-285 Perimeter, with a shorter Green line serving Downtown. There's only one transfer station: Five Points in Downtown.

There are nearly 40 total MARTA train stops, with one convenient to just about every notable tourist location. Generally speaking, trains run about every 15-20 minutes Monday-Friday 5am-1am; Saturdays, Sundays, and most holidays 6am-1am. There is full access for riders with disabilities, and bicycles are accommodated on trains and buses anytime.

One-way fares are $2.50 regardless of length of trip, which makes MARTA a remarkable bargain compared to other big-city transit systems. The best option is to purchase a reloadable BreezeCard at any MARTA station, which you just tap to a card reader to board.

Bus routes are fully integrated into MARTA. You can transfer to a bus line for free for one-way trips finished within three hours. The free transfer is automatically activated when used at the airport. Tap the card on the fare box on the bus.

The MARTA website features a handy downloadable "Rookie's Guide," which is worth a quick look.

BY BUS AND TRAIN

The Atlanta **AMTRAK** train station (1688 Peachtree St., 404/881-3060, www.amtrak.com) is smack dab Downtown.

Atlanta has two **Greyhound** bus stations to get in and out of town: one in Downtown (232 Forsyth St., 404/584-1728, www.greyhound.com) and another at Hartsfield-Jackson International Airport (404/765-9598, www.greyhound.com).

TAXI SERVICE

While not a taxi-centric town, there are plenty of cab companies to pick from. Try **Atlanta Checker Cab** (404/351-1111, www.atlantacheckercab.com) or **Atlanta Lenox Taxi Company** (404/872-2600, www.atlantalenoxtaxi.com).

Greater Atlanta

The idea of Greater Atlanta might seem funny, or at least redundant, to those who live in Atlanta, considering the city's notorious sprawl. But there are indeed several separate municipalities worth visiting, which though largely subsumed within the metro area still have managed to retain their individual identity. One of Georgia's most popular attractions, Stone Mountain, is just east of town, as is the happening little city of Decatur. North of Atlanta are Marietta and Gainesville, the latter a gateway to North Georgia. And southeast of Atlanta is the unique and well-preserved natural getaway of Arabia Mountain.

◖ DECATUR

Decatur is that rarest of birds: a place with a true small-town vibe directly adjacent to a massive metro area. Despite its proximity to the city, when you're here, you feel like you're away from Atlanta's sometimes-oppressive sprawl.

Decatur has had that feel from the beginning. Technically older than Atlanta, Decatur dates back to 1822. Citizens didn't want the rampant growth that would come with a major rail terminal, so they refused; the settlement

that would later be Atlanta was founded a bit west in 1837.

Today, Decatur (www.visitdecaturgeorgia.com) is known for the success of its downtown revitalization, which has resulted in one of the most vibrant café, restaurant, and shopping scenes in the South. It's also one of the most assertively progressive little cities in the region, a trait that showed itself with the recent grassroots effort against a new Walmart.

Waffle House Museum

The national chain boasts over 1,600 locations today, but the very first Waffle House was in little old Decatur, founded in 1955 when neighbors Joe Roger and Tom Forkner went into business together. The Waffle House Museum (2719 E. College Ave., 770/326-7086, www.wafflehouse.com, by appointment only, free) contains memorabilia from back in the day. Aside from a few annual open houses, it's only open by appointment, so call ahead and check the website.

Nightlife and Food

The draw in Decatur, other than its beautiful,

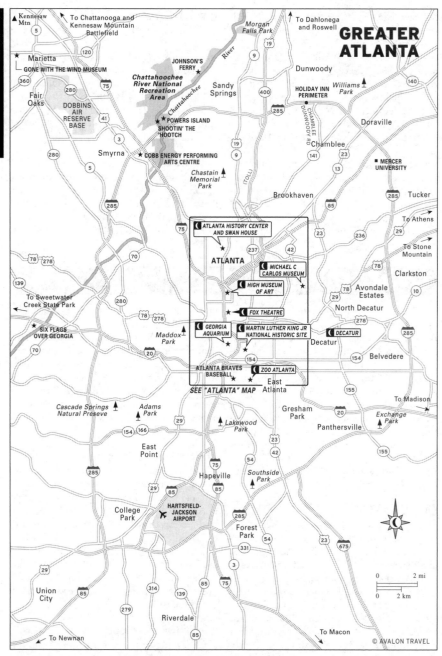

GREATER ATLANTA

Kennesaw Mtn
5
120
To Chattanooga and Kennesaw Mountain Battlefield
JOHNSON'S FERRY
Morgan Falls Park
19
9
To Dahlonega and Roswell
140
★ Marietta
GONE WITH THE WIND MUSEUM
360
280
75
Chattahoochee River National Recreation Area
Sandy Springs
400
285
HOLIDAY INN PERIMETER
Williams Park
CHAMBLEE DUNWOODY RD
Dunwoody
Fair Oaks
DOBBINS AIR RESERVE BASE
41
3
★ POWERS ISLAND SHOOTIN' THE 'HOOTCH
19
9
Chamblee
141
Doraville
280
Smyrna
★ COBB ENERGY PERFORMING ARTS CENTRE
Chastain Memorial Park
13
23
■ MERCER UNIVERSITY
5
Brookhaven
85
285
Tucker
78
278
237
42
▶ ATLANTA HISTORY CENTER AND SWAN HOUSE
ATLANTA
MICHAEL C CARLOS MUSEUM
23
236
29
To Athens
139
70
280
▶ HIGH MUSEUM OF ART
78
29
78
To Stone Mountain
Clarkston
10
To Sweetwater Creek State Park
78
278
★ FOX THEATRE
Avondale Estates
North Decatur
★ SIX FLAGS OVER GEORGIA
Maddox Park
▶ GEORGIA AQUARIUM
MARTIN LUTHER KING JR NATIONAL HISTORIC SITE
278
▶ DECATUR
285
70
20
154
Decatur
154
Belvedere
ATLANTA BRAVES BASEBALL
▶ ZOO ATLANTA
East Atlanta
155
SEE "ATLANTA" MAP
Cascade Springs Natural Preserve
Adams Park
29
Gresham Park
20
Pantherville
Exchange Park
155
To Madison
154
166
▲ Lakewood Park
23
42
East Point
54
285
75
Hapeville
85
Southside Park
To Newnan
College Park
29
85
HARTSFIELD-JACKSON AIRPORT
285
Forest Park
54
23
675
29
314
139
85
75
331
3
Union City
85
279
Riverdale
85
To Macon

0 — 2 mi
0 — 2 km

© AVALON TRAVEL

modernist town square, is its compelling food and nightlife, and the two pursuits are deeply intertwined here. Many of its hottest nightspots offer great food in addition to world-class craft beer selections, and many non-bars offer frequent live music.

It's fittingly Decatur-ish that its most famous nightspot, **Eddie's Attic** (515 N. McDonough St., 404/377-4976, www.eddiesattic.com, daily from 5pm) is located literally right next door to City Hall. One of the most influential folk-acoustic venues in the South, Eddie's upstairs performance space is where the Indigo Girls got their start. Other big names who honed their craft at Eddie's include Sugarland, John Mayer, Michelle Malone, Shawn Mullins and, believe it or not, Justin Bieber. Mayer, Mullins, and Sugarland's Jennifer Nettles are all past winners of Eddie's semi-annual songwriting contest. The main listening room isn't the place to get rowdy, or even to spend quality time with your smartphone, you're expected to pay attention to the performers. Mondays are standard open mic nights, and the quality is top-notch. For

a louder good time, there is rooftop patio seating.

With a name taken from a Shakespeare quote, **Cakes & Ale** (155 Sycamore St., 404/377-7994, www.cakesandalerestaurant.com, Tues.-Thurs. 6pm-11pm, kitchen closes 10pm, Fri.-Sat. 5:30pm-midnight, kitchen closes 10:30pm) recently moved into a larger space closer to the city center, the better to accommodate the crowds that come to enjoy their adventurous American farm-to-table style cuisine of Napa-trained lead chef Billy Allin, formerly of another great (and sadly now defunct) local spot, Watershed. The menus change too frequently to go over here, but a recent dinner included an oyster sampler, chicory salad, and a great halibut. The attached bakery is known for its actual cakes.

For an Irish pub atmosphere with that thing that most Irish pubs lack, really good food, try **The Marlay House** (426 W. Ponce de Leon Ave., 404/270-9950, www.themarlayhouse.com, Mon.-Thurs. 11:30am-10:30pm, bar until midnight, Fri. 11:30am-11:30pm, bar until 2am, Sat. 10:30am-11:30pm, bar until 2am,

© JIM MOREKIS

Eddie's Attic in Decatur

Sun. 10:30am-10:30pm, bar until midnight, $15), known to old-timers as former home of The Grange. They are known for their righteous roast and Yorkshire pudding. Of course they have a great beer-on-tap selection and pride themselves on pouring a pint of Guinness just as you would get in Dublin. Most nights there is live traditional Irish music.

An intriguing and beguiling mix of neighborhood bar, signature cocktail joint, craft brew headquarters, and farm-to-table restaurant, **Leon's Full Service** (131 E. Ponce de Leon Ave., 404/687-0500, www.leonsfullservice.com, Mon. 5pm-1am, Tues.-Thurs. 11:30am-1am, Fri.-Sat. 11:30am-2am, Sun. 11:30am-1am, kitchen closes an hour prior, $15-20) lives up to its name. The range of old school specialty cocktails, hovering around $10, is inspiring; check out the seasonal offerings. The main plate menu is small but finely honed; try the grilled flat iron steak or the veggie loaf. In any case, don't miss out on the "pub frites," with your choice of two sauces, such as goat cheese fondue or horseradish mayo.

The first spot to really put Decatur's downtown renaissance on the map, **Brick Store Pub** (125 E. Court Sq., 404/687-0990, www.brickstorepub.com, Mon. 11am-1am, Tues.-Sat. 11am-2am, Sun. noon-1am, $10) continues to offer a unique selection of amped-up yet affordable comfort food and pub fare, such as "Shepherd's Daughter's Pie," a great Cornish game hen, and an Italian-themed pierogi. The beer list includes a raft of great Belgians served in a dedicated space upstairs.

An outrageously popular tapas place, **Iberian Pig** (121 Sycamore St., 404/371-8800, www.iberianpigatl.com, Mon.-Thurs. 5pm-10pm, Fri.-Sat. 3pm-11pm, Sun. 5pm-9pm, tapas $5-15) offers great small plates and, as the name suggests, a remarkable variety of authentic Spanish pork dishes in a boisterous atmosphere. The best deal is the charcuterie sampler; don't miss the rare and incredible *jamón ibérico*.

For a more budget conscious, but still very gratifying, experience: **Raging Burrito and Taco** (141 Sycamore St., 404/377-3311, www.ragingburrito.com, Sun.-Thurs. 11am-10pm, Fri.-Sat. 11am-midnight, $7-10) offers fat and fresh Tex-Mex burritos and tasty tacos and

Leon's Full Service in Decatur

quesadillas in a sports bar atmosphere. Their hot sauce is outstanding.

For a real Italian wood-oven pizza experience, head to **No. 246** (129 E. Ponce de Leon Ave., 678/399-8246, www.no246.com, Mon.-Thurs. 11am-3pm and 5pm-10pm, Fri.-Sat. 11am-3pm and 5pm-11pm, Sun. 11am-3pm and 5pm-9pm, $12-24). They also offer a pasta and gnocchi menu and a special chicken scallopini for two.

For Continental-quality dining, get a table at **Cafe Alsace** (121 E. Ponce de Leon Ave., 404/373-5622, www.cafealsace.net, Tues.-Fri. 11:30am-2:15pm and 6pm-10pm, Sat. 6pm-10pm, Sun. 10am-2pm, $25). As the name tells you, this is French cuisine with a Germanic feel, including spaetzle and choucroute garnie, a sauerkraut-sausage combo.

There are several coffeehouses in Decatur, but my favorite is **Java Monkey** (425 Church St., 404/378-5002, www.javamonkeydecatur.com, Mon.-Fri. 6:30am-midnight). They have tasty goodies in addition to great coffee, and every Tuesday night they host a surprisingly dynamic open-mic night for musicians.

Decatur has two great farmers market options, chief among them is **Your Dekalb Farmers Market** (3000 E. Ponce de Leon Ave., www.dekalbfarmersmarket.com, daily 9am-9pm), an enormous collection of goods and produce not only from regional sources but literally from around the world. **The Decatur Farmers Market** (Wed. location 163 Clairemont Ave., Sat. 498 N. McDonough St., location www.decaturfarmersmarket.com, Wed. 4pm-7pm, Sat. 9am-1pm) is a more modest and typical collection of locally sourced organic produce.

Shopping

Decatur hosts numerous boutique-style retail establishments, including uber-trendy **Squash Blossom** (113 E. Court Sq., 404/373-1864, www.squashblossomboutique.com, Mon. 11am-7pm, Tues.-Thurs. 11am-8pm, Fri. 11am-9pm, Sat. 10am-9pm, Sun. 11am-6pm), a great place for hip women's apparel and accessories from companies like Free People, Michael

Stars, and Echo. There's fun and fresh **World of Collage** (114 E. Ponce de Leon Ave., 404/377-1280, www.worldofcollage.com, Mon.-Sat. 11am-9pm, Sun. noon-6pm), which actually has little to do with collage and is a boutique with hard-to-find designers like Desigual and Johnny Was. For a slightly more mature take but still a lot of color, browse **Boutique Karma** (145 Sycamore St., 404/373-7533, www.boutique-karma.com, Mon.-Sat. 10:30am-7:30pm, Sun. 12:30pm-6pm).

Their branch in Athens, Georgia, is much more famous, but only two years after that one opened in 1976 another branch of **Wuxtry Records** (2096 N. Decatur Rd., 404/329-0020, www.wuxtry-records.com, Mon.-Sat. 11am-8pm, Sun. noon-6pm) opened in Decatur. Like its sister store, it's a gathering place for local musicians and hipsters alike.

The local arts and crafts scene is well represented at two cooperative galleries: **Wild Oats and Billy Goats** (112 E. Ponce de Leon Ave., 404/378-4088, www.wildoatsandbillygoats.com, Wed.-Fri. 11am-6pm, Sat. 11am-7pm, Sun. 1pm-5pm) and **HomeGrown Decatur** (412 Church St., 404/373-1147, www.homegrowndecatur.com, Mon.-Sat. 10am-9pm, Sun. noon-8pm).

One of the most unique shops in town is **Houndstooth Road** (316 Church St., 404/220-8957, www.h2rd.com, Wed.-Sat. noon-7pm, Sun. noon-5pm, Tues. by appt.), an upper-end Euro-style bicycle retailer, which also offers a range of clothing and accessories for the upwardly mobile cyclist.

Getting There and Around

Getting to Decatur from Atlanta proper couldn't be easier. The dedicated Decatur MARTA station is literally yards away from the town center, something that was quite controversial at first. Conversely, you can just drive east on Ponce de Leon Avenue from the heart of Atlanta's midtown on Peachtree Street, and end up directly in downtown Decatur. Once in Decatur, a car isn't necessary at all. It's very walkable, with almost every place you might want to visit within a couple of blocks.

STONE MOUNTAIN

Stone Mountain is both an iconic feature of the Atlanta landscape, literally, and a fairly cheesy tourist destination. In any case, it's certainly unique. The massive outcropping itself is incredible and geologically fascinating, a nearly 1,700-foot dome of quartz and granite five miles around at the base. The bas-relief sculpture on the north side of Stone Mountain, of Confederate General Robert E. Lee flanked by General Stonewall Jackson and Confederate President Jefferson Davis, all on horseback, is also an impressive work, regardless of what you may think of the implied message. The nightly, narrated 45-minute laser shows, included with basic admission, have been a staple of the scene at **Stone Mountain Park** (1000 Robert E. Lee Blvd., 770/498-5690, www.stonemountain-park.com, daily 10am-10pm, $10 entrance fee, other attractions extra) for generations.

What is distinctly less unique about Stone Mountain is the theme park that has been built up around it since a major "upgrade" in the 1990s. A cynic might say that the Confederates in the rock have themselves become an afterthought, playing second, third, and fourth fiddles to the associated rides and seasonal attractions (extra ticket required) that have blossomed literally in the mountain's shadow, including an actual locomotive train that takes you, Magic Kingdom-style, around the park's periphery.

The Confederates on the rock look down on Memorial Hall, where you enter for the laser shows. Adjacent to Memorial Hall is where you hop on the Skyride tram to and from the top of the mountain (extra ticket required), which I must say is worth the price. Closer to the mountain are individual interpretive memorials to each state of the Confederacy, detailing their involvement and sacrifice in the Civil War. At the horses' feet lies a large reflective pool complete with fountains.

While summer brings a steady crowd, Christmastime is a really big deal at Stone Mountain Park, with a festival-of-lights style cordoned-off area with a show (extra charge) and even a fake "snow mountain" between Memorial Hall and the mountain. Perhaps understandably, the associated Confederate history museum has been shunted off to one side of the park, where you can park and take a hiking trail to the top of the mountain if you're so inclined.

Your $10 basic entrance fee also entitles you to the use of various picnic areas and walking-biking trails within the Park's vast expanse. There are over 400 tent and RV camping sites ($45-60) available within the Park, as well as the attached Stone Mountain Inn ($170-200) and Evergreen Marriott Conference Resort ($190-230).

Getting There and Around

When most folks talk about Stone Mountain, they're talking about the outcropping and theme park, not the separate small municipality. In any case, the best way to get to either is to take one of three routes east of Atlanta: Stone Mountain Parkway/U.S. Highway 78, Ponce de Leon Avenue, or Memorial Drive. There is no MARTA train service to Stone Mountain, but you can take a MARTA bus from the Kensington Station.

MARIETTA

One of the largest entities in the Atlanta metro area, Marietta (www.mariettasquare.com) is the Cobb County seat, with well over 50,000 residents within city limits alone. Sadly it has even less remaining antebellum history than Atlanta, given that General Sherman's troops left only four buildings intact during their torching of Marietta in 1864. A major battle was fought at nearby Kennesaw Mountain, now a Park Service-preserved national battlefield. During World War II, the city and Cobb County got a boost with the construction of the enormous Bell airplane factory (later Lockheed Martin), which produced B-29 bombers by the thousands for the strategic bombing campaign on Japan. Cultural life in Marietta today revolves around the charming town square.

Gone with the Wind Museum: Scarlett on the Square

Marietta doesn't play a role in Margaret Mitchell's novel, but the city does host one

STONE MOUNTAIN STORIES

© JIM MOREKIS

Stone Mountain carvings

"Let freedom ring from Stone Mountain of Georgia..."

When Dr. Martin Luther King Jr. included those famous words in his "I Have a Dream" speech in 1963, it wasn't a nod to the enormous carving of three Confederate figures on the face of the granite outcropping, the largest bas-relief sculpture in the world. Commissioned in 1916, the carving wasn't actually completed until 1972, several years after King's assassination.

King was almost certainly referring to the fact—not generally mentioned in the Atlanta area today—that the modern incarnation of the Ku Klux Klan was founded in November 1915 on the summit of Stone Mountain itself. Those "Knights of Mary Phagan," as the hooded group called itself, burned a cross and took an oath administered by the grandson of the first KKK Grand Wizard, Confederate General Nathan Bedford Forrest. Also present that night was Sam Venable, owner of Stone Mountain, who would oversee efforts by various sculptors to finish the carving, one of which was Gutzon Borglum of Mount Rushmore fame, all the while allowing the KKK to hold meetings here. Frustrated by a 30-year hiatus in the carving, the

state of Georgia finally purchased Stone Mountain from Venable in 1958 for a million dollars."

Today, the carving of Confederate generals Robert E. Lee and Stonewall Jackson and Confederate President Jefferson Davis forms the central attraction of Stone Mountain Park (1000 Robert E. Lee Blvd., 770/498-5690, www.stonemountainpark.com, daily 10am-10pm, $10 entrance fee, other attractions extra), one of Georgia's biggest tourist draws and a place where the KKK most certainly is not welcome anymore.

Truthfully, the most interesting history on Stone Mountain's summit happened long before the Civil War, when Creek and later Cherokee Indians held ceremonies up here. In the early 1800s, when it was called Rock Mountain, the summit was a frequent destination for daylong horseback trips. Contrary to what you might think, Stone Mountain was actually heavily quarried for granite throughout the history of white settlement of the area. Stone Mountain rock is in the U.S. Capitol in Washington, D.C., and was offered for use in the new Martin Luther King Jr. Memorial, but it was turned down in favor of granite from China.

of the few *Gone with the Wind* museums outside Atlanta proper. The Gone with the Wind Museum (18 Whitlock Ave., 770/794-5576, www.gwtwmarietta.com, Mon.-Sat. 10am-5pm, $7 adults, $6 children), also called "Scarlett on the Square," set within a restored 1875 cotton warehouse, offers a modest collection of memorabilia mostly from the movie, most notably the honeymoon gown worn by Vivien Leigh in the film.

Marietta Museum of History

The Marietta Museum of History (1 Depot St., 770/794-5710, www.mariettahistory.org, Mon.-Sat. 10am-4pm, $5 adults, $3 children) is on the second floor of the 1845 Kennesaw House, one of a handful of antebellum structures left in town. There are displays on Native Americans, the Gold Rush, and of course the localized aspects of the Civil War. A relatively new and separate **Aviation Wing** (corner of S. Cobb Dr. and Atlanta Rd. SE, 770/794-5710, www.mariettahistory.org, Thurs.-Sat. 10am-3pm) is on 15 acres of land and has vintage airplane displays focusing on Marietta's considerable contribution to the World War II production effort.

Marietta/Cobb Museum of Art

Dedicated purely to American art, mostly from the 19th and 20th centuries, the Marietta/Cobb Museum of Art (30 Atlanta St., 770/528-1444, www.mariettacobbartmuseum.org, Tues.-Fri. 11am-5pm, Sat. 11am-4pm, Sun. 1pm-4pm, $8 adults, $5 children) is housed in Marietta's first Post Office. They host frequent community-oriented art instruction workshops, such as plein air and figure drawing.

Kennesaw Mountain National Battlefield Park

In June 1864, General Sherman's advance on Atlanta was temporarily stopped by Confederate troops and artillery dug in along the top of Kennesaw Mountain outside of Marietta. The 3,000-acre Kennesaw Mountain National Battlefield Park (900 Kennesaw Mountain Dr., 770/427-4686, www.nps.gov,

daily 8:30am-5pm, free) preserves and interprets the vast battleground. There are four self-guided driving tour stops and an incredible 18 miles of hiking trails (no bikes) throughout the battlefield area, all interpreted. Go the website for info on a cell phone audio tour.

Marietta Confederate Cemetery

Over 3,000 Confederate veterans, including many killed in the Battle of Kennesaw Mountain, are laid to rest in Marietta Confederate Cemetery (395 Powder Springs St., 770/794-5606, www.mariettaga.gov, daily 8:30am-dusk, free), the largest Confederate cemetery south of Richmond, the Confederate capital. The graveyard was founded in 1863 when a local woman donated land on her plantation to bury 20 soldiers who died in a train wreck.

The Big Chicken

For generations of Atlantans, the main attraction in "May-retta" has been what is universally called "The Big Chicken" (U.S. 41 and GA-120). It's actually a vintage Kentucky Fried Chicken franchise started in 1956. The seven-story, 56-foot tall chicken was designed by a Georgia Tech architecture student and erected in 1963. Severe storm damage in 1993 nearly caused it to be demolished, but it was saved by a public outcry, which included Air Force pilots who use the Big Chicken as a navigation point while landing at a nearby base.

Accommodations and Food

Marietta's most beloved spot is the ◖ **Marietta Diner** (306 Cobb Pkwy. S., 770/423-9390, www.mariettadiner.com, daily 24 hours, $15), a 24-hour meet-and-eat place known to generations of locals. It's getting a good amount of national buzz these days for its well-crafted menu of Southern comfort food (with a few twists, like kebabs and Romanian Steak), all served in massive portions. Yes, they serve breakfast all day.

There's no shortage of good eats around Marietta's downtown square (www.eatonthesquare.com), but your best bets include the unusual but delicious Tex-Mex-Asian fusion of **Taqueria Tsunami** (70 S. Park Sq., 678/324-7491, www.taqueriatsunami.com, Mon.-Thurs. 11am-9pm, Fri.-Sat. 11am-10pm, Sun. 10:30am-9pm, $12-20); the Thai-Japanese blend at **Thaicoon & Sushi** (34 Mill St., 678/766-0641, www.thaicoonmarietta. com, Mon.-Thurs. 11:30am-2:30pm and 5pm-10pm, Fri. 11:30am-2:30pm and 5pm-11pm, Sat. 5pm-11pm, Sun. 5pm-10pm, $12-18); and the hearty pizzeria **Marietta Pizza Company** (3 Whitlock Ave., 770/419-0900, www.mariettapizza.com, Mon.-Thurs. 11am-10pm, Fri.-Sat. 11am-11pm, Sun. 12:30pm-10pm, $15), which offers a focused and well-conceived menu, including great subs and a gluten-free crust.

A favorite location to fuel up before or after a Kennesaw Mountain hike is **Mountain Biscuits** (1718 Old Hwy. 41, 770/419-3311, Mon.-Fri. 6am-2pm, Sat. 7am-2pm, $10), where all the namesake baked items are enormous, made from scratch, and served with delicious gravy and tasty country ham and eggs.

There are plenty of chain hotels in Cobb County, but for a more unique stay try the **Stanley House Bed & Breakfast** (236 Church St., 770/426-1881, www.thestanleyhouse.com, $125), housed in a beautiful Victorian a short walk from the main town square.

Getting There and Around

Unfortunately MARTA doesn't go directly to Marietta, but you can take a MARTA rapid transit train to the Holmes Station and then take a Cobb Community Transit bus (http:// dot.cobbcountyga.gov) to where you need to go. MARTA and Cobb Community Transit are both $2.50. By car from Atlanta, take I-75 north to exit 265; take a left on the North Marietta Parkway (GA-120).

LAKE LANIER

As the prime reservoir on the Chattahoochee River, Lake Lanier is the main drinking water source for Atlanta. It's also one of the most popular recreation spots in the metro area, a fact driven not only by its proximity to the big

city but by its sheer size: nearly 700 miles of shoreline. Rowing events in the 1996 Olympics were held here. The nearest city to Lake Lanier is Gainesville, known chiefly as the home of Confederate General James Longstreet and more recently as the "Poultry Capital of the World" for the large number of chicken processing plants on its outskirts, as well as being the alleged birthplace of Southern fried chicken.

The U.S. Army Corps of Engineers operates Lake Lanier and also runs over 70 recreation and boat access areas, over 40 of which are operated directly by the Corps with the rest leased out to various other government entities. In addition to the ubiquitous boat ramps, there are eight marinas.

Periodic draught in the region has also led to frequently low water levels. While there are over 100 boat ramp lanes in theory, in practice a percentage are often closed due to low water levels. The lowest level recorded since the lake's construction in the 1950s was during the severe drought of 2007.

By far the most upscale and comprehensive lodging on the lake is **⟨** **Lake Lanier Islands Resort** (7000 Lanier Islands Pkwy., 770/945-8787, www.lakelanierislands.com, $200-600). In addition to a variety of rooms, suites, lake houses, and villas, it has its own **golf course** (green fee starts at $50), **canopy-zipline tours** ($200 full day, $30 "express"), a boat landing, an **equestrian center** (rides start at $35), and even its own water park, **LanierWorld** ($35 adults, $20 children, lower prices after dark). Other amenities and activities include **miniature golf, tennis,** and **volleyball.** The main Legacy Lodge building features frequent live entertainment. Business travelers have use of the attached conference center. For those who want a more laidback or luxurious vibe, there is a campground and hiking trails, and of course a **full-service spa.** While the intent is to provide anything and everything for the whole family with full lake access, interestingly there are no pet-friendly facilities at the resort. You don't have to be a registered guest to enjoy many of the à la carte amenities; the $10 gate fee (which guests also have to pay) entitles you to entrance and parking.

The Corps of Engineers operates several reservable **campgrounds** (www.recreation.gov, $30) on Lake Lanier with nearly 500 campsites: Bald Ridge Creek; Bolding Mill; Duckett Mill; Old Federal; Sawnee; and Van Pugh South Campground. Keep in mind they are seasonal, mostly due to lower water levels in the winter; check the website in advance. While there are many islands strewn throughout the lake and accessible by boat, you're not supposed to camp on them.

GAINESVILLE

Gainesville is chiefly known for two things: Its supposed status as "Poultry Capital of the World," a nod to the many chicken processing plants in the area; and as the home of Confederate General James Longstreet, Robert E. Lee's second-in-command. Despite his Confederate bona fides, Longstreet was quick to embrace northern Reconstruction policies after the Civil War, even becoming an active Republican during a time when that was considered borderline traitorous for a white Southerner. Get to Gainesville from Atlanta via I-85 North; take I-985/Lanier Parkway into town.

Piedmont Hotel

Opened by General James Longstreet in 1876, the Piedmont Hotel (827 Maple St., 770/539-9005, www.longstreetsociety.org, Tues.-Sat. 10am-4pm, free) has been reduced over the years to only the ground floor of its former three-story opulence. It's a museum of sorts now and home to the Longstreet Society (www.longstreetsociety.org), dedicated to preserving the memory of the general. They have a good Longstreet-oriented walking tour at the website, which of course includes the hotel itself. President Woodrow Wilson's daughter Jesse was born in one of the rooms. Longtime *Atlanta Journal-Constitution* editor Henry Grady was a frequent guest, as was Joel Chandler Harris of "Uncle Remus" fame.

Local lore has it that what we now know as Southern fried chicken was first cooked in the Piedmont's kitchen.

Alta Vista Cemetery

General James Longstreet was laid to rest in Alta Vista Cemetery (1080 Jesse Jewell Pkwy.). Well-wishers often leave cigars at his gravesite, an homage to the general's favorite vice. You'll also find the graves of many other Confederate veterans, a Space Shuttle astronaut, and Daniel Boone, though not *that* Daniel Boone. The cemetery's name means "high view" in Spanish, and the scenic hilltop location certainly provides that. Download a walking tour at www.gainesville.org.

Northeast Georgia History Center

The little Northeast Georgia History Center (322 Academy St., 770/297-5900, Tues.-Sat. 10am-4pm, $5 adults, $3 children) has some modest exhibits from the Gainesville area's history, which includes Northeast Georgia Sports Hall of Fame and the restored circa-1780 log cabin of Chief White Path of the Cherokees. There's also a little Freedom Garden dedicated to veterans.

ARABIA MOUNTAIN NATIONAL HERITAGE AREA

Two wonderful areas of pristine nature right outside the concrete jungle of Atlanta are **Panola Mountain State Park** (2600 Hwy. 155, 770/389-7801, www.gastateparks.org, daily 7am-dusk, $5 parking fee), near the suburban town of Stockbridge, and **Davidson-Arabia Nature Preserve** (3787 Klondike Rd., 770/492-5231, www.arabiaalliance.org, daily dawn-dusk, free) near Lithonia. Both areas are part of the Arabia Mountain National Heritage Area, administered by a cooperative partnership of local groups, and both are centered on enormous granite outcroppings similar to the larger Stone Mountain but without the attendant tourism development.

Panola Mountain is known for its rich and

rare botanical treasure, such as yellow daisies and Diamorpha. Because of its fragile ecosystem, hiking is allowed only through guided tours (depart from the park's nature center, generally 8am on Wed. and Fri.-Sun., $7 pp). Hikers have full use of Davidson-Arabia, with trails accessible from Klondike Road or by trailheads on the paved, 20-mile Rockdale River-Panola Mountain PATH Trail, which is open to bicycles and leashed dogs.

Panola Mountain and Arabia Mountain are both easily accessible from Atlanta by taking I-20 East. For Panola Mountain, get off at exit 68 and take Highway 155. For Arabia Mountain get off at Klondike Road, exit 74.

SENOIA

At the very edge of metro Atlanta—about 25 miles south—is Senoia (pronounced "sen-oy"), better known to fans of the cable TV series *The Walking Dead* as Woodbury. In fact, shooting of the incredibly popular show is so integral to the economy of this 3,000-person burg that several buildings on Main Street, purpose-built for the show, simply bear the name of the fictional town, such as Woodbury Town Hall. Main Street itself is often closed for weeks during shooting, with on-camera lawns left unmowed in suitably apocalyptic style.

The unofficial hub of town activity is **Senoia Coffee & Café** (1 Main St., 770/599-8000, http://senoiacoffeeandcafe.com, Mon.-Thurs. 6:30am-3pm, Fri. 6:30am-9pm, Sat. 7:30am-9pm), also known as the Woodbury Coffee House from the show. Have a cup of Zombie Dark java and maybe overhear chatter from "Walker Stalkers"—admittedly obsessive fans—while the crew is in town filming.

For pub-style eats and entertainment, go to **Southern Ground Social Club** (18 Main St., 770/727-9014, www.southerngroundsocialclub.com, Tue.-Sat. 11a.m-2am, $15), owned by native son and country star Zac Brown. The limited menu is tasty. Try the fried green tomato BLT. As you'd expect, most nights feature live music.

© DOUG WEISS

the "Woodbury Town Hall" in Senoia

NORTH GEORGIA

The southern tip of the Appalachian Mountain chain pushes into the northern portion of Georgia like a boot heel. Though criss-crossed by gorges, rivers, creeks, and hollows, North Georgia is a distinctly accessible mountainous area, more logistically forgiving than many areas farther into the Blue Ridge, but with a similar culture of directness, faith, and self-sufficiency.

It's here where America's first real gold rush happened, here where the "Death Knell of the Confederacy" was sounded at the Georgia-Tennessee border, here where the great Appalachian Trail itself begins on Springer Mountain. It's also here where you can enjoy some of the South's best state parks, most peaceful camping, best trout fishing, and prettiest vistas.

North Georgia is both helped and hurt by its proximity to heavily populous Atlanta, a symbiotic relationship perhaps best symbolized by the fact that you can often make out the downtown skyline from the top of Brasstown Bald, the highest spot in the state. The local economy benefits from the number of Atlantans who take day trips or camping vacations a short drive away from the big city, but the amount of development, especially in the form of highways and dams, has come with a cost. Appreciating North Georgia comes with a sense of vigilance and stewardship for its natural beauty, which provides

HIGHLIGHTS

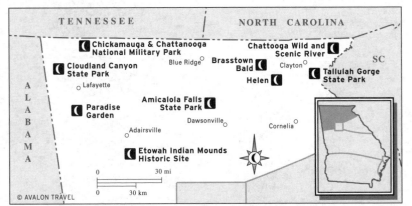

© AVALON TRAVEL

LOOK FOR ◖ TO FIND RECOMMENDED SIGHTS, ACTIVITIES, DINING, AND LODGING.

◖ **Chattooga Wild and Scenic River:** Take a raft ride on the Carolina border down through *Deliverance* country (page 99).

◖ **Tallulah Gorge State Park:** Hike way down into the deepest gorge in the eastern United States... or just hike around the rim (page 102).

◖ **Helen:** A little cheesy and a lot of fun, this "Alpine village" recreates *The Sound of Music* experience, but with beer (page 104).

◖ **Amicalola Falls State Park:** View the tallest waterfall east of the Mississippi River, near where the Appalachian Trail begins (page 110).

◖ **Brasstown Bald:** Hike or take the shuttle to Georgia's highest point. Look for the Atlanta skyline in the distance (page 116).

◖ **Etowah Indian Mounds Historic Site:** Climb to the top of an ancient Native American temple mound at this excellently preserved site and museum (page 125).

◖ **Chickamauga & Chattanooga National Military Park:** Take in the huge battlefield where the Confederacy won its last major victory (page 127).

◖ **Paradise Garden:** Immerse yourself in the eccentric, prolific vision of iconic folk artist Howard Finster (page 131).

◖ **Cloudland Canyon State Park:** Dotted with caves, this fascinating geological feature offers jaw-dropping views and great hiking and spelunking (page 132).

so much for so many and asks for so little in return.

PLANNING YOUR TIME

The single most important thing to keep in mind about North Georgia is that it's heavily seasonal. Many places, including most wineries and some restaurants, close for the winter after Christmas, not reopening until the spring

at the earliest. While occasionally state parks have limited access due to winter storm conditions, for the most part they stay open as usual throughout the cold season.

While Georgia is physically immense, the northern portion is much narrower than the rest of the state. It's theoretically possible to barnstorm through North Georgia in a day or two by car, just seeing the highlights.

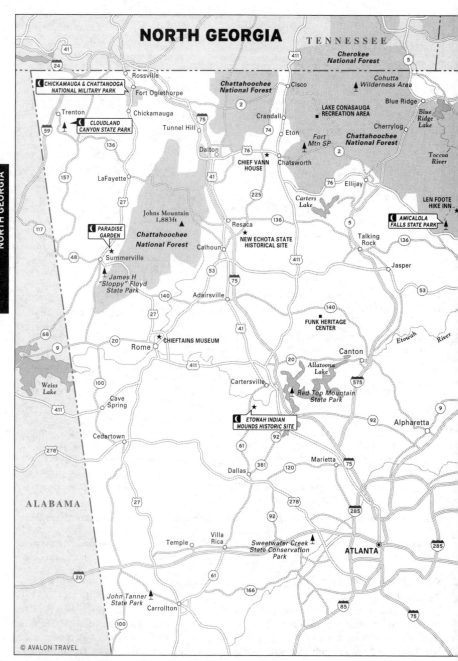

NORTH GEORGIA

TENNESSEE

Cherokee
National Forest

Cohutta
Wilderness Area

CHICKAMAUGA & CHATTANOOGA
NATIONAL MILITARY PARK

Rossville

Fort Oglethorpe

Chattahoochee
National Forest

Cisco

LAKE CONASAUGA
RECREATION AREA

Blue Ridge

Blue
Ridge
Lake

Trenton

Chickamauga

Crandall

Cherrylog

CLOUDLAND
CANYON STATE PARK

Tunnel Hill

Eton

Chattahoochee
National Forest

Toccoa
River

Dalton

Fort
Mtn SP

LaFayette

CHIEF VANN
HOUSE

Chatsworth

Johns Mountain
1,883ft

Carters
Lake

Ellijay

LEN FOOTE
HIKE INN

PARADISE
GARDEN

Chattahoochee
National Forest

Resaca

NEW ECHOTA STATE
HISTORICAL SITE

Talking
Rock

AMICALOLA
FALLS STATE PARK

Summerville

Calhoun

Jasper

James H
"Sloppy" Floyd
State Park

Adairsville

FUNK HERITAGE
CENTER

Etowah
River

CHIEFTAINS MUSEUM

Rome

Canton

Weiss
Lake

Allatoona
Lake

Cartersville

Red Top Mountain
State Park

Cave
Spring

ETOWAH INDIAN
MOUNDS HISTORIC SITE

Alpharetta

Cedartown

Marietta

Dallas

ALABAMA

Temple

Villa
Rica

Sweetwater Creek
State Conservation
Park

ATLANTA

John Tanner
State Park

Carrollton

© AVALON TRAVEL

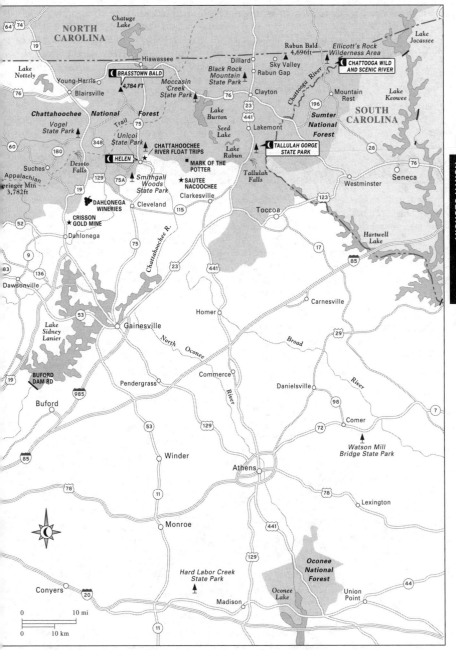

NORTH GEORGIA

Though, of course, a more relaxing approach is preferable.

The northeast section has more sights and more and better roads; that said, in the summer those two-lane roads, especially in the Helen area, can get pretty crowded with vacationers. Your actual progress might be slower than your map might indicate.

For those with more time to spend, I suggest making use of the plentiful state park facilities throughout North Georgia and extending your stay, perhaps with a couple of nights each in the northeast portion, the central Cohutta Mountains portion, and the Lookout Mountain portion on the northwest corner at the Tennessee border. A week of camping is plenty of time to enjoy the hiking, rafting, angling, and other outdoor activities in the entire North Georgia area.

Rabun County

In the northeast corner of the state on the border of the Carolinas, the Rabun County area (www.gamountains.com) is one of the most visited portions of North Georgia. It's where you'll find some of the state's most scenic vistas, all set amongst a collection of mountains, valleys, picturesque dairy farms, and delightful waterfalls along the Eastern Continental Divide in the Blue Ridge Mountains. Fittingly, Rabun is also chock-a-block with several well-maintained and attractive state parks catering to hikers, cyclists, campers, and anglers, most of which fill up early in the summer and especially during leaf-peeping season in October and November.

By the 1760s adventurous explorers came into this heavily Cherokee area; you can see a precious few small traces of Native American

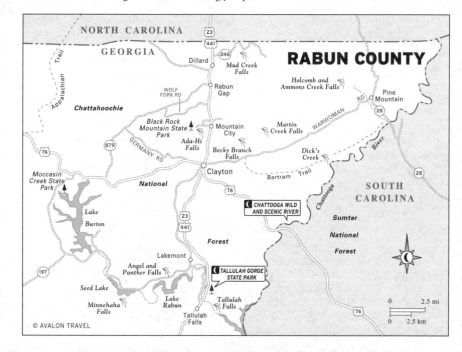

history today. The first high-profile visitor was naturalist William Bartram, who crossed the Chattooga River into Georgia at Warwoman Creek in 1775. The first white settler was John Dillard, who came in 1794 and gave his name to a town. By 1817 the Cherokee had been forced to cede the area permanently.

Along with only four other Georgia counties, Rabun voted not to secede from the Union. However, it did provide several regiments to the Confederate Army, though no real military action happened locally.

Rabun hit the global map in the 1890s, when the high Tallulah Falls Railway was constructed along the Tallulah Gorge, the deepest east of the Mississippi River. The Railway brought vacationers to various Victorian-style mountain resorts, and the area served as the scenic location for several movies, including *The Great Locomotive Chase*. In the 1970s it was a major location for the Burt Reynolds film *Deliverance*. Famed 1940s era actress Tallulah Bankhead got her name from a grandmother named after Tallulah Falls.

Dining in Clayton is a pleasure.

CLAYTON

The Rabun County seat is Clayton (www.downtownclaytonga.org), a diverse little mountain town with rustic charm to spare but still a full slate of offerings for the more sophisticated traveler. Adventurous food and nightlife in particular are readily available here, by no means a given in this otherwise very conservative part of the country.

The **Rabun County Welcome Center** (232 Hwy. 441, 706/782-4812, www.gamountains.com) is a good first stop. For a quick look at local history, go to the museum and research library at the **Rabun County Historical Society** (81 North Church St., Mon. 10am-2pm, Wed. 12:30pm-4:30pm, Fri. 10am-2pm) near the county courthouse.

There are plenty of shopping and gallery-browsing opportunities on the two primary avenues in Clayton: Main Street and Savannah Street. **Main Street Gallery** (51 N. Main St., 706/782-2440, www.mainstreetgallery.net, Mon.-Tues. and Thurs.-Sat. 10:30am-5pm)

specializes in mountain-style folk art, with three floors of arts and crafts, including plenty of jewelry.

A little ways out of downtown is the **Georgia Mountain Market** (811 Hwy. 441, 706/212-0523, Fri.-Sun. 8am-5pm), a huge warehouse with a bustling indoor flea market that folks drive to from many miles around.

My favorite restaurant in this part of North Georgia—and one of the few in the area that can go head-to-head with most any big-city spot—is ◖ **Zeppelin's** (88 Main St., 706/212-0101, www.zeppelinspastahouse.com, Mon.-Thu. 11:30am-9pm, Fri.-Sat. 11am-10pm, Sun. 11am-9pm, $12). As the name indicates, a classic rock-style decor greets you in this hip but tastefully appointed restaurant and tavern. A menu of perfectly crispy flatbread pizzas (about $15 and big enough for two) is their main claim to fame, but their burgers are incredible as well, including a bison option. Be sure to check out the specials, as Zeppelin's also has frequent seafood offerings that are hard to pass up. A cozy bar area greets you as you enter, and it's a hopping party spot at times, especially when the Georgia Bulldogs are playing on TV.

Right across the street from Zeppelin's is a fun tavern, **Universal Joint** (109 N. Main St., 706/782-7116, www.ujclayton.com, Mon.-Sat. 11:30am-midnight, Sun. noon-8pm, $10), which offers frequent live music and extensive outdoor seating, including around a fire pit. The bar-food type menu at this regional chain focuses on burgers and particularly-tasty tacos.

For a hearty traditional Italian meal, try **Mama G's** (777 Hwy. 441, 706/782-9565, www.loveisgoodfood.net, $10), where the pizza dough is made from scratch. In addition to their popular pizzas they have a full menu of pasta dishes, from basic spaghetti and 100 percent all-beef meatballs to linguini and clams.

Clayton's entry in the sustainable farm-to-table movement is **Grapes & Beans** (42 E. Savannah St., 706/212-0020, www.grapesandbeans.com, Fri.-Sat. 9am-4pm, lunch 11am-2:30pm, Sun.-Thurs. 9am-3pm, lunch 11am-2:30pm, $8), a combo coffeehouse and restaurant whose seasonal lunch menu focuses on fresh, healthy grab 'n' go sandwich items, such as portabella pita, gyro, and southwest chicken. They're open in the mornings for coffee and espresso, and they offer a good range of wine by the glass as well.

Another place for a good cuppa joe and something to read while you enjoy it is **Prater's Books** (34 N. Main St., 706/212-0017, www.praterbooks.com, Mon.-Tues. 10am-5pm, Thurs.-Fri. 10am-5pm, Sat. 10am-3pm), a full service bookstore and coffee shop.

A short drive north of Clayton is ◖ **Tomlin's Barbecue** (5030 Hwy. 441, 706/982-1750, www.tomlinbbq.com, May-Oct. Fri.-Sun. 10:30am-4:30pm, $7), set in a little red cabin adjacent to the Osage Farms Produce Market. Tomlin's is one of North Georgia's most highly regarded 'cue joints and offers some sublime smoked pulled pork and a distinctive vinegar sauce. While you're here you can pick up some tasty farm-fresh produce at the market.

Foxfire Museum & Heritage Center

For nearly 50 years, the *Foxfire* book and magazine series has chronicled and preserved the dwindling folkways of the Southern Appalachians in North Georgia. The Foxfire organization funds and runs the Foxfire Museum & Heritage Center (Black Mountain Pkwy., 706/746-5828, www.foxfire.org, Mon.-Sat. 8:30am-4:30pm, 11 and older $6, 7-10 $3, under six free) in Mountain City, a few minutes north of Clayton. This collection of vernacular log buildings just off Highway 441 contains a wealth of authentic displays and equipment portraying the often-grueling daily life of mountain people in this area for generations. Of the nearly two dozen structures, about half are completely intact and original. Highlights include the 1820s log home, which raised several generations of one family, and a 1790s tar grinder wagon, which was on the Trail of Tears. Adding to the fun are the frequent demonstrations from artisans and craftspeople. Of course at the gift shop you can pick up any number of rustic-themed items as well as the entire *Foxfire* oeuvre.

Each October in downtown Clayton, the community comes together for the **Foxfire Mountaineer Festival** (www.foxfire.org), which celebrates the area's heritage and the group's signature accomplishments.

Dillard

North of Clayton and Mountain City near the North Carolina border, the first settlement in the area is named after the founding family, whose legacy continues at ◖ **The Dillard House** (1158 Franklin St., 800/541-0671, www.dillardhouse.com, restaurant: daily, 7am-10:30am and 11:30am-8pm, $15-25), a grand bed-and-breakfast-style inn with a variety of rooms and cottages. Over the years the Dillard House has become something of a country resort, complete with riding stables, a petting zoo, and multiple adventure and special event packages. You don't have to be a guest to enjoy a nice meal here: The family-style community restaurant onsite features down-home Southern comfort food and plenty of it, drawing customers from many miles around.

Dick's Creek Falls

One of the more picturesque cascades in Rabun County is Dick's Creek Falls with a 60-foot drop into the Chattooga River. You get there by a 1.5-mile round-trip trail. Take Warwoman Road east out of Clayton and turn right on Sandy Ford Road, which will become unpaved. The trail parking area is right before the place where the creek washes over the road. Follow the trail along the creek and over a bridge to the falls.

◖ CHATTOOGA WILD AND SCENIC RIVER

If you've seen the 1972 film *Deliverance*, you've seen the Chattooga River (www.rivers.gov), the South's best whitewater rafting locale (in the movie it bore the fictional name "Cahulawassee"). The Chattooga River forms part of the Georgia-South Carolina border during its run from its origin at the base of Whiteside Mountain in North Carolina to its end at Lake Tugaloo in South Carolina. If you're whitewater rafting you'll likely be putting in farther upstream, but the easiest way to get to the Chattooga is to take U.S. 76 until you just cross the Chattooga River Bridge into South Carolina. On the Carolina side is a sizeable parking area, unfortunately with subpar restroom facilities. You can park in Georgia if you'd like, but there's a $2 parking fee and fewer spaces.

What greets you after a short walk down to the river is a sight straight out of a primordial era. Because of the river's federal Wild and Scenic designation in the 1970s, there is no development or damming along a sizeable portion of its length. The banks are so lush with ferns that you might expect a dinosaur to show up any minute and begin munching on them.

At this point the Chattooga forms the **Bull Sluice Falls**, a popular thrill-seeking point for rafters and kayakers at the end of Section III of the river, with a 14-foot drop when the river is at full level (Bull Sluice also had a starring role

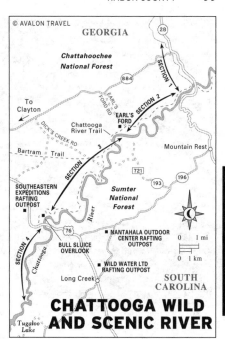

CHATTOOGA WILD AND SCENIC RIVER

in *Deliverance*). But you don't have to be a rafter or thrill-seeker to enjoy the Chattooga. Unless the water is particularly high when you go, you can make your way gingerly out on the rocks and find shallow pools away from the whitewater. If you're in your swimsuit you can relax in the water and even swim a short ways—just be aware of the strong current in the middle of the river. Bull Sluice is a popular, free place for area families to enjoy a dip in the cool water among the roaring sounds of the sluice. On a sunny weekend day bring your bathing suits and towels just like a day at the beach.

For recreational purposes the Chattooga is divided into four sections. Section I is primarily for anglers only and is off-limits to boating for the most part. Section II begins at Highway 28 and ends at Earl's Ford, where there's a quarter-mile hike to reach vehicles. This is a great little seven-mile run for families, tubers, and novice rafters, with only a single Class III rapid at Big Shoals.

The real action begins at Section III, a

A visitor enjoys the scenery at the Chattooga Wild and Scenic River.

© SUSAN LEGGETT/123RF.COM

14-mile run from Earl's Ford to the U.S. 76 bridge, with a quarter-mile walk to put in. Beginning with Warwoman Rapid, you'll get a lot of Class II, III, and IV rapids, including the final Class IV-V rapid at Bull Sluice, which concludes Section III. In all, Section III will take 6-8 hours from beginning to end.

The most challenging ride is Section IV, from the U.S. 76 bridge to the river's conclusion at Lake Tugaloo. It's a short but exciting five-mile run with a whole bunch of Class III and IV rapids, especially in the crazy Five Falls section.

For serious rafting the takeoff points are upriver on the South Carolina side. The main professional rafting tour company on the river is **Nantahala Outdoor Center** (888/905-7238, www.noc.com, prices vary). They run tours on several rivers in the region, including several packages on Sections III and IV of the Chattooga, some with lunch included. If you have kids ages 8-17, they offer a tour on Section III (Section IV is for ages 18 and over only due to its extreme rapids). Expect to pay at least $85

per person, more during the high season in the summer. While walk-ins are welcome, I recommend reserving your trip in advance. Another popular Chattooga rafting guide is **Wildwater Rafting** (800/451-9972, www.wildwaterrafting.com, prices vary). They run a similar series of guided tours on Sections III and IV, as well as a kid-friendly "mini trip" on Section III. To get to their put-in location, take U.S. 76 out of Westminster about 14 miles and take a right on Academy Road. Wildwater Rafting is about a mile down the road on the left. As with Nantahala Outdoor Center, reservations are strongly encouraged.

Ellicott Rock Wilderness Area

With roots in a scenic area designated in the 1960s, one of the oldest trails in the Southeast is the Ellicott Rock Wilderness Area (864/638-9568, www.fs.fed.us, daily dawn-dusk, free), which shares acreage with three states. It takes you through the Chattooga River gorge in the Sumter National Forest, with about half the trail in North Carolina and a small portion

DELIVERANCE SYNDROME

Before the 1972 film *Deliverance* brought the Chattooga River to the nation's consciousness, less than a thousand people a year went down the whitewater rapids of the largely unknown waterway up in the corner where Georgia and the Carolinas meet. The year after the film's release, that number skyrocketed to 21,000 a year.

Along with the dramatically increased traffic came an increase in foolhardiness and needless risk-taking, as rafters—many with little or no experience on the water—tried to emulate the crashing, adrenaline-filled rides from the movie. In the four years after the film's release, 24 people lost their lives on the river in displays of what came to be known as "*Deliverance* Syndrome." Today, the prevalence of professional raft trip guides means that even though up to 100,000 people a year raft the river these days, a lot fewer are getting hurt on the river.

While a casual glance would infer that the river's being granted official Wild and Scenic River status in 1974 had something to do with *Deliverance*, that's just coincidence. As early as 1969, a year before James Dickey's novel *Deliverance* was published, a congressional task force was studying the Chattooga for possible inclusion on the list. The river had to meet several criteria: It had to be "free flowing" long enough to provide a "meaningful experience"; it had to have enough volume to "allow full enjoyment of water-related activities"; its environment had to be "outstandingly remarkable"; the river had to be "generally inaccessible" and "essentially primitive"; and its waters had to be unpolluted. Technically speaking, 39.8 miles of the Chattooga have "wild" status, 2.5 miles "scenic" status, and 14.6 miles are "recreational," for a total of 56.9 miles.

in Georgia. (Ellicott Rock itself, once inaccurately considered the meeting point of the three states, is actually in North Carolina. You can reach it on one of the trails in the wilderness area.)

BLACK ROCK MOUNTAIN STATE PARK

The highest state park in Georgia and one of the most enjoyable, Black Rock Mountain State Park (3085 Black Rock Mountain Pkwy., 706/746-2141, www.gastateparks.org, Mar.-Nov. daily 7am-10pm, $5 parking fee; campsites $25-28, walk-in campsites $15, cottages $125-145) particularly attracts large crowds during leaf-turning season in the fall. From this vantage point way up in the Blue Ridge you can see the reds, yellows, and oranges vividly. Hikers will also enjoy the particularly challenging and visually appealing system of four wilderness trails. The Visitors Center at the summit of the mountain is a popular place in and of itself for its relaxing views and selection of merchandise. Campers will find 44 tent and RV sites, 10 cottages, two of which

are dog-friendly, and a dozen walk-in campsites. While not typically considered a hardcore angler's park, there is a small picturesque lake stocked with bass, trout, and catfish and good for kayaking (no rentals available, however).

MOCCASIN CREEK STATE PARK

Moccasin Creek State Park (3655 Hwy. 197, 706/947-3194, www.gastateparks.org, Mar.-Nov. daily 7am-10pm, $5 parking fee; campsites $25), nestled up against quiet, pretty Lake Burton, is focused on boating and fishing. Camping is a little snug here, with tent and RV gravel sites fairly close together. But it's a fine place from which to recreate on the water, with docks, a boat ramp, and a fishing pier open only to the handicapped, seniors, and children. It's also a reasonably centrally located state park, providing quick access to Tallulah Gorge to the southeast, Helen to the southwest, and the higher ground deeper up in the Blue Ridge. Sunrises and sunsets on the lake are particularly pleasant.

NORTH GEORGIA

© JIM MOREKIS

scenic views at Black Rock Mountain State Park

Wildcat Creek

Just around the corner from Lake Burton is the access road to one of North Georgia's hidden gems: Wildcat Creek (U.S. Forest Service Rd. 26, Chattahoochee-Oconee National Forest, www.fs.usda.gov, campsites $10, first come, first served, no water available). You'll find outstanding fishing in this delightful creek stocked with rainbow trout, along with a fun, natural rock slide into the water. Lining Wildcat Creek are two primitive campgrounds run by the U.S. Forest Service. Hikers can access the Appalachian Trail from this route as well. A sturdy four-wheel drive vehicle is strongly recommended for the rough gravel road; however, RVs will not be able to navigate the turns.

We all know that food tastes better when you're camping, but if you're roughing it around Lake Burton and want to splurge on a sit-down meal indoors, grab a steak or seafood dish at **The Chophouse** (25 Shoreline Trail, 706/947-0010, www.lapradesmarina.com, hours vary, $18-28) at LaPrade's Marina on the waterfront.

◖ TALLULAH GORGE STATE PARK

One of a handful of really widely recognized names in North Georgia, Tallulah Gorge State Park (338 Jane Hurt Yarn Dr., 706/754-7981, www.gastateparks.org, daily 8am-dark, $5 parking fee) has understandably been one of the state's most visited parks since its inception in the 1990s. Containing the eponymous and iconic Tallulah Falls themselves and covering a vast area on either side of the deepest gorge in the eastern United States (1,000 feet deep), the park has an expert infrastructure designed to balance maximum enjoyment for a maximum number of people while still preserving the inherent natural beauty and significance of the site itself.

Your first stop is the **Jane Hurt Yarn Interpretive Center** (daily 8am-5pm), a combined visitors center and museum explaining both the natural and human history of the area, including Tallulah Falls Victorian heyday as a national resort area. The rare Persistent Trillium is one of the life forms that exist in this very particular ecosystem. The Interpretive Center is also where you can get your free permit to hike the actual floor of the gorge (only permit holders can go all the way to the bottom and only 100 permits are given out each day; get there as early as you can). In the theater you can enjoy a high-quality video exploring the park from top to bottom and side to side, a particularly helpful offering considering not everyone has the time or stamina to fully explore it in person.

You can enjoy the park in different chunks. For the less adventurous or those with less time, a simple walk along the north rim includes several viewing points. You may choose to go down the 531-step staircase and across a suspension walking bridge to the bottom of the gorge (you'll need a permit to actually walk onto the rocky bottom). Along the way you'll see the old iron towers used to stage Karl

© JIM MOREKIS

at the bottom of Tallulah Gorge

Wallenda's famous tightrope walk across the gorge in 1970. But be forewarned: Climbing back up those steps is extremely strenuous and you must pace yourself. The most adventurous hikers can take the long trek from there to **Bridal Veil Falls,** where the only swimming in the park is allowed.

At 600 feet, the second tallest waterfall in the state is **Caledonia Cascade,** sometimes called Cascade Falls, near the beginning of Tallulah gorge. It's a tiered cascade with three drops. You can see it from the hiking trail around the rim.

The trail system within the park is extensive and includes 10 miles of hiking trails, a 10-mile mountain biking trail, and a 2-mile rails-to-trails bicycle and walking path. Lodging within the park is fairly limited considering its size, and includes 50 tent and RV sites and three backcountry shelters ($15).

As beautiful as the park is, much of its modern beauty is artificially constructed. While the various falls in the park are still quite impressive, they were quieted to a great extent by the damming of the Tallulah River to bring hydroelectric power to Atlanta in the early 20th century. The unsuccessful effort to fight the projects, led by the widow of Confederate General James Longstreet, was one of the first conservation movements in Georgia; one of the park's trails is named after her. The falls today are administered through the state and the massive utility Georgia Power. A few "aesthetic releases" of water each year increase kayaking and rafting opportunities; however, the tradeoff is that when this happens you can't visit the bottom of the gorge. Check the website for specific dates.

Minnehaha Falls

Not to be confused with a cascade in Minnesota with the same name, Minnehaha Falls are among the most picturesque you will see anywhere, despite not being particularly tall. The falls are near Lake Rabun on a half-mile Forest Service trail off Bear Gap Road a few miles northeast of Tallulah Gorge State Park. To get here take U.S. 441 north of the park for 2 miles, then turn onto "Old" Highway 441 and take that another 2.5 miles. Turn left onto Lake Rabun Road and take that for six miles before turning left onto the road below the dam. Bear left onto Bear Gap Road for about 1.5 miles. There's a very small parking area.

TOCCOA

Just south of Rabun County is the quiet hill town of Toccoa, famous as the hometown of the "world's strongest man," powerlifter Paul Anderson. Urban design mavens might be interested to know that from the 1960s to the early 2000s, a portion of downtown Toccoa was put entirely under concrete canopies to encourage foot traffic, a response to the flight to shopping malls on the outskirts. It didn't work, and downtown has been completely restored to its more realistic open-air state.

Toccoa Falls

While Toccoa Falls (107 N. Chapel Dr., 706/886-6831, daily 8:30am-dusk, adults $8, children $3) are by no means the most spectacular in north Georgia, the 190-foot cataract has the bonus of being extremely easy to get to. Indeed, the walk from your car to the Falls is shorter than the drive through the campus of Toccoa Falls College, within whose borders the Falls are located. There's a visitors center with a small gift shop and signage explaining the disastrous dam failure that killed 39 people in 1977.

Currahee Military Museum

Recently Toccoa's most dynamic attraction has been the Currahee Military Museum (160 N. Alexander St., 706/282-5055, www.toccoahistory.com, Mon.-Sat. 10am-4pm, Sun. 1pm-4pm), a modest but interesting memorial to the World War II-era training of U.S. Army paratroopers in and around the Toccoa area. One of the units that trained here, the 506th Parachute Infantry Regiment, included the "Easy Company" featured in the HBO series *Band of Brothers,* and the museum has enjoyed quite a boost in publicity and interest in the show's wake. The first Saturday of each October features a six-mile race emulating the old training runs of the paratroopers up Currahee Mountain and back; there's a companion "D-Day Run" in June.

Travelers Rest State Historic Site

A short drive east of Toccoa straddling the South Carolina border is Travelers Rest State Historic Site (4339 Riverdale Rd., 706/886-2256, www.gastateparks.org, hours vary, $4 parking), often called Jarrett Manor by locals. This large rustic building was built as a stagecoach inn by James Wyly around 1815. You can tour the house and see some original furnishings. The state of Georgia bought it in 1955 and runs the site as an attraction today. However, as of this writing budget cuts have severely impacted operating times; call ahead to check.

Helen and Vicinity

The area around Helen is picturesque, easily accessible, and offers plenty of tourist amenities. No wonder, then, that it's an extremely popular summer and fall vacation spot, especially for day-trippers from metro Atlanta.

The kitschy charm of Helen itself is the chief draw, but by no means the only one. There are other charming small towns, such as Sautee Nacoochee and Clarkesville, and a plethora of high-quality state parks, including the gateway to the legendary Appalachian Trail itself.

◖ HELEN

For generations of Georgians, the word "Helen" has either meant a fun place to get away in the mountains, a hilariously cheesy living theme park, or a combination of both. Situated in a neat little valley at the headwaters of the Chattahoochee River, this once-decrepit former logging town was literally rebuilt from scratch in the late 1960s specifically to mimic a stereotypical German-Swiss mountain village. Local zoning and building regulations require

© JIM MOREKIS

in the "Alpine village" of Helen

that every structure, including fast food restaurants, conform to the classic Alpine look and feel familiar to most people from *The Sound of Music.*

While the effect is often chuckle-inducing, you have to give Helen (www.helenga.org) credit for completely immersing itself—even the local cop cars bear the word "Polizei." For these few short blocks along Highway 17, you too can take the plunge, browsing impossibly-cute, well-stocked storefronts filled with Teutonic tchotchkes, sniffing colorful tulips, quaffing brew from enormous steins at one of many beer halls, or enjoying schnitzel and sauerkraut and Black Forest cake. In any case, the formula works, and Helen remains one of the top tourist destinations in the state. Motorcyclists in particular are drawn to the area, and the rumble of Harley engines never seems far away here.

The highlight of the year is the annual **Oktoberfest** centering around the city **Festhalle** (1074 Edelweiss Strasse, 706/878-1908, www.helenchamber.com, $8 Mon.-Fri.,

$9 Sat., free Sun.). Unlike many towns that hold similar events, Oktoberfest in Helen is no mere long weekend: It lasts from mid-September through the end of October. In true German style, the Festhalle is filled with rows of long tables for you to enjoy your beer and brats and listen to polka and oompah music.

Be forewarned: Helen is heavily seasonal. Much of it is closed down in the winter, but its surrounding roads can get very crowded during Oktoberfest and indeed on any pleasant weekend in the summer. This is not only due to its popularity but due to the fact that there is a single significant road through town. Make plans in advance and prepare to be patient anywhere in the vicinity of downtown, whether finding a parking space or a seat at a restaurant.

Sights

One of Georgia's most unique attractions, **Charlemagne's Kingdom** (8808 N. Main St., 706/878-2200, www.georgiamodelrailroad. com, Thurs.-Tues. 10am-5pm, $5) is the labor of love of a German couple who, over the course of the last two decades, have built an entirely self-contained little part of Germany traversed by an extensive model railroad in HO scale (the most popular model railway format), featuring over 400 feet of track, all indoors for your viewing enjoyment. The attention to detail and authenticity is stunning, and you don't have to be a child to enjoy the panorama, crowned by a 20-foot version of the Matterhorn summit. To find the Kingdom from the main road, look for the building with the huge mural of the eponymous medieval emperor; the owner Willi Lindhorst claims to be a descendant.

Sixteen bears are the attraction at the **Black Forest Bear Park** (8160 S. Main St., 706/878-7043, www.blackforestbearpark.com, Sun.-Fri. 10am-6pm, Sat. 10am-7pm, $5) smack downtown. An extra buck buys you a tray of apples and bread to feed them. While the bears are obviously well fed and will do tricks for snacks, their living conditions aren't exactly state of the art and might offend not only animal rights activists but a goodly portion of visitors. On the plus side, all the bears, including a grizzly, are rescues. Perhaps oddly, there's an associated display of snakes.

Just off the main drag you'll find the **Helen Arts and Heritage Center** (25 Chattahoochee Strasse, 706/878-3933, www.helenarts.org, Thurs.-Mon. noon-4pm, free) in the former City Hall building. The center exhibits a modest collection of regional art and local lore.

Helen Tubing and Water Park (9917 Hwy. 75 N., 706/878-1082, www.helentubing.com, water park summer Sun.-Thurs. 10am-6pm, Sat.-Fri. 10am-8pm, tubing summer daily 9am-6pm, weather permitting, all day tubing with waterpark $15, tubing only $8) is a little on the downscale side, but you can't beat the price and there is the modest, attached water park for those so inclined. There are four check-in locations to get on the Chattahoochee River. When water levels are low, it can be a fairly slow ride down the river.

Habersham Winery

The Helen-Sautee Nacoochee area hosts a couple of quality wineries. Habersham Winery (7025 S. Main St., 706/878-9463, www.habershamwinery.com, Mon.-Sat. 10am-6pm, Sun. 12:30pm-6pm) has its showroom and free sampling area just around the corner from downtown Helen. Their prime offerings include some good white wines, including a nice Riesling.

Shopping

You can get a little bit of everything at **Betty's Country Store** (18 Yonah St., 706/878-2943, www.bettysinhelen.com, daily 7am-9pm), from fresh groceries to baked goods to regionally produced wines in an old-fashioned country store atmosphere (the building is from 1937). Much of it is homemade, including their salsa and delicious signature carrot cake.

You wouldn't expect an Alpine village—even one in Georgia—to be without a **Christmas Shoppe** (8749 N. Main St., 706/878-1012, www.helenchristmasshoppe.com, spring-fall daily 10am-6pm). Here's where you can pick up your Yule-themed gifts, most with a Germanic feel.

The **Georgia Heritage Center for the Arts** (8016 S. Main St., 706/892-1033, Mon.-Fri. 10am-4pm) is a nonprofit representing local and regional artists.

Accommodations

Quality chain lodging in Helen is scarce, but you can try the entirely Alpine-themed **Hampton Inn** (147 Unicoi St., 706/878-3310, www.hamptoninn.com, $100) or the **Country Inn & Suites** (877 Edelweiss Strasse, 706/878-9000, www.countryinns.com, $110-150) for a cut above the typical chain experience. Both are within easy walking distance of the action on Main Street (Hwy. 17).

For a romantic, and yes, German-themed getaway, head to **Black Forest Bed & Breakfast** (8902 N. Main St., 706/878-3995, www.blackforestvacationrentals.com, $135-250), which offers four spacious rooms with separate entrances and whirlpool tubs, and three cottage rooms. There are five "couples-only" cabins as well. You can hang out and enjoy the peaceful, landscaped garden or walk the short distance to Main Street. They also offer vacation rental cabins worth checking out.

Food

The iconic **Old Heidelberg** (8660 N. Main St., 706/878-3273, spring-fall daily 11:30am-9pm, $20) calls itself the "most photographed building in Georgia." While this is almost certainly a stretch, its key location within well-traveled White Horse Square smack downtown, not to mention its evocative and quite handsome exterior, makes it unforgettable. The oldest German restaurant in Helen, dating back to 1975, pretty much concurrent with the town's rebirth, Old Heidelberg's menu has an entire page of schnitzel (about $20) and another for sausage dishes ($15). The bar is downstairs and you eat upstairs.

Off the Main Street hustle and bustle but also conveniently across the street from the town Festhalle, **◖ Bodensee** (64 Munichstrasse, 706/878-1026, spring-fall daily 11:30am-8pm, $15) is often considered

Helen's best German home-style restaurant. They serve a mean jaegerschnitzel along with all the other staples, such as spaetzle and stroganoff. If you're unsure what to get, they have various sampler platters, and the staff is particularly helpful.

While chiefly marketing itself as an authentically old-school German bakery and cafe, **Hofer's** (8758 N. Main St., 706/878-8200, www.hofers.com, spring-fall daily 8am-6pm, $12-18) has a full breakfast, lunch, and dinner menu, including schnitzel, knackwurst, and sauerbraten. They also sell a variety of hard-to-get German magazines.

The **Hansel & Gretel Candy Kitchen** (8078 S. Main St., 706/878-2443, daily 10am-6pm) is a popular stop for kids and adults alike, with all the chocolate concoctions you could reasonably ask for (fudge, truffles, and even sculptures), along with taffy, gummy bears, peanut brittle, and even pecan brittle, to take with you or eat on the spot.

SAUTEE NACOOCHEE

Directly adjacent to Helen is the somewhat more tasteful little community of Sautee Nacoochee. While it has clearly profited from its proximity to the tourism powerhouse of Helen, it maintains a quieter and generally more upscale feel.

Sights

Even the building is attractive at the **Folk Pottery Museum of Northeast Georgia** (283 Hwy. 255, 706/878-3300, www.folkpotterymuseum.com, Mon.-Sat. 10am-5pm, Sun. 1pm-5pm, $5 adults, $2 children), set within the Sautee Nacoochee Cultural Center. The picturesque setting and the outstanding rotating and permanent regional folk pottery exhibits combine for a very pleasant experience. Each September they hold their annual Pottery Show and Sale, a great opportunity to purchase their one-of-a-kind works of art. There's also a small history museum (Mon.-Sat. 10am-5pm, Sun. 1pm-5pm, free) within the Cultural Center.

In a huge, privately-owned, open field at the corner of Highways 75 and 17 is the **Nacoochee Mound,** or more accurately what's left of it. Completely excavated in the early 1900s and now topped with an incongruous Victorian-looking cupola, this restored Native American ceremonial temple mound is roughly what it might have looked like back in the 1500s when, according to legend, Spanish explorer Hernando DeSoto came through the area and met with the local chief. You can't get close to it but a helpful marker is roadside.

For the classic old-school country store experience, including the famous resident kitty "Wampus Cat," head to the **Old Sautee Store** (2315 Hwy. 17, 706/878-2281, www.oldsauteestore.com, Mon.-Sat. 10am-5:30pm, Sun. noon-5:30pm). This being around the corner from Helen, of course expect a dose of Nordic flavor. You can get most anything here, including fresh cheese, sandwiches, sodas, ice cream, and assorted gifts.

Sautee Nacoochee Vineyards

Sautee Nacoochee Vineyards (1299 Hwy. 17, 706/878-1056, www.sauteenacoocheevineyards.com, Mon.-Sat. noon-6pm) features a dedicated tasting room and deck overlooking the surrounding Appalachian foothills. They focus on classic reds, including a special blend called Red-Headed Stepchild.

Accommodations and Food

◖ **Lucille's Mountain Top Inn & Spa** (964 Rabun Rd., 706/878-5055, www.lucillesmountaintopinn.com, $200) is a far cry from Helen's tourist boom and offers a great place to get away from it all. The views from the balconies are stunning, the spa facilities are easily some of the best in the area, the gourmet breakfasts are delicious and filling, the 10 rooms are sumptuous and well-appointed, the staff is friendly, and the prices really aren't bad considering what you get.

If you need a break from all things German, head directly to the Italian-American-owned ◖ **Nacoochee Village Tavern & Pizzeria** (7275 S. Main St., 706/878-0199, www.villagetavernpizza.com, Mon.-Thurs. noon-10pm, Fri.-Sat. noon-11pm, Sun. 1pm-10pm, $15), known for wood-firing some of the best pizza in North Georgia. Subs and sandwiches are also excellent, the calzones are enormous and tasty, and they even offer a great antipasto platter. To finish things off with a great cup of coffee and a sweet treat, head down the road to **JumpinGoat Coffee Roasters** (7082 S. Main St., 706/892-1207, www.jumpingoatcoffee.com, daily 9am-5pm). They roast all their own beans and ship nationwide.

RAVEN CLIFF FALLS

Situated within the massive Raven Cliffs Wilderness Area (www.fs.usda.gov), itself a major trout-fishing and hiking mecca, Raven Cliff Falls on Dodd Creek is one of North Georgia's most popular cascades despite being a relatively long and strenuous five-mile round-trip hike. The falls, totaling a drop of 400 feet, are present in several sections along the hike. You can hear the roaring falls virtually the entire way, and nothing quite prepares you for the sight of the upstream 100-foot cascade literally splitting one of North Georgia's steepest cliffs in two.

While the Wilderness Area is itself a peaceful wildlife preserve, the actual area around the trail and falls is far from pristine due to heavy foot traffic. There is walk-in camping but it's not particularly recommended due to the crowds. To get here take Highway 75 north from Helen about a 1.5 miles and turn left onto Highway 356. From there go about 2.5 miles to the Richard B. Russell Scenic Highway, then turn right and go 3 miles to the well-marked trailhead and parking area.

SMITHGALL WOODS STATE PARK

With a focus on education, Smithgall Woods State Park (61 Tsalaki Trail, 706/878-3087, www.gastateparks.org, visitors center daily 8am-5pm, $5 parking) is a delightful gem a bit north of Helen nestled against the Chattahoochee National Forest and technically within the Raven Cliffs Wilderness Area. The rustically attractive main visitors center (daily 8am-5pm) contains displays on flora and fauna, with the highlight being the nearby raptor aviary, where rescued birds of prey live under care. As you might expect, there's a multitude of ranger-led programs and demonstrations of great interest. A system of hilly, fairly challenging trails takes you through quiet, heavily wooded areas with several accessible waterfalls and even an impressive covered bridge. Occasional ranger tours take you to the old Martin Mine site, complete with vertical shafts. Duke's Creek is the centerpiece of the park, running its length and attracting trout anglers from all around (catch-and-release only, advance reservations required). There is no camping at Smithgall Woods per se, but there are five reservable and perhaps surprisingly upscale cottages ($150-500) of various sizes; some even have hot tubs. Be aware that the area is closed for hunting some times throughout the year; check the website or call (the challenging Laurel Ridge trail is open all the time however). Sadly, state budget cuts have eliminated what was once one of the great draws of the park: the onsite restaurant that served guests at the cottages.

Duke's Creek Falls

Legendary as one of the first places in Georgia where gold was discovered, first by the Spanish in the 1500s and later by American settlers in 1828, the area around Duke's Creek Falls is in the Chattahoochee National Forest roughly equidistant between Smithgall Woods and Unicoi State Parks. The Duke's Creek Falls Recreation Area (www.fs.usda.gov, daily dawn-dusk, $3 per vehicle) is easily accessible via the Richard B. Russell Scenic Byway (Hwy. 348). From there take a two-mile round-trip hike to Duke's Creek Falls themselves, a great and quite popular place for a hike and a picnic, with several observation spots. The hike is fairly strenuous and steep, but you can take frequent breaks to enjoy the lush scenery throughout the trail area, as well as views of nearby Yonah Mountain. There's a much shorter ADA-compliant trail to an observation deck with a limited view.

UNICOI STATE PARK

One of the larger and more well-appointed state parks in Georgia, Unicoi State Park and Lodge (1788 Hwy. 356, 706/878-2201, www.gastate-parks.org, $5 parking, tents and RVs $29-35, walk-in campsites $25, cottages $80-100) offers something for everyone on a sprawling 1,000 acres packed with things to do, all within just a few miles of Helen. While there are nearly 100 camping spaces for tents and RVs and a couple dozen walk-in tent sites, there is also a vast array of tasteful, charming cottages; there are 30 of them, to be exact, in various multi-level clusters around the sloping, topographically diverse park. However, for many visitors the associated lodge (800/573-9659, rooms $75-100) is the highlight: 100 rooms at a modern, park-run lodge similar to a handful at state parks across Georgia. Don't miss the mountain trout at the nightly buffet! Outdoor enthusiasts will find no lack of opportunities at Unicoi, from the eight-mile mountain bike trail to the seven miles of hiking trails, one of which takes you directly to Helen. A clear mountain lake is available for recreation in the warmer months.

Anna Ruby Falls

Though contiguous with, and indeed within Unicoi State Park, Anna Ruby Falls (www.fs.usda.gov, daily 9am-6pm, entry gate closes 5pm, $3) is run by the U.S. Forest Service and requires a separate admission. However, it's very much worth the nominal fee, not only for the perfectly situated twin falls themselves—uniting to form Smith Creek at the bottom, which itself empties into Unicoi Lake and, much later, eventually to the Gulf of Mexico—but for the relaxing, scenic walk from the parking area and visitors center to the falls. The walk takes at least 10-15 minutes each way. The longer, nearly five-mile Smith Creek trail leads directly from Unicoi State Park to the falls and back again. The visitors center has a good exhibit on the geology of the falls and the surrounding area. While Unicoi and the falls both have separate admission, if all you're going to do is visit the falls, the state park will waive their entrance fee.

CLEVELAND

Helen is the best-known place in White County, but Cleveland is actually the county seat. However, visitors mostly know Cleveland for **Babyland General Hospital** (300 NOK Dr., 706/865-2171, www.cabbagepatchkids.com, Mon.-Sat. 9am-5pm, Sun. 10am-5pm, free), the "birthplace" of every Cabbage Patch Kid, where the little dolls are birthed, nursed, and adopted. There are even "C-sections" (for "Cabbage sections") and an ICU for "premature" Cabbage Patch Kids. Some find the overall effect creepy, but hardcore Cabbage Patch folks and their kids will love it.

If you're looking for a big hearty burger or fresh-baked biscuits in the Helen-Cleveland area, try **Yonah Burger** (2051 Helen Hwy., 706/865-4791, www.yonahburger.com, Mon.-Sat. 8am-8pm, $8), longtime local favorite for nearly 50 years running.

CLARKESVILLE

The seat of adjacent Habersham County, Clarkesville is primarily known for its tidy downtown shopping area and one of the premier B&B's in the state: **◖ Glen-Ella Springs Inn** (1789 Bear Gap Rd., 706/754-7295, www.glenella.com, $150-275). Set in a restored yet still rustic-feeling 1800s building on a scenic 12 acres complete with burbling brook, Glen-Ella's 16 rooms all boast covered porches with rocking chairs. Ed and Luci Kivett's place is a great spot to get away from it all, whether in your room, enjoying the grounds, or sitting in front of one of the huge stone fireplaces in the common areas. While there is free Wi-Fi, the rooms don't have TVs (though common areas have them). Four of the 16 rooms are designated as "family-friendly," meaning children are welcome. The attached restaurant (daily 6pm-10pm, $25) is considered one of Georgia's best, and it's open to the public as well as guests of the inn. For the restaurant menu and for the included grand breakfast for guests, Chef Marc Badon serves an upscale, refined take on traditional Southern inland and coastal classics.

For a great lunch in Clarkesville proper, go to **Sweet Breads** (129 E. Water St.,

706/754-3752, Mon.-Sat. 11am-3pm, Sun. 10am-2pm, $8), where as the name implies, the signature sandwiches are served on fresh-baked bread.

A few miles north of Clarkesville on Highway 197 is the venerable and charming pottery makers' collective **Mark of the Potter** (9982 Hwy. 197 N., 706/947-3440, www. markofthepotter.com, daily 10am-6pm), set within the historic, restored Watts gristmill. Their cast of artisans—four house potters and a rotating crew of invited regional potters—has created and sold high-quality stoneware at the same spot since 1969. The pottery on display is not only fine art; it's all food-safe, microwave-safe, and mostly oven-safe as well.

The Appalachian Trail

Following the lead of America's first conservationist president, Theodore Roosevelt, the first stirrings of the concept of a national "super trail" began making the rounds in the early 1920s. The original idea for an East Coast super trail was for a path from the highest point in the northern Appalachians at New Hampshire's Mt. Washington to the southern Appalachian's highest point at Mt. Mitchell in North Carolina. Within a year work began on what was then called "America's Footpath."

By 1925 the Appalachian Trail Conference was formed to discuss plans for completion, and they decided to extend both ends of the trail to Maine in the north and Georgia in the south. North Georgia was wild country then, and after extensive exploration Mt. Oglethorpe was chosen as the southern terminus. By 1937 the entire Appalachian Trail was finished on both ends. However, almost immediately a hurricane did heavy damage to the path, followed by the extension of Skyline Drive to the Blue Ridge Parkway in the 1940s, which destroyed a section of the trail 120 miles long.

Renewed interest in the Trail came in the post-war years. In the Peach State, this was manifested by the Georgia Appalachian Trail Club's move to relocate the southern terminus to Springer Mountain, where it remains today. The designation of the Appalachian Trail, or "AT" as it's often known, as a National Scenic Trail in 1968 cemented its status as a national treasure under federal protection.

◖ AMICALOLA FALLS STATE PARK

Home of the tallest cascade east of the Mississippi River, Amicalola Falls State Park and Lodge (418 Amicalola Falls State Park Rd., 706/265-8888, www.gastateparks.org, daily 7am-10pm, visitors center daily 8:30am-5pm, $5 parking) also happens to be a main gateway to the Appalachian Trail. Combine that with a wealth of lodging and activities, and the result is an extremely popular park, especially during leaf-watching season in the fall, when it can be almost uncomfortably crowded at times.

That said, the magnificent 730-foot falls themselves are one of the "Seven Natural Wonders of Georgia" and are well worth the crowds. Long before the throngs came each autumn, one of the first non-Indians to see the cascade was William Williamson, who famously said "in the Mountains I discovered a Water Fall perhaps the greatest in the World the most majestic Scene that I have ever witnessed or heard of."

Amicalola is fairly unique in that not only can you enjoy the view of the falls, you can enjoy views from the top of the falls themselves. There are several ways to do this: The most typically used is the very strenuous Falls Trail, essentially a 600-step staircase up to the top. Pace yourself and take frequent breaks to catch your breath. Alternatively, you can wind around on the East Ridge Trail to the top, and then take the Falls Trail back down. Finally, you can always cheat by driving up to an overlook parking lot and hiking a much shorter,

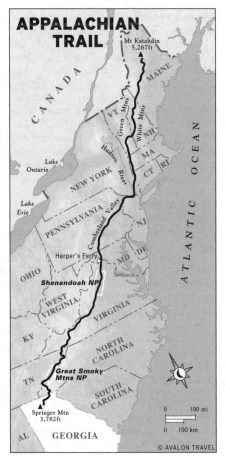

APPALACHIAN TRAIL

Mt Katahdin 5,267ft

CANADA

MAINE

VT Green Mtns

White Mtns NH

MA

RI

CT

Hudson River

NEW YORK

Lake Ontario

Lake Erie

PENNSYLVANIA

Cumberland Valley

NJ

DE

MD

Harper's Ferry

OHIO

Shenandoah NP

WEST VIRGINIA

VIRGINIA

KY

NORTH CAROLINA

TN

Great Smoky Mtns NP

SOUTH CAROLINA

Springer Mtn 3,782ft

AL

GEORGIA

ATLANTIC OCEAN

0   100 mi

0   100 km

© AVALON TRAVEL

lucky or extraordinarily proactive you can pick one of 24 tent and RV sites. However, the most unique accommodation at Amicalola is without doubt the ☾ **Len Foote Hike Inn** (www.hike-inn.com, $100-140), an eco-friendly hiker's lodge a five-mile trek from the main park area. Run by a non-profit, the inn has a staff that lives onsite and is happy to offer advice and answer questions. The 20 guest rooms are fairly Spartan, really only intended for sleeping, but the communal areas are charmingly appointed and the building itself perfectly designed for its surroundings. The non-profit is committed to a sustainable lifestyle, so much so that the goal of the communal kitchen is zero waste (especially important given that all supplies must come in by foot). From Hike Inn, it is another mile to reach the AT.

Good trout fishing is available on the park's streams, but the main focus, as you'd expect, is hiking. There are a total of 12 miles of trails on the park, with the most popular and famous being the 8.5-mile **Southern Terminus Approach Trail** from the falls to Springer Mountain itself, bottom tip of the AT.

Perhaps oddly given the extreme beauty of this area, the state park is of relatively recent vintage. The Georgia Appalachian Trail Club needed a new southern terminus when development threatened the old one at Mount Oglethorpe, so the park was built in the 1950s specifically to serve as the southern gateway to the Trail.

Cochrans Falls

Tied with Caledonia Cascade as second tallest waterfall in Georgia, 600-foot Cochrans Falls is close to the more famous Amicalola Falls. However, it's considerably more difficult to get to. A popular way for serious hikers is to go from the parking lot of the Amicalola Lodge to the Hike Inn Trail; at about three miles you make a right onto a trail going to a campsite near the top of the falls. Be aware the path is treacherous; in 2012 a hiker had to be rescued by helicopter after a bone-breaking fall onto the rocks.

flatter distance. The views aren't nearly as good, though. You can dine while enjoying the view at the onsite restaurant, though a picnic is always fun and advisable as well. The park's visitors center has a great exhibit on local geography, history, and wildlife, including a snake display.

Lodging at Amicalola (www.galodges.com) is varied, including of course the signature lodge itself near the top of the falls. Not quite as rustic as you might think, it's a 56-room facility with Wi-Fi. You can also opt to stay in one of 14 more rustic cottages. If you're either very

Clear mountain streams are all over North Georgia.

SPRINGER MOUNTAIN

Reached by the Southern Terminus Approach Trail from Amicalola Falls, the springboard of the south-north traverse of the Appalachian Trail is nearly 4,000 feet in elevation and about 2,100 miles from the Trail's other end in Maine. While the view is beautiful, perhaps the most stirring site is the simple weathered brass plaque marking the terminus itself, erected by the Georgia Appalachian Trail Club and bearing these words: "Georgia to Maine—a footpath for those who seek fellowship with the wilderness."

You don't have to be hiking the Trail to see Springer Mountain, of course. A day-use parking area below at Forest Service Road 42 allows you to take a hike up and around on top; many AT hikers begin here instead of Amicalola Falls, cutting almost nine miles off their total trip.

THE APPALACHIAN TRAIL THROUGH GEORGIA

Georgia's section of the AT (www.appalachiantrail.org) is 76 miles long from Springer Mountain to Bly Gap and on into North

Carolina. At its highest point in Georgia, Blood Mountain, the AT is 4,460 feet above sea level; its low spot is Dicks Creek Gap at 2,675 feet. White rectangular blazes mark the trail, with turns being marked with double blazes. Many of the views are truly beautiful, but be aware that extensive logging occurred throughout the area and virtually no place was immune. Whole lifetimes are spent learning every inch of the AT, and many detailed volumes have been written about every foot of its length. Following is a brief overview of Georgia's six sections of the Appalachian Trail.

Springer Mountain to Woody Gap: 20 Miles

A bit north of the southern terminus is the Spring Mountain Shelter, a simple lean-to construction with two levels, room for about 10 hikers, and dependable drinking water. A bit farther north still is the right turn onto the Benton MacKaye Trail, which briefly follows an original route of the AT. Benton MacKaye rejoins the AT for about a half-mile along Rich Mountain and then splits off for good. The MacKaye Trail shares a stretch with the Duncan Ridge Trail, commonly considered one of the most challenging hikes in the United States (it breaks off at Georgia Highway 60 and will eventually circle around to end at a different point on the AT). At mile 4 you'll hit Three Forks, a pretty area marking the confluence of Stover, Chester, and Long Creeks to form Noontootla Creek. The Appalachian Trail doesn't begin to be really challenging until about mile 7, when you enter a more mountainous area of Lumpkin County. Several more brushes with Forest Service Road 42 bring you to Woody Gap and the crossing of Highway 60, the first of six times the AT crosses a road in Georgia. Camping shelters along this section include Stover Creek at mile 2.5, Hawk Mountain Shelter at mile 7.6, and Gooch Gap Shelter at mile 16.

Woody Gap to Neels Gap: 11 Miles

This relatively short stretch features a lot of nice scenery and several intersections with

APPALACHIAN TRAIL THROUGH GEORGIA

NORTH CAROLINA
GEORGIA

Chatuge Lake

MILE 75.56

Southern Nantahala Wilderness

Hiawassee

19
129

76

BRASSTOWN BALD

DICKS CREEK GAP
MILE 66.80

76

Nottely Lake

515

Blairsville

75

Moccasin Creek State Park

Blue Ridge Lake

Chattahoochee

National Forest

180

Tray Mountain 4,430ft

MILE 56.26

UNICOI GAP
MILE 50.72

Lake Burton

60

Vogel State Park

348

Unicoi State Park

Blood Mountain 4,461ft

LAKE WINFIELD SCOTT

NEELS GAP
MILE 30.66

HOG PEN GAP
MILE 37.08

366

197

WALASI-YI CENTER

TESNATEE GAP
MILE 36.19

HELEN

Suches

WOODY GAP
MILE 20.02

BRASSTOWN RUSSELL SCENIC HWY

129

Approach Trail

Springer Mountain 3,782ft

52
Amicalola Falls State Park

MILE 8.27

MILE 0

19

Cleveland

115

Clarkesville

LEN FOOTE HIKE INN

52

Dahlonega

115

0   5 mi

0   5 km

365

© AVALON TRAVEL

other trails; therefore, you will rarely be alone for long on it. The first really nice spot is at Miller Gap, where you'll get nice views of Blood Mountain, the highest the AT gets in Georgia and which you'll be climbing soon enough. A little while longer takes you across the Slaughter Creek Trail, a popular trail from nearby Lake Winfield Scott. (The graphic place names in the area supposedly come from an epic clash between Indian tribes long ago.) From Slaughter Creek to the end of this section at Neels Gap is a no-campfire zone. A turn due east onto some rock steps marks the beginning of your relatively slow and easy ascent of Blood Mountain; as you climb, shortly you'll come across the end of the Duncan Ridge Trail. At "Picnic Rock," the summit of the mountain, you'll see a little cottage built by the Civilian Conservation Corps (CCC), a relic from the time of the Great Depression that's now on the National Register of Historic

Places. A steep descent takes you down into Neels Gap (known to old-timers as Frogtown Gap) and the AT's crossing of U.S. Highway 129 (Georgia 19).

This is where you'll find a delightful and welcome oasis for hikers: the legendary **Mountain Crossings at Walasi-yi**. A combination rest stop and provisioning point in a CCC-built structure, it is adjacent to the site of an old Cherokee village and was originally intended as a traveler's inn. However, parking at the Walasi-yi Center is for customers only, so don't be tempted to park your car here to hike the AT. Walasi-yi boasts a distinctive wraparound porch and a small breezeway marked with a white blaze—the only point on the Georgia AT where you pass through a building. Some scholarship indicates that because of the existence of an ancient Cherokee path in its footsteps here, this could be the single oldest stretch of the Appalachian Trail.

Neels Gap to
Hogpen Gap: 6.4 Miles

The shortest section of the Georgia AT begins with a 1.5-mile climb of nearly 1,000 feet in elevation to Levelland Mountain, featuring some great views. A campsite is another 1.5 miles ahead. A descent to Tesnatee Gap takes the AT along the Richard B. Russell Scenic Highway for a very brief bit before the steep, strenuous ascent up Wildcat Mountain and down to Hogpen Gap and its attached parking area. At mile 6.2 you can take a side trail about a mile to Whitley Gap Shelter.

Hogpen Gap to
Unicoi Gap: 13.6 Miles

This mostly easy section of trail runs through Wolfpen Stamp and along Strawberry Top, Poor Mountain, and Sheep Rock Top and down to the well-known shelter at Low Gap (mile 4.2), a popular place for AT hikers to spend their first night on the trail. Whether or not you break here, the next eight miles is taken up with a jaunt up and along Blue Mountain (there's a shelter at mile 11.4 of this section). At mile 9.2 of this section is the Chattahoochee Gap; look to your right and about 200 yards away you'll see the small spring that is actually the headwaters of the Chattahoochee River. It's somewhat surreal and daunting to realize the 'Hooch is a major source of drinking water for the massive metro Atlanta area, and indeed a lot of AT hikers take a drink from its waters right here. Chattahoochee Gap is also the intersection with Jack's Knob Trail, which takes you about 4.5 miles to the parking area at the summit of Brasstown Bald. A sharp descent from Blue Mountain takes you near the parking area at Unicoi Gap.

Unicoi Gap to
Dicks Creek Gap: 16.1 Miles

Starting at the Unicoi Gap parking area, this section climbs to the crown of Rocky Mountain at mile l.3. In a mile you'll intersect with the Rocky Mountain Trail junction to the left. On top of Rocky Mountain, look to the right to see Yonah Mountain. The section descends to Forest Service Road 283 in Indian Grave Gap at mile 2.7. Across the road, the AT enters an evergreen tunnel and then goes upward to cross Tray Mountain Road at mile 3.3, continues 0.2 miles to the ridge top, then hits the site of the "old cheese factory," a 19th-century farm. Tray Gap is next, on the way up to Tray's Summit, the second-highest point of the AT in Georgia and home to some beautiful panoramic views. At mile 5.5, a spur trail leads to the Tray Mountain Shelter. After Tray Mountain comes the traverse of several more gap-and-ridge combos until mile 12.6 when you come down into Deep Gap, with the Deep Gap Shelter off a spur on the right. The next high point will be Powell Mountain and a 90-degree turn onto an old road, whereupon you finish a mile down to Dicks Creek Gap.

Dicks Creek Gap to
Bly Gap: 8.8 Miles

This final, busy stretch of the AT in Georgia is trickier than it may seem, with some shorter but steeper grades. From the picnic tables at Dicks Creek Gap you'll make you way over the next mile to Little Bald Mountain and a series of up-down ridge climbs. At mile 8.4 you actually cross briefly into North Carolina before coming back into Georgia for a while, until ending at Bly Gap.

Blairsville and Brasstown Bald

The largest town in north central Georgia, but still pretty small, Blairsville is a good base of operations from which to enjoy the Union County-Brasstown Bald area.

BLAIRSVILLE
Sights
As is typical of most Georgia county seats, the old courthouse dominates the town square. But Blairsville (www.visitblairsvillega.com) has done a particularly nice job restoring the historic 1899 **Union County Courthouse** (One Town Square, 706/745-5493, www.unioncountyhistory.org, Mon.-Sat. 10am-4pm, $2 adults, $1 children), which now hosts a modest local history museum and a variety of concerts.

America's largest single 0-gauge model train display, **Misty Mountain Model Railroad** (4381 Misty Mountain Lane, 706/745-9819, www.mistymountainmodelrailroad.com, tour each Mon., Wed., Fri., Sat. beginning at 2pm, $5 per person) features 14 trains on a mile of track with a variety of bridges and tunnels. The display simulates various portions of North Georgia topography, including the mighty Tallulah Gorge. Overall, it's quite impressive and clearly a must-see for train buffs of all kinds.

Former Disney model-maker Art Millican used his experience to make **Sleepy Hollow Enterprises** (4339 Young Harris Hwy., 706/379-9622, www.whimsicalfairygarden.com, Mon.-Sat. 9:30am-4:30pm, free), a collection of fairies, hobbits, and the like gamboling in their own eccentric habitat. The key draws are the meticulous and beautifully detailed fairy houses Millican makes, many from found and salvaged material. He also produces handcrafted 'automata,' or simple mechanical toys, some fairy-themed and some not. Sleepy Hollow's gardens are free to visit, but of course you're encouraged to purchase artisan work by Millican and crew.

The combo attraction **Lardworks Studio and Lasso The Moon Alpaca Farm** (106 Agape Dr., 706/835-1837, www.alpacamoon.com, by appointment only, free) is where you can pet an alpaca raised right on the farm, purchase items made from alpaca fur, or watch some world-class glass bead-making in the studio. The studio and farm holds a couple of open houses each year, one in September for National Alpaca Days and another in December for the holidays.

Events
The main calendar event is the annual **Sorghum Festival** (sorghum.blairsville.com), happening each October and celebrating the robust, sweet local syrup. There's a big parade that Saturday, a car show, and of course lots of sorghum to pour on your biscuits.

Accommodations
People love the rocker on the front porch at **Granny's Cabin** (55 Old Beech Rd., 727/585-3132, www.grannyscabin.net, $95) about five miles out of Blairsville. It's all about relaxation here in this two-bedroom, two-bath cabin, with a sleeper sofa and two rollaways. Pets are not allowed.

Bonnie and Paul graciously run **Your Home in the Woods Bed & Breakfast** (2830 Timber Lane, 706/745-9337, www.yourhomeinthewoods.com, $80-100) near Blairsville, a getaway nestled up against a woodsy hillside with three rooms to choose from. The building itself isn't particularly expansive or historic, but the setting is hard to beat, the food is delicious, and the hosts sure are friendly.

Food
There are a couple of very good dining spots in town. ◖ **Dan's Grill** (305 Murphy Hwy., 706/745-0013, Tues.-Thurs. 10am-8pm, Fri.-Sat. 10am-9pm, Sun. 11am-4pm, $10) has an unusual specialty for this area: Cuban food. And Dan makes a killer Cuban sandwich, great plantains, succulent flank steaks, and even tasty Cuban tamales, all of which can go

toe-to-toe with similar dishes in South Florida. Seriously.

Get some outstanding pulled pork or ribs at **Jim's Smokin' Que** (4971 Gainesville Hwy. (Hwy. 129), 706/835-7427, www.jims-smokinque.com, Thurs.-Sat. 11am-8pm, $8-12), a classic family-run, weekend-only joint that slow-cooks with a "special blend" of woods. The recommended side is the sweet potato fries, but you can't go wrong with the Brunswick stew either.

You can also try the popular **Union County Farmers Market** (148 Old Smokey Rd., May-Oct. Tues. 4pm-8pm, Sat. 7am-1pm). Fresh produce, arts and crafts, and bluegrass music are all part of the fun.

TRACK ROCK PETROGLYPHS

Properly documented only a few years ago, Track Rock Gap (Track Rock Gap Rd., 706/745-6928, www.fs.usda.gov, daily dawn-dusk, free) with its ancient Indian rock carvings, or petroglyphs, is the only such site on public land in Georgia. The soapstone rocks feature over 100 depictions of wildlife, animal tracks, symbols, and footprints. While some are at least 3,000 years old, most were made within the last 1,000 years, probably by early Cherokees. Though some scholars maintain that the Creeks and Catawbas contributed.

Get to this recently-renovated site complete with historic marker from Blairsville by taking U.S. Highway 76 east about five miles. At Track Rock Gap Road, turn right for about two miles to the gap. Drive past the Track Rocks a short distance to the parking lot.

One of the lesser-known lodging gems of North Georgia is the nearby **Trackrock Campground** (141 Trackrock Camp Rd., 706/745-2420, www.trackrock.com, campsites $27-39, cabins $110-140), open year-round on a beautiful 300 acres a short drive south of the petroglyph site, nestled into the Chattahoochee National Forest. This dedicated Appalachian Botanical Sanctuary offers about 100 tent and RV sites, most shaded and roomy, plus a couple of large, fully furnished cabins complete with

fireplaces. **Trackrock Stables** (141 Trackrock Camp Rd., 706/745-5252, www.trackrock.com, one-hour ride $30: daily 9:15am, 1pm, 2:30pm, and 4pm; two-hour ride $60: daily 10am and 2:30pm) offers guided rides into and around the National Forest. The Stables are occasionally closed Sundays, so call ahead.

◖ BRASSTOWN BALD

At 4,784 feet, Georgia's highest point is the summit of Brasstown Bald (770/297-3000, www.fs.usda.gov, visitors center daily 10am-4pm, $3 pp). Deep in the Chattahoochee-Oconee National Forest and historic Cherokee country, the mountain is called Enotah by the Cherokee. Unlike other mountains in the Blue Ridge called "balds," Brasstown Bald is actually full of vegetation to the summit. While the ascent itself is not particularly dramatic, given that Brasstown Bald is more of a long ridge than a jutting mountaintop, the views are stunning and unmatched anywhere in the state, especially in autumn when the leaves change. On clear days, theoretically, you can see four states from the nostalgically charming and well-built observation deck: Georgia, Tennessee, and both Carolinas. You can even occasionally make out the Atlanta skyline. (The very top of the tower is for fire-spotting by the U.S. Forest Service, however, and is off limits.)

Hike up from the parking area, about a mile round-trip, or wait on the frequent but seasonal shuttle buses ($3) to chug you up the winding path to the top. The visitors center underneath the observation tower has a number of interesting exhibits, including a vintage train and a very informative exhibit on the geology of the mountain itself. Pack a lunch—the views from the picnic area are awesome. A popular way to extend your experience is to hike the ridgeline Wagon Train Trail, which if you follow all the way takes you to nearby Young Harris; two other trails emanate from Brasstown Bald as well.

The upscale lodging of note in the area is the fantastic ◖ **Brasstown Valley Resort and Spa** (6321 U.S. Hwy. 76, 706/379-9900, www.

brasstownvalley.com, $200) on a lush and scenic 500 acres near the town of Young Harris. The lodge itself might take your breath away, but the mountainside setting is of course an even more compelling draw. There are 102 rooms in the central lodge, 32 cottages, and a single spa suite. Wraparound balconies at the lodge take you out into nature. The cottages, each with four bedrooms, have a more rustic motif but are still relaxing and convenient, with fireplaces and full kitchens. The spa suite, if you can get it, is nearly 1,000 square feet of luxury complete with rooftop deck and of course a whirlpool tub. A golf course and excellent stable facilities round out the amenities.

HIAWASSEE

Hiawassee (www.mountaintopga.com) is primarily known for its **Georgia Mountain Fairgrounds** (1311 Music Hall Rd., 706/896-4191, www.georgiamountainfairgrounds. com), a sprawling place that hosts several very popular annual festivals, including the **Georgia Mountain Fair** (July) and the **Georgia Mountain Fall Festival** (Oct.). A highlight at the Fairgrounds is the **Fred Hamilton Rhododendron Garden**, where you cannot only enjoy thousands of the namesake plants but wonderful views of Lake Chatuge and Brasstown Bald itself. The Fairgrounds offer camping as well (706/896-4191, $21-34) with nearly 100 sites open year-round and nearly 200 open April-October, both paved and unpaved.

For a more rustic brush with nature stay at **Enota Mountain Retreat** (1000 Hwy. 180, 706/896-7504, www.enota.com, tents $25, RVs $35, cabins $110-165) near Hiawassee, which boasts no fewer than four waterfalls on its 60 acres. With a motel, cabins, and a tent and RV area, Enota combines a truly beautiful setting with no-frills, communal, pet-friendly living complete with attached 10-acre organic farm you can tour. The tent sites along the river are primitive and smallish and the cabins

humble, but the friendly vibe is relaxing and refreshingly unpretentious.

High Shoals Falls and the Blue Hole

Near Hiawassee are a couple of wonderful cascades that can be visited in tandem. Blue Hole Falls is a popular summertime swimming hole, where the water gets as deep as 10 feet at times, hence the swimming. But be aware even in summer it's pretty frigid. To get here look for Indian Grave Gap Road (Forest Service Rd. 283) off Highway 17. You'll park and hike High Shoals Trail for about a mile. A short distance downstream from the Blue Hole is taller, 100-foot High Shoals Falls. There's a modest observation deck.

VOGEL STATE PARK

The kind of state park that sees families returning year after year, Vogel State Park (405 State Rt. 129, 706/745-2628, www.gastateparks.org, daily 7am-10pm, $5 parking) is one of Georgia's oldest and most beloved, chiefly because of the sheer physical beauty and the perfection of its setting. There's plenty of hiking with lots to see, including a peaceful 22-acre lake (no motors allowed), complete with a little beachfront area, and the small but wonderful **Trahlyta Falls** within a short distance, which you can enjoy up close and personal. There's a 13-mile backcountry trail, and you can access the Appalachian Trail from the park as well. Perhaps the most unique aspect, however, is the museum dedicated to the Civilian Conservation Corps (CCC), the second such in the state. The CCC constructed Vogel (along with many other Southern state parks) in the 1930s. This is also one of the better Georgia parks for camping, with roomy, woodsy sites.

Just south of Vogel State Park is **Helton Creek Falls,** an easily accessible and attractive cascade. Turn east on Helton Creek Road and go two miles to the parking area; the trailhead for the quarter-mile hike is on your right.

Dahlonega

Epicenter of America's first gold rush, Dahlonega (www.dahlonega.org) still retains a fitting frontier vibe, centering mostly on its historic town square, joltingly reminiscent of mountain-fringed old West towns like Taos. Most everything in town revolves around either the town's literally golden history or the student and cultural life of North Georgia College and State University, the distinctive gold-leafed steeple of its administration building dominating the skyline. However, purple gold is making a big impact on the area these days in the form of a burgeoning wine region, which has gained national attention and is the area's fastest-growing economic sector.

This was raw country in the 18th and early 19th centuries, mostly Cherokee-dominated but also frequented by white trappers and deerskin traders. Everything changed in 1828 when, as local lore relates in several versions, a settler tripped over a fist-sized nugget. As embellished as the tales likely are, gold was indeed available in such large and relatively accessible quantities that the Lumpkin County area was quickly overrun with prospectors and miners. There was so much gold, in fact, that in 1838 the U.S. Mint opened a branch right in town to coin money.

As is the case with gold rushes, there were winners and losers. The winners were the large mining companies and the occasional lucky prospectors; the losers were the Cherokee tribe, forced to relinquish their ancestral lands by the 1831 Indian Removal Act and subsequent land lotteries awarded to gold prospectors. By 1838 the Trail of Tears had begun, taking the surviving Cherokee to an unwanted new life in the Oklahoma Territory.

SIGHTS
Dahlonega Gold Museum State Historic Site

The most important historical attraction in Dahlonega is in the dead center of the town square. The Dahlonega Gold Museum State Historic Site (1 Public Square, 706/864-2257, www.gastateparks.org, Mon.-Sat. 9am-5pm, Sun. 10am-5pm, $6 adults, $3.50 children) is in the old 1836 Courthouse building, itself of great significance as the oldest surviving courthouse in Georgia. The museum commemorates and explains the phenomenon of the Georgia gold rush and Dahlonega's role in it. The highlight for many visitors is the display of extremely rare gold coins minted in Dahlonega by the U.S. government; the ranger will proudly point out how much brighter the Georgia gold coins are because of their incredible 98 percent purity. Don't miss the excellent short film upstairs documenting the gold rush with oral history from Georgians who worked the mines and processing facilities, many still open well into the 20th century. The seats in the theater are the courthouse's original courtroom benches.

Crisson Gold Mine

The only honest-to-goodness working gold mine left in Georgia is the Crisson Gold Mine (2736 Morrison Moore Pkwy., 706/864-6363, www.crissongoldmine.com, daily 10am-6pm, price varies), which remained commercially viable from the 1840s until the 1980s. You can pan for gold or just shop for jewelry made from gold that is still mined onsite for the tourist market. You can also opt to buy their ore by the bucket at various concentration levels and prices and take it home with you to see if you get lucky. Those who purchase six buckets of ore can use the mine's own specialized trommel tools for a really authentic experience. Tours are given of the old stampmill on the grounds, where quartz is still crushed to separate it from attached gold flakes. While you can also "grub" for gems at Crisson, that particular ore is actually imported from North Carolina.

Consolidated Gold Mines

It's not a working mine anymore, but Consolidated Gold Mines (185 Consolidated

© JIM MOREKIS

Dahlonega Gold Museum State Historic Site

Gold Mine Rd., 706/864-8473, daily 10am-5pm, $15 adult, $9 children) is the actual site of what was once one of the largest gold processing plants in the world, only open for about 10 years at the turn of the 20th century. The enormous building is gone, but some of the old mine shafts, including the legendary "Glory Hole," have now been excavated and restored for public tours 200 feet underground, given by knowledgeable guides who in some cases actually are former gold miners. Consolidated offers the usual hokey tourist-oriented panning and gemming, but by taking the mine tour you will experience something virtually unheard of in this day and age: going safely down into a real gold mine. No flip-flops or sandals allowed though!

North Georgia College and State University

The state-supported military school North Georgia College and State University (82 College Circle, www.northgeorgia.edu) is a major economic bulwark of Lumpkin County,

and chiefly famous to visitors for its beautiful and unique administration building, specifically its gold-leafed steeple, visible from many places around town.

WINERIES

The Dahlonega area has made quite a name for itself over the past 10-15 years or so as a regional wine center. The combination of sloping elevation, well-draining clay soil, and a slightly drier harvest season than elsewhere in the region makes for a climate that most varietals seem to love. Today you can get something close to the classic Napa Valley wine-tasting experience here in the Appalachian foothills. The wine business is seasonal, however, so the wineries often take an extended hiatus from public visitation during the winter.

Wolf Mountain Vineyards (180 Wolf Mountain Trail, 706/867-9862, www.wolfmountainvineyards.com, tastings Thurs.-Sat. noon-5pm, Sun. 12:30pm-5pm, from $10) has rapidly established itself as Georgia's leading winemaker, recently winning the state's first-ever gold medal in the Los Angeles International Wine & Spirits competition. At 4,000 cases a year, they pride themselves on being a small-batch maker; however they bottle a full range of offerings, from whites to reds to ports to sparkling wine. Their food preparation and service are outstanding for this area, an experience enhanced by the beautiful views of the surrounding mountainside. There is the walk-in Vineyard Cafe, but the big draw is Sunday brunch (reservations required), which has a different theme each month (a recent theme was Wild Game & Red Wine). In addition to tastings, a winemaker's tour happens each Saturday and Sunday at 2pm, no reservations needed.

Frogtown Cellars (700 Ridge Pt. Dr., 706/865-0687, www.frogtownwine.com, Mon.-Fri. noon-5pm, Sat. noon-6pm, Sun. 12:30pm-5pm, tastings from $15) has 42 acres on the outskirts of Dahlonega as well as a satellite tasting room in Helen (7601 S. Main St., daily). They bottle about two dozen varieties of reds and whites, a couple of which have medalled at the San Francisco Chronicle Wine Competition. On weekends they run a "panini bar" for a tasty lunch to go with your vino.

Luxurious **Montaluce Estates** (946 Via Monteluce, 706/867-4060, www.montalucce. com, Tues.-Sat. 11am-5pm, Sun. noon-5pm) boasts a state-of-the-art, upscale facility where they make a narrow but tasteful range of wines, including a cab, a merlot, a chardonnay, and a viognier.

The first Dahlonega winery of the modern era, **Three Sisters Vineyards** (439 Vineyard Way, 706/865-9463, www.threesistersvineyards.com, Thurs.-Sat. 11am-5pm, Sun. 1pm-5pm, tastings $5-30) is a charming estate run by the Paul family. Their varietals planted in 1998 include a rare Cynthiana grape, with roots going back to Thomas Jefferson.

Blackstock Winery's (5400 Town Creek Rd., 706/219-2789, www.bsvw.com, Mon.-Sat. 10am-6pm, Sun. 12:30pm-6pm) chief vintner brings years of professional experience, and they specialize in tasty reds, including a spicy Sangiovese and a limited reserve. The

view is the draw here rather than the grounds themselves.

EVENTS

The highlight of the Dahlonega calendar is the **Gold Rush Days** festival (www.dahlonegajaycees.com) every October, which features food, fun, and music in the square, with cars banished from downtown so that everyone can walk around the streets freely.

Each November brings the **Dahlonega Literary Festival** (www.literaryfestival.org), which has brought in regional authors for talks and panel discussions for the past decade.

A bit north of town in the hills is the annual **HemlockFest** (www.hemlockfest.org), an interesting, all-ages, eco-friendly, music, arts, and crafts festival devoted to raising awareness to fight the spread of a parasitic insect that is killing many of the indigenous hemlock trees.

RECREATION

While the Chattahoochee gets most of the press up here, the scenic little Chestatee and Etowah rivers near Dahlonega have their own charms. Tube the Chestatee with **Appalachian Outfitters** (2084 S. Chestatee, 706/864-7117, www.canoegeorgia.com), a veteran local company that also runs extensive paddling trips on the Etowah.

For a one- or two-hour horseback ride through an available 250 acres in the hills, try **Sunny Farms** (Long Branch Rd., 706/867-9167, www.sunnyfarmsnorth.com), which also offers full board for horses.

ACCOMMODATIONS

Mountain Laurel Creek Inn & Spa (202 Talmer Grizzle Rd., 706/867-8134, www. mountainlaurelcreek.com, rooms $150-200, cottage $220) offers six rooms and the freestanding Dancing Bear Cottage, all in a well-maintained, scenic foothills setting. No kids are allowed though! Spa offerings include professional massage, various facial and skincare treatments, and relaxation packages. Just north of town, Mountain Laurel is close to all the area wineries, but you don't have to leave to enjoy

GOLD IN THEM THAR HILLS

An accident of geology put one of the world's largest, most accessible, and most pure veins of gold in North Georgia, a diagonal swath running northeast to southwest with its epicenter in Lumpkin County. Millions of years after being formed it would spur America's first and most tragic gold rush.

Georgia gold is legendary for its extraordinary purity: in some places as high as 98 percent (most miners are happy with 80 percent). While the quality was certainly part of its allure, most of the draw was its easy abundance. Indeed, local legend has it that a hunter began the rush in 1828 by literally tripping over a huge nugget.

The earliest method was placer mining ("plasser"), which involves sorting through alluvial deposits by an open-pit technique or by the old familiar "panning for gold." However, within a few years the most easily accessible gold in North Georgia had been discovered. Mining techniques became much more invasive, including hydraulic mining—essentially erasing entire mountainsides with very powerful hoses—or the classic dynamite-in-the-shaft method.

Above and below ground, the mines were everywhere, and the environmental devastation they caused can be seen to this day by the discerning eye. The human devastation included brutal Indian removal and the Trail of Tears.

The sheer volume of gold extracted from these Appalachian foothills was so impressive that the U.S. Mint decided it would be more efficient to just build a new branch in Dahlonega in 1838, which stayed open until the Civil War. You can see examples of the remarkably brilliant coins made at the Dahlonega Mint at the **Dahlonega Gold Museum State Historic Site** (1 Public Square, 706/864-2257, www.gastateparks.org, Mon.-Sat. 9am-5pm, Sun. 10am-5pm, $6 adults, $3.50 children) in the main square. Technically, Dahlonega wasn't America's first gold rush town, that honor belonged to nearby Auraria, which soon went extinct with hardly a trace remaining today.

As for the guy who first said "There's gold in them thar hills," he was Mint chief assayer M.F. Stephenson, and what he really said was "There's millions in it." Ironically he wasn't trying to kick off the Georgia gold rush, he was trying to convince prospectors to stay in Dahlonega instead of going to California, where another, and eventually much more famous, gold rush had just begun in 1849.

---

them; the onsite Copper Penny Pub offers an assortment to taste.

The **Mountain Top Lodge** (447 Mountain Top Lodge Rd., 706/864-5257, www.mountaintoplodge.net, $120-150) is a bit different from more typical B&Bs: The farmhouse-ranch-style main building is of a bit more modern provenance and the decor a bit more country-quilty. But the views on the 14 woodsy acres are nice. Try for the separate Hillside Lodge for a more romantic getaway.

FOOD

A big plus about Dahlonega is that there are over a dozen good and surprisingly diverse restaurants within quick walking distance of the town square. The following are a few highlights.

The signature shepherd's pie at ◖ **Shenanigan's Irish Pub** (87 N. Chestatee St., 706/482-0114, www.theshenaniganspub.com, Mon.-Thurs. 11am-10pm, Fri.-Sat. 11am-midnight, Sun. noon-7pm, $10) is just what the doctor ordered to warm you up from the inside on a brisk day in the foothills. Then again, you can't go wrong with the fish and chips either. This friendly, multi-roomed restaurant-tavern also boasts a happening Irish-style bar area that can get quite boisterous.

For a more classically Southern, family-style dining experience, similar to Mrs. Wilkes' in Savannah, try ◖ **Smith House Dining Inn and Country Store** (84 S. Chestatee St., 706/867-7000, www.smithhouse.com, Tues.-Thurs. 11am-3pm, Fri. 11am-3pm and 3:30pm-8pm, Sat.-Sun. 11am-8pm, $20). While sitting with people you don't know may take getting used to, you'll rapidly drop any awkwardness when you're confronted with the daunting variety of hearty Southern favorites like fried okra, creamed corn, mashed potatoes, and of course some fine fried chicken.

Caribbean in North Georgia? Yep, at **Dante's on the Square** (84 Public Square, 706/864-4091, daily 11am-2pm, $10), serving a variety of jerk and blackened dishes as well as tasty sandwiches with a tropical feel. Don't miss the plantains.

The Crimson Moon Cafe (24 N. Park St., 706/864-3982, www.thecrimsonmoon. com, Wed.-Thurs. 10am-9pm, Fri.-Sat. 8am-10:30pm, Sun. 8 a.m-9:30pm, $12-15) specializes in live music of the Americana and roots-folk variety, and is a popular nightspot on the square. They also offer a full and solid menu, including a great barbecue sandwich and my favorite, the falafel gyro.

OUTSIDE DAHLONEGA
Chestatee Wildlife Preserve

The Chestatee Wildlife Preserve (469 Old Dahlonega Hwy., 678/859-6820, www.

chestateewildlife.com, daily 10am-7pm, $10 adults, $5 children) markets itself as North Georgia's only zoo, but it's really more of a rescue sanctuary open to the public. The habitats aren't particularly large, but the selection of animals is pretty impressive. The highlights are the amazing white Siberian tigers and other big cats.

DeSoto Falls

Actually a series of three cascades, DeSoto Falls are on Rocky Mountain in a designated Scenic Area of the Chattahoochee National Forest north of Dahlonega. As the name indicates, according to legend the infamous Spanish explorer and his men passed through here in the 1500s; a sign on the trail to the falls says an armor plate was found here in the 19th century. Regardless, DeSoto Falls are beautiful and popular. There's a small, first-come, first-served campground ($12) along nearby Frogtown Creek. Get to the falls and campground by taking U.S. Highway 19 north of Dahlonega about 18 miles; the campground entrance is on your left. The nearby DeSoto Falls Trail is about 2.5 miles round-trip to the falls.

Cohutta Mountains

The central portion of North Georgia is dominated by the Cohutta Mountain range, which though technically not part of the Blue Ridge is for most purposes contiguous with it. The area is less populated than the Blue Ridge portion just to the east and almost completely dominated by the enormous Cohutta Wilderness Area.

ELLIJAY

For most of the year not much goes on in tiny, cute Ellijay, but in October it boasts one of Georgia's most popular annual festivals: the **Georgia Apple Festival** (www.georgiaapple-festival.org). Happening over two weekends each October, the Apple Festival celebrates the harvest of this area's chief crop—over 600,000 bushels a year—with food and arts and crafts

booths and vendors. For a scenic look at the farms where the apples are grown, take a drive down "Apple Alley," Highway 52. Many farms are open in the autumn harvest season for tours, hayrides, and u-pick-'em apples.

At the festival, the apple action mostly centers on the Lions Club Fairgrounds (1729 S. Main St., 706/636-4500), but the festival's popular **Classic Car Show** on the opening weekend is usually in the Civic Center (102 S. Main St.), a bit closer to town. The Apple Festival brings in folks from all over the region, so don't expect to roll into the Fairgrounds and get a great parking space. Frequent, free shuttle buses take you from organized parking areas into the festival area south of downtown Ellijay. Consult the festival website for maps and details.

Regardless of when you come to Ellijay, the folks at the main **Visitors Center** (696 First Ave., 706/635-7400, Mon.-Fri. 9am-5pm) are happy to help. For a great, locally-sourced lunch or Sunday brunch, try the **Tabor House Tearoom** (138 Spring St., 706/276-1861, Thurs.-Sat., 11am-2pm, Sun. 10am-2pm, $20). In the same historic building, the oldest in the county, is the **Gilmer County Historical Society and Civil War Museum** (138 Spring St., 706/276-1861, Thurs.-Sat., 11am-2pm, Sun. 10am-2pm, donations accepted).

About 20 miles north of Ellijay is the popular and versatile **Fort Mountain State Park** (181 Fort Mountain Park Rd., 706/422-1932, www.gastateparks.org, $5 parking, campsites $25-28, cottages $125-145), within the Chattahoochee National Forest and adjacent to the Cohutta Wilderness. The park's name might sound redundant, but actually refers to an 850-foot-long rock wall of uncertain provenance, usually credited to the work of ancient Native Americans. More recent CCC-era masonry work from the Depression era is also here, including an unusual stone tower. Fourteen miles of hiking opportunities through the forest abound and are particularly scenic and gratifying. However, the specialty here is mountain biking trails, 27 miles of them, with a nominal entrance fee. Other activities include 25 miles of equestrian trails, stables, a lake with swimming beach, and miniature golf. Fort Mountain has 70 campsites and 15 cottages, of which two are dog friendly.

COHUTTA WILDERNESS AREA

The most heavily used wilderness area in the region, the Cohutta Wilderness Area (706/695-6736, www.georgiawildlife.com, free) includes 36,000 acres in Georgia with another 1,000 or so in Tennessee. More to the point, it has about 100 miles of hiking trails of various description and skill levels, all through some very beautiful and extremely biologically interesting country, with over 100 species of birds, some black bears, and frequent wild boar sightings. Anglers come from all over to fly-fish on the numerous rivers cutting through. Perhaps surprisingly, three-quarters of the area was extensively logged in the early 20th century.

Hikers should watch the weather forecast; heavy rains can and do flash-flood area rivers and creeks, and you should pretty much count on getting your feet wet at some point regardless. Most trailheads have small parking areas. But as with many wilderness areas, actually getting to the trailhead is a process that occasionally benefits from the use of a four-wheel drive vehicle. While camping without a permit is allowed anywhere in Cohutta except directly on trails, usage regulations severely limit campfires; consult the website or call ahead.

There are several ways into Cohutta. To get to the southeast trailhead via Ellijay, travel west from town on Highway 52 for 9.5 miles to Forest Service Road 18. Turn right after the sign for Lake Conasauga Recreation Area; in about 1.5 miles the road becomes unpaved. At the fork, bear left over a one-lane bridge; at 3.5 miles turn right onto Forest Service Road 68. In another mile is a picnic area, and in another mile a check station. At six miles you can take a right onto Forest Service Road 64, which takes you to the Conasauga River Trail, actually the bed of an old logging railroad.

Cartersville to the Tennessee Border

Conveniently located roughly along I-75 from northwest metro Atlanta up to the Tennessee border at Chattanooga are several areas of historic and educational significance. Here they are, working northward from Atlanta.

CARTERSVILLE

Benefiting from its proximity to the Atlanta metro area, Cartersville is a fairly bustling old railroad town with an active town square and several notable attractions in and around. A distinctive bridge arches over part of the town square.

Booth Western Art Museum

North Georgia isn't where you'd expect to find a huge, shining new museum dedicated to cowboy-and-Indian art, but you'll find that and more at the 120,000-square-foot, limestone Booth Western Art Museum (501 Museum Dr., 770/387-1300, www.boothmuseum.org, Tues.-Wed. and Fri.-Sat. 10am-5pm, Thurs. 10am-8pm, Sun. 1pm-5pm, adults $10, students $7, under 12 free), which claims to be Georgia's biggest museum other than the High in Atlanta. While the highlight for many is the permanent and succinctly-named Cowboy Gallery, the entire multi-story edifice does a good job of being as inclusive as possible, with artwork by and about Native Americans, African Americans, and women, in addition to the more typically mainstream Western art by figures such as George Catlin, Charles M. Russell, and Frederic Remington. There's a solid effort to showcase modern working artists in the genre as well. The museum is very close to the downtown square and has plenty of parking.

Tellus Science Museum

The Tellus Science Museum (100 Tellus Dr., 770/606-5700, www.tellusmuseumorg, daily 10am-5pm, adults $14, children $10, planetarium shows $3.50) focuses on astronomy and geology, with mineral and fossil exhibits galore, specifically designed to interest children in an interactive manner. The building is constructed around a central observatory, which is open during monthly special events (check the website). The all-digital planetarium provides frequent shows with various themes every day at an added cost.

Rose Lawn House Museum

A very short walk from the town square is Rose Lawn House Museum (224 W. Cherokee Ave., 770/387-5162, www.roselawnmuseum.com, Tues.-Fri. 10am-noon and 1pm-5pm, adults $5, children $2), former home of influential Victorian evangelist Samuel Porter Jones of the "Second Great Awakening." The Union Gospel Tabernacle in Nashville, now the Ryman Auditorium, was built for him and would later host the Grand Ol' Opry. The museum features period furnishings and serves as a home for memorabilia of another famous Bartow County native, Rebecca Latimer Felton, the first female U.S. Senator.

Other Sights

The **Bartow History Museum** (4 E. Church St., 770/382-3818, www.bartowhistorymuseum.org, Mon.-Sat. 10am-5pm, adults $5.50, children $4.50) is in the old courthouse and is a particularly good little museum, including exhibits on the long Cherokee presence in the area and native son Joe Frank Harris, former governor. Around the corner is the official claimant to the title of **world's first outdoor Coca-Cola sign,** painted on the side of Young Brothers Pharmacy (2 Main St.). The sign dates from 1894 and is on the National Register of Historic Places.

Food

Tasty dining options downtown include **Appalachian Grill** (14 E. Church St., 770/607-5357, Mon.-Thurs. 11am-9pm, Fri. 11am-10pm, Sat. noon-10pm, $15) with its signature trout dishes and combo platters, and

The Etowah Indian Mounds are particularly well-preserved.

Jefferson's (28 W. Main St., 770/334-2069, www.jeffersonsrestaurant.com, Mon.-Wed. 11am-10pm, Thurs.-Sat. 11am-11pm, Sun. 11:30am-10pm, $10), known for its wings and oysters.

◖ ETOWAH INDIAN MOUNDS HISTORIC SITE

Of Georgia's three key mound-builder sites (Ocmulgee in Macon and Kolomoki near Blakely being the other two) the Etowah Indian Mounds Historic Site (770/387-3747, www.gastateparks.org, Wed.-Sat. 9am-5pm, $5) outside Cartersville is the most archaeologically significant, the most intact of all such sites in the Southeast, and takes its place among the premier remaining mound city-complexes in North America. On this 54 acres was one of the most influential communities of the Mississippian culture from about 1000-1500ad. Its six masterfully-constructed earthen mounds are in surprisingly good shape today, with full access to the top, providing a beautiful panorama of the surrounding area and the other mounds. The 63-foot-tall main temple mound was probably the home of the chief and his family. Etowah is often called the "Tumlin" site after the most recent landowner, who did an excellent job of stewardship before the state's acquisition of the site.

The small but well-curated visitors center has a nice museum with some stunning artifacts retrieved from the site. It provides information as to how the Etowah site interacted with other Mississippian mound cities around the country. Other aspects of Etowah still under archaeological research include the earthworks and moat and a possible palisade wall. Bring a picnic lunch and enjoy the tranquil serenity of the shaded picnic area on the banks of the Etowah River directly beside the mound site.

NEW ECHOTA HISTORICAL SITE

The beneficiary of a recent upgrade and renovation, New Echota Historical Site (1211

Chatsworth Hwy., 706/624-1321, www. gastateparks.org, Thurs.-Sat. 9am-5pm, adults $6.50, children $4.50) just outside Calhoun has an especially bittersweet nature, serving both as capital of the Cherokee Nation 1825-1838 and as the place where the Trail of Tears began. In its heyday, the town of New Echota was the site of the first Indian language newspaper. It eventually hosted the signing of the controversial New Echota Treaty in which the Cherokee essentially relinquished all claims to lands east of the Mississippi, laying the groundwork for their removal to Oklahoma along the infamous Trail of Tears.

Today there are a dozen original and reconstructed period buildings, including the council house and newspaper print shop, and the grounds also include several short, scenic, and easy trails. The visitors center plays a 17-minute film about the history of the site and hosts a Cherokee Research Library.

CHIEF VANN HOUSE HISTORIC SITE

A short drive east of Dalton is the Chief Vann House Historic Site (82 Hwy. 225 N., 706/695-2598, www.gastateparks.org, Thurs.-Sat. 9am-5pm, adults $6, children $3.50), the best-preserved remaining house of the Cherokee nation. Chief James Vann finished building the two-story brick mansion in 1804 on his thousand-acre estate in the Cherokee lands. The Chief was murdered in 1809, with ownership (and chiefdom) passing to his son Joseph. With the Trail of Tears in the 1830s, the Vanns were forced to give up their land and home. The state of Georgia officially took the estate over as a historic site in the late 1950s.

Admission includes a guided tour inside to view the quite ornate furnishings, including a unique floating staircase. Christmastime at the Vann House sees the delightful "Cherokee Christmas by Candlelight" special nighttime tour (regular admission), commemorating the time the Chief opened his house to Moravian missionaries. A nearby Moravian cemetery was recently included in the larger historic site.

TUNNEL HILL

As the name indicates, the chief attraction in this little mountain town is the **Historic Western & Atlantic Railroad Tunnel** (215 Clisby Austin Dr., 706/876-1571, www.tunnel-hillheritagecenter.com, Mon.-Sat. 9am-5pm, adults $7, children $5), opened to the public in 2000 after a long restoration effort. The oldest tunnel in the Southeast, the 1500-foot tunnel through the base of Chetoogeta Mountain was part of the first railroad through the Appalachians, intended to join the Tennessee River Valley with export centers east. It was in operation 1850-1928, and for a few minutes in 1862 it hosted part of the "Great Locomotive Chase." The tunnel itself, at the time considered one of the world's engineering marvels, is available to tour beginning at the top of each hour, and the small Heritage Center museum has a few modest displays. Each September on the weekend after Labor Day, Civil War reenactors once again fight the Battle of Tunnel Hill in a popular regional draw.

The nearby Clisby-Austin house is open for tours during the reenactment weekend, and boasts a bizarre history of its own. Before serving as General Sherman's headquarters at the onset of the Atlanta campaign, the house was a Confederate hospital and Confederate General John Bell Hood recuperated here after the amputation of his leg at the Battle of Chickamauga. His leg, which traveled with him from the battlefield, is buried in the family cemetery near the house! (The general himself lived on, sans leg, until 1879, when yellow fever claimed him in New Orleans.)

DALTON

Known as the "Carpet Capital of the World" for the area's signature export, which at one point created 90 percent of the globe's carpeting, Dalton got into the business in the early 20th century when Catherine Evans Whitener began making bedspreads using a technique called "candlewick embroidery." She and her family went on to form the Evans Manufacturing Company, first in a long line of family-run cottage industries along U.S.

"THE CRUELEST WORK I EVER KNEW"

It wasn't just the North Georgia gold rush that sealed the fate of the Cherokees and led to the infamous Trail of Tears. President Andrew Jackson, a son of the then-wild frontier on the border of the Carolinas, was strongly opposed to both the assimilation of Indians into society as well as their right to remain sovereign nations within state borders. His preference was for tribes to relocate altogether.

Soon after his election in 1828, he successfully pushed Congress to pass the Indian Removal Act, giving the president power to "negotiate" with tribes to essentially force them to give up ancestral lands and head west to federal lands. One of the most notorious such agreements was 1835's Treaty of New Echota, in which a minority of Cherokee, under duress after long and unsuccessful negotiations, without the signature of their main chief John Ross, and facing a rapacious gold rush, ceded all lands in Georgia, Tennessee, Alabama, and the Carolinas.

While many of their lands had already been effectively seized by the state-sponsored gold rush land lotteries, the Treaty of New Echota, ironically named for the ancient Cherokee capital in which it was signed, formed the legal basis for the actual physical removal of the Cherokee,

among the last of the indigenous tribes of the deep South to be forcibly removed.

The treaty allowed a two-year grace period for tribespeople to remove themselves. By then a new president, Martin Van Buren, was in the White House. He sent General Winfield Scott with 7,000 soldiers to remove the remaining Cherokee. For a month they were brutally rounded up and herded into camps. One soldier who would later serve in the Civil War recounted, "I fought through the War Between the States and have seen many men shot, but the Cherokee Removal was the cruelest work I ever knew."

Finally in the winter of 1838, the remaining Indian men, women, and children were forced west, on foot and by raft over the many waterways between them and the Oklahoma Territory. Scholars differ on the number of Cherokees who either died or were killed during this tragic episode of ethnic cleansing, but it is likely between two and five thousand.

The **New Echota Historical Site** near Calhoun details the vast archaeological work done to reveal the legacy of the old Cherokee capital. There's also a memorial to the Cherokees who died on the Trail of Tears.

Highway 41, called "Peacock Alley" for the dominant chenille motif made by the hardworking "tufters." However, the end of the housing boom marked major job losses in the area, which remains hard-hit by the downturn.

Dalton served as a major hospital and staging area for Confederate troops during the long campaigns for Chattanooga and Atlanta, but just about the only antebellum structure left is the old railroad depot famous for its role in the 1862 "Great Locomotive Chase," when the engine "Texas" chased the stolen engine "The General." The depot has been fully restored and now hosts a restaurant-tavern, the **Dalton Depot** (110 Depot St., 706/226-3160, www.thedaltondepot.net, Mon.-Sat. 11am-10pm, Sun. 10:30am-10pm, $15).

◖ CHICKAMAUGA & CHATTANOOGA NATIONAL MILITARY PARK

Directly south of Ft. Oglethorpe on Highway 1 (or off Exit 350 from I-75) is the Chickamauga & Chattanooga National Military Park (3370 LaFayette Rd., www.nps.gov, visitors center daily 8:30am-5pm, grounds daily dawn-dusk, free), preserving and interpreting one of the last major Confederate victories of the Civil War. The focus is primarily on the savage fighting around Chickamauga in September 1863. The Chattanooga portion came later as Union troops successfully defended the strategically important Tennessee city in what was later called the "death knell of the Confederacy." The key moment at Chickamauga came when

© JIM MOREKIS

Chickamauga National Battlefield

Confederate General James Longstreet, Robert E. Lee's closest confidante and a native of nearby Gainesville, Georgia, took advantage of an opportunity to exploit a gap in the Union line, driving nearly half the Federal troops from the field. By the time Union troops had retreated to Chattanooga, there were nearly 20,000 casualties on both sides.

There's a small and well-done visitors center and museum with a 20-minute video explaining the rather complicated actions involved in the battle. The museum features the Fuller Gun Collection, a massive array of U.S. military muskets and rifles from the 19th and early 20th centuries. But the main draw is the seven-mile walking tour over the expansive battlefield, culminating in a trip up an observation tower to view the entire vista. There are interpretive maps, or you can dial a number on your cell phone to listen to an audio tour as you drive and perhaps occasionally get out to walk around and see the sights up close at your leisure (get the number from the Park Service

rangers at the visitors center). While no real artifacts from the battle remain on the grounds, other than at the museum, the park has attempted to recreate the conflict by strategically positioned artillery batteries, with color-coded informational markers (red for rebels, blue for Yankees).

Perhaps most striking, especially to visitors not overly enamored with military hardware, are the over 1,000 handsome and often quite ornate monuments from the Victorian era spread all over the battlefield, commemorating the sacrifice of various states on both sides of the conflict as well as individual fighting units.

While most recreational activities at the park other than picnicking are limited out of respect for those who gave their lives here, there are about 14 miles of dedicated equestrian trails, with a horse trailer parking spot at a gravel lot on Dyer Road.

Just across the border into Tennessee, you can also visit the **Lookout Mountain Battlefield** (110 Point Park Rd., 423/821-7786, visitors center summer daily 9am-6pm, fall-spring daily until 5pm), also expertly administered by the National Park Service.

Fort Oglethorpe

Called Hargrave until 1902 when the U.S. Army bought out the inhabitants to build an army post, Fort Oglethorpe immediately north of the Chickamauga battlefield was the home of the U.S. Army 6th Cavalry Regiment (Gen. "Black Jack" Pershing being the unit's most famous alumnus) until its decommissioning after World War II in 1947, after which it became incorporated as a city with the same name. **The 6th Cavalry Museum** (6 Barnhardt Circle, 706/861-2860, www.6thcavalrymuseum. com, adults $3, children $2) on the old parade grounds and polo field interprets the unit's history in Georgia along with equipment, uniforms, and vehicles.

Ridge and Valley Country

The northwestern portion of Georgia is geologically and culturally somewhat different from the rest of North Georgia. It's often called the Ridge and Valley Country, an area to the west of the Cartersville-Great Smoky Fault and a clear differentiation from the Blue Ridge Mountains to the east. Rome is by far its biggest city.

Though northwest Georgia shares many of the Appalachian folkways typical of the entire northern section of the state, there are far fewer pockets of the type of tourism and retiree-driven affluence found nearer the Blue Ridge. It's a more culturally isolated, socioeconomically humble area that has more in common with east Tennessee than with North Carolina, with commensurately fewer tourist amenities but still plenty to offer lovers of the great outdoors.

ROME

Named of course for the great Italian capital, Rome, Georgia, was built on seven hills like its namesake. In front of City Hall (601 Broad St.) is a statue of Romulus and Remus nursing from a mother wolf, a nod to the creation story of the European city. A gift to the city from Italian dictator Benito Mussolini in 1929, the statue was taken down to prevent vandalism during World War II and put back in the 1950s. Today Rome is a center of regional higher education, healthcare, and manufacturing. You might first want to check out the **Rome-Floyd**

County Visitors Center (402 Civic Center Dr., 800/444-1834, www.romegeorgia.org).

Berry College

Rome's chief claim to fame is big and beautiful Berry College (2277 Martha Berry Hwy., 706/232-374, www.berry.edu), a liberal arts school with an inspiring history set on an expansive campus on the northern edge of town. Founder Martha Berry was the daughter of a wealthy area planter and was struck by the profound lack of educational opportunities for most young people in these hardscrabble foothills. She began an impromptu Sunday school at her home, which eventually expanded to a family log cabin, still on campus today. Her school also expanded to cover a variety of subject matters. From 1902-1909 she opened her own "Berry Schools," one boarding school each for boys and for girls. By 1930 Berry College was a four-year school, which continued after Berry's death in 1942.

At 26,000 acres, Berry is the largest contiguous college campus in the world. It's often used for film locations, most notably for *Sweet Home Alabama* and *Remember the Titans*. Fun fact: Perhaps odd given the Italian reference in Rome's name, the Berry College mascot is a Viking.

Much of the campus land is administered by the state as hunting and conservation areas; other parts are open to the public for walking and biking. The most popular multi-use trail on campus for students, residents, and visitors alike is the Viking Trail (daily dawn-dusk, free), a three-mile paved trail between the main campus and the mountain campus. There are also other designated trails for equestrians, mountain bikers, joggers, and hikers; go to the college website for more information.

The highlight is the **Oak Hill & The Martha Berry Museum** (24 Veterans Memorial Hwy., 706/368-6789, www.berry.edu, Mon.-Sat. 10am-5pm, tours 10am-3:30pm every 30 minutes, $5 adults, $3 children), Berry's Greek Revival home where you can learn much more about the school's fascinating history and the life and times of its philanthropic, pioneering founder. The specially designed Colonial Revival gardens and grounds are also beautiful, and you can walk them and see several historic outbuildings.

Clocktower Museum

Downtown Rome's most famous sight is the 1872 Clocktower (East Second St., Mon.-Fri. 9am-3pm, free), a massive clock atop the 100-foot old city water tower. The clock face is nine feet across, and the minute hand is more than four feet long. There's a small museum inside, and visitors can climb the stairs to see the view from the top.

Chieftains Museum and Major Ridge Home

One of the key remaining sites along the Trail of Tears, the Chieftains Museum (501 Riverside Pkwy., 706/291-9494, www.chieftainsmuseum.org, Fri.-Sat. 1pm-5pm, $5 adults, $3 children) is within the home of Major Ridge, who gathered a band of Cherokee Indians to fight alongside the colonists during the American Revolution. Out of gratitude, Andrew Jackson gave him the rank of major, which Ridge would adopt as his first name. However, by the 1830s pressure on his tribe to give up their lands was so intense he felt compelled to sign the controversial Treaty of New Echota, which resulted in the Trail of Tears. Ridge and his family went to Oklahoma with most of the remaining Georgia Cherokees, but he was soon assassinated by fellow Indians for his role in the treaty. The small museum inside the home has clothing, artifacts, and exhibits from Ridge's life and times.

Myrtle Hill Cemetery

Scenic Myrtle Hill Cemetery (Branham Ave. and South Broad St., daily dawn-dusk, free) is set on a six-tiered terraced hill, one of Rome's seven signature hills, and provides beautiful views of the surrounding area. The most famous perpetual resident is President Woodrow Wilson's first wife Ellen Axon Wilson, a Savannah native who grew up in Rome. The most controversial monument is the one to Confederate General Nathan Bedford Forrest, founder of the Ku Klux Klan; however, he is remembered locally for a successful defense of Rome against a much larger Union force, the "Lightning Mule Brigade." The most unusual grave is that of Private Charles Graves, who was supposed to lie in Arlington Cemetery as "America's Known Soldier" but whose mother strongly differed and petitioned to bury him in his hometown.

Accommodations and Food

The premier lodging in Rome is the **C Claremont House** (906 E. 2nd Ave., 706/291-0900, www.theclaremonthouse.net, $150-170), set in an absolutely stunning high Victorian masterpiece of a building. There are four charming rooms with 14-foot ceilings and canopy beds within the house and a cute cottage. The expansive front and back porches are pretty enticing in and of themselves.

A couple of good places to get a bite right downtown are **Harvest Moon Cafe** (234 Broad St., 706/292-0099, www.myharvestmooncafe.com, Mon. 11am-2:30pm, Tues.-Thurs. 11am-9pm, Fri.-Sat. 11am-10pm, $15), with its good steaks, salmon, and catfish, and **Jefferson's** (340 Broad St., 706/378-0222, www.jeffersonsrestaurant.com, Mon.-Wed. 11am-10pm, Thurs.-Sat. 11am-11pm, Sun. 11:30am-10pm, $10), a regional chain famous for its wings and oysters.

NEAR ROME
◖ Paradise Garden

You'd be forgiven for thinking that the late, great Georgia folk artist Howard Finster lived in Athens, Georgia, across the state. His collaborations on album cover art for the iconic Athens band R.E.M. and later with the Talking Heads put Finster on the global map, which suited Finster just fine, since all he said he wanted to do was spread the gospel through his art to as many people as possible. Finster became known as not only one of the South's greatest and certainly hippest outsider artists, but as a classic Southern showman-raconteur in the grand old style.

Finster's memory lives on in Athens, but the best place to view his fertile, almost feverish imagination in action is at Paradise Garden (200 N. Lewis St., 706/808-0800, www.paradisegardenfoundation.org, Wed.-Sun. 10am-4pm, Sun. 1pm-4pm, donations accepted), his Summerville studio on a swampy four-acres of land in a residential neighborhood off a side street. It's here among the double-wides and pickups, with a maximum security prison just down the way, that you viscerally sense the conflicted, paradoxical sources of Finster's outsider art.

Like the world's most eccentric theme park, Finster's drawing, painting, and craftwork cover just about every foot of available space on every structure: from the front porch of the main house; to the "Meditation Room" and its pews and angel altar overseeing Finster's unoccupied "casket"; to his bicycle repair shop; to the little handmade chapel in the west corner of the lot; to the unwieldy multi-story "World's Folk Art Church" overlooking the whole neighborhood like a bizarre Himalayan temple; to the gospel-festooned old Cadillac "art car" that Finster used to drive through Summerville. Here, you fully understand the provenance of the phrase, "one man's junk is another man's treasure."

Each May the town park at Summerville hosts "Finster Fest," an expansive celebration

NORTH GEORGIA

© JIM MOREKIS

Howard Finster's Paradise Garden in Summerville

not only of Finster's work but of regional folk artists from all around. Named to the National Register of Historic Places in 2012, Paradise Garden is finally getting both the public attention and at least some of the funding it deserves. It's not for everyone, but it is for those who want to immerse themselves into the robust, often quirky world of real Southern folk art, and have a lot of fun while they're at it.

To get to the Garden, head north through Summerville on U.S. Highway 27. Take a right on Rena Street, looking for the signs, and then a right onto North Lewis Street. You can't miss it!

If you need a bite to eat while you're in Summerville, head straight for the delectable fried catfish at **C Jim's Family Restaurant** (6 Lyerly St., 706/857-2123, daily 8am-8pm, $10). Camp for the night at little **James H. "Sloppy" Floyd State Park** (2800 Sloppy Floyd Lake Rd., 706/857-0826, www.gastateparks.org, $5 parking, campsites $25-28, cottages $135-145), one of Georgia's smaller yet still picturesque parks, with only 25 tent and RV sites and four cottages.

TAG CORNER

The extreme northwestern tip, sometimes called "TAG corner," an acronym referring to its position astride the borders of Tennessee, Alabama, and Georgia, is yet another geological substratum. Part of the Cumberland Plateau, it's a flat-topped highland area one of whose dominant features is limestone. Long story short, this means lots of caves and hence the exploration of them by spelunkers who come from all over the country.

Lookout Mountain

By far the main geological feature of the area is Lookout Mountain, chief local part of the Cumberland Plateau. Most of the 84-mile-long mountain is in Tennessee, including the remnants of a key Civil War battlefield and the popular Raccoon Mountain and Ruby Falls caves.

The East Coast's premier hang gliding location is **Lookout Mountain Flight Park and Training Center** (7201 Scenic Hwy., 800/688-5637, www.hanglide.com, Thurs.-Tues. 9am-6pm). Under the tutelage of certified staff, hang gliding customers launch from 1,340-foot McCarty's Bluff into the wild blue yonder off Lookout Mountain. Students of the school can take advantage of the park's lodgings right down in the landing zone, with choices ranging from upscale cabins to primitive camping.

C Cloudland Canyon State Park

Lookout Mountain's most dramatic feature is the thousand-foot canyon at Sitton's Gulch, renamed "Cloudland Canyon" in the 1930s during the park's construction by the Civilian Conservation Corps. Cloudland Canyon State Park (122 Cloudland Canyon Park Rd., 706/657-4050, www.gastateparks.org, daily 7am-10pm, $5 parking, backcountry trails $3 pp, campsites $25-28) is quite simply one of the most striking of all Southern state parks, and the place in Georgia most akin to the jaw-dropping geological features that are much more commonplace in the western United States. Its steep sandstone walls are the remnants of a 200-million-year-old shoreline. From the various lookout points along the West Rim Loop Trail skirting the edge of the main picnic area and parking lot along the canyon's edge, you can also see the entrances to some of the canyon's many interior limestone caves.

A great added plus at Cloudland is the fact that you can hike to the bottom of the canyon via some steep but well-maintained and staircase-augmented hiking trails. Ironically given the emphasis on sky and clouds in the park's name, when you get to the bottom it's a whole different world and one of my favorite places in Georgia: tranquil, heavily forested with large sedimentary boulders (talus), and hosting a pair of charming waterfalls cascading into blue pools.

Another bonus in the big picture is that because of the difficulty in moving equipment around this area, it is remarkably free of human development unlike many other supposedly "pristine" areas which in reality were quite heavily logged in previous centuries.

waterfall deep in the heart of Cloudland Canyon

Some quite old-growth botanical ecosystems still exist all around the canyon, including mountain laurel, hemlock, and Catawba Rhododendron.

In all, the Rim trail is about five miles and give you overlook opportunities into three canyon gorges. Be aware that at certain times of day when the sun is very low in the sky there will be a big "wash-out" effect bouncing off the canyon walls which will interfere not only with your own visibility but your camera's.

There is another five-mile network of backcountry trails, along which primitive camping is permitted, a particularly recommended option for those so inclined. There are another 72 tent and RV sites divided between the east and west rims, and 16 cottages along the west rim, two of which are dog friendly.

Don't forget: The park hosts frequent and fun guided hikes throughout the canyon and also into some of its many incredible caves for a small fee, at beginner and advanced levels; check the website for dates and times. The **Georgia Girl Guides** (www.georgiagirlguides. com) run many of them, as does the **Georgia Conservancy** (www.georgiaconservancy.org) and **Canyon Climbers Club** (www.gastateparks. org, $10), which you can join at Cloudland Canyon or at three other Georgia state parks with similar geology: Amicalola Falls, Tallulah Gorge, and Providence Canyon.

Pigeon Mountain

Adjoining with the larger Lookout Mountain, Pigeon Mountain closer to LaFayette, Georgia, was named for the massive flocks of now-extinct passenger pigeons that once made their home here. It's particularly rich spelunking ground and also boasts many rare species of plants and salamanders. Most of it is overseen by the Georgia Department of Natural Resources (706/295-6041, www.georgiawildlife.com) as part of a wildlife management area. The newly created Georgia Outdoor Recreation Pass (GORP, $3.50 for three days) is required to use the area; those with valid hunting and fishing licenses are exempt, however. To get here from Lafayette, take Highway 193 west for three miles to Chamberlain Road, then turn left and go another three miles to Rocky Lane Road, then turn right. The check station will be about a quarter mile ahead.

While Pigeon Mountain contains a vast network of limestone caves, some explored and some not, the most famous is Ellison's Cave, 12th deepest in the United States and containing over 13 miles of mapped caves. The two deepest drops in the continental United States are here, the "Fantastic" pit at 586 feet and the "Incredible" pit at 440 feet. Fantastic and another deep pit, the 490-foot Smokey I, lead down to TAG Hall, a long passage at the bottom of the cave. A spring fed by Ellison's Cave, the Blue Hole features its distinctive tint and year-round 56-degree temperatures. There's a parking area nearby with a kiosk to sign up to go down into the cave. Nearby Pettyjohn's Cave is nearly as deep, and some cavers say it's more interesting. It features a couple of underground waterfalls and the huge 100-by-200-foot "Echo Room." Only those with spelunking experience or expert guidance should enter the caves, preferably as part of a group-sponsored tour. Unfortunately, the mysterious bat-killing White Nose Sydnrome was just found in Georgia. Go to www.georgiawildlife.com for more on how this might affect your spelunking.

One of the most fun things non-cavers can do in the area is hike **Rocktown Trail,** named for its 150 acres of whimsical, all-natural sandstone-and-iron formations, some with boulders three stories tall. Though the trail is an easy two-mile round-trip, do reserve enough time to really explore the rocks; if you have kids with you they will certainly appreciate it. To get to Rocktown from U.S. Highway 27 in LaFayette, head west 3 miles on Highway 193 to Chamberlain Road; turn left and go another 3.5 miles, then turn right at the Crockford-Pigeon Mountain WMA sign. Pass the Department of Natural Resources check station and go straight; where the gravel road forks, veer right and then take the next gravel road on your left about 1.5 miles later. From there, it's another 0.5 miles or so to the trailhead.

Johns Mountain

On 25,000 acres within the Chattahoochee National Forest (706/695-6736, www.fs.usda.gov), the Johns Mountain Wildlife Management Area is a popular recreation ground roughly equidistant between the triangle formed by Dalton, LaFayette, and Calhoun. A particularly popular area here is just called **The Pocket** (camping Apr.-Oct., $10), so named because it lies between the ridges of the Horn and Hill mountains. On the site of a former CCC camp, this seasonal campground is a fairly accessible, scenic getaway, especially during leaf-watching season. From Dalton, head south until you get to Highway 136, then head west until you hit Pocket Road. Take a left and continue; the Pocket will be on your left. Continue on Pocket Road to find Lake Marvin, around which you'll find plenty of free camping, not to mention fishing on the lake itself.

PIEDMONT

The northeastern portion of Georgia between the great coastal plain to the south and the mountainous regions of the far north has been a hotbed of activity from the earliest days of the colony. Today, exurban Atlanta has encroached on its western edge. But for the most part communities in the Piedmont have steadfastly retained their small-town identity, which combines a respect for their well-preserved antebellum history with an enjoyment of the outdoors, chiefly in the form of the expansive lakes in the lush Savannah River valley that form the state's eastern border.

Physically, the Piedmont can be a breath of fresh air after the flat piney woods of the southern portion of the state. Rather than the larger agricultural concerns you'll see down south, the Piedmont's topography tends to lend itself to dairy farms and pastureland. And while there are rolling hills to spare, it's generally more inviting than the Blue Ridge, portions of which in the depth of winter can be literally impassable.

Packing more into a smaller space than anywhere else in the state except Atlanta itself, Georgia's Piedmont region hosts the state's largest university in Athens; indeed, red-and-black Georgia Bulldog paraphernalia is everywhere you look around here. On the South Carolina border is Augusta, Georgia's second-oldest city and today one of its largest.

Between Athens and Augusta are several of America's most charming and historic small towns in Madison, Greensboro, and Washington. Together they form a thoroughly delightful trifecta, which debunks the

© JIM MOREKIS

PIEDMONT

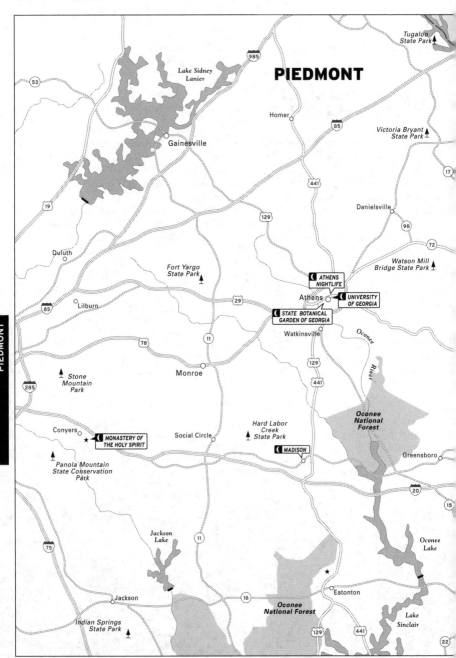

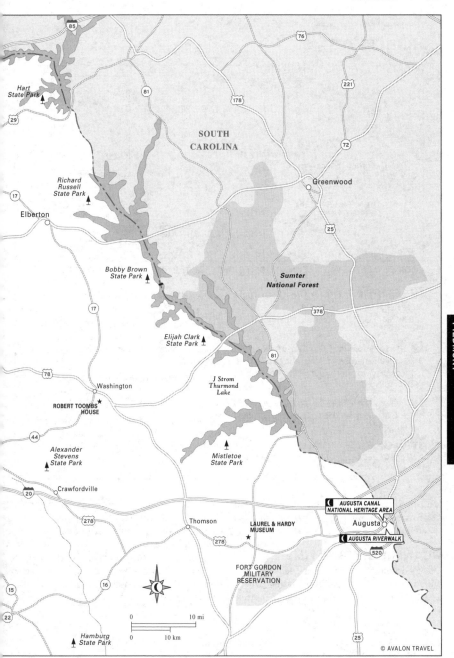

PIEDMONT

© AVALON TRAVEL

PIEDMONT

HIGHLIGHTS

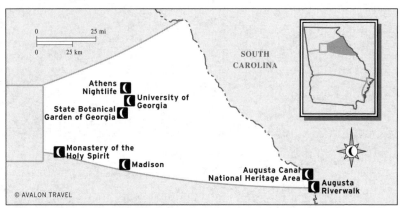

© AVALON TRAVEL

LOOK FOR █ TO FIND RECOMMENDED SIGHTS, ACTIVITIES, DINING, AND LODGING.

█ **University of Georgia:** The nation's oldest chartered university is on a beautiful shaded campus full of historic buildings (page 141).

█ **State Botanical Garden of Georgia:** Brilliantly themed landscaping and a huge tropical conservatory are highlights here (page 143).

█ **Athens Nightlife:** The legacy of the B-52s and R.E.M. live on in this college town's robust live music scene (page 146).

█ **Madison:** One of the most charming and well-preserved old Southern towns you'll find,

chock full of eclectic and interesting architecture (page 157).

█ **Monastery of the Holy Spirit:** Those of a spiritual bent will enjoy the museum and peaceful grounds of Georgia's only monastery (page 164).

█ **Augusta Riverwalk:** An expertly designed, terraced stroll runs along a scenic portion of the Savannah River (page 166).

█ **Augusta Canal National Heritage Area:** The South's only industrial canal still in use is now a recreation hub (page 170).

longstanding myth that General Sherman destroyed everything in his path during his "March to the Sea."

PLANNING YOUR TIME

The Piedmont can easily be experienced by car with a minimum of travel time. Using Athens as a base, you can take a fun day-trip circle

route from there to Madison, Greensboro, Washington, and back. To expand, hit the smaller towns of Conyers and Social Circle. The Augusta and Savannah River Lakes area are more of a destination in and of themselves if you're planning on getting out on the water, though the sights of Augusta itself can be fully enjoyed in a day or two.

Athens

One of the great American college towns, Athens is home to the University of Georgia, the oldest state university in the country. Athens is a heady and often quirky mix of culture, partying, football, and progressive thought in an otherwise conservative area. In that sense, it's not entirely unique, with any number of college towns having all of those qualities. But what makes Athens stand out, and clearly puts it head and shoulders above most college towns, is the fabled "Athens scene," a musical ethos that for the past 30 years has virtually defined, and in some cases directly authored, the sound of American indie rock 'n' roll. A blend of introspective artiness (R.E.M.), jam band virtuosity (Widespread Panic), and flamboyant dance party euphoria (B-52s), the Athens sound represents a perfect

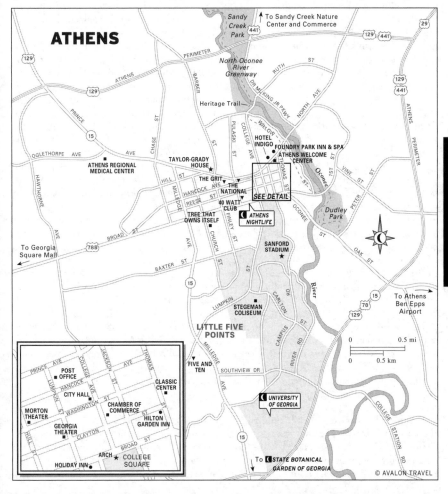

PIEDMONT

microcosm of the eclectic and spirited town in which it was born. While casual sightings of R.E.M. front man Michael Stipe, who still makes his home here, aren't quite as frequent as they used to be, the Athens spirit is alive and well every night of the week in the many, many clubs in and around the bustling downtown area. If you can't find a good time here, frankly there's something wrong with you.

College means parties and music, but in the South it also means football. The Athens music and arts scene exists in an interesting creative tension with the other important side of local life, the University of Georgia Bulldogs, a perennially powerful team with a passionately devoted fan base who turn out by the many thousands on home-game Saturdays, decked out in the school colors of red and black, to cheer on "them Dawgs."

HISTORY

With the U.S. Constitution still a gleam in James Madison's eye, a forward-thinking state legislature in 1785 made a bold step to endow a "college or seminary of learning," essentially giving birth to the idea of state-supported higher education in America. A site was eventually chosen on the Oconee River near Greensboro under the auspices of John Milledge, a close friend of Thomas Jefferson and soon to be Georgia governor. The site was eventually moved northward, and technically the first classes weren't held until 1801, which is why the University of North Carolina maintains that it is actually the first chartered state university, since they held classes earlier.

The surrounding town, created in 1806, was to be called Athens to channel the spirit of the great artistic, literary, and scientific accomplishments of the ancient Greeks. It quickly became an influential city, based not only on the fact that many of the state's leading citizens sent their young men to be educated here, but on the Oconee River's plentiful and profitable textile mills. Athens's most famous resident in the antebellum era was Henry W. Grady, who would go on to be a seminal editor of the *Atlanta Journal-Constitution* and founder of

the University of Georgia school of journalism, which bears his name to this day.

Athens escaped serious action during the Civil War, and Reconstruction was relatively mild. While the University closed its doors so its young men could go fight for the Confederacy, after the war Athens's academic importance led to a rapidly established freed black community and one of Georgia's largest black middle class sectors. Indeed, one of the state's wealthiest African American businessmen during the Victorian streetcar era, Monroe "Pink" Morton, built the historic and still operating theater that bears his name in downtown Athens today.

Buoyed by the growing university community, Athens stayed moderately prosperous through the end of the 20th century. Its next major chapter came in the late 1970s-early 1980s with two key events: the first house parties by the B-52s and the national football championship won in 1980 by the Georgia Bulldogs, mainly through the talents of Heisman Trophy-winner Herschel Walker. (That may sound strange, but since music and football are the two main pursuits in Athens, it makes perfect sense to anyone who's been here.)

While by no means the first band to tap into the eccentric local DIY dance vibe, the B-52s were the first to gain a national following and a record deal. They quickly decamped to New York City, but their contemporaries R.E.M. opted to keep deep roots in Athens long after they became international stars in the mid-1980s, virtually inventing the genre we now call "college radio." Some members of the band continue to live in Athens and are vital strands in the local cultural and economic fabric, contributing money, energy, and expertise to keeping Athens's quality of life high.

SIGHTS
Church-Waddel-Brumby House

The main Athens visitors center is within the restored Church-Waddel-Brumby House (280 E. Dougherty St., 706/353-1820, www.athenswelcomecenter.com, Mon.-Sat. 10am-5pm,

Sun. noon-5pm, free), a circa-1820 house museum alleged to be the oldest residence in the city. It moved to this spot in 1967. It's definitely worth a visit to load up on brochures, particularly for the various walking tours.

❰ University of Georgia

Founded in 1785, the University of Georgia (www.uga.edu), "Georgia" or UGA in common parlance, is the nation's oldest state-chartered university. (The University of North Carolina in Chapel Hill also claims that title, based on the fact that UGA didn't actually hold classes until 1801.)

As befitting its deep roots in the Deep South, UGA boasts not only a devotion to tradition, but a large (over 600 acres) and scenic campus which is worth exploring whether you're affiliated with the university or not. You can take free student-guided tours leaving from the Visitors Center on South Campus or download a walking tour map at http://visit.uga.edu. Here's a quick look at the highlights:

Every visit to UGA should begin with the

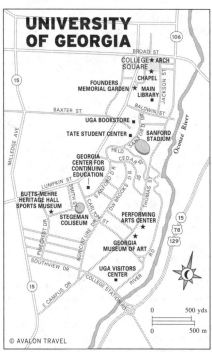

© JIM MOREKIS

The Arch is the introduction to the scenic UGA campus.

famous **Arch** at the old North Campus entrance on Broad Street. Old Bulldog etiquette demands that underclassmen only walk around the Arch, not under it. Visitors however, are under no such expectation, and you will likely see many people posing for pictures underneath and around the cast iron landmark. Just as you walk through the Arch you'll see the Greek Revival **Hunter Holmes Academic Building,** actually two antebellum buildings combined in the early 20th century. In 2001 it was renamed to honor the first two African American students admitted to UGA: Hamilton Holmes and Charlayne Hunter-Gault (later a renowned broadcast journalist), who began classes in 1961 after court-ordered integration.

Facing each other across the shady North Campus quad are twin debating society headquarters **Demosthenes Hall** and **Phi Kappa Hall,** the latter of which housed Union troops after the Civil War. Indeed, both buildings have changed little since antebellum days.

Right beside Demosthenes Hall is the 1832 **Chapel,** where students once attended services three days a week. These days, students take turns ringing the old chapel bell, now in a small tower nearby, until midnight after every Georgia football victory.

South of the Chapel and off to the right you'll run across verdant little **Herty Field,** where the Bulldogs played their first football game in 1892 (beating Mercer University 50-0) under the direction of Georgia's first coach, Charles Herty, also a chemist of national repute. A parking lot actually occupied this rectangle from the 1940s to 1999, when the hallowed athletic ground was reclaimed as relaxing green space for casual enjoyment.

Two buildings down from Phi Kappa Hall across the quad is the **Administration Building,** currently the university president's office and the home of the Georgia Museum of Art from 1948-82. The small building adjacent is **Old College,** the oldest building on campus. The 1806 building was based on Connecticut Hall at Yale University. Confederate Vice President Alexander Stephens lived here during his time as a student at UGA.

The imposing building ahead is the Ila Dunlap Little Library, usually just called the **"Main Library."** Its Hargrett Rare Book and Manuscript Library includes a copy of the original Confederate Constitution and some papers of Margaret Mitchell. The smaller building next to the Main Library is **Dean Rusk Hall,** part of the Law School complex and named for longtime UGA law professor Dean Rusk, who was also U.S. Secretary of State for presidents John F. Kennedy and Lyndon B. Johnson.

Continue down Sanford Drive until you get to the large, bricked pedestrian crossing at Baldwin Avenue, the demarcation between the original North Campus and the much newer South Campus. Ahead on your left in the large nondescript modernist building is the **Henry W. Grady School of Journalism and Mass Communication,** one of the nation's highest-ranked journalism schools.

Adjacent to the Grady School and impossible to miss is enormous **Sanford Stadium,** sixth largest college football stadium in the country (capacity 93,000) and where the Bulldogs play home games "between the hedges" growing all along the sidelines. The current hedges

Sanford Stadium, where the Georgia Bulldogs play

aren't the originals; those were removed to accommodate soccer games in the 1996 Summer Olympics. They are, however, direct descendants of the original plants. Right across the street is the huge **Tate Student Center** and campus bookstore, central gathering place for UGA's 30,000-plus undergrads.

Most of the rest of South Campus comprises nondescript academic buildings and athletic facilities. On the other side of East Campus Road is East Campus, notable chiefly for being the location of the **Georgia Museum of Art** and the two concert halls of the **Performing Arts Center.** At the extreme tip of South Campus at College Station Road is the **UGA Visitors Center** (Four Towers Building, 706/542-0842, http://visit.uga.edu), where the student-led campus tours begin.

◖ State Botanical Garden of Georgia

The very tastefully landscaped and interpreted State Botanical Garden (2450 S. Milledge Ave., 706/542-1244, www.botgarden.uga.edu, visitors center Tues.-Sat. 9:30am-4:30pm, Sun. 11:30am-4:30pm, grounds daily 8am-dusk,

modest donation requested), operated by UGA, eschews over-the-top displays of flora for a highly interesting and educational approach to the botanical arts. You enter through the Conservatory, which has a nice little tropical plant and orchid display. Just outside, arrayed around an inviting quad, is a series of geographically themed gardens, including a Native American garden, a Spanish garden, a nod to famed naturalist William Bartram, and a delightful-smelling herb garden. At the adjacent west ellipse is a beautiful classic garden divided into historically appropriate segments, such as the nod to Trustees' Garden in Savannah, the nation's first medicinal garden. In all, this is a must-stop for plant lovers.

Georgia Museum of Art

Once on old North Campus, the Georgia Museum of Art (90 Carlton St., 706/542-4662, www.georgiamuseum.org, Tues.-Wed. and Fri.-Sat. 10am-5pm, Thurs. 10am-9pm, Sun. 1pm-5pm, free, donations encouraged) is now in a purpose-built modern space on the East Campus. Run by the University, it is the official state art museum. It hosts a wide

PIEDMONT

© JIM MOREKIS

State Botanical Garden of Georgia, Athens

variety of rotating exhibits and its own collections are surprisingly eclectic, ranging from home-grown folk art by Howard Finster to Georgia O'Keefe to the Kress Collection of Italian Renaissance works. Note the late hours on Thursdays.

Butts-Mehre Heritage Hall Sports Museum

For fans of "the Dawgs," the Butts-Mehre Heritage Hall Sports Museum (1 Selig Circle, www.georgiadogs.com, Mon.-Fri. 8am-5pm, free) is a must-see. All University of Georgia athletic achievements are honored here through displays and video footage, but of course football takes center stage, including the two Heisman Trophies, won by UGA players Frank Sinkwich and Herschel Walker, and the National Championship trophy won by the Dawgs in 1980 during Walker's tenure.

Georgia Theatre

Athens's most beloved musical venue is also a piece of history as well. With a foundation dating from 1889, the circa-1935 Georgia Theatre (215 N. Lumpkin St., 706/850-7670, www.georgiatheatre.com) has hosted many bands of note over the past 30-plus years since its restoration as a music venue in 1978 (debut act: Sea Level!), with a brief hiatus as a carafe-and-draft movie theater in the 1980s. The Police played here on their first U.S. tour and the B-52s forged their reputation (and their first record deal) after a legendary show here. When the Georgia Theatre was severely damaged by fire in 2009, everyone feared the worst, some even seeing it as a symbolic omen of doom for the vaunted local music scene. But an extraordinary community reinvestment effort led to a total repair of the venue, and only two years later it was up and running again, hosting a full schedule of musical acts. A fun rooftop bar, added during the renovation, is a great bonus.

Morton Theatre

Just around the corner from the Georgia Theatre is the historic Morton Theatre (195

The Georgia Theatre was completely restored after a fire.

© JIM MOREKIS

W. Washington St., 706/613-3770, www. mortontheatre.com), which hosted signature acts such as Blind Willie McTell in the days of segregation. The larger edifice within which the theater resides, the Morton Building, was in the early 20th century the largest building owned by an African American in the country, and was the heart of the "Hot Corner" at Washington and Lumpkin, then the black business and entertainment district. Today it is fully restored and hosts regular events and shows.

City Hall and the Double-Barreled Cannon

Athens boasts one of the more attractive city halls (301 College Ave.) you're likely to find, with an extremely unique monument on the grounds. The double-barreled cannon on the northeast corner of the City Hall lot was built in Athens in 1862 as a Confederate "secret weapon." The idea was that the two cannonballs would be connected by an eight-foot chain and when fired the resulting spinning anti-personnel weapon would cause much damage. However, it didn't work so well in test firings and was never used in combat.

The Tree That Owns Itself

At South Finley and Dearing Streets you'll find the Jackson Oak, or the "tree that owns itself." Actually this white oak tree is a descendant of the original 300-year-old tree on the site, which was deeded to the land and eight feet all around it by former property owner William Jackson. Or so the story goes. Most legal experts insist the document has no legal bearing, with some going so far as to say there's no proof Jackson himself actually owned the land in the first place. In any case, the local government, knowing the value of a good story, now recognizes the tree's self-ownership and maintains the grounds. The first tree fell in 1942; the current tree is from one of its acorns and its self-ownership was officially passed down in a ceremony in 1946. Though situated in a residential area, the tree attracts many visitors.

PIEDMONT

© JIM MOREKIS

the double-barreled cannon beside Athens City Hall

Lyndon House Art Center

Operated by the local city and county government, the Lyndon House Art Center (293 Hoyt Ave., 706/613-3623, www.athensclarkecounty. com, Tues. and Thurs. noon-9pm, Wed. and Fri.-Sat. 9am-5pm, free) is a restored house museum, which offers various arts and cultural enrichment activities for the community. Check their calendar for frequent gallery openings and events.

T.R.R. Cobb House

Lawyer and Confederate officer Thomas Reade Roots Cobb is a key figure in Athens history, but interestingly the Greek Revival T.R.R. Cobb House (175 Hill St., 706/369-3513, www.trrcobbhouse.org, Tues.-Sat. 10am-4pm, $2) was at Stone Mountain Park near Atlanta for 20 years. It has since been returned to this site, about a block from the original location where it was first built in 1834. The ground floor is very expertly restored to antebellum furnishings. The second floor is more of a museum format, with a collection of papers, and standing and rotating exhibits on aspects of history reflected by the lives of the home's occupants.

Taylor-Grady House

Named for its two most notable owners, Confederate officer and Irish native Robert Taylor and *Atlanta Journal-Constitution* editor and UGA journalism school founder Henry W. Grady, the Taylor-Grady House (634 Prince Ave., 706/549-8688, www.taylorgradyhouse. com, Mon., Wed., and Fri. 9am-3pm, Tues. and Thurs. 9am-1pm, $3) was built in 1844 as a summer home for Taylor and his family. The Athens Junior League restored the house in the 1960s and now operates it as a house museum. Because it is the only surviving house in which Grady lived, it was declared a National Landmark in the 1970s.

Fraternity and Sorority Row

The vast bulk, but by no means all, of Greek fraternities and sororities in Athens are on Milledge Avenue from a stretch running roughly from College Avenue to South Lumpkin Avenue. These large, beautiful, and generally well-maintained houses, many with historic pedigree, are of course the sites of many a big party, especially during football season. On a nice spring or fall day it's pleasant to walk or drive down the road taking it all in.

ENTERTAINMENT AND EVENTS
《 Athens Nightlife

In a matter of great local pride, the University of Georgia is usually at or near the top of the annual lists of "Best Party Schools in America." Indeed, urban legend maintains that Athens has the highest per capita number of bars in the United States. Blend in the city's top-ranked status as a music hub and a last call at 2am, and you've got a drink recipe for a heady nightlife scene.

Generally speaking, the "hipster" or "townie" bars are near Washington Street on the western side of downtown and feature more and better live music. The frat-friendly or "bro" bars tend to be a couple of blocks eastward, and tend to focus on cheap drink specials, especially on football weekends. Word to the wise: There's not much serious crime in Athens, so the police have a lot of time on their hands to apprehend those driving under the influence.

First among equals, the legendary **40 Watt Club** (285 W. Washington St., 706/549-7871, www.40watt.com, open show nights only) has been at the forefront of the Athens music scene since 1978, when it was co-founded by Curtis Crowe, drummer with local legends Pylon (it's now owned by the ex-wife of R.E.M. guitarist Peter Buck). It's the CBGB of the South, but unlike that NYC club, it's still open for business, albeit in its fifth location. While it's been a long time since the 40 Watt was lit by a single light bulb, as local folklore says the first incarnation was, its reputation remains powerful, and it's still the case that no local band can say they've truly made it until they've played here. Unlike the sweaty, cramped vibe of some earlier 40 Watts, the current space is a good bit larger than previous locations, the cavernous space

the legendary 40 Watt Club

broken up by artfully placed couches around the perimeter. The only catch these days is the place is only open nights when a band is booked, so check ahead.

Despite its swank name, **Manhattan Cafe** (337 N. Hull St., 706/369-9767, Mon.-Sat. 4pm-2am) is one of Athens's most humbly charming bars, a cross between a dive, a hipster bar, and a Prohibition cocktail joint. Dark and quirkily decorated in throwback fashion, it features frequent liquor specials mixed by the skillful resident bartenders. The house cocktail is a refreshing blend of Maker's Mark and spicy Blenheim Ginger Ale. **Little Kings** (223 W. Hancock St., 706/369-3144, Mon.-Sat. 7pm-2am) is essentially Manhattan Cafe with an indoor and outdoor stage area, fitting given that both establishments share the same owner. Little Kings is a go-to for high-profile indie acts; local legend Pylon chose it to kickoff a reunion tour.

If you're into concerts where even the band wears earplugs, **Caledonia Lounge** (256 W. Clayton St., 706/549-5577, www.

caledonialounge.com, Mon.-Sat. 5pm-2am) is the place for you. This is where Athens's stable of hardcore-thrash bands plays at an eardrum-bashing (but always professionally mixed) volume. The focus here is on the music rather than the drink specials, but there is a rambling outdoor patio where you can actually hear yourself talk. Narrow little **Flicker Theatre and Bar** (263 W. Washington St., 706/546-0039, www.flickertheatreandbar.com, Mon.-Fri. 4pm-2am, Sat. 1pm-2am) is a favorite meet-up spot and also features occasional singer-songwriter music in a house party atmosphere. Even its sidewalk seating area is cozy.

You'll find Athens's own homegrown craft beer at **Terrapin Beer Co.** (265 Newton Bridge Rd., 706/549-3377, http://terrapinbeer.com, Mon.-Tues. 9am-5pm, Wed.-Fri. 9am-7:30pm, Sat. 5:30pm-7:30pm), as well as good music outdoors on the lawn. Bring a lawn chair or blanket and enjoy. Tastings (no reservation required) happen each Wednesday-Saturday 5:30pm-7:30pm. Craft brew lovers will also enjoy **Trappeze Pub** (269 N. Hull St.,

706/543-8997, www.trappezepub.com, Mon.-Sat. 11am-2am, Sun. 11am-midnight), a lively gastropub-style spot with a vast array of artisan hops, including many Terrapin offerings; a big plus is that it's open Sunday evenings, unlike many Athens nightspots. Cocktail lovers will enjoy **Allgood Lounge** (256 E. Clayton St., 706/549-0166, www.allgoodlounge.com, Mon.-Sat. noon-2am), which has over 50 whiskeys, nearly two dozen tequilas, and a build-your-own Bloody Mary bar.

The Max Canada (243 W. Washington St., 706/254-3392, Mon.-Sat. 4pm-2am), usually just called "Max," is a hybrid sports bar, pool, and air hockey spot, music venue, and late-night watering hole. It's warehouse-huge and you can always find a corner to hang out in. **Normal Bar** (1365 Prince Ave., 706/548-6186, Mon.-Sat. 4pm-2am) in Normaltown just west of downtown is a classic neighborhood-type hangout popular with the college crowd who want to get away from the downtown scene.

Known for hosting earlier and more well-behaved concerts than most local venues, the **Melting Point** (295 E. Dougherty St., 706/549-7051, www.meltingpointathens.com, show times vary) has become a go-to spot for music fans who actually have a job to go to the next morning. **Hendershot's Coffee Bar** (1560 Oglethorpe Dr., 706/353-3050, www.hendershotscoffee.com, Mon.-Fri. 6:30am-11pm, Sat.-Sun. 7:30am-11:45pm) is, well, a coffee bar. But it's notable for routinely hosting high-caliber jazz talent in its listening room.

Small and sweaty, **Go Bar** (195 Prince Ave., 706/546-5609, Mon.-Sat. 9pm-2am), next to the popular restaurant The Grit in a block restored and owned by R.E.M.'s Michael Stipe, is a popular spot to dance and enjoy live music. **New Earth Music Hall** (227 W. Dougherty St., 706/543-8283, www.newearthmusichall.com, Mon.-Sat. 9pm-2am) combines a hippie vibe with a rave-scene aesthetic, specializing in jam band shows.

While primarily known as a large-ish live music venue downstairs, the **Georgia Theatre** (215 N. Lumpkin St., 706/850-7670, www.georgiatheatre.com, bar hours Mon.-Thurs. 11:30am-midnight, Fri.-Sat. 11:30am-2am, show times vary) does allow you to bring libations into the mainstage area and also has a new rooftop bar with enjoyable views of downtown.

Film geeks will be glad to know that Athens has a cool theater with a liquor license. The **Cine BarCafe** (234 W. Hancock St., 706/353-7377, www.athenscine.com, Mon.-Fri. from 4:30pm, Sat.-Sun. from 2pm, show times vary) screens foreign, indie, and rare features and has a full bar area in the neo-industrial-looking lobby, which you can enjoy whether or not you're here to see a movie.

Events

When it was founded in 1980, the **Athens Twilight Criterium** (www.athenscriterium.com, Apr.) was the first pro nighttime cycling event in the modern era. Today it's grown to a vast competition with an associated festival. Events have expanded beyond the core Criterium races through town, men's 80K and women's 40K, and now include "extreme" competitions, kids' events, and a 5K run/walk for the non-cyclists. The festival component includes copious live music outdoors and plenty of food tents downtown for the 30,000 or so spectators.

The premier running event in town is the **AthHalf** (http://athhalf.com, Oct.), a half marathon, which happens each October. The course runs throughout downtown and all over the UGA campus, including through hallowed Sanford Stadium.

Of course Athens has a music festival: **AthFest** (www.athfest.com, June). Happening every June in a blocked-off portion of downtown, AthFest celebrates the local cultural scene and features plenty of free live outdoor concerts, film screenings, arts and crafts displays, and vendor product and food booths. The core experience, however, involves the ticketed bracelets ($17-20) which allow festivalgoers to club-crawl throughout various Athens music venues, enjoying a top-flight and more or less constant lineup of up-and-coming acts, most with a distinctive local or regional presence. All venues are of course

PARTY OUT OF BOUNDS

Athens is renowned for its contributions to rock 'n' roll, spawning names such as R.E.M., the B-52s, Widespread Panic, and Pylon, among many others. An entertaining 1987 documentary chronicling the scene, *Athens, GA: Inside/ Out,* is now available on DVD. Here's a brief tour of venues that played a role in forming Athens's rock 'n' roll legacy. Go to www.visitathensga. com for a full version courtesy of alt-weekly *The Flagpole*.

- **Automatic for the People:** The sign was stolen years ago, but Weaver D's Delicious Fine Foods restaurant is still in east Athens across the river.

- **40 Watt Club:** Named because its first incarnation was lit by a single light bulb, Athens's most legendary club has hosted every major name in local rock history. It's had several locations, in this order: second floor of 171 College Avenue (above The Grill); second floor of 100 College Avenue (above Starbucks); 382 E. Broad Street (now university offices), and 285 W. Washington Street, where it is now.

- **Georgia Theatre:** 215 N. Lumpkin Avenue. The century-old venue reopened after a 2009 fire; The Police played here on their first U.S. tour.

- **"Murmur" Railroad Trestle:** 270 South Poplar Street. The railroad trestle

on the back cover of R.E.M.'s "Murmur" album was recently restored through a community effort. Park at the lot near Dudley Park around the corner.

- **140 E. Washington Street:** This was once the Uptown Lounge, which in the 1980s hosted The Pixies, Jane's Addiction, R.E.M., and Black Flag. Now it's home to Copper Creek Brewing Co.

- **St. Mary's Steeple:** An Episcopal church was here until it was demolished in 1990, leaving only this steeple. R.E.M. rehearsed and played their first concert here, a birthday party for a friend in April 1980. It's now surrounded by condos but easily accessible from the street.

- **312 E. Broad Street:** The "Frigidaire" building was built in the 1880s as the Athens Opera House. For 10 years beginning in 1997, Tasty World operated here and hosted acts such as The Shins and Kings of Leon.

- **260 N. Jackson Street:** Now Jackson Street Books, it was record store Wax Jr. Facts in the early 1980s, managed by Pylon bassist Michael Lachowski, who now owns a local design firm.

- **Wuxtry Records:** 197 E. Clayton Street. R.E.M.'s Peter Buck once worked here among many other local musicians. It's been in business since 1975.

subject to capacity restrictions; so to avoid getting shut out of an already packed show, check out the *Flagpole*'s coverage to get up to speed on which bands to check out, and arrive early enough to get in. For those under 21, there are all-ages shows both inside and outside; check the schedule.

For those over 21 only, in early April is the **Classic City Brew Fest** (www.classiccitybrew. com, Apr., $40), featuring over 300 regional and world craft beers, with proceeds benefiting the local Humane Society.

The progressive spirit of this college town is celebrated each May with the **Athens Human Rights Festival** (www.athenshumanrightsfest. org, May, free), which offers a sprinkling of entertainment to go along with the politics-and-seminar heavy lineup.

And of course there's **University of Georgia Homecoming** (http://homecoming.uga.edu), held over a week each autumn (with that Saturday's game generally being against one of the Bulldogs' less highly-regarded opponents). There's tailgating galore, much of it sanctioned by various university departments and organizations, and tons of events (free for students) all around campus, from film screenings to street painting to the Homecoming Parade (free and open to the public), held the Friday evening before the game. The Homecoming King and Queen are crowned at halftime.

SHOPPING

Before he became a rock star, R.E.M.'s Peter Buck once managed **Wuxtry Records** (197 E. Clayton St., 706/369-9428, www.wuxtry-re-cords.com, Mon.-Fri. 10am-7pm, Sat. 11am-7pm, Sun. noon-6pm), and it remains one of the Southeast's best (and quirkiest) sources for vintage vinyl and hard to get recordings. As you'd expect, there's a large section devoted to Athens artists, new and old. Go upstairs to their even more eccentric cousin store **Bizarro Wuxtry Comics, Toys & Records** (197 E. Clayton St., 706/353-7938, Mon.-Fri. 10am-7pm, Sat. 11am-7pm, Sun. noon-6pm), which has an extensive collection of alternative 'zines as well as shirts and offbeat items.

Some collectors and local music aficionados will tell you that **Low Yo Yo Stuff Records** (261 W. Washington St., 706/227-6199, Mon.-Sat. noon-7pm, later on many Fri.-Sat. nights), with its expertly-curated inventory of vintage recordings and tight relationships with current Athens musicians, is even more of the real thing. They stay open late when there's a show next door at the 40 Watt Club.

Of course every great rock 'n' roll town needs a great music store, and here that would be **Chick Music** (240 W. Clayton St., 706/546-8742, www.chickmusic.net, Mon.-Fri. 9am-6pm, Sat. 10am-6pm), a 70-year-old Athens institution that has sold and rented instruments, amps, strings, and every other musical accessory to local luminaries such as Widespread Panic and the B-52s (as well as plenty of bands you've never heard of).

The best bookstore in town for the past 25 years has been **Jackson Street Books** (260 N. Jackson St., 706/546-0245, Mon.-Sat. 11am-6pm, Sun. noon-4pm), which deals in plenty of good-condition used and rare volumes.

For quality vintage clothes and accessories at a very high (but affordable) taste level, head straight to **Dynamite Clothing** (143 N. Jackson St., 706/543-1243, daily 12:30pm-6pm). For a newer range of nearly as hip clothes, go to **Fab'rik** (142 E. Clayton St., 706/353-8054, Mon.-Sat. 10am-7pm, Sun. noon-5pm).

Since 1975, **Masada Leather** (238 E. Clayton St., 706/546-5014, Mon.-Sat. 10am-6pm, Sun. noon-5pm) has sold high quality handmade leather items out of this small storefront downtown, with an emphasis on sandals and boots.

"Brother" store to the more famous version in Atlanta, **Junkman's Daughter's Brother** (458 E. Clayton St., 706/543-4454, Mon.-Sat. 11am-7pm, Sun. noon-6pm) deals in the same fun and funky mix of vintage-skater-hipster clothing, costume rental, and kitsch novelties in its 15,000 square feet of space.

Athens has any number of places to get your tacky red and black Bulldogs merch for game day, but two convenient locations downtown are **The Red Zone** (155 E. Clayton St., 706/353-8500, Mon.-Sat. 10am-6pm, Sun. 1pm-5pm) and **Dawg Fanz** (378 E. Broad St., 706/548-2700, daily 10am-6:30pm).

The main area mall is **Georgia Square Mall** (3700 Atlanta Hwy., www.georgiasquaremall. com, Mon.-Sat. 10am-9pm, Sun. noon-6pm), with Belk, JCPenney, Sears, and Macy's as anchor stores.

SPORTS AND RECREATION
Hiking, Biking, and Jogging

The premier overall outdoor activity in Athens these days is the new **North Oconee River Greenway** (70 Sunset Dr., www.athensclarkecounty.com, daily dawn-dusk), a well-done project which has reclaimed much of the north bank of the Oconee, once the home of a thriving mill industry. Four miles of multi-level walk, jog, and bike trails, including one along the river, meander through the peaceful wooded bank. Interpretive signage explains the rich heritage of the river's industry.

If you're in the South Campus area, you don't have to be a student to enjoy **Oconee Forest Park** (College Station Rd., 706/542-4287, http://warnell.forestry.uga.edu, daily dawn-dusk) which features 1.5 miles of hiking trails and a 1.2-mile mountain bike trail through green space maintained by the UGA forestry school, with roots back to the CCC era of the 1930s. The trails go through extensive forest as well as along the Lake Herrick shore (if you have a UGA student sponsor and $7, you can enjoy the beachfront on the lake; no swimming though). There's a 15-acre off-leash dog park as well.

Golf

The general public is strongly invited to play the **University Golf Course** (2600 Riverbend Rd., 706/369-5739, www.golfcourse.uga.edu, green fees $44-68). Green fees for 18 holes depend on the day of the week and whether you walk or ride. There's a full-service pro shop.

Swimming

The local city and county government runs **Sandy Creek Beach** (400 Bob Holman Rd., 706/613-3631, www.athensclarkecounty.com, Tues.-Sun. 9am-6pm, $2) on Lake Chapman, with a roped-off swimming area but no lifeguard.

Spectator Sports

Needless to say, the premier spectator sport in Athens involves the **Georgia Bulldogs football team** (www.georgiadogs.com, tickets from $55). They play in enormous Sanford Stadium on UGA's South Campus. The Dawgs are a huge deal around here, and for most big games tickets are hard to come by, though there are often tickets for sale by enterprising individuals on game day. For less competitive games, check online.

The home court of the Dawgs men's and women's **basketball team** (www.georgiadogs.com) is venerable Stegeman Coliseum (100 Smith St.). The baseball-playing Diamond Dawgs (www.georgiadogs.com) play at Foley Field.

The UGA **women's soccer team** (www.georgiadogs.com) consistently plays at the highest level of NCAA competition, and you can watch their games for free at their specially built soccer stadium. Ten-time national champs, the women's gymnastic team, the

Gym Dogs (www.georgiadogs.com) compete at Stegeman Coliseum (100 Smith St.).

ACCOMMODATIONS

For years, partying students, raucous football crowds, and a shortage of rooms combined for sub-par service and poorly maintained facilities in Athens-area hotels, at often-exorbitant rates bordering on extortion. Prices still spike uncomfortably on home football weekends, but a building boomlet over the past few years has brought a noticeable improvement in both the quality and the quantity of desirable lodging.

If you're coming to Athens on a graduation weekend or on one of the autumn Saturdays the Bulldogs play here, book your room *well in advance* or you'll be out of luck. Prices here are for non-football nights; they double (or triple!) for football weekends.

The newest addition, and Athens's first entry in the boutique category, is █ **Hotel Indigo** (500 College Ave., 706/546-0430, www.hotel-lindigoathens.com, $145-235). Its swank decor, frequent generous receptions, LEED-certified green attitude, and downtown location make it a no-brainer. It's pet-friendly to boot, and on game weekends there's shuttle service.

My favorite place to stay in Athens is the █ **UGA Hotel at the Georgia Center** (1197 S. Lumpkin St., 800/884-1381, www.georgia-center.uga.edu, $90-200). While constructed to serve as a lodging center for university-based conventions and for alumni, anyone can book a room. The central location on campus is unbeatable, the 200 rooms and various public spaces are top-notch and well-cared for, and there are plenty of amenities. Forget about staying here on a football weekend unless you've booked well in advance.

Athens has one B&B of note: **The Colonels** (3890 Barnett Shoals Rd., 706/559-9595, www.thecolonels.net, $115-200), a classic renovated seven-room antebellum farmhouse on historic Angel Oak Farm run by, yes, "Colonels" Marc and Beth. The breakfasts are magnificent. The location is about a 10-minute drive from downtown, but very convenient to the State Botanical Garden.

The **Foundry Park Inn & Spa** (295 E. Dougherty St., 706/549-7020, www.foundryparkinn.com, $130), as the name indicates, has an in-house spa facility. There's also a popular nightspot and music venue, the Melting Point, attached. This is a good "getaway" stay, though still technically downtown.

It's not downtown, but the **SpringHill Suites Athens** (3500 Daniels Bridge Rd., 706/353-8484, www.springhillsuitesathens.com, $90) is a clean, well-maintained, and professionally staffed new spot with a pleasant and contemporary design feel, all at a very competitive price. Their signature full breakfast is a value-added plus.

If you're looking for a total downtown base camp, the choice is **Hilton Garden Inn** (390 E. Washington St., 706/353-6800, www.hiltongardeninn3.hilton.com, $120), which couldn't be more centrally located. It's not the best hotel in town but it passes most standards. The only catch is a $10 parking fee for the separate deck, but that beats trying the impossible task of finding convenient on-street parking downtown.

FOOD
Burgers, Barbecue, and Steak
One of Athens's great food traditions, **◖ The Grill** (171 College Ave., 706/543-4770, www.thegrillathensga.com, daily 24 hours, breakfast served daily midnight-noon, $7) is open 24/7 right on the town's most traveled block, so there's no excuse not to check it out. They serve traditional diner food in a retro-tinged, 1950s decor, with a wide menu of big, juicy, perfectly cooked burgers and the same signature fries they've cooked for decades. And of course milkshakes! Upstairs is where the first incarnation of local music venue 40 Watt Club opened in the late 1970s.

Generally considered the best barbecue in town, **Harry's Pig Shop** (2425 Jefferson Rd., 706/612-9219, www.harryspigshop.com, daily 11am-9pm, $8) outside of downtown, just across "the Loop," offers a few creative menu items in addition to their regular succulent pulled pork, such as a barbecue quesadilla and

tenderloin or tofu sliders. Don't miss the sweet potato fries.

If you've just got to have a steak while you're in town, hit **Porterhouse Grill** (459 E. Broad St., 706/369-0990, www.porterhouseathens.com, Mon.-Fri. 11am-3pm and 5pm-10pm, Sat. 5pm-10pm, Sun. 11:30am-2pm, $25-35), generally considered Athens's best old-school fine dining spot. Since they can't really afford the prices themselves, students often go here with their parents when they're in town. Be prepared to wait, especially on a game day and at Sunday brunch.

Coffeehouses
An expanding local chain, **◖ Jittery Joe's** (www.jitteryjoes.com) has several locations around town and all of them offer a delicious variety of expertly roasted beans, prepared by extraordinarily well-trained baristas in the big-city tradition. The main "tasting room" location (780 E. Broad St., 706/227-2161, Mon.-Fri. 7am-6pm, Sat.-Sun. 8am-6pm), just east of the main downtown area, is a nice getaway inside a rustic former warehouse. There's a smaller location further into downtown (297 E. Broad St., 706/613-7449, Mon.-Fri. 6:30am-midnight, Sat.-Sun. 7:30am-midnight) and one south of downtown in the Five Points neighborhood (1230 S. Milledge Ave., 706/208-1979, Mon.-Fri. 6:30am-midnight, Sat.-Sun. 7:30am-midnight), along with several others around town.

Walker's Pub & Coffee (128 College Ave., 706/543-1433, www.walkerscoffee.com, Mon.-Sat. 7am-2am, Sun. 7am-9pm), ironically a couple of doors down from a Starbucks, is, as the name indicates, a hybrid spot. During the day it's a lounge-worthy coffeehouse, with big roomy wooden booths. After about 10pm, it turns into a full-service bar.

Indian
A convenient and tasty option in the heart of downtown, **Taste of India** (131 E. Broad St., 706/559-0000, www.indiaathens.com, Mon.-Fri. 11:30am-2:30pm and 5pm-10pm, Sat.-Sun. noon-3pm and 5pm-10pm, $12-18)

features a perhaps-surprising range of authentic menu options considering its smallish size. Lunch buffets, cheap and delicious, are especially popular.

Mexican and Southwestern

Unassuming (it's attached to a gas station) **Sr. Sol** (2455 W. Broad St., 706/850-7112, Mon.-Thu. 11am-10pm, Fri.-Sat. 11am-11pm, Sun. 11am-10pm, $8) is a fun place to get authentically Mexican food that's a cut above the usual hyper-Americanized fare, including hard-to-find south of the border delicacies like tongue, tripe, and menudo.

A strong Southwestern flavor dominates the menu at **Last Resort Grill** (174-184 W. Clayton St., 706/549-0810, www.lastresort-grill.com, lunch Mon.-Sat. 11am-3pm, dinner Sun.-Thu. 5-10pm, Fri.-Sat. 5-11pm, $15), including a good hanger steak and shrimp quesadilla. A great veggie option is the Southwestern roll. They have some good seafood dishes as well, such as pecan trout and crab cakes.

Organic and Vegetarian

The kind of vegetarian and vegan place that even a carnivore could love, **◖ The Grit** (199 Prince Ave., 706/543-6592, www.thegrit.com, Mon.-Fri. 11am-10pm, Sat.-Sun. 10am-3pm and 5pm-10pm, $10) offers fresh, lovingly prepared, and *extremely affordable* meatless delicacies. Most are locally sourced, such as the grilled seitan steak, scintillating noodle bowls, and their signature must-try black bean chili. Be sure to check the chalkboard for their always-changing menu of specials and daily veggie offerings. Truthfully, you could just order a bunch of vegetable side dishes à la carte and it will be a better meal than you'll find in most other restaurants.

A main local exponent of farm-to-table cuisine **Farm 255** (255 W. Washington St., 706/549-4660, www.farm255.com, Tues.-Thurs. 5:30pm-10pm, Fri.-Sat. 5:30pm-10:30pm, Sun. 10:30am-2pm and 5:30pm-9:30pm, Tues.-Sun. bar stays open later, $20-30) prides itself on using produce and meat from within a small radius in the

© JIM MOREKIS

The Grit, a vegetarian foodie's paradise

surrounding area (though a recent visit did feature Alaskan salmon). The focus is on the central dish of an entrée, rather than weighing it down with too many extraneous flavors. Two starter dishes, the butcher board and the cheese board, are popular alternatives to the pricey main dishes.

A combination of natural food mecca and fine dining date spot, **(The National** (232 W. Hancock St., 706/549-3450, www.thenationalrestaurant.com, Mon.-Thurs. 11am-3pm and 5pm-10pm, Fri.-Sat. 11am-3pm and 5pm-11pm, Sun. 5pm-10pm, $15-25) has perhaps the most tightly focused rotating menu in the city, all changing with the seasons. A recent visit featured pan-roasted North Carolina trout and a grilled hanger steak with marinated roasted peppers. There are always great veggie and vegan options. Or you could just content yourself with two or three starters, the "pizzettes" being particularly good choices. On Sunday-Tuesday nights they offer a combo dinner and a movie deal with the Cine BarCafe theater right next door.

Pizza

As the often-long line at both locations indicates, the most popular pizza place in town is **(Transmetropolitan,** almost always just called "Transmet." There's a downtown location (145 E. Clayton St., 706/613-8773, daily 11am-11pm, pizza $10) and a location northwest of downtown (1550 Oglethorpe Ave., 706/549-5112, daily 11am-11pm, pizza $10). The vibe is combination college pizza joint, hipster bar, and sports bar. Any of the signature pizzas are great and affordable, with some adventurous options including, yes, the Hungry Sasquatch.

Another great pizza spot is **Ted's Most Best** (254 W. Washington St., 706/543-1523, www.tedsmostbest.com, Mon.-Wed. 11am-10pm, Thurs.-Sat. 11am-11pm, Sun. noon-10pm, $10), which serves up a tasty thin-crust style pie with fresh, artfully arranged, and satisfying toppings. Their salads are quite excellent as well. Did I mention the bocce ball court?

Seafood

Athens has very few genuine seafood restaurants, but the one to try is **Square One Fish Co.** (414 N. Thomas St., 706/353-8862, www.squareonefishco.com, Mon.-Thurs. 4pm-10pm, Fri.-Sat. 4pm-11pm, Sun. 11am-9pm, $10-20), a classic Key West-style spot with lots of aged wood, outdoor seating, umbrellas, a nice raw bar, and of course tried-and-true seafood dishes like blackened tuna and a good snapper.

Southern

There are definitely better restaurants in Athens, but none that can claim to have provided a title for an R.E.M. album. Sadly Dexter Weaver's original "Automatic for the People" sign was stolen a few years back, but **Weaver D's Delicious Fine Foods** (1016 E. Broad St., 706/353-7797, daily 9am-10pm, $15) is an important piece of local history as well as where you can find some solid soul food, including very good fried chicken.

For Southern comfort food and a wide menu available throughout most of the day, head straight to **Five Star Day Cafe** (229 E. Broad St., 706/543-8552, www.fivestardaycafe.com, Mon.-Fri. 7:30am-9:30pm, Sat.-Sun. 9am-9:30pm, $10) right in the downtown bustle. You can do a burger, barbecue, or a fried green tomato sandwich, or try their signature stuffed meatloaf. Popular local coffee roasters Jittery Joe's provides all their java.

Sushi

For your sushi fix, head to **Shokitini** (251 W. Clayton St., 706/353-7933, www.shokitini.com, Mon.-Sat. 5pm-2am, Sun. 5pm-midnight, $10-15). The rolls are imaginative and fresh, and if you sit at the sushi bar itself, definitely my recommendation, you'll get a few treats, including a fried Oreo.

INFORMATION AND SERVICES
Hospitals

The main hospital in town is **Athens Regional Medical Center** (1199 Prince Ave., 706/475-7000, www.athenshealth.org), with a Level

II emergency room. Their Regional FirstCare clinic (485 Hwy. 29 N.) offers walk-in service for non-emergencies. **St. Mary's Hospital** (1230 Baxter St., 706/389-3000, www.st-marysathens.com) is the official healthcare provider of UGA athletics and has an emergency room.

Media

The newspaper of record in Athens is the *Athens Banner-Herald* (www.onlineathens.com). However, a more popular media outlet and certainly the one to consult for music and entertainment is the *Flagpole* (www.flagpole.com), the independent alt-weekly. Now weekly, *The Red and Black* (www.redandblack.com) is run by University of Georgia students, most of them in the journalism school. However it is independent from the school administration.

The most unique radio station in town is the student-staffed and university-run **WUOG 90.5FM,** which airs the usual eclectic and quirky blend of indie college rock, Americana, blues, and jazz. The local Georgia Public Broadcasting public radio station is **WUGA 91.7/97.9FM,** and also broadcasts from campus.

Libraries

As you'd expect, the University of Georgia has a rich collection of archived material. Perhaps most unique is the **Walter J. Brown Media Archives and Peabody Awards Collection** (Waddell St., www.libs.uga.edu), the only public archive in the state devoted just to audiovisual material. The Peabody Awards, sponsored by the Henry W. Grady School of Journalism, are given for excellence in broadcasting. Also in the Russell Building is the **Hargrett Rare Book & Manuscript Library** (www.libs.uga.edu), with six million historical documents, over 100,000 rare books, and over 1,000 historical maps.

On the third floor of the Georgia Museum of Art on East Campus is the **Louis T. Griffith Library** (www.georgiamuseum.org), a smallish collection of art history and art appreciation

volumes and material. While it's open to the public, books are not allowed to be checked out.

And of course the **Main Library** at UGA (www.libs.uga.edu) offers a copious selection of liberal arts and humanities volumes, collections, and periodicals. As with most college libraries, non-students can't check out books without special permission; UGA does have an agreement with the Athens-Clarke County library system to recognize those library cards.

GETTING THERE AND AROUND
By Car

The main route to Athens from Atlanta is Highway 78, the old "Atlanta Highway." It turns into Broad Street when you reach town. The main route into Athens from the south is Highway 441, which runs into the Athens Perimeter (Hwy. 10), often called "The Loop" or the "Ten Loop," before you hit town.

By Air

Athens's airport is **Ben Epps Airport** (1010 Ben Epps Dr., www.athensclarkecounty.com, airport code AHN). As of this writing the only airline operating there is **GeorgiaSkies** (www.flygeorgiaskies.com), which runs flights to and from Atlanta's Hartsfield-Jackson International Airport.

Public Transit

The Athens city and county government runs a good bus system called simply **The Bus** (www.athenstransit.com, $1.60 per ride, free for UGA students). The Bus runs a UGA football shuttle ($5 round-trip, purchase ticket at airport) on home game Saturdays from Ben Epps Airport to the Arch on North Campus.

Also free to UGA students, the university runs a very comprehensive and active **Campus Transit System** (www.transit.uga.edu), from early morning well into the evening and technically limited to student use. Weekend service sees more limited hours, with no service at all on home football Saturdays in the fall.

PIEDMONT

OUTSIDE ATHENS
Watkinsville

A short drive south of Athens, Watkinsville is gaining a reputation as a welcoming oasis for regional art and crafts. Oconee County, of which Watkinsville is the seat, is the Georgia county with the highest per capita income, due to its large UGA faculty presence.

First stop should be the **Eagle Tavern Museum & Welcome Center** (21 N. Main St., 706/769-5197, www.visitoconee.com, Mon.-Fri. 10am-4pm, donations welcome), probably the oldest building in Oconee County. This 1801 stagecoach stop was built on the site of the frontier outpost of Fort Edward, on the dangerous border between white settlers and Creek Indian lands. Legend has it that a Confederate soldier hid in the tavern's attic after a Union victory at nearby Sunshine Creek. Eagle Tavern now hosts exhibits on local antebellum life and history as well as the county visitors center.

In addition to its variety of fun pottery, craft shops, and galleries, historic downtown Watkinsville features many buildings of note, including the 1893 ◖ **Ashford Manor** (5 Harden Hill Rd., 706/769-2633, www. ambedandbreakfast.com, $85-100), which isn't only the town's premier B&B, with six romantically appointed rooms, it's a center of local cultural life as well, hosting frequent free public concerts on its expansive lawns. The 1827 **Haygood House** (25 S. Main St., 706/769-8129, Mon.-Sat. 10am-5:30pm, free) is open for tours and was the home of Atticus Haygood, an early president of Atlanta's Emory University. The Chappelle Gallery is now located inside.

The **Georgia Nature Center** (3001 Salem Rd., 800/800-2099, www.naturecenter.com, $15 adults, $10) is a fun place for everyone not only to explore nature but also to learn about the cutting edge ways in which people interact with it. There's an organic farm, an orchid preserve hiking trail, a clean energy exhibition, and a "next generation" home. The only catch is that guided tours are available and you need to reserve in advance.

Outside Watkinsville

Fans of old-timey covered bridges will want to see the 1897 **Elder Mill Covered Bridge** over little Rose Creek, which benefited from an extensive renovation in the 1970s. Head south of town on Highway 441, take a left on State Route 15 and then a right on unpaved Elder Mill Road.

Fort Yargo State Park (210 Broad St., 770/867-3489, www.gastateparks.org, daily 7am-10pm, $5 parking fee, campsites $25-29, cottages $120, yurts $70) near little Winder between Atlanta and Athens has a wide variety of activities on its scenic grounds. Mountain bikers and hikers will enjoy the nearly 20 miles of trails. A rather large lake has a boat ramp, good fishing, and a swimming beach. The icing on the cake is a disc golf course. There are 52 tent and RV sites, three cottages, and—wait for it—six honest-to-goodness yurts. Frequent programs include reenactments at the still-standing little colonial log fort from which the park got its name, and guided kayak tours.

Madison and Vicinity

There are winners and losers in the recent economic downturn, and Madison (www.madisonga.org) is clearly one of the winners. About a half-hour south of Athens, this altogether charming and well-kept little burg named for founding father James Madison routinely tops the lists of "Best Small Town in America" in travel magazines and provides location sets for movies seeking old South authenticity. Visitor traffic is steady, driven not only by the nostalgically picturesque, safe, and friendly town itself but also by an upscale real estate boom on nearby Lake Oconee.

Madison was settled in the early 1800s, largely by Revolutionary War veterans who'd been awarded lots for their service. It was an early center of education, hosting several influential private academies; future Confederate Vice President Alexander Stephens was a notable alumnus.

Madison likes to market itself as "the town Sherman refused burn." While technically true—Madison was the home of staunchly Unionist Senator Joshua Hill, a friend of Sherman's brother—the truth is there are plenty of Georgia towns Union troops spared from the torch that boast about as much fine pre-Civil War architecture; nearby Washington and Milledgeville are good examples. In any case, Madison is well worth a visit, not only to see its eclectic historic district but to enjoy its trim, pleasant vibe, at once very Southern and very all-American. Nearby Lake Oconee, long a recreation center, is rapidly becoming an off-the-radar playground of the rich and famous, complete with a Ritz-Carlton resort on its shore.

◖ MADISON

The best way to enjoy Madison's sizeable historic district, comprising a surprisingly diverse collection of beautiful restored homes, is to pick up the official walking tour brochure at the **Madison Visitors Center** (115 E. Jefferson St., 706-342-4454, www.madisonga.org,

Mon.-Fri. 9:30am-4pm, Sat. 10am-5pm, Sun. 1pm-4pm), which is itself inside the 1887 old firehouse and original city hall. You can easily spend a solid hour or two walking the perimeter of downtown, enjoying the occasionally quirky mix of antebellum and Victorian architecture. In Southern style, these are private homes without public access, but you are free to admire and take photos from the sidewalk.

Highlights include the magnificent 1811 Greek Revival **Heritage Hall** (277 S. Main St., 706/342-9627, www.friendsofheritagehall.org, Mon.-Sat. 11am-4pm, Sun. 1:30pm-4:30pm, $7 adults, $3 children), now home of the Morgan County Historical Society and open for tours daily. Other homes of aesthetic and historical significance, now private residences, are the Queen Anne gingerbread-style **Hunter House** (580 S. Main St.); **Joshua Hill Home** (485 Old Post Rd.), home of the senator credited with saving Madison from Sherman; the 1810 **Stagecoach House** (549 Old Post Rd.), oldest surviving building in Madison; and the charming, Italianate-inspired estate of **Boxwood** (357 Academy St.).

The **Morgan County Courthouse** (149 E. Jefferson St.) is a classic and particularly well-preserved example of the grand Beaux Arts courthouse-on-the-square found throughout Georgia's older county seats.

Built as one of the South's first "graded schools," a Victorian innovation and modern alternative to the traditional rural one-room schoolhouse, the gloriously Romanesque Revival **Madison Morgan Cultural Center** (434 S. Main St., 706/342-4743, www.mmcc-arts.org, Tues.-Sat. 10am-5pm) now hosts community cultural events, classes, and performances in a friendly environment.

The **Madison Museum of Art** (300 Hancock St., 706/485-4530, mmofa.org, call ahead for hours, donations encouraged) has a small but intriguing collection of European work and regional artists. There's also outdoor sculpture in the relaxing garden. Highlights of

© JIM MOREKIS

Madison's remarkable Heritage Hall

the permanent collection include originals by Picasso, Calder, and Dalí. The best way to visit is to take one of the docent's tours, held each Saturday at 11:30am and 2pm; call ahead to reserve a space.

The vast and well-manicured **Town Park** (between W. Washington and Jefferson Sts.) is an impressively landscaped green space and where the annual **Chili Cookoff** (www.madisonga.com), Madison's main festival, happens each October.

Madison Presbyterian Church (382 S. Main St., 706/342-2813, call ahead for hours to visit the sanctuary) is where President Woodrow Wilson's first wife, Ellen Axson, attended services as daughter of the pastor. Sunday services are at 11am.

The **Rogers House and Rose Cottage** (179 E. Jefferson St., 706/343-1090, Mon.-Sat. 10am-4:30pm, Sun. 1:30-4:30pm, $5 adults, $3 children) are Madison's two house museums, side-by-side and adorably hard-to-resist from the outside. The former is a rarely seen Piedmont Plain cottage from the early 1800s,

charmingly restored, and the latter is the restored home of Adeline Rose, who built the home after being emancipated from slavery.

The **Morgan County African American Museum** (154 Academy St., 706/342-9191, www.mcaam.org, Tues.-Sat. 10am-4pm, $5) is actually more of an arts and crafts co-op focusing on African American artists and culture. It features several small but well-curated collections in an adorable 1895 cottage.

Entertainment

The newest addition to Madison's entertainment scene is the fun **Retro Cinema and Books** (139 E. Jefferson St., 772/215-2757, www.retrocinema.net, show times vary), recently relocated from Washington, Georgia. Here you can read and purchase books about movies, watch the movies, and enjoy a beer or glass of wine.

Shopping

There are several good antique stores near each other in the town center, making for a great afternoon of browsing. Some highlights are three stores owned by the same folks and within shouting distance of each other: sprawling, fascinating **J&K Fleas An'Tiques** (184 S. Main St., 706/342-3009, www.j-and-k-enterprises.com, Mon.-Fri. 10:30am-5:30pm, Sat. 10:30am-6pm, Sun. 1pm-5:30pm), **J&K Antiques Etc.** (159 S. Main St., 706/752-0009, www.j-and-k-enterprises.com, Mon.-Sat. 10:30am-5:30pm), and the consignment shop **Just Out of the Kloset** (179 S. Main St., 706/752-1960, www.j-and-k-enterprises.com, Tues.-Sat. 10:30am-5:30pm).

Accommodations

The small and plush boutique hotel **James Madison Inn** (260 W. Washington St., 706/342-7040, www.jamesmadisoninn.com, $190-220) is right off the big town park and offers full concierge service. The guest rooms are remarkably well appointed, both in terms of decor and technological compatibility. Book early: These rooms are in high demand.

There are two excellent and somewhat unique B&Bs of note: The ◖ **Farmhouse Inn** (1051 Meadow Lane, 706/342-7933, www.thefarmhouseinn.com, guestrooms $100-170, farmhouse $400-500) offers a delightful get-away-style experience in a charmingly rustic (but not *too* rustic) farm setting on 100 green and glorious acres outside of town. It has three guestrooms in the main building, two in an adjacent restored barn, and a five-bedroom separate farmhouse. The **Southern Cross Guest Ranch** (1670 Bethany Church Rd., 706/342-8027, www.southcross.com, $160-300) is a Georgia-style dude ranch focusing on equestrian pursuits on an all-inclusive basis, with over 150 horses onsite. Expect to pay roughly $1,000 per person for lodging with the full meal plan and riding privileges.

Food

Madison's fine dining spot is ◖ **Town 220** (220 W. Washington St., 706/752-1445, www.town220.com, Tues.-Thurs. 11am-2:30pm and 5pm-9pm, Fri.-Sat. 11am-2:30pm and 5pm-10pm, $15-30), just behind the James Madison Inn, featuring Chef Fransisco De La Torre's hip take on fusion-style cuisine, with creative steak and seafood entrées and hearty pasta dishes.

Your best bet for casual dining is **Madison Chop House Grille** (202 S. Main St., 706/342-9009, daily 7am-10am and 11:30am-9:30pm, $10-15), on the main drag, for killer burgers and fresh salads.

Amici Italian Cafe (113 S. Main St., 706/342-0000, www.amici-cafe.com, Mon.-Wed. 11am-9:30pm, Thurs. 11am-10pm, Fri. 11am-10:30pm, Sat. 11am-10pm, Sun. 11am-9pm, $10-15), part of a regional chain, offers solid Italian dishes and pizza in a café atmosphere.

For a spot of afternoon tea in a high Victorian atmosphere, try **Madison Tea Room** (290 Hancock St., 706/688-9832, www.madisontearoom.com, Tues.-Sat. 11am-4pm, reservations required).

Information and Services

The **Madison Visitors Center** (115 E. Jefferson St., 706-342-4454, www.madisonga.org, Mon.-Fri. 9:30am-4pm, Sat. 10am-5pm, Sun. 1-4pm) is the place to go for brochures and information. Madison is served by the small newspaper *Morgan County Citizen* (www.morgancountycitizen.com).

Getting There and Around

Madison is very conveniently located just north of I-20. However, a popular way to get into town is U.S. Highway 278, which becomes the unavoidable Main Street as it passes through town. There is no public transportation in Madison, but the town is one of the most walkable you'll find.

EAST ALONG I-20
Lake Oconee

At 19,000 acres it's the second largest body of water in Georgia. Created for hydroelectric energy by Georgia Power Co., Lake Oconee is now benefitting from a gated community boom and robust recreational tourism, including an internationally-ranked Ritz-Carlton resort, mostly along the east side of the lake. Most residents live "behind the gates," as locals refer

PIEDMONT

"I WILL MAKE GEORGIA HOWL"

Scorched-earth campaigns have been a part of war for centuries. But the first formal targeting of civilian infrastructure in modern times was **General William T. Sherman**'s infamous **"March to the Sea"** from Atlanta to Savannah during the Civil War. It only took a little more than a month, but by the time Sherman "gave" Savannah to President Abraham Lincoln as a Christmas present in December 1864, the March would enter Southern mythology as one of the war's most bitter memories, with Sherman himself regarded as Satanic.

To keep the Confederates guessing, Sherman originally split his forces, 60,000 strong, into two wings deep in enemy territory with no supply lines, a daring, some said foolhardy, move which defied conventional military theory. The right wing pointed toward Macon, while the left wing farther north pointed to Augusta. Ironically, Sherman himself rode with a bodyguard unit made up entirely of Southerners, the Unionist 1st Alabama Cavalry Regiment.

Sherman's goal wasn't to starve Georgians into submission, but to break their will to resist and destroy confidence in the Confederate Army, to "make Georgia howl," as he told his boss, General Ulysses S. Grant. Sherman wanted his soldiers to feed on the move with local supplies. Foraging Union troops were called "bummers," and their behavior ranged from professional to atrocious. The destruction Sherman intended was to anything Confederates might use for military purposes: mills, manufacturing, bridges, and especially railroads, the tracks heated intensely and twisted into "Sherman's neckties."

So how much destruction did Sherman actually cause? If you travel today in the footsteps of his army, from Madison to Milledgeville, from Forsyth to Swainsboro, you'll see plenty of antebellum structures still standing, used for anything from bed-and-breakfasts to law offices to private homes. Contrary to reputation, the March's swath of destruction was actually quite narrow. (South Carolina, however, as the cradle of secession, would feel Northern vengeance intensely.)

Also contrary to opinion, Sherman never saw emancipating slaves as a chief goal. As crowds of freed slaves began following his army, Sherman just saw more mouths to feed: In his own orders, "Negroes who are able-bodied and can be of service to the several columns may be taken along, but each army commander will bear in mind that the question of supplies is a very important one and that his first duty is to see to them who bear arms."

to the plethora of exclusive, upscale communities (many of them second or third homes). A good first stop for general tourism information is the **Lake Oconee Welcome Center** (5820 Lake Oconee Pkwy., Mon.-Fri. noon-8pm, Sat. 10am-5pm).

By far the premier property on Lake Oconee is the ◖ **Ritz-Carlton Lodge, Reynolds Plantation** (1 Lake Oconee Trail, 706/467-0600, www.ritzcarlton.com, $260-450), one of the nation's top resorts. While more casual in approach than other properties in the brand, the level of attentiveness is everything you'd expect, with a nice retro feel to the buildings themselves, somewhat akin to the much older but similarly-styled Jekyll Island Club. Most guests rave about the immaculate and vast grounds, which include full lakeside access complete with a sandy beach. While technically closed to everyone but guests, you can generally get on the grounds if you are dining at one of the facilities. You can book an upscale, inclusive golf vacation package (starting around $300 per night) at **Reynolds Plantation** (800/800-5250, www.reynoldsplantation.com), which offers 99 holes of golf on five world-class courses (there's a sixth, private course as well), including the legendary Plantation Course and the Jack Nicklaus-designed Great Waters.

There are fishing and hunting opportunities

© JIM MOREKIS

Greensboro's Old Gaol

galore in the well-stocked lake and in the portions of **Oconee National Forest** (www.fs.usda.gov) that border it. Chief draws include Georgia Power-run recreational areas (www.georgiapower.com/lakes, modest fees) for hiking, camping, bird-watching, boat ramp access, and various outdoor pursuits, including **Parks Ferry Recreational Area, Old Salem Park Recreational Area,** and **Lawrence Shoals Recreational Area.** There are three other public access boat ramps, one on the west side of the lake closer to Eatonton, one near the Ritz-Carlton, and the other at the extreme southern tip. Marinas include **Blue Springs Marina** (1271 Blue Springs Dr., 706/342-9442) and **Sugar Creek Marina** (353 Parks Mill Rd., 706/342-2231).

Greensboro

Named for Revolutionary War hero Nathanael Greene, little Greensboro (www.visitlakeoconee.com), closest municipality to Lake Oconee, isn't as energetically marketed as Madison but offers much of the same friendly confidence. It occupies a unique niche in state history in that the University of Georgia was originally intended to go here, a plan canceled when the powers-that-be discovered Greensboro had a boisterous tavern (ironic considering the volume of bars at the University of Georgia in Athens today). This area was also the original location of Mercer University, which has since moved to Macon.

The highlight at Greensboro as far as I'm concerned is the historic 1807 **Old Gaol** (E. Greene St., 706/453-7592), the oldest jail still standing in Georgia. This sturdy, two-story little fortress with granite walls two feet thick has actual dungeons inside and includes an ominous hanging area with a trapdoor where convicts were executed, complete with hangman's noose. The tour is self-guided, so be careful on the stairs. You have to get the key from the nice folks around the corner at the **Greensboro Chamber of Commerce** (111 N. Main St., 706/453-7592, www.greenec-coc.org, Mon.-Sat. 10am-5pm) on the main drag.

For a closer look at local history, a stone's throw from the Old Gaol you'll find the **Greene County Historical Society Museum** (201 E. Greene St., 706/453-7592, Sat. 11am-2pm), a small collection of exhibits on local history.

Greensboro was a center of black political power for a brief period during Reconstruction, and a legacy of that is recounted at the **Calvin Baber Museum and African-American Resource Center** (1415 N. East St., 706/342-4412, Tues.-Fri. 9am-4pm, Sat. by appointment), within the 1920's Craftsman bungalow owned by that pioneering local African American physician.

Across the street from the Chamber office is the **Greensboro Florist and Gift Shop** (120 N. Main St., 706/453-7534, Mon.-Sat. 10am-5pm), where the owner can regale you with tales of local lore.

Nearby is the **Genuine Georgia Artisan Marketplace** (101 N. Main St., 706/453-1440, www.genuinegeorgia.com, Mon.-Sat. 10am-5pm), where you can browse regional arts and crafts, including artisan pottery.

You can have a delightful B&B experience two short blocks from downtown at **Goodwin Manor** (306 S. Main St., 706/453-6218, www.goodwinmanor.com, $150), a five-guestroom, two-story restored Greek Revival mansion still in Goodwin family hands, surrounded by a pecan orchard.

Get a bite to eat a few doors down at **Yesterday Cafe** (114 N. Main St., 706/453-0800, Mon.-Tues. 11am-3pm, Wed.-Sat. 11am-9pm, $10), where the house specialty is an Angus rib eye.

Penfield Historic District

North of Greensboro on Highway 15 is the Penfield Historic District, a small collection of buildings comprising the original campus of Mercer University. Chief among them is the huge 1846 **Penfield Chapel** (1051 Mercer Circle), an excellent masonry Classical Revival building. It's not generally open to the public but it's worth a visit to take a look at the grand construction. This original campus was made possible in 1833 by a grant from Savannah jeweler Josiah Penfield. The school moved to Macon in 1871.

The Iron Horse

Up Highway 15 in a cornfield about 11 miles north of Greensboro is the Iron Horse, a one-ton modernist equine metal sculpture made in 1954 by Abbott Pattison. Originally placed on the UGA campus in Athens, it was stolen only a few days later and eventually loaned to an agriculture professor, who now has it on his private property. When the corn is high you can't see it from the road.

Scull Shoals Mill Village

For a rare glimpse at what little is left of an extinct mill village, head farther north of Greensboro to Scull Shoals Mill Village (www.scullshoals.org, daily dawn-dusk, free) within the Oconee National Forest. This circa-1810 company town thrived through the 1840s, when a major fire, the Civil War, and a huge flood all conspired to cease operations. Only a few traces remain, but archaeology is ongoing. Get here from Greensboro by heading 12 miles north on Highway 15, then make a right on Macedonia Road. Take a left onto gravel Forest Service Road 1234 for three miles.

Buckhead

Not to be confused with the neighborhood in Atlanta of the same name, little Buckhead's chief claim to fame is the **Steffen Thomas Museum of Art** (4200 Bethany Rd., 706/342-7557, www.steffenthomas.org, Tues.-Sat. 11am-4pm, $5), dedicated entirely to the life's work of Georgia artist Steffen Thomas, an Expressionist painter, sculptor, and printmaker who emigrated from Germany in the 1930s.

WEST ALONG I-20

For a quick jaunt, you can head west of Madison and Lake Oconee along I-20 and make stops in the following modest but interesting locales, each of them either directly off the interstate or a very short drive from it.

Hard Labor Creek State Park

Between Madison and Social Circle is Hard Labor Creek State Park (5 Hard Labor Creek Rd., 706/557-3001, www.gastateparks.org, $5 parking, equestrian campsites $18, tent and RV sites $25-28, cottages $95-120), known for its challenging and well-maintained 18-hole golf course, The Creek, and its focus on equestrian activities. There are more than 20 miles of horse and hiking trails, and horse owners can camp near the stalls in 11 equestrian campsites. For lodging, there are 46 tent and RV sites and 19 cottages. There's also a seasonal swimming beach.

Social Circle

There's not much to see in tiny Social Circle, but folks come from miles around to enjoy fried chicken, fried green tomatoes, fried catfish, peanut butter pie, lemon pie, and many more hearty Southern delicacies at the sumptuous all-you-can-eat buffet in the friendly, Greek Revival confines of the **C Blue Willow Inn** (294 N. Cherokee Rd., 770/464-2131, www.bluewillowinn.com, lunch Mon.-Sat. 11:30am-2:30pm, $15, $19 on Sat.; dinner Tues.-Thurs. 5pm-8pm, $17, Fri. 5pm-9pm, $24, Sat. 4:30pm-9pm, $24, Sun. 11am-7pm, $20). You eat this rich comfort food off classic China in the "Blue Willow" pattern, hence the inn's name. The nationally renowned restaurant first came to modern fame in the 1990s, when the *Atlanta Journal-Constitution* columnist Lewis Grizzard penned an ode to their fried green tomatoes. Margaret Mitchell was a visitor here when it was the residence of Berrien Upshaw, who partially inspired her creation of Rhett Butler.

Fans of vintage Americana will want to know that just a few blocks out of town is a series of old "Burma Shave" signs. But while you're driving around, rigidly keep to the posted speed limit: The police in Social Circle are especially social about handing out speeding tickets!

A restored wishing well along its main drag explains the entertaining and possibly apocryphal story about how the town got its name.

Covington

If you ever watched Reese Witherspoon's film *Sweet Home Alabama, The Dukes of Hazzard, In the Heat of the Night* with Carroll O'Connor, or *The Vampire Diaries,* you've probably seen Covington. The cute little town has made quite a name for itself standing in as other cute little towns in dozens of movies and TV shows. A combination of aggressive marketing to film companies and its proximity to Atlanta has made it and Newton County a regular stop for film and TV crews, from Tyler Perry to *The Walking Dead.*

Stop by the **Visitors Center** (2101 Clark St., 770/787-3868, www.gocovington.com, Mon.-Fri. 10am-5pm, Sat. 10am-4pm) and they can hook you up with some good self-guided walking tour information of the various film and TV locations downtown, set in a number of quaint historic districts. *Vampire Diaries,* for example, spent a lot of time filming in the Worthington Manor on East Street off the main square.

Conyers

Though most of Conyers is sprawl on either side of I-20, they do promote their **Olde Town** (visit.conyersga.com), which centers on a single smallish but attractively restored alleyway near the old train depot, now populated with shops and cafés. Train buffs will enjoy the 1905 "Dinky" locomotive at the depot. A highlight of the local calendar is the Olde Town Fall Festival each October, with food and live music.

The **Old Jail Museum** (967 Milstead Ave., 770/922-3740, http://rockdalehistory.org, tours second Sat. of month 10am-2pm, free) in the Olde Town features an old-timey "hanging room"; the Rockdale County Historical Society leads free tours. **The Lewis Vaughn Botanical Garden** (daily 8am-dusk, free), also right downtown, is a nice little urban acre of green, with a pond fed by the town's historic water tower.

All the equestrian activities at the 1996 Summer Olympics were held at the **Georgia International Horse Park** (1996 Centennial Olympic Pkwy., 770/860-4190, www.georgia-horsepark.com, Mon.-Fri. 8am-5pm, fees vary), or just "the Horse Park," which now offers a range of mountain biking trails—first ever in the Olympics—in addition to its miles of horse trails. On its grounds is the Big Haynes Creek Nature Center, which features five miles of trails and a wetlands canoe launch.

While Conyers does promote the **Rockdale County Covered Bridge** (Haralson Mill Rd.) as an attraction, keep in mind this wooden bridge, while attractive, isn't historic: It was built in 1997.

◄ Monastery of the Holy Spirit

Outside of town is the Monastery of the Holy Spirit (2625 Hwy. 212, www.trappist. net, daily 4am-8pm), the only monastery in Georgia. It's open to casual day visitors as well as retreat participants. The new and actually fairly plush Visitors Center has exhibits on the history of monasticism in general. In the restored Historic Barn (the first home of the monastery), there's an exhibit on the history of this particular monastery. You can watch a video explaining the rigorous daily schedule and activities of the resident monks. For many, though, the chief attraction of the monastery are the grounds: tranquil, attractively maintained, and featuring the monastery's own famous Bonsai nursery.

Augusta

Don't be fooled by Augusta's charmingly deceptive ways. Yes, this is the home of the affluently aloof Augusta National Golf Club, which has refused to admit U.S. presidents on more than one occasion. But this is also where you'll find Tobacco Road, as in the *actual* Tobacco Road of Erskine Caldwell's eponymous novel about hardscrabble life in the old South during the Great Depression. There it is, right there, on the outskirts of town when you come in on Highway 25.

Behind the dogwoods, the fox hunts, the yearly obsession with the Masters golf tournament, and the seemingly endless shrines to Augusta National founder Bobby Jones, this remains a city with a bit of the free-for-all frontier spirit of its founding—if you know where to look. For every nod to the genteel Jones is a nod to Augusta's other favorite son, the "Godfather of Soul," James Brown, who knew quite a different Augusta, one marked by segregation and often stunning levels of poverty.

Official segregation is long gone, and while pockets of poverty remain, both in the African American section of town called "the Terry" as well as in the poor white sections chronicled in *Tobacco Road,* Augusta has worked hard to make its downtown area an active and attractive showcase. (There's even a James Brown Boulevard now to go along with the Bobby Jones Expressway.) But you still won't be able to play Augusta National unless you're a member...

HISTORY

A scant two years after General James Edward Oglethorpe founded Savannah on the coast in 1733, he sent a contingent 120 miles up the Savannah River to establish an outpost on the fall line, at the farthest northward navigable point. While Savannah was a planned city intended both as social experiment and as military buffer against the Spanish, the new town of Augusta (named after the wife of Frederick, Prince of Wales) initially served a much less glamorous purpose: to be a key center of the deerskin trade, procured from the hinterland. From Augusta the deerskins were sent in barges down the river for export to Europe, where deerskin was in high demand. What this meant in practice was that Augusta's first settlers gained a reputation for frontier toughness. Augusta wasted little time in pushing its main trade rival Ft. Moore, over the river in South Carolina, out of the way.

Life in Augusta during the American Revolution was turbulent, if not particularly violent. When Savannah was captured by the British in 1778, Augusta became the state capital. In 1779 it was briefly taken by the British and then retaken by colonial forces, thus becoming state capital again, before being taken yet again by the British, who held it until 1781.

The period between the Revolution and the Civil War was a time of great enterprise in Augusta. The building of the Augusta Canal (which you can visit today) and the Georgia Railroad were huge elements of Augusta's commercial success. While Augusta was never threatened by the Union torch—a 1917 fire claimed more antebellum homes than the Yankees ever did—life here during the latter period of the Civil War was made quite difficult by the huge influx of refugees from other parts of Georgia that were not so lucky.

President Woodrow Wilson, though born in Virginia and today strongly identified with the Ivy League, actually spent most of his childhood in Augusta, during the Civil War as well its tumultuous run-up.

Once again proving the efficacy of the old adage, "Location, location, location," Augusta quickly recovered its commercial prominence during the Victorian era in the aftermath of the Civil War. As cotton production moved westward, Augusta was well positioned to become an important inland port for the cotton trade.

A sprawling nuclear weapons factory in nearby South Carolina, the Savannah River Site, became a major regional employer during the Cold War, boosting Augusta's population significantly. Today Augusta is primarily known to the world for the Masters golf tournament and its key role in golf history; indeed, the two major world manufacturers of golf carts are both headquartered in Augusta.

PIEDMONT

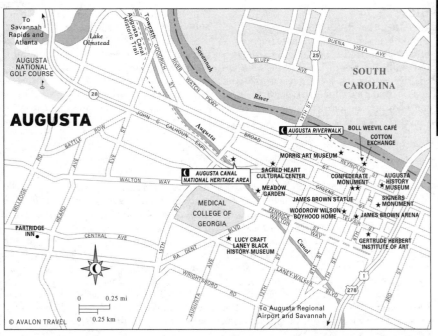

© JIM MOREKIS

old railroad bridge over the Savannah River in Augusta

SIGHTS
🄲 Augusta Riverwalk

Ironically given the extraordinary importance of the Savannah River to Augusta's commercial well-being over the decades, the stretch of the river at Augusta is quite serene, pleasant, and free of the ugly industrial sprawl typical of some downstream locations, such as Savannah itself.

There are few better places to enjoy the natural vistas of the river than the Augusta Riverwalk (daily dawn-dusk, free), which stretches for about five city blocks, from 6th to 10th Streets. Because this is the south bank of the river, it's shielded from the intensity of the afternoon sun (the South Carolina side on the north bank, however, isn't so lucky).

In order for you to better negotiate the steepness of the bluff, the Riverwalk actually comprises two bricked walkways. Access the upper level by ramps at the ends of 10th Street, 8th Street Plaza, and 6th Street; get to the lower level via RiverWalk Marina (5th Street), 8th Street Plaza, the Jessye Norman Amphitheatre,

and 10th Street Plaza (in front of the Marriott and where the Morris Museum of Art is located). You'll find many contemplative pleasures during your shaded walk, including a Japanese garden with a waterfall sunk into a shaded nook (courtesy of Augusta's sister city Takarazuka), historical markers (including one detailing the visit of naturalist and writer William Bartram), and little Oglethorpe Park with playground equipment for the kids.

Train buffs will find the **6th Street Railroad Bridge,** a historic iron rail trestle (still in use), most interesting. Before it crosses the river, the tracks run parallel to 6th Street; every few years an auto driver accidentally turns onto the train tracks and ends up stuck on the bridge.

The influence of the river also extended to the many disastrous floods that periodically inundated Augusta prior to the damming and flood control of the Savannah River. The dates and high-water marks of each historic flood are clearly marked on the "bulkheads" and walkways of the Riverwalk. It's a sobering thought exercise to examine these markings and visualize the incredible height of the flooding.

Morris Museum of Art

Considering how hard his industry was hit in the economic downturn, regional newspaper tycoon William Morris might occasionally regret putting so much of his money into the Morris Museum of Art (1 10th St., 706/724-7501, http://themorris.org, Tues.-Sat. 10am-5pm, Sun. noon-5pm, $5 adults, $3 children). But his expenditure is your gain, and since its opening in 1992 this venue has quickly become one of the most important second-tier art museums in the South. (The Morris's aesthetic commitment is strictly an interior thing; the museum itself is housed in a fairly nondescript corporate office building.)

The core of its all-Southern collections is the life's gatherings of Robert P. Coggins, whose collection was acquired by the nascent Morris board in the late 1980s. Building on Coggins's Southern-centric sensibilities, the Morris now has a full range of antebellum portraiture, outsider art, landscapes, and a small but lively contemporary collection. Recent rotating exhibits have included works by acclaimed Gullah culture chronicler Mary Whyte and photographs by author Eudora Welty.

Augusta Museum of History

Though it's one of the better small-city museums I've come across, I wouldn't call the Augusta Museum of History (560 Reynolds St., 706/722-8454, www.augustamuseum.org, Thurs.-Sat. 10am-5pm, Sun. 1pm-5pm, $4 adults, $3 children) a must-see unless you're a huge James Brown fan or a railroad buff, in which case you simply must go.

Standouts among the well-curated exhibits include the Civil War section; the exhibit of Savannah River Edgefield Pottery, including works by the renowned Dave "The Slave" Drake; an homage to Augusta's golf heritage; and a small but intriguing exhibit on Augusta native and posthumous Medal of Honor recipient Jimmie Dyess. Railroad buffs will be thrilled to know that the largest room of this restored mill warehouse contains basically an *entire train* on its own track, including a 1914 locomotive, a coal tender, and a fully restored 1927 passenger car.

As for the extensive James Brown wing, which features not only several of his famous performance costumes and listening niches to hear his music, it delves into aspects of local life that Brown would have been familiar with.

Just across the atrium from the museum entrance is the official **Augusta Visitor Center** (560 Reynolds St., 706/724-4067, Mon.-Sat. 10am-5pm, Sun. 1pm-5pm), where you can get a ton of brochures about Augusta and the rest of the state.

James Brown Statue

It took awhile, but a bronze commemoration of the Godfather of Soul in his hometown was erected in 2005 in the median of Broad Street between 8th and 9th Streets, within sight of the Imperial Theatre where Brown rehearsed and performed and a block from the portion of 9th Street renamed James Brown Boulevard, where he shined shoes as a child.

The life-size statue (on the smallish side, since Brown was small of stature himself) depicts the singer grinning and holding an old-fashioned microphone. It's at ground level to make it easier for fans to pose for photos. In fact, the **James Brown Cam,** installed by the Augusta Arts Council, enables you to dial a number on your cell phone and have a picture taken for download later! Interestingly, Brown's likeness, sculpted by John Savage, directly faces the statue of Augusta founder James Oglethorpe across the way in the Augusta Common green space, which hosts many community events.

Broad Street Historic District

It's seen better days in some parts, but Broad Street is reckoned to be the second-widest downtown boulevard in the entire nation and is still the heart and soul of Augusta. The Historic District runs from 5th to 13th Streets, and the 1000-1100 blocks are the core of the local cuisine and nightlife scene. The

© JIM MOREKIS

the Imperial Theatre, where James Brown often rehearsed

less-thriving sections are an intriguing mix of imposing Victorian architecture and nostalgic kitschy Americana.

For most visitors, the most important single structure on Broad (other than James Brown's statue of course) is the circa-1918 **Imperial Theatre** (749 Broad St., 706/722-8341, www. imperialtheatre.com), where Brown himself often rehearsed with his notoriously micro-managed bands prior to going on tour. These days it hosts a full calendar of various musicals and film screenings. Across the street is the 1940 *Art Moderne* **Miller Theater,** currently under renovation.

No longer the tallest building in Augusta, the 17-story, circa-1918 **Lamar Building** (753 Broad St.) is still pretty impressive. Famed architect I.M. Pei designed the penthouse level, added in 1976 as his firm was working on other revitalization projects on Broad Street. Perhaps the most poignant sight on Broad is the 76-foot-tall **Confederate Monument.** The 1878 obelisk at 7th Street features the requisite

"Our Confederate Dead" on one side, and this mind-blowing inscription on the other: "No Nation Rose So White and Fair, None Fell So Pure of Crime."

At 5th Street you'll see the **Haunted Pillar,** all that remains of a former farmer's market. Local lore has it that the pillar was cursed by a preacher who wasn't allowed to preach here, and that any effort to move it would result in death. The ghost story has actually prevented city leaders from moving the pillar on at least one occasion, so here it stands. By the way, the somewhat garish and sprawling modern architecture occupying a large portion of the median at 6th Street is the Chamber of Commerce building.

Laney-Walker Historic District

In the days of segregation, many Southern cities featured separate white and black business districts, and Augusta was no exception. The old African American business district is commemorated today in the

Laney-Walker Historic District north of Laney-Walker Boulevard (formerly Gwinnett Street), bounded on the west by Phillips and Harrison Streets and on the east by 7th and Twiggs Streets (Twiggs Street was the boyhood neighborhood of James Brown).

The most notable renovation is the formerly black-owned **Penny Savings Bank** (1114 James Brown Blvd.). The key community site is the **Tabernacle Baptist Church** (1223 Laney-Walker Blvd., 706/724-1230, www.tb-caugusta.org). The largest African American church in Augusta and one of the nation's oldest black congregations, Tabernacle's first pastor was Charles T. Walker, the other part of the historic district's hyphenated name.

The key attraction in Laney-Walker is the **Lucy Craft Laney Museum of Black History** (1116 Phillips St., 706/724-3546, www.lucy-craftlaneymuseum.com, Tues.-Fri. 9am-5pm, Sat. 10am-4pm, $5 adults, $2 children). Ms. Laney herself, whose former home hosts the museum named for her, was one of the first black educators in the South. Born into slavery, she could read by the time she was four and attended the first class of Atlanta University right after the Civil War. In 1883 she opened Augusta's first dedicated school for black children.

St. Paul's Episcopal Church

Most older Southern cities have an original Anglican-Episcopal congregation that traces its roots back to the city's founding, and Augusta's "mother church" is St. Paul's Episcopal Church (605 Reynolds St., 706/724-2485, www.stpauls.org). The congregation began with a church built in 1750. As is often the case with older churches, a succession of churches burned to the ground in wars and conflagrations before this one, the fifth on the site, was completed in 1919. The red brick church is complimented by the expansive grounds and attached cemetery, all within historic walls. A pamphlet with a walking tour is available at the church or at the Visitors Center on the ground floor of the Augusta Museum of History.

Sacred Heart Cultural Center

One of the best examples of a respectfully re-purposed church you're likely to see, Sacred Heart Cultural Center (1301 Greene St., 706/826-4700, www.sacredheartaugusta.org, Mon.-Fri. 9am-5pm, show times vary) is an 1897 Roman Catholic sanctuary which now hosts the activity, both performance and administrative, of various local nonprofits, such as the Augusta Ballet, Augusta Players, and the annual Garden Festival. Sacred Heart's last mass was held in 1971. After decades of neglect, Sacred Heart was fully restored and reopened in the late 1980s. A gorgeous example of Victorian church architecture influenced by classic Gothic tastes, the church features twin spires, 94 stained glass windows, and Italian marble altars. Not only is the beautiful sanctuary preserved, but you can also see the rectory, the convent, and the school, most of which now comprise nonprofit office space for organizations from the Girl Scouts to the Red Cross.

Meadow Garden

Smack-dab in a somewhat incongruous location (a rehabilitative hospital campus), Meadow Garden (1320 Independence Dr., 706/724-4174, www.historicmeadowgarden.org, Mon.-Fri. 9am-4pm, last tour at 3:30pm, Sat. by appointment, $4 adults, $1 children) is the preserved homesite of George Walton, one of Georgia's three signers of the Declaration of Independence and the youngest of any who signed that august document, at the ripe old age of 26. After the Revolution, this Savannah lawyer settled down at this circa-1790 estate then on the outskirts of Augusta. One of Georgia's oldest dwellings, this charming house is restored with 18th- and 19th-century American and English furnishings, porcelains, and paintings. The grounds, herb garden, and outbuildings are also engaging and well-kept, and between Meadow Garden and the entrance to the hospital (named after Walton) is a shaded green space with a playground. Parking for Meadow Garden on this hospital campus off 13th Street is marked and free.

© JIM MOREKIS

The Augusta Canal is lined with repurposed mills.

◖ Augusta Canal National Heritage Area

Fairly unique among American canals in that it wasn't built for commercial transport but for hydromechanical power, the Augusta Canal is the South's only industrial canal in continuous use. Built in 1845, the Canal played a major role in Augusta's prominence before, during, and after the Civil War. Enormous textile mills, many of which have been repurposed, lined its length. The South's largest gunpowder factory was on its banks. An arm of the Savannah River, the Canal provided the city's drinking water until recently. It began producing electrical power in the 1890 heyday of Augusta's Victorian-era resurgence. But the textile mills wasted away, and the "urban redevelopment" kick in the 1960s almost led to the Canal being drained and turned into a roadway. Cooler heads prevailed, and by the 1990s a special authority had been created to oversee its preservation.

It isn't the only place to see the lengthy historic waterway, Georgia's first National Heritage Area, but the **Augusta Canal Interpretive Center** (1450 Greene St., 706/823-0440, www.augustacanal.com, Apr.-Nov. Mon.-Sat., 9:30am-5:30pm, Sun. 1pm-5:30pm, Dec.-Mar. Tues.-Sat. 9am-5:30pm, $6 adults, $4 children, free admission with $12.50-25 boat tour) at the well-restored Enterprise Mill building is the only place to see related exhibits and artifacts and take boat tours on it. Most tours on the uncovered boats, very similar to ones that might have historically plied the canal, last an hour, but longer sunset and music cruises are available Friday and Saturday nights.

Technically the Canal is in three sections but only one is navigable today, the eight-mile stretch from the headgates in Columbia County to 13th Street in downtown Augusta (adjacent to Meadow Garden). The headgates area is best explored at **Savannah Rapids Park** (3300 Evans to Locks Rd., 706/868-3349, www.columbiacountyga.gov, daily dawn-dusk, free) in the next county over. Launch your own canoe or kayak from a low point along the bank at the launch dock at Petersburg Boat Dock at the headgate, or just enjoy the view from the pavilion area.

As you paddle be careful around the mill intake gates. Tour boats have the right of way and motorboats are not allowed. You can rent a canoe or kayak at **Broadway Tackle & Canoe Rentals** (1730 Broad St., 706/738-8848, www. broadwaytackle.com). The old towpath runs alongside this entire section and can be walked or biked. Get a free self-guided tour map at the Interpretive Center. Occasional "Discovery Walks" happen on weekends in the spring and fall; call the Interpretive Center for details. Rent a bike from **The Bicycle Peddler** (706/373-4519) at the headgates in Columbia County. Along the Canal's length, vehicle parking and access is at Savannah Rapids Park; Sibley Mill (site of the former Confederate Powderworks) at Eve Street; the water pump station at Eisenhower Drive; and the Lake Olmstead Pedestrian Bridge at the end of Milledge Road.

Confederate Powderworks

The South had a catastrophic disadvantage in industry and manufacturing during the Civil War, but one notable exception was in gunpowder. Confederate troops always seemed to have plenty of it, and the main reason was Augusta's Confederate Powderworks (1717 Goodrich St.), the world's second-largest such facility and by far the Confederacy's main—indeed, virtually only—supplier. Comprising over two dozen separate buildings (to lessen risk of explosion) and stretching two miles along the Augusta Canal, the Powderworks was built in 1862 and thus was technically the largest project ever purpose-built by the Confederacy.

While occasionally you'll hear a local tell a tall tale about how the old Powderworks blew up, the truth is more mundane: It was deemed obsolete after the war and demolished in the 1870s. All that remains of this impressive facility—which in a very real sense helped change the course of history—is a towering 150-foot chimney obelisk, to which was added a commemorative inscription to honor Confederate veterans. The enormous and vaguely Harry Potter-esque building all around it is actually the circa-1880 Sibley Mill, originally a cotton mill. Its turbines are still in use and produce electrical power. The Sibley Mill isn't open for tours, but you can drive right up to the old Confederate chimney. While at the chimney, look for the bright and ornate Sibley family coat-of-arms high up on the rampart of the fortress-like mill building.

Gertrude Herbert Institute of Art

A nonprofit contemporary art space within a beautifully-restored 1818 Federal-style mansion, the Gertrude Herbert Institute of Art (506 Telfair St., 706/722-5495, www.ghia.org, Tues.-Fri. 10am-5pm, free) features five galleries. The juxtaposition of the more modern pieces with the classic interior is particularly nice. And it's free!

Woodrow Wilson Boyhood Home

A native of Virginia, the future president led a peripatetic life before occupying the White House, never staying in one place for very long. Apparently the Woodrow Wilson Boyhood Home (419 Seventh St., 706/722-9828, www. wilsonboyhoodhome.org, Tues.-Sat. 10am-5pm, tours on the hour, $5 adults, $3 students) is the place where he stayed the longest, a 10-year stint from 1860 to 1870 while his father was pastor of the local First Presbyterian Church and before the family's move to Columbia, South Carolina (which boasts a Wilson home of its own). The 14 rooms are furnished with period pieces, including about a dozen originals that the Wilsons owned and used.

Signers Monument

One of Augusta's claims to fame is the fact that all three of Georgia's signers of the Declaration of Independence had ties to the city. Two of the three, Lyman Hall and George Walton, were exhumed (or what could be salvaged, anyway) from their respective tombs elsewhere and buried under the large obelisk of the Signers Monument in the median of the 500 block of

PIEDMONT

Greene Street, which was dedicated in 1848. The third signer, Button Gwinnett, is alleged to have been buried in Savannah after his death in a duel, his bones still at large.

Signal Corps Museum

Military buffs might want to visit the small but dedicated U.S. Army Signal Corps Museum (Conrad Hall Bldg. 29807, Fort Gordon, 706/791-2818, www.signal.army.mil, Tues.-Fri. 7:30am-5pm, Sat. 10am-4pm, free) on post at sprawling Fort Gordon southwest of town, where the Signal Corps is based. Artifacts display the history of the Corps going back to before the Civil War.

Tours and Information

The main city tour is the **Historic Trolley Tour** (560 Reynolds St., 706/724-4067, $12) on board the Lady Liberty trolley. You'll see the Canal, the Wilson home, several historic homes, and more. It leaves from the Augusta Museum of History each Saturday at 1:30pm, is roughly two hours, and they do ask for 24-hour advance reservations. Admission to the Museum is included with the price of the tour, which is a good deal. In the atrium of the Augusta Museum of History is the **Augusta Visitor Center** (560 Reynolds St., 706/724-4067, Mon.-Sat. 10am-5pm, Sun. 1pm-5pm) and gift shop, where you'll find a large rack of Augusta and Georgia-centric brochures and some decent swag.

ENTERTAINMENT AND EVENTS

Most large shows in Augusta happen at the **Augusta Entertainment Complex** (706/722-3521, www.augustaentertainmentcomplex.com), which comprises the larger **James Brown Arena** (601 7th St.) and the smaller **Bell Auditorium** (712 Telfair St.). The **Sacred Heart Cultural Center** (1301 Greene St., 706/826-4700, www.sacredheartaugusta.org, Mon.-Fri. 9am-5pm, show times vary) hosts a variety of performances, including shows by **Augusta Ballet** (706/261-0555, www.augustaballet.org), **Symphony Orchestra Augusta**

(706/826-4705, www.augustasymphony.org), and **Augusta Choral Society** (706/826-4713, www.augustachoralsociety.org).

Nightlife

The most hallowed nightspot in Augusta is **The Soul Bar** (984 Broad St., 706/724-8880, www.soulbar.com, Mon.-Sat. 4pm-3am), a cavernous and charming old-school rock-punk-hipster dive just down from the Imperial Theatre and well known for hosting local musicians including James Brown's band, even fairly recently before the singer's death. There's no guarantee that you'll see anyone famous, but the tunes are awesome as are the frequent live acts most evenings.

The larger **Sky City** (1157 Broad St., 706/945-1270, www.skycityaugusta.com, Mon.-Sat. 6pm-3am) down the road is where to go for bigger-name touring acts such as Drive-By Truckers and Justin Townes Earle. There's a smaller bar area in front and a larger dance floor-concert space in the back.

If only an Irish pub will do, head straight for **Tipsey McStumble's** (214 7th St., 706/955-8507, Mon.-Sat. 11:30am-3am), where the name says it all. Local legend has it that Tipsey's is on the site of Augusta's first strip club, and the current staff respects that spirit by the females wearing naughty Catholic schoolgirl outfits.

Festivals

Without question Augusta's premier event is **The Masters** golf tournament (www.themasters.com, May), which takes place each year on the first full weekend in May and fills up hotel rooms throughout northeast Georgia and into South Carolina. While tickets to the actual weekend competition are notoriously hard to come by, tickets to the qualifying rounds during the week are actually not so hard to score. Lucky members of the general public can score tickets to the Masters through a lottery system (apply at the website) nearly a full year prior.

Augusta's other event of note is the **Westobou Festival** (www.westiboufestival.

© JIM MOREKIS

The Soul Bar, Augusta's favorite watering hole

com, Oct., ticket prices vary), which takes place the first week in October at various downtown venues and features a ton of regional and national performing and artistic talent. Though named after the first Indian tribe known to have inhabited the Savannah River area, the Westobou Festival is actually more of a cultural event than a history-celebrating one. Past performers have included Roseanne Cash and Sharon Jones & The Dap-Kings, who hail from the area.

SHOPPING

Head straight to **Artists Row** (www.artistsrowaugusta.com), a delightful consortium of galleries within restored Victorian storefronts, many complete with lofts and wrought-iron balconies, clustered in and around the 1000 block of Broad Street. The roster includes **Art on Broad** (1028 Broad St., 706/722-1028, Mon. 10am-4pm, Tues.-Sat. 10am-6pm), **OddFellows Gallery** (301 8th St., 706/513-0916, Mon.-Sat 10am-5pm), **Tire City Potters** (210B 10th St., 706/828-0334, Tues. and

Fri.-Sat. 6pm-11pm), and **Schweitzer Art Glass** (980 Broad St., 706/722-8959, Tues.-Sat. 10am-5pm). Participating galleries often sponsor public art projects, and the first Friday of each month sees an evening of openings and entertainment on the Row until 11pm.

One of Broad Street's most classically Augustan establishments is the kitschy antique and bric-a-brac nostalgia market called **Merry's Trash & Treasures** (1236 Broad St., 706/722-3244, www.merrystrashandtreasures. com, Mon.-Fri. 9am-5:30pm, Sat. 9am-5pm). Forty years of history and 25,000 square feet of display space mean you can get a lot here amongst the various furniture and home goods offerings.

If only a big mall will do, that would be **Augusta Mall** (3450 Wrightsboro Rd., 706/733-1001, www.augustamall.com, Mon.-Sat. 10am-9pm, Sun. noon-6pm), west of downtown off I-520 and one of the Peach State's largest malls. Anchor stores include Dillard's, JCPenney, Sears, Macy's, and Dick's Sporting Goods.

SPORTS AND RECREATION
Spectator Sports
The minor league **Augusta GreenJackets** (www.milb.com), a single-A farm team of the San Francisco Giants, play at Lake Olmstead Stadium (78 Milledge Rd.). The great and infamous Ty Cobb, who was born near town, once played ball in Augusta.

The **Augusta RiverHawks** (www.augustariverhawks.pointstreaksites.com) minor league ice hockey team skates at James Brown Arena, as part of the Southern Professional Hockey League.

Golf
If you're a member of **Augusta National Golf Club** (www.masters.com) or an invitee of a member, and hence eligible to play here, you already know who you are. Even to members, it's open for play only a few weeks out of the year.

Area public courses include the renovated, links-style **Augusta Municipal** (2023 Highland Ave., 706/731-9344, www.thepatchaugusta.com, $20 green fees), aka "The Patch," and a very good state park course over the Savannah River in South Carolina, **Hickory Knob State Resort Park** (1591 Resort Dr., McCormick, S.C., 864/391-1764, www.hickoryknobresort.com, $30-35 green fees).

ACCOMMODATIONS
With few exceptions, the Augusta hotel scene is dominated by national chains. If that fits the bill for you, there are dozens of examples within close proximity to I-20. Keep in mind that during Masters week in early April accommodations in Augusta and the surrounding area are not only *extremely* difficult to obtain at the last minute, they are *extraordinarily* expensive, with rates often quadrupling during that week-long period.

The **Queen Anne Inn** (406 Greene St.,

THE MASTERS AND AUGUSTA

Seldom has one place been so intimately identified with such an iconic event. Indeed, to most of the rest of the world, The Masters golf tournament and Augusta, Georgia, are virtually synonymous. Interestingly, the immaculately, almost religiously tended course that hosts this king of all golf tourneys, the Augusta National Golf Club, designed by Georgia native Bobby Jones, is only open for play a few weeks out of the year.

Augusta National is one of the world's most exclusive organizations. They have refused the request of presidents to join. They told another president who was a member, Dwight Eisenhower, that they refused to remove a tree that was interfering with his shot.

The rarified exclusivity extends to those who want to watch The Masters as well. Tickets for the tournament proper, while not particularly expensive at all in dollar terms, are nearly priceless in reality. They're only sold to members already on a list that is rarely opened: Once the wait between openings was 22 years.

There has been controversy, most recently in Augusta National's refusal to admit women as members, but even that has seemed to only enhance the luster of The Masters, which began in 1934 and has changed almost not at all since then, one of the last truly authentic things left in this increasingly over-processed world. The old-school vibe goes deep, down to the pimento cheese sandwiches (still only a buck fifty!) and the grounds-keeping (the roots of the azaleas are frozen until it's time for them to bloom during the first full week of each April in time for the tournament).

The Masters' impact on Augusta is truly incalculable. During the tournament and its run-up, the entire city and its outskirts seemingly exist for that one reason. Forget getting a hotel room within a 100-mile radius unless you've booked it years in advance, and if you do manage to get a room expect to pay three or four times the rate for the rest of the year. Bed-and-breakfasts many cities away make their profit margins for the entire year based just on stays during The Masters.

706/723-0045, www.queenanneinnaugusta. com, $80-150) is a charming B&B located in, yes, a restored Queen Anne Victorian mansion. The 10 rooms are sumptuous but tasteful, and several go the Victorians one better by featuring whirlpool tubs; inquire at booking. Another interesting twist: A continental breakfast is served on-site, or you can choose a full breakfast at the nearby Whistlestop Cafe, included in the price of your stay.

Augusta's premier accommodation is the **◖Partridge Inn** (2110 Walton Way, 706/737-8888, www.partridgeinn.com, $130-150). This AAA-rated hotel and attached spa in an over-century-old building features 144 rooms, many with a nice view of downtown. Many of the rooms feature access to the hotel's distinctive, beautiful wraparound balconies; if this is important to you make a point to seek out those rooms. A recent renovation makes this an even more luxurious and user-friendly experience. While most rooms will top out at over $150 a night after taxes and fees, you can find a simple room without balcony access for under $150.

For maximum ease of access to the Riverwalk and downtown sights, go straight to the **Augusta Marriott at the Convention Center** (2 10th St., 706/722-8900, www.marriott.com, $150). This location features all the usual amenities and design sensibilities of the Marriott chain with total immediate access to downtown; the Riverwalk, for example, is mere feet away, and you can throw a baseball and hit the Morris Museum of Art. You will pay a premium for the location, however.

FOOD
Barbecue
Most Augustans will tell you the best barbecue in town is at **◖Sconyer's** (2250 Sconyers Way, 706/790-5411, www.sconyersbar-b-que. com, Thurs.-Sat. 10am-10pm, $10). It's certainly the most interesting such experience in the area, given the top-of-the-hill location of the restaurant and the memorabilia tucked into every corner of the place. The hickory-smoked 'cue itself is delicious, with a tangy sauce a cut above the usual too-sweet variety you'll find

in other parts of Georgia. The sides are noteworthy as well. Like many 'cue spots in the Savannah River valley, Sconyers deals in that variety of gravy-over-rice called "hash," which is common in South Carolina but fairly rare in the Peach State. Also, this: You can get a beer here, not a given with most authentic barbecue joints in the Bible Belt.

Classic Southern
While strolling near the Riverwalk, take a slight detour a few feet down 9th Street to find **◖Boll Weevil Cafe & Sweetery** (10 9th St., 706/722-7772, http://thebollweevil.com, daily 11am-9pm, $20), Augusta's newish nod to traditional, classic Southern cuisine. Here you'll find all the favorites, like shrimp, grits, and fried green tomatoes, in addition to some distinctly non-Augusta dishes such as jambalaya and Creole chicken. Their sumptuous desserts, a multitude of cakes, cheesecakes, and pies, are famous for miles around, so save some room.

The best hush puppies—those addictive fried cornmeal fritters renowned throughout the South—I've ever had were at **T's Restaurant** (3416 Mike Padgett Hwy., 706/798-4145, www.tsrestaurant.com, Tues.-Thurs. 11am-9pm, Fri. 11am-10pm, Sat. 4:30pm-10pm, $10). This 60-year-old family concern specializes in those incredible hush puppies as well as perfect fried catfish. Fresh seafood lovers will also find whatever is in season to crack or shell.

Mexican
For an enormous, tasty burrito washed down with a margarita in an informal, quirky atmosphere, head straight to **Nacho Mama's** (976 Broad St., 706/724-0501, Mon.-Sat. 11:30am-10pm, $8). You step up to the counter, order your burrito, quesadilla, or nachos, and they make it to order and call your name when it's ready. Margaritas, frozen or on the rocks, are available by the pitcher.

Tapas
For a more leisurely swank experience downtown, go to **Bee's Knees** (211 10th St., 706/828-3600, www.beeskneestapas.com,

Tues.-Thurs. 5pm-11pm, Fri.-Sat. 5pm-midnight, Sun. 11am-3pm and 5pm-midnight, $15), a couple of doors down from the Boll Weevil Cafe. Their tapas stretch beyond the usual Costa del Sol variety and delve into Polynesian, Thai, and Cajun flavors, among others. And they do offer "big tapas," essentially regular entrées.

INFORMATION AND SERVICES

The newspaper of record is the *Augusta Chronicle* (www.augustachronicle.com), but for a more street-level look at what's going on around town, check out the local independent weekly, *Metro Spirit* (www.metrospirit.com).

No one wants to get sick, but if you've got to get sick, Augusta is one of the best places to do it. The prestigious Medical College of Georgia and its **Georgia Health Sciences Medical Center** (1120 15th St., 706/721-2273, www.mcghealth.org) provides high quality medical expertise.

GETTING THERE AND AROUND

Augusta is very conveniently located near east-west I-20. A loop highway, I-520, circles the city. Keep in mind that just north of the Savannah River is North Augusta, South Carolina, part of the greater Augusta metro area.

The city is served by **Augusta Regional Airport** (1501 Aviation Way, 706/798-3236, www.flyags.com, airport code AGS), which hosts flights by Delta and US Airways Express.

Greyhound (1128 Greene St., 706/722-6411, www.greyhound.com) offers bus service into and out of town. As for public transit, the city runs **Augusta Public Transit** (www.augustaga.gov, $1.25 per ride), with frequent routes around town.

OUTSIDE AUGUSTA
Harlem

At first glance, little Harlem, Georgia, has little to do with the famous neighborhood of the

Harlem's Laurel & Hardy Museum

© JIM MOREKIS

PIEDMONT

same name in New York City. However, it is named after the more well-known locale, and it also has a link with the entertainment world. Harlem was the birthplace in 1892 of Oliver Hardy, member of the famed Laurel & Hardy comedy team of the 1920s and 1930s. He wasn't here long, but Harlem really plays it up.

The main stop is the **Laurel & Hardy Museum** (250 N. Louisville St., 706/556-0401, www.harlemga.org, Tues.-Sat. 10am-4pm, free) on the main road, where the man's youth and life and times are celebrated in an exhibit and video. Old-timey cars and costumes abound the first weekend of each October as the entire town celebrates their native son's legacy at the **Oliver Hardy Festival** (http://harlemga.org), which brings as many as 30,000 people to this town that normally holds less than 2,000 residents. There's a wonderful Laurel & Hardy mural on the side of the historic **Columbia Theatre** (134 N. Louisville St.), a 1940s-era movie house currently in a state of restoration.

Louisville

Not many people know that one of Georgia's capitals was little Louisville. But from 1796 to 1806, Louisville did indeed succeed Augusta's brief tenure as center of state government. Despite being named for King Louis XVI in honor of France's contributions to American independence, it's pronounced "Lewisville." Louisville entered the world stage as launching ground for the Yazoo Fraud, in which bogus land titles were sold for property in the Louisiana Purchase. The incriminating records were burned in Louisville.

These days not much goes on in its depressed downtown, but there are a few sites of note for those with a historical bent. The **Old Market** is a restored circa-1790 structure that served as the central town marketplace (recent research indicates that slaves were never auctioned here, as some old information attests). The 1904 **Jefferson County Courthouse** on Highway 1 is on the site of the original state capitol. The 1923 **Old Jefferson Hotel** across the highway has been restored, with the upstairs serving as headquarters of the regional Queensborough Bank and the downstairs serving as Louisville's premier dining spot, **Foster's** (203 E. Broad St., 478/625-3260, Mon.-Thurs. 11am-2pm, Fri. 11am-2pm and 5pm-10pm, $15).

Washington

The first city in America named after George Washington (the nation's capital didn't bear his name until nearly 20 years later), stately, sleepy Washington is in some ways the very picture of the genteel Georgia courthouse-on-the-square county seat. Its proud, history-minded residents insist there are more antebellum homes per capita here than anywhere else in Georgia. It's also possibly the resting place of the legendary missing Confederate gold!

Preceded by intrepid trappers, white settlers first came into the area in the 1770s after a treaty ceded Creek and Cherokee lands. Built on the site of Fort Heard—the Wilkes County Courthouse reputedly sits on that very spot today—the settlement, named Washington in the midst of the Revolution, played a major role in that conflict. The most important Patriot victory in Georgia happened at nearby Kettle Creek, where Elijah Clarke and South Carolina guerrilla leader Andrew Pickens defeated a Redcoat force.

With the coming of a rail line in Washington's antebellum heyday, it became a major cotton exporting center, boasting the South's first cotton mill. In addition to the mythical lost Confederate treasure, the city figures large in Southern symbolism as one-time home of Alexander Stephens, vice president of the Confederacy, and as the place where Jefferson Davis convened the last meeting of his cabinet on May 5, 1865.

© JIM MOREKIS

the Robert Toombs House in Washington

SIGHTS
Robert Toombs House

A hugely influential figure in U.S. and Georgia politics, Robert Toombs was a staunch Unionist for most of his political career (though also a slave-owning planter) who morphed into the state's most vocal advocate of secession. As a U.S. senator he made a fiery, prescient speech with the famous line "Defend yourselves; the enemy is at your door!" A year later Georgia would leave the Union. Toombs was immediately named the Confederacy's first Secretary of State, which was a problem only because he really wanted to be its first President. As a result, he feuded with Jefferson Davis for the rest of the war. He only served in Davis's cabinet for half a year before taking up arms as a general in Robert E. Lee's Army of Northern Virginia. Toombs was the major architect of the Georgia Constitution, adopted in 1877 largely through his authorship and insistence. The Robert Toombs House (216 E. Robert Toombs Ave., 706/678-2226, www.gastateparks.org,

Tues.-Sat. 9am-5pm, tours 10am-4pm, $5 adults, $3 children) brings his life, well, to life with guided tours in this antebellum Greek Revival mansion, first built in 1797 and added onto significantly through the 1830s. In addition to period furnishings there are exhibits on Toombs and a short video.

Washington Historical Museum

Run by the Washington-Wilkes Historical Foundation, the Washington Historical Museum (308 E. Robert Toombs Ave., 706/678-5001, www.historyofwilkes.org, Tues.-Sat. 10am-5pm, $3) is particularly interesting to Civil War buffs, chiefly because Wilkes County was so well connected at that time. The primary draw of this restored 1835 house is a large collection of Civil War relics gathered by the Last Cabinet chapter of the United Daughters of the Confederacy. Among other items you'll see General Robert Toomb's general's uniform, a great period firearm collection, and the chest given to Jefferson

Davis by British sympathizers, left behind in Washington during his flight to refuge.

Callaway Plantation

Run by the City of Washington, the "living history museum" of Callaway Plantation (2160 Lexington Rd., 706/678-7060, www.washingtongeorgia.net, Tues.-Sat. 10am-5pm, $4 adults, $2 children) is a collection of restored historic buildings representing a slice of antebellum life on one of the larger cotton plantations in the area, which at one time stretched 3,000 acres. Indeed, the land surrounding the city's 50 acres still belongs to the original settling family. The focal point is the 1868 great house, which you can go inside. The oldest building onsite is a hand-hewn log cabin dating from the Revolution. Most of the buildings have exhibits and period artifacts inside.

Tours

Washington has about 100 antebellum buildings, with the grandest of them displayed along Robert Toombs Avenue east of the courthouse square. They're all private residences, but the ones with the most historic pedigree have easy-to-read interpretive plaques in the front yard near the street. There are two eagerly-anticipated **Tours of Homes** (http://wwtourofhomes.com, $30), one each April and a holiday edition in December.

The delightful **"Miss Fanny,"** actually her name's Elaine, gives very entertaining and informative tours (706/318-3128, http://missfanny.com, $20), which cover dozens of key homes and usually include a few invitations to come inside. And yes, you'll no doubt hear about the lost Confederate gold.

PRACTICALITIES

The 17-room **Fitzpatrick Hotel** (16 W. Square, 706/678-5900, www.thefitzpatrickhotel.com, $120-225), now more of a B&B, was built on the courthouse square in 1898 and stayed in business until 1952. "The Fitz" wasn't reopened until 2004, and the renovation is both stunning and respectful of the building's history.

They're oriented to weekend guests, so if you'd like to stay on a weekday give them a call well ahead of time.

The premier B&B in town is the circa-1828 **Washington Plantation Bed & Breakfast** (15 Lexington Ave., 877/405-9956, www.washingtonplantation.com, $160-230), known for its gourmet breakfasts and beautiful seven-acre grounds, used as campsites for both Union and Confederate troops.

You don't have to look too hard for the best place to eat in town. The **◖ Washington Jockey Club** (5 E. Square, 706-678-1672, www.washingtonjockeyclub.com, Wed.-Thurs. 5pm-9:30pm, Fri.-Sat. 11am-2pm and 5pm-9:30pm, $10-30) is right on the courthouse square, the kind of place where everyone knows everyone else and they'll quickly make you feel right at home, yet with a professional style of service unusual in these parts. Signature entrées are the pecan chicken and the shrimp and grits. There's also a full-service bar, pretty much the only watering hole in this sleepy, conservative town.

The **Washington-Wilkes Chamber of Commerce** (22 W. Square, 706/678-5111, www.washingtonwilkes.org, Mon.-Fri. 10am-4pm) right on the main courthouse square is where to get your brochures and other information.

Most people get to Washington via U.S. 78/Hwy. 10, which for a stretch in town becomes Robert Toombs Avenue. Access via I-20 to the south is by Highways 47 and 80.

SOUTH OF WASHINGTON
Battle of Kettle Creek

War Hill (daily dawn-dusk, free), the generally accepted site of the Battle of Kettle Creek on Valentine's Day 1779, is on a 12-acre parcel a few miles outside of town. A monument, marker, and several graves are about all there is to see, though there are occasional reenactments. Take Highway 44 south out of Washington, make a right on County Road 68, another right on Court Ground Road, and a left on War Hill Road.

PIEDMONT

Crawfordville

Crawfordville was the birthplace of Alexander H. Stephens, vice president of the Confederacy. These days its handsomely restored block of downtown serves as the backdrop of frequent movies, including Reese Witherspoon's *Sweet Home Alabama,* in which you can also see the Taliaferro County Courthouse. It's pronounced "Tollifer," by the way, and incidentally the county is the least populous east of the Mississippi River, with under 2,000 residents.

Stephens's home, **Liberty Hall** (456 Alexander St., 706/456-2602, www.gastateparks.org, Fri.-Sun. 9am-5pm), is preserved as a house museum and is on the grounds of nearby **A. H. Stephens Historic Park** (456 Alexander St., 706/456-2602, www.gastateparks.org, parking $5, campsites $24, cottages $115-125), a state-run site with a campground, cottages, a couple of cute little fishing lakes, and 12 miles of equestrian trails (horse campsites are available for roughly the same price as the regular ones).

Savannah River Lakes

The mighty Savannah River forms the border of Georgia and South Carolina, and since the 1950s the U.S. Army Corps of Engineers has controlled its flow through the use of dams. Dams make lakes, and millions of Georgians and Carolinians come to frolic on three of them on the Savannah River each year, from north to south, Lake Hartwell, Lake Russell, and Clark's Hill-Lake Thurmond, putting this 120-mile chain of freshwater waterways near the top of most-visited Corps recreation sites in the country.

The main focus is boating, fishing, camping, and swimming, largely in that order. Despite the lakes' artificially constructed provenance, there are also wildlife-viewing opportunities in this otherwise semi-rural corner of the state, from waterfowl to deer to wild turkeys to the occasional black bear.

Planning Your Visit

You'll find a mix of Corps-run and state-run facilities, in addition to private efforts. For a general overview go to www.sas.usace.army.mil. Lakes Hartwell and Thurmond have campgrounds (877/444-6777, www.ReserveUSA.com) operated by the Corps. Generally speaking, public boat ramps are plentiful, even at campgrounds. The general websites for reservations and info on Georgia and South Carolina state parks are www.gastateparks.org and www.discoversouthcarolina.com.

Always keep in mind that many recreation areas and campgrounds close in the off-season after Labor Day, though most boat ramps stay open all year. Drought conditions can also affect water levels, sometimes seriously, on Lakes Hartwell and Thurmond (Lake Russell is kept near full at all times). Check the Corps websites for up-to-date info.

LAKE HARTWELL

Of the three lakes, northernmost Lake Hartwell (www.sas.usace.army.mil), named after Revolutionary war heroine Nancy Hart, has the most upscale feel and is focused more on private docks and private vacation rentals.

There are five marinas on the lake. The Corps of Engineers runs 54 recreation areas here, Georgia and South Carolina run 4 recreation areas, and local governments run 23. For full information, stop by the Hartwell Dam, Lake Office & Visitor Center (5625 Anderson Hwy., Hartwell, 706/856-0300, Mon.-Fri. 8am-4:30pm, summer weekends 9am-5:30pm, off-season weekends 8am-4:30pm).

Optimized for serious anglers, **Tugaloo State Park** (1763 Tugaloo State Park Rd., 706/356-4362, www.gastateparks.org, office hours daily 8am-5pm, RV and tent sites $23-30, primitive campsites $15, cottages $135) has one of the biggest boat ramps in the area, with six lanes. There are over 100 RV and tent sites, 5 primitive campsites, and 20 cottages, 3 of which are dog friendly ($40 per dog, max two). The primitive sites are rustically fun and spacious, but occasionally the noise from private residences directly across the lake gets loud.

Hart Outdoor Recreation Area (330 Hart Park Rd., 706/213-2045, http://gastateparks.org, campsites $19-26, walk-in campsites $19) is a good base of operations for fishing, and also offers self-registration seasonal camping with nice views of the lake (62 sites), as well as 16 walk-in campsites. The boat ramp is open year-round.

Royston

Nestled near the South Carolina line, Royston is a typical hardscrabble foothills town. Its main contribution to history is being the hometown of baseball legend Ty Cobb, the "Georgia Peach," whose impressive and often-controversial career is memorialized at the **Ty Cobb Museum** (461 Cook St., 706/245-1825, www.tycobbmuseum.org, Mon.-Fri. 9am-5pm, Sat. 10am-4pm, $5 adults, $3 children).

Don't think you took a wrong turn when you find yourself driving up to a health care clinic; the museum is actually inside the Ty Cobb Healthcare Center, a philanthropic legacy of Cobb himself, an astute investor who amassed a large personal fortune. With its entrance in the lobby, the little museum is actually quite well curated, including Cobb's 1907 American League batting champion trophy, various uniform items, and of course "Cobb-lehead" bobblehead figures. (Note: While there is a Ty Cobb Avenue nearby, the Museum is not on Ty Cobb Avenue.)

If you're in the area on a weekend, head straight to **◖ Vanna's Country Barbecue** (Hwy. 17 S., 706/246-0952, Fri.-Sat. 11am-9pm, Sun. 11am-3pm, $5) to get a bite in "beautiful downtown Vanna," a bit south of Royston. While the pulled pork is delectably soft and the Brunswick stew most excellent, I'd head straight for their legendary ribs. You can dine in the friendly, wood-paneled interior or drive-thru.

Victoria Bryant State Park

Commonly known as one of the best lesser-known state parks in Georgia, Victoria Bryant State Park (1105 Bryant Park Rd., 706/245-6270, www.gastateparks.org, $5 parking, campsites $25-28) is a small but delightful treat. A nice creek runs through the camping area of 27 tent and RV sites. But the highlight is the selection of eight raised-platform tenting sites. The adjacent **Highland Walk golf course** (706/245-6770, http://georgiagolf.com, daily from 8am) offers 18 holes in a hilly and fairly challenging environment.

LAKE RUSSELL

Named after long-serving Georgia Senator Richard B. Russell, Lake Russell (www.sas.usace.army.mil) is the youngest of the three lakes, created in the 1980s. Because it was made after the Water Projects Act of 1974, exclusive private development on its shores is prohibited, making Lake Russell great for a quiet getaway and very different from its sister lakes on either end.

The Corps runs 2 recreation areas here, and Georgia and South Carolina operate 21 recreation areas. There is a single marina, Beaverdam Marina (1155 Marina Dr., 706/213-6462). For more information, stop by the **Russell Dam & Lake Office & Visitor Center** (4144 Russell Dam Dr., 706/213-3400, Mon.-Fri. 8am-4:30pm, Sat.-Sun. 8am-4pm).

Along Lake Russell is one of the gems in the Georgia state park system, **Richard B. Russell State Park** (2650 Russell State Park Rd., 706/213-2045, www.gastateparks.org, $5 parking, tent and RV sites $25-28, cottages $130-140). It offers pretty much something for everyone, all in a scenically rustic setting. There's the 18-hole Arrowhead Pointe Golf Course ($45-50), as well as a well-regarded disc golf course. There's a swimming beach lakeside with canoe and paddleboat rental, beach volleyball, and six miles of trails. There are only 28 RV and tent sites and no primitive sites at all, but there are 20 very nice lakefront cottages, 2 of which are dog friendly ($40 per dog, max two).

CLARK'S HILL LAKE

First off, to clear up any confusion: Clark's Hill Lake is technically called Lake Strom Thurmond (www.sas.usace.army.mil); in 1988 Congress renamed it in honor of the long-serving, controversial South Carolina politician. Angry Georgia politicians refused to honor the change, and on Georgia maps it's still called Clark's Hill, which in any case is what most everyone in both states still calls it regardless. Created in the mid-1950s, it is the oldest of the three Corps lakes on the Savannah River and its 70,000 acres make it the largest such project east of the Mississippi.

Clark's Hill/Lake Thurmond has five marinas. There are 37 Corps-run recreation areas on both sides of the lake, 7 recreation areas run by Georgia and South Carolina, and 6 locally-run recreation areas. For more info go across the border into South Carolina and visit the **Thurmond Lake Office & Visitors Center** (510 Clarks Hill Hwy., Clarks Hill SC, 864/333-1147, daily 8am-4:30pm).

A great way to enjoy the lake with the family is **Elijah Clark State Park** (2959 McCormick Hwy., 706/359-3458, www.gastateparks.org, $5 parking, tent and RV sites $25, walk-in campsites $15, Pioneer campground $35, cottages $120). There are 165 RV and tent sites, 10 walk-in tent sites, Pioneer campground, and 20 lakefront cottages, 2 of which are dog friendly ($40 per dog, max two). There's also a log cabin museum, a fishing pier, and even a little swimming beach on the lake.

Bass anglers should head straight to **Mistletoe State Park** (3725 Mistletoe Rd., 706/541-0321, www.gastateparks.org, $5 parking, tent and RV sites $25, walk-in campsites $15, backcountry sites $10, cottages $140), with three boat ramps from which to launch for a usually successful fishing trip. There are 12 miles of hiking trails, nearly 100 RV and tent sites, four walk-in campsites, three backcountry tent sites, and 10 cottages, 2 of which are dog friendly ($40 per dog, max two).

For a more barebones stay, try **Bobby Brown Outdoor State Recreation Area** (2509 Bobby Brown State Park, 706/359-3458, www.gastateparks.org, $5 parking, campsites $25). It has a seasonal self-reserve campground (61

NANCY HART: WARWOMAN

The local Indians called her "Wahatchee" or "Warwoman." She was six feet tall, red-haired, hot-tempered, and an excellent shot despite her crossed eyes. Despite her simple mountain ways, Nancy Hart was one of Georgia's most effective and colorful Revolutionary War figures and a spy of great ingenuity and repute.

During the war, while her husband, Benjamin, was away fighting with Elijah Clarke's militia, she not only raised their eight children by herself, she often dressed as a man and wandered the Tory camps looking for information. Reportedly she took part in the Battle of Kettle Creek to the south.

Legend has it that one day a group of Tories from a nearby British army camp came to her cabin demanding food. When Nancy told them she only had one turkey left because the last Tories to visit had killed her other ones, a Tory shot the last turkey and demanded Nancy cook it. She did as ordered, biding her time, plying them with whiskey, and sending her daughter to warn the male neighbors.

As the Tories bragged of killing the Harts' friend Colonel Dooley, Nancy began quietly stealing their muskets. When confronted, she killed one Tory outright and held the others hostage until her husband came home. When she heard that Benjamin planned to shoot a Tory for his role in Dooley's death, his wife supposedly said, "Shootin's too good for him. Hang him!"

You can visit a 1930s replica of that log cabin today just north of Elberton. It was built using some original chimney stones from her actual home.

sites), year-round boat ramp, and two miles of trails. It's built near the dead town of circa-1790 Petersburg, and if water levels are low you can occasionally see some of the old foundations.

Elberton

The town of Elberton prides itself on being the "Granite Capital of the World" for the remarkable amount of stone quarried here, shipped to all corners of the globe. So, fittingly its chief attraction is made out of granite as well, specifically the **Georgia Guidestones** (Guidestones Rd.) off Highway 77 north of town, known as "America's Stonehenge" because of the vague resemblance of the 19-foot-tall stones to the Druid monument. The Guidestones, erected in 1980, feature an assortment of New-Agey exhortations in 12 languages, including 4 ancient tongues. The exhortations are rumored by some to be conspiratorial in nature and in any case not typical of this area's strongly conservative character.

A more classic bit of Elberton history can be found at the **Nancy Hart Cabin** (off River Rd., daily dawn-dusk), a replica of the home of the colonist woman who according to legend singlehandedly captured a war party of Tories who accosted her and her family. The cabin, a 1930s project of the Daughters of the American Revolution and the Civilian Conservation Corps, uses chimney stones from the original house.

GETTING THERE AND AROUND

The lake country is sparsely developed for the most part and access is by a few roads of mediocre quality. Bridge access to and from South Carolina is by Georgia Highways 8, 28, 72, and 150, and U.S. Highway 378, and of course I-75 and I-20.

PIEDMONT

MIDDLE GEORGIA

Middle Georgia is full of surprises. Besides being the home of the Allman Brothers and Otis Redding, Macon also has one of the most beautifully ornate cathedrals you'll see outside Europe. Columbus is where the inventor of Coca-Cola was born. President Franklin Roosevelt was inspired by the healing properties of Warm Springs to found the March of Dimes. America's first state park was at Indian Springs. And polite Milledgeville once housed the largest insane asylum on the planet.

It's the most far-ranging area of Georgia, both in subject matter as well as sheer physical size. It encompasses the lush riverine environment of Columbus on the Alabama border, the breezy heights of Pine Mountain, the old South mannerisms of Milledgeville, and the sandy stretches on the coastal plain on the way to Savannah.

You just never know what you're going to come across here in this rolling countryside. But most will tell you this is where the real soul of Georgia lives.

PLANNING YOUR TIME

Driving around Middle Georgia can be a bit time-consuming given the large east-west distances involved. Visiting the fairly nearby cities of Macon and Milledgeville can be done in a day apiece. To fully enjoy the scenic and invigorating area in the Pine Mountain-Warm Springs-Columbus area, I do suggest slowing your pace down and spending more than just a quick pass-through for the day.

HIGHLIGHTS

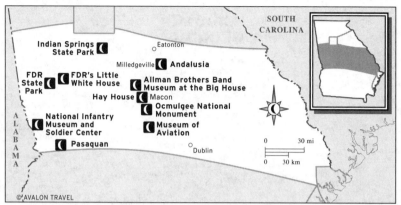

© AVALON TRAVEL

LOOK FOR ☾ TO FIND RECOMMENDED SIGHTS, ACTIVITIES, DINING, AND LODGING.

☾ **Hay House:** One of the South's grandest house museums is also fascinatingly individualistic (page 190).

☾ **Ocmulgee National Monument:** Tour the enormous mounds, which are remnants of a once-glorious Native American civilization (page 194).

☾ **Allman Brothers Band Museum at the Big House:** One of America's favorite bands has a lovingly curated collection of unique memorabilia (page 197).

☾ **Museum of Aviation:** A vast and significant collection of American military aircraft encompasses WWI to the present day (page 202).

☾ **Indian Springs State Park:** The first state park in the United States is also a charming getaway (page 203).

☾ **Andalusia:** Visit the farm where the great Flannery O'Connor authored most of her classic Southern Gothic novels and short stories (page 208).

☾ **FDR's Little White House:** A bittersweet look into the life of a pioneering figure is enriched with amazing memorabilia from his transformative presidency (page 214).

☾ **FDR State Park:** Georgia's largest state park is also among its most scenic, with great hiking and picnicking on breezy Pine Mountain (page 218).

☾ **National Infantry Museum and Soldier Center:** A stirring look at the exploits of the American fighting soldier comes with state-of-the-art technology (page 222).

☾ **Pasaquan:** Find inspiration in the eccentric and ambitious visionary folk art project of the man called "St. EOM" (page 228).

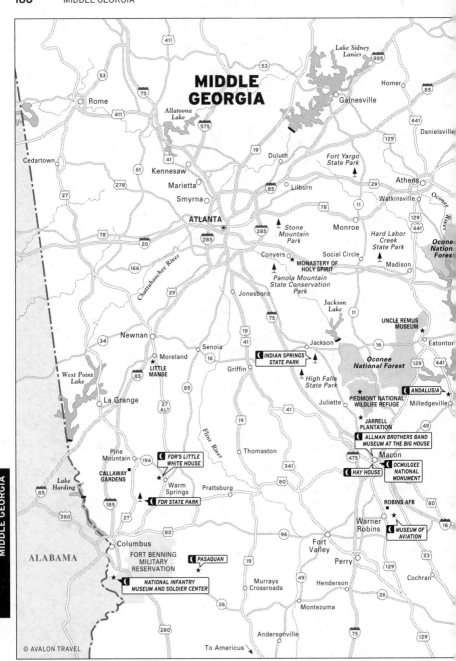

MIDDLE
GEORGIA

© AVALON TRAVEL

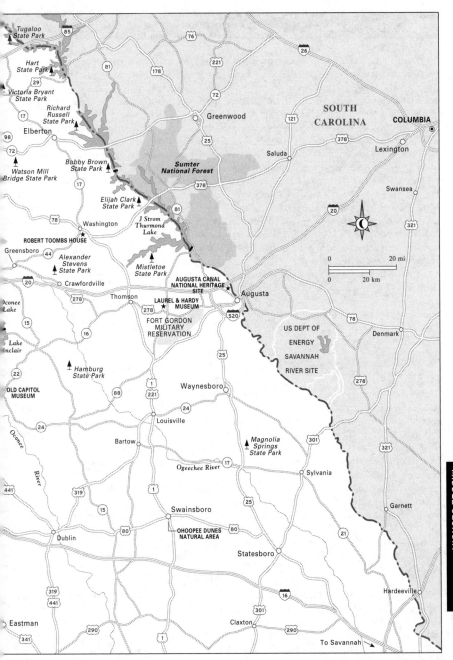

Macon

It's fitting that Macon is pretty much dead center in the middle of Georgia, since in many ways it's the archetypal Georgia town: laid-back, churchified, heavy on fried food, built by the railroad, surrounded by seemingly endless farmland, and a center of cross-pollinating musical traditions.

Much to city leaders' chagrin, Macon's proximity to metro Atlanta, within an hour's drive on fast-moving I-75, has turned out to be as much a detriment than a help. Atlanta's size, diversity, and vast range of entertainment options means that Macon is perennially in the capital's shadow. Even locals will tell you that many fewer people come *to* Macon than drive *through* it on the way to Atlanta.

That said, Macon's physical closeness to Atlanta is an advantage. Unlike some of the more out-of-the-way parts of Georgia, there's really no good excuse to skip centrally located Macon entirely and fortunately a short visit is all you'll need to soak in the often-surprising pleasures here.

HISTORY

Thousands of years before Europeans came to Middle Georgia, Native Americans had already built a prosperous society in this gently rolling landscape. The Mississippian culture flourished from about 900 AD-1100 AD and built a complex network of earthwork mounds on what would be known to early explorers and archaeologists as the "Ocmulgee Old Fields," among other places. Their immediate descendents, the Muscogee Creek tribe, were the Native Americans who inhabited the area when European settlement began in earnest.

Along with Augusta and Columbus, Macon is another Georgia city straddling the fall line and serving as farthest-inland navigable point on a key waterway. While Hernando de Soto's expedition crossed the Ocmulgee in Creek territory near Macon, the first permanent white settlement didn't come until 1806. At the behest of President Thomas Jefferson, Benjamin

Hawkins was sent to establish a fort to guard the frontier and initiate trade with the local Creeks. Unfortunately for the Creeks, they were required to cede their lands east of Fort Hawkins to the white settlers and tradesmen. The village that sprang up around Fort Hawkins took the name Macon in 1823.

Macon became one of the South's major cotton trading centers. The Central of Georgia railroad was not only a key element in this commercial success before the Civil War, it would also be the underpinning of the city's renaissance after the war and lead to its eventual, unsuccessful bid to compete with Atlanta as the state's prime transportation hub. With the Union capture and sack of Atlanta in 1864 by General William T. Sherman, Macon briefly served as capital of the state. While Sherman's troops passed close by Macon on their march to the sea, the city was spared the torch.

The World Wars of the 20th century brought major economic and social change. The Wellston Air Depot, built in 1941 south of Macon, would become Warner Robins Army Air Depot, one of the largest stateside facilities during World War II. Robins Air Force Base is still a massive economic presence in the region.

While many Macon fortunes were built on slavery, the civil rights era went fairly smoothly in the area, unlike other Georgia towns such as Albany. Perhaps one reason is because Macon hosted several very successful African American companies in the years after the Civil War and became a major center of Southern black culture. Macon was the central stop on Georgia's so-called "Chitlin Circuit" of segregated theaters, featuring such musical titans as James Brown, Little Richard, and Otis Redding.

SIGHTS

As far as most visitors are concerned, there are four basic areas of Macon: Intown, featuring the city's grandest homes and churches arrayed on the area's highest hills; downtown and its museum district; east Macon across

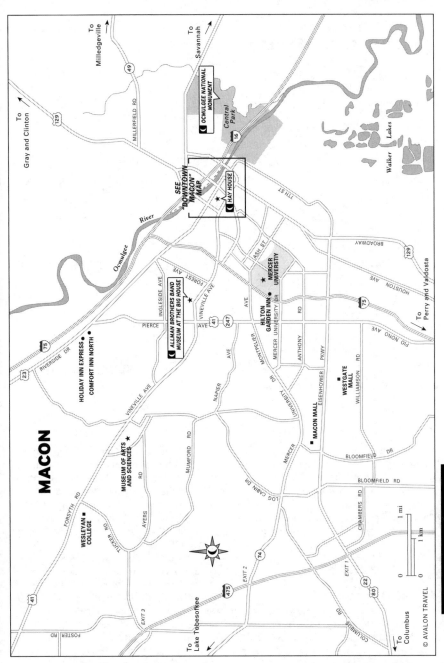

MACON

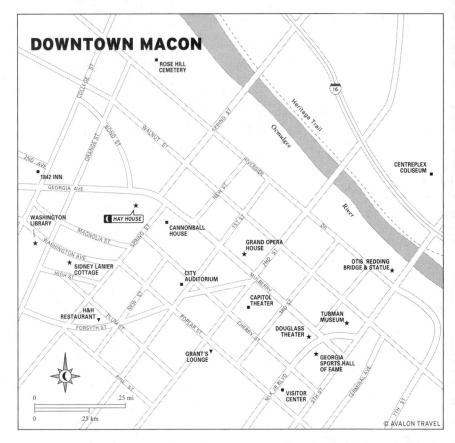

DOWNTOWN MACON

ROSE HILL CEMETERY

CENTREPLEX COLISEUM

1842 INN

WASHINGTON LIBRARY

HAY HOUSE

CANNONBALL HOUSE

GRAND OPERA HOUSE

SIDNEY LANIER COTTAGE

CITY AUDITORIUM

OTIS REDDING BRIDGE & STATUE

CAPITOL THEATER

H&H RESTAURANT

TUBMAN MUSEUM

DOUGLASS THEATER

GRANT'S LOUNGE

GEORGIA SPORTS HALL OF FAME

VISITOR CENTER

0   .25 mi

0   .25 km

© AVALON TRAVEL

the river, where you'll find Ocmulgee National Monument; and the area along and adjacent to Riverside Drive and the Ocmulgee River, where you'll find two historic cemeteries, a waterfront trail, and, a bit farther away from the city center, the Allman Brothers Museum at the Big House. Cherry Street is the main drag of downtown, famous for its central role in Macon's biggest annual event, the Cherry Blossom Festival each March.

Hay House

Easily one of the most splendid and splendidly restored antebellum mansions in the South, the Hay House (934 Georgia Ave., 478/742-8155, www.georgiatrust.org, Tues.-Sat. 10am-4pm,

Sun. 1pm-4pm, closed Sun. Jan.- Feb. and July-Aug., last tour 3pm, $9 adults, $5 students) in the stately Intown neighborhood is worthy of a tour. Built in the Italian Renaissance Revival style and completed a scant five years before the outbreak of the Civil War, the Hay House was built by William Butler Johnston. It passed into the hands of insurance magnate Parks Lee Hay during the 1920s. The magnificent abode stayed in Hay hands until 1977, when it was given to the Georgia Trust for Historic Preservation, which not only still administers and restores the property, it makes its head-quarters here, too.

Touring the multiple, often overlapping levels of the 18,000-plus-square-foot Hay

© JIM MOREKIS

the magnificent Hay House

House today brings to mind less a classic Southern mansion than a film set, perhaps even Shangri-La from *Citizen Kane*. However, the taste level is still remarkably high and consistent throughout, from the incredible plasterwork to the extensive faux finishes, which actually cost more in their day than the real materials they imitated.

Not only an aesthetic and decorative wonder, the Hay House is an amazing technological specimen as well. It had an early intercom system to communicate with servants, and a form of central heat and air was employed: Heat from a fire pit dispersed heat through ductwork throughout the house, and cooling ran through a sophisticated ventilation system keyed on the cool wine cellar beneath the front porch. For purposes of authenticity, the Hay House to this day lacks modern air-conditioning. It does get warm in the summertime, but tour patrons are given a fan to wave in front of their faces while inside.

The docent-led tours are not only informative, keeping you up-to-date on which sections are undergoing restoration and what era of the house's history the renovations reflect, their stories are engaging as well. Unlike many house museum tours, children will enjoy the Hay House both for its eccentric opulence and its secrets, including the alleged hiding place for Confederate gold behind a false wall.

In addition to the standard guided tour, the Hay House offers numerous specialty tours, for example a trip to the tippy-top of the cupola if it's not too hot. Christmas time and the annual Cherry Blossom Festival also see expanded hours and frequent special tours. Inquire by phone, website, or at the check-in desk at the visitor entrance, which is actually in the rear of the home.

St. Joseph Catholic Church

Oddly for this rigidly Baptist area of the country, one of the most beautiful and ornate Roman Catholic churches pretty much anywhere is right in Macon's Historic Intown neighborhood. That said, St. Joseph Catholic Church (830 Poplar St., 478/745-1631, www.

MIDDLE GEORGIA

© JIM MOREKIS

St. Joseph Catholic Church

stjosephmacon.com, office hours Mon.-Fri. 9:30am-4:30pm) views itself as the direct heir of a remarkably old and vital tradition: Lore has it that Spanish explorer Hernando de Soto baptized two Indian boys on the banks of the Ocmulgee River near present-day Macon, the first Christian baptisms east of the Mississippi River.

This incredible Gothic Romanesque edifice was completed at the turn of the 20th century, though it hearkens back to a much older tradition of grand European cathedrals. Its physical location makes it even more spectacular: On the top of a hill, its 200-foot spires seem to touch the heavens and they can be seen for miles around; in the old days they could be seen from the countryside as travelers approached the remote outskirts of town.

Inside you'll find over 60 stained glass windows, most crafted in Bavaria. While most decorative marble is Italian in origin, the columns are made of Georgia marble. The Schlicker organ, though technically dating from 1985,

incorporates portions of the original 1903 Pilchers & Sons instrument.

At the top of the church's left tower, as you face the sanctuary from Poplar Street, you'll see three huge bronze bells, named Jesus, Mary, and Joseph. You can hear them at 6am, noon, and 6pm every day.

Sidney Lanier Cottage

Just around the corner from St. Joseph, the Sidney Lanier Cottage (935 High St., 478/743-3851, Mon.-Sat. 10am-4pm, last tour 3:30pm, $5 adults, $3 children) is where that great American man of letters was born in 1842; this was actually his grandparents' home at the time. While he didn't live in this house most of his life, he did spend much of his time in the Macon area. He volunteered for the Confederate Army at the outbreak of the Civil War, eventually catching consumption as a prisoner of war at a Maryland camp. While Lanier is best known as a poet and influential literature professor, he was actually quite an accomplished flutist as well. You can see one of his flutes at this charming and charmingly-appointed little cottage in a very attractive neighborhood of Historic Intown Macon.

Cannonball House

While General Sherman and his troops pretty much left Macon alone, an exchange of artillery fire led to some random shells hitting and embedding themselves into the antebellum Cannonball House (856 Mulberry St., 478/745-5982, www.cannonballhouse.org, Jan.-Feb. Mon.-Fri. 11am-last tour begins 4:15pm, Sat. 10am-last tour 4:15pm, Mar.-Dec. Mon.-Sat. 10am-last tour 4:15pm, $6 adults, $3 students, under age 4 free). Tours last 45 minutes and include the main house, with its furnishings and Civil War memorabilia, and the historically notable two-story brick kitchen building with servants' quarters.

Grand Opera House

The thousand-seat Grand Opera House (651 Mulberry St., 478/301-5470, www.thegrand-macon.com, Mon.-Fri. 10am-5pm, show times vary), built in 1883, represents the height of Macon's opulent Victorian heyday. While Reconstruction and its aftermath was particularly difficult throughout the South, Macon fared noticeably better than most Southern cities, and "the Grand" is proof. Designed by the flamboyant W.R. Gunn, who designed about 100 such structures throughout the country, the Grand was the largest playhouse in the South when built (seating nearly double the number that it does today) and hosted such luminaries as Charlie Chaplin, Will Rogers, Sarah Bernhardt, George Burns, and Gracie Allen. While the Grand was renovated along the way and isn't totally vintage, it's still not only a throwback to the age of Vaudeville and traveling roadshows (a 1908 production of *Ben Hur* included a chariot race with live horses), it continues to host a wide variety of touring Broadway shows and high-quality performances.

Museum District

While not all offerings have worked out—the Georgia Music Hall of Fame was forced to close in 2011—Macon does boast its own fledgling museum district with some nice facilities clustered in a walkable, renovated section of downtown near Martin Luther King Boulevard.

MUSEUM OF ARTS AND SCIENCES

Billing itself as Georgia's largest general-purpose museum, the Museum of Arts and Sciences (4182 Forsyth Rd., 478/477-3232, www.masmacon.org, Tues.-Sat. 10am-5pm, Sun. 1pm-5pm, $10 adults, $7 students, $5 children 2-17) features a wide range of natural history exhibits and regionally oriented historical artifacts. Highlights include the "mini-zoo" of live animals and the Planetarium-Observatory. Also on the grounds is the rustic Kingfisher Cabin, writing retreat of poet Henry Stillwell Edwards.

GEORGIA CHILDREN'S MUSEUM

Four floors of enriching, educational children's activities, some still under development, are the attraction in this handsome building in the heart of downtown, which also includes a decent café for the refreshment of the adults. Highlights of the Georgia Children's Museum (382 Cherry St., 478/755-9539, www.georgia-childrensmuseum.com, Tues.-Sat. 10am-5pm, $4) include a hands-on TV studio and a Creek Indian exhibit.

GEORGIA SPORTS HALL OF FAME

Georgia has a rich sports legacy and that's celebrated at the Georgia Sports Hall of Fame (301 Cherry St., 478/752-1585, www.gshf.com, Tues.-Sat. 9am-5pm, $8 adults, $3.50 children). Fans of the Atlanta Braves and the state's premier college football program, the University of Georgia, will be particularly pleased with the memorabilia on display in the 14,000 square feet of exhibits. There's also a NASCAR race simulator and several interactive sports exhibits for the children. And needless to say there's lots of team merchandise at the gift store!

TUBMAN AFRICAN AMERICAN MUSEUM

Actually more of an art and art-history destination than strictly a historical museum, the Tubman African American Museum (340 Walnut St., 478/743-8544, www.tubmanmuseum.com, Tues.-Fri. 9am-5pm, Sat. 11am-5pm, $8 adults, $4 children) explores the intersection between African American experience and culture. Of particular interest is the Inventors Gallery, documenting the often-surprising and little-known contributions of African American patent holders. The museum also contains a memorial to Sergeant Rodney Davis Jr., who won a posthumous Medal of Honor for jumping on top of a live grenade at age 25 to save his fellow soldiers during the Vietnam War. His uniform and Medal of Honor are inside. A memorial to Sgt. Davis is in the plaza across the street from Macon City Hall on Poplar Street downtown.

Fort Hawkins

A replica of the blockhouse that established the first white settlement in the area, Fort Hawkins (Emery Hwy. and Maynard St., 478/742-3003, www.forthawkins.com, Sat. 10am-4pm, Sun.

noon-4pm, free) hosts frequent living-history demonstrations and features a small display about the site's history and significance to Macon.

◖ Ocmulgee National Monument

There are a couple of sites in America with somewhat better-preserved Native American mounds, but none quite so extensive as the sprawling and entirely fascinating Ocmulgee National Monument (1207 Emery Hwy., 478/752-8257, www.nps.gov, daily 9am-5pm, free). To early white settlers of the region they were simply called the "Old Fields," but to the Mississippian culture that lived here from about 900ad-1650ad, it was a bustling center of activity, from the enormous temple mound (from the top you can see most of downtown Macon) to the intimate and striking Earth Lodge, which though being completely restored does boast the only original and unchanged lodge floor in North America.

Begin and end your visit at the charming art moderne visitors center, begun in the 1930s and completed in 1952. Inside you'll find an extensive and interesting series of displays illustrating not only artifacts from the area, but the scope of Native American life and experience in the region covering at least 17,000 years of human habitation. From the visitors center you take the trails through the actual mounds, which may not look like much more than grassy knolls until you fully digest the spectrum of history and life that happened throughout the vast site; some scholars say at its peak it the same or greater population than modern-day Macon.

There are several spurs, some along wetland boardwalks, for those who want more of a natural experience in addition to the mounds themselves. Of particular non-Native American historical note is the section of trail upon which the great naturalist William Bartram trod during his visit to the "Ocmulgee Old Fields" in 1774. Perhaps the most amazing offering at the monument is actually some distance away from the rest of the mounds at the younger Lamar Mound. Built around 1350ad during a later

Go inside an ancient ceremonial mound at Ocmulgee National Monument.

ON THE CHITLIN' CIRCUIT

In the days of segregation, there was even a color line for music. Thus began the legendary "Chitlin' Circuit" of African American entertainers playing to black audiences. While technically it featured cities all across the eastern seaboard, in practice the circuit was most active in the segregated South, and Macon was a key stop.

Indeed, when I mentioned Augusta's James Brown to a Macon resident, she was quick to point out that Brown actually became famous in Macon and without Macon's thriving black music scene, "James Brown never would have left Augusta."

While an actual chitlin' is an ingredient in soul food, specifically a fried pig's intestine, or "chitterling," the chitlin' circuit is best exemplified by four enormously influential Georgia artists: **Ray Charles, James Brown,** and two who grew up blocks apart in Macon's Pleasant Hill neighborhood, **Little Richard** and **Otis Redding.**

Richard "Little Richard" Penniman is considered in some circles the real father of rock 'n' roll, emulated by white artists such as Elvis Presley and Jerry Lee Lewis. Little Richard wrote "Long Tall Sally" while working as a dishwasher at Ann's **Tic-Toc Room** (408 Broadway, now Martin Luther King Jr. Blvd.) in honor of a waitress there. It's now a swank bar, but

it's still the Tic-Toc Room and a plaque outside explains the history of the building. A stone's throw away is the restored circa-1921 **Douglass Theatre** (355 Martin Luther King Jr. Blvd.), a major chitlin' circuit venue that continues to host a full calendar of shows. Contrary to what many assume, the venue isn't named after early abolitionist Frederick Douglass but rather local black entrepreneur Charles Henry Douglass.

Otis Redding, though born in nearby Dawson came of age in Macon. It's said that he won so many teen talent shows at the Douglass that he was eventually barred from competing. He sang at the Baptist church (850 Armory Dr.) where his father was pastor.

Though idolizing fellow Macon resident Little Richard, Redding took soul and R&B to the next level. After an association with groundbreaking Stax Records in Memphis, Redding became one of the first soul artists to play a white club on the West Coast, L.A.'s Whisky a Go Go. Redding then nearly single-handedly brought chitlin' circuit R&B to a white counterculture audience with his short but electrifying headlining appearance at the Monterey Pop Festival in 1967. Redding died in a plane crash only six months later, but his memory lives on at Macon's **Gateway Park,** where he is memorialized with a statue and plaza.

---

incarnation of the Mississippian culture, the Lamar site is the only known example of a spiral mound in North America. It is accessible only during low water levels of the Ocmulgee River, and only by a Ranger-led tour that is held frequently throughout the year. Call ahead or check with the Ranger at the visitors center.

The calendar at Ocmulgee National Monument stays active, with several special events throughout the year at a slight added charge. Keep two things in mind: It can get *very* hot here during the middle of the day in the warm months, so I recommend coming here first thing in the morning during the height of summer; and be aware there's a lot of

distance to cover, so hydrate yourself and wear proper walking shoes.

Otis Redding Statue

Just as you cross the bridge over the Ocmulgee from downtown into east Macon, on your left you'll see Gateway Park and the beginning of the Ocmulgee Heritage Trail. The key landmark here, however, is the small but well-done memorial plaza to the late great Otis Redding, Macon native and beloved R&B-soul musician who influenced an entire generation before dying in a plane crash at the age of 26. While the bronze statue of Redding seems a little smallish (he was

© MACON-BIBB COUNTY CONVENTION & VISITORS BUREAU

Otis Redding Sittin' on the Dock of the Bay (artist: Bronze by Cooley)

actually a large and statuesque man himself), it is charming in its depiction of his trademark broad smile and casually confident performing style. A particularly nice touch is the buried, vandalism-proof speakers surrounding the statue, which play a steady 24-hour diet of Redding songs.

Rose Hill Cemetery

One of two adjacent historic cemeteries along Riverside Drive, Rose Hill Cemetery (1071 Riverside Dr., 478/751-9119, www.historicrosehillcemetery.org, daily dawn-dusk, free) is generally of more interest to visitors. This is where Duane Allman and Berry Oakley are buried side-by-side; they died in separate motorcycle accidents about a year and three blocks apart. While tall wrought iron fencing now keeps admirers (and potential vandals) away from the actual tombs, you can get close enough to read the inscriptions and take a good photo. Allman Brothers fans can also see the poignant graves of "Little Martha" Ellis and

Elizabeth Reed, both of which inspired band tunes.

Many other Macon historical figures are buried at this circa-1840 cemetery. Perhaps the most striking non-Allmans feature at Rose Hill is "Soldiers Square," the extensive burial plot of over 600 Confederate Civil War casualties and veterans, which you'll find down the steepest hill near the railroad tracks. This is one of the few places in the United States where the official flag of the Confederate States of America, the familiar battle flag emblem set against an all-white background, still waves 24 hours a day on public land, proudly overseeing this collective war memorial. While technically cars can enter Rose Hill, its steep hills and narrow roadways aren't designed for auto traffic. I strongly recommend parking at or near the entrance and hiking through the cemetery instead. Wear good walking shoes.

Riverside Cemetery

While adjacent Rose Hill Cemetery tends to get more attention, Riverside Cemetery (1301 Riverside Dr., 478/742-5328, www.riverside-cemetery.com, daily dawn-dusk, free) is much more walkable, as well as more noteworthy in the careful and deliberate design of its 125 acres by the Calvert Vaux firm in 1887 and the inclusion of many plants taken directly from New York's Central Park, itself an icon of landscape design. Interestingly, there are no graves of Confederate war casualties; though many Confederate veterans were eventually laid to rest here.

A few notable sites include the poignant "Babyland" (a Victorian area plot where small children are buried) and the graves of Charles Reb Messenburg (buried standing up at his request), WWI-veteran Ernest McWilliams (a machine gun is carved on his tombstone), and USAF Major Bobby Marvin, who was Missing in Action in Vietnam and whose memorial does not feature his actual remains, which have never been found. There is an excellent and quite detailed walking tour map of Riverside available at the entrance or at the Macon Visitors Center downtown.

◖ Allman Brothers Band Museum at the Big House

If you're any kind of a fan of The Allman Brothers Band, or if the idea of vintage tube amps, beautiful guitars, well-used drums, handwritten set lists, and flamboyant 1970s outfits gets you excited, head straight to the new, long-anticipated and wonderfully-done Allman Brothers Band Museum at The Big House (2321 Vineville Ave., 478/741-5551, www.thebighousemuseum.com, Thurs.-Sun. 11am-6pm, $8 adults, $4 children). The rambling Tudor mansion, or "Big House," a very short drive northwest of downtown, where the band lived as an extended community from 1970-73, and where many of their iconic hits were written, has been beautifully and tastefully restored. In some cases the intent is to replicate rooms where the Allmans and friends hung out, in other cases to create light-filled and joyously celebratory display areas for the enormous volume of Allmans-related memorabilia and vintage instruments.

You'll see the "casbah," the band's hippiefied songwriting and relaxing room, complete with patchouli incense. You'll see Duane Allman's restored bedroom (Gregg Allman's bedroom now houses a series of display cases). The little cubbie hole where roadies occasionally crashed now suitably contains a collection of beat-up amps. You'll even see the gorgeous Gibson Les Paul on which Duane Allman recorded "Layla" with Derek & the Dominoes, among many other vintage instruments.

Make sure you get the printed guide to the museum, which matches up with numbers posted throughout the rooms. An audio tour guides you through the stops (at no extra cost) or you can follow the numbers yourself.

Pleasant Hill Historic District

Just north of the Vineville Avenue location of the Big House museum is the city's traditional African American middle class district, Pleasant Hill. Bounded by Rogers Avenue on the west and Neal Avenue on the north and bisected by the Interstate (an unfortunately typical fate of traditional black neighborhoods in Southern cities), it's on the National Register of Historic Places and boasts a number

© JIM MOREKIS

Allman Brothers Band Museum at the Big House

ALLMAN BROTHERS TOUR

graves of Duane Allman and Berry Oakley at Rose Hill

Though their family roots are actually in north Florida, perhaps no other musical name is so associated with Macon and middle Georgia as the Allman Brothers Band. Far ahead of their time musically in their sinuous and rhythmic blend of rock, blues, soul, and even country, they were also one of the first true multi-racial bands.

Duane and Gregg Allman grew up as competing siblings, with Duane's fiery personality and virtuosic slide guitar work driving their early success. Touring with what would become a close-knit bunch of friends in various incarnations through the mid-to-late 1960s, the whole bunch ended up in Macon as the Allman Brothers Band. With the 1969 release of their eponymous debut album, nothing in the rock world, or Macon for that matter, was ever the same.

The city is chock-full of Allman sites that have inspired pilgrimages for decades. The band had various residences, including **309 College Street** and **315 College Street,** which was on the cover of the band's first album. The most famous was the "Big House," a large Tudor rented by bassist Berry Oakley and his wife Linda, and memorialized today in the **Allman Brothers Band Museum at the Big House** on Vineville Avenue, which opened in 2010.

Alas, the Allmans' heyday was short-lived. In October 1971 Duane perished in a motorcycle crash at **Hillcrest and Bartlett.** Barely a year later, Oakley died in another motorcycle crash at **Napier and Inverness.** Both were only 24. Both are buried side-by-side at **Rose Hill Cemetery.** At Rose Hill you can also see two gravesites that inspired Allman songs, "Little Martha" Ellis and Elizabeth Napier Reed. The Bond tomb at Rose Hill was on the back cover of the band's debut record.

Not all is gloom and doom, however. Down the road from the Big House you can have the best fried chicken and collard greens for miles around at **H&H Restaurant** (807 Forsyth St.), where the band frequently ate and which features much of the Allman Brothers' memorabilia.

While in Macon the band's label was **Capricorn Record** (535 D.T. Walton Sr. Way/ Cotton Ave.), which though now in other hands still retains the old signage and exterior. The actual Capricorn studios were at **536 Martin Luther King Jr. Blvd.;** that exterior can be seen on the *Allman Brothers Band at Fillmore East* album.

of Queen Anne and Craftsman cottages. The childhood home of "Little Richard" Penniman is at 1437 Woodliff Street. Otis Redding, another Pleasant Hill resident, is honored at the **Otis Redding Memorial Library** within the **Booker T. Washington Community Center** (391 Monroe St.).

Tours and Information

Easily the most unique tour in town is **Lights on Macon** (www.lightsonmacon.com). This free, self-guided illuminated nighttime walking tour is available every night of the year. A neighborhood of historic Intown Macon leaves its lights on every night so tour-goers can view at their leisure. Download the tour guide from the website or get the brochure at the **Downtown Macon Visitor Information Center** (450 Martin Luther King Jr. Blvd., Mon.-Fri. 9am-5pm, Sat. 10am-4pm). Begin your tour at one of two iconic Macon locations, the Hay House (934 Georgia Ave.) or 1842 Inn (353 College St.). The trip covers about 60 homes and gardens and takes anywhere from 30 minutes to about two hours depending on how quickly you go. Download a handy, free daytime walking tour of downtown Macon at www.maconwalkingtours.com.

ENTERTAINMENT AND EVENTS
Nightlife

The premier rock club in town and a key part of Georgia's music history is **Grant's Lounge** (576 Poplar St., 478/746-9191, www.grantslounge.com, Mon.-Sat. noon-2am), the "original home of Southern rock," which still hosts regular live music after over four decades of nourishing the budding careers of Southern names like Lynyrd Skynyrd, Tom Petty, and the Marshall Tucker Band.

For another neat bit of Southern music history, have a cocktail at the **Tic-Toc Room** (408 Broadway, 478/744-0123, Mon.-Sat. 5pm-2am). It's more of a martini bar and swank café these days, but in the days before integration it was a key venue on the "Chitlin' Circuit"

of African American entertainment. James Brown, Little Richard, and Otis Redding all performed here. (Little Richard also worked here, and it's said he wrote "Long Tall Sally" about a co-worker.)

Another good spot downtown is **The Rookery Restaurant & Bar** (543 Cherry St., 478/746-8658, www.rookerymacon.com, Tue.-Sat. 11am-2am, Sun. 11:30am-midnight), which pretty much has it all: friendly and lively bar scene, sports on the tube, a great kitchen, and plenty of tables at which to enjoy the good food that comes out of it.

Theater

Macon has two well-regarded theater companies: the venerable, nearly 80-year-old **Macon Little Theatre** (4220 Forsyth Rd., 478/471-7529, http://maconlittletheatre.org), which performs in a newly renovated and historic building, and **Theatre Macon** (438 Cherry St., 478/746-9485, www.theatremacon.com), which performs in the heart of downtown.

Entertainment Venues

The largest concert and event venue in Georgia outside metro Atlanta is the **Macon Centreplex** (200 Coliseum Dr., 478/751-9232, www.maconcentreplex.com), formerly just the Coliseum, which also straddles the border between downtown and east Macon over the river. The grandly ornate 1925 **Macon City Auditorium** (415 First St., 478/751-9232, www.maconcentreplex.com) is now operated as part of the Centreplex.

The historic **Grand Opera House** (651 Mulberry St., 478/301-5470, www.thegrandmacon.com), or "the Grand," hosts a full slate of concerts and traveling musicals and plays. The **Douglass Theatre** (355 Martin Luther King Jr. Blvd., 478/742-2000, www.douglasstheatre.com), in the days of segregation the premier African American venue in town, is now owned by the city, fully restored, and hosts many an event throughout the year. Despite its opulence, the 1916 movie house **Cox Capitol Theatre** (382 Second St., 478/257-6391, www.

coxcapitoltheatre.com) was neglected for decades until a 2006 renovation brought it back to its former prominence as a fun performance venue.

Local institutions **Mercer University** (www.mercer.edu) and **Wesleyan College** (www.wesleyan.edu) host a variety of college-oriented productions and presentations on their respective beautiful campuses.

Festivals

Without question Macon's premier event is the "pinkest party on earth," the **Cherry Blossom Festival** (www.cherryblossom.com, Mar.) that takes place in mid-to-late March to take advantage of the annual flowering of the city's estimated 300,000-plus Yoshino cherry trees, which are actually not indigenous but were originally Japanese imports. Events are varied, from a Bed Race to nightly concerts to of course the Cherry Blossom Parade, and take place at various venues from Cherry Street downtown to Central City Park (Willie Smokie Glover Dr.) to Mercer University and Wesleyan College. A free trolley takes festival-goers from spot to spot. While some events and concerts are ticketed, the majority are free and open to the public.

A beloved event in early May is the **Secret Garden Tour** (www.georgiatrust.org, May) in which many of Macon's finest private residences open their doors and gates to display their grounds and gardens. The historic Hay House is not only the beneficiary of this fundraising effort but is the hub of activity, usually hosting a flower and plant market concurrent with the tours.

African heritage is celebrated at the **Tubman Pan African Festival** (www.tubmanmuseum.com, late Apr.), which features Reggae, African music, and lots of dance and cultural displays. Easily the most unique event in the area is the **Ocmulgee Indian Celebration** (www.nps.gov, Sept.), which takes place on the grounds of the National Park Service-operated Ocmulgee National Monument and celebrates the heritage and culture of the descendants of the Creek Indians who built the enormous mound complex there.

Visitors in February will be glad to know there's something to do in the dead of winter: the **Macon Film Festival** (www.maconfilmfestival.com, Feb.), a fun event nearly a decade old which brings new and notable films to town at various historic venues downtown.

SPORTS AND RECREATION
Hiking and Biking

With the recent departure of both the local minor league baseball team, the Macon Braves, and a minor league hockey team with the awesome name Macon Whoopee, locals and visitors have more participatory activities in which to engage. The centerpiece is the Ocmulgee River, which runs beside the city.

The newly completed **Ocmulgee River Heritage Trail** is essentially a paved path for hiking and biking on the banks of the slow brown river, with occasional put-ins for a canoe or kayak. Its main terminus is at Gateway Park at the foot of the Otis Redding Bridge, where the statue of Otis Redding resides.

ACCOMMODATIONS
Under $150

Due to its very central location at the confluence of three Interstate highways, I-75, I-475, and I-16, Macon offers a vast range of budget chain accommodations that tend to group in large clusters.

The I-75 cluster is just north of downtown and about a five-minute drive away. I'd recommend the **Comfort Inn & Suites** (3935 Arkwright Rd., 478/757-8688, www.comfortinn.com, $75-100) or the pet-friendly **Candlewood Suites** (3957 River Place Dr., 478/254-3531, www.ichotelsgroup.com, $75-100). The most crowded cluster is off I-475 on the western edge of Macon, with downtown about 10 minutes away. Try **Comfort Inn West** (4951 Eisenhower Pkwy., 478/788-5500, www.comfortinn.com, $75-100) with renovated rooms or the pet-friendly **Sleep Inn West** (140 Plantation Inn Dr., 48/476-8111, www.sleepinn.com, $75-100).

A good budget choice a bit closer to downtown is the **Hilton Garden Inn** (1220 Stadium Dr., 478/741-5527, www.hilton.com, $130) adjacent to the tranquil Mercer University campus.

$150-300

By far the premier lodging in Macon is the (**1842 Inn** (353 College St., 478/741-1842, www.1842inn.com, $140-255) and I urge you to make every effort in securing a room if you're planning to visit the city. It's in a particularly striking Greek Revival building that was once the home of a mayor, with "opulent" being a fair word to describe its interior. Ten of the inn's 19 rooms are in the main building, which boasts a classic wraparound veranda with 17 columns. There's a separate "Victorian Cottage," which was actually moved onto this parcel of land in the 1980s and offers nine guest rooms featuring 12-foot ceilings and heart pine flooring. Both buildings share a verdant common courtyard. You can enjoy your full breakfast in your room, in the parlor, or in the courtyard. There's also a generous hospitality hour each evening.

Another option is the **Marriott Macon City Center** (240 Coliseum Dr., 800/228-9290, www.marriott.com, $150-175), the city's premier convention and business lodging and a very central and convenient base from which to explore the area. Rooms are well appointed and spacious and the hotel offers a full range of amenities. Off-season rates are lower. While there is free parking in the lot, the hotel does charge about $10 a day for wireless Internet access.

Camping

The **Tobesofkee Recreation Area** (6600 Moseley Dixon Rd., 478/474-8770, www.co.bibb.ga.us, parking $3, campsites $18-22) is a large county park off I-475 where you'll find fishing, swimming, and lake-style boating opportunities along with a campground.

FOOD

Because of Macon's central location to several Interstate highways, pretty much every type

of fast food or upscale fast-food chain you can think of has an outpost in town. Instead, here are some of the more unique and recommended local and regional offerings.

American

With an active bar scene to go along with its well-received menu, (**The Rookery Restaurant & Bar** (543 Cherry St., 478/746-8658, www.rookerymacon.com, Mon. 11am-3pm, Tue.-Thu. 11am-9:30pm, Fri.-Sat. 11am-10pm, Sun. 11:30am-9pm, $8-15) is a great, all-purpose stop in the most happening area of Macon's restored downtown, with a history going back to 1976. Specialties include Betsy's Grilled Pimento Cheese, a Southern delicacy, and a range of great burgers, all half a pound and all named after famous Georgians, from the Allman Brothers (Swiss cheese and mushrooms) to Jerry Reed (pepperjack cheese and jalapeños) to Jimmy Carter (peanut butter and bacon). Most everything is very reasonable.

Perhaps the most unique restaurant in Macon is **Nu-Way Weiners** (430 Cotton Ave., 478/743-1368, www.nu-wayweiners.com, Mon.-Fri. 6am-7pm, Sat. 7am-6pm, $2-4), which has grown to nine locations in its nearly 100-year history. At all of them you'll find the same inexpensive menu of hot dogs built around Nu-Way's "secret" chili topping. They have decent burgers too, as well as a breakfast menu. Combo plates include a mix of burgers and dogs.

Barbecue

With 75 years in operation, **Fincher's** (891 Gray Hwy., 478/743-5866, www.finchersbqga.net, $5) is one of two longtime local 'cue joints considered the city's best, and it's the most out of the ordinary. The sauce is sharper and tangier than the usual Georgia variety, a variant of the North Carolina vinegar-based sauce, along with Tarheel-style coleslaw topping. There's another location at 3947 Houston Avenue.

If tang isn't your thing, head to **Satterfield's** (120 New St., 478/742-0352, www.satterfieldscatering.com, Mon.-Fri.

© JIM MOREKIS

the legendary Tic-Toc Room

10:30am-3pm, $7), which offers dependably good hickory-smoked pulled pork as well as solid fried catfish.

Soul Food

Allman Brothers fans will know ◖ **H & H Restaurant** (807 Forsyth St., 478/742-9810, www.mamalouise.com, Mon.-Sat. 6:30am-4pm, $12) as the band's favorite hangout in Macon, but "Mama Louise" Hudson's place is also one of the best soul food diners anywhere. It's very informal: When you're ready to leave, you come back behind the counter and pay the cook, who also runs the register. The menu is as simple as it's been for the last 50 years; the offerings are listed by day, and you pick a meat (go with the fried chicken) and three veggies, such as perfect collard greens and their signature squash. There is a full breakfast as well. The walls are covered with memorabilia of Southern rock, particularly the Allman Brothers, who were taken under Mama Louise's wing during their early days as starving artists.

Steaks

Widely regarded as perhaps Macon's best fine-dining restaurant and one of the few in town that can compete with bigger-city offerings, the ◖ **Tic-Toc Room** (408 Broadway, 478/744-0123, Mon.-Sat. 5pm-10 pm, $20) is also an important part of Georgia music history, hosting performers such as Little Richard and Otis Redding back when this was an African American nightspot in the days of segregation. Today it's part swank martini bar, part steakhouse. The bone-in rib eyes are the stuff of legend. There are tapas, too, and even the sides, such as the famous lobster mashed potatoes, are great.

SOUTH OF MACON
◖ Museum of Aviation

There's one very worthwhile reason to visit the town of Warner Robins, 14 miles south of Macon, and that's the excellent Museum of Aviation (Russell Pkwy., 478/926-6870, www.museumofaviation.org, daily 9am-5pm, free) on the massive Robins Air Force Base.

Comprising several very large buildings with roughly outlined chronological themes, the core collection of the Museum is its impressive array of many, many dozens of military aircraft from all eras of American aviation. Airplane buffs of all ages will go nuts seeing these beauties up close, from WWII classics like the P-51 Mustang to the host of Cold War and Vietnam era jets to the starkly elegant U-2 and SR-71 spy planes. Some of the aircraft are within exhibits chronicling some aspect of their use; others are simply in large warehouse areas you can walk around.

Their historical exhibits are solid, featuring uniforms, memorabilia, and breakdowns of various air campaigns in U.S. military history. As you'd expect, there's an extensive display on the history and construction of the sprawling Robins AFB itself. In one of the buildings is the **Georgia Aviation Hall of Fame,** honoring the Peach State's contributions to human flight. A nice plus with the Museum is that, despite being on a military installation, it's in an area where you don't have to go through the usual checkpoints for drivers license and proof of insurance. You just drive right up, park, and enjoy.

INFORMATION AND SERVICES

The centrally located **Downtown Macon Visitor Information Center** (450 Martin Luther King Jr. Blvd., 478/743-3401, www.

maconga.org, Mon.-Sat. 9am-5pm, Sat. 10am-4pm) is in the offices of the local Convention and Visitors Bureau and is a must-stop. They not only have every possible local, regional, and state brochure you could want, they have a video of local life and culture and a fun timeline exhibit of interesting Macon history.

For those who prefer a visitors center off the Interstate highway, go to the I-75 **Southbound Rest Area** (478/994-8181, info kiosk Mon.-Fri. 9am-5pm), a mile south of Exit 181.

The **Medical Center of Central Georgia** (777 Hemlock St., 478/633-1000, www.mccg. org) is the state's largest hospital and provides a full range of emergency care.

The newspaper of record is the *Macon Telegraph* (www.macon.com).

GETTING THERE AND AROUND

Macon is extraordinarily well-served by the Interstate Highway system. I-75 passes through town north-south, and the western terminus of I-16 is here.

The small **Middle Georgia Regional Airport** (1000 Terminal Dr., 478/788-3760, www.cityofmacon.net, airport code MCN) hosts flights by GeorgiaSkies to and from Atlanta.

Macon is served by a **Greyhound** (65 Spring St., 478/743-5411, www.greyhound.com) station. In town, the **Macon Transit Authority** (www.mta-mac.com, $1.25 fare) runs buses and trolleys in various routes.

Indian Springs and Juliette

The short but often congested drive north from Macon on I-75 doesn't have to be a headlong rush into Atlanta's sprawl. There are several very interesting stops and stays along the way, including America's oldest state park.

INDIAN SPRINGS AND FLOVILLA

◖ Indian Springs State Park

There's truth in advertising at Indian Springs State Park (678 Lake Clark Rd., 770/504-2277,

www.gastateparks.org, daily 7am-10pm, $5 parking, campsites $25-28, cottages $115-125), which in fact centers on a natural spring well known to Native Americans for its heady taste and healing properties. A Civilian Conservation Corps masonry "spring house" from the 1930s showcases a rustic drinking fountain for guests to sample, as well as members of the public, who often come and fill up jugs to take with them.

Georgia makes the persuasive case that

this is technically the first state park in the country. The land was first acquired in 1825 through the shady and controversial Second Treaty of Indian Springs, in which some Creek Indians were persuaded to sign over the entire tribe's rights to remaining area land. A second, somewhat more legit treaty was signed in 1828, calling the land "Indian Springs Reserve," a remarkably early appearance of the concept of land conservation. By 1927 it was a "State Forest Park," and in 1931 it and Vogel became the first two state parks in Georgia.

Across the street from the entrance to the state park is the circa-1823 **Chief McIntosh House** (Memorial Day-Labor Day Sat.-Sun. 10am-2pm), the handsome two-story home of the local half-white Creek Indian leader who was assassinated by his own people for his role in signing the Second Treaty. The building would later become Indian Springs Hotel, one of 10 serving a large population of resort tourists to the springs in antebellum years (a "mineral bath" would set you back two bucks). It's now a seasonal museum about the history of the park and the area.

Today, the sulfur-smelling spring feeds 100-acre, stocked Lake McIntosh, named for the unfortunate chief, and there is a charming waterfall and creek area to explore. The park has 60 tent and RV campsites and 10 cottages, 2 of which are dog friendly.

Flovilla

Unlike many Georgia state parks in more remote locations, the cute little town of Flovilla is a few blocks down the road from Indian Springs State Park. Next to the park entrance are the **Whimsical Botanical Gardens** (1834 Hwy. 42, www.thevillageatindiansprings.com, daily 10am-7pm, free), a meandering eight-acre site with a rose garden and an "enchanted garden."

A bit north of Flovilla is one of Georgia's oldest restaurants and certainly one of its best, if not the best, 'cue joints, **◖ Fresh Air Barbecue** (1164 Hwy. 42, Jackson,

770/775-3182, www.freshairbarbecue.com, Mon.-Thurs. 8am-7:30pm, Fri.-Sat. 8am-8:30pm, Sun. 8am-8pm, $3-7), in business since before the Great Depression. The building hasn't changed much since then, with prices to match: $7 gets you the full pulled pork plate with Brunswick stew, coleslaw, pickle, and crackers. The pit-cooked barbecue is generally served with a tangy, North Carolina-style sauce. Significantly, they're open seven days a week, so there's no excuse not to drop by!

Dauset Trails Nature Center

Dauset Trails Nature Center (360 Mt. Vernon Church Rd., 770/775-6798, www.dausettrails.com, Mon.-Sat. 9am-5pm, Sun. noon-5pm, free) is a laid-back and tranquil place to hike or stroll around while learning about colonial farm life in middle Georgia. There's a barnyard animal area as well as an "animal trail" with various raptors and four-legged creatures in various states of recovery, a nod to Dauset Trail's original role in the 1980s as a rehab center for injured animals who couldn't be returned to the wild. As for the "trails" in their name, there are 17 miles of hiking and biking trails, plus another 10 miles of dedicated equestrian trails. You can use the trails after the park closes at 5pm by taking the trailhead near the entrance.

JULIETTE AND VICINITY

Juliette was pretty beat until a Hollywood scout decided it might be a great location for the 1991 film *Fried Green Tomatoes at the Whistlestop Café*. So the town became a stand-in for Irondale, Alabama, with the old hardware store transformed into the titular café.

The film crew is long gone, but somebody had the bright idea to keep the **◖ Whistlestop Café** (443 McCrackin St., 478/992-8886, www.thewhistlestopcafe.com, daily 11am-4pm, $10) going, and it became the centerpiece of a minor tourist renaissance in the little town. Clearly, you must have the fried green tomatoes, either as an appetizer or in their signature sandwich. But save room for their decadent shortcake afterwards. Yup, Juliette has a **Fried Green Tomato Festival** (Oct., www.themiddleofeverywhere.com/GreenTomatoFestival.html).

In the wake of the movie, Juliette decided to open its own tiny **Opry House** (342 McCrackin St.) down the street from the Café, hosting mostly bluegrass shows generally on the first Saturday night of the month, with occasional "Pickin' on the Porch" jam sessions.

High Falls State Park

Want to camp in a yurt? Then High Falls State Park (76 High Falls Park Dr., 478/993-3053, www.gastateparks.org, daily 7am-10pm, $5 parking, yurts $65, tent and RV sites $25-28) is your place. In addition to six of the Mongolian-style accommodations, there are 100 more traditional tent and RV sites. As for the eponymous "falls," that is a humble cascade on the Towaliga River within the park, along which also lie the remains of an old power plant. But for many visitors the highlight here is the 650-acre lake, designed for maximum boater enjoyment. With two boat ramps, it's fully stocked and known for its great bass fishing, and unlike many other state park lakes, private motorboats are allowed.

Jarrell Plantation Historic Site

A popular teaching destination for educators seeking to impart a lesson in the ways of the old South, Jarrell Plantation Historic Site (711 Jarrell Plantation Rd., 478/986-5172, Thurs.-Sat. 9am-5pm, $4-6.50) near Juliette, is centered on the historic and rustically compelling heart pine house built by John Fitz Jarrell in 1847. The 600 acres saw a lot of crazy stuff over the years, including Sherman's March, typhoid, and the boll weevil. It also saw slavery; the Jarrells at one point had about 40 slaves, some of whom stayed on to work for pay after emancipation. There's also a saw mill, gristmill, a cotton gin, and many other implements added in the Victorian era when the farm business was rejuvenated after John's son Dick took over. The Jarrells eventually donated the site

to the state in the 1970s. There's usually a fun Christmas program each December.

Piedmont National Wildlife Refuge

The vast majority of federally run wildlife refuges in Georgia are on the coastal flyway, but a key exception is the 35,000-acre Piedmont National Wildlife Refuge (718 Juliette Rd., 478/986-5441, www.fws.gov, daily dawn-dusk, free). The backstory is interesting: With the land exhausted by the boll weevil and poor farming practices, this was nearly a wasteland by the time of the Dust Bowl. In the 1930s President Franklin Roosevelt made it a wildlife refuge, and since then the loblolly pine stands are back, along with a resident population of endangered red-cockaded woodpeckers, among many other flora and fauna. The attached Visitors Center (Mon.-Fri. 8am-4:30pm, Sat.-Sun. 9am-5pm, free) has exhibits on the refuge's ecosystem and history.

Gray

Not much goes in the town of Gray, but folks drive from many miles around to enjoy what many connoisseurs consider Georgia's best barbecue: ◼ **Old Clinton BBQ** (4214 Gray Hwy., 478/986-3225, www.oldclintonbbq.com, Mon.-Thurs. 10am-8pm, Fri.-Sat. 10am-9pm, Sun. 10am-4pm, $5). This original location (there's another in nearby Milledgeville) has been dishing out masterfully smoked pork and ribs since 1958, and it looks every bit its age, with memorabilia and kitsch appeal to burn. Like most of the better 'cue joints in Georgia, Old Clinton eschews the Peach State's indigenous cloying tomato-based sauce for a tangier, almost North Carolina-style sauce, which is ridiculously good. Not only that, but it's inexpensive: The full platter meal with Brunswick stew, pickle, bread, and slaw is under seven bucks! Save room for the also incredible homemade layer cake. Perhaps surprisingly for a place that's the very definition of old school, they're open seven days a week, unusual for the more serious barbecue restaurants in the South.

Milledgeville

Milledgeville may not get as much attention as some other cities in Georgia, but it's well worth a visit and is actually vital to the state's history. It served as state capital during the antebellum era—Atlanta didn't get that title until after the Civil War—and so boasts more than its share of intriguing political shenanigans.

The Marquis de Lafayette ate barbecue here during his visit in 1825. And while General Sherman famously stayed here during his March to the Sea, thankfully much of the city's distinctive architecture, including the home-grown style called "Milledgeville Federal," was spared the torch.

A cynic would say it's only fitting that a town famous for hosting so many politicians would also be famous as the site of one of the nation's earliest hospitals for the mentally ill. While the facility itself, now called Central State Hospital, dramatically downsized, it was once the largest mental hospital in the United States; in old Georgia lore "going to Milledgeville" was often slang for losing one's mind.

Milledgeville's eccentric combination of lively social gatherings and Southern gothic darkness meant that it was the perfect breeding ground for writer Flannery O'Connor's brand of darkly humorous symbolic fiction. Fans of O'Connor in particular will find lots to see and appreciate about a visit to Milledgeville, where she wrote all of her major works and which undoubtedly influenced their tone.

But life in modern Milledgeville is marked primarily by the dynamic downtown presence of Georgia College and State University, O'Connor's alma mater and one of the state's premier educational institutions.

HISTORY

Along with Macon, Augusta, and Columbus, Milledgeville (www.visitmilledgeville.org) is one of Georgia's cities on the fall line. Unlike those other cities, however, Milledgeville was much more of a purpose-built proposition. In 1803 the Georgia legislature specifically called for the creation of a brand-new capital city to replace nearby Louisville. They even decided on the name in advance, honoring the governor at the time, John Milledge.

The Creek Indians had long lived in this land of plenty along the Oconee River, and indeed left some unique monuments that exist to this day. But not at all coincidentally, the Creeks had been forced to vacate their traditional lands a year prior to the creation of Milledgeville by the Treaty of Fort Wilkinson. By 1807 the legislature was convening in the state house, which was still under construction. It was still wild country, and early life in the fledgling capital was frontier-tough. Gambling and drinking were commonplace, and formal duels between political rivals were regular occurrences.

During the cotton boom of the classic antebellum era, however, money and power began flowing freely to Milledgeville. Much cotton from interior plantations was gathered here in preparation for barging downriver to the port of Darien. The cotton boom also meant a dramatic increase in the importation of slave labor to the local economy.

Milledgeville's heyday came in 1825, when Revolutionary War hero the Marquis de Lafayette, then in his waning days, visited town during a tour of the Southern states. The associated fete, complete with country barbecue, entered local legend. In the 1840s, riding a progressive wave of reform, Milledgeville erected the Georgia Lunatic Asylum, which exists to this day as Central State Hospital and was at one time the largest mental hospital in the country.

As Georgia's capital, Milledgeville was front and center during the move towards secession. Rowdy, all-night parties on the state house grounds celebrated the vote to join the Confederacy on January 19, 1861, when the special Secession Convention meeting inside ratified the formal break with the union.

Perhaps surprisingly given Milledgeville's rebel credentials, General Sherman and his troops went comparatively easy on them. While several important military buildings were burned, most of the city, including the state house, was spared (Sherman himself stayed in the governor's mansion, which stands today).

SIGHTS
Old Capital Museum

Despite the ominously fortress-like countenance of this Gothic Revival building on the quad of Georgia Military College, the Old Capital Museum (201 E. Greene St., 478/453-1803, www.oldcapitalmuseum.org, Tues.-Fri. 10am-4pm, Sat. noon-4pm, $5.50 adults, $4.50 children) was never a military site, but did serve as the meeting place for the state legislature and was political center of Georgia for the most contentious period of its history, 1807-1868. Largely due to activities of Sherman's troops in 1864, none of the original furnishings and layout are present. Your visit

is limited to the ground-floor exhibits and displays chronicling the history of Milledgeville, from native times through the present day. The sections detailing the area's often frightfully-bloody early colonial history are the most interesting, as is the exhibit devoted to the building of the Georgia Lunatic Asylum, now Central State Hospital.

Stetson-Sanford House

A great example of the local "Milledgeville Federal" architectural style, the Stetson-Sanford House (601 W. Hancock St., 478/453-1803, www.oldcapitalmuseum.org, Thurs.-Sat. visit via Milledgeville Trolley Tours) was originally on North Wilkinson Street and acted as a hotel to house visiting legislators and dignitaries during Milledgeville's tenure as state capital. From 1951-1966 the house was the popular Sanford House Tea Room. The owners then donated it to the Old Capital Historical Society, which also runs the Old Capital Museum; the Society moved the entire house to the current address in 1966. You visit this

© JIM MOREKIS

Old Capital Museum

by taking a trolley tour; go to the Milledgeville Visitors Center (200 W. Hancock St.) to catch the trolley.

Old Governor's Mansion

One of the preeminent examples of Greek Revival architecture in the country, the Old Governor's Mansion (120 S. Clark St., 478/445-4545, www.gcsu.edu, Tues.-Sat. 10am-4pm, Sun. 2pm-4pm, $10 adults, $2 children) was built in Georgia's antebellum heyday in the late 1830s. It hosted 10 Georgia governors and their families, until Atlanta became the state capital in 1868. It also briefly hosted General Sherman himself, who made it his headquarters during a portion of his March to the Sea. It survived the war and in 1891 became home to the president of Georgia Normal and Industrial College, precursor to today's Georgia College and State University, which currently owns and operates the mansion as a house museum. (It was traditionally the college president's home up until the 1980s, and remains the college's oldest structure.) A series of renovations in the first years of the 21st century have made the mansion a worthwhile visit to tour its many grand rooms. Tours begin at the top of each hour and no self-guided tours are available. There's a cute gift shop in a well-restored outbuilding to the mansion's rear.

◖ Andalusia

On a 550-acre plot of wooded land north of the city center, Andalusia (Hwy. 441, 4 miles northwest of Milledgeville, 478/454-4029, www.andalusiafarm.org, Mon.-Tues. and Thurs.-Sat. 10am-4pm, $5 donation requested) is the name given to the family dairy farm of the O'Connor family, where iconic Southern writer Flannery O'Connor lived most of her adult life. She wrote all her major works in a bedroom on the ground floor of the main house, actually a parlor converted so that the ailing Flannery, suffering from lupus, wouldn't have to climb the stairs (her crutches are right there by the bed).

Five rooms are open for viewing: Flannery's bedroom, the kitchen area, the dining room,

O'Connor family farm at Andalusia

MIDDLE GEORGIA

© JIM MOREKIS

FINDING FLANNERY

Georgia College & State University hosts an excellent Flannery O'Connor collection.

Though born and raised in Savannah, Flannery O'Connor attended college in Milledgevillle and did the bulk of her writing here. Her family had deep roots in the area and their imprint is felt all over town. Here are some related sites:

Her first home here is the **Cline-O'Connor-Florencourt House** (311 W. Greene St.), now a private residence, where she lived until her beloved father's early death from lupus (a hereditary disease which would later claim Flannery herself). As an aside, this handsome building briefly served as the governor's residence in the 1830s; indeed, it's a stone's throw away from the grand old governor's mansion itself.

Flannery and family faithfully attended **Sacred Heart Catholic Church,** which was actually built on land donated to the church by her great-grandmother. After her father died, Flannery became quite close with her mother, Regina Cline O'Connor, and the two often lunched at the tearoom and enjoyed peppermint chiffon pie in the **Stetson-Sanford House,** now a house museum.

During World War II, Flannery attended Georgia State College for Women, now Georgia College and State University. Visit the **Flannery O'Connor Room** of the college museum to see vintage photos and personal items, including the manual typewriter on which those amazing novels and short stories were written.

The major stop is at **Andalusia,** the ancestral Cline-O'Connor family dairy farm. After studying at the prestigious University of Iowa Writer's Workshop writing program and a brief stay at the Yaddo writer's retreat in New York, O'Connor was diagnosed, as she feared, with lupus. She returned to Milledgeville under the burden of a pessimistic prognosis to live out her days with her mother and write in the downstairs parlor converted into a bedroom.

However, Flannery defied expectations and lived another 14 years at Andalusia before passing away at the age of 39. Visit her simple gravesite at **Memory Hill Cemetery.** Well-wishers often leave a single peacock feather at her tomb in memory of Flannery's well-known fondness for "The King of the Birds."

MIDDLE GEORGIA

a porch area with displays and a video, and an upstairs bedroom, plus there's a small reception area with a small but delightful selection of unique O'Connor-related items, some of them created by family members still in the area. Most of the furnishings are original, even the refrigerator. Flannery's mother, Regina O'Connor, owned and operated the farm and her stitchwork can still be seen on some of the drapes.

Several outbuildings in various states of disrepair are also here to see, including a charming stable area where Flannery's beloved horse Flossie once roamed, and the restored cottage of the Hill family, African American workers featured in some of Flannery's letters. Not far from the main house, a small dam has made a pond area circled by a walking trail. Of course, there's a pen for a family of peacocks, which have become living signatures of Flannery's life and works. Indeed, while walking the house and grounds, aficionados of O'Connor's work will no doubt find echoes of particular scenes, whether involving the milk-chilling room or the dilapidated barn or just the overall feel of romantic isolation.

As evidenced by the huge Walmart adjacent to the O'Connor parcel, Andalusia has to had to fend off much development pressure over the years. While its future seems assured, they can always use more funding for basic repairs and upkeep of this important piece of American literary history. The entrance to Andalusia isn't particularly obvious; heading north out of Milledgeville, pass the Walmart on your left, then look for a Babcock furniture store on your right. The driveway entrance is directly across Highway 441 on your left.

Central State Hospital

Fans of poignant abandoned sites will find themselves drawn to the evocative decay of the sprawling 1700-acre Central State Hospital, one of the oldest in the United States and at one time the biggest. However, while you can drive around the buildings you may not trespass within them. Instead you'll have to content yourself with a visit to the Central State

Hospital Museum (620 Broad St., 478/445-4878, www.centralstatehospital.org, appointment only) in the old 1891 depot on the hospital campus, which chronicles the history of this darkly fascinating institution.

In 1837 the state legislature, then conveniently based in Milledgeville, authorized a "State Lunatic, Idiot, and Epileptic Asylum," which admitted its first patient in 1842. While standards of treatment were primitive by modern standards, at the time it represented a spirit of real reform. However, with the end of the Civil War came new pressures, as the Asylum began admitting those with profound wartime injuries as well as the mentally ill. By 1897 it had changed its name to the Georgia State Sanitarium, and throughout the 20th century was a notorious symbol of oppressive bureaucracy.

By the time it was renamed again in 1967 as Central State Hospital, it was the largest mental hospital in America, with the world's largest kitchen feeding over 12,000 patients several times a day. Shock therapy was common, as was outright neglect and abuse. All told, over 20,000 deceased patients were buried somewhere on the grounds, with tomb markers long since removed.

The trend towards a more humane and sophisticated treatment model eroded "Central State's" mission, and in 2010 the state of Georgia reduced it to a much more limited program. The vast bulk of the century and a half's worth of buildings, some of them oddly ornate, are vacant and unused, except for the tortured ghosts that many swear walk the halls and stairwells each night.

Lockerley Arboretum

Landscaped in 1965, the 50-acre Lockerley Arboretum (1534 Irwinton Rd., 478/452-2112, www.lockerly.org, Mon.-Fri. 8:30am-4:30pm, Sat. 9am-1pm, free) is a charming place to spend an hour or two, walking the grounds and maybe having a picnic. You can also tour the Greek Revival antebellum Lockerley Hall, formerly known as Rose Hill, furnished with historic pieces.

Memory Hill Cemetery

Flannery O'Connor isn't the only famous person interred at the circa-1804 Memory Hill Cemetery (Liberty and Franklin Sts., www.friendsofcems.org, daily 8am-5pm), but her gravesite is the most visited. Native son, former Congressman, and aircraft carrier namesake Carl Vinson, "father of the two-ocean navy" is also buried here, as is famed chemist and first University of Georgia football coach Charles Herty, not to mention plenty of Georgia state political figures due to Milledgeville's long tenure as state capital. The cemetery provides an excellent free walking tour brochure, available at the kiosk inside the front gate.

Georgia College & State University Museums

Georgia's dedicated liberal arts university, which has a variety of buildings all over downtown, offers a trio of small but solid museums, all free of charge. **Georgia College Museum** (221 N. Clark St., 478/445-4391, www.gcsu.edu, Mon.-Sat. 10am-4pm, free) is primarily known for its standing Flannery O'Connor Room, a repository of personal items specific to the Milledgeville-based author, including mementos from her time at the college itself. The highlight is the actual manual typewriter on which she typed most of her works. The **Natural History Museum and Planetarium** (Herty Hall, corner W. Montgomery and N. Wilkinson, 478/445-2395, www.gscu.edu, Mon.-Fri. 8am-4pm, first Sat. of month 10am-4pm, free) opened in 2004 and features a region-leading collection of fossils and other paleontology-related artifacts as well as a state-of-the-art digital planetarium. The **Museum of Fine Arts** (102 S. Columbia St., 478/445-4572, www.gcsu.edu, by appointment, free) is housed in the beautiful restored 1935 Napier-Underwood house.

John Marlor Art Center

This handsome antebellum building was once in "The Strip," Milledgeville's historically African American area through segregation. The John Marlor Art Center (201 N. Wayne St., 478/ 452-8676, www.milledgvilleallied-arts.com, Mon.-Fri. 9am-4:30pm, free) is now a hub of the local nonprofit arts scene and an art gallery.

NIGHTLIFE

While Milledgeville is nowhere near the league of Atlanta or Athens when it comes to a college party scene, local students do occasionally call it "Millyvegas" for the plethora of college-oriented watering holes here. Indeed, Milledgeville's raucous nightlife briefly gained national notoriety for an alleged incident involving NFL quarterback Ben Roethlisberger, who had a home in the nearby lake country.

On Hancock Street downtown there's a trio of nightspots that do double duty as good restaurants. **The Brick** (136 W. Hancock St., 478/452-0089, www.thebrick.info, Mon.-Sat. 11am-2am, Sun. noon-midnight) gets louder and rowdier as the night wears on, morphing from a gastropub atmosphere to more of a sports bar. A couple of doors down is **Buffington's** (120 W. Hancock St., 478/414-1975, www.eatinthebuff.com, Mon.-Fri. 11am-2am, Sat. 11:30am-2am). On the other side of Wilkinson Street you'll find **Velvet Elvis** (113 W. Hancock St., 478/453-8226, Mon.-Sat. 4pm-2am), which gets packed with students late at night after the dinner burger crowd has gone home.

RECREATION

Though it's technically in the county next door to Milledgeville, **Lake Sinclair** (478/452-4687, www.lakesinclair.org) is by far the biggest recreational draw in the area and a major economic driver. This artificially constructed lake was created in the 1950s to produce hydroelectric power, and the proof is in the hulking power plant, which dominates the view from most of the lake. That said, plenty of folks live, vacation, fish, and boat on Lake Sinclair. There are eight full-service marinas and campgrounds at **Oconee Springs Park** (706/485-8423, www.campgroundcomputerheroes.com) and **USFS Park** at opposite ends of the lake. Catfish and largemouth bass are the preferred quarry for anglers on Lake Sinclair.

ACCOMMODATIONS AND FOOD

The premier accommodation in Milledgeville is the **C Antebellum Inn** (200 N. Columbia St., 478-453-3993, www.antebelluminn.com, rooms $110-150, cottage $170), which has five rooms in the Greek Revival main house plus an adorable pool cottage with a full-size pool, quite a rarity for B&Bs in these parts. Standard hotels in the area aren't very impressive, but you might try the **Holiday Inn Express** (1839 N. Columbia St., 877/859-5095, www.hiexpress.com, $80-110).

The "satellite location"—if that phrase can be used for such an old-school institution—of the original location in Gray, **C Old Clinton BBQ** (2645 N. Columbia St., 478/454-0084, www.oldclintonbbq.com, Mon.-Thurs. 10am-8pm, Fri.-Sat. 10am-9pm, Sun. 10am-4pm, $5) is considered one of Georgia's top-tier barbecue spots. Their sauce, atypical for Georgia, is of the tangier North Carolina variety. A full platter with the works is under $7, a no-frills pulled pork sandwich less than $3!

You can get a very good gyro and fresh Greek salad at **Metropolis Cafe** (138 N. Wayne St., 478/452-0247, Mon.-Sat. 11am-10pm, Sun. 11am-9pm, $12), which like most every Milledgeville restaurant also has a well-stocked bar. **The Brick** (136 W. Hancock St., 478/452-0089, www.thebrick.info) offers an excellent range of brick-oven pizzas, with an emphasis on the things you wash it down with.

NORTH OF MILLEDGEVILLE
Eatonton

A short drive from Milledgeville in Putnam County is the small, neat town of Eatonton (http://eatonton.com), whose main claim to fame is being the birthplace of writers Joel Chandler Harris and Alice Walker. Don't be deceived by the moribund main drag of Highway 441 through town; Eatonton has

some magnificent antebellum architecture one block west on Madison Avenue.

The **Uncle Remus Museum** (214 Oak St., 706/485-6856, www.uncleremusmuseum.org, Mon.-Sat. 10am-5pm, Sun. 2pm-5pm, free) is right on the main drag on the site of the original homestead of Joseph Sidney Turner, the "Little Boy" in the classic folk tales told by Uncle Remus and chronicled by Joel Chandler Harris. The small but charming museum is within a log cabin, which actually comprises three slave cabins moved from a nearby location, and intended to simulate the cabin of Remus himself. Don't miss the two original watercolor prints from the movie *Song of the South,* donated by Walt Disney himself when the museum opened in the early 1960s. There's also a delightful collection of regionally made shadow box art depicting scenes from the tales, and an extensive display of Uncle Remus books translated into different languages and published all over the world.

There isn't a museum to Alice Walker, but Eatonton markets the **Alice Walker Driving Trail** that includes her girlhood church, Wards Chapel A.M.E. Church. Get the tour brochure at the **Eatonton-Putnam Chamber of Commerce** (305 N. Madison Ave., 706/485-7701, Mon.-Fri. 9am-5pm).

A few miles north of Eatonton off Highway 441 within the grounds of the Georgia 4-H center is the **Rock Eagle Effigy** (350 Rock Eagle Rd., 706/484-2899, www.rockeagle4H.org, daily 9am-5pm, free), an ancient Mississippian stone sculpture between 1,000 and 3,000 years old, one of the oldest native sites found in the state. Partially excavated and then restored during the 1930s by the Civilian Conservation Corps, the rock eagle—intended to depict the bottom of the bird as it flies over one's head—can be viewed from a 1930s era tower. Accompanying signage does a good job of explaining the site's history and significance, as well as its shifting shape over the centuries since white settlers encountered it. Turn off Highway 441 at the Georgia 4-H Center entrance and follow signs along the short drive to the effigy site.

The Uncle Remus Museum

INFORMATION AND SERVICES

Pick up your brochures and tour info at the friendly **Milledgeville Visitors Center** (200 W. Hancock St., 478/452-4687, Mon.-Fri. 9am-5pm, Sat. 10am-4pm). While you're picking up brochures, make sure you get the Milledgeville Historic Walking Tour brochure, a particularly well-done, user-friendly, and attractive little document. This is also where you can catch the **guided trolley tour** (Mon.-Fri. 10am, Sat. 2pm, $12 adults, $5 children), including visits to the Old State Capitol and Lockerly Hall.

The paper of record in town is the *Union Recorder* (www.unionrecorder.com). Georgia College and State University has a high-quality, informative student newspaper: the *Colonnade* (www.gsunade.com).

Oconee Regional Medical Center (821 N. Cobb St., 478/454-3505, www.oconeeregional. com) provides a full range of emergency care.

GETTING THERE AND AROUND

Highway 441 is the key route in and out of Milledgeville, and it can get crowded in the more sprawl-dominated northern and southern approaches to downtown. There is no public transit to speak of, but you don't really need it because of the town's walkability.

MIDDLE GEORGIA

FDR Country

The Pine Mountain-Warm Springs area north of Columbus would be worth visiting just for its natural beauty and lush landscape along the Flint River and its tributaries. The town of Pine Mountain itself is cute and friendly, and just down the road from there you'll find renowned Callaway Gardens Preserve and its famous butterfly collection.

But more importantly to the world at large, as you'll quickly notice from all the things named after him here, the entire area retains enormous impact to this day because of President Franklin D. Roosevelt (FDR). As governor of New York, FDR began visiting the town now called Warm Springs, eventually building his picturesque Little White House there, today a state historic site and museum. The expansive FDR State Park near Pine Mountain isn't only a mecca for area hikers, it also commemorates the president's legacy of community building and conservation, with some particularly well-preserved Depression-era CCC-built structures enjoyed by visitors to this day.

Collectively, the Roosevelt-oriented spots in the Warm Springs-Pine Mountain area represent a slice of American history that is as interesting and enriching as it is comparatively little-known.

WARM SPRINGS

While Warm Springs owes its fame to FDR, the healing properties of its natural spring were well known to the Creek Indians. In the 18th and 19th centuries, the town, originally called Bullochville, was a familiar name to Southerners seeking relief from various ills and escape from the mosquito-borne miasmas of the coast.

Franklin D. Roosevelt, then-governor of New York, began visiting the therapeutic springs in 1924, purchasing the historic Meriwether Inn and the 1700 acres the now-demolished building stood on. The 88-degree

water from ancient sources deep within the surrounding hills (milder than the near-scalding water that some natural spas are known for) gave the town its more descriptive modern name at that time. The gently warming, mineral-infused springs aided the management of Roosevelt's polio, and the surrounding countryside extending north to Pine Mountain—much of which FDR also purchased—provided a restful getaway during the unprecedented four terms of his presidency, during which he faced the twin challenges of the Depression followed by World War II.

This relatively isolated area in the Deep South also had the advantage of making it easier to hide FDR's affliction from prying eyes. But while the White House and the national media essentially conspired to keep the president's polio and reliance on a wheelchair from public knowledge, FDR himself worked strenuously behind the scenes to advance research in the field, not just for himself but for all the similarly afflicted people of the world.

Warm Springs had its own effect on FDR and his policies. Many of his New Deal projects, such as the Rural Electrification Program, came directly from his experiences in this little-visited rural corner of the nation. Besides its charming buildings and some very kitschy shops, Warm Springs today offers several FDR-oriented sites, chief among them the Little White House, an eighth of a mile from the town's main block. Within a short drive are two other sites, both affiliated with the area's healing waters. For more of FDR's impressive legacy in the area or just to have some outdoor fun you'll want to visit nearby Pine Mountain and vicinity.

◖ FDR's Little White House

While Franklin D. Roosevelt began visiting Warm Springs in 1924, it wasn't until 1932—the year he was first elected president—that he had the charming six-room Little White House

(401 Little White House Rd., 706/655-5870, www.gastateparks.org, daily 9am-4:45pm, $10 adults, $6 children) built from Georgia pine in a wooded area down the road from *the* town center. (The first building you'll see when walking toward the Little White House from the entrance building and museum is actually a servants' quarters.)

While the president enjoyed all the amenities you'd expect, including a cook, live-in secretary, servants, and constant U.S. Marine and Secret Service protection, there's a cozy and rustic nature to the humble cottage that is easily felt today as you walk through the small rooms. (History buffs won't be surprised to learn that FDR and First Lady Eleanor Roosevelt had separate bedrooms.)

Fascinating memorabilia are on hand, all arranged as they might have been during FDR's 16 visits here during his presidency (usually a couple of weeks at a time, since it was a day's train ride from Washington). You'll see the leash and collar of little Fala, his beloved

terrier. You'll see a unique Victrola that was an early dictation device; the president recorded some of his "fireside chats" on it, sending them directly to vinyl.

While the Little White House itself is well worth seeing, the state of Georgia in 2004 completed the extensive **FDR Memorial Museum** on site, contiguous with the entrance building and gift shop. Here you'll learn not only about FDR's political career but about his life and times in Warm Springs and how that community shaped some of his domestic policies. There are rooms full of nostalgic memorabilia, mostly gifts to the president, including a huge collection of intricately carved wooden canes (while FDR's wheelchairs were carefully concealed, apparently everyone knew he walked with a cane).

The highlight, however, is the separate memorial area featuring the famous "Unfinished Portrait" of the president by Elizabeth Shoumatoff, which he was posing for in the Little White House when he died of cerebral

© JIM MOREKIS

FDR's Little White House in Warm Springs

hemorrhage on April 12, 1945. Seeing this striking portrait in person—an incredible work of art in its own right, all the more poignant given its incomplete nature—is a moving experience. (Shoumatoff also painted a full version based on memory; it is a few feet away.)

This is a state-administered site, not a National Park Service site, so the rangers and staff tend to be more local in origin and hence a little on the chatty side. They will happily answer questions at length. As befitting this memorial to a man who did so much for the cause of the handicapped, there is an extraordinary level of handicapped accessibility throughout the site.

Roosevelt Warm Springs Institute for Rehabilitation

Right around the corner from the Little White House on Highway 27 is the Roosevelt Warm Springs Institute for Rehabilitation (6135 Roosevelt Hwy., 706/655-5670, www. rooseveltrehab.org, daily 9am-5pm, free), on the site of FDR's first land purchase in the Warm Springs area. It's a working hospital, not a tourist attraction, but you can take a free self-guided tour of the grounds. At the time of FDR the Meriwether Inn stood on this site, but it was soon demolished and replaced with the main entrance building at the Institute, Georgia Hall. Utilizing the great natural gift of the area's famous healing spring water, the Roosevelt Warm Springs Institute became a key center in the advancement of the concept of modern physical therapy as we know it, and it still practices that mission today.

The beautiful campus comprises an enormous quad surrounded by red brick buildings, each with its own story to tell. Highlights include the "Polio Hall of Fame," actually a display of modern sculpture commemorating key figures in the fight against that disease, and views into some of the historic therapy pool areas. For a self-guided tour ask for the brochure at the welcome desk in the lobby area of Georgia Hall. They also offer guided tours

Tuesdays at 10am and 2pm and Wednesdays at 10am.

Note the Roosevelt Warm Springs Institute is *not* the same as the FDR Historic Pools site. Both are on Highway 27 and both have entrances on the same side of the road, which confuses a lot of visitors, but they aren't one and the same.

FDR Historic Pools and Springs

Just down the road from the Roosevelt Warm Springs Institute are the FDR Historic Pools and Springs (Hwy. 27, 706/655-5870, www. gastateparks.org, daily 9am-4:45pm, $10 but that includes admission to the Little White House). At this simple, lovingly curated site you can walk around the famous pools (usually empty) in which the president himself enjoyed the healing spring waters from beneath the nearby hills. He also invited others, especially afflicted children, to undergo therapy here. A small but well-done series of displays chronicles the geological history of the springs, FDR's influence on the area, and the changing face of physical therapy through the years.

In case you're wondering: Yes, the pools are occasionally used, specifically on Labor Day of each year when they are open to the public. You do have to sign up in advance, though, and swim time is limited to 90 minutes per person.

Please note the historic pools are *not* on the campus of the Roosevelt Warm Springs Institute just down the road. Though both sites use the same spring water, they are unaffiliated and have completely separate entrances. If you visit the Little White House you don't have to pay admission here also.

Accommodations and Food

The classic Warm Springs experience is a stay at the C Hotel Warm Springs (47 Broad St., 706/655-2114, www.hotelwarmspringsbb.org, $65-160) on the little main block. During the Roosevelt era, this circa-1907 inn hosted luminaries from all over the world who came to visit the president at the Little White House, including the King and Queen of Spain. The

© JIM MOREKIS

the classic Hotel Warm Springs

rooms are cute and come in all sizes, hence the wide range in rates. They're well appointed with vintage items, and the inn recently became pet-friendly. The associated Tuscawilla Soda Shop downstairs is a great place for a cool drink or some tasty ice cream and fudge, in addition to being historic in its own right: FDR snacked here often.

For other dining I strongly recommend heading north a few minutes to Pine Mountain, which offers a much better and wider variety of food options. However, if you simply must eat in Warm Springs, I suggest **Mac's Barbecue** (5711 Spring St., 706/655-2472, daily 11am-8pm, $5) about a minute walk from the Warm Springs Hotel.

PINE MOUNTAIN

The thoroughly charming little burg of Pine Mountain, while owing much of its current success to the nearby Callaway Gardens attraction, is worth of a visit in and of itself. The main town area consists of a couple of well-restored blocks of shops and cafés, two very good barbecue spots, and the friendly little **Visitors Center** (101 Broad St., 706/663-4000, www.pinemountain.org, Mon.-Sat. 10am-5pm).

Callaway Gardens

It's a bit hard to describe Callaway Gardens (17800 Hwy. 27, 800/225-5292, www.callawaygardens.com, daily 9am-5pm, $18 adults, $9 children) to those who don't know anything about it. Part nature preserve, part kids' theme park, part retiree playground, and part sportsman's dream, its 13,000 acres encompass all those pursuits as gracefully as could reasonably be expected. This major tourist attraction actually has fairly humble roots, literally.

The story goes like this: Local resident and gardener Cason Callaway found a rare azalea growing on his land and began cultivating it. By the early 1950s the gardens had grown to the extent that Cason and his wife, Virginia, formed Callaway Gardens with the main intent of protecting native azalea species. Their son Bo Callaway, who also helped manage the gardens, would gain fame as the first Republican that Georgia voters sent to the U.S. House of Representatives since Reconstruction.

Most visits start with a walk through the $12 million **Virginia Hand Callaway Discovery Center,** which features info kiosks and an orientation video in the big theater. A particular highlight at Callaway is the **Cecil B. Day Butterfly Center,** one of the largest butterfly observatories in North America. This LEED-certified building hosts at least 1,000 butterflies at any given time. The **John A. Sibley Horticultural Center** is a five-acre designed landscape featuring a hybrid garden-greenhouse-indoor waterfall area. Other offerings include a regular bird of prey show, a zipline, a beach, stocked fishing lakes, a nearly 10-mile bike trail, and miles of themed nature and garden walking trails. The annual Christmas light show is always a huge hit.

Callaway Gardens' famous **Mountain View Course** has hosted PGA events in the past and is a consistently high-rated course at the national level. The older course, **Lake View,** is less challenging but more scenic and quietly enjoyable.

Callaway Gardens' well-stocked lakes are known far and wide among anglers. **Mountain Creek Lake** is particularly known for its bass fishing; you can rent a boat or even go on a guided fishing trip. **Robin Lake** at Callaway Gardens bills itself as the world's largest artificially made white sand beach, stretching a mile around the huge lake. The beach is a central part of summer fun at Callaway and hosts the park's Summer Adventure programs, as well as a popular annual waterski tournament.

◖ FDR State Park
It's fitting that Franklin D. Roosevelt State Park (2970 Hwy. 190, 706/663-4858, www.gastateparks.org, daily 7am-10pm, $5 parking) would bear the president's name, since the circa-1935 park is one of the first built under the auspices of his now-legendary Civilian Conservation Corps. Of course, it had a head start; Roosevelt owned most of the land the park now sits on.

Georgia's largest state park, this 9,000-acre preserve is a huge regional draw for the excellent hiking opportunities on its 40 acres of mostly shaded trails through the hardwood and pine forest, complete with occasional waterfall. The centerpiece is the 23-mile **Pine Mountain Trail** traversing the topographical feature of the same name. The historic main building and ranger station offers numerous trail maps; you'll need one if you plan on doing any serious hiking.

Pay a visit to **Dowdell's Knob,** highest point in the park, where the president enjoyed picnics, the scenic vista, and a relaxing time away from his pressures. A life-size sculpture of FDR sitting on his customized removable car seat is near the overlook; you can even sit next to him and take your picture with him.

Several of the cottages in the park are original CCC-era constructions. Take a dip in the historic **Liberty Bell Swimming Pool,** also a CCC project and a very enjoyable pool fed by natural springs.

Horseback Riding
The Pine Mountain area offers terrain perfectly suited for comfortable but fun horseback riding along the trails and ridges. The best bet is **Roosevelt Stables** (1063 Group Camp Rd., 706/628-7463, www.rooseveltstables.com, $40-200 pp). They have a wide range of guided rides, including an overnight "Cowboy Trail" ride.

Accommodations
Callaway Gardens (www.callawaygardens.com) offers a variety of lodging, mostly geared for family getaways and often offering packages that include park admission. For larger families and groups, cottage and villa stays are available from about $300 a night. The 150-room ◖ **Lodge at Callaway Gardens** (4500 Southern Pine Dr., 706/489-3300, www.callawaygardens.com, $220 and up), actually a Marriott property, is the choice for swank upscale lodging, complete with a large, beautiful pool area and the onsite Spa Prunifolia. They offer packages including park admission. Less recommended is the more generic hotel experience at the older, 300-room **Mountain Creek Inn** (17800 Hwy. 27, 706/663-2281, www.callawaygardens.com, $99-150) across from one of the park entrances.

A surprisingly good stay for a low price can be found at the **Days Inn & Suites** (368 S. Main Ave., 706/663-2121, www.daysinn.com, under $100) in Pine Mountain near Callaway Gardens. A nice B&B experience is in the heart of Pine Mountain proper at the charming **Chipley Murrah House** (207 W. Harris St., 706/663-9801, www.chipleymurrah.com, $95-150), with four rooms in the main house and three cottages.

If camping or cabin life is your thing, choose among the 22 cottages and 140 tent and RV campsites offered at historic **FDR State Park** (2970 Hwy. 190, 706/663-4858, www.gastateparks.org, $5 parking, primitive campsites $9 pp, tent and RV sites $25; cottages $100-135, five-night minimum). Many of the tent and RV sites are on scenic Lake Delanor, which also has canoe rental. There are 16 primitive campsites as well in the Pine Mountain Trail network; these are strenuous hike-in sites with no facilities and no water.

Food

I recommend dining in town rather than at the Callaway Gardens facilities if you can help it. If barbecue's your thing, head straight to **◖ The Whistlin' Pig Cafe** (572 S. Main Ave, 706/663-4647, Mon.-Sat. 10:30am-3pm, $7), a real locals' favorite that's also known far and wide for its pulled pork, its absolutely out-of-this-world ribs, and its excellent Brunswick Stew. Their slightly sweet, slightly tangy sauce is particularly nice. Don't confuse them with **Three Lil Pigs** (146 S. Main Ave., 706/307-7109, daily 11am-7pm, $7 cash only), which is not far away on the same side of the road, and also has a local following. I would stick with the pig that whistles.

For a more elegant experience, try the fare at **The Bakery and Cafe at Rose Cottage** (111 Broad St., 706/663-7877, www.rosecottagega. com, Mon.-Fri. 9am-6pm, dinner Fri.-Sat. 6pm-8:30pm, brunch Sun. 11am-3pm, $25), which despite its name actually deals in big-city, high-end cuisine on the dinner menu, such as pan-seared snapper or crab cakes.

If you must eat at Callaway proper, the best bet is the **Country Kitchen** (17800 Hwy. 27, 800/225-5292, www.callawaygardens.com, Sun.-Thurs. 8am-8pm, Fri.-Sat. 8am-9pm, $12) inside the Country Store, which offers a cut above the usual meat 'n' three style Southern fare at diners like this all over Georgia.

SPREWELL BLUFF WILDLIFE MANAGEMENT AREA

One of the great hidden gems of Georgia is the Sprewell Bluff Wildlife Management Area (www.georgiawildlife.org, daily dawn-dusk, free), about a half-hour drive from Warm Springs. Once considered for the site of a dam—vetoed by then-Governor Jimmy Carter—the area is now one of the best ways to enjoy the scenic and unique Flint River, whether by kayak and canoe, fly-fishing, or hiking along several miles of trails. Continuing downstream you will hit the fall line and some serious whitewater rapids, including some Class III and IV rapids, which are for the serious rafter. The most notorious stretch is the mile called "Yellow Jacket Shoals," featuring a total 40-foot drop.

From April-September, **Flint River Outdoor Center** (4429 Woodland Rd., 706/647-2633, www.flintriveroutdoorcenter.com) runs frequent half-day guided water tours that are just right. To get to Sprewell Bluff WMA from Warm Springs take Highway 85 north to Woodbury. Take Highway 74 until you see Old Alabama Road; turn right and follow the signs.

INFORMATION AND SERVICES

The **Pine Mountain Visitors Center** (101 Broad St., 706/663-4000, www.pinemountain. org) provides a range of information for the entire area. The tiny **Warm Springs Welcome Center** (1 Broad St., 706/655-3322, hours vary) is in a restored train depot.

Oconee Regional Medical Center (821 N. Cobb St., 478/454-3505, www.oconeeregional. com) provides a full range of emergency care.

GETTING THERE AND AROUND

U.S. Highway 27 is the main route into and out of Warm Springs. The Pine Mountain area and all other FDR-related sites are along Highway 190.

MIDDLE GEORGIA

Columbus

Unlike some of the more visually monotonous rural areas of Georgia, the state's western edge is scenically inviting with a gently rolling landscape. The area also has a lot of sites well worth visiting, and a key base of operations here is by far its largest city, Columbus. Billing itself as the last city founded of the original 13 colonies and site of the last engagement of the Civil War, Columbus has retained a robust presence into the 21st century, due in no small part to its very close association with the massive U.S. Army installation at Fort Benning.

The sprawling base is directly adjacent to Columbus, and since World War II has provided the city's main economic engine, in addition to training many thousands of Army infantry over the decades. Fort Benning's influence and size have only increased in the post-9/11 era, and you can learn more about its history and exploits at the new National Infantry Museum on post.

That said, there's no particular reason for visitors to interact heavily with the military-industrial complex if they don't want to. The city's vibrant downtown and Riverwalk area are well restored and active at all times of day and night, and Columbus boasts an excellent little art museum, which might surprise you with its offerings.

HISTORY

The classic Southern mill town built on the fall line of a river, Columbus (www.visitcolumbusga.com) was supposedly the last city founded among the original 13 colonies in 1828 and named for Christopher Columbus himself. Columbus wasted no time in exerting its financial muscle. Its location on the key waterway of the Chattahoochee River and at the nexus of many railroad lines made Columbus a major industrial center. Indeed, during the Civil War the city was second only to Richmond, Virginia, as a manufacturing hub for the Confederacy.

The torching of most of the town by the

Union Army at war's end turned out to be a small blessing in disguise in that it gave city fathers a good excuse to rebuild bigger and better. The city's restored Uptown district is a good example of this robust commercial architecture during Columbus's heyday in the Victorian era, when none other than the great Oscar Wilde was among the luminaries who performed at the famous Springer Opera House.

The huge presence of Fort Benning has been an enormous boost to the city's economy since World War II up to the present day. In recent years, downtown revitalization and the long, scenic Riverwalk on the Chattahoochee have sparked visitor interest. To the world at large, however, Columbus is best known as the hometown of several key figures in Southern arts and commerce: author Carson McCullers *(The Heart is a Lonely Hunter)*, "Mother of the Blues" Ma Rainey, Coca-Cola inventor John Pemberton, and longtime Coca-Cola president and philanthropist extraordinaire Robert Woodruff.

SIGHTS
National Civil War Naval Museum

It surprises many people to hear that the National Civil War Naval Museum (1002 Victory Dr., 706/327-9798, www.portcolumbus.org, Tues.-Sat. 10am-4:30pm, Sun.-Mon. 12:30pm-4:30pm, $7.50 adults, $6 children) is located far away from the nearest ocean, but any Civil War buff will tell you that naval warfare during that conflict was mostly of a riverine nature, not out on the deep blue sea. That said, all maritime phases of the war are well represented here, from coastal to blue water.

The first thing you'll see, dominating the entrance to the parking lot, is a replica of the Confederate steamer and blockade runner *Water Witch*, captured in a famous engagement in Savannah. But the main exhibit, comprising at least half the museums' physical space, is devoted to the remains of the massive Confederate ironclad CSS *Jackson*, which was

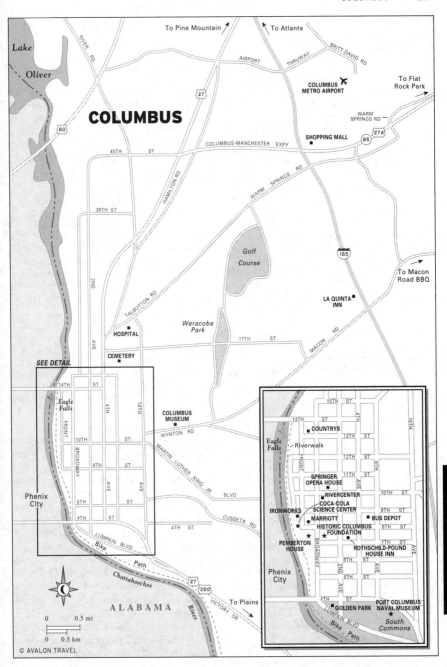

© AVALON TRAVEL

REBELS AT SEA

The Civil War is known primarily for its brutal, large-scale land battles. What's lesser known is its key naval component, one that would have far-reaching effects on world history. Though the Union blockaded the Southern coast almost immediately with war's outbreak, that didn't stop the Confederacy from embarking on a crash course to build its own navy. At its peak, the Confederate Navy counted only about 5,000 personnel—outnumbered literally 10-to-1 by the U.S. Navy in both ships and sailors. However, what the rebels lacked in numbers they made up for in innovation and bravery.

Confederate subs made the first submarine attacks in history. The rebel raider CSS *Alabama* sank Federal shipping as far away as the coast of France. A particularly feared Southern innovation—as represented by CSS *Virginia* or "Merrimac" in its epic fight with the USS *Monitor*—was the ironclad, basically a regular wooden warship stripped to its berth deck and topped with an impenetrable iron superstructure.

These and other innovations quickly caught on, and by war's end a menagerie of bizarre looking contraptions was the norm in both fleets. As awkward as some vessels were—many were simply too underpowered to drag around that extra metal—they were the forerunners of the sophisticated warships to come. (There were even aircraft carriers, in this case hot-air balloons.)

The best place to find out more is at the **National Civil War Naval Museum** (1002 Victory Dr., 706/327-9798, www.portcolumbus.org, Tues.-Sat. 10am-4:30pm, Sun.-Mon. 12:30pm-4:30pm, $7.50 adults, $6 children) in Columbus. You'll leave not only with a certain admiration for the ragtag but plucky Confederate Navy, but also with an appreciation of the profound paradigm shift in naval technology, which echoes in the present day.

based at Columbus and partially destroyed by Union troops at war's end. All that remains are the wooden components of the ship's keel and hull, whose oaky, ashen scent wafts strongly throughout every corner of the museum. A metal framework hanging from the football field-sized ceiling outlines the imposing iron superstructure of the ship when it was still afloat. In the other half of the museum you'll find a walk-in mockup of the Confederate ironclad CSS *Albemarle* and a detailed chronicle of the entire naval aspect of the Civil War, from before Fort Sumter to the final engagement at Columbus itself.

Both the Civil War Naval Museum and the U.S. Infantry Museum at Fort Benning are located off Victory Parkway, a short drive away from each other, so one can easily make an afternoon of visiting the pair.

◖ National Infantry Museum and Soldier Center

The brand-new National Infantry Museum and Soldier Center (1775 Legacy Way, 706/685-5800, www.nationalinfantrymuseum.org, Tues.-Sat. 9am-5pm, Sun. 11am-5pm, $5 donation requested) is a well-funded and well-designed extended love letter to the soldiers, paratroopers, and Rangers of the U.S. Army Infantry, a large portion of whom received their training at Fort Benning, where the museum resides.

The grand entrance, featuring a giant statue of a WWII-era squad leader exhorting his men to attack, sets the tone. From there you enter a series of stimulating multimedia vignettes highlighting notable small-unit infantry actions from the Revolutionary War to Vietnam. From there, the bulk of the museum comprises separate galleries, each dealing with a specific period of U.S. Army history. As of this writing the Colonial-Revolutionary and Civil War galleries weren't completed, but the other galleries are well assembled and informative, featuring a range of uniforms, armament, memorabilia, and instructional multimedia about individual

replica of the *Water Witch* outside the National Civil War Naval Museum

campaigns and engagements through the present day.

A large portion of the museum is set aside for exhibits detailing not only the history of Fort Benning itself and its contribution to the area, but the strenuous daily life of the enlisted soldiers and officers who train there. Military families in particular will enjoy these displays. An affiliated IMAX theater shows thematic movies in the IMAX format, in addition to special seasonal films. Check the website for show times and charges.

While the museum is located on post, thankfully you will not have to show ID or insurance papers upon entry, as is often the case with other attractions on military bases; though do be aware that you should always follow the speed limit while on post.

Coca-Cola Space Science Center

The iconic soft drink and outer space may not seem to have much to do with each other, but of course the name of the Coca-Cola Space Science Center (701 Front Ave., 706/649-1470, www.ccssc.org, Mon.-Fri. 10am-4pm, Sat. 10:30am-8pm, $6 adults, $4 children) is more a nod to the drink company's roots in Columbus. The site is currently operated by Columbia State University and has a fitting emphasis on education and research and is still a lot of fun. Major components include the Omnisphere Theater, which shows various films about space and space exploration, and the Mead Observatory, which holds numerous public-viewing sessions of the night sky. Kids in particular will enjoy the Challenger Center's emphasis on hands-on astronomy and flight simulation activity.

Riverwalk

Aside from Fort Benning, the greatest civic pride in Columbus is the Riverwalk, a lit, paved, extensive multi-level trail along the banks of the Chattahoochee, with Front Avenue as the nearest parallel street Uptown. The Riverwalk is part of the nearly 15-mile

the stirring National Infantry Museum in Columbus

Chattahoochee River Trail, which extends south through Fort Benning, ending at Oxbow Meadows Educational Center. The upper levels of the Riverwalk feature more scenic views, while the lower levels take you right along the river. In fact, at the base of Woodruff Park, near the Columbus State University Uptown campus, you can take steps down to the edge and literally put your feet in the river. While there, look directly across the river to see (and very often hear) the civic amphitheater of Phenix City, Alabama.

Uptown Columbus

Most cities would call this "downtown," but in Columbus it's Uptown (www.uptown-columbusga.com). It's a National Historic District and the center of Columbus social and nightlife. The bulk of the activity centers on Broadway, which has a grassy median with a fountain.

Just a couple of blocks off Broadway is the renowned **Springer Opera House** (103 10th St., 706/324-5714, www.springeroperahouse. org), a handsome, cast iron balcony-bedecked Victorian venue of 700 seats that has hosted luminaries from Oscar Wilde to Will Rogers to Tom Thumb to Franklin Roosevelt to Garrison Keilor (a "walk of stars" is on the sidewalk in front of the building). Built in 1871, the Springer was declared the official state theater of Georgia in the 1970s by then-Governor Jimmy Carter. It continues to host a regular schedule of performances by its in-house theater company.

Directly adjacent to Uptown and overlooking the Chattahoochee is the well-manicured RiverPark Campus of **Columbus State University** (www.columbusstate.edu), home of the university's art, music, and theater departments. The associated events, not to mention expenditures by students and faculty, are a big part of Uptown's revival and current success. Architecture buffs might appreciate the pleasantly ornate, circa-1930 Mediterranean-style **Ledger-Enquirer Building** (17 W. 12th St.), which is headquarters of the local daily paper and on the National Register of Historic Places.

Columbus Museum

The Columbus Museum (1251 Wynnton Rd., 706/748-2562, www.columbusmuseum.com, Tues.-Wed. and Fri.-Sat. 10am-5pm, Thurs. 10am-8pm, Sun. 1pm-5pm, free) is among the best-curated museums I've seen in a medium-to-small market city, with the not-trivial added benefit of having free admission every day. The space itself is bright, inviting, clean, and contemporary in feel, but without the sense of lonely emptiness that many such modern museums tend to evoke. The permanent collection boasts an excellent variety of stimulating American impressionists, and the third floor hosts rotating exhibits of national and international value and interest. There's a standing exhibit on Columbus history as well, with a particular focus on the Native American presence.

Keep in mind it is not within walking

The Springer Opera House hosted some pretty big names back in the day.

distance of Uptown Columbus, where the restaurants and cafés are; but the drive is a short one.

Carson McCullers Center for Writers and Musicians

Columbus State University now owns and operates the Carson McCullers Center for Writers and Musicians (1519 Stark Ave., 706/565-4021, www.mccullerscenter.org, appointment only, $5) based in the Smith-McCullers House, childhood home of the Columbus-born novelist. In a nice twist that McCullers herself would no doubt appreciate, not only is there a museum devoted to her life and an archive of her works and letters, there are continuing workshops and residencies for up-and-coming writers.

Oxbow Meadows Environmental Learning Center

A project of Columbus State University, Oxbow Meadows Environmental Learning Center (3535 South Lumpkin Rd., 706/507-8550, oxbow.columbusstate.edu, Tues.-Fri. 9am-4pm, Sat. 10am-4pm, Sun. noon-4pm, free) is a hands-on learning center whose main claim to fame is the "Treetop Trail," a tour through the grounds on a high suspension footbridge, the better to see the birds and critters in their natural habitats. The 30-minute guided tours include binocular rental. Oxbow also offers numerous lectures and informative programs by certified naturalists. It's also one terminus of the long Chattahoochee River Trail, which includes the scenic Riverwalk at Uptown Columbus.

Linwood Cemetery

It's not as evocative as Savannah's Bonaventure or Macon's Rose Hill, but Columbus's Linwood Cemetery (721 Linwood Blvd., www.linwood-cemetery.org, daily dawn-dusk, free) is quite historic, literally going back to the city's founding in the late 1820s. Notables buried here include Coca-Cola inventor John Pemberton

MIDDLE GEORGIA

(who was wounded in the last battle of the Civil War, fought in Columbus); Francis Springer, who built the Springer Opera House; and Henry Benning, the Confederate general for whom Fort Benning is named.

PERFORMING ARTS

Columbus has something of a theater district in the historic Uptown area along the river. The key venue is the **RiverCenter for the Performing Arts** (Broadway and 10th St., 706/256-3612, www.rivercenter.org), which is where most cool concerts and shows happen, from Bonnie Raitt to *Seussical the Musical*. Just around the corner is the historic **Springer Opera House** (103 10th St., 706/327-3688, www.springeroperahouse.org), which hosts a professional theater company and its regular season schedule. Very nearby at its Uptown campus, Columbus State University holds a regular series of performances at the **Riverside Theatre** (901 Front Ave., 706/507-8400, http://theatre.columbusstate.edu) in the new Theatre and Art Complex overlooking the Chattahoochee River. The historic 1924 **Liberty Theatre Cultural Center** (823 8th Ave., 706/653-7566), the premier African American showcase during the years of segregation and now on the National Register of Historic Places, hosts shows and concerts on a regular basis.

RECREATION

Most recreation in Columbus centers along the Chattahoochee River. The most obvious choice is a walk or ride along the **Chattahoochee River Trail,** that long trail which now extends roughly 15 miles from Uptown Columbus all the way down to Fort Benning itself, concluding at Oxbow Meadows. The Trail includes the Riverwalk section adjacent to the popular Uptown area of restaurants and nightlife.

But by far the biggest news in Columbus outdoors life is the pending completion of the **Whitewater Project** (www.columbusgawhite-water.com), more popularly known as "River City Rush." Two antiquated earthen dams near the falls of the river have been demolished to

reveal a magnificent 2.5-mile whitewater run that goes from Class I all the way to Class IV. The city, which bills the Whitewater Project as the longest urban whitewater course in the world, hopes it will be a major spur for ecotourism development.

ACCOMMODATIONS

The vast military presence in Columbus means there is plenty of inexpensive lodging. While quality can vary, generally speaking you can book a brand-name hotel for well under what you'd pay in many other markets.

Under $150

The pet-friendly **C Staybridge Suites Columbus** (1678 Whittlesley Rd., 706/507-7700, www.sbscolumbus.com, $100) is close to I-185 and has a nice kitchen in each suite, though there is free hot breakfast each morning. The **Hampton Inn Columbus** (7390 Bear Lane, 706/256-2222, www.hamptoninn.com, $100) is also off I-185 and is one of the least expensive Hampton Inns you'll find, with all the guarantee of quality typical of the chain. There are no hidden charges here and the Wi-Fi and parking really are free.

$150-300

The **C Rothschild-Pound House Inn** (201 Seventh St., 706/322-4075, www.thepound-houseinn.com, $185-365) is the premier B&B in Columbus, set in an ornately appointed Second Empire-style home. There are four sumptuous suites in the main house itself, with another six spread out in three cottages that are part of the whole enterprise. Breakfast is in the grand (and rich) Southern style, with the added modern twist of Fair Trade coffee. Rates depend on the season and the size of the cottage. Do keep in mind that occupancy is capped at two guests with the exception of the Garrett Suite in the main house, which has two queen beds.

FOOD

Every imaginable chain restaurant is available in the Columbus area. Otherwise, your best bet is to stick with pub food, which seems to set the standard here.

American

Also known for its lively bar scene, **The Cannon Brewpub** (1041 Broadway, 706/653-2337, www.thecannonbrewpub.com, Mon.-Thurs. 11am-10pm, Fri.-Sun. 11am-11pm, $15) is a linchpin of Uptown nightlife. All of the burgers are excellent, and you can get them with their signature sweet potato "sunspots." Of course, you have your selection of hand-crafted beers brewed onsite. Try the sampler flight of beers if you can't quite decide. Just down the street, a boisterous gastropub atmosphere is also the order of the day at **The Loft** (1032 Broadway, 706/596-8141, www.theloft.com, Tues.-Fri. 11:30am-2:30pm and 5pm-11pm, Sat. 5pm-11pm, $12), one of the best all-around locally-owned restaurants in town. They have live jazz every Friday night.

Barbecue

There are two major purveyors of Columbus 'cue, and each has their fan base. The most well known and the one with the longest tradition is **Country's** (3137 Mercury Dr., 706/563-7604, www.countrysbarbecue.com, Sun.-Thurs. 11am-10pm, Fri.-Sat. 11am-11pm, $8-12), which has a well-rounded menu featuring equally good pulled pork, grilled chicken, ribs, and brisket. Seasonal favorites are always welcomed by regular patrons. Tuesday night is all-you-can-eat BBQ chicken night, and Friday and Saturday nights bring live bluegrass to the original location. They have an Uptown location too (1329 Broadway), a little closer to the action.

However, some aficionados will tell you that the humble **Pepper's** (4620 Warm Springs Rd., 706/569-0051, Mon.-Tue. and Sat. 10:30am-2:30pm, Wed.-Fri. 10:30am-8pm, $7) is at least as good, with a leaner cut of meat, and offers a particularly tasty take on that Georgia side dish known as Brunswick Stew.

Coffee

When I'm in Columbus I never miss a stop at **Fountain City Coffee** (1007 Broadway, 706/494-6659, www.fountaincitycoffee.com, Mon.-Thurs. 6:30am-10:30pm, Fri. 6:30am-2am, Sat. 8am-2am, Sun. 9am-8pm), the best of the small number of uptown java joints. It's a cool place to hang out, and the friendly baristas really know what they're doing. Notice the extraordinarily late weekend hours.

Deli

Middle Georgia isn't known for its delicatessen activity, but by far the best deli for miles around is **Jason's Deli** (5555 Whittlesey Blvd., 706/494-8857, www.jasonsdeli.com, daily 8am-10pm, $10), known for its robust sandwiches, very fresh salads, and particularly tasty desserts. However, they do offer lighter portions on some menu items for those watching the calories.

INFORMATION AND SERVICES

The spacious and well-done **Columbus Visitor Center** (900 Front Ave., 706/322-1613, www.visitcolumbusga.com, Mon.-Fri. 8:30am-5:30pm, Sat. 10am-2pm) is conveniently located.

For emergencies go to **The Medical Center** of the Columbus Regional Healthcare System (710 Center St., 706/571-1000, www.columbusregional.com).

The newspaper of record is the *Ledger-Enquirer* (www.ledger-enquirer.com).

GETTING THERE AND AROUND
By Car

Columbus is on the Georgia-Alabama border and several highways lead directly to and from both states over the Chattachoochee River. A major interstate doesn't pass through, however a spur of I-75, I-185, does take you directly to Columbus. When driving in Columbus always keep in mind that Fort Benning in effect surrounds the city on the Georgia side. While highways going through that military facility are fully accessible to the public, traffic laws tend to be more tightly enforced there.

By Air
Columbus Metropolitan Airport (3250 W. Britt David Rd., 706/324-2449, www.flycolumbusga.com, airport code CSG) hosts flights by Delta and American Eagle.

By Bus
Columbus is served by a **Greyhound** (818 Veterans Pkwy., 706/322-7391, www.greyhound.com) station. There's a good public transportation service, **METRA** (www.columbusga.org, fare $1.30) with extensive routes throughout the metro area. They run a charming trolley service through the Uptown-downtown-historic areas.

OUTSIDE COLUMBUS
◖ Pasaquan
On the outskirts of Buena Vista about 20 miles outside Columbus is one of the most unique places anywhere, the folk art compound of Pasaquan (238 Eddie Martin Rd., 229/649-9444, www.pasaquan.blogspot.com, Apr.-Nov. first Sat. of the month 10am-4pm, $5). The sprawling collection of almost psychedelic pagoda-like temples, statues, and masonry walls, all of them brightly painted, is the product of the late visionary artist Eddie Owens Martin, or St. EOM. The inspiration came while Martin was living in New York City following a dream sparked by a high fever. In the vision several "people of the future" from a place they called Pasaquan selected Martin to devote his life to spreading peace through art. He moved down to his mother's parcel of land and began work, supporting his endeavor through fortunetelling.

Now run by a nonprofit organization, Pasaquan was put on the National Register of Historic Places in 2008. In all, there are over 2,000 works by Martin on the seven acres, which also include an 1880s farmhouse. Sadly, Martin committed suicide in 1986. Note the very limited hours; though for a $100 donation you can make an appointment for a private visit. To get here from the Buena Vista town square, drive north 1.5 miles on Highway 41, then veer left onto Highway 137. Go about 4.5 miles and take a right on Eddie Martin Road. Pasaquan is a half-mile north.

Along I-16: Statesboro to Swainsboro

The stretch of I-16 between Macon and Savannah is relatively unexciting. While not really much less exciting than any other drive through a heavily rural area, there is a certain lonesome, nondescript feel to it. In any case, there are actually a few interesting things to do and see in the area. For a break, there's a state-run rest area at around mile marker 45 near Laurens.

POINTS NORTH
Statesboro
Cynics might say there's a good reason Blind Willie McTell wrote "Statesboro Blues" about his hometown, a tune later famously covered by the Allman Brothers. While it's true there's not much to do in "the 'Boro" (www.visitstatesboroga.com), the huge presence of **Georgia Southern University** (www.georgiasouthern.edu) does give this town, about 15 miles off I-16, a leg up on most in this often-overlooked area. Things have also spiced up a bit recently thanks to a referendum allowing the sale of alcoholic beverages in this formerly totally dry county.

The most interesting thing open to the public at GSU is the Center for Wildlife Education, specifically its **Lamar Q. Ball Jr. Raptor Center** (1461 Forest Dr., 912/478-0831, Mon.-Fri. 9am-5pm, Sat. 1pm-5pm, free), a research facility that stages frequent wildlife programs, generally each afternoon at 3:30pm. (Georgia Southern sports teams are called the Eagles. Get it?) Highlights are the Thursday "Flight Show" in the amphitheater, involving various birds of prey from the Center.

Friday afternoons usually bring a show devoted to the Center's hawks.

Other offerings on the sprawling campus include the **Georgia Southern University Museum** (2142 Southern Dr., 912/478-5444, Tues.-Fri. 9am-5pm, Sat.-Sun. 2pm-5pm, $2), which might surprise with the depth and variety of its historical and archaeological exhibits. A paleontological highlight is the 40-million-year-old "Vogtle Whale," oldest whale fossil found in North America. The newly upgraded **Georgia Southern Planetarium** (Math & Physics Building, 912/478-5292, by reservation), part of the university's physics and astronomy department, has a state of the art digital full dome projector. Non-student visitors need reservations.

GSU has been a perennial football power in the Football Championship Subdivision (formerly Division I-AA), and the Eagles play in Paulson Stadium to fanatical crowds of 20,000, which fill area hotels and restaurants on football weekends during the fall. Their bald eagle mascot "Freedom" makes a flight from press box to field before every home game. There's been talk recently of moving the team up to the more competitive Football Bowl Subdivision.

Downtown Statesboro has seen an attractive Main Street-style revitalization recently. The key piece of the puzzle is the **Averitt Center for the Arts** (33 E. Main St., 912/212-2787, www.averittcenterforthearts.org), located in a historic bank building. The Averitt Center hosts frequent performances and houses the Emma Kelly Theater, named after the Statesboro songstress and pianist featured in *Midnight in the Garden of Good and Evil*.

One of the biggest things to happen in this neck of the woods was the $10 million **Splash in the 'Boro** (1388 Hwy. 24, 912/489-3000, www.splashintheboro.com, Mon.-Sat. 10am-6pm, Sun. noon-6pm, $10-12), a waterpark that comes in very handy during Statesboro's extremely hot summers. There is a variety of slides for different age groups and a lazy river. There's an off-season when it's closed

during the cooler months, so check ahead on the website.

ACCOMMODATIONS AND FOOD

A favorite downtown spot to get a tasty bite from breakfast on through dinner is **⟨ Sugar Magnolia** (106 Savannah Ave., 912/764-2090, www.sugarmagnoliabakery.com, Tues.-Wed. 7am-4pm, Thurs.-Fri. 7am-8pm, Sat. 7am-9pm, Sun. 10am-2pm, $15). While their claim to fame is baked goods, they have a great all-around menu with no weak links. Pizza nights on Thursdays and burger nights on Saturdays in particular are big hits, with locals packing the place.

Another fun stop is **Manny's Neighborhood Grille** (230 S. Main St., 912/489-1004, www.mannysgrills.com, Mon.-Wed. 11am-10pm, Thurs.-Sat. 11am-11pm, Sun. 11am-9pm, $15), which has a solid Greek menu served late, including lots of pita choices. They also have very good pizzas and what are commonly considered the best burgers in town.

Statesboro is a college football town, so you'll find plenty of chain lodging all around, the better to accommodate all those parents and fans. But for a classier choice try **Georgia's Bed & Breakfast** (123 S Zetterower Ave., 912/489-6330, $100), set in a historic Federal-style home. The hospitality is everything you'd expect and the breakfasts in particular are outstanding.

Ohoopee Dunes Natural Area

The entire coastal plain between Macon and Savannah was underwater 60 million years ago. For evidence, go to the Swainsboro vicinity and check out the Ohoopee Dunes Natural Area (www.georgiawildlife.com), white sandy deposits built up by wind as the water receded. This 3,000-acre co-managed tract is but part of a 22,000-acre sandhill ecosystem stretching over 60 miles along the Ohoopee and Little Ohoopee Rivers to their junction with the Altamaha River. In addition to the low dunes themselves, interesting wildlife include thriving groups of sand-burrowing gopher tortoises, threatened species like the eastern indigo snake and striped newt, and the Ohoopee Dunes moth, which lives only in this area. Botanical hallmarks include the distinctive stunted turkey oak, longleaf pine stands, wiregrass, and threatened plants like the sandhill milk vetch and sandhill rosemary.

There are three separate tracts. To get to the McLeod Bridge Tract, go 1.5 miles west of Swainsboro on U.S. 80, then right on county road 456/McLeod Bridge Road. To get to the U.S. 80 tract, go west of Swainsboro 4.1 miles on U.S. 80 until you see a small unpaved parking area and kiosk. To get to the Halls Bridge tract, take U.S. 80 west of Swainsboro about a mile, then make a left on county road 160/Halls Bridge Road to the crossing. You can launch a canoe or kayak from there if you'd like.

George L. Smith State Park
Paddlers and birders will especially enjoy the boat-ramp-equipped George L. Smith State Park (371 George L. Smith State Park Rd., 478/763-2759, www.gastateparks.org, daily 7am-10pm, $5 parking, campsites $24-26, cottages $110-120), which offers 10 miles of canoe trails and a rich variety of wading birds such as blue heron and ibis along the lake, complete with 1880s gristmill and covered bridge. There are also hiking trails and a campground with 25 tent and RV sites and eight cottages.

Magnolia Springs State Park
One of the more interesting parks in Georgia, Magnolia Springs State Park (1053 Magnolia Springs Dr., 478/982-1660, www.gastateparks.org, daily 7am-10pm, $5 parking, campsites $25-28, cottages $125-145) is named for a unique natural feature, a natural spring which still flows about seven million gallons per day and helps support a robust wetlands environment, which you can enjoy either from the boardwalk over the spring or by kayak and canoe. There's also a stocked 28-acre lake fed by the spring.

The spring is also indirectly responsible for the other really interesting thing about the park: its former role as the location of the largest POW camp in the Confederacy, **Camp Lawton,** put here because the spring would provide water for the thousands of Union prisoners kept within its high wooden walls. Founded specifically to relieve overcrowding at the much more notorious camp at Andersonville farther southwest, Camp Lawton actually held more prisoners during its brief six weeks of operation before the arrival of Sherman's forces provoked a hasty evacuation. Archaeology, mostly through ground-penetrating radar, is still going on; in 2010 a team from Georgia Southern finally found the long-rumored location of the stockade wall. Despite its fairly large size (1,000 acres), Magnolia Springs has comparatively few accommodations: only 26 tent and RV sites and eight cottages, one of which is dog friendly.

POINTS SOUTH
Vidalia Onion Museum
One of Georgia's main exports is the delectable sweet onion. While Vidalia isn't the only place it's grown, the little town gave its name to the vegetable, memorialized at the new Vidalia Onion Museum (100 Vidalia Sweet Onion Dr., 912/537-1918, www.vidaliaonion.org, Mon.-Fri. 9am-5pm), opened in 2011. Interactive displays explain the science behind the onions' sweetness and the economic benefits of the crop to the region. There's an onsite onion patch where you can see the little sweeties growing in the sandy soil, and of course onions are for sale!

Claxton
For reasons unknown to science, fruitcakes are a popular Christmas gift in some quarters, most often as fundraisers for various groups and civic organizations. The acknowledged headquarters of this acquired taste is the little town of Claxton, "Fruitcake Capital of the World," specifically **Claxton Bakery** (203 W. Main St., 912/739-3441, www.claxtonfruitcake.com, Mon.-Sat. 8am-5pm), established over 100 years ago by an Italian immigrant.

Magnolia Springs State Park

While you can't actually tour the facility, you can watch them being made through some large windows. And of course you can sample and buy them!

Gordonia-Alatamaha State Park

The comparatively full-service Gordonia-Alatamaha State Park (322 Park Lane, Hwy. 280 W., 912/557-7744, www.gastateparks. org, daily 7am-10pm, $5 parking, campsites $19-30, cottages $105-115) near Reidsville—note the spelling is slightly different from the nearby Altamaha River—offers 29 tent and RV sites, five cottages, one of which is dog friendly, the 18-hole **Brazell's Creek Golf Course** (www.georgiagolf.com), miniature golf, and fishing and paddleboat rental on the stocked 12-acre lake.

SAVANNAH

Rarely has a city owed so much to the vision of one person than Savannah owes to General James Edward Oglethorpe. Given the mission by King George II of England to buffer Charleston from the Spanish, this reformer had a far more sweeping vision in mind. After befriending a local Creek people, Oglethorpe laid out his settlement in a deceptively simple plan that is still studied the world over as a model of nearly perfect urban design. Many of his other progressive ideas—such as prohibiting slavery and hard liquor, to name two—soon went by the wayside. But the legacy of his original plan lives on to this day.

Savannah was built as a series of rectangular "wards," each built around a central square. As the city grew, each square took on its own characteristics, depending on who lived on the square and how they made their livelihood. It is this individuality that is so well documented in John Berendt's *Midnight in the Garden of Good and Evil*. The squares of Savannah's downtown—since 1965 a National Landmark Historic District—are also responsible for the city's walkability, another defining characteristic. Just as cars entering a square must yield to traffic already within, pedestrians are obliged to slow down and interact with the surrounding environment, both constructed and natural. You become participant and audience simultaneously, a feat made easier by the local penchant for easy conversation.

In an increasingly homogenized society, Savannah is one of the last places left where eccentricity is celebrated and even encouraged. This outspoken, often stubborn determination

HIGHLIGHTS

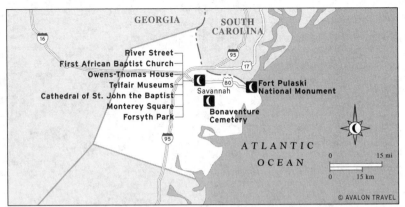

LOOK FOR ◖ TO FIND RECOMMENDED SIGHTS, ACTIVITIES, DINING, AND LODGING.

◖ **River Street:** Despite River Street's tourist tackiness, there's still nothing like strolling the cobblestones amid the old cotton warehouses, enjoying the cool breeze off the river, and watching the huge ships on their way to and from the bustling port (page 238).

◖ **First African Baptist Church:** The oldest black congregation in the United States still meets in this historic sanctuary, a key stop on the Underground Railroad (page 242).

◖ **Owens-Thomas House:** Possibly the country's best example of Regency architecture and definitely an example of state-of-the-art historic preservation in action, this is Savannah's single greatest historical home (page 248).

◖ **Telfair Museums:** Old school meets new school in this museum complex that comprises the traditional collection of the Telfair Academy of Arts and Sciences and the ultra-modern Jepson Center for the Arts, both within a stone's throw of each other (page 250).

◖ **Cathedral of St. John the Baptist:** This soaring Gothic Revival edifice is comple-mented by its ornate interior and its matchless location on verdant Lafayette Square, stomping ground of the young Flannery O'Connor (page 254).

◖ **Monterey Square:** Perhaps Savannah's quintessential square, with some of the best examples of local architecture and world-class ironwork all around its periphery (page 256).

◖ **Forsyth Park:** A verdant expanse ringed with old live oaks, with chockablock memorials. The true center of downtown life, it is Savannah's backyard (page 262).

◖ **Bonaventure Cemetery:** This historic burial ground is the final resting place for some of Savannah's favorite citizens, including the great Johnny Mercer, and makes great use of its setting on the banks of the Wilmington River (page 265).

◖ **Fort Pulaski National Monument:** This well-run site, built with the help of a young Robert E. Lee, is not only historically significant, its beautiful setting makes it a great place for the entire family (page 270).

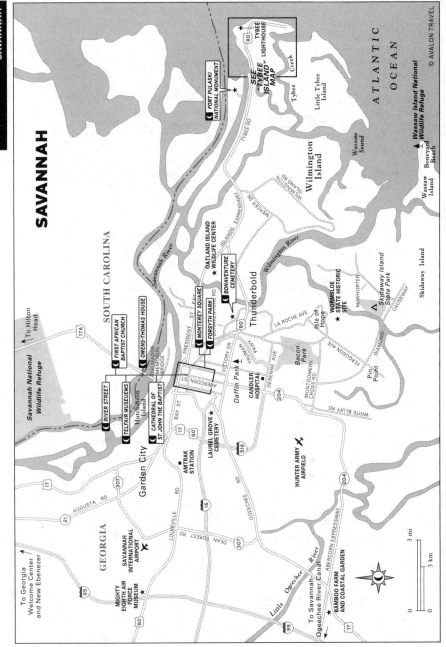

SAVANNAH

SOUTH CAROLINA

GEORGIA

To Hilton Head

To Georgia Welcome Center and New Ebenezer

Savannah National Wildlife Refuge

ATLANTIC OCEAN

SEE "TYBEE ISLAND" MAP

TYBEE LIGHTHOUSE

FORT PULASKI NATIONAL MONUMENT

Tybee Creek

Little Tybee Island

Tybee Island

Wassaw Island National Wildlife Refuge

Boneyard Beach

Wassaw Island

Wassaw Sound

Savannah River

TYBEE RD

WILMINGTON ISLAND RD

MERCER DR

Wilmington Island

Wilmington River

RIVER STREET

TELFAIR MUSEUMS

Hutchinson Island

TALMADGE MEMORIAL BRIDGE

FIRST AFRICAN BAPTIST CHURCH

OWENS-THOMAS HOUSE

CATHEDRAL OF ST. JOHN THE BAPTIST

PRESIDENT ST. EXT.

MONTEREY SQUARE

FORSYTH PARK

OATLAND ISLAND WILDLIFE CENTER

BONAVENTURE CEMETERY

SKIDAWAY RD

Thunderbolt

LA ROCHE AVE

WORMSLOE STATE HISTORIC SITE

Isle of Hope

DIAMOND CAUSEWAY

McWHORTER

Skidaway Island State Park

Skidaway Island

BAY ST

17

80

VICTORY DR

TRUMAN PKWY

ABERCORN ST

Daffin Park

CANDLER HOSPITAL

DERENNE AVE

BACON AVE

FERGUSON AVE

Bacon Park

Pin Point

MONTGOMERY CROSS RD

204

WHITE BLUFF RD

LAUREL GROVE CEMETERY

AMTRAK STATION

Garden City

AUGUSTA RD

17

307

21

LOUISVILLE RD

DEAN FOREST RD

16

OGEECHEE RD

516

204

HUNTER ARMY AIRFIELD

MIGHTY EIGHTH AIR FORCE MUSEUM

95

80

SAVANNAH INTERNATIONAL AIRPORT

307

ABERCORN EXPRESSWAY

Ogeechee River

Little Ogeechee River

To Savannah-Ogeechee River Canal

BAMBOO FARM AND COASTAL GARDEN

95

17

0   3 mi

0   3 km

© AVALON TRAVEL

to make one's own way in the world is personified by the old Georgia joke about Savannah being the capital of "the state of Chatham," a reference to the county in which it resides. In typical contrarian fashion, Savannahians take this nickname, ostensibly a pejorative, as a compliment.

Savannah is also known for being able to show you a rowdy good time, and not only during its massive, world-famous St. Patrick's Day celebration. Savannahians, like New Orleanians, will use any excuse for a party, and any excuse to drink in the full flavor of natural beauty here—whether in the heady glory of a spring day with all the flowers blooming, or the sweet release of the long-awaited autumn, brisk and bracing but not so crisp that you can't wear shorts.

HISTORY

By the early 1700s, the land south of Charleston was a staging area for attacks by the Spanish and Native Americans. So in 1732, King George II granted a charter to the Trustees of Georgia, a proprietary venture that was the brainchild of a 36-year-old general and member of parliament, General James Edward Oglethorpe. On February 12, 1733, the *Anne* landed with 114 passengers along the high bluff on the south bank of the Savannah River. Oglethorpe bonded with Tomochichi, the local Creek Indian chief, and the colony prospered. (Contrary to what locals might tell you, Savannah did not get its name because it resembles a grassy savanna. The city is named for the Savannah River, which itself is named for a wandering, warring offshoot of a local Shawnee people.)

Ever the idealist, Oglethorpe had a plan for the new "classless society" in Savannah that prohibited slavery, rum, and—wait for it—lawyers! But as the settlers enviously eyed the dominance of Charleston's slave-based rice economy, the Trustees bowed to public pressure and relaxed restrictions on slavery and rum. By 1753, the crown reclaimed the charter, making Georgia America's 13th colony. Though part of the new United States in 1776, Savannah was captured by British forces in 1778, who held the city against a combined assault a year later. After the Revolution, Savannah became the first capital of Georgia, a role it had until 1786.

Despite hurricanes and yellow fever epidemics, Savannah's heyday was the antebellum period from 1800 to 1860, when for a time it outstripped Charleston as a center of commerce. By 1860, Savannah's population doubled after an influx of European immigrants, chief among them Irish workers coming to lay track on the new Central of Georgia line.

Blockaded for most of the Civil War, Savannah didn't see much action other than the fall of Fort Pulaski in April 1862, when a Union force successfully laid siege using rifled artillery, a revolutionary new technology that instantly rendered the world's masonry forts obsolete. War came to Savannah's doorstep when General William T. Sherman's March to the Sea concluded with his capture of the town in December 1864. Sherman sent a now-legendary telegram to President Lincoln granting him the city as a Christmas present with these words: "I beg to present you as a Christmas gift, the City of Savannah with 150 heavy guns and plenty of ammunition and also about 25,000 bales of cotton."

After a lengthy Reconstruction period, Savannah began reaching out to the outside world. From 1908 to 1911 it was a national center of road racing. In the Roaring '20s, native son Johnny Mercer rose to prominence, and the great Flannery O'Connor was born in downtown Savannah. World War II provided an economic lift, with Savannah being a major center for the building of Liberty Ships to transport soldiers and equipment overseas. But the city was still known as the "pretty woman with a dirty face," as Britain's Lady Astor famously described it in 1946. Almost in answer to Astor's quip, city leaders in the 1950s began a misguided program to retrofit the city's infrastructure for the automobile era. This frenzy of demolition cost such civic treasures as Union Station, the City Auditorium, and the old DeSoto Hotel. Savannah's preservation movement had its seed in the fight by

OGLETHORPE: VISIONARY ARISTOCRAT

One of the greatest products of the Enlightenment, James Edward Oglethorpe was a study in contrasts, embodying all the vitality, contradiction, and ambiguity of that turbulent age. A stern moralist yet an avowed liberal, an aristocrat with a populist streak, an abolitionist and an anti-Catholic, a man of war who sought peace—the founder of Georgia would put his own inimitable stamp on the new nation to follow, a legacy personified to this day in the city he designed.

After making a name for himself fighting the Turks, the young London native and Oxford graduate would return home only to serve a two-year prison sentence for killing a man in a brawl. The experience was a formative one for Oglethorpe, scion of a large and upwardly mobile family now forced to see how England's underbelly really lived. Upon his release, the 25-year-old Oglethorpe ran for the "family" House of Commons seat once occupied by his father and two brothers, and won. He made a name for himself as a campaigner for human rights and an opponent of slavery. Another jail-related epiphany came when Oglethorpe saw a friend die of smallpox in debtors prison. More than ever, Oglethorpe was determined to right what he saw as a colossal wrong in the draconian English justice system. His crusade took the form of establishing a sanctuary for debtors in North America.

To that end, he and his friend Lord Perceval established the Trustees, a 21-member group who lobbied King George for permission to establish such a colony. The grant from the king—who was more interested in containing the Spanish than in any humanitarian concerns—would include all land between the Altamaha and Savannah Rivers and from the headwaters of these rivers to the "south seas." Ironically, there were no debtors among Savannah's original colonists. Nonetheless, the new settlement was indeed a reflection of its founder's core values, banning rum as a bad influence (though beer and wine were allowed), prohibiting slavery, and eschewing lawyers on the theory that a gentleman should always be able to defend himself.

Nearing 40 and distracted by war with the Spanish, Oglethorpe's agenda gradually eroded in the face of opposition from settlers, who craved not only the more hedonistic lifestyle of their neighbors to the north in Charleston but the economic advantage that city enjoyed in the use of slave labor. In nearly the same hour as his greatest military victory, crushing the Spanish at the Battle of Bloody Marsh on St. Simons Island, Oglethorpe also suffered an ignominious defeat: being replaced as head of the 13th colony, which he had founded.

He went back to England, never to see the New World again. But his heart was always with the colonists. After successfully fending off a political attack and a court-martial, Oglethorpe married and commenced a healthy retirement. He supported independence for the American colonies, making a point to enthusiastically receive the new ambassador from the United States, one John Adams. The old general died on June 30, 1785, at age 88. Fittingly for this lifelong philanthropist and humanitarian, his childhood home in Godalming, Surrey, is now a nursing home.

---

seven Savannah women to save the Davenport House and other buildings from similar fates.

Savannah played a pioneering, though largely unsung, role in the civil rights movement. Ralph Mark Gilbert, pastor of the historic First African Baptist Church, launched one of the first black voter registration drives in the South, which led the way for the historic integration of the police department in 1947.

Gilbert's efforts were kept alive in the 1950s and 1960s by the beloved W. W. Law, a letter carrier who was head of the local chapter of the NAACP for many years. Savannah's long-standing diversity was further proved in 1970, when Greek American John P. Rousakis began his 21-year stint as mayor. During Rousakis' tenure, the first African American city alderman was elected, the movie industry discovered the area, and Atlanta was awarded the 1996 Summer Olympics, which brought several events venues to Savannah. Once-decrepit River Street and Broughton Street were revived. The opening of the Savannah College of Art and Design (SCAD) in 1979 ushered another important chapter in Savannah's renaissance.

After the publication of John Berendt's *Midnight in the Garden of Good and Evil* in 1994, nothing would ever be the same in Savannah. Old-money families cringed as idiosyncrasies and hypocrisies were laid bare in "The Book." Local merchants and politicians, however, delighted in the influx of tourists. A more recent driver of tourism to the area has been the arrival of Paula Deen, whose ubiquitous presence on the Food Channel has convinced many thousands of visitors to come eat at her world-famous, if overrated, Lady & Sons restaurant.

Savannah's first African American mayor, Floyd Adams Jr., was elected in 1995. Succeeding him was Otis Johnson, the first black Savannahian to graduate from the University of Georgia. Savannah's first female African American mayor, Edna Jackson, was elected in 2011 (the first female mayor was Susan Weiner, who served one term in the early 1990s).

PLANNING YOUR TIME

Much more than just a parade, St. Patrick's Day in Savannah—an event generally expanded to include several days before and after it—is also a time of immense crowds, with the city's usual population of about 150,000 doubling with the influx of partying visitors. Be aware that lodging on and around March 17 fills up well in advance. Unless you know someone that lives here, it's best not to just spontaneously show up in Savannah on St. Patrick's weekend.

Like Charleston, you don't need a car to have a great time and see most sights worth enjoying. A strong walker can easily traverse the length and breadth of downtown in a day, although less energetic travelers should consider a central location or use of the free downtown shuttle. To fully enjoy Savannah, however, you'll need access to a vehicle so you can go east to Tybee Island and south to various historical sights with spottier public transportation. You'll appreciate downtown all the more when you can get away and smell the salt air.

And also like Charleston, it's hard to imagine fully enjoying Savannah in a single day. Plan on two nights at an absolute minimum—not only to enjoy all the sights, but to fully soak in the local color and attitude.

ORIENTATION

It's tempting for newcomers to assume that Savannah jumps across the river into South Carolina. But this is not the case, as Savannah emanates strictly southward from the river and never crosses the state line. (Don't be confused by the spit of land you see across the main channel of the Savannah River, the one bearing the squat Trade and Convention Center and the towering Westin Savannah Harbour hotel. That's not South Carolina, it's Hutchinson Island, Georgia, annexed by the city of Savannah for development. South Carolina begins farther north, after you cross the river's Back Channel.)

The downtown area is bounded on the east by East Broad Street and on the west by Martin Luther King Jr. Boulevard (formerly West Broad St.). For quick access to the south, take the one-way streets Price (on the east side of downtown) or Whitaker (on the west side of downtown). Conversely, if you want to make a quick trip north into downtown, three one-way streets taking you there are East Broad, Lincoln, and Drayton. Technically, Gwinnett Street is the southern boundary of the National Historic Landmark District, though in practice locals extend the boundary several blocks southward. When you're driving downtown and come to a square, the law says traffic within the square *always* has the right of way. In other words, if you haven't yet entered the square, you must yield to any vehicles already in the square.

Many of the following neighborhood designations, like City Market and the Waterfront, are well within the National Historic Landmark

District, but locals tend to think of them as separate entities, and we'll follow their lead. While largely in private hands, the Victorian District—with certification and protection of its own—contains some wonderful architecture that unfortunately is often overshadowed by the more ornate buildings in the Historic District proper.

Sights

It's best to introduce yourself to the sights of Savannah by traveling from the river southward. It's no small task to navigate the nation's largest contiguous Historic District, but when in doubt it's best to follow James Oglethorpe's original plan of using the five "monumental" squares on Bull Street (Johnson, Wright, Chippewa, Madison, and Monterey) as focal points.

WATERFRONT

It's only natural to start one's adventures in Savannah where Oglethorpe's adventures themselves began: on the waterfront, now dominated by scenic and historic River Street. Once the bustling center of Savannah's thriving cotton and naval stores export industry, the waterfront is also generally thought of as including Factor's Walk and Bay Street.

◖ River Street

It's much tamer than it was 30 years ago, when muscle cars cruised its cobblestones and a volatile mix of local teenagers, sailors on shore leave, and soldiers on liberty made things less than family-friendly after dark—but energetic pub crawling remains a favorite pastime for locals and visitors alike.

If you have a car, park it somewhere else and walk. The cobblestones—actually old ballast stones from some of the innumerable ships that docked here over the years—are tough on the suspension, and much of River Street is dedicated to pedestrian traffic anyway.

THE WAVING GIRL

Begin your walking tour of River Street on the east end, at the statue of Florence Martus, a.k.a. *The Waving Girl,* set in the emerald green expanse of little Morrell Park. Beginning at the age of 19, Martus—who actually lived several miles downriver on Elba Island—took to greeting every passing ship with a wave of a handkerchief by day and a lantern at night, without fail for the next 40 years. Ship captains returned the greeting with a salute of their own on the ship's whistle, and word spread all over the world of the beguiling woman who waited on the balcony of that lonely house. Was she looking for a sign of a long lost love who went to sea and never returned? Was she trying to get a handsome sea captain to sweep her off her feet and take her off that little island? No one knows for sure, but the truth is probably more prosaic. Martus was a life-long spinster who lived with her brother the lighthouse keeper, and was by most accounts an eccentric, if delightful, person—which of course makes her an ideal Savannah character. After her brother died, Martus moved into a house on the Wilmington River, whiling away the hours by—you guessed it—waving at passing cars. Martus became such an enduring symbol of the personality and spirit of Savannah that a U.S. Liberty ship was named for her in 1943. She died a few months after the ship's christening at the age of 75.

ROUSAKIS PLAZA

Continue walking west to Rousakis Plaza (River Street behind City Hall), a focal point for local festivals. It's a great place to sit, feed the pigeons, and watch the huge container ships go back and forth from the Georgia Ports Authority's sprawling complex farther upriver (you can see the huge Panamax cranes in the distance). The **African American Monument** at the edge of Rousakis Plaza was erected in 2002 to controversy for its stark tableau of a dazed-looking African American family with

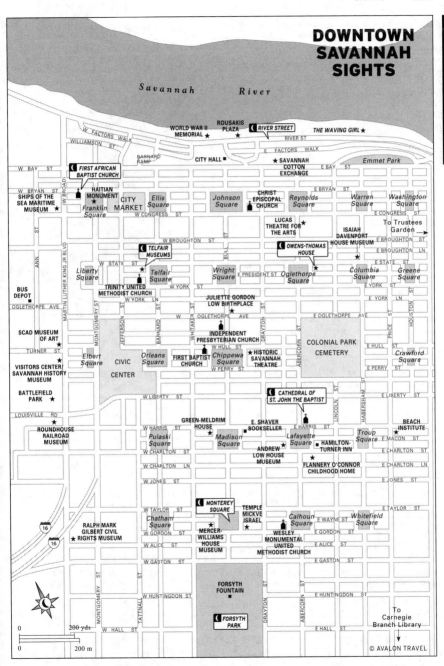

DOWNTOWN SAVANNAH SIGHTS

Savannah River

WORLD WAR II MEMORIAL ★
ROUSAKIS PLAZA
☾ RIVER STREET
THE WAVING GIRL ★

W FACTORS WALK
WILLIAMSON ST
RIVER ST
E FACTORS WALK

BARNARD RAMP
CITY HALL ■
★ SAVANNAH COTTON EXCHANGE
Emmet Park

W BAY ST
☾ FIRST AFRICAN BAPTIST CHURCH
E BAY ST

W BRYAN ST
SHIPS OF THE SEA MARITIME MUSEUM ★
HAITIAN MONUMENT ★
CITY MARKET
Ellis Square
Johnson Square
CHRIST EPISCOPAL CHURCH
Reynolds Square
E BRYAN ST
Warren Square
Washington Square

Franklin Square
W CONGRESS ST
LUCAS THEATRE FOR THE ARTS ★
E CONGRESS ST
To Trustees Garden →

W BROUGHTON ST
ISAIAH DAVENPORT HOUSE MUSEUM ★
E BROUGHTON ST
E BROUGHTON LN

☾ TELFAIR MUSEUMS
Liberty Square
W STATE ST
Telfair Square
Wright Square
E PRESIDENT ST
☾ OWENS-THOMAS HOUSE
Oglethorpe Square
E STATE ST
Columbia Square
Greene Square

TRINITY UNITED METHODIST CHURCH
W YORK ST
W YORK LN
E YORK ST
E YORK LN

BUS DEPOT ■
OGLETHORPE AVE
JULIETTE GORDON LOW BIRTHPLACE
W OGLETHORPE AVE
E OGLETHORPE AVE

SCAD MUSEUM OF ART ★
TURNER ST
Elbert Square
CIVIC CENTER
Orleans Square
INDEPENDENT PRESBYTERIAN CHURCH
W HULL ST
FIRST BAPTIST CHURCH
Chippewa Square
★ HISTORIC SAVANNAH THEATRE
COLONIAL PARK CEMETERY
E HULL ST
Crawford Square

VISITORS CENTER/ SAVANNAH HISTORY MUSEUM ★
W PERRY ST
E PERRY ST

BATTLEFIELD PARK ★
LOUISVILLE RD
W LIBERTY ST
☾ CATHEDRAL OF ST. JOHN THE BAPTIST
E LIBERTY ST

ROUNDHOUSE RAILROAD MUSEUM ★
GREEN-MELDRIM HOUSE ★
E. SHAVER BOOKSELLER ★
BEACH INSTITUTE ★

W HARRIS ST
Pulaski Square
Madison Square
Lafayette Square
E HARRIS ST
Troup Square
E MACON ST

W CHARLTON ST
ANDREW LOW HOUSE MUSEUM
■ HAMILTON-TURNER INN
E CHARLTON ST

W CHARLTON LN
FLANNERY O'CONNOR CHILDHOOD HOME ★
E CHARLTON LN

W JONES ST
E JONES ST

W TAYLOR ST
☾ MONTEREY SQUARE
TEMPLE MICKVE ISRAEL ★
E TAYLOR ST

Chatham Square
MERCER-WILLIAMS HOUSE MUSEUM ★
Calhoun Square
E WAYNE ST
Whitefield Square

RALPH MARK GILBERT CIVIL RIGHTS MUSEUM ★
W GORDON ST
WESLEY MONUMENTAL UNITED METHODIST CHURCH
E GORDON ST

W ALICE ST
E ALICE ST

W GASTON ST
E GASTON ST

FORSYTH FOUNTAIN ■

W HUNTINGDON ST
E HUNTINGDON ST
To Carnegie Branch Library ↓

☾ FORSYTH PARK

0   200 yds
0   200 m
W HALL ST
E HALL ST

© AVALON TRAVEL

broken shackles around their feet. Adding to the controversy was the graphic content of the inscription at the base of the 12-foot statue, written especially for the monument by famed poet Maya Angelou. It reads:

> We were stolen, sold and bought together from the African continent. We got on the slave ships together. We lay back to belly in the holds of the slave ships in each other's excrement and urine together, sometimes died together, and our lifeless bodies thrown overboard together. Today, we are standing up together, with faith and even some joy.

Nearby you can't miss the huge, vaguely cubist Hyatt Regency Savannah, another controversial local landmark. The modern architecture of the Hyatt caused quite a stir when it was first built in 1981, not only because it's so contrary to the area's historic architecture but because its superstructure effectively cuts off one end of River Street from the other. "Underneath" the Hyatt—actually still River Street—you'll find elevators to the hotel lobby, the best way to get up off the waterfront if you're not up for a walk up the cobblestones. Immediately outside the west side of the Hyatt up toward Bay Street is another exit and entry point, a steep and solid set of antebellum stairs that, despite its decidedly pre-Americans with Disabilities Act aspect, is nonetheless one of the quicker ways to leave River Street for those with strong legs and good knees.

WORLD WAR II MEMORIAL
Near the foot of the new Bohemian hotel on River Street, the newest addition to Savannah's public monuments, the World War II Memorial—fairly modernist by local standards—features a copper and bronze globe torn in half to represent the European and Pacific theaters of the war. The more than 500 local people who gave their lives in that conflict are memorialized by name.

FACTOR'S WALK
One level up from River Street, Factor's Walk has nothing to do with math, though a lot of money has been counted here. In arcane usage,

statue of Florence Martus, *The Waving Girl*, by sculptor Felix de Weldon

© JIM MOREKIS

a "factor" was a broker, i.e., a middleman for the sale of cotton, Savannah's chief export during most of the 1800s. Factors mostly worked in Factor's Row, the traditional phrase for the actual buildings on River Street, most all of which were used in various import-export activities before their current transformation into a mélange of shops, hotels, restaurants, and taverns. Factor's Walk is divided into Lower Factor's Walk, comprising the alleys and back entrances behind Factor's Row, and Upper Factor's Walk, the system of crosswalks at the upper levels of Factor's Row that lead directly to Bay Street.

BAY STREET
Because so few downtown streets can accommodate 18-wheelers, Bay Street unfortunately has become the default route for industrial traffic in the area on its way to and from the industrial west side of town. In front of the Hyatt Regency is a concrete bench marking the spot on which Oglethorpe pitched his first tent. But

THE TWO PAULAS

It's odd that this conservative Southern city's two biggest empire-builders are women who overcame contentious divorces to get where they are today. Odder still is the fact that they both share the same first name. In any case, the empires that **Paula Deen** and **Paula Wallace** have built are two of the major reasons people enjoy Savannah today. Deen's empire centers on The Lady & Sons restaurant in City Market and her high profile on the Food Network. Wallace's empire centers on the Savannah College of Art and Design (SCAD), one of the largest art schools in the nation (and growing, now with campuses in Atlanta and Hong Kong). Their names are similar, but that's about the only similarity. These two powerhouse women and the stories of how they rose to the top could not be more different in every other way.

Deen, a native of Albany, Georgia, came to Savannah after divorcing her first husband in 1989, arriving with only $200 and her two teenage sons, Jamie and Bobby, now Food Network stars in their own right. Severely agoraphobic (fearing crowds), Deen gradually increased her public presence first with a job cooking at a local hotel and then with her own restaurant, Lady & Sons, initially on West Congress Street. Her gregarious "aw, shucks" style caught the attention of producer Gordon Elliott, formerly with the seminal tabloid show *A Current Affair*. His first cooking show pilot with Deen fizzled in 1999. But soon after the 9/11 attacks, Elliott spotted an opportunity to market a good old-fashioned comfort-food show, *Paula's Home Cooking*, to the Food Network. In 2013, Deen's contract with the Food Network was canceled after a controversy in which Deen allegedly made racist remarks.

Petite, soft-spoken, and often surrounded by a coterie of devoted assistants, Paula Wallace is Deen's polar opposite in temperament. She arrived in Savannah in 1979 with her then-husband Richard Rowan to establish an art school. The two 20-somethings, young children in tow, came armed with the guts to take a chance on depressed downtown real estate, the willingness to roll up their sleeves, and her parents' deep pockets. The power couple soon became the toast of the town. Then came a bitter divorce. After the smoke cleared, Paula became the clear and undisputed *presidente* of SCAD. It's hard to overstate the college's impact on Savannah. It has renovated nearly 100 historic properties and is estimated to own at least $200 million in assets, returning nearly $100 million a year into the local economy and employing over 1,000 people.

dominating Bay Street is **City Hall** (2 E. Bay St.) next door, with its gold-leaf dome. The 1907 building was designed by acclaimed architect Hyman Witcover and erected on the site of Savannah's first town hall.

The large gray Greek Revival building directly across from City Hall is the **U.S. Custom House** (1 E. Bay St.), not "customs" regardless of what the tour guides may say. Built on the spot of Georgia's first public building in 1852, the Custom House was also Georgia's first federal building and was the first local commission for renowned New York architect John Norris, who went on to design 22 other buildings in

Savannah. Within its walls was held the trial of the captain and crew of the notorious slave ship *Wanderer*, which illegally plied its trade after a national ban on the importation of slaves. Local newspaper publisher and educator John H. DeVeaux worked here after his appointment as the first African American U.S. Collector of Customs.

Directly adjacent to City Hall on the east is a small canopy sheltering two cannons, which together comprise the oldest monument in Savannah. These are the **Chatham Artillery Guns,** presented to the local militia group of the same name by President George

Washington during his one and only visit to town in 1791. Today, locals use the phrase "Chatham Artillery" differently, to refer to a particularly potent local punch recipe that mixes several hard liquors.

Look directly behind the cannons and you'll see the ornate **Savannah Cotton Exchange** (100 E. Bay St.), built in 1886 to facilitate the city's huge cotton export business. Once nicknamed "King Cotton's Palace" but now a Masonic lodge, this delightful building by William Gibbons Preston is one of Savannah's many great examples of the Romanesque style. You'll become well acquainted with Preston's handiwork during your stay in Savannah—the Boston architect built many of Savannah's finest buildings. The fanciful lion figure in front—sometimes mistakenly referred to as a griffin—represents Mark the Evangelist. However, it isn't original—the first lion was destroyed in 2009 in a bizarre traffic accident.

CITY MARKET

In local parlance, the phrase "City Market" refers not only to the refurbished warehouses that make up this tourist-friendly area of shops and restaurants in the Historic District's western portion but also its bookend squares as well—both of which had close scrapes with the bulldozer and wrecking ball before their current renaissance.

Ellis Square

Just across Bay Street on the western edge of the Historic District, Ellis Square has a history as Savannah's main open-air marketplace that goes back to 1755, when there was actually a single City Market building in the square itself. Three market buildings would come and go until the building of the fourth City Market in 1872, an ornate Romanesque affair with a 50-foot roofline. In 1954, the city, in the thrall of auto worship then sweeping the country, decided a parking garage in the square was more important than fresh food or a sense of community. So the magnificent City Market building—and Ellis Square—simply ceased to exist. Several large warehouses surrounding

City Market survived, however. They carried with them the seed of real renewal, which grew with the nascent preservation movement in the 1950s and 1960s.

The eyesore that was the Ellis Square parking garage is now gone, and the square has been literally rebuilt as a pedestrian hangout, complete with a fountain, all atop a huge underground parking garage. It cost taxpayers millions of dollars, but as any Savannahian will tell you, the return of one of their precious squares is priceless. Be sure to check out the smallish bronze of native Savannahian and Oscar-winning lyricist Johnny Mercer on the square's western edge.

Franklin Square

Just west of City Market is Franklin Square, once known simply as "Water Tank Square" because that's where the city reservoir was back in the day. Don't be alarmed by the numbers of men hanging out in the square. Scruffy heirs to an old Savannah tradition, most of them are day laborers for hire. Until recently, Franklin Square was, like Ellis Square, a victim of "progress," this time in the form of a highway going right through the middle of it. But as part of the city's effort to reclaim its history, Franklin Square was returned to its integral state in the mid-1980s.

◖ FIRST AFRICAN BAPTIST CHURCH

Without a doubt the premier historic attraction on Franklin Square—and indeed one of the most significant historic sites in Savannah—is the First African Baptist Church (23 Montgomery St., 912/233-2244, www.oldestblackchurch.org, tours Tues.-Sun. 11am and 2pm, $5). It's the oldest black congregation in North America, dating from 1777. The church also hosted the first African American Sunday school, begun in 1826. The church's founding pastor, George Liele, was the first black Baptist in Georgia and perhaps the first black missionary in the country. He baptized his successor, Andrew Bryan, a slave who opted to stay in Savannah and preach the Gospel instead of leaving with many other blacks after the British

THE REBIRTH OF ELLIS SQUARE

One of the great tragedies of Savannah's 1950s love affair with "urban renewal" was the paving over of Ellis Square, site of the original City Market, replaced by a squat, drab parking garage. Savannah has finally made amends for its bad karma by bringing Ellis Square back from the grave. In the massive $22 million Ellis Square Project–also called "The Big Dig" in a nod to a similarly ambitious project in Boston–city taxpayers funded a complete facelift that boasts a new, modern landscape design, including a colorful fountain.

While not everyone in town is enamored of the new look–many local landscape architects see its self-conscious modernity as a slap in the face to Oglethorpe's original design–there's no doubt that Savannah welcomes the return of one of its most beloved squares. There's also no doubt that the city welcomes the 1,000 or so new parking spaces available in the massive Whitaker Street Garage under the new Ellis Square.

Ellis Square is not the only one to have been partially or completely destroyed, however. A small plot of worn grass on the west side of the Savannah Civic Center is all that remains of Elbert Square, eviscerated by the construction of the block-long building. And, ironically, Liberty Square was annihilated to make room for a place where some people lose their liberty–the new Chatham County Courthouse and Jail.

---

vacated the city. Third pastor Andrew Marshall was an ardent supporter of American independence and purchased his freedom shortly after the end of the Revolution. He served as George Washington's personal servant during his visit here. This founding trio is immortalized in stained-glass windows in the sanctuary.

The present building dates from 1859 and was built almost entirely by members of the congregation themselves, some of whom redirected savings intended to purchase their freedom toward the building of the church. It houses the oldest church organ in Georgia. A key staging area for the fabled Underground Railroad, First African Baptist still bears the scars of that turbulent time. In the floor of the fellowship hall—where many civil rights meetings were held, because it was safer for white citizens to go there instead of black activists going outside the church—you'll see breathing holes, drilled for use by escaped slaves hiding in a cramped crawlspace.

HAITIAN MONUMENT

This monument in the center of the square commemorates the sacrifice and service of "Les Chasseurs Volontaires de Saint-Dominigue," the 750 Haitian volunteers who fought for American independence and lost many of their number during the unsuccessful attempt to wrest Savannah back from the British in 1779.

HISTORIC DISTRICT
Johnson Square

Due east of City Market, Oglethorpe's very first square is named for Robert Johnson, governor of South Carolina at the time of Georgia's founding. It was here that Savannah's Liberty Pole was erected in 1774 to celebrate a new nation. And it was here that a gathering in 1861 celebrated Georgia's secession, ironically with a huge banner draped over the Greene Monument bearing the words "Don't Tread on Me"—a slogan used in the founding of the very union they sought to dissolve.

The roomy, shady square, ringed with major bank branches and insurance firms, is dominated by the **Nathanael Greene Monument** in honor of George Washington's second-in-command, who was granted nearby Mulberry Grove plantation for his efforts. Marquis de Lafayette dedicated the towering obelisk during his one and only visit to Savannah in 1825. At the time it did not honor any one person. Its dedication to Greene came in 1886, followed by the reinterment of Greene's remains directly underneath the monument in 1901. (In typically maddening Savannah fashion, there is a separate square named for Greene, which has no monument to him at all.)

A much smaller but more charming and personable little monument in Johnson Square is the **William Bull Sundial** at the south side. Bull Street was named for this South Carolinian who accompanied Oglethorpe on his first journey to the new colony, helping him choose and survey the site—hence a sundial is an appropriate remembrance.

CHRIST EPISCOPAL CHURCH

The southeast corner of Johnson Square is dominated by Christ Episcopal Church (18 Abercorn St., 912/232-4131, www.christchurchsavannah.org), a.k.a. Christ Church, a historic house of worship also known as the "Mother Church of Georgia" because its congregation traces its roots to that first Anglican service in Savannah, held the same day Oglethorpe landed. While this spot on Johnson Square was reserved for the congregation from the very beginning, this is actually the third building on the site, dating from 1838. Much of the interior is more recent than that, however, since a fire gutted the interior in 1895. In the northeast bell tower is a bell forged in 1919 by Revere and Sons of Boston.

Reynolds Square

Walk directly east of Johnson Square to find yourself at Reynolds Square, named for John Reynolds, the first (and exceedingly unpopular) royal governor of Georgia. First called "Lower New Square," Reynolds originally served as site of the filature, or cocoon storage warehouse, during the fledgling colony's ill-fated flirtation with the silk industry (a federal building now occupies the site). As with Johnson Square, the monument in Reynolds Square has nothing to do with its namesake, but is instead a likeness of John Wesley dedicated in 1969 near the spot believed to have been his home. On the northeast corner of the square is the parish house of Christ Church, Wesley's congregation.

A Reynolds Square landmark, the **Olde Pink House** (23 Abercorn St.), is not only one of Savannah's most romantic restaurants but quite a historic site as well. It's the oldest Savannah mansion from the 18th century still standing as well as the first place in Savannah where the Declaration of Independence was read aloud. Pink inside as well as out, the Georgian mansion was built in 1771 for rice planter James Habersham Jr., one of America's richest men at the time and a member of the notorious "Liberty Boys" who plotted revolution. The building's pink exterior was a matter of serendipity, resulting from its core redbrick seeping through the formerly white stucco outer covering.

LUCAS THEATRE FOR THE ARTS

The other major Savannah landmark on Reynolds Square is the Lucas Theatre for the Arts (32 Abercorn St., 912/525-5040, www.lucastheatre.com). Built in 1921 as part of Arthur Lucas's regional chain of movie houses, the Lucas also featured a stage for road shows. Ornate and stately but with cozy warmth to spare, the venue was a hit with Savannahians for four decades, until the advent of TV and residential flight from downtown led to financial disaster. In 1976, the Lucas closed after a screening of *The Exorcist.* Several attempts to revive the venue followed, including a comedy club in the 1980s, but to no avail. When the building faced demolition in 1986, a group of citizens created a nonprofit to save it. Despite numerous starts and stops, the 14-year campaign finally paid off in a grand reopening in 2000, an event helped immeasurably by timely donations from *Midnight* star Kevin Spacey and the cast and crew of the locally shot *Forrest Gump.* Once inside, be sure to check out the extensive gold-leaf work throughout the interior, all painstakingly done by hand.

Columbia Square

Named for the mythical patroness of America, this square features at its center not an expected portrait of that female warrior figure but the original fountain from Noble Jones's Wormsloe Plantation, placed there in 1970.

ISAIAH DAVENPORT HOUSE MUSEUM

Columbia Square is primarily known as the home of the Isaiah Davenport House Museum (324 E. State St., 912/236-8097, www.davenporthousemuseum.org, Mon.-Sat. 10am-4pm, Sun. 1pm-4pm, $8 adults, $5 children). The house museum is a delightful stop in and of itself because of its elegant simplicity, sweeping double staircase, and near-perfect representation of the Federalist style. But the Davenport House occupies an exalted place in Savannah history as well, because the fight to save it began the preservation movement in Savannah. In 1955 the Davenport House, then a tenement, was to be demolished for a parking lot. But Emma Adler and six other Savannah women, angered by the recent destruction of Ellis Square, refused to let it go down quietly. Together they formed the Historic Savannah Foundation in order to raise the $22,500 needed to purchase the Davenport House. By 1963 the Davenport House—built in 1820 for his own family by master builder Isaiah Davenport—was open to the public as a museum.

Most Octobers, the Davenport House hosts living history dramatizations based on Savannah's yellow fever plague of the 1820s. Despite the grim subject matter, the little playlets are usually quite entertaining.

Across the corner from the Davenport House is the Classical Revival masterpiece **Kehoe House** (123 Habersham St.), designed for local ironworks owner William Kehoe in 1892 by DeWitt Bruyn, now one of Savannah's premier bed-and-breakfasts.

WARREN AND WASHINGTON SQUARES

Warren Square and its neighbor Washington Square formed the first extension of Oglethorpe's original four and still boast some of the oldest houses in the Historic District. Both squares are lovely little garden spots, ideal for a picnic in the shade. Two houses near Washington Square were restored by the late Jim Williams of *Midnight* fame: The **Hampton Lillibridge House** (507 E. St. Julian St.), which once hosted an Episcopal exorcism,

and the **Charles Oddingsells House** (510 E. St. Julian St.). Now a hotel, the **Mulberry Inn** on Washington Square was once a cotton warehouse and subsequently one of the nation's first Coca-Cola bottling plants.

GREENE SQUARE

Named for Revolutionary War hero Nathanael Greene, but bearing no monument to him whatsoever, this square is of particular importance to local African American history. At the corner of Houston (pronounced "HOUSE-ton") and East State Streets is the 1810 **Cunningham House,** built for Henry Cunningham, former slave and founding pastor of the **Second African Baptist Church** (124 Houston St., 912/233-6163) on the west side of the square, in which General Sherman made his famous promise of "40 acres and a mule." In 1818, the residence at 542 East State Street was constructed for free blacks Charlotte and William Wall. The property at 513 East York Street was built for the estate of Catherine DeVeaux, part of a prominent African American family.

Old Fort

One of the lesser-known aspects of Savannah history is this well-trod neighborhood at the east end of Bay Street, once the site of groundbreaking experiments and piratical intrigue, then a diverse melting pot of Savannah citizenry.

TRUSTEES GARDEN

At the east end of Bay Street where it meets East Broad Street rises a bluff behind a masonry wall—at 40 feet off the river, still the highest point in Chatham County. This is Trustees Garden, the nation's first experimental garden. Modeled on the Chelsea Botanical Garden in London, it was intended to be the epicenter of Savannah's silk industry. Alas, the colonists had little knowledge of native soils or climate—they thought the winters would be milder—and the experiment was not as successful as hoped. Soon Trustees Garden became the site of Fort Wayne, a defensive installation overlooking the river named after General "Mad Anthony" Wayne of Revolutionary War fame, who retired to a plantation near Savannah. The Fort Wayne area—still called the "Old Fort" neighborhood by old-timers—fell from grace and became associated with the "lowest elements" of Savannah society, which in the 19th and early 20th centuries were Irish and African Americans. It also became known for its illegal activity and as the haunt of sea salts such as the ones who frequented what is now the delightfully schlocky Pirates' House restaurant. That building began life in 1753 as a seamen's inn and was later chronicled by Robert Louis Stevenson in *Treasure Island* as a rogue's gallery of pirates and nautical ne'er-do-wells.

Find the **Herb House** on East Broad Street, the older-looking clapboard structure next to the Pirates' House entrance. You're looking at what is considered the single oldest building in Georgia and one of the oldest in the United States. Constructed in 1734, it was originally the home of Trustees Garden's chief gardener.

To the rear of Trustees Garden is the 1881 Hillyer building, now the **Charles H. Morris Center,** a mixed-use performing arts and meeting space that is heavily used during the springtime Savannah Music Festival.

EMMET PARK

Just north of Reynolds Square on the north side of Bay Street you'll come to Emmet Park, first a Native American burial ground and then known as "the Strand" or "Irish Green" because of its proximity to the Irish slums of the Old Fort. In 1902 the park was named for Robert Emmet, an Irish patriot of the early 1800s, who was executed by the British for treason. Within it is the eight-foot **Celtic Cross,** erected in 1983 and carved of Irish limestone. The Celtic Cross is the center of a key ceremony for local Irish Catholics during the week prior to St. Patrick's Day.

Close by is one of Savannah's more recent monuments, the **Vietnam War Memorial** at East Bay Street and Rossiter Lane. The reflecting pool is in the shape of Vietnam itself, and the names of all 106 Savannahians killed in

the conflict are carved into an adjacent marble tablet.

Walk a little farther east and you'll find my favorite little chapter of Bay Street history, the **Beacon Range Light.** Tucked into a shady corner, few visitors bother to check out this masterfully crafted 1858 navigation aid, intended to warn approaching ships of the old wrecks sunk in the river as a defense during the Revolutionary War.

Broughton Street

Downtown's main shopping district for most of the 20th century, Broughton Street once dazzled shoppers with decorated gaslights, ornate window displays, and fine examples of terrazzo, a form of mosaic that still adorns many shop entrances. Postwar suburbs and white flight brought neglect to the area by the 1960s, and many thought Broughton was gone for good. But with the downtown renaissance brought about largely by the Savannah College of Art and Design (SCAD), Broughton was able not only to get back on its feet but to thrive as a commercial center once again.

Around the corner from the Lucas Theatre on Reynolds Square is the art moderne **Trustees Theatre** (216 E. Broughton St., 912/525-5051, www.scad.edu), a SCAD-run operation that seats 1,200 and hosts concerts, film screenings, and the school's much-anticipated spring fashion show. It began life in the postwar boom of 1946 as the Weis Theatre, another one of those ornate Southern movie houses that took full commercial advantage of being the only buildings at the time to have air conditioning. But by the end of the 1970s it followed the fate of Broughton Street, lying dormant and neglected until its purchase and renovation by SCAD in 1989.

This block of Broughton in front of Trustees Theatre is usually blocked off to mark the gala opening of the Savannah Film Festival each fall. Searchlights crisscross the sky, limos idle in wait, and Hollywood guests strike poses for the photographers.

Across the street is SCAD's **Jen Library** (201 E. Broughton St.), a state-of-the-art

THE IRISH IN SAVANNAH

It seems Savannah's close connection to St. Patrick's Day was ordained from the beginning. The very first baby born here, Georgia Close, came into the world on March 17, 1733. Two hundred and fifty years later, Savannah holds the second-largest St. Patrick's Day celebration in the world, second only to New York City's. Three presidents have visited during the shindig—William Howard Taft, Harry Truman, and Jimmy Carter. With its fine spring weather and walkability—not to mention its liberal "to-go cup" rules allowing you to carry an adult beverage on the street—Savannah is tailor-made for a boisterous outdoor celebration. But most of all, what makes it a perfect fit is the city's large Irish-American population.

The earliest Irish in Georgia were descendants of the Calvinist Scots who "planted" Ireland's northern province of Ulster in the 1600s. Often called "crackers"—perhaps from the Gaelic *craic*, "enjoyable conversation"—these early Irish entered Georgia from upstate South Carolina and made their living trading, trapping, or soldiering. One such "cracker" was Sergeant William Jasper, mortally wounded leading the charge to retake Savannah from the British in 1779.

The main chapter in local Irish history began in the 1830s with the arrival of the first wave of Irish to build the Central of Georgia Railway. The story goes that Irish were employed on the railroad because, unlike slaves, their bodies had no commercial value and could be worked to exhaustion with impunity. A second wave of Irish immigration followed two decades later when the potato famine in the old country forced many to seek new shores.

Though the Irish were initially subject to prejudice, their willingness to work long hours for low pay soon made them irreplaceable in Savannah's economy. And as in New York, in short order the Irish became major players in politics and business. In the early days, Irish neighborhoods were clustered around East Broad Street in the Old Fort area, and on the west side near West Broad Street (now MLK Jr. Boulevard). It's no coincidence that those areas also had large African American populations. Because of their shared links of poverty and prejudice, in the early days Savannah's Irish tended to live near black neighborhoods, often socializing with them after-hours—much to the chagrin of Savannah's elite.

Ironically, given St. Patrick's Day's current close association with the Catholic faith, the first parade in Savannah was organized by Irish Protestants. Thirteen members of the local Hibernian Society—the country's oldest Irish society—took part in a private procession to Independent Presbyterian Church in 1813. The first public procession was in 1824, when the Hibernians invited all local Irishmen to parade through the streets. The first recognizably modern parade, with bands and a "grand marshal," happened in 1870.

Today's parade is a far cry from those early beginnings. Organized by a "committee" of about 700 local Irishmen—with but a tiny sprinkling of women—the three-hour procession includes marchers from all the local Irish organizations, in addition to marching bands and floats representing many local groups. Rain or shine, the assembled clans march—*amble* is perhaps a more accurate word—wearing their kelly green blazers, brandishing their walking canes and to-go cups, some pushing future committee members in strollers, fair skin gradually getting redder in the Georgia sun.

---

facility set in the circa-1890 Levy and Maas Brothers department stores. An important piece of Broughton Street history happened farther west at its intersection with Whitaker Street. Tondee's Tavern was where the infamous "Liberty Boys" met over ale and planned Savannah's role in the American Revolution. Only a plaque marks the site's contribution to Savannah's colonial history.

Wright Square

By now you know the drill. The big monument in Wright Square, Oglethorpe's second square, has nothing to do with James Wright, royal governor of Georgia before the Revolution, for whom it's named. Instead the monument honors **William Gordon,** former mayor and founder of the Central of Georgia Railway, which upon completion of the Savannah-Macon run was the longest railroad in the world. Gordon is in fact the only native Savannahian honored in a city square. But more importantly, Wright Square is the final resting place for the great Yamacraw chief **Tomochichi,** buried in 1737 in an elaborate state funeral at James Oglethorpe's insistence. A huge boulder of north Georgia granite honoring the chief was placed in a corner of the square in 1899 under the auspices of William Gordon's daughter-in-law. However, Tomochichi is not buried under the boulder, but rather somewhere underneath the Gordon monument. So why not rename it Tomochichi Square? Old ways die hard down here...

JULIETTE GORDON LOW BIRTHPLACE

Around the corner from Wright Square at Oglethorpe and Bull is the Juliette Gordon Low Birthplace (10 E. Oglethorpe Ave., 912/233-4501, www.juliettegordonlowbirthplace.org, Mar.-Oct. Mon.-Sat. 10am-4pm, Sun. 11am-4pm, Nov.-Feb. Mon.-Tues. and Thurs.-Sat. 10am-4pm, Sun. 11am-4pm, $8 adults, $7 children, $6 Girl Scouts under age 19), declared the city's very first National Historic Landmark in 1965. The founder of the Girl Scouts of the USA lived here from her birth in 1860 until her marriage, returning home to stay until her mother's death. The house was completed in 1821 for Mayor James Moore Wayne, future Supreme Court Justice, but the current furnishings, many original, are intended to reflect the home during the 1880s.

Also called the Girl Scout National Center, the Low birthplace is probably Savannah's most festive historic site because of the heavy traffic of Girl Scout troops from across the United States. They flock here year-round to take part in programs and learn more about their organization's founder, whose family sold the house to the Girl Scouts in 1953. You don't have to be affiliated with the Girl Scouts to tour the home. Tours are given every 15 minutes, and

tickets are available at the Oglethorpe Avenue entrance. Be aware the site is closed most holidays, sometimes for extended periods; be sure to check the website for details.

Oglethorpe Square

Don't look for a monument to Georgia's founder in the square named for him. That would be way too easy, so of course his monument is in Chippewa Square. Originally called "Upper New Square," Oglethorpe Square was created in 1742.

◖ OWENS-THOMAS HOUSE

The square's main claim to fame, the Owens-Thomas House (124 Abercorn St., 912/233-9743, www.telfair.org, Mon. noon-5pm, Tues.-Sat. 10am-5pm, Sun. 1pm-5pm, last tour 4:30pm, $15 adults, $5 children, $20 multi-site ticket), lies on the northeast corner. Widely known as the finest example of Regency architecture in the United States, the Owens-Thomas House was designed by brilliant young English architect William Jay. One of the first professionally trained architects in the United States, Jay was only 24 when he designed the home for cotton merchant or "factor" Richard Richardson, who lost the house in the depression of 1820 (all that remains of Richardson's tenure are three marble-top tables). The house's current name is derived from Savannah Mayor George Owens, who bought the house in 1830. It remained in his family until 1951, when his granddaughter Margaret Thomas bequeathed it to the Telfair Academy of Arts and Sciences, which currently operates the site.

Several things about the Owens-Thomas House stand out. First, it's constructed mostly of tabby, a mixture of lime, oyster shells, and sand. Its exterior is English stucco while the front garden balustrade is a type of artificial stone called Coade stone. Perhaps most interestingly, a complex plumbing system features rain-fed cisterns, flushing toilets, sinks, bathtubs, and a shower. When built, the Owens-Thomas House in fact had the first indoor plumbing in Savannah.

While inside the house, notice the little

SCOUT'S HONOR: JULIETTE GORDON LOW

Known as "Daisy" to family and friends, Juliette Magill Kinzie Gordon was born to be a pioneer. Her father's family took part in the original settlement of Georgia, and her mother's kin were among the founders of Chicago. Mostly known as the founder of the Girl Scouts of the USA, Daisy was also an artist, adventurer, and healer. Born and raised in the house on Oglethorpe Avenue in Savannah known to Girl Scouts across the nation as simply "The Birthplace," she was an animal lover with an early penchant for theater, drawing, and poetry.

After school she traveled, returning home to marry wealthy cotton heir William Mackay Low, son of the builder of Savannah's exquisite Andrew Low House. A harbinger of her troubled marriage happened on her wedding day on the steps of Christ Church. A grain of rice, thrown for good luck, struck her eardrum and led to a painful infection and loss of hearing. Daisy and her husband moved to England, using the Andrew Low House as a rental property and winter residence. She maintained a home in England until her death, spending much of the year traveling in the United States and abroad.

Daisy returned to Savannah with the outbreak of the Spanish-American War in 1898. Because of the city's proximity to Cuba, one of the main theaters of the war, it became a staging area for U.S. Army troops from all over the country. For Savannah, taking such an active role was an opportunity to make amends for the alienation of the Civil War and effectively rejoin the Union again. For the first time since Sherman's March to the Sea, Savannahians proudly displayed the Stars and Stripes in an honest show of patriotism of which Daisy was a part, tending to wounded soldiers returning from Cuba. After the war, Daisy returned to England to spend the last days of her marriage, which existed in name only until her husband's death in 1905. After settling his estate, she used the proceeds to fund some traveling.

In 1911 while in England, she met another man who would change her life: Robert Baden-Powell, founder of the Boy Scouts and Girl Guides in Britain. Struck by the simplicity and usefulness of his project, she carried the seeds of a similar idea back with her to the United States. "I've got something for the girls of Savannah, and all of America, and all the world, and we're going to start it tonight," were her famous words in a phone call to a cousin after meeting Baden-Powell. So on March 12, 1912, Daisy gathered 18 girls to register the first troop of American Girl Guides, later the Girl Scouts of the USA.

Juliette "Daisy" Gordon Low died of breast cancer in her bed in the Andrew Low House on January 17, 1927. She was buried in Laurel Grove Cemetery on the city's west side. Girl Scout troops from all over the United States visit her birthplace, the Andrew Low House, and her gravesite to this day, often leaving flowers and small personal objects near her tombstone as tokens of respect and gratitude.

---

touches like the unusual curved walls, with doors bowed to match, and the recessed skylights. While many Owens family furnishings are part of the collection, much of it is representative of American and European work from 1750 to 1830. On the south facade is a beautiful cast-iron veranda from which Revolutionary War hero Marquis de Lafayette addressed a crowd of starstruck Savannahians during his visit in 1825. The 1990s marked the most intensive phase of restoration for the home, which began with a careful renovation of the carriage house and the associated slave quarters—discovered in a surprisingly intact state, including the original "haint blue" paint. The carriage house, where all tours begin, is now the home's gift shop.

Telfair Square

One of the few Savannah squares to show consistency in nomenclature, Telfair Square was indeed named for Mary Telfair, last heir of a family that was one of the most important in Savannah history. A noted patron of the arts, Mary bequeathed the family mansion to the Georgia Historical Society upon her death in 1875 to serve as a museum. Originally called St. James Square after a similar square in London, Telfair is the last of Oglethorpe's original four squares.

TELFAIR MUSEUMS

Also consistent with its name, Telfair Square indeed hosts two of the three buildings operated by the Telfair Museums (912/790-8800, www.telfair.org, $20 adults, $5 children, $12 Jepson Center and Telfair Academy, $15 Owens-Thomas House, free under age 5), an umbrella organization that relies on a combination of private and public funding and has driven much of the arts agenda in Savannah for the last 125 years. The original part of the complex and in fact the oldest public art museum in the South, the **Telfair Academy of Arts and Sciences** (121 Barnard St., Mon. noon-5pm, Tues.-Sat. 10am-5pm, Sun. 1pm-5pm) was built in 1821 by the great William Jay for Alexander Telfair, scion of that famous Georgia family. The five statues in front are of Phidias, Raphael, Rubens, Michelangelo, and

Rembrandt. Inside, the sculpture gallery and rotunda were added in 1885, the year before the building's official opening as a museum. As well as displaying Sylvia Judson Shaw's now-famous *Bird Girl* sculpture, originally in Bonaventure Cemetery (actually the third of four casts by the sculptor), the Telfair Academy features an outstanding collection of primarily 18th- and 20th-century works, most notably the largest public collection of visual art by Khalil Gibran. Major paintings include work by Childe Hassam, Frederick Frieseke, Gari Melchers, and the massive *Black Prince of Crécy* by Julian Story.

The latest and proudest addition to the Telfair brand is the striking, 64,000-square-foot **Jepson Center for the Arts** (207 W. York St., Tues.-Wed. and Fri.-Sat. 10am-5pm, Thurs. 10am-8pm, Sun.-Mon. noon-5pm), whose ultramodern exterior sits catty-corner from the old Telfair. Promoting a massive, daringly designed new facility devoted to nothing but modern art was a hard sell in this traditional town, especially when renowned architect

© JIM MOREKIS

Jepson Center for the Arts

A CITY OF ART

There are more art galleries per capita in Savannah than in New York City—one gallery for every 2,191 residents, to be exact. The no-brainer package experience for the visitor is the combo of the **Telfair Academy of Arts and Sciences** (121 Barnard St., 912/790-8800, www.telfair.org) and the **Jepson Center for the Arts** (207 W. York St., 912/790-8800, www.telfair.org). These two affiliated arms of the Telfair Museums run the gamut, from the Academy's impressive collection of Khalil Gibran drawings to the 2012 visit by priceless works from the Uffizi Gallery in Florence, one of only four museums in the U.S. chosen for the honor.

Naturally, Savannah College of Art & Design (SCAD) galleries (www.scad.edu) are in abundance all over town, displaying the handiwork of students, faculty, alumni, and important national and regional artists. The SCAD outposts with the most consistently impressive exhibits of visiting artists—along with the occasional thesis show—are the **Pei Ling Chan Gallery** (324 MLK Jr. Blvd.), **Gutstein Gallery** (201 E. Broughton St.), and **Pinnacle Gallery** (320 E. Liberty St.). The college also runs its own museum, the **SCAD Museum of Art** (227 MLK Jr. Blvd.), which recently doubled in size to

accommodate a massive new wing devoted to the huge Walter O. Evans Collection of African American Art.

While they don't get as much press, Savannah also has plenty of non-Telfair, non-SCAD galleries as well, ranging from the cutting edge to pedestrian acrylics of seagulls. An adventurous indie cooperative in town that focuses on local artists is **Kobo Gallery** (33 Barnard St., http://kobogallery.com), on Ellis Square near City Market. Another cutting edge effort is The Butcher (19 E. Bay St., www.whatisthebutcher. com), which also houses a tattoo parlor, the gallery proprietors being devoted to body ink.

Other neat locally focused spots include the fairly avant-garde **Desotorow Gallery** (2427 DeSoto Ave., 912/335-8204, www.desotorow. org); **Gallery Espresso** (234 Bull St.,. galleryespresso.com), actually a coffeehouse; and **Daedalus Gallery** (129 E. Liberty St., http:// daedalus-art.com), where you'll find a nice selection of impressionist works in the French tradition, a rarity in Savannah.

An interesting, newish gallery in town, **Liquid Sands Glass Gallery** (5 W. York St., www.liquidsandsglassgallery.com), deals in intricate blown studio glass from North American artists.

Moshe Safdie insisted on building a glassed-in flyover across a lane between two buildings. After a few delays in construction, Jepson opened its doors in 2006 and has since wowed locals and visitors alike with its cutting-edge traveling exhibits and rotating assortment of late-20th-century and 21st-century modern art. If you get hungry, you can enjoy lunch in the expansive atrium café, and, of course, there's a nice gift shop.

Paying admission to one site also gets you a one-time visit to the other two sites for a week following purchase.

TRINITY UNITED METHODIST CHURCH
Directly between the Telfair and the Jepson stands Trinity United Methodist Church (225 W. President St., 912/233-4766, www.trinitychurch1848.org, sanctuary daily 9am-5pm, services Sun. 8:45am and 11am), Savannah's first Methodist church. Built in 1848 on the site of the Telfair's family garden, its masonry walls are of famous "Savannah Gray" bricks— a lighter, more porous, and elegant variety— under stucco. Virgin longleaf pine was used for most of the interior, fully restored in 1969. Call ahead for a tour.

Chippewa Square
Named for a battle in the War of 1812, Chippewa Square has a large monument not to the battle, natch, but to James Oglethorpe, clad in full soldier's regalia. Notice the general is still facing south, toward the Spanish.

© JIM MOREKIS

statue of General James Oglethorpe in Chippewa Square

Yes, the bench on the square's north side is in the same location as the one Tom Hanks occupied in *Forrest Gump,* but it's not the same bench that hosted the two-time Oscar winner's backside—that one was donated by Paramount Pictures to be displayed in the Savannah History Museum on MLK Jr. Boulevard.

HISTORIC SAVANNAH THEATRE

At the northeast corner is the Historic Savannah Theatre (222 Bull St., 912/233-7764, www.savannahtheatre.com), which claims to be the oldest continuously operating theater in the United States. Designed by William Jay, it opened in 1818 with a production of *The Soldier's Daughter.* In the glory days of gaslight theater in the 1800s, some of the nation's best actors, including Edwin Booth, brother to Lincoln's assassin, regularly trod the boards of its stage. Other notable visitors were Sarah Bernhardt, W. C. Fields, and Oscar Wilde. Due to a fire in 1948, little remains of Jay's original design except a small section of exterior

wall. It's currently home to a semiprofessional revue company specializing in oldies shows.

INDEPENDENT PRESBYTERIAN CHURCH

Built in 1818, possibly by William Jay—scholars are unsure of the scope of his involvement—Independent Presbyterian Church (207 Bull St., 912/236-3346, www.ipcsav.org, services Sun. 11am, Wed. noon) is called the "mother of Georgia Presbyterianism." A fire destroyed most of Independent Presbyterian's original structure in 1889, but the subsequent rebuilding was a very faithful rendering of the original design, based on London's St. Martin-in-the-Fields. The marble baptism font survived the fire and is still used today. Note also the huge mahogany pulpit, another original feature. The church's steeple made a cameo appearance in *Forrest Gump* as a white feather floated by.

Lowell Mason, composer of the hymn "Nearer My God to Thee," was organist at Independent Presbyterian. In 1885 President Woodrow Wilson married local parishioner Ellen Louise Axson in the manse to the rear of the church. Presiding was her grandfather, minister at the time. During the Great Awakening in 1896, almost 3,000 people jammed the sanctuary to hear famous evangelist D. L. Moody preach. Call ahead for a tour.

FIRST BAPTIST CHURCH

The nearby First Baptist Church (223 Bull St., 912/234-2671, services Sun. 11am) claims to be the oldest original church building in Savannah, with a cornerstone dating from 1830. Services were held here throughout the Civil War, with Union troops attending during the occupation. The church was renovated by renowned local architect Henrik Wallin in 1922. Call ahead for a tour.

COLONIAL CEMETERY

Just north of Chippewa Square is Oglethorpe Avenue, originally called South Broad and the southern boundary of the original colony. At Oglethorpe and Abercorn Streets is Colonial Cemetery, first active in 1750. You'd be forgiven for assuming it's the "DAR" cemetery;

© JIM MOREKIS

Green-Meldrim House

the Daughters of the American Revolution contributed the ornate iron entranceway in 1913, thoughtfully dedicating it to themselves instead of the cemetery itself.

Unlike the picturesque beauty of Bonaventure and Laurel Grove cemeteries, Colonial Cemetery has a morbid feel. The fact that burials stopped here in 1853 plays into that desolation, but maybe another reason is because it's the final resting ground of many of Savannah's yellow fever victims. Famous people buried here include Button Gwinnett, one of Georgia's three signers of the Declaration of Independence. The man who reluctantly killed Gwinnett in a duel, General Lachlan McIntosh, is also buried here. The original burial vault of Nathanael Greene is in the cemetery, although the Revolutionary War hero's remains were moved to Johnson Square over a century ago. Vandalism through the years, mostly by Union troops, took a toll on the old gravestones. Many line the east wall of the cemetery, with no one alive able to remember where they originally stood.

Madison Square

Named for the nation's fourth president, Madison Square memorializes a local hero who gave his life for his city during the American Revolution. Irish immigrant Sergeant William Jasper, hero of the Battle of Fort Moultrie in Charleston three years earlier, was killed leading the American charge during the Siege of Savannah, when an allied army failed to retake the city from the British. The monument in the square honors Jasper, but he isn't buried here; his body was interred in a mass grave near the battlefield along with other colonists and soldier-immigrants killed in the one-sided battle.

The two small, suitably warlike cannons in the square have nothing to do with the Siege of Savannah. They commemorate the first two highways in Georgia, today known as Augusta Road and Ogeechee Road.

GREEN-MELDRIM HOUSE

Given the house's beauty and history, visitors will be forgiven for not immediately realizing that the Green-Meldrim House (1 W. Macon

St., 912/232-1251, tours every 30 minutes Tues. and Thurs.-Fri. 10am-4pm, Sat. 10am-1pm, $7 adults, $2 children) is also the rectory of the adjacent St. John's Episcopal Church, which acquired it in 1892. Though known primarily for serving as General William T. Sherman's headquarters during his occupation of Savannah, visitors find the Green-Meldrim House a remarkably calming, serene location in and of itself, quite apart from its role as the place where Sherman formulated his ill-fated "40 acres and a mule" Field Order Number 15, giving most of the Sea Islands of Georgia and South Carolina to freed blacks. A remarkably tasteful example of Gothic Revival architecture, this 1850 design by John Norris features a beautiful external gallery of filigree ironwork. The interior is decorated with a keen and rare eye for elegant minimalism in this sometimes rococo-minded town.

Nearby, the old **Scottish Rite Temple** at Charlton and Bull Streets was designed by Hyman Witcover, who also designed City Hall. A popular drugstore with a soda fountain for many years, it currently houses the Gryphon Tea Room, run by the Savannah College of Art and Design.

Directly across from that is SCAD's first building, **Poetter Hall,** known to old-timers as the Savannah Volunteer Guards Armory. With its imposing but somewhat whimsical facade right out of a Harry Potter movie, this brick and terra-cotta gem of a Romanesque Revival building was built in 1893 by William Gibbons Preston. It housed National Guard units (as well as a high school) until World War II, when the USO occupied the building during its tenant unit's service in Europe.

At the north side of Madison Square is the **Hilton Savannah DeSoto.** Imagine occupying that same space the most glorious, opulent, regal building you can think of, a paradise of brick, mortar, and buff-colored terra-cotta. That would have been the old DeSoto Hotel, which from its opening in 1890 was known as one of the world's most beautiful hotels and the clear masterpiece in Boston architect William Gibbons Preston's already-impressive Savannah

portfolio. Alas, it didn't have air-conditioning, so the Hilton chain demolished it in 1968 to build the current nondescript box.

Lafayette Square

Truly one of Savannah's favorite squares, especially on St. Patrick's Day, verdant Lafayette Square boasts a number of important sights and attractions.

◖ CATHEDRAL OF ST. JOHN THE BAPTIST

Spiritual home to Savannah's Irish community and the oldest Catholic church in Georgia, the Cathedral of St. John the Baptist (222. E. Harris St., 912/233-4709, www.savannahcathedral.org, daily 9am-noon and 12:30pm-5pm, mass Sun. 8am, 10am, 11:30am, Mon.-Sat. noon, Latin mass Sun. 1pm) was initially known as Our Lady of Perpetual Help. It's the place to be for mass the morning of March 17 at 8am, as the clans gather in their green jackets and white dresses to take a sip of communion wine before moving on to harder stuff in honor of St. Patrick.

Despite its overt Celtic character today, the parish was originally founded by French Catholics who arrived after an uprising in the colony of Haiti in the late 1700s. They were joined by other Gallic Catholics when some nobles fled from the French Revolution. The first sanctuary on the site was built in 1873, after the diocese traded a lot at Taylor and Lincoln Streets to the Sisters of Mercy in exchange for this locale. In a distressingly common event back then in Savannah, fire swept through the edifice in 1898, leaving only two spires and the external walls. In an amazing story of determination and skill, the cathedral was completely rebuilt within a year and a half. In the years since, many renovations have been undertaken, including an interior renovation following the Second Vatican Council to incorporate some of its sweeping reforms, for example, a new altar allowing the celebrant to face the congregation. The most recent renovation, from 1998 to 2000, involved the intricate removal, cleaning, and

© JIM MOREKIS

Cathedral of St. John the Baptist

the Girl Scouts of the USA, who was married to cotton heir William "Billow" Low, Andrew Low's son. Despite their happy-go-lucky nicknames, the union of Daisy and Billow was a notably unhappy one. Still, divorce was out of the question, so the couple lived separate lives until William's death in 1905. The one good thing that came out of the marriage was the germ for the idea for the Girl Scouts, which Juliette got from England's "Girl Guides" while living there with her husband, Savannah being the couple's winter residence.

Designed by the great New York architect John Norris, the Low House is a magnificent example of the Italianate style. Check out the cast-iron balconies on the long porch, a fairly rare feature in historic Savannah homes. Antiques junkies will go nuts over the furnishings, especially the massive secretary in the parlor, one of only four of this type in existence (a sibling is in the Metropolitan Museum of Art). Author William Makepeace Thackeray ate in the dining room, now sporting full French porcelain service, and slept in an upstairs room; he also wrote at the desk by the bed. Also on the second floor you'll see the room where Robert E. Lee stayed during his visit and the bed where Juliette Gordon Low died.

releading of more than 50 of the cathedral's stained-glass windows, a roof replacement, and an interior makeover.

When inside the magnificent interior, look for the new 9,000-pound altar and the 8,000-pound baptismal font, both made of Italian marble. In 2003 an armed man entered the cathedral and set the pulpit and bishop's chair on fire, resulting in nearly $400,000 of damage. The pulpit you see now is an exact replica carved in Italy. The arsonist claimed he did it as a statement against organized religion.

ANDREW LOW HOUSE MUSEUM

Another major landmark on Lafayette Square is the Andrew Low House Museum (329 Abercorn St., 912/233-6854, www.andrewlowhouse.com, Mon.-Wed. and Fri.-Sat. 10am-4:30pm, Sun. noon-4:30pm, last tour 4pm, $8 adults, $4.50 children), once the home of Juliette "Daisy" Gordon Low, the founder of

FLANNERY O'CONNOR CHILDHOOD HOME

On the other corner of Lafayette Square stands the rather Spartan facade of the Flannery O'Connor Childhood Home (207 E. Charlton St., 912/233-6014, www.flanneryoconnorhome.org, Fri.-Wed. 1pm-4pm, $6 adults, $5 students, free under age 15). The Savannah-born novelist lived in this three-story townhome from her birth in 1925 until 1938 and attended church at the cathedral across the square. Once a fairly nondescript attraction for so favorite a native daughter, a recent round of renovations has returned the two main floors to the state Flannery would have known, including an extensive library. A nonprofit association sponsors O'Connor-related readings and signings. While the current backyard garden dates to 1993, it's the place where five-year-old Flannery is said to have taught a chicken to walk backward, foreshadowing the eccentric, Gothic flavor of her writing.

Across from the O'Connor house is the **Hamilton-Turner Inn** (330 Abercorn St., 912/233-1833, www.hamilton-turnerinn.com). Now a privately owned bed-and-breakfast, this 1873 Second Empire mansion is best known for the showmanship of its over-the-top Victorian appointments and its role in "The Book" as the home of Joe Odom's girlfriend "Mandy Nichols" (real name Nancy Hillis). In 1883 it was reportedly the first house in Savannah to have electricity.

Troup Square

This low-key square boasts the most modern-looking monument downtown, the **Armillary Sphere.** Essentially an elaborate sundial, the sphere is a series of astrologically themed rings with an arrow that marks the time by shadow. It is supported by six tortoises.

Troup Square is also the home of the historic **Unitarian Universalist Church of Savannah** (313 E. Harris St., 912/234-0980, www.jinglebellschurch.org, services Sun. 11am). This original home of Savannah's Unitarians, who sold the church when the Civil War came, was recently reacquired by the congregation. It is where James L. Pierpont first performed his immortal tune "Jingle Bells." When he did so, however, the church was actually on Oglethorpe Square. The entire building was moved to Troup Square in the mid-1800s.

Just east of Troup Square, near the intersection of Harris and Price Streets, is the **Beach Institute** (502 E. Harris St., 912/234-8000, www.kingtisdell.org, Tues.-Sun. noon-5pm, $4). Built as a school by the Freedmen's Bureau soon after the Civil War, it was named after its prime benefactor, Alfred Beach, editor of *Scientific American.* It served as an African American school through 1919. Restored by SCAD and given back to the city to serve as a museum, the Beach Institute houses the permanent Ulysses Davis.

JONES STREET

There aren't a lot of individual attractions on Jones Street, the east-west avenue between Taylor and Charlton Streets just north of Monterey Square. Rather, it's the small-scale, throwback feel of the place and its tasteful, dignified homes, including the former home of Joe Odom (16 E. Jones St.), that are the attraction. The **Eliza Thompson House** (5 W. Jones St.), now a bed-and-breakfast, was the first home on Jones Street. Cotton factor Joseph Thompson built the house for his wife, Eliza, in 1847. The carriage house is not original to the structure, having been built almost from scratch in 1980.

◖ Monterey Square

For many, this is the ultimate Savannah square. Originally named "Monterrey Square" to commemorate the local Irish Jasper Greens' participation in a victorious Mexican-American War battle in 1846, the spelling morphed into its current version somewhere along the way. But Monterey Square remains one of the most visually beautiful and serene spots in all of Savannah. At the center of the square is a monument not to the victory for which it is named but to Count Casimir Pulaski, killed while attempting to retake the city from the British, and whose remains supposedly lie under the 55-foot monument. As early as 1912, people began noticing the disintegration of the monument due to substandard marble used in some key parts, but it wasn't until the 1990s that a full restoration was accomplished. The restoration company discovered that one of the monument's 34 sections had been accidentally installed upside down. So in the true spirit of preservation, they dutifully put the section back—upside down. The *Goddess of Liberty* atop the monument, however, is not original; you can see her in the Savannah History Museum. Fans of ironwork will enjoy the ornate masterpieces in wrought iron featured at many houses on the periphery of the square.

MERCER-WILLIAMS HOUSE MUSEUM

Many visitors come to see the Mercer-Williams House Museum (429 Bull St., 912/236-6352,

THE STORY OF "JINGLE BELLS"

Long after the Civil War, a North-South feud of a more harmless kind still simmers, as Boston and Savannah vie over bragging rights as to where the classic Christmas song "Jingle Bells" was written. The song's composer, James L. Pierpont, led a life at times as carefree as his song itself. Born in Boston as the son of an abolitionist Unitarian minister, Pierpont's wanderlust manifested early, when he ventured from his new wife and young children to follow the 1849 gold rush to San Francisco, coming back east after one of that city's periodic enormous fires. When his brother John was named minister of the new Unitarian congregation in Savannah in 1853—a novelty down south at the time—Pierpont followed him, becoming music director and organist, again leaving behind his wife and children in Boston. During this time Pierpont became a prolific composer of secular tunes, including polkas, ballads, and minstrel songs.

Pierpont's first wife died of tuberculosis in 1856. By August 1857 he had remarried the daughter of the mayor of Savannah. That same month, a Boston-based publisher, Oliver Ditson and Co., published his song "One Horse Open Sleigh." Two years later it was rereleased with the current title, "Jingle Bells." At neither time, however, was the song a popular hit. In 1859, with slavery tearing the country apart, the Unitarian Church in Savannah closed due to its abolitionist stance. By the outbreak of war, Pierpont's brother John had gone back up north. James Pierpont, however, opted to stay in Savannah with his second wife, Eliza Jane, going so far as to sign up with the Isle of Hope Volunteers (he served as a company clerk) of the Confederate Army.

It took action by his son Juriah in 1880 to renew the copyright to what would become one of the most famous songs of all time. Pierpont died in 1883 in Winter Haven, Florida, and by his own request was buried in Savannah's Laurel Grove Cemetery. The provenance of his now-famous song is more in doubt. In Massachusetts, they swear Pierpont wrote the song while at the home of one Mrs. Otis Waterman. In Georgia, scholars assure us a homesick Pierpont wrote the tune during a winter at a house at Oglethorpe and Whitaker Streets, long since demolished. The Savannah contingent's ace in the hole is the fact that "Jingle Bells" was first performed in public at a Thanksgiving program at the local Unitarian Universalist Church in 1857. And despite persistent claims in Massachusetts that he wrote the song there in 1850, Southern scholars point out that Pierpont was actually in California in 1850. So in this case, at least, it appears the South can claim victory over the Yankees.

In one of those delightful happenstances of serendipity, Pierpont's old church—moved to Troup Square from its original site on Oglethorpe Square—went on the market in the 1990s, and the local Unitarian Universalist congregation was able to raise enough money to buy it. It remains there to this day.

www.mercerhouse.com, Mon.-Sat. 10:30am-4pm, Sun. noon-4pm, $12.50 adults, $8 students). While locals never begrudge the business Savannah has enjoyed since "The Book," it's a shame that this grand John Norris building is now primarily known as a crime scene involving antiques dealer Jim Williams and his lover. Therefore it might come as no surprise that if you take a tour of the home, you might hear less about "The Book" than you may have expected. Now proudly owned by Jim Williams's sister Dorothy Kingery, an established academic in her own right, the Mercer-Williams House deliberately concentrates on the early history of the home and her brother's prodigious talent as a collector and conservator of fine art and antiques. That said, Dr. Kingery's mama didn't raise no fool, as we say down here. The house was known to generations of Savannahians as simply the Mercer House until *Midnight in the Garden of Good and Evil* took off, at which time the eponymous nod to the late Mr. Williams was added.

Built for General Hugh W. Mercer, Johnny

© JIM MOREKIS

Mercer-Williams House Museum on Monterey Square

Mercer's great-grandfather, in 1860, the war interrupted construction. General Mercer—descendant of the Revolutionary War general and George Washington's close friend Hugh Mercer—survived the war, in which he was charged with the defense of Savannah. But he soon fell on hard times and was forced to sell the house to John Wilder, who moved in after completion in 1868. Just so you know, and despite what any tour guide might tell you, the great Johnny Mercer himself never lived in the house. Technically, no member of his family ever did either.

Tours of the home's four main rooms begin in the carriage house to the rear of the mansion. They're worth it for art aficionados even though the upstairs, Dr. Kingery's residence, is off-limits. Be forewarned that if you're coming just to see things about the book or movie, you might be disappointed.

TEMPLE MICKVE ISRAEL

Directly across Monterey Square from the Mercer House is Temple Mickve Israel (20 E. Gordon St., 912/233-1547, www.mickveisrael. org), a notable structure for many reasons: It's Georgia's first synagogue; it's the only Gothic synagogue in the country; and it's the third-oldest Jewish congregation in North America (following those in New York and Newport, Rhode Island). Notable congregants have included Dr. Samuel Nunes Ribeiro, who helped stop an epidemic in 1733; his descendant Raphael Moses, considered the father of the peach industry in the Peach State; and current Mickve Israel Rabbi Arnold Mark Belzer, one of Savannah's most beloved community leaders. A specialist in the study of small, often-persecuted Jewish communities around the world, Belzer met Pope John Paul II in 2005 as a part of that pontiff's historic rapprochement between the Catholic Church and Judaism.

Mickve Israel offers 30-45 minute tours of the sanctuary and museum (Mon.-Fri. 10am-1pm and 2pm-4pm, closed Jewish holidays).

Calhoun Square

The last of the 24 squares in Savannah's

original grid, Calhoun Square is also the only square with all its original buildings intact—a rarity indeed in a city ravaged by fire so many times in its history.

Dominating the south side of the square is Savannah's first public elementary school and spiritual home of Savannah educators, the **Massie Heritage Center** (207 E. Gordon St., 912/201-5070, www.massieschool.com, Mon.-Fri. 9am-4pm, self-guided tour $7 adults, $3 children). In 1841, Peter Massie, a Scots planter with a populist streak, endowed the school to give poor children as good an education as the children of rich families, like Massie's own, received. Another of Savannah's masterpieces by John Norris—whose impressive oeuvre includes the Low House, the Mercer House, and the Green-Meldrim House—the central portion of the trifold building was completed in 1856 and is a great example of Greek Revival architecture. The two large wings on each side were added later. After the Civil War, the "Massie school," as it's known locally, was designated as the area's African American public school. Classes ceased in 1974, and it now operates as a living history museum, centering on the period-appointed one-room "heritage classroom." A recent million-dollar renovation includes an interactive model of Oglethorpe's urban design and several interesting exhibits on aspects of Savannah architecture and history.

Catty-corner to the Massie School is the **Wesley Monumental United Methodist Church** (429 Abercorn St., 912/232-0191, www.wesleymonumental.org, sanctuary daily 9am-5pm, services Sun. 8:45am and 11am). This home of Savannah's first Methodist parish was named not only for movement founder John Wesley but for his musical younger brother Charles. Built in 1875 on the model of Queen's Kirk in Amsterdam and the fourth incarnation of the parish home, this is another great example of Savannah's Gothic churches. Its acoustically wonderful sanctuary features a magnificent Noack organ, which would no doubt please the picky ears of Charles Wesley himself, author of the lyrics to "Hark! The Herald Angels Sing."

Martin Luther King Jr. Boulevard

Originally known as West Broad Street (you'll still hear old-timers refer to it that way), Martin Luther King Jr. Boulevard is the spiritual home of Savannah's African American community, though it has gone through several transformations. In the early 1800s, West Broad was a fashionable address, but during the middle of that century its north end got a bad reputation for crime and blight as thousands of Irish immigrants packed in right beside the area's poor black population.

West Broad's glory days as a center of black culture happened in the first half of the 20th century, beginning and ending with the late, great Union Station terminal. Built in 1902, the terminal was the main gateway to the city and ushered in a heyday on West Broad that saw thriving black movie theaters like the Star. Here were packed venues on the "chitlin circuit" such as The Dunbar, hosting such legends as Little Richard. The great number of African American-owned banks on the street gave it the name "the Wall Street of black America." The end came with the razing of the gorgeous Union Station in 1963 to make way for an on-ramp to I-16. The poorly planned project cut the historic boulevard in two, with several entire neighborhoods being destroyed to make way. While the hideous on-ramp remains, every now and then talk surfaces of moving it in an attempt to recreate the magic of old West Broad.

Renamed for the civil rights leader in 1990, MLK Jr. Boulevard currently is undergoing another renaissance. During his visit for the 2007 Savannah Music Festival, jazz great Wynton Marsalis dedicated a plaque to Louis Armstrong's mentor King Oliver in front of the building at 514 MLK Jr. Boulevard, where Oliver spent his last days.

RALPH MARK GILBERT CIVIL RIGHTS MUSEUM

One of the former black-owned bank buildings on MLK Jr. Boulevard is now home to the Ralph Mark Gilbert Civil Rights Museum (460 MLK Jr. Blvd., 912/231-8900, www.

savcivilrights.com, Mon.-Sat. 9am-5pm, $8 adults, $4 children). Named for the pastor of the First African Baptist Church and a key early civil rights organizer, the building was also the local NAACP headquarters for a time. Three floors of exhibits here include photos and interactive exhibits, the highlight for historians being a fiber-optic map of nearly 100 significant civil rights sites. The first floor features a re-creation of the Azalea Room of the local Levy's department store, an early boycott diner where blacks were not allowed to eat, though they could buy goods from the store. The second floor is more for hands-on education, with classrooms, a computer room, and a video and reading room. A film chronicles mass meetings, voter registration drives, boycotts, sit-ins, kneel-ins (the integration of churches), and wade-ins (the integration of beaches).

SHIPS OF THE SEA MARITIME MUSEUM

One of Savannah's more unique museums is the quirky Ships of the Sea Maritime Museum (41 MLK Jr. Blvd., 912/232-1511, http://shipsofthesea.org, Tues.-Sun. 10am-5pm, $8 adults, $6 students). The stunning Greek Revival building in which it resides is known as the Scarbrough House because it was initially built in 1819 by the great William Jay for local shipping merchant William Scarbrough, owner of the SS *Savannah,* the first steamship to cross the Atlantic. After the Scarbroughs sold the property, it became the West Broad School for African Americans from Reconstruction through integration.

One of the Historic Savannah Foundation's key restoration projects in the 1970s, the museum got another major facelift in 1998, including a roof based on the original Jay design and a delightful enlargement of the mansion's garden out back. Inside, children, maritime buffs, and crafts connoisseurs can find intricate and detailed scale models of various historic vessels, such as Oglethorpe's *Anne,* the SS *Savannah,* and the NS *Savannah,* the world's first nuclear-powered surface vessel. There's even a model of the *Titanic.*

BATTLEFIELD PARK COMPLEX

Three important sites are clustered together on MLK Jr. Boulevard under the auspices of the Coastal Heritage Society: the Savannah History Museum, the Roundhouse Railroad Museum, and the Siege of Savannah battlefield.

The **Savannah History Museum** (303 MLK Jr. Blvd., 912/651-6825, www.chsgeorgia.org, Mon.-Fri. 8:30am-5pm, Sat.-Sun. 9am-5pm, $5 adults, free for children), first stop for many a visitor to town because it's in the same restored Central of Georgia passenger shed as the visitors center, contains many interesting exhibits on local history, concentrating mostly on colonial times. Toward the rear of the museum is a room for rotating exhibits, as well as one of Johnny Mercer's two Oscars and, of course, the historic "*Forrest Gump* bench" that Tom Hanks sat on during his scenes in Chippewa Square.

The **Roundhouse Railroad Museum** (601 W. Harris St., 912/651-6823, www.chsgeorgia.org, daily 9am-5pm, $10 adults, $4 students) is an ongoing homage to the deep and strangely underreported influence of the railroad industry on Savannah. Constructed in 1830 for the brand-new Central of Georgia line, the Roundhouse's design was cutting-edge for the time, the first facility to put all the railroad's key facilities in one place. Spared by Sherman, the site saw its real heyday after the Civil War. But as technology changed, so did the Roundhouse, which gradually fell further into neglect until the 1960s, when preservation-minded buffs banded together to raise enough money to save it. There's a large collection of various period locomotives and rail cars. Some of Savannah's greatest artisans have contributed their preservation skills to bring back much of the facility's muscular splendor. The real highlight of the Roundhouse is the thing in the middle that gave it its name, a huge central turntable for positioning rolling stock for repair and maintenance. Frequent demonstrations occur with an actual steam locomotive firing up and taking a turn on the turntable.

Right off MLK Jr. Boulevard is the

Battlefield Park off MLK Jr. Boulevard

Battlefield Park (dawn-dusk, free), a.k.a. the Spring Hill Redoubt, a reconstruction of the British fortifications at the Siege of Savannah with an interpretive site. Note that the redoubt is not at the actual location of the original fort; that lies underneath the nearby Sons of the Revolution marker. Eight hundred granite markers signify the battle's casualties, most of whom were buried in mass graves soon afterward. Sadly, most of the remains of these brave men were simply bulldozed up and discarded without ceremony during later construction projects.

SCAD MUSEUM OF ART

The Savannah College of Art and Design recently concluded a massive expansion of this handsome building into an old railroad facility immediately behind it, more than doubling exhibition space and adding the impressive Walter O. Evans Collection of African American Art. The SCAD Museum of Art (601 Turner Blvd., 912/525-5220, www.scad.edu, Tues.-Wed. and Fri. 10am-5pm, Thurs.

10am-8pm, Sat.-Sun. noon-5pm, $10, $5 students) now hosts a rotating series of exhibits, from standard painting to video installations, many of them commissioned by the school itself.

VICTORIAN DISTRICT

Boasting 50 blocks of fine Victorian and Queen Anne frame houses, Savannah's Victorian district gets nowhere near the media attention that the older, more stately homes closer to the river get. But it is truly magnificent in its own right, and nearly as expansive. The city's first suburb, built between 1870 and 1910, it runs from roughly Gwinnett Street south to Anderson Street, with Montgomery and Price Streets as eastern and western boundaries.

In addition to the glories of Forsyth Park, some key areas for connoisseurs of truly grand Victorian architecture are the residential blocks of East Hall Street between Lincoln and Price Streets—one of the few street sections in town with the original paving. Some other nice examples are in the 1900-2000 blocks of Bull

Street near the large Bull Street Public Library, including the famous "Gingerbread House" at 1917 Bull Street, now a private bridal design studio.

🄲 Forsyth Park

A favorite with locals and visitors alike, the vast, lush expanse of Forsyth Park is a center of local life, abuzz with activity and events year-round. The park owes its existence to William B. Hodgson, who donated its core 10 acres to the city for use as a park. Deeply influenced by the then-trendy design of green-space areas in France, Forsyth Park's landscape design by William Bischoff dates to 1851. Named for Georgia Governor John Forsyth, the park covers 30 acres, and its perimeter is about a mile. The park is a center of activities all year long, from free festivals to concerts to Ultimate Frisbee games to the constant circuit around the periphery of walkers, joggers, dog owners, and bicyclists. The only time you shouldn't venture into the park is after midnight; otherwise, enjoy.

A WALKING TOUR OF FORSYTH PARK

Here's a walking tour of Savannah's backyard, the one-of-a-kind Forsyth Park, beginning at the north end at Gaston and Bull Streets: As you approach the park, don't miss the ornate ironwork on the west side of Bull street marking the **Armstrong House,** designed by Henrik Wallin. Featured in the 1962 film *Cape Fear* as well as 1997's *Midnight in the Garden of Good and Evil,* this Italianate mansion was once home to Armstrong Junior College before its move to the south side. When he's not practicing law in this building, Sonny Seiler, one of the characters in "The Book," still raises the University of Georgia's signature bulldog mascots. Directly across Bull Street is another site of *Midnight* fame, the Oglethorpe Club, one of the many brick and terra-cotta designs by local architect Alfred Eichberg.

It's easy to miss, but as you enter the park's north side, you encounter the **Marine Memorial,** erected in 1947 to honor the 24 Chatham County Marines killed in World War II. Subsequently, the names of Marines killed

Forsyth Fountain

© JIM MOREKIS

in Korea and Vietnam were added. Look west at the corner of Whitaker and Gaston Streets; that's **Hodgson Hall,** home of the Georgia Historical Society. This 1876 building was commissioned by Margaret Telfair to honor her late husband, William Hodgson, chief benefactor of the park the house overlooks. The Georgia Historical Society (912/651-2125, www.georgiahistory.com) administers a treasure of books, documents, maps, photos, and prints that has been a boon to writers and researchers since it was chartered by the state legislature in 1839.

Looking east at the corner of Drayton and Gaston Streets, you'll see the old **Poor House and Hospital,** in use until 1854, when it was converted to serve as the headquarters for the Medical College of Georgia. During the Civil War, General Sherman used the hospital to treat Federal soldiers. From 1930 to 1980 the building was the site of Candler Hospital. Behind Candler Hospital's cast-iron fence, you can soak in the venerable beauty of Savannah's most famous tree, the 300-year-old **Candler Oak.** During Sherman's occupation, wounded Confederate prisoners were treated within a barricade around the oak. The tree is on the National Register of Historic Trees and was the maiden preservation project of the Savannah Tree Foundation, which secured the country's first-ever conservation easement on a single tree.

Walking south into the park proper, you can't miss the world-famous **Forsyth Fountain,** an iconic Savannah sight if there ever was one. Cast in iron on a French model, the fountain was dedicated in 1858. Its water is typically dyed green a few days before St. Patrick's Day. Interestingly, two other versions of this fountain exist—one in Poughkeepsie, New York, and the other in, of all places, the central plaza in Cusco, Peru. Various acts of vandalism and natural disaster took its toll on the fountain until a major restoration in 1988 brought it to its present level of beauty.

Continuing south, you'll encounter two low buildings in the center of the park. The one on the east side is the so-called "Dummy Fort,"

circa 1909, formerly a training ground for local militia. Now it's the **Forsyth Park Café** (daily 7am-dusk, open later on festival evenings) managed by the hotel Mansion on Forsyth Park just across Drayton Street. To the west is the charming **Fragrant Garden for the Blind.** One of those precious little Savannah gems that is too often overlooked in favor of other attractions, the Fragrant Garden was initially sponsored by the local Garden Club and based on others of its type throughout the United States.

The tall monument dominating Forsyth Park's central mall area is the **Confederate Memorial,** which recently received a major facelift. Dedicated in 1875, it wasn't finished in its final form until several years later. A New York sculptor carved the Confederate soldier atop the monument. A copy of it is in Poughkeepsie, New York, as a memorial to the Federal dead—with the "CSA" on the soldier's rucksack changed to "USA." The Bartow and McLaws monuments surrounding the Confederate Memorial were originally in Chippewa Square.

We'll close the walking tour with my favorite Forsyth Park landmark, at the extreme southern end. It's the Memorial to Georgia Veterans of the Spanish-American War, more commonly known as *The Hiker* because of the subject's almost casual demeanor and confident stride. Savannah was a major staging area for that conflict, and many troops were bivouacked in the park. Sculpted in 1902 by Alice Ruggles Kitson, more than 50 replicas of *The Hiker* were made and put up all over the United States; because the same bronze formula was used for all 50 of them, the statues are used by scientists today to gauge the effects of acid rain across the nation.

Carnegie Branch Library

Looking like Frank Lloyd Wright parachuted one of his buildings into Victorian Savannah, the Carnegie Branch Library (537 E. Henry St., 912/652-3600, Mon. 10am-8pm, Tues.-Thurs. 10am-6pm, Fri. 2pm-6pm, Sat. 10am-6pm) is the only example of prairie architecture in town, designed by Savannah architect Julian de Bruyn Kops and built, as the name implies, with funding from tycoon-philanthropist Andrew Carnegie in 1914. But more importantly, the Carnegie Library was for decades the only public library for African Americans in Savannah. One of its patrons was a young Clarence Thomas, who would of course grow up to be a U.S. Supreme Court justice.

EASTSIDE
Old Fort Jackson

The oldest standing brick fort in Georgia, Old Fort Jackson (Fort Jackson Rd., 912/232-3945, http://chsgeorgia.org, daily 9am-5pm, $6, free under age 7), named for Georgia Governor James Jackson, is also one of eight remaining examples of the so-called Second System of American forts built prior to the War of 1812. Its main claim to fame is its supporting role in the saga of the CSS *Georgia,* a Confederate ironclad now resting under 40 feet of water directly in front of the fort. Built with $115,000 in funds raised by the Ladies Gunboat Society, the *Georgia*—wrapped in an armor girdle of railroad ties—proved too heavy for its engine. So it was simply anchored in the channel opposite Fort Jackson as a floating battery. With General Sherman's arrival in 1864, Confederate forces evacuating to South Carolina scuttled the vessel where it lay to keep it out of Yankee hands.

Maritime archaeology on the *Georgia* continues apace, with dive teams bringing up cannons, ammunition, and other artifacts. Unlike Charleston's CSS *Hunley* submarine, no lives were lost in the *Georgia* incident, therefore there are no concerns about disrupting a grave site. Every now and then, talk surfaces of raising the ironclad—both for research and because the port views it as an impediment to dredging the channel even deeper—but most experts say it's unlikely to survive the stress.

Operated by the nonprofit Coastal Heritage Society, Fort Jackson is in an excellent state of preservation and provides loads of information for history buffs as well as for kids, who will enjoy climbing the parapets and running on the large parade ground (this area was once a rice field). Inside the fort's casemates underneath the ramparts you'll find well-organized exhibits on the fort's construction and history. Most visitors especially love the daily cannon firings during the summer. If you're really lucky, you'll be around when Fort Jackson fires a salute to passing military vessels on the river—the only historic fort in the United States that does so.

To get to Fort Jackson, take President Street Extension (Islands Expressway) east out of downtown. The entrance is several miles down on the left.

Oatland Island Wildlife Center

The closest thing Savannah has to a zoo is the vast, multipurpose Oatland Island Wildlife Center (711 Sandtown Rd., 912/898-3980, www.oatlandisland.org, daily 10am-5pm, $5 adults, $3 children). Set on a former Centers for Disease Control site, it has undergone an extensive environmental cleanup and is now owned by the local school system, although supported purely by donations. Families by the hundreds come here for a number of special Saturdays throughout the year, including an old-fashioned cane-grinding in November and a day of sheep-shearing in April.

The main attractions here are the critters, located at various points along a meandering two-mile nature trail through the woods and along the marsh. All animals at Oatland are there because they're somehow unable to return to the wild. Highlights include a tight-knit pack of Eastern wolves, a pair of bison, cougars (once indigenous), some cute foxes, and an extensive raptor aviary.

The massive central building was designed by noted local architect Henrik Wallin as a retirement home for railroad conductors. Inside, check out the display of a huge set of whalebones, the remains of a 50-foot-long endangered fin whale that washed ashore on Tybee Island in 1989.

To get here from downtown, take President Street Extension (Islands Expressway) about five miles. Begin looking for the Oatland Island sign on the right. You'll go through part of a residential neighborhood until you take a bend to the right; Oatland's gate is then on the left. To get here from Bonaventure Cemetery, go straight out the gate on Bonaventure Road and take a right on Pennsylvania Avenue. As you dead-end on Islands Expressway, take a right and look for the entrance farther along on the right.

◖ Bonaventure Cemetery

On the banks of the Wilmington River just east of town lies one of Savannah's most unique sights, Bonaventure Cemetery (330 Bonaventure Rd., 912/651-6843, daily 8am-5pm). John Muir, who went on to found the Sierra Club, wrote of Bonaventure's Spanish moss-bedecked beauty in his 1867 book *A Thousand-mile Walk to the Gulf,* marveling at the screaming bald eagles that then frequented the area. While its pedigree as Savannah's premier public cemetery goes back 100 years, it was used as a burial ground as early as 1794. In the years since, this achingly poignant vista of live oaks and azaleas has been the final resting place of such local and national luminaries as Johnny Mercer, Conrad Aiken, Wormsloe Historic Site founder Noble Jones, and, of course, the Trosdal plot, former home of the famous *Bird Girl* statue (the original is now in the Telfair Academy of Arts and Sciences). Fittingly, the late, great Jack Leigh, who took the *Bird Girl* photo for the cover of *Midnight in the Garden of Good and Evil,* is interred here as well.

While strolling through Bonaventure, you might see some burial sites lined with reddish-brown tiles, their tops studded with half circles. Mistakenly known as "slave tiles," these are actually a rare type of Victorian garden tile that has nothing whatsoever to do with slaves.

Several local tour companies offer options that include a visit to Bonaventure. If you're doing a self-guided tour, go by the small visitors center at the entrance and pick up one of the free guides to the cemetery, assembled by the local volunteer Bonaventure Historical Society. By all means, do the tourist thing and pay your respects at Johnny Mercer's final resting place, and go visit beautiful little "Gracie" in Section

© JIM MOREKIS

memorial to "Gracie" in Bonaventure Cemetery

E, Lot 99. But I also suggest doing as the locals do: Bring a picnic lunch and a blanket and set yourself beside the breezy banks of the Wilmington River, taking in all the lazy beauty and evocative bygone history surrounding you.

To get here from downtown, take President Street Extension east and take a right on Pennsylvania Avenue, then a left on Bonaventure Road. Alternately, go east on Victory Drive (U.S. 80) and take a left on Whatley Road in the town of Thunderbolt. Veer left onto Bonaventure Road. The cemetery is one mile ahead on the right.

Daffin Park

A century spent in Forsyth Park's more genteel shadow doesn't diminish the importance of Daffin Park (1500 E. Victory Dr.) as Savannah's second major green space. Designed by John Nolen in 1907 and named for a former local parks commissioner, Daffin not only hosts a large variety of local athletes on its fields and courts, it's also home to Historic Grayson

JOHNNY MERCER'S BLACK MAGIC

Visitors might be forgiven for thinking Paula Deen is Savannah's most famous native, but the Food Network star, born 200 miles away in Albany, Georgia, technically cannot claim that title. The great Johnny Mercer is not only without a doubt Savannah's most noteworthy progeny, he is also one of the greatest lyricists music has ever known. He grew up in southside Savannah on a small river then called the Back River but since renamed Moon River in honor of his best-known song. Armed with an innate talent for rhythm and a curious ear for dialogue—both qualities honed by his frequent boyhood contact with Savannah African American culture and musicians during the Jazz Age—Mercer moved away from Savannah to New York when he was only 19 to try his hand in Tin Pan Alley, then the world center of popular music.

There he met the woman who would be his wife, Ginger Meehan (real name Elizabeth Meltzer). This Brooklyn Jewish chorus girl—once Bing Crosby's lover—would be both muse and foil for Mercer in the decades to follow. Mutual infidelity and a partying lifestyle combined for a stormy marriage, yet both remained together until Mercer's death from a brain tumor in 1976 (Ginger died in 1994). In a few years he was an established success in New York. By 1935, however, the show business center of gravity was moving toward Hollywood, and Mercer—ahead of his time as usual—sensed the shift early and moved to the West Coast to write musicals for RKO. The advent of high-quality microphones was tailor-made for Mercer's nuanced lyrics.

During his long and productive Hollywood career in the 1930s and 1940s, he wrote such classics as "Jeepers Creepers," "That Old Black Magic," "Come Rain or Come Shine," "Skylark," and "Ac-Cent-Tchu-Ate the Positive."

Mercer embarked on an affair with the young Judy Garland in 1941, a dalliance which he later said inspired the song "I Remember You." While the advent of rock and roll in the postwar era signaled the decline of Mercer's career, he wrote what is arguably his greatest song, "Moon River," in 1961. The song, debuted by Audrey Hepburn in the film *Breakfast at Tiffany's*, won an Academy Award for Best Original Song. In addition to "Moon River," Mercer won three other Oscars, for "On the Atchinson, Topeka and the Santa Fe" (1946), "In the Cool, Cool, Cool of the Evening" (1951), and "Days of Wine and Roses" (1962).

Today you can pay your respects to Mercer in three places: his boyhood home (509 E. Gwinnett St., look for the historical marker in front of this private residence); the bronze sculpture of Mercer in the newly revitalized Ellis Square near City Market, erected in 2009 in honor of the centennial of his birth; and, of course, at his gravesite in beautiful Bonaventure Cemetery. And regardless of what anyone tells you, neither Johnny Mercer nor any member of his family ever lived in the Mercer-Williams House on Monterey Square, of *Midnight in the Garden of Good and Evil* fame. Although it was built for his great-grandfather, the home was sold to someone else before it was completed.

Stadium on the park's east end. Recently given a serious face-lift, Grayson Stadium hosts the minor league Savannah Sand Gnats. One of the great old ballparks of America, this venue dates from 1941 and has hosted greats such as Babe Ruth, Jackie Robinson, and Mickey Mantle.

Most picturesque for the visitor, however, is the massive fountain set in the middle of the expansive central pond on the park's west side. Originally built in the shape of the continental United States, the pond was the backdrop

for a presidential visit by Franklin D. Roosevelt in 1933 that included a speech to an African American crowd. On the far west end of Daffin Park along Waters Avenue is a marker commemorating the site of the Grandstand for the Great Savannah Races of 1911.

WESTSIDE
Laurel Grove Cemetery

Its natural vista isn't as alluring as Bonaventure's, but Laurel Grove Cemetery boasts its own exquisitely carved memorials and a distinctly Victorian type of surreal beauty that not even Bonaventure can match. In keeping with the racial apartheid of Savannah's early days, there are actually two cemeteries: **Laurel Grove North** (802 W. Anderson St., daily 8am-5pm) for whites, and **Laurel Grove South** (2101 Kollock St., daily 8am-5pm) for blacks. Both are well worth visiting.

By far the most high-profile site in the North Cemetery is that of Juliette Gordon Low, founder of the Girl Scouts of the USA. Other historically significant sites there include the graves of 8th Air Force founder Frank O. Hunter, Central of Georgia Railway founder William Gordon, and "Jingle Bells" composer James Pierpont. But it's the graves of the anonymous and near-anonymous that are the most poignant sights. The various sections for infants, known as "babylands," cannot fail to move. "Mr. Bones," a former Savannah Police dog, is the only animal buried at Laurel Grove. There's an entire site reserved for victims of the great yellow fever epidemic. And don't blink or you'll miss the small rock pile, or cairn, near Governor James Jackson's tomb, the origin and purpose of which remains a mystery. Make sure to view the otherworldly display of Victorian statuary, originally from the grand Greenwich Plantation, which burned in the early 20th century. As with Bonaventure, throughout Laurel Grove you'll find examples of so-called "slave tiles," actually Victorian garden tiles, lining gravesites. Laurel Grove South features the graves of Savannah's early black Baptist ministers, such as Andrew Bryan and Andrew Cox Marshall.

To get to Laurel Grove North, take MLK Jr. Boulevard to Anderson Street and turn west. To get to Laurel Grove South, take Victory Drive (U.S. 80) west to Ogeechee Road. Take a right onto Ogeechee, then a right onto West 36th Street. Continue on to Kollock Street.

Mighty Eighth Air Force Museum

Military and aviation buffs mustn't miss the Mighty Eighth Air Force Museum (175 Bourne Ave., 912/748-8888, www.mightyeighth.

org, daily 9am-5pm, $10 adults, $6 children and active duty military) in Pooler, Georgia, right off I-95. The 8th Air Force was born at Hunter Field in Savannah as the 8th Bomber Command in 1942, becoming the 8th Air Force in 1944; it is now based in Louisiana.

A moving testament to the men and machines who conducted those strategic bombing campaigns over Europe in World War II, the museum also features later 8th Air Force history such as the Korean War, the Linebacker II bombing campaigns over North Vietnam, and the Persian Gulf. Inside you'll find not only airplanes like the P-51 Mustang and the German ME-109, there's also a restored B-17 bomber, the newest jewel of the collection. Outside are several more aircraft, including a MiG-17, an F-4 Phantom, and a B-47 Stratojet bomber like the one that dropped the fabled "Tybee Bomb" in 1958. The nearby Chapel of the Fallen Eagles is a fully functioning sanctuary to honor the more than 26,000 members of the Mighty Eighth that died during World War II.

To get to the Mighty Eighth Museum from downtown, take I-16 west until it intersects I-95. Take I-95 north, take exit 102, and follow the signs.

Savannah-Ogeechee River Canal

A relic of the pre-railroad days, the Savannah-Ogeechee River Canal (681 Ft. Argyle Rd., 912/748-8068, www.savannahogeecheecanal. com, daily 9am-5pm, $2 adults, $1 students) is a 17-mile barge route joining the two rivers. Finished in 1830, it saw three decades of prosperous trade in cotton, rice, bricks, guano, naval stores, and agriculture before the coming of the railroads finished it off. You can walk some of its length today near the Ogeechee River terminus, admiring the impressive engineering of its multiple locks to stabilize the water level. Back in the day, the canal would continue through four lift locks as it traversed 16 miles before reaching the Savannah River. Naturalists will enjoy the built-in nature trail that walking along the canal provides. Be sure to check out the unique sand hills on a nearby trail, a vestige of a bygone geological era when this area was an offshore sandbar. Kids will enjoy the impromptu menagerie of gopher turtles near the site's entrance. Do bring mosquito repellent, although often there's a community spray can at the front door of the little visitor center-museum where you pay your fee.

To get here, get on I-95 south and take exit 94. The canal is a little over two miles west.

SOUTHSIDE
Wormsloe State Historic Site

The one-of-a-kind Wormsloe State Historic Site (7601 Skidaway Rd., 912/353-3023, www.gastateparks.org/info/wormsloe, Tues.-Sun. 9am-5pm, $6 adults, $3.50 children) was first settled by Noble Jones, who landed with Oglethorpe on the *Anne* and fought beside him in the War of Jenkin's Ear. One of the great renaissance men of history, this soldier was also an accomplished carpenter, surveyor, forester, botanist, and physician. Wormsloe became famous for its bountiful gardens, so much so that the famed naturalist William Bartram mentioned them in his diary after a visit in 1765

with father John Bartram. After his death, Noble Jones was originally buried in the family plot on the waterfront, but now his remains are at Bonaventure Cemetery. Jones's descendants donated 822 acres to The Nature Conservancy, which transferred the property to the state. The house, dating from 1828, and 65.5 acres of land are still owned by his family, and no, you can't visit them.

The stunning entrance canopy of 400 live oaks, Spanish moss dripping down the entire length, is one of those iconic images of Savannah that will stay with you forever. A small interpretive museum, a one-mile nature walk, and occasional living history demonstrations make this a great site for the entire family. Walk all the way to the Jones Narrows to see the ruins of the original 1739 fortification, one of the oldest and finest examples of tabby construction in the United States. No doubt the area's abundance of Native American shell middens, where early inhabitants discarded their oyster shells, came in handy for its construction. You can see one nearby.

© DNDAVIS/123RF.COM

Wormsloe State Historic Site

To get to Wormsloe, take Victory Drive (U.S. 80) to Skidaway Road. Go south on Skidaway Road for about 10 miles and follow the signs; you'll see the grand entrance on the right.

Isle of Hope

A charming, friendly seaside community and National Historic District, Isle of Hope is one of a dwindling number of places where parents still let their kids ride around all day on bikes, calling them in at dinnertime. It doesn't boast many shops or restaurants—indeed, the marina is the only real business—but the row of waterfront cottages on Bluff Drive should not be missed. You might recognize some of them from movies such as *Forrest Gump* and *Glory*. Built from 1880 to 1920, they reflect Isle of Hope's reputation as a healing area and serene Wilmington River getaway from Savannah's capitalist hustle.

To get to Isle of Hope, take Victory Drive (U.S. 80) east and take a right on Skidaway Road. Continue south on Skidaway Road and take a left on Laroche Avenue. Continue until you hit Bluff Drive.

Pin Point

Off Whitfield Avenue (Diamond Causeway) on the route to Skidaway Island is tiny **Pin Point, Georgia,** a predominantly African American township better known as the boyhood home of Supreme Court Justice Clarence Thomas. Pin Point traces its roots to a community of former slaves on Ossabaw Island. Displaced by a hurricane, they settled at this idyllic site overlooking the Moon River, itself a former plantation. Many new residents made their living by shucking oysters at the Varn Oyster Company, the central shed of which still remains and forms the basis of the new **Pin Point Heritage Museum** (9924 Pin Point Ave., www.pinpointheritagemuseum.com). The museum tells the story of the Pin Point community through exhibits, a film, and demonstrations of some of the maritime activities at the Varn Oyster Company through the decades, such as crabbing, canning, shucking and shrimp net making.

Skidaway Island

Though locals primarily know Skidaway Island as the site of The Landings, the first gated community in Savannah, Skidaway Island is notable for two beautiful and educational nature-oriented sites. The first, the **University of Georgia Marine Educational Center and Aquarium** (30 Ocean Science Circle, 912/598-3474, www.uga.edu/aquarium, Mon.-Fri. 9am-4pm, Sat. 10am-5pm, $6 adults, $3 children, cash only) shares a scenic 700-acre campus on the scenic Skidaway River with the research-oriented **Skidaway Institute of Oceanography,** also University of Georgia (UGA) affiliated. It hosts scientists and grad students from around the nation, often on trips on is research vessel, the RV *Sea Dawg*. The main attraction of the Marine Center is the small but well-done and recently upgraded aquarium featuring 14 tanks with 200 live animals. Don't expect Sea World here; remember you're essentially on a college campus and the emphasis is on education, not flash. There's also a range of natural history exhibits.

The second site of interest to visitors is **Skidaway Island State Park** (52 Diamond Causeway, 912/598-2300, www.gastateparks.org/info/skidaway, daily 7am-10pm, parking $2). Yeah, you can camp here ($25-28), but the awesome nature trails leading out to the marsh—featuring an ancient Native American shell midden and an old whiskey still—are worth a trip just on their own, especially when combined with the Marine Education Center Aquarium. To get here, take Victory Drive (U.S. 80) until you get to Waters Avenue and continue south as it turns into Whitfield Avenue and then the Diamond Causeway. The park is on your left after the drawbridge. An alternate route from downtown is to take the Truman Parkway all the way to its dead end at Whitfield Avenue; take a left and continue as it turns into Diamond Causeway into Skidaway.

PIN POINT ON THE MOON RIVER

On Ossabaw Island off the Georgia coast, former slaves had settled into freedom as subsistence farmers after the Civil War. But when a massive hurricane devastated the island in 1893, many moved to the mainland, finding themselves south of Savannah along what would later be known as Moon River, at a place called Pin Point. While many continued farming on the long, skinny lots particular to the area, plenty of them gained employment at local packing factories on the marsh-front, where crabs and oysters were packed and sold. By far the largest and longest-lived of those factories was A. S. Varn & Son, which during its heyday employed nearly 100 Pin Point residents—about half of the adult population. There they shucked oysters and picked crabs for five cents a pound and tended to the various machinery of a seafood factory operation, down to sewing the crab nets (itself a vanishing art).

Because so many local people worked at the same place, Pin Point developed an extraordinarily strong community bond, one that was instrumental in forging the life and career of future Supreme Court Justice Clarence Thomas, who was born at Pin Point in 1948. Until he was seven, Thomas lived in a tiny house there with his parents, one without plumbing and insulated with newspapers in the old Southern vernacular tradition. After a house fire, Thomas moved to Savannah with his grandparents, attending a Catholic school where he was for a time the only African American student. He often studied at the Carnegie Library on Henry Street, then the only library where blacks were allowed. Savannah's more active intellectual and social life no doubt influenced his choice of career, and his grandfather, a successful businessman, was his greatest role model. But Thomas's heart was always in Pin Point.

While times have certainly changed here—paved roads finally came in the 1970s, and most of the old shotgun shacks have been replaced with mobile homes—Pin Point remains a small, closely-knit community of about 300 people, with most property still owned by descendants of the freedmen who bought it after Reconstruction. (Pin Point hasn't been immune to big-city problems, however, including a high-profile drug bust in the 1990s that claimed none other than Thomas's nephew.) The Varn factory remained the economic heart of Pin Point until it shut down in 1985, a victim of changing economic and environmental fortunes. Today, the old factory forms the heart of an ambitious new project, the Pin Point Heritage Museum (www.pinpointheritagemuseum.com), which conveys the spirit and history of that community, including its most famous native son, through a series of exhibits and demonstrations.

TYBEE ISLAND

Its name means "salt" in the old Euchee tongue, indicative of the island's chief export in those days. And Tybee Island—"Tybee" to locals—is indeed one of the essential seasonings of life in Savannah. First incorporated as Ocean City and then Savannah Beach, the island has since reclaimed its original name. Eighteen miles from Savannah, in truth Tybee is part and parcel of the city's social and cultural fabric. Many of the island's 3,000 full-time residents, known for their boozy bonhomie and quirky personal style, commute to work in the city. And those living "in town" often reciprocate by visiting Tybee to dine in its few but excellent restaurants, drink in its casual and crazy watering holes, and frolic on its wide, beautiful beaches lined with rare sea oats waving in the Atlantic breeze.

◀ Fort Pulaski National Monument

There's one must-see before you get to Tybee Island proper. On Cockspur Island you'll find Fort Pulaski National Monument (U.S. 80 E., 912/786-5787, www.nps.gov/fopu, fort Sept.-May daily 9am-5pm, June-Aug. daily 9am-6:30pm, visitors center Sept.-May daily 9am-5pm, June-Aug. daily 9am-6:45pm, $5 pp, free under age 16). Not only a delight for any history buff, the fort's also a fantastic place to take the kids. They can climb on the parapets, earthworks, and cannons, and burn off calories on the great nature trail nearby. Along the way they'll no doubt learn a few things as well.

HISTORY

Synchronicity and irony practically scream from every brick. Perhaps prophetically named for Count Casimir Pulaski, who died leading an ill-fated charge on the British in 1779, Fort Pulaski is also symbolic of a catastrophic defeat, this one in 1862 when Union forces using new rifled cannons reduced much of it to rubble in 30 hours. Robert E. Lee—yes, *that* Robert E. Lee—helped build the fort while a lieutenant with the U.S. Army Corps of Engineers. And the Union general who destroyed the fort, Quincy A. Gillmore, was in the Corps of Engineers himself, helping to oversee its construction.

Fort Pulaski's construction was part of a broader initiative by President James Madison in the wake of the disastrous War of 1812, which dramatically revealed the shortcoming of U.S. coastal defense. Two hundred new forts were planned, but by the beginning of the Civil War only 30 were complete. Based on state-of-the-art European design forged in the cauldron of the Napoleonic Wars, Fort Pulaski's thick masonry construction used 25 million bricks, many of them of the famous "Savannah Gray" variety handmade at the nearby Hermitage Plantation. At its unveiling, Fort Pulaski was considered to be invincible—indeed, perhaps the finest fortress ever made.

When Georgia seceded from the Union in January 1861, a small force of 134 Confederates

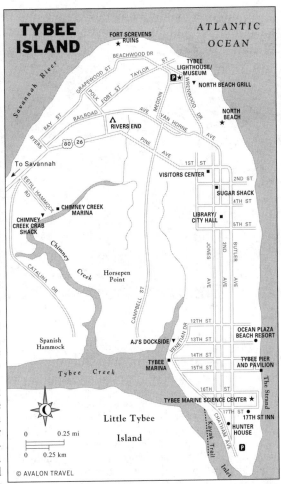

immediately took control of two Savannah area fortifications, Fort Pulaski and Fort Jackson. However, in early 1862 a Union sea-land force under General Quincy Gillmore came to covertly lay the groundwork for a siege of Fort Pulaski to ensure the success of Lincoln's naval blockade. (Besides being one of the North's most brilliant officers, Gillmore had a built-in advantage: Like Robert E. Lee, he also helped build the fort before the war.) The siege would rely on several batteries secretly set up across the Savannah River. Some of the Union guns

© JIM MOREKIS

Fort Pulaski, on the way to Tybee Island

utilized new rifled chamber technology, which dramatically increased the muzzle velocity and penetrating power of their shells. The Union barrage began at 8:15am on April 10, 1862, and Fort Pulaski's walls immediately began to crumble under the withering Union fire. At least one shell struck a powder magazine, igniting an enormous explosion. After a mere 30 hours, Confederate general Charles Olmstead surrendered the "invincible" fortress.

But it was not only Fort Pulaski that was rendered obsolete—it was the whole concept of masonry fortification. From that point forward, military forts would rely on earthwork rather than brick to withstand artillery bombardment. In fact, the section of earthworks you see as you enter Fort Pulaski, the "demilune," was added after the Civil War—an ironic nod to the fort's own premature demise.

Fort Pulaski's new commander, General David Hunter, immediately issued an order freeing all local slaves and guaranteeing them a wage working at the fort. The fort was occupied mostly by troops of the 48th New York Volunteers, who sometimes relieved the boredom of garrison duty by playing the brand-new game of baseball on the fort's vast, grassy parade ground. One of the first photographs of a baseball game was taken at Fort Pulaski in 1863.

VISITING THE FORT

By all means, visit the visitors center, a few hundred yards from the fort itself—but the palpable pleasure starts when you cross the drawbridge over the moat and see a cannon pointed at you from a narrow gun port. Enter the inside of the fort and take in just how big it is—Union occupiers regularly played baseball on the huge, grassy parade ground. Take a walk around the perimeter, underneath the ramparts. This is where the soldiers lived and worked, and you'll see re-creations of officer's quarters, meeting areas, sick rooms, and prisoners' bunks among the cannons, where Confederate prisoners of war were held after the fort's surrender. Cannon firings happen most Saturdays.

And now for the pièce de résistance: Take the steep corkscrew staircase up to the ramparts themselves and take in the jaw-dropping view of the lush marsh, the Savannah River and Tybee Island spreading out in the distance. Stop and sit near one of the several remaining cannons and contemplate what went on here a century and a half ago. (Warning: There's no railing of any kind on the inboard side of the ramparts. Keep the kids well back from the edge, because it's a lethal fall to the fort interior.) Afterward, take a stroll all the way around the walls and see the power of those Yankee guns. Though much of the devastation was soon repaired, some sections of the wall remain in their damaged state. You can even pick out a few cannonballs still stuck in the masonry, like blueberries in a pie.

Save some time and energy for the extensive palmetto-lined nature trail through the sandy upland of Cockspur Island on which the fort is located. There are informative markers, a picnic area, and, as a bonus, there's a coastal defense facility from the Spanish-American War, Battery Hambright.

Cockspur Beacon

Continue east on U.S. 80, passing over Lazaretto Creek, named for the quarantine or "lazaretto" built in the late 1700s to make sure newcomers, mostly slaves, were free of disease. As you cross, look to your left over the river's wide south channel. On a tiny oyster shell islet, find the little Cockspur Beacon lighthouse, in use from 1848 to 1909, when major shipping was routed through the deeper north channel of the river. The site is now preserved by the National Park Service, and is accessible only by boat or kayak. You have to time your arrival with the right tide; Check with a local rental place for advice.

Tybee Lighthouse

Reaching Tybee proper on U.S. 80, you'll soon arrive at the intersection with North Campbell Avenue. This is the entrance to the less-populated, more historically significant north end of the island, once almost entirely taken up

by Fort Screven, a coastal defense fortification of the early 1900s. Take a left onto North Campbell Avenue then left again on Van Horne Street. Take an immediate right onto Meddin Drive. Continue until you see a lighthouse on the left and a parking lot on the right.

Rebuilt several times in its history, the Tybee Island Light Station and Museum (30 Meddin Ave., 912/786-5801, www.tybeelighthouse.org, Wed.-Mon. 9am-5pm, last ticket sold 4:30pm, $8 adults, $6 children) traces its construction to the first year of the colony, based on a design by the multitalented Noble Jones. At its completion in 1736, it was the tallest structure in the United States. One of a handful of working 18th-century lighthouses today, the facility has been restored to its 1916-1964 incarnation, featuring a nine-foot-tall first order Fresnel lens installed in 1867.

The entrance fee gives you admission to the lighthouse, the lighthouse museum, and the nearby Tybee Island Museum. All the outbuildings on the lighthouse grounds are original, including the residence of current lighthouse keeper and Tybee Island Historical Society Director Cullen Chambers, which is also the oldest building on the island. If you've got the legs and the lungs, definitely take all 178 steps up to the top of the lighthouse for a stunning view of Tybee, the Atlantic, and Hilton Head Island.

Old Fort Screven

All around the area of the north end around the lighthouse complex you'll see low-lying concrete bunkers. These are remains of Fort Screven's coastal defense batteries, and many are in private hands. Battery Garland is open to tours, and also houses the **Tybee Island Museum** (30 Meddin Ave., 912/786-5801, Wed.-Mon. 9am-5:30pm, last ticket sold 4:30pm, $8 adults, $6 children, includes admission to lighthouse and lighthouse museum), a charming, almost whimsical little collection of exhibits from various eras of local history.

On nearby Van Horne Avenue is a key part of Fort Screven, the **Tybee Post Theater** (912/323-7727, www.tybeeposttheater.org).

THE TYBEE BOMB

On a dark February night in 1958 at the height of the Cold War, a USAF B-47 Stratojet bomber based at Homestead, Florida, made a simulated nuclear bombing run somewhere over southeast Georgia. A Charleston-based F-86 fighter on a mock intercept came too close, clipping the big bomber's wing. Before bringing down the wounded B-47 at Savannah's Hunter Airfield—then a Strategic Air Command base—Commander Howard Richardson decided he first had to jettison his lethal cargo: a 7,000-pound Mark 15 hydrogen bomb, serial number 47782. We know for sure that he jettisoned it over water; Richardson, who won the Distinguished Flying Cross for his efforts that night, said so himself. What no one knows is exactly where. And thus began the legend of "the Tybee bomb." Go in any Tybee watering hole and ask 10 people where they think it is and you'll get 10 different answers. Some say it's in the north side of Wassaw Sound, some say the south. Some say it's in the shallows, some in deep water. Many locals who work in shrimping, crabbing, and fishing have claimed at various times to have ripped their nets on the bomb. Or on something...Speculation ran wild, with some locals fearing a nuclear explosion, radioactive contamination, or even that a team of scuba-diving terrorists would secretly retrieve the ancient weapon.

Former Army colonel and present-day raconteur and soldier of fortune Derek Duke took it as his personal mission to find the bomb. He says the Air Force could easily find it but won't do so either because they don't want to go to the expense of finding it or they don't want to admit they lost a thermonuclear weapon for half a century. Duke claims to have found a radiation-emitting object off Little Tybee Island during a search in 2004.

Commander Richardson, now retired and living in Jackson, Mississippi, says the point is moot because the bomb wasn't armed when he jettisoned it. Environmentalists say that doesn't matter, because the enriched uranium the Air Force admits was in the bomb is toxic whether or not there's the risk of a nuclear detonation. People who work in the fishing industry on Tybee say the fact that the bomb also had 400 pounds of high explosive "nuclear trigger" is reason enough to get it out of these waterways, which hosted the 1996 Olympic yachting competition. And what of the owners of the Tybee Bomb, the Air Force? In 2000, they sent a team to Savannah to find the bomb, concluding it was buried somewhere off the coast in 5-15 feet of mud. In 2005, in another attempt to find the weapon—and also to shut down the rampant conspiracy theories, most of them propagated by Duke—they sent another team of experts down to look one last time. Their verdict: The bomb's still lost. That won't stop local speculation about its whereabouts, however. Who can resist a real-life cloak-and-dagger story? Certainly few people around here.

Postscript: No one was injured that night in 1958, except for some frostbite the F-86 pilot suffered as a result of ejecting from his damaged plane. In an interesting bit of synchronicity, the fighter pilot, Clarence Wilson, and the B-47 commander, Howard Richardson, grew up miles away from each other in Winston County, Mississippi.

Once a site for Army entertainment such as movies, concerts, and theatrical productions, the Post Theater is currently undergoing extensive renovation. It occasionally hosts events; check the website for details.

Continue on Van Horne around the delightful Jaycee Park to the row of ornate mansions with expansive porches facing the Atlantic. This is **Officer's Row,** former home of Fort Screven's commanding officers and now a mix of private residences, vacation rentals, and B&Bs.

South End

Next, scoot out Van Horne Street to Butler Avenue and take a left. This is Tybee's main drag, the beach fully public and accessible from any of the numbered side streets on the left.

Go all the way down to **Tybrisa Street** (formerly 16th St.) to get a flavor of old Tybee. Here's where you'll find the old five-and-dimes like T. S. Chu's, still a staple of local life, and little diners, ice cream spots, and taverns. The new pride of the island is the large, long pier structure called the **Tybrisa Pavilion II,** built in 1996 in an attempt to recreate the lost glory of the Tybrisa Pavilion, social and spiritual center of the island's gregarious resort days. Built in 1891 by the Central of Georgia Railway, the Tybrisa hosted name entertainers and big bands on its expansive dance floor. Sadly, fire destroyed it in 1967, an enormous blow to area morale.

Literally at the foot of the Pavilion you'll find the little **Tybee Island Marine Science Center** (1510 Strand Ave., 912/786-5917, www.tybeemarinescience.org, daily 10am-5pm, $4 adults, $3 children), with nine aquariums and a touch tank featuring native species. Here is the nerve center for the Tybee Island Sea Turtle Project, an ongoing effort to document and preserve the local comings and goings of the island's most beloved inhabitant and unofficial mascot, the endangered sea turtle.

TOURS

Savannah's tourist boom has resulted in a similar explosion of well over 50 separate tour services, ranging from simple guided trolley journeys to horse-drawn carriage rides to specialty tours to ecotourism adventures. There's even an MP3-player walking tour. Fair warning: Although local tour guides technically must pass a competency test demonstrating their knowledge of Savannah history, in practice whatever they learned is often thrown out the window in favor of whatever sounds good to them at the time. I've heard the craziest, most untrue things said from passing trolleys and horse carriages. By all means go on a tour, but do so with the knowledge that much of what you're likely to hear won't be true at all.

Here's a listing of the key categories with the most notable offerings in each. Don't forget to tip your guide if you were satisfied with the tour.

Trolley Tours

The vehicle of choice for the bulk of the masses visiting Savannah, trolley tours allow you to sit back and enjoy the views in reasonable comfort. As in other cities, the guides provide commentary while attempting, with various degrees of success, to navigate the cramped downtown traffic environment. The main trolley companies in town are **Old Savannah Tours** (912/234-8128, www.oldsavannahtours.com, basic on-off tour $25 adults, $11 children), **Old Town Trolleys** (800/213-2474, www.trolleytours.com, basic on-off tour $23 adults, $10 children), **Oglethorpe Trolley Tours** (912/233-8380, www.oglethorpetours.com, basic on-off tour $22.50 adults, $10 children), and **Gray Line Tours** (912/234-8687, www.graylineofsavannah.com, basic on-off tour $15). All embark from the Savannah Visitors Center on Martin Luther King Jr. Boulevard about every 20-30 minutes on the same schedule, daily 9am-4:30pm.

Frankly there's not much difference between them, as they all offer a very similar range of services for similar prices, with most offering pickup at your downtown hotel. While the common "on-off privileges" allow trolley riders to disembark for a while and pick up another of the same company's trolleys at marked stops, be aware there's no guarantee the next trolley will have enough room to take you on board. Or the one after that.

Specialty Tours

Besides the standard narrated Historic District tours, all the above companies also offer a number of spin-off tours. Samples include the Pirate's House Dinner & Ghost Tour, Belles of Savannah, the Evening Haunted Trolley, and multiple Paula Deen tours.

The copious ghost tours, offered by all the companies, can be fun for the casual visitor who wants entertainment rather than actual history. Students of the paranormal are likely to be disappointed by the cartoonish, Halloween aspect of some of the tours. A standout in the ghost field is the **Hearse Ghost Tours** (912/695-1578, www.

hearseghosttours.com), a unique company that also operates tours in New Orleans and St. Augustine, Florida. Up to eight guests at a time ride around in the open top of a converted hearse, painted all black, of course, and get a 90-minute, suitably over-the-top narration from the driver-guide. It's still pretty cheesy, but a hip kind of cheesy. Two very popular ghostly walking tours are found with **Cobblestone Tours** (912/604-3007, www.cobblestone-tours.com, $20), a "Haunted History" tour and a "Haunted Pub Crawl." Another fun paranormal/ghost tour is at **Blue Orb Tours** (912/665-4258, www.blueorbtours.com, $25-50), which offers a - you guessed it - "Zombie Tour."

Storyteller and author Ted Eldridge leads **A Walk Through Savannah Tours** (912/921-4455, www.awalkthroughsavannah.bravehost.com, $15 adults, $5 6-12, free under age 6) and offers all kinds of specialty walking tours. To learn about Savannah's history of filmmaking and to enjoy the best of local cuisine, try a **Savannah Movie Tour** (912/234-3440, www.savannahmovietours.net, $25 adults, $15 children), taking you to various film locations in town, and a newer **Savannah Foody Tour** (912/234-3440, www.savannahmovietours.net, $48) featuring 6-9 local eateries.

For a more enlightened take than you'll usually get on a local tour, contact licensed guide **Orlando Montoya** (912/308-2952, $20) for a personalized walking tour. His regular job is as a journalist with Georgia Public Radio, so expect a higher level of taste and information with this journey. Another offbeat tour option is **Savannah's Uncommon Walk** (912/358-0700, www.sellersandhiggins.com, $20), a two-hour exploration of little-known Savannah leaving at 9:30am and 1:30pm daily from Chippewa Square.

To see downtown Savannah by bicycle—quite a refreshing experience—try **Savannah Bike Tours** (41 Habersham St., 912/704-4043, www.savannahbiketours.com, $15 adults, $10 under age 12), two-hour trips through all 19 squares and Forsyth Park with your "rolling concierge." They leave daily at 9:30am, 12:30pm, and 4pm Rent bikes from them or ride your own.

The unique **Negro Heritage Trail Tour** (912/234-8000, $19 adults, $10 children) takes you on a 90-minute air-conditioned bus tour of over 30 of Savannah's key African American history sites. Pick up the Negro Heritage Tour at the Visitors Center downtown (301 MLK Jr. Blvd.) Tuesday-Saturday at 10am and noon.

Carriage Tours

Ah, yes—what could be more romantic and more traditional than enjoying downtown Savannah the way it was originally intended to be traveled, by horse-drawn carriage? Indeed, this is one of the most fun ways to see the city, for couples as well as for those with horse-enamored children. Yes, the horses sometimes look tired, but the tour operators generally take great care to keep the horses hydrated and out of the worst of the heat. There are three main purveyors of equine tourism in town: **Carriage Tours of Savannah** (912/236-6756, www.carriagetoursofsavannah.com, pickup in City Market), **Historic Savannah Carriage Tours** (888/837-1011, www.savannahcarriage.com, pickup at the Hampton Inn), and **Plantation Carriage Company** (912/201-0001, pickup in City Market). As with the trolleys, the length of the basic tour and the price is about the same for all—45-60 minutes, about $20 adults and $10 children. All offer specialty tours as well, from ghost tours to evening romantic rides with champagne. Some will pick you up at your hotel.

Water Tours

The heavy industrial buildup on the Savannah River means that the main river tours, all departing from the docks in front of the Hyatt Regency hotel, tend to be disappointing in their unrelenting views of cranes, docks, storage tanks, and smokestacks. Still, for those into that kind of thing, narrated trips up and down the river on the *Georgia Queen* and the *Savannah River Queen* are offered by **Savannah Riverboat Cruises** (912/232-6404, www.savannahriverboat.com, $19 adults, $10 ages 4-12).

If you've just *got* to get out on the river for a short time, by far the best bargain is to take one of the three little **Savannah Belles** (daily 7:30am-10:30pm, free) water ferries, which shuttle passengers from River Street to Hutchinson Island and back every 15-20 minutes. Pick up one of them on River Street in front of City Hall or at the Waving Girl landing a few blocks east.

Ecotours

The 35-year-old nonprofit **Wilderness Southeast** (912/897-5108, www.wilderness-southeast.org, $10-35) offers guided trips, including paddles to historic Mulberry Grove, birding trips, and beach explorations. Regularly scheduled "Walks on the Wild Side" run the gamut from "Alligators to Anhingas" to the "Urban Forest" to "Explore the Night Sky" to the "Blackwater River Float." Custom tours are also available.

The most highly-regarded local canoe and kayak tour operator and rental house is **Savannah Canoe & Kayak** (912/341-9502, www.savannahcanoeandkayak.com), run by the husband-wife team of Nigel and Krstin Law. They offer several kayak trips, including a short jaunt to Little Tybee Island. On U.S. 80 just as you get on Tybee is another quality tour service, **Sea Kayak Georgia** (1102 U.S. 80, 888/529-2542, www.seakayakgeorgia.com, half-day tour $55). Run by locals Marsha Henson and Ronnie Kemp, Sea Kayak offers many different types of kayak tours. Run by Captain Mike Neal, an experienced local boatman and conservationist, **Moon River Kayak Tours** (912/898-1800, www.moonriverkayak.com, $50) focuses on 2.5-hour tours of the Skidaway Narrows and scenic Moon River, departing from the public boat ramp at the foot of the bridge to Skidaway Island. No kayaking experience required.

Entertainment and Events

If you like to have a good time, you're in the right place. Savannah is known for its heavy year-round schedule of festivals, many of them outdoors, as well as its copious variety of watering holes hosting a diverse range of local residents and adventurous visitors.

NIGHTLIFE

Savannah is a hard-drinking town, and not just on St. Patrick's Day. Visitors expecting a Bible Belt atmosphere are sometimes surprised—often, it must be said, pleasantly so—at Savannah's high tolerance for intoxication and its associated behavior patterns. A few years ago a city councilman decided he'd had a few too many and simply got a ride home from an on-duty cop. The ability to legally walk downtown streets with beer, wine, or a cocktail in hand also contributes to the overall *joie de vivre.* Bars close in Savannah at 3am, a full hour later than in Charleston. A city-wide indoor smoking ban is in effect and you may not smoke cigarettes in any bar in Savannah.

Bars and Pubs

Uncharacteristically, Savannah now sports several good hotel bars, and chief among them is no doubt **Rocks on the Roof** (102 W. Bay St., 912/721-3800, daily 11am-3pm) atop the Bohemian Hotel Savannah on the waterfront. In good weather the exterior walls are opened up to reveal a large wraparound seating area with stunning views of downtown on one side and of the Savannah River on the other. The crowd is a fun mix of locals and visitors.

Savannah's best dive—and I mean that in the nicest way—is **Pinkie Masters** (318 Drayton St., 912/238-0447, Mon.-Fri. 4pm-3am, Sat. 5pm-3am). Named for a legendary local political kingmaker, Pinkie's is a favorite not only with students, artists, and professors but also with lawyers, journalists, and grizzled war vets. This is where Jimmy Carter, ironically a teetotaler, stood on the bar and announced his candidacy for Georgia governor. The service is very informal; bartenders often finish their shift and simply take their place on a barstool

THE TO-GO CUP TRADITION

Arguably the single most civilized trait of Savannah, and certainly one of the things that most sets it apart, is the glorious old tradition of the "to-go cup." True to its history of hard-partying and general open-mindedness, Savannah, like New Orleans, legally allows you to walk the streets downtown with an open container of your favorite adult beverage. Of course, you have to be 21 and over, and the cup must be Styrofoam or plastic, never glass or metal, and no more than 16 ounces. While there are boundaries to where to-go cups are legal, in practice this includes almost all areas of the Historic District frequented by visitors. The quick and easy rule of thumb is, keep your to-go cups north of Jones Street.

Every other election year, some local politician tries to get the church folk all riled up and proposes doing away with to-go cups in the interest of public safety, and he or she is inevitably shouted down by the outcry from the tourism-conscious Chamber of Commerce and from patriotic Savannahians defending their way of life. Every downtown watering hole has stacks of cups at the bar for patrons to use. You can either ask the bartender for a to-go cup—alternately a "go cup"—or just reach out and grab one yourself. Don't be shy; it's the Savannah way.

with the customers. Think of **Hang Fire** (27 Whitaker St., 912/443-9956, Mon.-Sat. 5pm-3am) as Pinkie's, the new generation. Only a few years old, this Whitaker Street haunt, occupying the site of downtown's last strip bar, is already one of the most popular bars in town and, like Pinkie's, caters to a wide range of people who seem to get along in more or less perfect harmony. Trivia nights on Tuesdays are a hoot.

One of the hottest hangouts downtown is

The Distillery (416 W. Liberty St., 912/236-1772, www.distillerysavannah.com), located in, yes, a former distillery. As such, the atmosphere isn't exactly dark and romantic—it's sort of one big open room—but the excellent location at the corner of MLK Jr. Boulevard and Liberty Street, the long vintage bar, and the great selection of beers on tap combine to make this a happening spot. The real hipsters hang out in ironic fashion drinking PBRs at the **American Legion Bar** (1108 Bull St., 912/233-9277, http://alpost135.com), located in, yes, an actual American Legion post. While the Legionnaires themselves are a straight-laced patriotic bunch, the patrons of "the Legion," as the bar is colloquially known, tend toward the counterculture. The drinks are some of the cheapest in town. Fun historical fact: The building housing the Legion was the birthplace of the U.S. 8th Air Force during World War II.

The main landmark on the west end of River Street is the famous (or infamous, depending on which side of "The Troubles" you're on) **Kevin Barry's Irish Pub** (117 W. River St., 912/233-9626, www.kevinbarrys.com, daily 11am-3am), one of Savannah's most beloved establishments. KB's keeps alive the spirit of Irish independence. It's open seven days a week, with evenings seeing performances by a number of Irish troubadours, all veterans of the East Coast trad circuit. An eclectic mix of travelers, local Irish, military, and sailors keeps this place always interesting and alive. While no one in their right mind goes to an Irish pub for the food, Kevin Barry's offers a good, solid range of typical fare, including serviceable corned beef and cabbage. Check out the view of the river from the second-floor "Hall of Heroes," featuring tons of military memorabilia and 9/11 tributes.

Don't get too excited about the "rooftop dining" advertised at **Churchill's Pub & Restaurant** (13-17 W. Bay St., 912/232-8501, www.thebritishpub.com, Mon.-Fri. 5pm-3am, Sat. 10am-3am, kitchen until 10pm Sun.-Thurs., 11pm Fri.-Sat.), unless you enjoy looking at the sides of other buildings.

The fish-and-chips here are among the best in town. The "other" English pub in town, **Six Pence Pub** (245 Bull St., 912/233-3151, daily 11:30am-midnight), is centrally located off Chippewa Square downtown, and though more popular with visitors than with locals, it is still a good place to stop in for a pint on a rainy day. Look for the big red London telephone booth out front.

The only brewpub in Savannah, **Moon River Brewing Company** (21 W. Bay St., 912/447-0943, www.moonriverbrewing.com, Mon.-Thurs. 11am-11pm, Fri.-Sat. 11am-midnight, Sun. 11am-10pm) directly across from the Hyatt Regency, offers half a dozen handcrafted beers—from a pale ale to a stout and all points between.

Live Music and Karaoke

Despite its high-volume offerings, the hardcore and heavy metal club **The Jinx** (127 W. Congress St., 912/236-2281, www.thejinx.net, Mon.-Sat. 4pm-3am) is a friendly watering hole and probably the closest thing Savannah has to a full-on Athens, Georgia, music club. Shows start *very* late here, never before 11pm and often later than that. If you're here for the show, bring earplugs.

Savannah's undisputed karaoke champion is **McDonough's** (21 E. McDonough St., 912/233-6136, www.mcdonoughsofsavannah. com, Mon.-Sat. 8pm-3am, Sun. 8pm-2am), an advantage compounded by the fact that a lot more goes on here than karaoke. The kitchen at McDonough's is quite capable, and many locals swear you can get the best burger in town. Despite the sports bar atmosphere, the emphasis here is on the karaoke, which ramps up every night at 9:30pm, and a very competent group of regulars never fails to entertain. The crowd here is surprisingly diverse, racially and socioeconomically mixed, featuring lawyers and students, rural folks and Rangers in equal numbers.

Gay and Lesbian

Any examination of gay and lesbian nightlife in Savannah must, of course, begin with **Club One Jefferson** (1 Jefferson St., 912/232-0200, www.clubone-online.com) of *Midnight in the Garden of Good and Evil* fame, with its famous drag shows, including the notorious Lady Chablis, upstairs in the cabaret, and its rockin' 1,000-square-foot dance floor downstairs. Cabaret showtimes are Thursday-Saturday 10:30pm and 12:30am, Sunday 10:30pm, and Monday 11:30pm Call for Lady Chablis's showtimes. As with all local gay nightclubs, straights are more than welcome.

A friendly, kitschy little tavern at the far west end of River Street near the Jefferson Street ramp, **Chuck's Bar** (301 W. River St., 912/232-1005, www.myspace.com/chucks_bar, Mon.-Wed. 8pm-3am, Thurs.-Sat. 7pm-3am) is a great place to relax and see some interesting local characters. Karaoke at Chuck's is especially a hoot, and they keep the Christmas lights up all year.

PERFORMING ARTS
Theater

The multiuse venue **Muse Arts Warehouse** (703D Louisville Rd., 912/713-1137, www. musesavannah.org) hosts a variety of community-based plays and performances within a well-restored historic train depot. Get there by taking Liberty Street west from downtown, where it turns into Louisville Road.

The semipro troupe at the **Historic Savannah Theatre** (222 Bull St., 912/233-7764, www.savannahtheatre.com) performs a busy rotating schedule of oldies revues (a typical title: *Return to the '50s*), which make up for their lack of originality with the tightness and energy of their talented young cast of regulars.

There are few things to recommend Savannah's south side to the visitor, but one of them is the **Armstrong Atlantic State University Masquers** (11935 Abercorn St., 912/927-5381, www.finearts.armstrong.edu), the second-oldest college theater group in the country (only Harvard's Hasty Pudding Theatricals is older). Now marking their 75th anniversary, the Masquers boast a newly restored performance space at the Jenkins Theatre, and might surprise you with the high quality of their performances despite being a student program. Parking is never a problem.

Music

The **Savannah Philharmonic** (800/514-3849, www.thesavannahphil.org) is a professional troupe that performs concertos and sonatas at various venues around town and is always worth checking out.

CINEMA

The closest multiplex to downtown is the **Victory Square Stadium 9** (1901 E. Victory Dr.). The historic **Lucas Theatre for the Arts** (32 Abercorn St., 912/525-5040, www.lucas-theatre.com) downtown is a great place to see a movie, and the Savannah Film Society hosts screenings there throughout the year. Check the website for scheduling. The **Sentient Bean Coffeehouse** (13 E. Park Ave., 912/232-4447, www.sentientbean.com) hosts counterculture and political documentaries and kitsch classics.

FESTIVALS AND EVENTS

Savannah's calendar fairly bursts with festivals, many outdoors. Dates shift from year to year, so it's best to consult the listed websites for details.

January

Floats and bands take part in the **Martin Luther King Jr. Day Parade** downtown to commemorate the civil rights leader and Georgia native. The bulk of the route is on historic MLK Jr. Boulevard, formerly West Broad Street.

February

Definitely not to be confused with St. Patrick's Day, the **Savannah Irish Festival** (912/232-3448, www.savannahirish.org) focuses on Celtic music. A regular performer and Savannah's most popular "Irishman at large" is folk singer Harry O'Donoghue, a native of Ireland who regularly plays at Kevin Barry's Irish Pub on River Street and hosts his own Celtic music show, "The Green Island,"

on local public radio 91.1 FM Saturday evenings.

Hosted by the historically black Savannah State University at various venues around town, the month-long **Black Heritage Festival** (912/691-6847) is tied into Black History Month and boasts name entertainers like the Alvin Ailey Dance Theatre (performing free!). This event also usually features plenty of historical lectures devoted to the very interesting and rich history of African Americans in Savannah.

Also in February is the **Savannah Book Festival** (www.savannahbookfestival.org), modeled after a similar event in Washington DC and featuring many local and regional authors at various venues.

March

One of the most anticipated events for house-proud Savannahians, the **Tour of Homes and Gardens** (912/234-8054, www.savannahtou-rofhomes.org) offers guests the opportunity to visit six beautiful sites off the usual tourist-trod path. This is a great way to expand your understanding of local architecture and hospitality beyond the usual house museums.

More than just a day, the citywide **St. Patrick's Day** (www.savannahsaintpatricks-day.com) celebration generally lasts at least half a week and temporarily triples the population. The nearly three-hour parade—the second-biggest in the United States—always begins at 10am on St. Patrick's Day (unless that falls on a Sunday, in which case it's generally on the previous Saturday) and includes a mix of bands, wacky floats, and sauntering local Irishmen in kelly green jackets. The appeal comes not only from the festive atmosphere and generally beautiful weather but from Savannah's unique law allowing partiers to walk the streets with a plastic cup filled with an adult beverage. While the parade itself is very family-friendly, afterward hardcore partiers generally head en masse to River Street, which is blocked off for the occasion and definitely not where you want to take small children. If you want to hear traditional Celtic music on St. Patrick's Day in Savannah, River Street also isn't the place to go, with the

CINEMA IN SAVANNAH

The first high-profile film made in Savannah was 1962's *Cape Fear,* starring Gregory Peck and Robert Mitchum (who was arrested and briefly jailed years before for public indecency while wandering in a drunken state through Savannah). But 1975's *Gator,* directed by and starring Burt Reynolds, really put the city on the Hollywood map, due in no small part to the then-mega star power of Reynolds himself, whose filmmaking mission was, in his words, to "say some nice things about the South."

In short order, parts of the landmark 1970s TV miniseries *Roots* were filmed in and around Savannah, as were part of the follow-up *Roots: The Next Generation.*

Film aficionados fondly remember the 1980 TV movie *The Ordeal of Dr. Mudd,* starring Dennis Weaver. In addition to the infamous story from "The Book" where Jim Williams unfurls a swastika banner to ruin a shot on Monterey Square, there are other reasons to remember the film. *Dr. Mudd* also expertly uses interiors of Fort Pulaski to tell this largely sympathetic account of the physician accused of aiding Abraham Lincoln's assassin John Wilkes Booth. In a chilling bit of synchronicity, Booth's brother Edwin, the most famous actor in the United States during the 1800s, played in Savannah often.

A key chapter in local filmography came with the filming of 1989's *Glory.* River Street was the set for parade scenes, and as Colonel Shaw, Matthew Broderick delivered his address to the troops a block west of Mrs. Wilkes' Boarding House. The railroad roundhouse off MLK Jr. Boulevard stood in for a Massachusetts training ground.

Another brush with Hollywood came with the filming of 1994's *Forrest Gump* in and around Savannah. Look for Tom Hanks on a bench in Chippewa Square—and note how the traffic runs the wrong direction around the square! The bench itself now resides in the Savannah History Museum on MLK Jr. Boulevard. The steeple in the shot of the floating white feather is of nearby Independent Presbyterian Church.

Ben Affleck and Sandra Bullock filmed many scenes of 1999's *Forces of Nature* on Tybee Island and in Savannah (yours truly's house is in the final scene for about two seconds). Longtime Hollywood producer and Savannah native Stratton Leopold, who also owns Leopold's Ice Cream on Broughton Street, helped Savannah land 1999's *The General's Daughter* starring John Travolta (look for the grand exterior of the main building at Oatland Island). Trotting out a serviceable Southern accent for a Brit, Kenneth Branagh came to town to play a disgruntled Savannah lawyer in Robert Altman's *Gingerbread Man.*

Though quite a few downtown art students had no idea what the fuss was about, Robert Redford still turned female heads when he came to town to direct 2000's *The Legend of Bagger Vance,* with Will Smith as the eponymous caddie. In the film, watch for the facsimile of a Depression-era storefront specially built around City Market. Redford returned to Savannah in late 2009 to film *The Conspirator,* another locally shot film about the Lincoln assassination. (Savannah stands in for Washington DC.) Cate Blanchett and Katie Holmes starred in 2000's *The Gift,* one of the few movies to take full advantage of the beauty of Bonaventure Cemetery.

Ironically, considering the impact of "The Book" on Savannah, Clint Eastwood's *Midnight in the Garden of Good and Evil* (1997) is arguably the worst movie ever filmed here. Eastwood's famously laissez-faire attitude toward filmmaking—reportedly there were no rehearsals before cameras rolled—did not work well, perhaps because Savannah's already a pretty darn laissez-faire kind of place to begin with.

But the biggest stir of them all came in summer 2009, when Disney star Miley Cyrus of *Hannah Montana* fame came to Tybee Island to film *The Last Song.*

exception of Kevin Barry's on the west end. For authentic Irish music wander around the pubs on the periphery of City Market.

Savannah's answer to Charleston's Spoleto, the three-week **Savannah Music Festival** (912/234-3378, www.savannahmusicfestival. org) is held at various historical venues around town and begins right after St. Patrick's Day. Past festivals have featured Wynton Marsalis, the Beaux Arts Trio, and Diane Reeves. The jazz portion is locked down tight, thanks to the efforts of festival director Rob Gibson, a Georgia native who cut his teeth as the founding director of Jazz at Lincoln Center. The classical side is equally impressive, helmed by one of the world's great young violinists, Daniel Hope, acting as associate director. Other genres are featured in abundance as well, including gospel, bluegrass, zydeco, world music, and the always-popular American Traditions vocal competition. The most economical way to enjoy the Music Festival is to purchase tickets online before December of the previous year at a 10 percent discount. However, if you just want to take in a few events, individual tickets are available at a tiered pricing system that allows everyone to enjoy this popular event. You can buy tickets to individual events in town at the walk-up box office beside the Trustees Theatre on Broughton Street.

April

Short for "North of Gaston Street," the **NOGS Tour of Hidden Gardens** (912/961-4805, www. gcofsavnogstour.org, $30) is available two days in April and focuses on Savannah's amazing selection of private gardens selected for excellence of design, historical interest, and beauty.

Everyone loves the annual free **Sidewalk Arts Festival** (912/525-5865, www.scad.edu) presented by the Savannah College of Art and Design in Forsyth Park. Contestants claim a rectangular section of sidewalk on which to display their chalk art talent. There's a noncontest section with chalk provided.

May

The SCAD-sponsored **Sand Arts Festival**

(www.scad.edu) on Tybee Island's North Beach centers on a competition of sand castle design, sand sculpture, sand relief, and wind sculpture. You might be amazed at the level of artistry lavished on the sometimes-wondrous creations only for them to wash away with the tide.

If you don't want to get wet, don't show up at the **Tybee Beach Bum Parade,** an uproarious event held the weekend prior to Memorial Day weekend. With a distinctly boozy overtone, this unique 20-year-old event features homemade floats filled with partiers who squirt the assembled crowds with various water pistols. The crowds, of course, pack their own heat and squirt back.

July

Two key events happen around **Fourth of July,** primarily the large fireworks show on River Street, always on July 4, and also an impressive fireworks display from the Tybee Pier and Pavilion, which is sometimes on a different night. A nice bonus of the Tybee event is that sometimes you can look out over the Atlantic and see a similar fireworks display on nearby Hilton Head Island, South Carolina, a few minutes away by boat (but nearly an hour by car).

September

The second-largest gay and lesbian event in Georgia (only Atlanta's version is larger), the **Savannah Pride Festival** (www.savannah-pride.org, various venues, free) happens every September. Crowds get pretty big for this festive, fun event, which usually features lots of dance acts and political booths.

Though the quality of the acts has been overshadowed lately by the Savannah Music Festival in the spring, the **Savannah Jazz Festival** (www.savannahjazzfestival.org) has two key things going for it: It's free, and it's outside in the glorious green expanse of Forsyth Park. Generally spread out over several nights, the volunteer-run festival draws a good crowd regardless of the lineup, and concessions are available.

October

Area musicians unite to play a free evening at **Picnic in the Park** (www.savannahga.gov), a concert in Forsyth Park that draws thousands of noshers. Arrive early to check out the ostentatious, whimsical picnic displays, which compete for prizes. Then set out your blanket, pop open a bottle of wine, and enjoy the sweet sounds.

The combined aroma of beer, sauerkraut, and sausage that you smell coming from the waterfront is the annual **Oktoberfest on the River** (www.riverstreetsavannah.com), which has evolved to be Savannah's second-largest celebration (behind only St. Patrick's Day). Live entertainment of varying quality is featured, though the attraction, of course, is the aforementioned beer and German food. A highlight is the Saturday morning "Weiner Dog races" involving, you guessed it, competing dachshunds.

If pickin' and grinnin' is your thing, don't miss the low-key but always entertaining **Savannah Folk Music Festival** (www.savannahfolk.org). The main event of the weekend is held on a Sunday night in the historic Grayson Stadium in Daffin Park, but a popular Old-Time Country Dance is usually held the previous Saturday. Members of the Savannah Folk Music Society will help you learn how to do the dance, so don't be shy!

It's a fairly new festival, but the **Tybee Island Pirate Festival** (http://tybeepiratefest.com) is a fun and typically rollicking Tybee event in October featuring, well, everybody dressing up like pirates, saying "Arr" a lot, eating, drinking, and listening to cover bands. It may not sound like much, and it's really not, but it's typically very well-attended.

Sponsored by St. Paul's Greek Orthodox Church, the popular **Savannah Greek Festival** (www.stpaulsgreekorthodox.org) features food, music, and Greek souvenirs. The weekend event is held across the street from the church at the parish center—in the gym, to be exact, right on the basketball court. Despite the pedestrian location, the food is authentic and delicious, and the atmosphere convivial and friendly.

Despite its generic-sounding name, the **Fall Festival** (www.bamboo.caes.uga.edu) is actually quite interesting, given its location in the unique Bamboo Farm and Coastal Garden. A joint project of the University of Georgia and Chatham County, the Bamboo Farm features a wide array of native species, all lovingly tended. The festival features tours, displays, arts and crafts, food, and lots of kids' activities. The event is free, but parking is $1. To get here, take exit I-95 exit 94 and take Highway 204 east toward Savannah. Turn right on East Gateway Boulevard, then left on Canebrake Road. Enter at the Canebrake gate.

Hosted by the Savannah College of Art and Design, the weeklong **Savannah Film Festival** (www.scad.edu) beginning in late October is rapidly growing not only in size but in prestige. Lots of older, more established Hollywood names appear as honored guests for the evening events, while buzz-worthy up-and-coming actors, directors, producers, writers, and animators give excellent workshops during the day. Many of these usually jaded showbiz types really let their hair down for this festival, because, as you'll see, Savannah is the real star. The best way to enjoy this excellent event is to buy a pass, which enables you to walk from event to event.

One of Savannah's most unique events is late October's **"Shalom Y'all" Jewish Food Festival** (912/233-1547, www.mickveisrael.org), held in Forsyth Park and sponsored by the historic Temple Mickve Israel. Latkes, matzo, and other nibbles are all featured along with entertainment.

November

Generally kicking off the month is the popular **Telfair Art Fair** (www.telfair.org), a multiday annual art show and sale outside in Telfair Square between its two museums, the Telfair Academy and the Jepson Center. Browse or buy; either way it's a culturally enlightening good time.

The name says it all: The **Savannah Seafood Festival** (www.riverstreetsavannah.

com) on River Street offers mouthwatering fare from a variety of local vendors, plus live entertainment.

December

Arts and crafts and holiday entertainment highlight the **Christmas on the River and Lighted Parade** (www.riverstreetsavannah. com), which happens on River Street.

Another beloved local tour, the annual **Holiday Tour of Homes** (912/236-8362, www.dnaholidaytour.net), sponsored by the Downtown Neighborhood Association, is a great way to get up close with a half-dozen or so of some of Savannah's best private homes, all dolled up in their finest for the holidays. There's an afternoon tour and a candlelight tour by trolley.

Shopping

Downtown Savannah's main shopping district is Broughton Street, which is included here along with several other key shopping areas of note.

BROUGHTON STREET

The historic center of downtown shopping has recently seen a major renaissance and is once again home to the most vibrant shopping scene in Savannah, just like it was in the 1940s and 1950s. While several chain stores have made inroads onto the avenue, here are some of the most notable independent shops.

Clothes and Fashion

Perhaps Broughton's most beloved old shop is **Globe Shoe Co.** (17 E. Broughton St., 912/232-8161), a Savannah institution and a real throwback to a time of personalized retail service. They have no website and no Facebook page—they're all about simple one-to-one service, like in the old days. Easily one of the coolest women's stores in town is **Go Fish** (106 W. Broughton St., 912/231-0609, www.gofishretail.com). This regional franchised operation provides for a lot of independence on the part of the owners; Debbie and Lloyd Ryysylainen offer a sharply curated range of upscale-looking clothes and shoes at reasonable prices. **Gaucho** is another popular choice for women, with a strong emphasis on accessories, jewelry, and shoes. There are two locations: 18 East Broughton Street (912/234-7414, Mon.-Sat. 10am-6pm) and the original location at 250 Bull Street (912/232-7414, Mon.-Sat.

10am-6pm, Sun. 1pm-5pm). **Copper Penny** (22 W. Broughton St., 912/629-6800, www. shopcopperpenny.com) is easily the premier women's shoe showcase on the historic avenue. Vintage shoppers will enjoy **Civvies** (22 E. Broughton St., 912/236-1551), a second-floor shop with a nice selection of previously owned clothing.

Home Goods

While Savannah is an Anglophile's dream, Francophiles will enjoy **The Paris Market & Brocante** (36 W. Broughton St., 912/232-1500, www.theparismarket.com, Mon.-Sat. 10am-6pm, Sun. 11am-4pm) on a beautifully restored corner of Broughton Street. Home and garden goods, bed and bath accoutrements, and a great selection of antique and vintage items combine for a rather opulent shopping experience. Plus there's an old-school Euro café inside where you can enjoy a coffee, tea, or hot chocolate.

Those looking for great home decorating ideas with inspiration from both global and Southern aesthetics, traditional as well as sleekly modern, should check out **24e Furnishings at Broughton** (24 E. Broughton St., 912/233-2274, www.twentyfoure.com, Mon.-Thurs. 10am-6pm, Fri.-Sat. 10am-7pm, Sun. noon-5pm), located in an excellent restored 1921 storefront. Be sure to check out the expansive second-floor showroom.

One of the more unique Savannah retail shops is the **Savannah Bee Company** (104

© JIM MOREKIS

The Paris Market & Brocante is one of Broughton's most interesting stores.

W. Broughton St., 912/233-7873, www.sa-vannahbee.com, Mon.-Sat. 10am-7pm, Sun. 11am-5pm), which, as the name implies, carries an extensive line of honey-based merchandise, from foot lotion to lip balm. All the honey comes from area hives owned by company founder and owner Ted Dennard. The company now has a sizeable national presence since being picked up for the Williams-Sonoma catalogue 10 years ago. The flagship Broughton location provides plenty of sampling opportunities at the little café area and even boasts a small theater space for instructional films.

Outdoor Outfitters
Outdoors lovers should make themselves acquainted with **Half Moon Outfitters** (15 E. Broughton St., 912/201-9313, www.half-moonoutfitters.com, Mon.-Sat. 10am-7pm, Sun. noon-6pm), a full-service camping, hiking, skiing, and kayaking store. Half Moon is part of a regional chain that also has two locations in Charleston.

WATERFRONT
Amid the T-shirt shops, candy stores, and tchotchke places, Savannah's waterfront area does have a handful of quality shopping options.

Antiques
One of the coolest antiques shops in town is **Jere's Antiques** (9 N. Jefferson St., 912/236-2815, www.jeresantiques.com, Mon.-Sat. 9:30am-5pm). It's in a huge historic warehouse on Factor's Walk and has a concentration on fine European pieces.

Clothes
Clothe your inner biker at **Harley-Davidson** (503 E. River St., 912/231-8000, Mon.-Sat. 10am-6pm, Sun. noon-6pm).

CITY MARKET
A borderline tourist trap, City Market strongly tends toward more touristy, less unique items. Here are a couple of exceptions: The whimsical **A. T. Hun Gallery** (302 W. St. Julian St.,

912/233-2060, www.athun.com, Mon.-Thurs. 10am-6pm, Fri.-Sat. 10am-10pm, Sun. 11am-5pm) is one of the first true art galleries in town and features a variety of adventurous art from local and regional favorites. **Kobo Gallery** (33 Barnard St., 912/201-0304, http://kobogallery. com, Mon.-Sat. 10:30am-5:30pm, Sun. 11am-5pm) is Savannah's newest local artist cooperative and offers a nice range of adventurous artwork in a variety of media.

DOWNTOWN DESIGN DISTRICT

Focusing on upscale art and home goods, this small but chic shopping area runs for three blocks on Whitaker Street downtown beginning at Charlton Lane and ending at the Mercer-Williams House on Monterey Square.

Antiques

Arcanum Antiques and Interiors (422 Whitaker St., 912/236-6000, Mon.-Sat. 10am-5pm) deals in a tasteful range of vintage items with a chic twist. For a more European take, try **The Corner Door** (417 Whitaker St., 912/238-5869, Tues.-Sat. 10am-5pm). Perhaps the most eclectic antiques shop in the Downtown Design District is **Peridot Antiques and Interiors** (400 Whitaker St., 912/596-1117).

Clothes

Custard Boutique (414 Whitaker St., 912/232-4733) has a cute, fairly cutting-edge selection of women's clothes. **Mint Boutique** (413 Whitaker St., 912/341-8961, Mon.-Fri. 10am-6pm) right next door brings a similarly modern style to this often very conservative town.

Home Goods

An eclectic European-style home goods store popular with locals and visitors alike is **One Fish Two Fish** (401 Whitaker St., 912/484-4600, Mon.-Sat. 10am-5pm, Sun. noon-5pm). Owner Jennifer Beaufait Grayson, a St. Simons Island native, came to town a decade ago to set up shop in this delightfully restored old dairy building on the corner of Whitaker and Jones and has been getting rave reviews since.

Madame Chrysanthemum (101 W. Taylor St., 912/238-3355) is technically a florist, and a fine one at that, but they also deal with fun home items and gift ideas.

BOOKS

The fact that **E. Shaver Bookseller** (326 Bull St., 912/234-7257, Mon.-Sat. 9am-6pm) is one of the few locally owned independent bookstores left in town should not diminish the fact that it is also one of the best bookstores in town. Esther Shaver and her friendly, well-read staff can help you around the rambling old interior of their ground-level store and its generous stock of regionally themed books. Don't miss the rare map room, with some gems from the 17th and 18th centuries.

Specializing in "gently used" books in good condition, **The Book Lady** (6 E. Liberty St., 912/233-3628, Mon.-Sat. 10am-5:30pm) on Liberty Street features many rare first editions. Enjoy a gourmet coffee while you browse the stacks. The beautiful Monterey Square location and a mention in *Midnight in the Garden of Good and Evil* combine to make **V&J Duncan** (12 E. Taylor St., 912/232-0338, www.vj-duncan.com, Mon.-Sat. 10:30am-4:30pm) a Savannah "must-shop." Owner John Duncan and his wife Virginia ("Ginger" to friends) have collected an impressive array of prints, books, and maps over the past quarter-century, and are themselves a treasure trove of information.

OTHER UNIQUE STORES

Not only a valuable outlet for SCAD students and faculty to sell their artistic wares, **shopSCAD** (340 Bull St., 912/525-5180, www.shopscadonline.com, Mon.-Wed. 9am-5:30pm, Thurs.-Fri. 9am-8pm, Sat. 10am-8pm, Sun. noon-5pm) is also one of Savannah's most unique boutiques. You never really know what you'll find, but whatever it is, it will be one-of-a-kind. The jewelry in particular is always cutting-edge in design and high-quality in craftsmanship. The designer T-shirts are a hoot too.

Possibly the most beloved antiques store in town is **Alex Raskin Antiques** (441 Bull

St., 912/232-8205, Mon.-Sat. 10am-5pm) in Monterey Square, catty-corner from the Mercer-Williams House. Set in the historic Hardee mansion, a visit is worth it just to explore the home. But the goods Alex lovingly curates are among the best and most tasteful in the region.

A delightful little slice of Manhattan's Fashion District on Liberty Street, **Fabrika Fine Fabrics** (2 E. Liberty St., 912/236-1122, www.fabrikafinefabrics.com) has provided high-quality supplies for local luminaries such as former *Project Runway* contestant April Johnston. Run by two SCAD grads, the hip space is jammed with high-quality, buzz-worthy bolts of fabric, oodles of beads, and lots of sewing paraphernalia. They offer custom sewing and sewing lessons.

And in this town so enamored of all things Irish, a great little locally owned shop is **Saints and Shamrocks** (309 Bull St., 912/233-8858, www.saintsandshamrocks.org, Mon.-Sat. 9:30am-5:30pm, Sun. 11am-4pm). Pick up your St. Patrick's-themed gear and gifts to celebrate Savannah's highest holiday along with high-quality Irish imports

Set in a stunningly restored multi-level Victorian within a block of Forsyth Park, the globally conscious **Folklorico** (440 Bull St., 912/232-9300, Mon. -Sat. 10am-5pm, Sun. 1pm-5pm) brings in a fascinating and diverse collection of sustainably made jewelry, gifts, and home goods from around the world, focusing on Central and South America and Asia.

MALLS

The mall closest to downtown—though not that close, at about 10 miles south—is **Oglethorpe Mall** (7804 Abercorn St., 912/354-7038, www.oglethorpemall.com, Mon.-Sat. 10am-9pm, Sun. noon-6pm). Its anchor stores are Sears, Belk, J. C. Penney, and Macy's.

Much farther out on the south side is the **Savannah Mall** (14045 Abercorn St., 912/927-7467, www.savannahmall.com, Mon.-Sat. 10am-9pm, Sun. noon-6pm). Its anchor stores are Dillard's, Target, and Bass Pro Shops Outdoor World.

GROCERIES AND MARKETS

Savannah's first and still premier health-food market, **Brighter Day Natural Foods** (1102 Bull St., 912/236-4703, www.brighterdayfoods.com, Mon.-Sat. 10am-7pm, Sun. 12:30pm-5:30pm) has been the labor of love of Janie and Peter Brodhead for 30 years, all of them in the same location at the southern tip of Forsyth Park. Boasting organic groceries, regional produce, a sandwich and smoothie bar in the back, and an extensive vitamin, supplement, and herb section, Brighter Day is an oasis in Savannah's sea of chain supermarkets.

Fairly new but already thriving, the **Forsyth Park Farmers Market** (www.forsythfarmersmarket.org, Sat. 9am-1pm) happens in the south end of Forsyth Park. You'll find fresh fruit and produce, as well as organic dairy and meat products, from a variety of fun and friendly regional farmers.

If you need some good quality groceries downtown—especially after-hours—try **Parker's Market** (222 E. Drayton St., 912/231-1001, daily 24 hours). In addition to a pretty wide array of gourmet-style victuals inside, there are gas pumps outside to fuel your vehicle.

A local tradition for 20 years, **Keller's Flea Market** (5901 Ogeechee Rd., I-95 exit 94, 912/927-4848, www.ilovefleas.com, Sat.-Sun. 8am-6pm, free) packs in about 10,000 shoppers over the course of a typical weekend, offering a range of bargains in antiques, home goods, produce, and general kitsch. There are concessions on-site.

Sports and Recreation

Savannah more than makes up for its sad organized sports scene with copious outdoor options that take full advantage of its temperate climate and the natural beauty of its marshy environment next to the Atlantic Ocean.

ON THE WATER
Kayaking and Canoeing

Maybe the single best kayak or canoe adventure in Savannah is the run across the Back River from Tybee to **Little Tybee Island,** an undeveloped State Heritage Site that despite its name is actually twice as big as Tybee, albeit mostly marsh. Many kayakers opt to camp on the island. You can even follow the shoreline out into the Atlantic, but be aware that wave action can get intense offshore. Begin the paddle at the public boat ramp on the Back River. To get here, take Butler Avenue all the way to 18th Street and take a right, then another quick right onto Chatham Avenue. The parking lot for the landing is a short way up Chatham Avenue on your left. Warning: Do not attempt to swim to Little Tybee no matter how strong a swimmer you think you are—the currents are exceptionally vicious. Also, do not be tempted to walk far out onto the Back River beach at low tide. The tide comes in very quickly and often strands people on the sandbar.

One of the great overall natural experiences in the area is the massive **Savannah National Wildlife Refuge** (912/652-4415, www.fws.gov/savannah, daily dawn-dusk, free). This 30,000-acre reserve—half in Georgia, half in South Carolina—is on the Atlantic Flyway, so you'll be able to see birdlife in abundance, in addition to alligators and manatee. Earthen dikes crisscrossing the refuge are vestigial remnants of paddy fields from plantation days. You can kayak on your own, but many opt to take guided tours offered by **Wilderness Southeast** (912/897-5108, www.wilderness-southeast.org, two-hour trips from $37.50 for two people), **Sea Kayak Georgia** (888/529-2542, www.

seakayakgeorgia.com, $55 pp), and **Swamp Girls Kayak Tours** (843/784-2249, www.swampgirls.com, $45). To get here, take U.S. 17 north over the big Talmadge Bridge, over the Savannah River into South Carolina. Turn left on Highway 170 south and look for the entrance to Laurel Hill Wildlife Drive on the left.

Another pleasant kayaking route is the **Skidaway Narrows.** Begin this paddle at the public boat ramp, which you find by taking Waters Avenue all the way until it turns to Whitefield Avenue and then Diamond Causeway. Continue all the way over the Moon River to a drawbridge; park at the foot of the bridge. Once in the water, paddle northeast. Look for the osprey nests on top of the navigational markers in the narrows as you approach Skidaway Island State Park. Continuing on, you'll find scenic Isle of Hope high on a bluff to your left, with nearly guaranteed dolphin sightings around marker 62.

Farther out of town but worth the trip for any kayaker is the beautiful blackwater **Ebenezer Creek,** near the tiny township of New Ebenezer in Effingham County. Cypress trees lining this nationally designated Wild and Scenic River hang overhead, and wildlife abounds on this peaceful paddle. Look for old wooden sluice gates, vestiges of the area's rice plantation past. To get here, take exit 109 off I-95. Go north on Highway 21 to Rincon, Georgia, then east on Highway 275 (Ebenezer Rd.). Put in at the Ebenezer Landing ($5).

The best guided water tour in the area is Capt. Rene Heidt's **Sundial Nature Tours** (912/786-9470, www.sundialcharters.com). Rene is an expert in local marine life and offers a variety of tours, including dolphin watches, fossil hunts, and trips to various barrier islands. Rates start at about $160 for two people. A great one-stop shop for local kayaking information, tours, and equipment is **Savannah Canoe & Kayak** (414 Bonaventure Rd., 912/341-9502, www.savannahcanoeandkayak.com), run by the husband-wife team of Nigel and

Kristin Law. To rent an ocean-worthy kayak on Lazaretto Creek, stop by **North Island Surf and Kayak** (1C Old Hwy. 80, 912/786-4000, www.northislandkayak.com, Mon.-Fri. 10am-5pm, Sat.-Sun. 9am-6pm, $45), located at Tybee Marina. Reservations are recommended.

Fishing

Savannah is a saltwater angler's paradise, rich in trout, flounder, and king and Spanish mackerel. Offshore there's a fair amount of deep-sea action, including large grouper, white and blue marlin, wahoo, snapper, sea bass, and big amberjack near some of the many offshore wrecks.

Perhaps the best-known local angler is Captain Judy Helmey, a.k.a. "Miss Judy." In addition to her frequent and entertaining newspaper columns, she runs a variety of well-regarded charters out of **Miss Judy Charters** (912/897-2478, www.missjudycharters.com). Four-hour trips start at $500. To get there, go west on U.S. 80, take a right onto Bryan Woods Road, a left onto Johnny Mercer Boulevard, a right onto Wilmington Island Way, and a right down the dirt lane at her sign. Another highly regarded local fishing charter is the Tybee-based **Amick's Deep Sea Fishing** (912/897-6759, www.amicksdeepseafishing.com). Captain Steve Amick and crew run offshore charters daily starting at $120 pp. Go east on U.S. 80 and turn right just past the Lazaretto Creek Bridge. Another charter service is offered from **Lazaretto Creek Marina** (1 U.S. 80, 912/786-5848, www.tybeedolphins.com). Half- and full-day inshore and offshore fishing charters are available, starting at $250 for four hours. Go east on U.S. 80 and turn right just past the Lazaretto Creek Bridge. Turn right at the dead end.

Shallow-water fly fishers might want to contact **Savannah Fly Fishing Charters** (56 Sassafras Trail, 912/308-3700, www.savannahfly.com). Captain Scott Wagner takes half- and full-day charters both day and night from Savannah all the way down to St. Simons Island. Half-day rate starts at $300. Book early.

Diving

Diving is a challenge off the Georgia coast because of the silty nature of the water and its mercurial currents. Though not particularly friendly to the novice, plenty of great offshore opportunities abound around the many artificial reefs created by the Georgia Department of Natural Resources (www.coastalgadnr.org).

Certainly no underwater adventure in the area would be complete without a dive at **Gray's Reef National Marine Sanctuary** (912/598-2345, www.graysreef.noaa.gov). Administered by the National Oceanic and Atmospheric Administration, this fully protected marine sanctuary 17 miles offshore is in deep enough water to provide divers good visibility of its live-bottom habitat. Not a classic living coral reef but rather one built by sedimentary deposits, Gray's Reef's provides a look at a truly unique ecosystem. Some key dive charter operators that can take you to Gray's Reef are Captain Walter Rhame's **Mako Dive Charter** (600 Priest Landing Dr., 912/604-6256), which leaves from the Landings Harbor Marina; **Georgia Offshore** (1191 Lake Dr., Midway, 912/658-3884); and **Fantasia Scuba** (3 E. Montgomery Cross Rd., 912/921-8933). The best all-around dive shop in town is **Diving Locker and Ski Chalet** (74 W. Montgomery Cross Rd., 912/927-6603, www.divinglockerskichalet.com, Mon.-Fri. 10am-6pm, Sat. 10am-5pm) on the south side.

Surfing and Boarding

Other than some action around the pier, the surfing is poor on Tybee Island, with its broad shelf, tepid wave action, and lethal rip currents. But board surfers and kite boarders have a lot of fun on the south end of Tybee beginning at about 17th Street. The craziest surf is past the rock jetty, but be advised that the rip currents are especially treacherous there.

The best—and pretty much only—surf shop in town is **High Tides Surf Shop** (405 U.S. 80, 912/786-6556, www.hightidesurfshop.com). You can get a good local surf report and forecasts at their website.

ON THE LAND
Golf

There are a couple of strong public courses in Savannah that are also very good bargains. Chief among these has to be the **Henderson Golf Club** (1 Al Henderson Blvd., 912/920-4653, www.hendersongolfclub.com), an excellent municipal course with very reasonable green fees (Mon.-Fri. $28, Sat.-Sun. $33) that include a half-cart. Another local favorite and unbeatable bargain is the circa-1926 **Bacon Park Golf Course** (Shorty Cooper Dr., 912/354-2625, www.baconparkgolf. com, green fees about $20), comprising three nine-hole courses with a choice of three 18-hole combinations and some very small, fast greens. A relatively new course but not one you'd call a bargain is the **Club at Savannah Harbor** (2 Resort Dr., 912/201-2007, www. theclubatsavannahharbor.com, green fees $135, $70 for twilight) across the Savannah River on Hutchinson Island, adjacent to the Westin Savannah Harbor Resort. Home to the Liberty Mutual Legends of Golf Tournament each spring, the Club's tee times are 7:30am-3pm, with half-light play 2pm-5pm The **Wilmington Island Club** (501 Wilmington Island Rd., 912/897-1612, green fees about $70) has arguably the quickest greens in town and is unarguably the most beautiful local course, set close by the Wilmington River amid lots of mature pines and live oaks.

Tennis

The closest public courts to the downtown area are at the south end of **Forsyth Park** (912/351-3850), which features four free lighted courts. They are unsupervised, and as you might expect, they get serious use. Farther south in **Daffin Park** (1001 E. Victory Dr., 912/351-3850), there are six clay courts and three lighted hard courts ($3). On the south side, **Bacon Park** (6262 Skidaway Rd., 912/351-3850) has 16 lighted hard courts ($3). If you get the tennis jones on Tybee, there are two free courts at **Tybee Island Memorial Park** (Butler Ave. and 4th St., 912/786-4573, www.cityoftybee.org).

Hiking

Though hiking in Savannah and the Lowcountry is largely a 2-D experience given the flatness of the terrain, there are plenty of good nature trails from which to observe the area's rich flora and fauna up close. My favorite trails are at **Skidaway Island State Park** (52 Diamond Causeway, 912/598-2300, www. gastateparks.org, daily 7am-10pm, parking $2 per vehicle per day). The three-mile Big Ferry Trail is the best overall experience, taking you out to a wooden viewing tower from which you can see the vast expanse of the Skidaway Narrows. A detour takes you past a Native American shell midden, Confederate earthworks, and even a rusty old still—a nod to Skidaway Island's former notoriety as a bootlegger's sanctuary. The shorter but still fun Sandpiper Trail is wheelchair-accessible.

An interesting, if hardly challenging, trail is the **McQueen Island Trail,** more commonly known as "Rails to Trails." This paved, palm-lined walking trail along the Savannah River was built on the old bed of the Savannah-to-Tybee railroad, which operated during Tybee's heyday as a major East Coast vacation spot in the 1930s and 1940s. To get here, cross the long, low, Bull River Bridge and take an immediate left into the small parking area, being very mindful of fast-moving inbound traffic on U.S. 80.

Biking

Most biking activity centers on Tybee Island, with the **McQueen Island Trail** being a popular and simple ride. Many locals like to load up their bikes and go to **Fort Pulaski** (912/786-5787, www.nps.gov, fort daily 8:30am-5:15pm, visitors center daily 9am-5pm, closed Christmas Day, $2 pp, free under age 16). From the grounds you can ride all over scenic and historic Cockspur Island.

Plenty of folks ride their bikes downtown, and it is particularly enriching and fun to pedal around the squares. Legally, however, you're not allowed to ride through the squares; you're supposed to stay on the street around them. And always yield to traffic already within the

The McQueen Island Trail is more commonly known as the "Rails to Trails."

square as you enter. For a guided two-hour tour of downtown, try **Savannah Bike Tours** (41 Habersham St., 912/704-4043, www.savannahbiketours.com, $15 adults, $10 under age 12), leaving every day at 9:30am, 12:30pm, and 4pm

Bird-Watching

Birding in the Savannah area is excellent at two spots on the **Colonial Coast Birding Trail** (http://georgiawildlife.dnr.state.ga.us). The main site is **Skidaway Island State Park** (52 Diamond Causeway, 912/598-2300, www.gastateparks.org, daily 7am-10pm, parking $2 per vehicle per day). Spring and fall bring a lot of the usual warbler action, while spring and summer feature nesting osprey and painted bunting, always a delight. The other trail spot is Tybee Island's **North Beach** area (parking $5 per day, meters available). You'll see a wide variety of shorebirds and gulls, as well as piping plover, northern gannets, and purple sandpipers (winter).

Wading birds in particular are in wide abundance at the **Savannah National Wildlife Refuge** (912/652-4415, www.fws.gov/savannah, daily dawn-dusk, free). The views are excellent all along the Lauren Hill wildlife drive, which takes you through the heart of the old paddy fields that crisscrossed the entire area. To get here, take U.S. 17 north over the big Talmadge Bridge, over the Savannah River into South Carolina. Turn left on Highway 170 south and look for the entrance to Laurel Hill Wildlife Drive on the left.

SPECTATOR SPORTS

Topping the list of local spectator sports is the **Savannah Sand Gnats** (912/351-9150, www.sandgnats.com, season Apr.-Sept.) baseball franchise, currently a single-A affiliate of the New York Mets. The attraction here is not the level of play but the venue itself: Grayson Stadium (1401 E. Victory Dr.) in Daffin Park in the city's midtown area, a historic venue that has hosted such greats as Babe Ruth, Jackie Robinson, and Mickey Mantle over the years. There's not a bad seat in the house, so your best bet by far is to just buy a $7 general admission ticket. The games never sell out, so there's no need to stress. Entertainment runs the usual gamut of minor league shenanigans, including frequent fireworks displays after the games.

For sports action that's a good bit more hard-hitting and comes with a certain hipster kitsch

SAVANNAH BASEBALL

Savannah has a long and important history with the national pastime. In fact, the first known photograph of a baseball game was taken in Fort Pulaski, of Union occupation troops at play on the parade ground.

A pivotal figure in baseball history also has a crucial association with Savannah. Long before gaining notoriety for his role on the infamous Chicago "Black Sox" that threw the 1919 World Series, baseball legend **Shoeless Joe Jackson** was a stalwart on the South Atlantic or "Sally" League circuit. Playing for the Savannah Indians in 1909, Joe played ball predominantly at Bolton Street Park, off what's now Henry Street. After retirement Joe returned to town, began a thriving dry-cleaning business, and lived with his wife at 143 Abercorn Street and then on East 39th Street.

Another early great who played in Savannah was Georgia native Ty Cobb, who visited in 1905 with an Augusta team. He's remembered, typically enough, for getting into a fistfight with a teammate who voiced his displeasure at Cobb eating popcorn in the outfield and muffing an easy catch.

Savannah got a proper ballpark in 1926, named Municipal Stadium. After a hurricane destroyed it in 1940, rebuilding began but abruptly stopped when Pearl Harbor was attacked the next year and all the laborers rushed off to enlist. So abruptly did they drop their tools, in fact, that to this day behind third base you can still clearly see the jagged line indicating where construction halted.

The great **Babe Ruth** played in the stadium once in 1935 in his final year as a major leaguer, as his Boston Braves beat the South Georgia Teachers College (now Georgia Southern University) 15-1 in an exhibition game. Ruth, of course, hit a home run.

Mickey Mantle and the defending world champion New York Yankees played the Cincinnati Reds in a 1959 exhibition game in Savannah. The switch-hitting slugger hit two of his trademark mammoth home run shots during the game—both left-handed and each over 500 feet, according to witnesses.

Atlanta Braves great **Hank Aaron**, then a skinny second baseman with a Jacksonville club, played in Grayson's first game with both black and white players in 1953. Jackie Robinson stole home base in an exhibition game.

But in a way, all these names pale in comparison to one Savannah player whose influence can be felt to this day, not only in sports but in the business world at large: **Curt Flood**, who gave the world free agency. Flood, who played for the Savannah Redlegs in 1957, refused to report to the Phillies after the Cardinals traded him in 1969. Flood sued Major League Baseball the next year, saying the so-called "reserve clause" allowing the trade violated antitrust laws. While Flood would lose the lawsuit in the U.S. Supreme Court, the narrowly worded decision left the way open for collective bargaining and today's massive free agent salaries.

The **Savannah Braves**, a double-A team, began a successful run in 1971 (including a 12-game winning season by pitcher and controversial *Ball Four* writer Jim Bouton), followed in 1984 by the Savannah Cardinals.

The current single-A team, the **Savannah Sand Gnats**, had their name chosen by a poll of daily newspaper readers. While their level of play rarely conjures mental images of Shoeless Joe or the Babe, Grayson Stadium itself has just been given an impressive new facelift courtesy of the city, with a new scoreboard and upgraded seating. By far the Sand Gnats' most famous face so far has been Cy Young Award-winning pitcher Éric Gagné, who pitched his very first professional game with the local club.

quotient, check out the bruising bouts of the women of the **Savannah Derby Devils** (www. savannahderby.com), who bring the Roller Derby thunder against other regional teams.

They skate downtown at the Savannah Civic Center (301 W. Oglethorpe Ave., 912/651-6556), and the matches are usually quite well attended.

Accommodations

The hotel scene in Savannah, once notorious for its absurdly high price-to-service ratio, has improved a great deal in the past couple of years. Perhaps ironically, several stylish new downtown hotels opened concurrently with the recent economic downturn. Their appearance means increased competition, and therefore marginally lower prices, across the board. Savannah's many historic bed-and-breakfasts are competitive with the hotels on price, and often outperform them on service and ambience. If you don't need a swimming pool and don't mind climbing some stairs every now and then, a B&B is usually your best bet. And the breakfasts, of course, are great too.

CITY MARKET
$150-300
A Days Inn property, the **Inn at Ellis Square** (201 W. Bay St., 912/236-4440, www.innatellissquare.com, $189) is smack-dab between City Market and Bay Street—in other words, the heart of the tourist action. Set in the renovated 1851 Guckenheimer Building, the inn is one of the better-appointed chain hotels in town.

Providing a suitably modernist decor to go with its somewhat atypical architecture for Savannah, the new **Andaz Savannah** (14 Barnard St., 912/233-2116, www.savannah.andaz.hyatt.com, $200 and up) overlooks restored Ellis Square and abuts City Market with its shopping, restaurants, and nightlife. The guest rooms and suites feature top-of-the-line linens, extra-large and well-equipped baths, in-room snack bars, and technological features such as MP3 docking stations, free Wi-Fi, and, of course, the ubiquitous flat-screen TV. Off the lobby is a very hip lounge-wine bar that

attracts locals as well as hotel guests. Keep in mind things can get a little noisy in this area at night on weekends.

WATERFRONT
$150-300
The **Mulberry Inn** (601 E. Bay St., 912/238-1200, www.holidayinn.com, $189) is a long-time favorite with travelers to Savannah, with a charming central courtyard and with peaceful little Washington Square on the back of the building. Don't miss the genuine English teatime, complete with jazz piano accompaniment, observed in the lobby each afternoon at 4pm (as if there's another English teatime). Another nifty touch is a dedicated parking garage—an amenity only someone who has spent half an hour looking for a parking space in downtown Savannah will truly appreciate. Parking is free for Holiday Inn "priority members" (you can sign up for membership at check-in). The building formerly housed one of the first Coca-Cola bottling plants in the United States; look for the historical photos all around the building.

Although it's new, **The Bohemian Hotel** (102 W. Bay St., 912/721-3800, www.bohemianhotelsavannah.com, $279-350) is already gaining a reputation as one of Savannah's premier hotels, both for the casual visitor as well as visiting celebrities. Located between busy River Street and bustling City Market, this isn't the place for peace and quiet, but its combination of boutique-style retro-hip decor and happening rooftop bar scene (swank and quite popular with local scenesters) make it a great place to go for a fun stay that's as much Manhattan as Savannah. Valet parking is available, which you will come to appreciate.

DOWNTOWN SAVANNAH ACCOMMODATIONS, FOOD AND ENTERTAINMENT

Savannah   River

Savannah River

W FACTORS WALK
WILLIAMSON ST
W BROAD
CHUCK'S BAR
KEVIN BARRY'S IRISH PUB
RIVER STREET
RIVER ST
E FACTORS WALK
VIC'S ON THE RIVER
THE BOHEMIAN HOTEL
HYATT REGENCY
W BAY ST
Emmet Park
MULBERRY INN
CLUB ONE JEFFERSON
MOON RIVER BREWING CO
CHURCHILL'S PUB & RESTAURANT
E BAY ST
B. MATTHEW'S EATERY
W BRYAN ST
VINNIE VANGOGO'S
AVIA SAVANNAH
CHRIST EPISCOPAL CHURCH
OLDE PINKHOUSE/ PLANTER'S TAVERN
E BRYAN ST
PIRATE'S HOUSE
FIRST AFRICAN BAPTIST CHURCH
Franklin Square
CITY MARKET
Ellis Square
THE LADY & SONS
Johnson Square
Reynolds Square
Warren Square
Washington Square
W CONGRESS ST
SAPPHIRE GRILL
E CONGRESS ST
LULU'S CHOCOLATE BAR
GARIBALDI CAFÉ
SAIGON
CASBAH
LEOPOLD'S ICE CREAM
CHA BELLA
W BROUGHTON ST
E BROUGHTON ST
WASABI'S
W STATE ST
OWENS-THOMAS HOUSE
E STATE ST
Liberty Square
TELFAIR MUSEUMS
Telfair Square
Wright Square
Oglethorpe Square
THE KEHOE HOUSE
Columbia Square
Greene Square
OGLETHORPE AVE
W YORK ST
ZUNZI'S
E YORK ST
THE GREEN PALM INN
WRIGHT SQUARE CAFÉ
BALLASTONE INN
TURNER ST
ANGEL'S BBQ
E OGLETHORPE AVE
Elbert Square
CIVIC CENTER
Orleans Square
FOLEY HOUSE INN
Chippewa Square
COLONIAL PARK CEMETERY
Crawford Square
W HULL ST
W PERRY ST
GALLERY ESPRESSO
E PERRY ST
W LIBERTY ST
CATHEDRAL OF ST. JOHN THE BAPTIST
E LIBERTY ST
LOUISVILLE RD
PINKIE MASTERS
BRASSERIE 529
W HARRIS ST
E HARRIS ST
Pulaski Square
Madison Square
Lafayette Square
Troup Square
E MACON ST
W CHARLTON ST
E CHARLTON ST
RANCHO ALEGRE
W CHARLTON LN
E CHARLTON LN
ELIZA THOMPSON HOUSE
W JONES ST
E JONES ST
MRS. WILKES' DINING ROOM
W TAYLOR ST
E TAYLOR ST
Chatham Square
MONTEREY SQUARE
Calhoun Square
Whitefield Square
W GORDON ST
E WAYNE ST
WESLEY MONUMENTAL UNITED METHODIST CHURCH
E GORDON ST
W ALICE ST
E ALICE ST
GASTONIAN INN
W GASTON ST
E GASTON ST
BLOWIN' SMOKE BBQ
DRESSER-PALMER HOUSE
W HUNTINGDON ST
MANSION ON FORSYTH PARK
E HUNTINGDON ST
FORSYTH PARK
LEOCI'S TRATTORIA
0   200 yds
0   200 m
W HALL ST
E HALL ST
To Green Truck Neighborhood Pub and Al Salaam Deli
To Elizabeth on 37th
© AVALON TRAVEL

© JIM MOREKIS

The Bohemian is one of Savannah's favorite new hotels.

Over $300

For years critics have called it an insult to architecture and to history. That said, one of the few name-brand hotels in Savannah worth the price and providing a consistent level of service is one of its original chain hotels, the **(** **Hyatt Regency Savannah** (2 E. Bay St., 912/238-1234, www.savannah.hyatt.com, $379). It is more than three decades old, but a competent renovation means that the Hyatt—a sort of exercise in cubism straddling an entire block of River Street—has avoided the neglect of many older chain properties downtown. While the price may seem daunting, consider the location: literally smack-dab on top of River Street, mere blocks from the bulk of the important attractions downtown and some of its best restaurants. Three sides of the hotel offer views of the bustling Savannah waterfront, with its massive ships coming in from all over the world.

HISTORIC DISTRICT
$150-300

Easily the best bed-and-breakfast for the price in Savannah is **The Green Palm Inn** (546 E. President St., 912/447-8901, www. greenpalminn.com, $159-189), a folksy and romantic little Victorian number with some neat gingerbread exterior stylings and four cute guest rooms, each named after a species of palm tree. It's situated on the very easternmost edge of the Historic District—hence it's reasonable rates—but let's face it, being right next to charming little Greene Square is far from the worst place you could be. Delightful innkeeper Diane McCray provides a very good and generous breakfast plus a pretty much constant dessert bar.

One of Savannah's original historic B&Bs, the **(** **Eliza Thompson House** (5 W. Jones St., 912/236-3620, www.elizathompson-house.com, $180-225) is a bit out of the bustle on serene, beautiful Jones Street but still close enough to get involved whenever you feel the urge. You can enjoy the various culinary offerings—breakfast, wine and cheese, nighttime munchies—either in the parlor or on the patio overlooking the house's classic Savannah garden. One of the half-dozen lodging properties owned by the locally based HLC group, the Eliza Thompson House hews to their generally high standard of service.

The circa-1896 **(** **Foley House Inn** (14 W. Hull St., 912/232-6622, www.foleyinn. com, $199-375) is a four-diamond B&B with some rooms available at a three-diamond price. Its 19 individualized, Victorian-decor guest rooms, in two town houses, range from the smaller Newport overlooking the "grotto courtyard" to the four-poster, bay-windowed Essex room, complete with a fireplace and a whirlpool bath. The location on Chippewa Square is pretty much perfect: well off the busy east-west thoroughfares but in the heart of Savannah's active theater district and within walking distance of anywhere.

One of Savannah's favorite bed-and-breakfasts, **The Kehoe House** (123 Habersham St., 912/232-1020, www.kehoehouse.com, $215-315) is a great choice for its charm and attention to guests. Its historic location, on quiet little

Columbia Square catty-corner to the Isaiah Davenport House, is within walking distance to all the downtown action, but far enough from the bustle to get some peace out on one of the rocking chairs on the veranda.

Once a bordello, the 1838 mansion that is home to the 16-room **Ballastone Inn** (14 E. Oglethorpe Ave., 912/236-1484, www.ballastone.com, $235-355) is one of Savannah's favorite inns. Highlights include an afternoon tea service and one of the better full breakfasts in town. Note that some guest rooms are at what Savannah calls the "garden level," meaning sunken basement-level rooms with what amounts to a worm's-eye view.

VICTORIAN DISTRICT
$150-300

A short walk from Forsyth Park, the **Dresser-Palmer House** (211 E. Gaston St., 912/238-3294, www.dresserpalmerhouse.com, $189-319) features 15 guest rooms in two wings but still manages to make things feel pretty cozy. Garden-level rooms go for a song (under $200).

The 1868 **C Gastonian Inn** (220 E. Gaston St., 912/232-2869, www.gastonian.com, $245-455) got a major renovation in 2005 and remains a favorite choice for travelers to Savannah, mostly for its 17 sumptuously decorated guest rooms and suites, all with working fireplaces, and the always outstanding full breakfast. They pile on the epicurean delights with teatime, evening nightcaps, and complimentary wine. This is one of the six properties owned by the local firm HLC, which seems to have consistently higher standards than most out-of-town chains.

Over $300

How ironic that a hotel built in a former mortuary would be one of the few Savannah hotels not to have a resident ghost story. But that's the case with **Mansion on Forsyth Park** (700 Drayton St., 912/238-5158, www.mansiononforsythpark.com, $339-419), which dominates an entire block alongside Forsyth Park, including partially within the high-Victorian

former Fox & Weeks Mortuary building. Its sumptuous guest rooms, equipped with big beds, big baths, and big-screen TVs, scream "boutique hotel," as does the swank little bar and the alfresco patio area. The Mansion's Addams Family decor of thick velvet and vaguely dadaist artwork isn't for everyone, but still, it certainly beats seagulls and pink flamingos.

TYBEE ISLAND

Most of the hotels on the main drag, Butler Avenue, are what we describe in the South as "rode hard and put away wet," meaning that they see a lot of wear and tear from eager vacationers. For that reason it's difficult for me to recommend any of them in good conscience. Also be aware that any place on Butler Avenue, even the substandard places, charges a premium during the high season (Mar.-Oct.). For long-term stays, weekly rentals are the name of the game. Though not cheap—expect to pay roughly $1,000 per week in the summer—they provide a higher level of accommodations than some hotels on the island. For weekly rentals, try **Oceanfront Cottage Rentals** (800/786-5889, www.oceanfrontcottage.com), **Tybee Island Rentals** (912/786-4034, www.tybeeislandrentals.com), or **Tybee Vacation Rentals** (866/359-0297, www.tybeevacationrentals.com).

Here are a few other places that are a cut above. One of Tybee's most worthwhile lodging experiences for the money, the single-suite **C Bluebird Bed and Breakfast** (1206 Venetian Dr., 912/786-0786, www.tybeebandb.com, $125) is tucked away on Horsepen Creek and the Back River, away from the general beach-town hubbub—but that's what makes it all the more romantic, in a whimsical sort of way. Its spacious and charming interior comprises a master bedroom, a large kitchen-den area, and a delightful breakfast nook overlooking the marsh. There's even a resident dock if you want to put in your kayak or canoe. There is a two-night minimum on weekends.

Available for daily or weekly rentals, the delightful and well-appointed upstairs apartment of **The Octopus Lair** (12th St., 912/660-7164, www.octopuslair.com, $125) is tucked away on the south side of the island, equidistant from both the beach and the more active areas. There's even a propane grill on the porch so you can cook out. Another good B&B-style experience can be found at **The Georgianne Inn** (1312 Butler Ave., 912/786-8710, $125-235), a short walk off the beach.

CAMPING

The best overall campground in town is at the well-managed and rarely crowded **Skidaway Island State Park** (52 Diamond Causeway, 912/598-2300, www.gastateparks.org, parking $2 per vehicle per day, tent and RV sites $24, group camping $35). There are 88 sites with 30-amp electric hookups.

There's one campground on Tybee Island, the **River's End Campground and RV Park** (915 Polk St., 912/786-5518, www.cityoftybee. org, water and electric sites $34, 50-amp full hookup sites $45) on the north side. Owned by the city of Tybee Island, River's End offers 100 full-service sites plus some primitive tent sites.

Totally wilderness camping can be done on state-owned Little Tybee, accessible across the Back River by boat only; there are no facilities. The best camping and wilderness resource locally is **Half Moon Outfitters** (15 E. Broughton St., 912/201-9393, www.halfmoonoutfitters. com).

Food

Although Charleston's cuisine scene is clearly a cut or two above Savannah's, the Georgia city is still a foodie's paradise, with a big-city selection of cuisine concocted by a cast of executive chefs who despite their many personal idiosyncrasies tend to go with what works rather than experimenting for the sake of experimentation. Here's a breakdown of the most notable offerings, by area and by type of cuisine. You'll note there's rarely a separate *Seafood* section listed; that's because seafood is an intrinsic part of most restaurant fare in Savannah, whether through regular menu offerings or through specials.

CITY MARKET
Classic Southern

Every year, thousands of visitors come to Savannah for the privilege of waiting for hours outside in all weather, the line stretching a full city block, for a chance to eat at **The Lady & Sons** (102 W. Congress St., 912/233-2600, www.ladyandsons.com, lunch Mon.-Sat. 11am-3pm, dinner Mon.-Sat. from 5pm, buffet Sun. 11am-5pm, $17-25) and sample some of local celebrity Paula Deen's "home" cooking—actually a fairly typical Southern buffet with some decent fried chicken, collard greens, and mac-and-cheese. For the privilege, you must begin waiting in line as early as 9:30am for lunch and as early as 3:30pm for dinner in order to be assigned a dining time. You almost assuredly will never see Paula, who has precious little to do with the restaurant these days. Eating at this Savannah landmark provides a story that visitors will be able to tell friends and family for the rest of their lives, and far be it from me to look down on them for doing so. That being said: If it were me, I'd take that four hours spent waiting in line and instead go to one of Savannah's many other excellent eating establishments, leaving lots of time for an afternoon beer or coffee or dessert, and leaving yet more time to see one of Savannah's many interesting and beautiful sights. A chef friend of mine puts it best: When food sits out under a heat lamp too long, it all tastes the same anyway.

Coffee, Tea, and Sweets

Combine a hip bar with outrageously tasty dessert items and you get **Lulu's Chocolate Bar** (42 MLK Jr. Blvd., 912/238-2012, www. luluschocolatebar.net). While the whole family is welcome before 10pm to enjoy chocolate chip cheesecake and the like, after that it's strictly 21-and-over. The late crowd is younger and trendier and comes mostly for the unique specialty martinis, including the pineapple upside-down martini.

Italian

One would never call Savannah a great pizza town, but the best pizza here is **⚓ Vinnie VanGoGo's** (317 W. Bryan St., 912/233-6394, www.vinnievangogos.com, Mon.-Thurs. 4pm-11:30pm, Fri. 4pm-1am, Sat. noon-1am, Sun. noon-11:30pm, $3-13, cash only) at the west end of City Market on Franklin Square. Featuring some of the best local characters both in the dining area and behind the counter, Vinnie's is a classic Savannah hangout, due in no small part to its excellent beer selection and late hours on weekends. Their pizza is a thin-crust Neapolitan style—although the menu claims it to be New York style—with a delightful tangy sauce and fresh cheese. Individual slices are huge, so don't feel obliged to order a whole pie. The waiting list for a table can get pretty long, but take heart: Vinnie's offers free delivery throughout downtown, delivered by bicycle courier. Remember, cash only.

Many Savannahians recall a time when the charmingly old-school **Garibaldi Café** (315 W. Congress St., 912/232-7118, daily 5-10pm, $11-33) was the only fine-dining restaurant downtown, and it's still great. More like a spot you'd find in Little Italy than Savannah, Garibaldi features the over-the-top decor typical of the genre, from Roman busts to massive brocade curtains and the huge chandelier in the "Grand Ballroom." But longtime master chef Gerald Green's food is still the draw, a dependable northern Italian menu known for its well-made veal dishes, its raw bar offerings, and the signature dish, the popular crispy scored flounder with apricot glaze.

New Southern

Accomplishing the difficult task of being achingly hip while also offering some of the best food in town, **⚓ Sapphire Grill** (110 W. Congress St., 912/443-9962, www.sapphiregrill.com, Fri.-Sat. 5:30pm-11:30pm, Sun.-Thurs. 6pm-10:30pm, $25-40) comes closer than any other Savannah restaurant to replicating a high-class trendy Manhattan eatery—at prices to match. With its bare stone walls, lean ambience, and romantically dark interior, you'd be tempted to think it's all sizzle and no steak. But executive chef Chris Nason, former exec at Charleston's Anson Restaurant, has a way with coastal cuisine, relying on the freshest local seafood. His classic meat dishes like lamb, filet mignon, and veal are equally skillful. The lobster bisque is a must-have.

WATERFRONT
Breakfast

If you're downtown and need something more than your hotel breakfast—and you will!—go to **⚓ B. Matthew's Eatery** (325 E. Bay St., 912/233-1319, www.bmatthewseatery.com, Mon.-Thurs. 8am-9pm, Fri.-Sat. 8am-10pm, brunch Sun. 9am-3pm, $15), widely considered the best breakfast in the entire Historic District. The omelets—most under $10—are uniformly wonderful, and the sausage & bacon excellent and most ungreasy. There is a range of more healthy selections as well, and you can actually get a decent bowl of oatmeal—but I suggest something more decadent. Sunday brunch is incredible, as you might imagine. And they don't just do breakfast—lunch sandwiches and salads are of similarly high quality, and dinner entrées (from $17) include killer osso buco, lamb, and seafood.

Classic Southern

Locals rarely eat at the Savannah institution called the **Pirate's House** (20 E. Broad St., 912/233-5757, www.thepirateshouse.com, lunch daily 11am-4pm, dinner Sun.-Thurs. 4pm-9:30pm, Fri.-Sat. 4-10pm, $17-26), known primarily for its delightfully kitschy pre-Jack Sparrow pirate decor and its dependably pedestrian food. Still, the history here is undeniable: One of the country's oldest buildings, built in 1753, the Pirate's House hosted many a salty sea dog—though perhaps few actual pirates—in its day as a seamen's inn. And any place that rates a shout-out in Robert Louis Stevenson's *Treasure Island* might be worth a visit. The "Southern Buffet" (daily 11am-3pm) features the Pirate House's signature honey pecan fried chicken.

Very few restaurants on River Street rise above tourist schlock, but a standout is **Vic's on the River** (16 E. River St., 912/721-1000, www.vicsontheriver.com, Sun.-Thurs. 11am-10pm, Fri.-Sat. 11am-11pm, $22-40). Hewing more to Charleston-style fine dining than most Savannah restaurants—with dishes like wild Georgia shrimp, stone-ground grits, and blue crab cakes with a three-pepper relish—Vic's combines a romantic old Savannah atmosphere with an adventurous take on Lowcountry cuisine. Note the entrance to the dining room is not on River Street but on the Bay Street level on Upper Factor's Walk.

Greek

Another worthwhile place to stop for a relaxing and tasty meal on River Street is **Olympia Café** (5 E. River St., 912/233-3131, www.olympia-cafe.net, $15), which serves a variety of Greek dishes such as dolmades, spanokopita, seafood and lemon chicken in a friendly atmosphere.

The standard menu items aren't particularly cheap, but the daily specials often offer a surprisingly good deal for your money.

HISTORIC DISTRICT
Barbecue

A great local barbecue joint tucked away in a lane is **Angel's BBQ** (21 W. Oglethorpe Lane, 912/495-0902, www.angels-bbq.com, Tues. 11:30am-3pm, Wed.-Sat. 11:30am-6pm, $5-9), which was featured on a recent episode of Travel Channel's *Man v. Food*. Get there by finding Independent Presbyterian Church at the northwest corner of Chippewa Square and walking down the lane next to the church. Angel's offers a particularly Memphis-style take on barbecue, but you might try the unique house specialty, the barbecued bologna. Don't miss the peanuts-and-greens on the side. Vegetarians can opt for the "Faux-Q," barbecue-flavored tofu.

Classic Southern

The meteoric rise of Paula Deen and her Lady

© JIM MOREKIS

Angel's BBQ is hard to find, but well worth the effort.

& Sons restaurant has only made local epicures even more exuberant in their praise for **Mrs. Wilkes' Dining Room** (107 W. Jones St., 912/232-5997, www.mrswilkes.com, Mon.-Fri. 11am-2pm, $13), Savannah's original comfort-food mecca. President Obama's impromptu lunchtime visit with the local mayor in 2010 has further raised the restaurant's already legendary profile. The delightful Sema Wilkes herself has passed on, but nothing has changed—not the communal dining room, the cheerful service, the care taken with take-out customers, and, most of all, not the food—a succulent mélange of the South's greatest hits, including the best fried chicken in town, snap beans, black-eyed peas, and collard greens. While each day boasts a different set menu, almost all of the classics are on the table at each meal.

Once the home of General James Habersham and the first place the Declaration of Independence was read aloud in Savannah, the **Olde Pink House** (23 Abercorn St., 912/232-4286, Sun.-Thurs. 5:30pm-10:30pm, Fri.-Sat. 5:30-11pm, $15-30) is still a hub of activity in Savannah, as visitors and locals alike frequent the classic interior of the dining room and the downstairs Planter's Tavern. Regularly voted "Most Romantic Restaurant in Savannah"—but make no mistake, they pack you in pretty tight here—the Pink House is known for its savvy (and often sassy) service and the uniquely regional flair it adds to traditional dishes, with liberal doses of pecans, vidalia onions, shrimp, and crab. The she-crab soup and lamb chops in particular are crowd-pleasers, and the scored crispy flounder stacks up to similar versions of this dish at several other spots in town. Reservations are recommended.

Coffee, Tea, and Sweets

He helped produce *Mission Impossible III* and other Hollywood movies, but Savannah native Stratton Leopold's other claim to fame is running the 100-year-old family business at **Leopold's Ice Cream** (212 E. Broughton St., 912/234-4442, www.leopoldsicecream.com, Sun.-Thurs. 11am-10pm, Fri.-Sat. 11am-11pm).

Leopold's Ice Cream is in the heart of the theater district.

© JIM MOREKIS

Now in a new location but with the same delicious family ice cream recipe, Leopold's also offers soup and sandwiches to go with its delicious sweet treats. Memorabilia from Stratton's various movies is all around the shop, which stays open after every evening performance at the Lucas Theatre around the corner. You can occasionally find Stratton himself behind the counter doling out scoops.

A coffeehouse before coffeehouses were cool, Savannah's original java joint **Gallery Espresso** (234 Bull St., 912/233-5348, www.galleryespresso.com, Mon.-Fri. 7:30am-10pm, Sat.-Sun. 8am-11pm) currently occupies a prime corner lot on beautiful Chippewa Square. Of course, there's the requisite free Wi-Fi, and while you sip and surf you can also enjoy the regular rotating modern art exhibits by well-known local artists, all curated by owner Jessica Barnhill.

For a more upscale take on sweets, check out the chocolate goodies at **Wright Square Cafe** (21 W. York St., 912/238-1150). While they do offer tasty wraps and sandwiches, let's not kid ourselves; the draw here is the outrageous assortment of high-quality European-style brownies, cookies, cakes, and other sweet treats.

French

One of only two honest-to-goodness French restaurants in town is (**Brasserie 529** (529 E. Liberty St., 912/238-0045, Tues.-Sat. 11am-3pm and 5-10pm, from $20). The interior is renovated in contemporary bistro. The food is splendid and authentically French in both flavor and cost. House specialties include the côtes de boeuf (a bone-in rib eye for two), the rabbit stew, and the steak frites, featuring a hanger steak and the best french fries you'll ever enjoy. My favorite dish, however, is the Fish Normande, a succulently cooked piece of halibut that is the best whitefish entrée I've eaten anywhere. As mundane as this sounds after all that buildup, the fact that Brasserie 529 has a dedicated parking lot is another huge plus given the general dearth of parking spaces in downtown Savannah.

Italian

The hot Italian place in town is **Leoci's Trattoria** (606 Abercorn St., 912/335-7027, www.leocis.com, daily 11am-10pm, $10-20), named for its skillful and personable young executive chef, Roberto Leoci. His compact but diverse menu offers delights such as a crispy delicious pizza, excellent paninis, and a wild-mushroom risotto. The room is small and intimate, and the restaurant is quite popular, so a wait is not unusual.

South African

Look for the long lunchtime line outside the tiny storefront that is **Zunzi's** (108 E. York St., 912/443-9555, Mon.-Sat. 11am-6pm, $5-10). This takeout joint is one of Savannah's favorite lunch spots, the labor of love of South African expatriates Gabby and Johnny DeBeer, who've gotten a lot of national attention for their robust, rich dishes like the exquisite South African-style sausage.

Southwest

Situated in a large downstairs space on busy Broughton Street, **Taco Abajo** (217 W. Broughton St., www.tacoabajo.com, Mon.-Wed. 11 a.m.-10 p.m., Thu.-Sat. 11 a.m.-3 a.m., Sun. 11 a.m.-2 a.m., under $5 per taco) is *the* go-to spot for Tex/Mex and Southwestern when you're downtown, at just about any time of day or night. In addition to delicious spicy faves like chorizo, carne asada, and of course fish tacos, there's a full bar for those of age and frequent live music for an all-ages crowd.

VICTORIAN DISTRICT

This pretty, quiet, but up-and-coming area—occasionally referred to by the somewhat precious new term SoFo, for South of Forsyth—spans Forsyth Park south to Victory Drive (U.S. 80).

Burgers

Cozy (**Green Truck Neighborhood Pub** (2430 Habersham St., 912/234-5885, http://greentruckpub.com, Tues.-Sat. 11am-11pm, $10) earns its raves on the basis of delicious regionally sourced meat and produce offered at reasonable prices. (The large selection of craft beers on tap is a big draw too). The marquee item is the signature five-ounce grass-fed burger. A basic burger is $7, but several other, increasingly more dressed-up versions are offered, none over $12.50. Burgers are also offered with chicken or veggie patties. Salads here are also particularly awesome, all with the added option of burger, chicken, or veggie patty to any salad for $4.50 extra. It's a small room that often has a big line, and they don't take reservations, so be prepared.

Coffee, Tea, and Sweets

The coffee at **The Sentient Bean** (13 E. Park Ave., 912/232-4447, www.sentientbean.com, daily 7:30am-10pm) is all fair-trade and organic, and the all-vegetarian fare is a major upgrade above the usual coffeehouse offering. But "The Bean" is more than a coffeehouse—it's a community. Probably the best indie film venue in town, the Bean regularly hosts screenings of cutting-edge left-of-center documentary and kitsch films, as well as rotating art exhibits. When there's no movie, there's usually some low-key live entertainment or spoken word open mike action.

Primarily known for its sublime sweet treats, **Back in the Day Bakery** (2403 Bull St., 912/495-9292, www.backinthedaybakery.com, Tues.-Fri. 9am-5pm, Sat. 8am-3pm, $7) on the southern edge of the Victorian District also offers a small but delightfully tasty (and tasteful) range of lunch soups, salads, and sandwiches (11am-2pm) Lunch highlights are the baguette with camembert, roasted red peppers, and lettuce; and the *caprese,* the classic tomato, mozzarella, and basil trifecta on a perfect *ciabatta.* But whatever you do, save room for dessert, which runs the full sugar spectrum: red velvet cupcakes, lemon bars, macaroons, carrot cake, Cosmopolitan Cake, Nana's Pudding, and my favorite, Omar's Mystic Espresso Cheesecake.

Hard to define easily, and perhaps successful precisely because of that, **Form** (1801 Habersham St., 912/236-7642, www.form-cwg.com, Mon.-Fri. 10am-7pm, Sat. 11am-6pm) is part winery, part bakery, and part foodie gathering place. Form is the kind of place you can pick up an amazing made-from-scratch cheesecake and get advice on which bottle of wine might go with said cheesecake. They also host a variety of special events, from dinners and wine tastings to guest chef demos.

For a quick coffee or a panini, stop by the **Forsyth Park Café** (621 Drayton St., 912/233-7848, daily 7am-dusk, open later on festival evenings) located in what was once the circa-1920 "dummy fort."

Middle Eastern

For a falafel fix, travel well off the beaten path to **Al Salaam Deli** (2311 Habersham St., 912/447-0400, daily 9am-9pm, $5-10). The signature falafel at this humble little storefront is big-city quality, and the gyros are almost as good. While it's not in the most elegant of neighborhoods, Al Salaam—run by a family of Jordanian expatriates—has a devoted local following, and deservedly so. In a nod to the cosmopolitan background of the owner and his cuisine, the walls are decorated with *National Geographic* magazine covers.

New Southern

Before there was Paula Deen, there was Elizabeth Terry, Savannah's first well-known high-profile chef and founder of this most elegant of all Savannah restaurants, **C Elizabeth on 37th** (105 E. 37th St., 912/236-5547, daily 6-10pm, from $25). Terry has since sold the place to two of her former waiters, Greg and Gary Butch, but this restaurant has, for the most part, continued to maintain her high standards. In a beautifully restored Victorian mansion just outside the Historic District, with its own lovingly tended herb garden and emphasis on local suppliers, Elizabeth on 37th continues to be—a quarter-century after its founding—where many Savannahians go when the evening calls for something really memorable. Executive chef Kelly Yambor uses eclectic, seasonally shifting ingredients that blend the South with the south of France. Along with generally attentive service, it makes for a wonderfully old-school fine dining experience. Reservations are recommended.

Soul Food

Savannah's hottest new soul food purveyor is tiny **C Cafe Florie** (1715 Barnard St., 912/236-3354, Tue.-Fri. 11am-8pm, Sat. 9am-8pm, $10), a family effort of cousins Latoya Rivers and Theo Smith. From this charming and colorful little shack they've gained national attention for their deeply authentic takes on soul food classics based on old family recipes, such as Verna's Fried Chicken and Tillie's Meatloaf. In an interesting twist not often found with traditional Southern places, they strive to use organic ingredients whenever possible. Save room for some sweet potato pie or pecan pie for dessert.

EASTSIDE
Classic Southern

Located just across the Wilmington River from the fishing village of Thunderbolt,

© JIM MOREKIS

Elizabeth on 37th remains one of Savannah's best restaurants.

C Desposito's (187 Old Tybee Rd., 912/897-9963, www.despositosseafood.com, Tues.-Fri. 5-10pm, Sat. noon-10pm, $15-25) is a big hit with locals and visitors alike, although it's not in all the guidebooks. The focus here is on crab, shrimp, and oysters, and lots of them, all caught wild in local waters and served humbly on tables covered with newspapers.

Mexican

There aren't too many authentic Mexican places in Savannah, and frankly the situation has become worse with the recent passage of immigration legislation in Georgia that has caused an exodus from area Hispanic communities. A survivor is the family-operated **La Xalapena** (2308 Skidaway Rd., 912/234-8076, www.la-xalapena.com, Mon.-Thurs. 10am-9pm, Fri.-Sat. 10am-10pm, Sun. 10am-8pm, $10), which is still patronized by many local Mexican Americans. Note that this restaurant is not to be confused with a lesser but more heavily marketed local chain called Jalapeno's.

The menu is strong on tamales, empanadas, and pork-skin gorditas, everything much lighter and more agile in flavor than the usual fatty stuff that passes for Mexican elsewhere. The only drawback is that they have no liquor license, so you won't be able to enjoy a margarita or cerveza.

SOUTHSIDE
Asian

It's not pretty and it's not fancy, but hands-down the best Vietnamese cuisine in town is at **C Saigon Flavors** (6604 Waters Ave., 912/352-4182, daily 11am-9pm, $6-9), a humble little place in a nondescript storefront. The food is anything but nondescript—excellent, authentic, inexpensive, and tasty. I usually get the pork and noodles dish with a side order of delicious fried spring rolls, but any of their shrimp dishes are great too.

Southwestern

Should you find yourself shopping at Oglethorpe Mall on Savannah's ugly paved-over south side, take a quick jaunt across Abercorn to **Moe's Southwestern Grill** (7801 Abercorn St., 912/303-6688, daily 11am-10pm, $5-10) in the Chatham Plaza shopping center. This regional franchise offers made-to-order Southwestern fare in a boisterous atmosphere. Local vegetarians and vegans love this spot, since you tell the counter staff exactly what you want in your burrito and you can always substitute tofu for any meat.

WHITEMARSH ISLAND

Pronounced "WIT-marsh," this overwhelmingly residential area is on the way from the city of Savannah to Tybee Island's beaches. It's notable for the presence of two outstanding barbecue joints, right across U.S. 80 from each other.

Barbecue

Though relatively new, **《 Wiley's Championship BBQ** (4700 U.S. 80 E., 912/201-3259, www.wileyschampionshipbbq. com, lunch Mon.-Sat. 11am-3pm, dinner Wed.-Thurs. 5pm-8pm, Fri.-Sat. 5pm-9pm, $8-25) has what is already widely considered the best pulled pork in Savannah. In addition—and unusually for this area—they smoke a mean brisket too. Save room for the great sides, such as mac-and-cheese and sweet-potato casserole.

Papa's Bar-B-Q (4700 U.S. 80, 912/897-0236, www.papasbar-b-que.com, Mon.-Wed. 11am-9pm, Thurs.-Sat. 11am-10pm, Sun. noon-9pm, $6-15) has a very wide-ranging menu in addition to its signature pulled pork sandwiches, including shrimp, tilapia, and flounder cooked in a variety of ways, and cold plates that include chef, shrimp, and chicken salads. Their house barbecue sauce is very smooth and a clear cut above the generally poor-quality sauce in this area.

TYBEE ISLAND
Breakfast and Brunch

Considered the best breakfast in the Savannah area for 30 years and counting, **《 The Breakfast Club** (1500 Butler Ave., 912/786-5984, http://tybeeisland.com/breakfast-club, daily 6:30am-1pm, $5-15), with its brisk diner atmosphere and hearty Polish sausage-filled omelets, is like a little bit of Chicago in the South. Lines start early for a chance to enjoy such house specialties as Helen's Solidarity, the Athena Omelet, and the Chicago Bear Burger, but don't worry—you'll inevitably strike up a conversation with someone interesting while you wait.

Casual Dining

One of Tybee's most cherished restaurants is on the north end in the shadow of the Tybee Lighthouse. Like a little slice of Jamaica near the dunes, the laid-back **《 North Beach Grill** (33 Meddin Ave., 912/786-4442, lunch and dinner daily, $8-17) deals in tasty Caribbean fare such as its signature jerk chicken, fish sandwiches, and, of course, delicious fried plantain, all overseen by chef-owner "Big George" Spriggs. Frequent live music adds to the island vibe.

If you're hanging out near the Pier, you can't miss the three-story pink building with the open decks and the words "Time to Eat" in six-foot letters across the top of the facade. That's not the name of the restaurant—it's actually **Fannie's on the Beach** (1613 Strand Ave., 912/786-6109, www.fanniesonthebeach. com, Mon.-Thurs. 11am-10pm, Fri.-Sun. 11am-11pm, brunch Sun. noon-3pm, $8-24) a great-for-all-ages restaurant and bar with a menu that's a cut above the usual tavern fare. Sunday brunches noon-3pm are a local favorite.

For a leisurely and tasty dinner, try **Tybee Island Social Club** (1311 Butler Ave., 912/472-4044, http://tybeeislandsocialclub.com, Tues. 5pm-9:30pm, Wed.-Fri. noon-9:30pm, Sat.-Sun. 11:30am-10pm, brunch Sun. 11:30am-2pm, $15). Their menu is somewhat unusual for this seafood-heavy island: Primarily an assortment of gourmet-ish tacos, including fish, duck, and lime- and tequila-marinated steak, all under $10 each. The beer and wine list is accomplished, and the live entertainment usually very good—which is fortunate, since the service here can be on the slow side.

Known far and wide for its sublime pizza is **《 Huc-a-Poo's Bites & Booze** (1213 E. Hwy

80, 912/786-5900, http://hucapoos.com, daily 11am-11pm, $10). Individual slices run about four bucks, can easily feed two, and are quite delicious. Out of the tourist ruckus and tucked away within a small shopping center just as you arrive onto Tybee proper, Huc-a-Poo's also has a lively bar scene.

Set in a large former fishing camp overlooking Chimney Creek, **The Crab Shack** (40 Estill Hammock Rd., 912/786-9857, www.thecrab-shack.com, Mon.-Thurs. 11:30am-10pm, Fri.-Sun. 11:30am-11pm, $6-30) is a favorite local seafood place and also something of an attraction in itself. Don't expect gourmet fare or quiet seaside dining; the emphasis is on mounds of fresh, tasty seafood, heavy on the raw-bar action. Getting there is a little tricky: Take U.S. 80 to Tybee, cross the bridge over Lazaretto Creek, and begin looking for Estill Hammock Road to Chimney Creek on the right. Take Estill Hammock Road and veer right. After that, it's hard to miss.

For a typically rough and rowdy Tybee experience alongside locals and visitors alike, there's always **Stingray's** (1403 Butler Ave., 912/786-0209, http://stingraysontybee.com, Sun.-Thurs. 11am-9pm, Fri.-Sat. 11am-11pm, $20), located in a quaint but usually crowded semi-historic seafood shack on the main drag. This is the sort of place that has live entertainment and often a live remote from a local radio station, all for your drinking and dining pleasure. They got some national exposure when Miley Cyrus played and sang onstage here briefly while she was in town filming the otherwise forgettable *The Last Song.*

Information and Services

VISITORS CENTERS

The main clearinghouse for visitor information is the downtown **Savannah Visitors Center** (301 MLK Jr. Blvd., 912/944-0455, Mon.-Fri. 8:30am-5pm, Sat.-Sun. and holidays 9am-5pm). The newly revitalized Ellis Square features a small visitors kiosk (Mon.-Fri. 8am-6pm), at the northwest corner of the square, with public restrooms and elevators to the underground parking garage beneath the square.

Other visitors centers in the area include the **River Street Hospitality Center** (1 River St., 912/651-6662, daily 10am-10pm), the **Tybee Island Visitor Center** (S. Campbell Ave. and U.S. 80, 912/786-5444, daily 9am-5:30pm), and the **Savannah Airport Visitor Center** (464 Airways Ave., 912/964-1109, daily 10am-6pm).

Visit Savannah (101 E. Bay St., 877/SAVANNAH—877/728-2662, www.savannahvisit.com), the local convention and visitors bureau, maintains a list of lodgings on its website.

HOSPITALS

Savannah has two very good hospital systems. Centrally located near midtown, **Memorial Health University Hospital** (4700 Waters Ave., 912/350-8000, www.memorialhealth.com) is the region's only Level-I Trauma Center and is one of the best in the nation. The St. Joseph's-Candler Hospital System (www.sjchs.org) has two units, **St. Joseph's Hospital** (11705 Mercy Blvd., 912/819-4100) on the extreme south side and **Candler Hospital** (5401 Paulsen St., 912/819-6000), closer to midtown.

MEDIA
Newspapers

The daily newspaper of record is the **Savannah Morning News** (912/525-0796, www.savannahnow.com). It puts out an entertainment insert, called "Do," on Thursdays. The free weekly newspaper in town is **Connect Savannah** (912/721-4350, www.connectsavannah.com), hitting stands each Wednesday. Look to it for culture and music coverage as well as an alternative take on local politics and issues.

Two glossy magazines compete: the hipper **The South** magazine (912/236-5501, www.thesouthmag.com) and the more establishment **Savannah** magazine (912/652-0293, www.savannahmagazine.com).

Radio and Television

The National Public Radio affiliate is the Georgia Public Broadcasting station WSVH (91.1 FM). Savannah State University offers jazz, reggae, and Latin music on WHCJ (90.3 FM). Georgia Public Broadcasting is on WVAN. The local NBC affiliate is WSAV, the CBS affiliate is WTOC, the ABC affiliate is WJCL, and the Fox affiliate is WTGS.

LIBRARIES

The **Live Oak Public Library** (www.liveoakpl. org) is the umbrella organization for the libraries of Chatham, Effingham, and Liberty Counties. By far the largest branch is south of downtown Savannah, the **Bull Street Branch** (222 Bull St., 912/652-3600, Mon.-Tues. 9am-8pm, Wed.-Fri. 9am-6pm, Sun. 2pm-6pm, closed Sat.). In midtown Savannah is the historic **Carnegie Branch** (537 E. Henry St., 912/231-9921, Mon. 10am-8pm, Tues.-Thurs. 10am-6pm, Fri. 2pm-6pm, Sat. 10am-6pm).

The **Georgia Historical Society** (501 Whitaker St., 912/651-2128, www.georgiahistory.com, Tues.-Sat. 10am-5pm) has an extensive collection of clippings, photos, maps, and other archived material at its headquarters at the corner of Forsyth Park in Hodgson Hall.

The **Jen Library** (201 E. Broughton St., 912/525-4700, www.scad.edu, Mon.-Fri. 7:30am-1am, Sat. 10am-1am, Sun. 11am-1am, shorter hours during school breaks), run by the Savannah College of Art and Design, features 3,000 Internet connections in its cavernous 85,000-square-foot space. Its main claim to fame is the remarkable variety of art periodicals to which it subscribes, nearly 1,000 at last count. The public can use it as well with photo ID (you just can't check anything out).

GAY AND LESBIAN RESOURCES

Visitors often find Savannah to be surprisingly cosmopolitan and diverse for a Deep South city, and nowhere is this truer than in its sizeable and influential gay and lesbian community. In line with typical Southern protocol, the community is largely apolitical and more concerned with integration than provocation. But they're still very much aware of their growing impact on the local economy and are major players in art and commerce.

The **Savannah Pride Festival** is held every September at various venues in town. Top-flight dance-oriented musical acts perform, restaurants show off their creativity, and activists staff information booths. The chief resource for local gay and lesbian information and concerns is the First City Network, whose main website (www.firstcitynetwork.org) features many useful links, though many might find its MySpace page (www.myspace.com/firstcitynetwork) useful as well. Another great Internet networking resource is Gay Savannah (www.gaysavannah. com). For specifically gay-friendly accommodations, try the **Under the Rainbow Inn** (104-106 W. 38th St., 912/790-1005, www.under-the-rainbow.com, $109-155), a great B&B in the historic Thomas Square district, a former streetcar suburb of Savannah.

Getting There and Around

BY AIR

Savannah is served by the fairly new and efficient **Savannah/Hilton Head International Airport** (SAV, 400 Airways Ave., 912/964-0514, www.savannahairport.com) directly off I-95 at exit 104. The airport is about 20 minutes from downtown Savannah and an hour from Hilton Head Island. Airlines with routes to SAV include American Eagle (www.aa.com), Continental (www.continental.com), Delta (www.delta.com), United Express (www.ual.com), and US Airways (www.usairways.com).

Taxi stands provide taxi transportation to Savannah at the following regulated fares and conditions: The cost is $2 for the first one-sixth of a mile and $0.32 per sixth of a mile thereafter, not to exceed $3.60 for the first mile and $1.92 per mile thereafter. Waiting charge is $21 per hour. No charge for baggage. The maximum fare for destinations in the Historic District is $25.

BY CAR

Savannah is the eastern terminus of I-16, and that interstate is the most common entrance to the city. However, most travelers get to I-16 via I-95, taking the exit for downtown Savannah (Historic District). Once on I-16, the most common entry points into Savannah proper are via the Gwinnett Street exit, which puts you near the southern edge of the Historic District near Forsyth Park, or more commonly, the Montgomery Street exit farther into the heart of downtown.

Paralleling I-95 is the old coastal highway, now U.S. 17, which goes through Savannah. U.S. 80 is Victory Drive for most of its length through town; after you pass through Thunderbolt on your way to the islands area, however, including Tybee, it reverts to U.S. 80.

BY TRAIN

Savannah is on the New York-Miami *Silver Service* of Amtrak (2611 Seaboard Coastline Dr., 912/234-2611, www.amtrak.com). To get to the station on the west side of town, take I-16 west and then I-516 north. Immediately take the Gwinnett Street-Railroad Station exit and follow the Amtrak signs.

BY BUS

Chatham Area Transit (www.catchacat. org, Mon.-Sat. 5:30am-11:30pm, Sun. 7am-9pm, $1.25, includes one transfer, free for children under 41 inches tall, exact change only), Savannah's publicly supported bus system, is quite thorough and efficient considering Savannah's relatively small size. Plenty of routes crisscross the entire area.

Of primary interest to visitors is the free **Dot Express Shuttle** (daily 7am-9pm), which travels a continuous circuit route through the Historic District with 11 stops at hotels, historic sites, and the Savannah Visitors Center. The Shuttle is wheelchair-accessible.

If you're on River Street, a neat experience is to jump on the free **River Street Trolley** (www.catchacat.org, Thurs.-Sun.). This restored historical trolley moves on the old trolley lines on River Street, and while it only goes a short distance, serving six stops, it's certainly fun.

BY RENTAL CAR

The majority of rental car facilities are at the Savannah/Hilton Head International Airport, including **Avis** (800/831-2847), **Budget** (800/527-0700), **Dollar** (912/964-9001), **Enterprise** (800/736-8222), **Hertz** (800/654-3131), **National** (800/227-7368), and **Thrifty** (800/367-2277). Rental locations away from the airport are **Avis** (7810 Abercorn St., 912/354-4718), **Budget** (7070 Abercorn St., 912/355-0805), **Enterprise** (3028 Skidaway Rd., 912/352-1424; 9505 Abercorn St., 912/925-0060; 11506-A Abercorn Expressway, 912/920-1093; 7510 White Bluff Rd., 912/355-6622).

BY TAXI

Taxi services in Georgia tend to be less regulated than in other states, but service is plentiful in Savannah. The chief local provider is **Yellow Cab** (866/319-9646, www.savannahyellowcab.com). For wheelchair accessibility, request cab number 14. Other providers include **Adam Cab** (912/927-7466), **Magikal Taxi Service** (912/897-8294), and **Sunshine Cab** (912/272-0971). If you like some local flavor to go with your cab ride, call **Concierge Taxi Services** (912/604-8466), the one-man show of local author Robert S. Mickles. He's very friendly and always has a great Savannah story to tell.

If you're not in a big hurry, it's always fun to take a **Savannah Pedicab** (912/232-7900, www.savannahpedicab.com) for quick trips around downtown. Your friendly driver will pedal one or two passengers anywhere within the Historic District for a reasonable price.

PARKING

Parking is at a premium in downtown Savannah. Traditional coin-operated meter parking is available throughout the city, but more and more the city is going to self-pay kiosks where you purchase a stamped receipt to display inside your car's dashboard. The city operates several parking garages at various rates and hours: the **Bryan Street Garage** (100 E. Bryan St., daily 24 hours, rates Mon.-Fri. 7am-6pm $1 per hour, Mon.-Fri. 6pm-7am $2 flat rate, Sat.-Sun. $3 flat rate), the **Robinson Garage** (132 Montgomery St., daily 24 hours, rates Mon.-Fri. 7am-6pm $1 per hour, Mon.-Fri. 6pm-7am $2 flat rate, Sat.-Sun. $3 flat rate), the **State Street Garage** (100 E. State St., open Sun.-Fri. 5am-1am, Sat. 5am-Sun. 5am, rates Mon.-Fri. 5am-6pm $1 per hour, Mon.-Fri. 6pm-1am $2 flat rate, Sat.-Sun. $3 flat rate), the **Liberty Street Garage** (401 W. Liberty St., open Mon.-Fri. 5am-1am, Sat. 5am-Sun. 5am, rates Mon.-Fri. 5am-6pm $1 per hour, Mon.-Fri. 6pm-1am $2 flat rate, Sat.-Sun. $1 flat rate), and the new **Whitaker Street Garage** (daily 24 hours, $2 per hour) underneath revitalized Ellis Square. Special events sometimes incur rates of $5-20.

Outside Savannah

As is the case with Charleston, Savannah's outlying areas still bear the indelible marks of the plantation era. The marsh still retains traces of the old paddy fields, and the economics of the area still retain a similar sense of class and racial stratification. While history is no less prominent, it is more subtle in these largely semirural areas, and the tourist infrastructure is much less well-developed than Savannah proper. This area contains some of the most impoverished communities in Georgia, so keep in mind that the locals may have more on their minds than keeping you entertained—though certainly at no point will their Southern manners fail them. And also keep in mind that you are traveling in one of the most unique ecosystems in the country, and natural beauty is never far away.

MIDWAY AND LIBERTY COUNTY

Locals will tell you that Midway is named because it's equidistant from the Savannah and Altamaha Rivers on Oglethorpe's old "river road," which it certainly is, but others say the small but very historic town is actually named after the Medway River in England. In any case, we know that in seeking to pacify the local Creek people, the Council of Georgia in 1752 granted a group of Massachusetts Puritans then residing in Dorchester, South Carolina, a 32,000-acre land grant as incentive to move south. After moving into Georgia and establishing New Dorchester, they soon founded a nearby settlement that would later take on the modern spelling of Midway. Midway's citizens were very aggressive early on in the cause for American independence, which is why the area's three original parishes were combined and named Liberty County in 1777—the only Georgia county named for a concept rather than a person. Two of Georgia's three signers of the Declaration of Independence, Lyman Hall and Button Gwinnett, resided primarily in Midway, and both attended the historic Midway Church. A key part of Liberty County history is no more: The once-thriving seaport of Sunbury, which formerly challenged Savannah for economic supremacy in the region, no longer exists.

The main highways in Midway are I-95, U.S. 17, and U.S. 84, also called Oglethorpe Highway, which becomes Highway 38 (Islands Hwy.) east of I-95.

Sights

Tourism in this area has been made much more user-friendly by the liberal addition of signage for the "Liberty Trail," a collection of key attractions. When in doubt, follow the signs.

In Midway proper is the charming **Midway Museum** (U.S. 17, 912/884-5837, Tues.-Sat. 10am-4pm, Sun. 2pm-4pm, $3) and the adjacent **Midway Church,** sometimes called the Midway meetinghouse. The museum contains a variety of artifacts, most from the 18th and 19th centuries, and an extensive genealogy collection. The Midway Church, built in 1756, was burned during the Revolution but rebuilt in 1792. Both Button Gwinnett and Lyman Hall attended services here, and during the Civil War some of Sherman's cavalry set up camp. The cemetery across the street is wonderfully poignant and is the final resting place of two Revolutionary War generals; Union cavalry kept horses within its walls. The museum, church, and cemetery are easy to find: take exit 76 from I-95 South, and take a right on U.S. 84 (Oglethorpe Highway). Turn right on U.S. 17, and they're just ahead on the right.

Farther west off Islands Highway is **Seabrook Village** (660 Trade Hill Rd., 912/884-7008, Tues.-Sat. 10am-4pm, $3), a unique living-history museum chronicling the everyday life of Liberty County's African

the historic Midway Church
© JIM MOREKIS

Americans, with a direct link to Sherman's famous "40 acres and a mule" Field Order No. 15. There are eight restored vernacular buildings on the 100-acre site, including the simple but sublime one-room Seabrook School.

Youmans Pond (daily, free) is a prime stop for migratory fowl. Its main claim to fame is that it was visited in 1773 by the great naturalist William Bartram on one of his treks across the Southeast. Youmans Pond has changed little since then, with its tree-studded pond and oodles of owls, ospreys, herons, egrets, wood storks, and many more. To get here, take I-95 south from Savannah to exit 76. Take a left onto Highway 38 (Islands Hwy.) and then a left onto Camp Viking Road. About one mile ahead, take a right onto Lake Pamona Drive. About 0.75 miles ahead, look for the pond on the right. It's unmarked, but there's a wooden boardwalk.

Less easy to find is **LeConte-Woodmanston Botanical Garden** (912/884-6500, www.hist.armstrong.edu/publichist/LeConte/leconte-home.htm, Feb. 15-Dec. 17 Tues.-Sat.

THE DEAD TOWN OF SUNBURY

If you spend much time in Liberty County, you'll probably hear someone mention that a certain place or person is "over near Sunbury." Such is the lasting legacy of this long-gone piece of Georgia history on the Midway River that locals still refer to it in the present tense, though the old town itself is no more.

Founded soon after Midway in 1758, by 1761 Sunbury rivaled Savannah as Georgia's main commercial port, with a thriving trade in lumber, rice, indigo, corn, and, unfortunately, slaves. At one time, one writer recalls, seven square-rigged vessels called on the port in a single day. At various times, all three of Georgia's signers of the Declaration of Independence—Button Gwinnett, Lyman Hall, and George Walton—had connections to Sunbury.

The beginning of the end came with those heady days of revolution, however, when Sun-bury was the scene of much fighting between colonists and the British army in 1776-1779. A British siege in 1778 culminated in this immortal reply from the colonial commander, Colonel John McIntosh, to a redcoat demand for surrender: "Come and take it." By the beginning of 1779, a separate British assault did indeed "take it," adding to the increasingly violent pillage of the surrounding area. After U.S. independence, Sunbury remained the Liberty County seat until 1797, but it was never the same, beset by decay, hurricanes, and yellow fever outbreaks. (Fort Morris, however, would defend the area against the British one more time, in the War of 1812, as Fort Defiance.) By 1848, nothing of the town remained but the old cemetery, which you can find a short drive from the Fort Morris State Historic Site; ask a park employee for directions.

9am-5pm, call first to verify hours and road conditions, $2). Part of William Bartram's historic nature trail, this was the home of Dr. Louis LeConte, renowned 19th-century botanist, and his sons John LeConte, first president of the University of California, Berkeley; and Joseph LeConte, who founded the Sierra Club with John Muir. The highlight here is the rare tidally influenced freshwater wetland, featuring the blackwater Bulltown Swamp. This visit is best done in a 4WD vehicle. From Savannah, take I-95 south to exit 76. Turn right on U.S. 84, then left on U.S. 17. Turn right on Barrington Ferry Road until the pavement ends at Sandy Run Road. Continue until you see the historic markers. Turn left onto the dirt road, then drive another mile.

Dorchester Academy and Museum (8787 E. Oglethorpe Hwy., 912/884-2347, www. dorchesteracademy.com, Tues.-Fri. 11am-2pm, Sat. 2pm-4pm, free) was built as a boarding and day school for freed African Americans after the Civil War. Liberty County was one of the earliest integrated school districts in Georgia, and Martin Luther King Jr. came to Dorchester

in 1962 to plan the march on Birmingham. In 1997 an extensive renovation brought the multiple-building facility to its current state. The museum is small but features an interesting display of memorabilia. Take exit 76 off I-95 and go west on U.S. 84, about two miles past the intersection with U.S. 17.

Built to defend the once-proud port of Sunbury, **Fort Morris State Historic Site** (2559 Ft. Morris Rd., 912/884-5999, www. gastateparks.org/info/ftmorris, Tues.-Sat. 9am-5pm, Sun. 2pm-5:30pm, $3) was reconstructed during the War of 1812 and was an encampment during the Civil War. It was here that Colonel John McIntosh gave his famous reply to the British demand for his surrender: "Come and take it." The museum has displays of military and everyday life of the era. Reenactments and cannon firings are highlights. There's a visitors center and a nature trail. To get here, take exit 76 off I-95 south. Go east on Islands Highway and take a left on Fort Morris Road; the site is two miles down.

A little way south of Midway on the Liberty Trail in tiny Riceboro is **Geechee Kunda** (622

© JIM MOREKIS

re-enactors at Fort Morris

Ways Temple Rd., Riceboro, 912/884-4440, www.geecheekunda.net), a combination museum-outreach center dedicated to explaining and exploring the culture of Sea Island African Americans on the Georgia coast. (Don't be confused: *Geechee* is the Georgia word for the Gullah people. Both groups share similar folkways and history, and the terms are virtually interchangeable.) There are artifacts from slavery and Reconstruction, including authentic Geechee-Gullah relics.

Liberty County is also home to part of the sprawling Fort Stewart army installation, home of the U.S. Army "Rock of the Marne" 3rd Infantry Division. The only thing open to the public is the **Fort Stewart Museum** (Bldg. T904, 2022 Frank Cochran Dr., Fort Stewart, 912/767-7885, Tues.-Sat. 10am-4pm, free), which chronicles the division's activity in World War II, Vietnam, Korea, Desert Storm, and Iraq. All visitors must stop at the main gate and provide proof of registration, insurance, and a driver's license to receive a visitor's pass. To get here, take exit 87 off I-95 south. Take a

left on U.S. 17, then veer right onto Highway 196 west. Turn right at U.S. 84. Turn right onto General Stewart Way, and follow directions to the main gate.

Accommodations and Food

While industry is coming quickly to Liberty County, it's still a small self-contained community with not much in the way of tourist amenities (many would say that is part of its charm). A great choice for a stay is **Dunham Farms** (5836 Islands Hwy., Midway, 912/880-4500, www.dunhamfarms.com). The B&B ($165-205) is in the converted 1940s Palmyra Barn, and the self-catered circa-1840 Palmyra Cottage ($300) nearby is right on the river, with plenty of kayaking and hiking opportunities. Your hosts, Laura and Meredith Devendorf, couldn't be more charming or informed about the area, and the breakfasts are absurdly rich and filling in that hearty and deeply comforting Southern tradition.

Restaurants of note include the **Sunbury Crab Company** (541 Brigantine Dunmore

Rd., Midway, 912/884-8640, lunch Sat.-Sun., dinner Wed.-Sun., $10-30), providing, you guessed it, great crab cakes in a casual atmosphere on the Midway River. Get here by taking Highway 38 east of Midway and then a left onto Fort Morris Road. Many locals eat at least once a week at **Holton's Seafood** (13711 E. Oglethorpe Hwy., Midway, 912/884-9151, daily lunch and dinner, $7-17), an unpretentious and fairly typical family-run fried seafood place just off I-95 at the Midway exit.

RICHMOND HILL AND BRYAN COUNTY

Known as the "town that Henry Ford built," Richmond Hill is a growing bedroom community of Savannah in adjacent Bryan County. Sherman's March to the Sea ended here with much destruction, so little history before that time is left. Most of what remains is due to Ford's philanthropic influence, still felt in many place names around the area, including the main drag, Highway 144, known as Ford Avenue. After the auto magnate and his wife Clara made the area, then called Ways Station, a summer home, they were struck by the area's incredible poverty and determined to help improve living conditions, building hospitals, schools, churches, and homes. The Fords eventually acquired over 85,000 acres in Bryan County, including the former Richmond plantation. What is now known as Ford Plantation—currently a private luxury resort—was built in the 1930s and centered on the main house, once the central building of the famous Hermitage Plantation on the Savannah River, purchased and moved by Ford south to Bryan County.

Sights

The little **Richmond Hill Historical Society and Museum** (Ford Ave. and Timber Trail Rd., Richmond Hill, 912/756-3697, daily 10am-4pm, donation) is housed in a former kindergarten built by Henry Ford.

Perhaps the main attraction here, especially for Civil War buffs, is **Fort McAllister State Historic Site** (3894 Ft. McAllister Rd.,

Richmond Hill, 912/727-2339, www.gastate-parks.org/info/ftmcallister, daily 7am-10pm, $5 adults, $3.50 children). Unlike the masonry forts of Savannah, Fort McAllister is an all-earthwork fortification on the Ogeechee River, the site of a short but savage assault by Sherman's troops in December 1864 in which 5,000 Union soldiers quickly overwhelmed the skeleton garrison of 230 Confederate defenders. After the war, the site fell into disrepair until Henry Ford funded and spearheaded restoration in the 1930s, as he did with so many historic sites in Bryan County. The fort, which features many reenactments throughout the year, has a well-run new **Civil War Museum** (Mon.-Sat. 9am-5pm, Sun. 2pm-5pm). An adjacent recreational site features a beautiful oak-lined picnic ground, a nature trail, and the nearby 65-site Savage Island Campground. To get here from I-95, take exit 90 and go 10 miles east on Highway 144.

Practicalities

There's no end to the chain food offerings here, but one of the better restaurants in town is **The Upper Crust** (1702 U.S. 17, 912/756-6990, lunch Mon.-Sat., dinner Mon.-Sun., $7-12), a casual American place with great pizza in addition to soups, salads, and hot sandwiches. Another popular place, also on U.S 17, is **Steamers Restaurant & Raw Bar** (4040 U.S. 17, 912/756-3979, daily 5-10pm, $10-20), home of some good Lowcountry boil.

To get to Richmond Hill, drive south of Savannah on I-95 and take exit 90. Most lodgings in the area are clustered off I-95 at exit 87 (exit 90 also takes you to Richmond Hill). Keep in mind the two most important thoroughfares are the north-south U.S. 17 and the east-west Highway 144, also known as Ford Avenue.

NEW EBENEZER

Few people visit New Ebenezer today, west of Savannah in Effingham County. Truth is, there's not much there anymore except for one old church. But oh, what a church. The **Jerusalem Evangelical Lutheran Church**

(2966 Ebenezer Rd., Rincon, 912/754-3915, www.effga.com/jerusalem) hosts the oldest continuous congregation in the United States. Built of local clay brick in 1769, its walls are 21 inches thick. Some original panes of glass remain, and its European bells are still rung before each service (Sun. 11am). Several surrounding structures are also heirs to New Ebenezer's Salzburg legacy. Around the corner from the church is a much newer spiritually themed site, the **New Ebenezer Retreat and Conference Center** (2887 Ebenezer Rd., Rincon, 912/754-9242, www.newebenezer. org). Built in 1977, the Retreat provides acres of calm surroundings, lodging, and meals in an ecumenical Christian setting.

Scenic blackwater **Ebenezer Creek** is best experienced by putting in at the private Ebenezer Landing ($5). To get to New Ebenezer, take exit 109 off I-95. Go north on Highway 21 to Rincon, Georgia, then east on Highway 275 (Ebenezer Rd.). The New Ebenezer Retreat and Conference Center offers a range of very reasonably priced lodgings, most including meals, in a beautiful setting. The extremely fast-growing town of Rincon, through which you will most likely drive on your way to New Ebenezer, offers an assortment of the usual chain food and lodging establishments.

WASSAW ISLAND NATIONAL WILDLIFE REFUGE

Totally unique in that it's the only Georgia barrier island never cleared for agriculture or development, the 10,000-acre Wassaw Island National Wildlife Refuge (www.fws.gov/wassaw) is accessible only by boat. There are striking driftwood-strewn beaches, and the interior of the island has some beautiful old-growth stands of longleaf pine and live oak. Wassaw is a veritable paradise for nature lovers and birdwatchers, with migratory activity in the spring and fall, waterfowl in abundance in the summer, and manatee and loggerhead turtle activity (about 10 percent of Georgia's transient loggerhead population makes use of Wassaw for nesting). There are also about 20 miles of

trails and a decaying Spanish-American War-era battery, Fort Morgan, on the north end. National Wildlife Refuge Week is celebrated in October.

Because of its comparatively young status—it was formed only about 1,600 years ago—Wassaw Island also has some unique geographical features. You can still make out the parallel ridge features, vestiges of successive ancient shorelines. A central ridge forms the backbone of the island, reaching an amazing (for this area) elevation of 45 feet above sea level at the south end. Native Americans first settled the island, whose name comes from an ancient word for sassafras, which was found in abundance here. During the Civil War, both Confederate and Union troops occupied the island successively. In 1866 the wealthy New England businessman George Parsons bought the island, which stayed in that family's hands until it was sold to the Nature Conservancy in 1969 for $1 million. The Conservancy in turn sold Wassaw to the U.S. government for $1 to be managed as a wildlife refuge.

It's easiest to get to Wassaw Island from Savannah. Charters and scheduled trips are available from **Captain Walt's Charters** (Thunderbolt Marina, 3124 River Dr., 912/507-3811, www.waltsadventure.com/charters), the **Bull River Marina** (8005 E. U.S. 80, 912/897-7300), **Delegal Marina** (1 Marina Dr., 912/598-0023), **Captain Joe Dobbs** (Delegal Marina, 1 Marina Dr., 912/598-0090, www.captjdobbs.com), and **Isle of Hope Marina** (50 Bluff Dr., 912/354-8187, www.isleofhopemarina.com). Most docking is either at the beaches on the north and south ends or in Wassaw Creek, where the U.S. Fish and Wildlife Service dock is also located (temporary mooring only). There's no camping allowed on Wassaw Island; it's for day use only.

OSSABAW ISLAND

Owned and operated by Georgia as a heritage and wildlife preserve, the island was a gift to the state in 1978 from Eleanor Torrey-West and family, who still retain some property on the island. All public use of the island is managed

NEW EBENEZER AND THE SALZBURGERS

Perhaps the most unsung chapter in Europe's great spiritual diaspora of the 1700s, the Salzburgers of New Ebenezer—a thrifty, peaceful, and hard-working people—were Georgia's first religious refugees and perhaps the most progressive as well. The year after Oglethorpe's arrival, a contingent of devout Lutherans from Salzburg in present-day Austria arrived after being expelled from their home country for their beliefs. Oglethorpe, mindful of Georgia's mission to provide sanctuary for persecuted Protestants and also wishing for a military buffer to the west, eagerly welcomed them. Given land about 25 miles west of Savannah, the Salzburgers named their first settlement Ebenezer ("stone of help" in Hebrew). Disease prompted them to move the site to better land nearer to the river and call it—in pragmatic Germanic style—New Ebenezer, and so it remains to this day.

Because they continued to speak German instead of English, the upriver colony maintained its isolation. Still, the Salzburgers were among Oglethorpe's most ardent and loyal supporters. Their pastor and de facto political leader, Johann Martin Boltzius, seeking to build an enlightened agrarian utopia of small farmers, was an outspoken foe of slavery and the exploitative plantation system of agriculture. His system largely worked: The fragile silk industry thrived in New Ebenezer while it had failed miserably in Savannah, and the nation's first rice mill was built here. However, don't get the idea that the Salzburgers were all work and no play. They

enjoyed their beer, so much so that Oglethorpe was forced to send regular shipments, rationalizing that "cheap beer is the only means to keep rum out."

For 10 years, Georgia hosted another progressive Lutheran sect, the Moravians, whom John Wesley called the only genuine Christians he'd ever met. Despite their professed pacifism, however, they had to leave New Ebenezer because they didn't get along with the Salzburgers, and their communal living arrangements led to internal discord.

The Trustees' turnover of Georgia back to the crown in 1750 signaled the final victory of pro-slavery forces—so much so that even Pastor Boltzius acquired a couple of slaves as domestic servants. New Ebenezer's influence began a decline that rapidly accelerated when British forces pillaged much of the town in the Revolution, even burning pews and Bibles. Fifty years later, nothing at all remained except the old Jerusalem Church, now the Jerusalem Evangelical Lutheran Church. Built in 1769, it still stands today and hosts regular worship services. Right around the corner is the New Ebenezer Retreat, nestled along the banks of the Savannah River, providing an ecumenical meeting and natural healing space for those of all faiths.

Although New Ebenezer is often called a "ghost town," this is a misnomer. Extensive archaeological work continues in the area, and the Georgia Salzburger Society works hard to maintain several historic buildings and keep the legacy alive through special events.

by the **Ossabaw Island Foundation** (www.ossabawisland.org).

The 12,000-acre island is much older than Wassaw Island to its north and so has traces of human habitation back to 2000 BC The island's name comes from an old Muskogean word referring to yaupon holly, found in abundance on the island and used by Native Americans in purification rituals to induce vomiting. Wading birds and predators such as bald eagles make their homes on the island, as

do feral horses and a transient population of loggerhead turtles, who lay eggs in the dunes during the summer. There are several tabby ruins on the island, along with many miles of walking trails. Unlike the much-younger Wassaw, Ossabaw Island was not only timbered extensively but hosted several rice and cotton plantations, particularly on the north end. The first property transfer in Georgia involved Ossabaw, St. Catherine's, and Sapelo Islands, which were ceded to the Yamacraws in exchange for the English getting the coastal region. The Yamacraws then granted those islands to Mary Musgrove, who began the modern era on the island by planting and introducing livestock.

Descendants of the island's slaves moved to the Savannah area after the Civil War, founding the community of Pin Point. Similarly to Jekyll Island to the south, Ossabaw was a hunting preserve for wealthy families in the Roaring '20s. Even today, hunting is an important activity on the island, with lotteries choosing who gets a chance to pursue its overly large populations of deer and wild hogs, the latter of which are descended from pigs brought by the Spanish.

Now reserved exclusively for educational and scientific purposes, the island is accessible only by boat. Georgia law ensures public access to all beaches up to the high-tide mark—which simply means that the public can ride out to Ossabaw and go on the beach for day use, but any travel to the interior is restricted and you must have permission first. Contact the Ossabaw Island Foundation (info@ossabawisland.org) for information. Day trips can be arranged with charter operators at the marinas in Savannah.

SOUTH GEORGIA

Considering it's the least populous part of the state and unquestionably the hottest during the summer, one might be tempted to ask, "Why go to South Georgia?" The answer is that there are some things to see here that you simply can't find anywhere else.

Where else can you find an entire town devoted almost entirely to celebrating the life and times of a president born there, as is the case with Plains and native son Jimmy Carter? Where else can you find a swamp the size of Delaware, filled with black water that is as clean as what comes out of your tap at home, as is the case with the Okefenokee? Where else can you walk in the footsteps of Civil War POWs and visit a stirring national museum devoted to the memory of American POWs from all wars, as you can at Andersonville?

It's certainly true that there are more pecans and peanuts down here than people. It's also true that you've got a lot of room to spread out and a lot of friendly people to meet here, where the pace of life is slow and easy.

PLANNING YOUR TIME

Time management is a real challenge in this portion of Georgia, a truly vast swath of land, which, though served by an excellent road system, is simply too big to traverse quickly. While theoretically you could hit all the major sights in a three-day-long weekend, realistically unless you have four or five days to spare you will have to prioritize.

Basically, there are three routes of particular interest in South Georgia. The area occasionally called "Presidential pathways" includes

HIGHLIGHTS

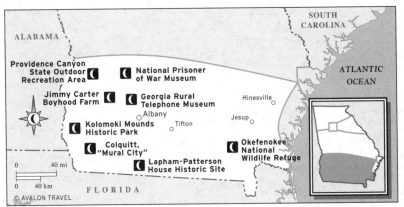

LOOK FOR **(** TO FIND RECOMMENDED SIGHTS, ACTIVITIES, DINING, AND LODGING.

(Georgia Rural Telephone Museum: More than just a quirky labor of love, this is the largest collection of vintage telephone memorabilia in the country (page 321).

(Jimmy Carter Boyhood Farm: Take in a nostalgic and insightful look into the Depression-era experiences of the Georgia-born president just outside his hometown of Plains (page 323).

(National Prisoner of War Museum: The site of the notorious Andersonville Civil War POW camp also hosts a deeply affecting exploration of cruelty and bravery during wartime (page 324).

(Providence Canyon State Outdoor Recreation Area: This geological feature of high white walls and a deep floor, surprisingly

developed by human impact, has been called "Georgia's Grand Canyon" (page 327).

(Kolomoki Mounds Historic Park: An enormous temple mound and an excellent museum are the highlights of this ancient Native American site (page 330).

(Colquitt, "Mural City": World-class murals can be found on just about every flat surface in this tiny farm town (page 331).

(Lapham-Patterson House Historic Site: This whimsical Victorian folly combines incredible workmanship with an eccentric vision (page 337).

(Okefenokee National Wildlife Refuge: Visit a vast and wholly fascinating natural feature the likes of which can't be found anywhere else on the planet (page 343).

sites related to Jimmy Carter, as well as the Andersonville POW camp and museum and the Kolomoki Mounds and Providence Canyon sights. This is by far the most interesting and well-traveled part of South Georgia away from the coast.

Then there's the southern band along the

Florida border, with Thomasville as the main stop, and finally the huge Okefenokee Swamp, taking up virtually the entire southeastern corner of Georgia. The Okefenokee is something of a special case, as you can easily spend several days exploring it or simply confine it to a day trip.

SOUTH GEORGIA

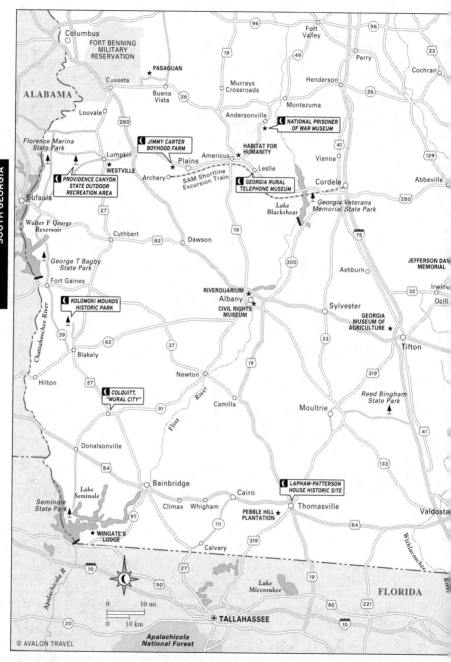

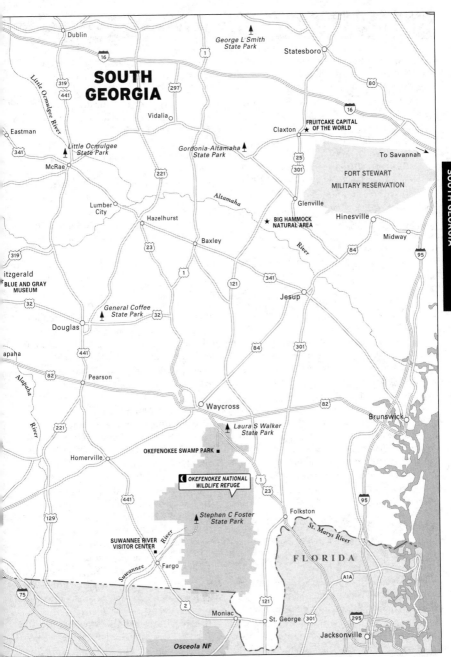

Dublin

George L Smith
State Park

Statesboro

16

319
441

**SOUTH
GEORGIA**

297

Vidalia

Claxton FRUITCAKE CAPITAL
OF THE WORLD

Eastman

341

Little Ocmulgee
State Park

McRae

Gordonia-Altamaha
State Park

25
301

To Savannah

FORT STEWART
MILITARY RESERVATION

221

Altamaha

Glenville

Hinesville

Lumber
City

Hazelhurst

BIG HAMMOCK
NATURAL AREA

Midway

95

Baxley

23

River

84

319

1

121

341

Jesup

itzgerald

**BLUE AND GRAY
MUSEUM**

32

General Coffee
State Park

32

Douglas

84

301

apaha

82

Pearson

441

Waycross

82

Brunswick

221

Alapaha

River

Homerville

Laura S Walker
State Park

OKEFENOKEE SWAMP PARK ■

441

OKEFENOKEE NATIONAL
WILDLIFE REFUGE

1

23

95

129

Stephen C Foster
State Park

Folkston

St. Marys River

**SUWANNEE RIVER
VISITOR CENTER** ■

River

Fargo

F L O R I D A

75

Suwannee River

A1A

2

75

Moniac

St. George

301

121

295

Jacksonville

Osceola NF

Jimmy Carter Country

With the notable exception of Providence Canyon, the deeply rural farm country around Americus isn't very scenically stimulating, but it contains some of the nation's most important and interesting history.

Many come just to see tiny Plains, population under 700, birthplace of the 39th president, Jimmy Carter. The president and his wife Rosalynn still live on the main road in the only house they've ever owned, and Carter himself still teaches Sunday School (open to the public) many times a year at his church on the outskirts of town. Even for those who don't care for Carter's politics, a visit to Plains is stimulating for anyone who believes in the American dream, where a peanut farmer from a tiny town in the middle of nowhere can become president.

Every American should visit the National Prisoner of War Museum, at the site of the notorious Andersonville POW Camp. The Civil War site itself is grimly fascinating, and the adjacent museum is deeply moving in its portrayal of the plight and ingenuity of U.S. prisoners of war throughout history.

Plains is geared for the day visitor to the various Carter-related sites. The Andersonville area is similarly suitable mainly for day visitors. The only thing approaching a metropolitan area in the vicinity is Americus, where you'll find much more variety and availability of food and lodging, as well as the global headquarters of Habitat for Humanity and its associated enterprise, Koinonia Farms.

AMERICUS

Americus is your best base of operations from which to explore Carter Country, and this cute town perched on a little hill offers a few things of its own worth seeing as well. Because it's home to Georgia Southwestern University and is the international headquarters of Habitat for Humanity, Americus is a little more resistant to the ups and downs of the economy than many comparatively hard-hit rural towns.

Habitat for Humanity Global Village and Discovery Center

The brainchild of Millard and Linda Fuller, who founded the organization in 1976 (the same year Jimmy Carter was elected president), Habitat for Humanity International has expanded into a major global force for good, promoting the construction of safe, affordable housing. Though the Fullers were ousted in 2005, the organization continues its mission unabated and has helped build over half a million homes all over the world.

Administrative offices are in Atlanta, but the global operations center for Habitat for Humanity and the associated Global Village and Discovery Center (721 W. Church St., 229/410-7937, www.habitat.org, Mon.-Fri. 9am-5pm, Sat. 10am-2pm, $4 adults, $3 children) is in its hometown of Americus. The centerpiece of the experience is seeing replicas of typical Third World housing, along with tours of 15 of the special low-cost, sustainable buildings that Habitat for Humanity seeks to build in those areas, each design customized for the particular area's climate and terrain.

Koinonia Farms

Before founding Habitat for Humanity, Millard and Linda Fuller met at Koinonia Farms (1324 Hwy. 49, 877/738-1741, www. koinoniapartners.org, Mon.-Sat. 9am-5pm, Sun. 1pm-5pm, free). This 70-year-old agricultural and ministerial institution was established by two couples, Clarence and Florence Jordan and Martin and Mabel England, specifically to embody what they saw as the ideals of early Christianity. By growing and providing food and spreading fellowship, they aimed to overcome the then-ingrained racism and economic disparity endemic to the South Georgia region and be an example to other "intentional communities."

Today, visitors are always welcome at this working farm, especially at the weekday noon community lunches. The emphasis is on *working,* however, and Koinonia is mainly a place where people come to volunteer their labor on the farm or their trade skills, or even their musicianship, in exchange for a stay at the attached RV and lodging area, where people can stay for up to two weeks (longer during harvest time). Koinonia goods can be purchased on site or at shops around the Americus and Plains area.

(Georgia Rural Telephone Museum

About 20 minutes south of Americus in a restored cotton warehouse in tiny Leslie is one of the quirkiest and most fun little museums around, the Georgia Rural Telephone Museum (135 N. Bailey Ave., 229/874-4786, www. grtm.org, Mon.-Fri. 9am-3:30pm, nominal fee). We're not just talking rotary phones here, we're talking the old-timey phone exchanges with live operators who manually connected your call. In fact, this labor of love of Mr. Tommy Smith comprises the largest collection of such memorabilia in the country, with gear dating back to the very invention of the telephone in 1876, including the last operating old-fashioned switchboard of the Southern Bell company. Not only a humorously educational experience for younger folks raised on cell phones, the museum is a thought-provoking look back into the past, where in some ways communication was more difficult, but in other ways more genuine.

Accommodations and Food

Your best bet for lodging in Americus is the historic (**Windsor Hotel** (125 Lamar St., 229/924-1555, www.windsor-americus.com, $200), itself a landmark worth visiting. Now a Best Western property, it's a stirring image of Victoriana with its imposing turrets and broad balcony. It was extensively renovated in 2010, but its diverse, individualized rooms and splendid common areas remain redolent of the Victorian high period. Book in advance, as the Windsor usually hosts any foreign dignitaries in the area to visit President Carter and family and Habitat for Humanity.

Another recommended lodging option is the well-run, clean, and recently upgraded **Jameson Inn** (1605 E. Lamar St., 229/924-2726, www.jamesoninns.com, $100), several blocks away, which offers a free full breakfast.

The Windsor also happens to be your best bet for food and adult beverages in this corner of the Bible Belt. The Windsor has two excellent dining options, the sit-down, farm-to-table **Rosemary & Thyme** (125 Lamar St., 229/924-1555, www.windsor-americus.com, Mon.-Fri. 6:30am-9:30am and 5pm-9pm, Sat. 6:30am-10am and 5pm-9pm, Sun. 6:30am-10am, $20) and the upstairs (**Floyd's Pub** (125 Lamar St., 229/924-1555, www.windsor-americus.com, Mon.-Sat. from 5pm, $15), named after a longtime bellman. My favorite meal in Americus consists of sitting down at the bar at Floyd's and ordering the sublime gyro wrap; but any of their sandwiches are excellent. And, as the bar staff jokingly points out, Floyd's is pretty much the only nightlife for miles around. They have live music most Friday nights.

PLAINS

Plains (www.plainsgeorgia.com) itself is little more than a single block of businesses and a few houses and churches. For most intents and purposes, the entire town comprises the Jimmy Carter National Historic Site and can be enjoyed within a single day. It's surrounded by intensively cultivated farmland, which includes the exceptionally well-interpreted Jimmy Carter Boyhood Farm. All the Carter-oriented sites are free of charge.

As you'd expect from the place where a peanut farmer became president, the big annual event is the **Plains Peanut Festival** (www. plainsgeorgia.com) happening each September, which almost always features appearances by the President and Mrs. Carter.

Jimmy Carter National Historic Site

Start your visit at the Victorian-era **Plains Depot Museum and Presidential Campaign Headquarters** (Main St., 229/824-4104,

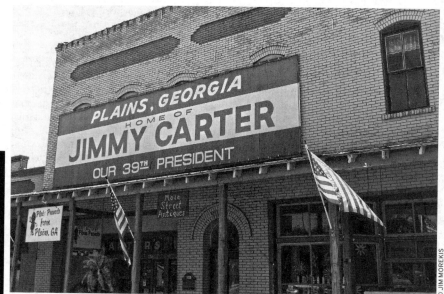

Tiny Plains features several Carter-oriented sites.

www.nps.gov, daily 9am-4:30pm, free) on Main Street next to the block of shops comprising Plains' "downtown." Not just the train depot and oldest building in the area, it was where Jimmy Carter symbolically based his presidential campaign and is a must-stop for any political junkie. The interior of the depot (warning: no air-conditioning) features much memorabilia about Carter's insurgent run in the post-Watergate years, shocking not only the Democratic Party establishment but the entire globe, which marveled at a peanut farmer becoming leader of the free world.

Technically the **Plains High School Visitors Center and Museum** (300 N. Bond St., 229/824-4104, www.nps.gov, daily 9am-5pm, free), housed in the old Plains High School, is the premier Carter-oriented site in Plains, but for those expecting an in-depth interpretation of his legacy and influential post-presidential activity it might be underwhelming (for that, go to the Carter Center in Atlanta). But certainly it's neat to walk around in the same school where both the future president and his

future wife Rosalynn attended classes, and the museum does a good job in explaining the social and political circumstances of the times in which Carter grew up and his motivations for running for office after a successful career in the U.S. Navy submarine service.

There's not much to see at **Billy Carter's Gas Station** on Main Street except, well, a restored gas station. But it's a hoot for those who remember the upstaging antics of the president's younger brother, which in today's reality TV world look remarkably tame but were quite scandalous in the 1970s.

Maranatha Baptist Church (148 Hwy. 45 N., 229/824-7896, www.mbcplains.com) isn't nearly the largest church in Plains (that honor goes to Plains Baptist, which Jimmy and Rosalynn left decades ago in protest of their now-repudiated policy of refusing African American congregants). But it's where the Carters still attend church each Sunday. Dozens of times a year the president himself gives an hour-long Sunday School lesson right before the regular 11am service. You can stay for the service or just attend the lesson; all you have to do is show up about 8am or 9am, get checked out quickly by the Secret Service, take a seat at a pew, listen to an orientation, and enjoy.

You won't be able to tour the **Carter Family Compound** on the town's main road, but you'll spot it instantly by the tall fence and the Secret Service checkpoint at the entrance. The simple 1961 ranch home is on 4.5 acres of land and is the only home the president and his wife have ever owned. There's a video tour at the museum in the old Plains High School.

🅒 Jimmy Carter Boyhood Farm

It's not in Plains proper—it's actually in even smaller Archery—but the impeccably maintained Jimmy Carter Boyhood Farm (Old Plains Hwy., 229/824-4104, www.nps.gov, daily 10am-5pm, free) a few miles out of town is a must-see, not only to get a better perspective on the president's boyhood but for a charming and educational slice-of-life of rural and agricultural Americana gone by.

While the centerpiece is the well-restored one-story farmhouse where Earl and Lillian Carter raised the future president and his siblings during the Depression era, there's plenty more to see, from the lovingly tended native-plant gardens to the old Carter general store to the domestic animals to the restored home of the Clarks, an African American family who were often employed by the Carters and who provided a window on the real need for social justice in the Jim Crow-era South.

The farm itself is expertly maintained by the National Park Service, but keep in mind that there's no air-conditioning onsite, just like when the Carters lived here. There are restrooms and a water fountain at the entrance by the parking lot, and a park ranger is always around if you have any questions. Stay hydrated and use sunscreen. Walking tours of the farm are led on Saturdays and Sundays at 11:30am and 3:30pm.

Get there by taking Highway 280 west out of Plains for half a mile, then bearing left on Old Plains Highway for 1.5 miles. The farm is

The Jimmy Carter Boyhood Farm provides the best glimpse into his life.

© JIM MOREKIS

SOUTH GEORGIA

on the right side of the road. The family burial ground in Lebanon Cemetery is along the same road; the president's parents and brother and sister are interred there.

SAM Shortline

The railroads are still very active in this part of Georgia, and the tracks through Plains host the tourist-oriented passenger shuttle SAM Shortline (877/427-2457, www.samshortline.com). These 1949 vintage cars are a fun way to get around from the Boyhood Farm with stops in Plains, Americus, and Leslie (site of the Georgia Rural Telephone Museum). Check the website for schedules and prices.

Shopping

On the main block of Plains, pick up your souvenirs at the **Plains Trading Post** (229/824-5207, www.plainstradingpost.com, daily 9am-6pm), which bills itself as the largest private collection of political memorabilia in the country. Pins, bumper stickers, signed books, and all kinds of campaign items from a wide range of U.S. history are on sale, with apparently even more in storage. This is also where to pick up your Plains peanut items, many of them from nearby Koinonia Farms.

Accommodations

You can rent a wonderful, one-of-a-kind room, each one is themed after a particular decade, at the **Plains Historical Inn** (106 W. Main St., 229/824-4517, www.plainsinn.net, $75-110). It has seven suites in this building historically owned by members of the extended Carter family. There's a fun antiques store on the ground floor. The sidewalk a few feet away is where President Carter made his first statement after receiving the Nobel Peace Prize in 2002.

◖ NATIONAL PRISONER OF WAR MUSEUM

First off, don't be confused: The National Prisoner of War Museum (760 POW Rd., 229/924-0343, www.nps.gov, museum daily 9am-5pm, grounds and cemetery daily 8am-5pm, free) about 12 miles north of Americus is

also where you'll find the infamous Civil War prison camp now called Andersonville as well as Andersonville National Cemetery. The multiple nature of the site is deliberate and entirely appropriate.

The museum not only describes the history, atmosphere, and ensuing controversy of the Andersonville POW camp (called Camp Sumter at the time) through exhibits and an excellent short film, it also delves into the poignant human chronicle of American prisoners of war from all conflicts, from the Revolution to the World Wars, and through Korea and Vietnam to the Iraq War. Young children might find some of the exhibits disturbing, but I consider the museum a must-visit for any American high schooler or older. While often quite unsettling in its depictions of man's inhumanity to man, you'll leave with a profound admiration for the extraordinary bravery and resourcefulness of imprisoned U.S. servicemen and women, many of whose stories are conveyed through interactive video. And candidly, perhaps you'll also leave with a less-than-charitable attitude toward some of their enemies in particular conflicts who in no way recognized the Geneva Convention guidelines for humane treatment of POWs.

Behind the air-conditioned and fully-appointed museum is the entrance to **Camp Sumter,** demarcated by a memorial wall and sculpture. You're greeted by an expanse of open space, bifurcated by a still-existing creek. At one point nearly 40,000 Union POWs were confined here completely open to the elements, using the creek as both a toilet and for drinking water. The site was picked clean of artifacts decades ago, but the National Park Service has done a great job of maintaining replicas of the 18-foot stockade wall and associated "deadline," as well as facsimiles of the "she-bangs," or makeshift tents, of the otherwise sun-blasted prisoners. There are a series of ornate monuments erected by various Northern states to memorialize their citizens' sacrifices while in captivity.

You can drive a small loop road around the entire Andersonville camp, but unless the

The National Prisoner of War Museum is on the grounds of the notorious Andersonville camp (sculpture by Donna L. Dobberfuhl).

afternoon sun is just too intense, I recommend walking the site to get the full impact of what actually went on here 150 years ago. Adjacent to Camp Sumter is **Andersonville National Cemetery,** which contains graves of POWs and Civil War veterans and was established specifically to keep the lessons of Andersonville in public memory.

Andersonville Village

This small collection of shops, a museum, and a visitors center (109 E. Church St., 229/924-2558, www.andersonvillegeorgia.com) should in no way be considered affiliated with the National Park Service-administered National Prisoner of War Museum and Civil War site directly across the highway. The highlight is the **Drummer Boy Museum** (109 E. Church St., 229/924-2558, www.andersonvillegeorgia.com, daily 9am-5pm, $5 adults, $1 children), which features 15 mannequins in various authentic Civil War uniforms, including of course a drummer boy from each side.

Outside is a somewhat controversial monument to Colonel Henry Wirz, camp commandant and the first person executed for war crimes, but who many feel was wrongly demonized.

Food

Really good food is hard to find in this area, but one notable exception is ◖ **Yoder's Deitsch Haus** (5252 Hwy. 26, 478/472-2024, Tue., Thu.-Sat. 11:30am-2pm and 5pm-8:30pm, Wed. 11:30am-2pm, $8) near the otherwise bereft town of Montezuma a few miles from Andersonville. Yoder's menu—cooked and served by local Mennonites, a sizeable contingent in the surrounding area—draws people from miles around. The delectable, hearty Southern-meets-German cuisine is served in a clean, open, community-style buffet atmosphere. Do save room for the amazing pies and other desserts, which are signature items here. The only drinks are iced tea, coffee, and water. Dress conservatively.

AMBIGUITY AND ANDERSONVILLE

© JIM MOREKIS

POWs made their own shelters in the shadow of the stockade wall.

The very word "Andersonville" is synonymous with harsh cruelty to captives, one reason the National Prisoner of War Museum was established a stone's throw from the notorious Confederate camp. From February 1864 to May 1865, 45,000 Union prisoners lived on this bare 26-acre plot, with no roof or shelter of any kind to shield them from the blistering South Georgia sun, nor from the winter cold. Nearly 13,000 died.

Within Andersonville's 20-foot stockade walls was a grotesque city all its own, with its own rules and rulers. Food was thrown into the compound to be fought over, sold, and resold by prisoners. The only drinking water was a fetid creek through the middle of the camp, with the downstream portion the camp's only latrine.

The world's first war crimes trial came out of the Andersonville experience, as camp commandant Colonel Henry Wirz was hanged for his role after the war in a court martial presided over by Union General Lew Wallace, who would later write *Ben-Hur*.

As horrible as Andersonville was, however, the only reason the camp existed at all was because of a decision by Union General Ulysses S. Grant to stop the practice of POW exchanges,

previously the norm throughout the war. The concept was simple: regular agreements were made to trade roughly equal numbers of prisoners, thus relieving the burden on both sides of feeding and caring for them. But the sudden halt in exchanges and the deterioration of Southern military and civilian standards meant that Confederates suddenly found themselves responsible for thousands of prisoners, but with dwindling supplies and people to devote to them.

None other than Colonel Wirz himself sent a petition north asking that POW exchanges be reinstated. It was denied. By late 1864 the Confederacy even offered to release all prisoners if the Union would provide transportation. It refused.

So as awful as it was, we see that Andersonville represented a deeply flawed and imperfect response to a nearly impossible situation, a situation mirrored by similarly horrific POW camps in the north such as Camp Elmira, New York.

Southerners were far from immune to the degrading effect of the prisoners' plight. Many Andersonville prison guards themselves broke down under the strain and guilt.

POINTS WEST
◖ Providence Canyon State Outdoor Recreation Area

While at first glance it looks like a cluster of little canyons parachuted in from out west, the truth about Providence Canyon State Outdoor Recreation Area (8930 Canyon Rd., 229/838-6870, www.gastateparks.org, mid-Sept.-mid-Apr. daily 7am-6pm, mid-Apr.-mid-Sept. daily 7am-9pm, $5, backcountry campsites $9), aka "Georgia's Grand Canyon," is a bit more complicated. Though it doesn't look that way when you wander among these steep, white walls dotted with trees and patrolled overhead by circling hawks, the canyons are actually products of human activity. Poor farming practices in the early 1800s in this soft-soil area led to topsoil erosion followed by dramatic washouts, carving the deep gulches that now form a picturesque attraction.

There are plenty of opportunities to drive or walk around the rim and look down into the fingers of Providence Canyon, but the best way to enjoy the 16 separate canyons that form the park is to take the short, pleasant hike onto the canyon floor. (However, it's strictly forbidden to climb the fragile walls once you're down there.) The floor, though occasionally a bit wet and muddy, is quite pleasant, and you definitely get an exotic, faraway feel that's pretty unusual for this part of the state. Adding to the mystique is the fact that the largest wild colony of the very rare plumleaf azalea blooms here from mid to late summer. You might consider joining the Canyon Climbers Club (www.gastateparks.org, $10), which coordinates activity in Providence Canyon and two other Georgia parks with similar topography, Tallulah Gorge and Cloudland Canyon. Backpackers can camp on the seven-mile backcountry trail.

While the visitors center (Sept. 1-Nov. 30 and Mar. 1-May 31 Sat.-Sun. 8am-5pm) at Providence Canyon is back in operation after an extended hiatus due to budget cuts, the attached museum remains closed for budgetary reasons.

SOUTH GEORGIA

© JIM MOREKIS

Providence Canyon's dramatic features are actually manmade.

Florence Marina State Park

The closest park ranger to Providence Canyon during the week is in nearby Florence Marina State Park (218 Florence Rd., 229/838-6870, www.gastateparks.org, daily 7am-10pm, $5 parking, tent and RV sites $25-28, cottages $115), itself a very good recreational area. Set on the huge Lake Walter F. George on the Chattahoochee River, Florence Marina is known for its water-based recreational activities; at one time this was actually a flourishing trading center on the Alabama border. They have 43 tent and RV sites and six furnished cottages, two of which are dog friendly. The park marina has 66 slips for rent, which is good since this is one of the premier cat-fishing spots in the region: The state record blue cat was caught on Lake George in 2010.

Westville

Between Plains and Providence Canyon is the town of Lumpkin, and a very short drive south of the downtown area is the living history village of Westville (9294 Singer Rd., 888/733-1850, www.westville.org, Thurs.-Sat. 10am-5pm, $10 adults, $5 children), a compound of genuine 1850s buildings attended by volunteers in period dress doing all sorts of period things in true Williamsburg, Virginia, style. In a remarkable bargain, your admission entitles you to not one but three separate 40-minute guided tours (each beginning at 15 minutes after the hour; call ahead to make sure they will be given that day though). One deals with the history and origin of the village, the other is on slavery and the cotton era, and the last delves into the business of farming at the time. There's an onsite restaurant, the **Kiser House** (9294 Singer Rd., 888/733-1850, www.westville.org, 229/838-4655, Thurs.-Sat. 10am-4:30pm) which occasionally serves delicious sausage biscuits and gingerbread and unlike the rest of Westville is air-conditioned.

Westville was created by John West, a Victorian era teacher dismayed by the deterioration of Georgia's rural folkways after the Civil War. Determined to keep them alive, he built "The Fair of 1850" in Jonesboro outside Atlanta. The whole kit and kaboodle was moved way down here in the late 1960s when Stewart County decided to encourage heritage tourism.

INFORMATION AND SERVICES

The **Plains Welcome Center** (1763 Hwy. 280 W., 229/824-7477) is a short ways outside the tiny town and as of this writing was facing budget issues. The best bet for information in Plains is at the **Plains High School Visitors Center and Museum** (300 N. Bond St., 229/824-4104, www.nps.gov, daily 9am-5pm, free), also the main portal for exploring all Jimmy Carter-related sights.

If you pass through Americus, check out the **Americus Welcome Center** (123 W. Lamar St., 229/928-6059, www.visitamericusga.com) on the first floor of the city Municipal Building.

The **Phoebe Putney Health System** (www.phoebeputney.com) is the largest health care provider in the region, serving several counties. The **North Campus** (2000 Palmyra Rd., 229/434-2000) in nearby Albany provides the nearest emergency care to the Americus-Plains area.

GETTING THERE AND AROUND

This part of South Georgia is very well served by roads and is fairly easy to get around in by car. Americus, the best base of operations, is easily accessible from I-75 south of Atlanta. U.S. Highway 280/Highway 27 heads due west out of Americus and takes you right through Plains, and on to Westville and Providence Canyon. To get to Andersonville, head north out of Americus on Highway 49.

A unique way to get around Carter County is by the **SAM Shortline** (877/427-2457, www.samshortline.com), a light passenger rail running a route from Plains to Cordele and points between. Check the website for frequently changing schedules and fares.

Southwest Georgia

Agriculture is the name of the game down here in this sparsely populated area, from peanuts to pecans to cotton, including the state's dedicated agricultural college. Though largely free of fighting in the Civil War, this is where the Confederacy ended for good with the capture of Confederate President Jefferson Davis. The city of Albany played a key role in national civil rights, chiefly with the groundbreaking "Albany Movement," orchestrated in part by Martin Luther King Jr. The main natural attraction is the scenic and intriguing Flint River.

ALBANY

South Georgia's largest city, Albany (www.visitalbanyga.com) owes its history to the scenic Flint River, one of the South's great waterways. The Flint's bounty helped support a large population of Native Americans before white settlement and sparked the city's founding as a trade center, named after the capital of New York state in case anyone didn't get the hint. During the heyday of the cotton era, it was one of Georgia's busiest export centers.

Though the Food Network icon moved her operations to Savannah long ago, Paula Deen is actually an Albany native. By the way, locals like Paula pronounce it "All-Benny," not "ALLbunny." It ain't the capital of New York, y'all!

Sights

Learn about the area's human and natural history at the **Thronateeska Heritage Center** (100 W. Roosevelt Ave., 229/432-6955, www.heritagecenter.org, Thurs.-Sat. 10am-4pm, free), named for the ancient Native American word for the area. There's a Museum of History, a Science Discovery Center, and a good model train layout within its cavernous interior—the main building is the repurposed 1913 rail depot—but for many the highlight is the Wetherbee Planetarium ($3, show times vary) in the adjacent building, which holds various themed shows on the night sky.

Albany's chief claim to fame to the world at large is as the boyhood home of the great Ray Charles, one of the first performers to move traditional gospel into the realm of popular R&B. He is commemorated in the neat **Ray Charles Plaza** (Front St.) on the Flint riverwalk. The elaborate memorial features Charles at a rotating baby grand piano. He "plays" music through a discreet sound system, and each evening there is a light and fountain show. The audience sits in the round on huge piano keys.

The centerpiece of a recent public-private effort to revitalize downtown Albany is the **Flint RiverQuarium** (117 Pine Ave., 229/639-2650, www.flintriverquarium.com, Tues.-Sat. 10am-5pm, Sun. 1pm-5pm, $9 adults, $6.50 children), a 175,000-gallon, 22-foot-deep "Blue Hole" aquarium on the river—one of the few open-air such facilities you'll find—exploring the area's interesting riverine ecosystem. Next door is the three-story **Imagination Theater** (117 Pine Ave., 229/639-2650, www.flintriverquarium.com, Sat.-Sun., $6 adults, $4.50 children, combo tickets available), which while not an IMAX facility is a state-of-the-art digital surround entertainment venue with 3D capability.

Another way to enjoy local flora and fauna is at the **Parks on Chehaw** (229/430-5275, www.chehaw.org, park daily 8am-7pm, zoo daily 9:30am-5pm, park and zoo $8.75 adults, $5.75 children, park only $2 adults, $1 children), a former state park now repurposed into a small, fully accredited zoo and attached campground (tent sites $15, RV sites $20-28). The newest arrivals are a family of red wolves; other animals include black rhinos, black bears, cheetahs, and zebras, among others. Other recreational activities include disc golf, mountain bike trails, and a BMX course.

Albany's key role in the national struggle for equal rights is documented at the **Albany Civil Rights Institute** (326 Whitney Ave., 229/432-1698, www.albanycivilrightsinstitute.org, Tues.-Sat. 10am-4pm, $6 adults, $5 students), a new facility right next to the historic 1906

SOUTH GEORGIA

Mt. Zion Baptist Church, where Martin Luther King Jr. made speeches during the push to integrate Albany public facilities in the early 1960s. The entire history of the Albany Movement is chronicled in fascinating detail. The second Saturday of the month you can hear a performance by the Freedom Singers, a group with roots going back to 1962.

The **Albany Museum of Art** (311 Meadowlark Dr., 229/439-8300, www.albany-museum.com, Tues.-Sat. 10am-5pm, $4 adults, $2 children) has a solid collection of European and American art, but they're chiefly known for the Davis collection of sub-Saharan African art, one of the largest in the country. The museum recently began hosting a performance series by the Albany Symphony Orchestra.

One of the original "Seven Natural Wonders of Georgia," **Radium Springs** (Radium Springs Rd., 229/317-4760, Tues.-Sat. 9am-5pm, Sun. 1pm-5pm, free) is the largest natural spring in the state, feeding 70,000 gallons per minute into the Flint River at a constant 68 degrees. Its reputation for healing—yes, it does contain natural traces of radium—led to the building of a spa and casino during the Prohibition era. Sadly, flooding led to the old casino's demolition in 2003, but the city has used its foundation as the building block for an attractive and peaceful walking garden area near the pools, which unfortunately you aren't allowed to swim in.

Accommodations and Food

Albany is almost totally a chain-hotel kind of place. If you want to stay within view of the great statue of native son Ray Charles, book a room at the **Hilton Garden Inn Albany** (101 S. Front St., 229/888-1590, www.hiltongardeninn3.hilton.com, $120). Another good choice is the **Jameson Inn** (2720 Dawson Rd., 800/526-3766, www.jamesoninns.com, $85).

Native daughter Paula Deen long ago moved to Savannah, but the closest thing to her cooking and some would say a heck of a lot better is at ◖ **Pearly's Famous Country Cooking** (814 N. Slappey Dr., 229/432-0141, Mon.-Fri. 6am-2pm, Sat. 6am-noon, $10). Think hearty

biscuits, sausage, and cheese grits served in huge portions in a boisterous but friendly atmosphere. Mr. "Pearly" Gates, his real name is Carey, has run this local legend for half a century, and his standards remain as high as ever. The best barbecue in town is at **Riverfront BBQ** (105 W. Broad St., 229/888-4647, Mon.-Thu. 10:30am-2:30pm, Fri. 10:30am-9pm, Sat. noon-9pm, $5), and somewhat unusually for a 'cue joint, they also have great burgers and dogs as well.

WEST OF ALBANY
◖ Kolomoki Mounds Historic Park

One of the best-preserved pre-Columbian mound-builder sites in America, Kolomoki Mounds Historic Park (205 Indian Mounds Rd., 229/724-2150, www.gastateparks.org, daily 7am-10pm, $5 parking, campsites $25-27) is also Georgia's oldest, its sprawling complex inhabited from 350 AD-750 AD, nearly 1,000 years older than the Etowah Mounds up in Cartersvillle.

You'll see the mounds on the drive in, but you'll first want to go to the end of the road to the visitors center, which incorporates a theater and boardwalk within a partially excavated mound, opened up in the less-enlightened era of the 1930s. The film explores the history of the site and the culture of the Woodland Indians who built it, part of a thriving network of similar compounds across the Southeast. The mound was for burial, and there are two very realistic skeleton replicas in the exact positions of the dead elite tribesmen buried here (the actual remains have since been buried properly). The museum in the visitors center is small but quite informative and has some beautifully crafted Native American artisanal artifacts from around the site.

But the real highlight is your trip up the stairs to the top of the enormous great temple mound, tallest in Georgia at 57 feet over the surrounding vista, and feeling much higher than that because of its dominant view overlooking a broad plain featuring two smaller burial mounds and several ceremonial mounds,

© JIM MOREKIS

stunning view from the top of the Kolomoki temple mound

smaller still. Because of the relatively isolated area where Kolomoki is, there are times you can have the entire top of the mound all to yourself, quite a powerful experience.

Unlike Etowah and the other big mound site in Georgia, Macon's Ocmulgee, Kolomoki offers 27 tent and RV sites. There are a couple of small lakes to boat and fish on, a boat ramp, and a swimming beach. Hikers have five miles to enjoy on two trails: a lake trail and a forest trail.

George T. Bagby State Park

A "full-service" state park, George T. Bagby State Park (330 Bagby Pkwy., 229/768-2571, www.gastateparks.org, daily 7am-10pm, $5 parking, cottages $125-150) is known not only for its recreational opportunities at the southern tip of huge Lake Walter F. George on the Alabama border (the state record blue catfish was caught on the lake), it has an entire 60-room lodge (877/591-5575, $65-125) and a large marina with its own seafood restaurant. In addition to the fully-appointed lodge, there are five cottages, one of which is dog friendly. However, there are no tent or RV sites. The attached 18-hole **Meadow Links Golf Course** (229/768-3714, $40 green fees with cart) is actually quite well regarded; the lodge offers stay-and-play packages.

◖ Colquitt, "Mural City"

With not even 2,000 residents and tucked away deep into some of Georgia's most productive farmland, Colquitt (www.colquitt-georgia.com) wouldn't seem to merit much attention from visitors. But over the last decade the tiny town has written an important how-to chapter on rejuvenation through cultural tourism.

The most obvious aspect is the nearly 20 large-scale murals throughout the downtown area, seemingly on every flat surface. Initiated with the Millennium Mural Project and representing some aspect of regional life and history, the murals are uniformly of extremely high artistic quality and a photographer's dream. So much so in fact that in 2010 Colquitt hosted the bi-annual Global Mural Conference.

© JIM MOREKIS

Down at the Depot is one of many amazing murals in Colquitt (artist: Chris Moore).

Painted during the Conference, Colquitt's largest mural, *Spirit Farmer* by Charles Johnston, wraps around the entire surface of an enormous silo at the corner of Main Street and Second Avenue at a peanut harvesting plant. To give you an idea of its scale, each peanut being harvested by the farmer is itself six feet long. Other murals around town depict images related to farming, to the railroad, to simple rural life, to soldiers leaving town for WWII battlefields, and to the bobby-sox era.

The other component of Colquitt's vibrant cultural scene for its small size is **Swamp Gravy** (229/758-5450, www.swampgravy.com, $27), Georgia's "official folk-life play" performed at the historic **Cotton Hall** (158 E. Main St.), a renovated cotton warehouse turned into a 300-seat venue, which also hosts other productions throughout the year. *Swamp Gravy* is a humorous musical performed by a huge volunteer cast. A new edition premieres each October, portraying segments of local life, history, and culture, and is reprised each March.

Colquitt also hosts the annual **Mayhaw**

Festival (229/758-2400, www.colquitt-georgia.com, Apr.) celebrating the local flora from which delicious homemade jellies are made (other towns throughout the Southeast have a similar version). Coinciding with the festival each April, and again in January, the Cotton Hall hosts a performance of the variety show *May-Haw* (229/758-5450, www.swampgravy.com).

There's only one place to stay in Colquitt, the restored, historic ❰ **Tarrer Inn** (155 S. Cuthbert St., 229/758-2888, www.tarrerinn.com, $100) right on the main square. Somewhat nondescript on the outside, inside is a different story: very well-appointed and friendly with a patio area and a full-service Southern comfort food restaurant (call the hotel for table reservations during runs of *Swamp Gravy,* when things get pretty crowded). Continental breakfast is included with your stay, which can be in one of 11 rooms in the main building or 5 rooms in the Kimbrel-Bush House across the square.

The other restaurant of note in town is **Moby Dick** (627 Hwy. 27, 229/758-8141, Tues.-Fri.

11am-2pm and 5pm-9pm, Sat. 5pm-9pm, $15), which as the name implies specializes in seafood served buffet-style. The fried catfish and fried oysters are the can't-miss items here.

EAST OF ALBANY
Tifton

It may seem strange that the epicenter of Georgia agriculture was modeled on the New England seaport of Mystic, Connecticut, but that's the case with Tifton (www.tiftontourism.com). Founder Henry Tift, a man from Mystic who went South to get into the logging business, ended up laying out the city named after him along the city plan of his hometown. By the early 1900s it was quite active, complete with opera house, and still remains a viable commercial location thanks to its proximity to I-75.

Today it is best known as the home of the state university system's only dedicated agricultural school, **Abraham Baldwin Agricultural College** (ABAC, 2802 Moore Hwy., 229/391-5001, www.abac.edu). The main stop in town is the ABAC-run **Georgia Museum of Agriculture & Historic Village** (1392 Whiddon Rd., 229/391-5200, Tues.-Sat. 9am-4:30pm, $7 adults, $4 children), formerly "Agrirama." It's a living history demonstration, with costumed interpreters, of traditional farming techniques and home life, in addition to touches like a Masonic lodge, a country store, and a working steam train on Saturdays. Though agriculture is now a big corporate business for the most part in South Georgia, this gives an interesting and fun look back in time.

If you want a real taste of Tifton life, however, attend one of the seasonal **Truck and Tractor Pulls** (American Legion fairground on Hwy. 82, Fri.-Sat. from 7pm, www.tiftontourism.com), where assorted high-powered vehicles perform various feats of strength. The engines usually get fired up at 7pm on Friday and Saturday nights, and it is the center of town activity during that time.

Due to Tifton's proximity to I-75, there is plenty of mediocre chain lodging. Two B&B-style exceptions are the classic four-room B&B **Three Graces at the Lankford Manor** (401 N. Love Ave., 229/238-2534, www.threegracesmanor.com, $125) near downtown, with a full-service restaurant for lunch and dinner in addition to the included breakfasts, and the rustic-feeling yet fully-furnished **Shalom House** (7 Ross Rd., 229/386-0513, www.shalomhousebnb.com, $110) in the nearby countryside, which has the "pond house" cabin plus rooms in the main house.

Irwinville

Technically speaking, the end of the Civil War didn't happen with Lee's surrender at Appomattox but instead with the capture of Confederate President Jefferson Davis in Irwinville under fairly unflattering circumstances (though he wasn't disguised as a woman, as Northern propaganda claimed at the time). While fleeing to link up with remaining Confederate forces and continue the fight in the Western theater of battle, on May 9, 1865, Davis and his party were surrounded by two groups of Union cavalry who were unaware of each other. Two horsemen died of friendly fire, and Davis was taken prisoner.

The incident is commemorated at the **Jefferson Davis Memorial Historical Site** (338 Jeff Davis Park Rd., 229/831-2335, www.gastateparks.org, Wed.-Sun. 9am-5pm, $2.75-4), a bit southeast of Tifton. It has a small but detailed museum and a marker at the site of his arrest, as well as a picnic area on the relaxing and scenic grounds. Once a state park, the facility was recently handed over to Irwin County; I strongly suggest calling ahead to confirm hours. Note: This isn't to be confused with the site of a similar name in Kentucky, which marks Davis's birthplace.

Fitzgerald

Ironically, Fitzgerald (www.fitzgeraldga.org), less than 10 miles from the site of Davis's capture, was designed and founded after the Civil War by a former Union Army drummer. Its other main Civil War-themed claim to fame is the **Blue and Gray Museum** (116 N. Johnston St., 229/426-5069, www.fitzgeraldga.org,

HOW DO YOU SAY PECAN?

Pecan orchards dot South Georgia, the global center of pecan production.

PEA-can or pe-CON? The debate continues in South Georgia, where the meadows are dotted with picturesque pecan orchards and roadside stands sell bushels of the freshly harvested nut each autumn.

What's the right way to pronounce pecan?

Old-timers insist it ain't French, and the emphasis should be on the first syllable: PEA-can.

More recent arrivals—perhaps enamored of the nut's newly acquired foodie cachet as a key part of reinvented Southern cuisine—say it's the more refined pe-CON.

The Georgia Department of Agriculture has actually come up with a Solomonic answer to the debate. The official pronunciation of "pecan" for state agricultural purposes is with the emphasis on the first syllable: PEA-can.

However, the Agriculture Department also says the original pronunciation of the word, derived from an ancient Native American tongue, was almost certainly pe-CON.

So you're not nuts. You can say it any way you like.

Tues.-Sat. 10am-4pm, Sun. 1pm-5pm, $3 adults, $2 children) in the baggage room of the ornate and historic train depot downtown, other portions of which also house the city hall. The museum delves a bit into local history as well as having various Civil War artifacts of interest.

Architecture buffs might enjoy Fitzgerald's unusual house designs. Primarily settled by migrating Midwesterners, the town boasts many examples of non-Southern styles such as the "T-house." Downtown Fitzgerald is also worth an architecture tour; go to the **Welcome Center** (116 N. Johnston St., 229/426-5033, Mon.-Fri. 10am-5pm) near the museum for more friendly information. The highlight is the **Grand Theater** (115 S. Main St., 229/426-5090), an ornate art deco building, burned in the 1920s and rebuilt in the 1930s, which still hosts productions, including the locally-themed musical about the unique circumstances of Fitzgerald's founding, *Our Friends, the Enemy.*

Walking around town, however, you'll see that Fitzgerald's real signature item is the horde of Burmese chickens wandering around, legacies of an ill-fated introduction by the state in the 1960s. Intended to stock the area as game birds, the plump, colorful fowl for whatever reason migrated to downtown Fitzgerald and don't want to leave, even blocking the street on occasion. So of course there's a **Wild Chicken Festival** (www.wildchickenfestival.com, Mar.) to honor them!

The best place to stay in town is the historic **Dorminy-Massee House Bed & Breakfast** (516 W. Central Ave., 229/423-3123, www.dorminymasseehouse.com, $95), which is still in the original family's hands. There are six gorgeous guest rooms in this stately two-story Greek Revival manor built in 1915, with plenty of heart pine furnishings.

INFORMATION AND SERVICES

The **Albany Visitors Center** (112 N. Front St., 229/317-4760, www.visitalbanyga.com, Mon.-Fri. 9am-5pm, Sat. 10am-4pm, Sun. noon-4pm) in the historic Bridge building downtown is the best place in the area to get tourist info.

The paper of record in town is the *Albany Herald* (www.albanyherald.com).

The **Phoebe Putney Health System** (www.phoebeputney.com) is the largest health care provider in the region, serving several counties. The **North Campus** (2000 Palmyra Rd., 229/434-2000) provides emergency care in Albany.

GETTING THERE AND AROUND

Albany is easily accessible from I-75 via numerous exits from Cordele down to Tifton. **Greyhound** (300 W. Oglethorpe Blvd., 229/432-0511, www.greyhound.com) has a bus station downtown a couple of blocks from the Flint River. The **Albany Transit System** (www.albany.ga.us, fare $1.25) has bus routes around town.

SOUTH GEORGIA

Thomasville and Vicinity

This area borders the balmy, piney woods of north Florida, and has a different feel from most other parts of Georgia. Indeed, down here folks are more likely to root for the Seminoles of Florida State University in nearby Tallahassee than for the Bulldogs of the University of Georgia.

But the main difference about Thomasville in particular—despite energetically marketing its plantation past—is that it's more of a high Victorian city, a legacy of the time when affluent Northerners came down to this railroad terminus seeking good weather, good relaxation, and good hunting. (President Eisenhower also enjoyed quail hunts down here.) Many of their flamboyant "winter cottages" exist today and are part of the town's historic district.

Founded in 1825 on part of the old Pebble Hill Plantation, which you can still visit, Thomasville today offers a busy downtown, the most vibrant cultural life for many miles, some beautiful architecture both pre- and post-Civil War, and its popular annual Rose Festival. Its most famous native is actress Joanne Woodward, wife of the late Paul Newman.

SIGHTS

I recommend a stop at the **Visitors Center** (144 E. Jackson St.) at the side entrance of the circa-1940 Municipal Auditorium building to get brochures and information from the friendly folks there. They have a very well-done, handsome walking tour brochure which I highly recommend for a self-guided walking tour of downtown; or download it yourself at www.thomasvillega.com.

THE BIG OAK
Thomasville, Ga.

AGE	351 YRS.
SPREAD	162 FEET
HEIGHT	68 FEET
TRUNK	24 FT CIRC.
VARIETY	LIVE OAK

Thomasville's "Big Oak" occupies an entire corner lot downtown.

The "Big Oak"

Yup, it's a live oak tree that's really big, and really old, over 300 years. It occupies its own lot at the corner of North Crawford and East Monroe Streets. When live oaks get old, they don't necessarily get taller, they get wider and take up more space. The Big Oak measures nearly 30 feet in circumference, and its sprawling branches are now so long and heavy that they have to be suspended in some places with steel cables to keep them off the ground. While climbing on them is quite tempting, it's not allowed. However, you can have your picture taken with the tree through the **"Big Oak Cam";** you dial 229/236-0053 on your cell phone, look at the camera across the street, and follow the audio instructions. Find the photo online at www.bigoak.rose.net.

All Saints' Episcopal Church

Oldest standing church in town, All Saints' Episcopal Church (443 S. Hansell St., 229/228-9242, www.allsaintsthomasville.org, open to public Mon.-Fri. 9am-4pm) is most famous for

hosting former First Lady Jacqueline Kennedy at a service soon after President Kennedy's assassination.

Thomas County Museum of History

The Thomas County Museum of History (725 N. Dawson St., 229/226-7664, www.thomascountyhistory.org, tours Mon.-Sat. 10am-11:30am and 2pm-3:30pm, closed late Aug., $5 adults, $1 children) has preserved local history for over a half century. This is a great place to learn about the area's somewhat unique background for this part of the country.

Jack Hadley Black History Museum

On the campus of a former black high school during the days of segregation, the Jack Hadley Black History Museum (214 Alexander St., 229/226-5029, www.jackhadleyblackhistorymuseum.com, Tues.-Sat. 10am-5pm, $5 adults, $3 children) is named for a leading local black historian whose copious collection of memorabilia is on display. There are exhibits about key local and regional African Americans. You can get info here on other key black history sites in Thomasville.

Lt. Henry O. Flipper Burial Site

The first black graduate of the West Point Military Academy was Henry Ossian Flipper, born into slavery in Thomasville and buried on Crawford Street in a graveyard across the street from "Flipper Park," not to be confused with the nearby, larger "Old Cemetery." Eldest of five brothers, Flipper was appointed to attend West Point during Reconstruction and served with distinction as a "Buffalo Soldier" in the Indian wars out west, becoming the first black officer to command troops in the U.S. Army (prior to that, black soldiers were always commanded by white officers). He was court-martialed under questionable circumstances, receiving a posthumous pardon to clear his name from President Clinton in 1999.

◖ Lapham-Patterson House Historic Site

The whimsically handsome Lapham-Patterson House Historic Site (626 N. Dawson St., 229/226-7664, www.gastateparks.org, Fri. 1pm-5pm, Sat. 10am-5pm, Sun. 2pm-5pm, $5) is a great example of the "winter cottage" homes built by wealthy Victorians as resort homes in the temperate climate of Thomasville. In this case, Chicago shoe merchant C.W. Lapham built this three-story gem in 1885, and it features some amazing artisan work, from longleaf pine floors to fishscale shingles, and a double-flue chimney with walk-through stairway. The stained glass windows are oriented to maximize sunlight during the spring and fall equinoxes. Oddly, there are about 50 ways to get out of the house. In addition to possibly being an occult devotee, the eccentric Mr. Lapham barely survived the Great Chicago Fire and retained a lifelong phobia about house fires.

Pebble Hill Plantation

Pebble Hill Plantation (1251 Hwy. 319 S., www.pebblehill.com, Tues.-Sat. 10am-5pm,

© JIM MOREKIS

SOUTH GEORGIA

the whimsical Lapham-Patterson House

Sun. noon-5pm, plantation admission $5 adults, $2 children, including house tour adults $15, children $6) is a remarkable collection of a dozen early-1900s buildings—ranging from an ornate main house open for tours to a log cabin school to a dog hospital—all in the service of the Hanna and Ireland families. While the original plantation covered over 10,000 acres, it's down to a still-huge 3,000 acres now, of which about 75 well-manicured acres are open for relaxed visitation.

You enter down a classic allée of live oaks; gardeners will particularly enjoy the collection of flora all over the plantation. Indeed, touring the main house isn't even a must-do to get a lot of enjoyment out of Pebble Hill. Of course there are animals too, chiefly horses that live in the wonderful historic stables, once home to many prize family competitive horses. The 26,000-square-foot, 40-room main house (actually mostly rebuilt in the 1930s after a fire) is known for its exquisite antique and art collection, all from the original family, making it almost a museum in its own right. The paintings, such as the Audubon, generally reflect nature or hunting.

Power of the Past Museum

Serious aviation buffs should check out Power of the Past Museum (Hwy. 122, 229/226-3010, www.powerofthepast.org, usually Sat.-Sun afternoons or by appt., free), the labor of love of collector James Dekle. You'll see vintage civilian aircraft, and for those so inclined, an extensive collection of vintage airplane engines. It's at the airport seven miles northeast of town on Highway 122. The second weekend of October the airport hosts the annual **Thomasville Fly-In event** (www.thomasvilleflyin.com) for regional civil pilots.

ENTERTAINMENT AND EVENTS

Thomasville is famous for its roses, and the best place to find about 500 gorgeous rose bushes is at the city **Rose Garden** (Smith Ave. and Covington Dr., 866/228-7977) along scenic Cherokee Lake. The entire town celebrates this heritage annually at the **Thomasville Rose Show & Festival** (www.downtownthomasville. com, late Apr.), which has been going on for nearly a century, of course crowning a "Rose Queen" each year. The town celebrates its sumptuous Victorian architectural and cultural heritage one weekend each December with the **Victorian Christmas** (www.downtownthomasville.com, Dec.), complete with costumed carolers, carriage rides, candlelight, and a live Nativity.

The **South Georgia Ballet** (www.southgeorgiaballet.org) is the only full-on ballet company in the area. Of course they perform a well-received *Nutcracker* each holiday season, held in the historic Thomasville Auditorium. They also perform smaller shows at the **Thomasville Center for the Arts** (600 E. Washington St., 229/226-0588, www.thomasville.org), which itself hosts a variety of rotating arts and crafts shows.

Performing in a restored storefront on the main drag, **Thomasville On Stage and Company** (Storefront Theater, 117 S. Broad St.,

229/226-0863, www.tosac.com), is the local community theater group. They put on four shows a year.

ACCOMMODATIONS AND FOOD

The premier B&B in Thomasville is the **❰ 1884 Paxton House Inn** (445 Remington Ave., 229/226-5197, www.1884paxtonhouseinn.com, $175-275), an exquisitely restored, flamboyant Victorian that was one of the first and still best example of homes built by wealthy Northerners for Thomasville's resort "Winter season." In this case, Colonel J.W. Paxton of West Virginia had this house built complete with circular staircase, 13-foot ceilings, and 12 coal fireplaces, along with several outbuildings that also host guests today. There are four rooms in the main house, three in the garden cottage, and a suite in the carriage house and the pool house. It's located several blocks from downtown.

Another great B&B is **Freedom Oaks Bed 'n' Breakfast** (429 N. Crawford St., 229/227-1749, www.freedomoaksbb.com, $140-170), around the corner from the "Big Oak" and itself on a corner lot festooned with magnificent live oaks. Set in the 1908 Fannie Bottoms House, Freedom Oaks only has four guest rooms, all upstairs, which means all the more enjoyment of the expansive and sumptuous public areas, including of course the huge wraparound porch. You're a very short walk from downtown Thomasville's shops and restaurants.

Wherever you stay in Thomasville, remember its proximity to Tallahassee means many rooms are booked well in advance on Florida State University home football game weekends in the autumn.

The most popular restaurant in town is **❰ Jonah's Fish and Grits** (109 E. Jackson St., 229/226-0508, www.jonahsfish.com, Mon.-Fri. 11am-2pm and 5pm-9pm, Sat. 11am-9pm, $12-15), which offers a signature parmesan grouper entrée along with, of course, fish 'n' chips and shrimp 'n' grits on its expansive seafood menu.

But the most unique place in town is **Billiard Academy** (121 South Broad St., 229/226-9981, Mon.-Fri. 8am-7pm, Sat. 8am-5:30pm, pool room Mon.-Fri. until 9pm), open since 1949. Besides offering pool tables, their real claim to fame is their signature $2 chili dogs, either inside at the counter or at a walk-up window on the main drag. Another hot spot is the interesting **George & Louie's** (217 Remington Ave., 229/226-1218, www.georgeandlouies.com, Mon.-Sat. 11am-9pm, $10-17) and their adventurous seafood menu, not just grilled items like grouper and salmon, but a mullet dinner and their signature "Crab Louie" deviled crab.

If you need a big city-style coffee shop, hit **Grassroots Coffee** (123 S. Broad St., 229/226-3388, www.grassrootscoffee.com, Mon.-Thurs. 6:30am-9pm, Fri. 6:30am-10pm, Sat. 7:30am-10pm). They have a wide menu of hot and cold brewed treats, plus sandwiches, bagels, and scones. To pick up some artisanal goodies, head to **C Sweet Grass Dairy Cheese Shop** (106 N. Broad St., 229/228-6704, www.sweetgrassdairy.com, Mon.-Sat. 11am-2pm), where the farmstead products of their New Zealand-style "rotational grazing" lands are sold. Sample their crazy-delicious cheeses with wine and craft beer.

WEST OF THOMASVILLE
Bainbridge

At the deepest corner of Georgia lies Bainbridge (www.visitbainbridgega.com), named for Commodore William Bainbridge, captain of the U.S.S. *Constitution*. (Decatur County, for which Bainbridge serves as county seat, was named after another War of 1812 hero, Stephen Decatur.) One of two inland ports in Georgia (Columbus is the other one), Bainbridge's lifeblood is the Flint River, by which it connects to the Gulf of Mexico. As a marker in downtown's Willis Park explains, DeSoto's men traveled through on their journey through the Southeast; soon the area would be on the "Camino Real," the Spanish "king's highway" built on an old Indian trail.

You can access the Flint at another center of city activity, the **Earle May Boat Basin Park**

ornate gingerbread house in Bainbridge

(101 Boat Basin Circle, 229/248-2010, daily dawn-dusk, free, campsites $14). Besides providing a riverwalk for pedestrians, a fishing pier, and full boat access to the river, including kayaks and canoes, this is where the town's Christmas parade of boats on the river starts. There are 10 riverfront campsites. And, there's even a petting zoo!

The **Decatur County Historical and Genealogical Society Museum** (110 Broughton St., 229/515-5761, Tues. and Thurs. 1pm-4pm, Sat. 10am-2pm, free) is the place to go for a quick hit of local history. Most of downtown Bainbridge is a historical district, with some handsome homes. **Oak City Cemetery** is older than the city itself; built on an old Indian burial grounds, it was also home to the first Jewish cemetery in south Georgia and has the gravesite of Oscar-nominated 1930s actress Miriam Hopkins, who auditioned for the role of Scarlett O'Hara. Download walking tours at www.bainbridgecity.com.

Lake Seminole

Bainbridge has profited from its proximity to huge 37,000-acre Lake Seminole (corpslakes. usace.army.mil), a Corps of Engineer-run lake at the confluence of the Flint, Chattahoochee, and Apalachicola Rivers where Georgia meets Alabama and Florida. Sometimes called the "Bass Capital of Georgia," Lake Seminole offers every amenity for both the casual boater and the serious competitive angler and hosts frequent state and national tournaments. The Corps runs 10 recreational areas all around the lake; there are about two dozen more run by other entities. There are over a dozen separate campgrounds on the lake; the Corps-run Eastbank Campground is reservable online (www.recreation.gov) as is Seminole State Park.

The most famous facility on Lake Seminole is **Wingate's Lodge & Marina** (139 Wingate Rd., 229/246-0658, www.wingatelodge.com, rooms $50, cabins $75, trailers $50, RV sites $25, tent sites $20), founded by the late, legendary bass fisherman Jack Wingate, who was actually mentioned in an early Mark Trail comic strip decades ago. The "Sage of

Seminole" passed away in 2011 but is remembered fondly throughout the area. The Lodge offers humble, brick, motel-style rooms; log cabins; and pre-fab modular trailers. There are also RV spots and a dedicated tents-only campground. There's an onsite restaurant (Thurs. 11am-8pm, Fri. 11am-9pm, Sat. 6am-9pm, Sun. 6am-6pm, $10), which has some pretty good barbecue.

Many folks opt to stay and fish or camp at the popular **Seminole State Park** (7870 State Park Dr., 229/861-3137, www.gastateparks.org, daily 7am-10pm, $5 parking, tent and RV sites $25-28, cottages $125-135, treehouse camping $25), situated in a sheltered cove on the lake and providing a bit more of a laidback experience, though there are five boat ramps and several fishing piers. There are 50 tent and RV sites, 14 cottages, 2 of which are dog friendly, and even treehouse camping for groups up to 15.

The adjacent and also enormous 10,000-acre **Silver Lake Wildlife Management Area** (229/430-4254, www.georgiawildlife.com, daily dawn-dusk, $3.50), bordering the lake and Flint River, provides extensive hunting and fishing opportunities. It's also a significant habitat for the endangered red-cockaded woodpecker and contains some century-old tracts of longleaf pine, a direct legacy of a time when much of the Southeast was covered in massive longleaf pine forests. Cypress-lined Silver Lake itself has several families of osprey and hosts numerous waterfowl rookeries. Get there by taking Highway 253 south of Bainbridge three miles and then make a left onto Ten Mile Still Road. After another six miles turn right onto Silver Lake Road, then three miles until you turn left onto the access road.

Cairo

It may be named after the Egyptian capital, but this Cairo is pronounced "KAY-ro." The chief local product is sweet cane syrup, so much so that the local high school football team is called the Syrupmakers, or more commonly just the 'Makers. Cairo's main contribution to history was being the birthplace of Jackie Robinson, first African American to play major league baseball. However, he and his family left town when he was a toddler. Precious little legacy of him in Cairo remains other than the solitary chimney of what is thought to be his home on Hadley Ferry Road (County Route 154), with nearby historical marker.

EAST OF THOMASVILLE
Valdosta
Considering its size, the 14th largest city in the state, there's comparatively little for visitors to do in Valdosta. Its trio of main economic drivers consists of the world's largest turpentine industry; nearby Moody Air Force Base; and large Valdosta State University, a perennial Division II college football power. Indeed, football is something of a religion here; Valdosta High School has the winningest high school football program in the country, and its rival Lowndes High School isn't far behind. The area's athletic prowess caused ESPN to dub Valdosta "Titletown USA," up against some stiff national competition.

Two historical figures are associated with Valdosta: James Pierpont, writer of "Jingle Bells," taught music for awhile here; gunfighting gambler Doc Holliday, of OK Corral fame, spent much of his youth here.

For most travelers, though, Valdosta is a stop on busy I-75 en route to Florida. So its chief tourist attraction is wisely located along I-75, **Wild Adventures** (3766 Old Clyattville Rd., 229/219-7080, www.wildadventures.com, $46 adults, $41 children). This combination roller coaster mecca, zoo, and waterpark covers over 160 acres. Highlights include the massive "Cheetah" old-school rollercoaster, the "Splash Island" seasonally-open waterpark (especially desirable during the intensely hot Valdosta summers), and the fairly impressive collection of mammals such as zebras, giraffes, rhinos, and even a Siberian tiger.

The **Lowndes County Historical Society & Museum** (305 W. Central Ave., 229/247-4780, www.valdostamuseum.com, Mon.-Fri. 10am-5pm, Sat. 10am-2pm, free) is located in a historic Carnegie Library building. The

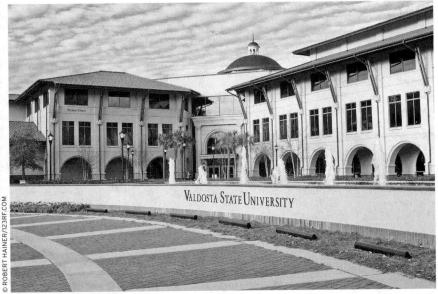

Valdosta State University

remarkable 1905 **Lowndes County Courthouse** on the town square, while far from the oldest in the state, is one of the most splendid.

The cityscape is largely dominated by the sprawling campus of Valdosta State University, and there is fast food galore. But a revitalized section of North Patterson Street is where the quality spots to eat are located, a clear stand-out being C **Bleu Cafe** (125 N. Patterson St., 229/244-2248, www.thebluegroup.com, daily 11am-2pm and 6pm-10pm, $15). What you want to do is get the tacos, which are truly delicious. They also have great artisan pizza.

Grand Bay

About 10 miles north of Valdosta is Grand Bay, second-largest wetland in the state after the great Okefenokee Swamp itself. About half of this 13,000-acre ecosystem is run by the state as a wildlife management area; hunting, fishing, hiking, and particularly bird-watching are all worthwhile pursuits here. Its cluster of Carolina Bays, or elliptical sunken wetlands, provide extraordinary bird habitat. To visit the **Grand Bay Wetland Education Center** (4661 Knights Academy Rd., 229/333-0052, www.georgiawildlife.com, Mon.-Fri. 8am-4pm, free) take Highway 221 north out of Valdosta and take a left onto Knights Academy Road, then a right onto Coastal Plains Trail.

Banks Lake National Wildlife Refuge

More or less contiguous with Grand Bay is the federally-run Banks Lake National Wildlife Refuge (Hwy. 122, 912/496-7836, www.fws.gov, daily 24 hours, free). This blackwater wetland system comprises 1,500 acres of cypress swamp, and about twice that much water and freshwater marsh. But the centerpiece is the *pocosin,* or sinkhole-like bog similar to a Carolina Bay. There's a boat ramp, walking trail, and viewing boardwalk.

INFORMATION AND SERVICES

The **Thomasville Visitors Center** (144 E. Jackson St., 229/228-7977, www.thomasvillega.com, Mon.-Fri. 8am-5pm, Sat. 10am-3pm) is at the side entrance of the Municipal Auditorium building. There's a good state-run **Georgia Visitors Center** (5584 Mill Store Rd., Lake Park, 229/559-5828, www.exploregeorgia.org) near Valdosta.

The **Archbold Medical Center** (915 Gordon Ave., 229/228-2000, www.archbold.org) provides care in the Thomasville area. The **South Georgia Medical Center** (2501 N. Patterson St., 229/333-1000, www.sgmc.org) is the go-to hospital in the Valdosta area.

GETTING THERE AND AROUND

I-75 bisects deep South Georgia, heading nearly due south from Macon to Valdosta. A useful east-west route for the entire southern and southwest tier of Georgia is U.S. Highway 82/State Route 520.

The Okefenokee Swamp

Scientists often refer to Okefenokee as an "analogue," an accurate representation of a totally different epoch in the earth's history. In this case it's the Carboniferous Period, about 350 million years ago, when the living plants were lush and green and the dead plants simmered in a slow-decaying peat that would one day end up as the oil that powers our civilization. But for the casual visitor, Okefenokee might also be simply a wonderful place to get almost completely away from human influence and witness firsthand some of the country's most interesting wildlife in its natural habitat. Despite the enormous wildfires of the spring of 2007 and the summer of 2011—some of the largest the Southeast has seen in half a century, so large they were visible from space—the swamp has bounced back, for the most part, and is once again hosting visitors to experience its timeless beauty.

◖ OKEFENOKEE NATIONAL WILDLIFE REFUGE

It's nearly the size of Rhode Island and just a short drive off I-95, but the massive and endlessly fascinating Okefenokee National Wildlife Refuge (912/496-7836, www.fws.gov, Mar.–Oct. daily dawn–7:30pm, Nov.–Feb. daily dawn–5:30pm, $5 per vehicle) is one of the lesser-visited national public lands. Is it that very name "swamp" that keeps people away, with its connotations of fetid misery and lurking danger? Or simply its location, out of sight and out of mind in South Georgia? In any case, while it long ago entered the collective subconscious as a metaphor for the most untamed, darkly dangerous aspects of the American South, as well as the place where Pogo the Possum lived, the Okefenokee remains one of the most intriguing natural areas on the planet. The nearby old rail town of Folkston is the gateway to the swamp for most visitors off I-95, which is to say most of them. In true Georgia fashion, the town is insular but friendly, slow but sincere.

History

The Okefenokee Swamp was created by an accident of geology. About 250,000 years ago, the Atlantic Ocean washed ashore about 70 miles farther inland from where it does today. Over time, a massive barrier island formed off this primeval Georgia coastline, running from what is now Jesup, Georgia, south to Starke, Florida. When the ocean level dropped during the Pleistocene Era, this sandy island became a topographical feature known today as the Trail Ridge, its height effectively creating a basin to its west. Approximately 90 percent of the Okefenokee's water comes from rainfall into that basin, which drains slowly via the Suwannee and St. Marys Rivers.

Ordinarily, what the summer heat evaporates from the Okefenokee is more than replenished by rain, unless there's a severe drought like the one that caused the recent wildfires. But even the fires can't hold the swamp back. In fact, the Okefenokee is a fire ecosystem, meaning some plant species, like the cypress, depend on heat generated by wildfires to open their seed cones and perpetuate their lifecycle. Indeed, because of the particularly combustible nature of the peat that forms most of the swamp, fire is never far away; sometimes it's right under your feet!

Portions of the massive Honey Prairie Fire of 2011 in the swamp's southwestern area, caused by a lightning strike, still smolder to this day under the surface. Because of constant rejuvenation by water and fire, biologists estimate that the oldest portion of this supposedly "ancient" swamp is actually no older than 7,000 years, the faintest blink of an eye in geological terms. Unlike Florida's Everglades, which are actually a single large and very slow-moving river, the Okefenokee is a true swamp.

Native Americans used the swamp as a hunting ground and gave us its current name, which means "Land of the Trembling Earth," a reference to the floating peat islands, called "houses," that dominate the landscape. The Spanish arrived about 1600, calling the swamp Laguna de Oconi (Lake Oconi) and establishing at least two missions in the area near two Timucuan villages. During the Seminole Wars of the 1830s, the Timucua took refuge within the swamp for a time before continuing south into Florida. While trade had occurred on the outskirts for nearly a century before, it wasn't until the 1850s that the first nonnative settlers set up camp inside the swamp itself.

It's a common mistake to call the Okefenokee "pristine" because, like much of the heavily timbered and farmed southeastern coast, it is anything but. The swamp's ancient cypress stands and primordial longleaf pine forests were heavily harvested in the early 20th century. About 200 miles of old rail bed through the swamp remain as a silent testament to the scope of that logging operation. But the pace of logging gradually slowed to a stop as the cost of the operation became prohibitive. In 1918 the Okefenokee Society, the first organized attempt to protect the habitat, was formed in nearby Waycross, Georgia. In 1937, President Franklin Roosevelt brought the area within the federal wildlife refuge system.

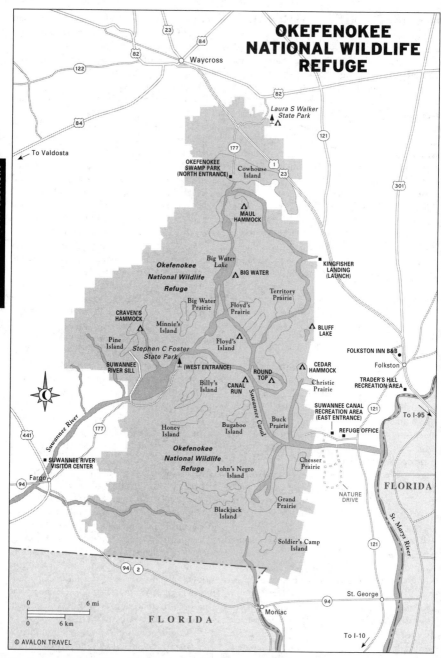

OKEFENOKEE NATIONAL WILDLIFE REFUGE

SOUTH GEORGIA

great blue heron on the banks of the Suwanee River

In recent years, large deposits of titanium prompted several mining interests, including DuPont, to exercise rights in the area, to great outcry from conservationists who worried that the intrusive 24-hour mining operations would destroy the swamp's habitat. A series of transactions involving the state and conservation trusts, however, have so far resulted in halting those mining efforts.

Sights and Wildlife

Contrary to the popular image of a nasty, dank swamp, the Okefenokee is anything but a monoculture. It features a wide variety of ecosystems, including peat bogs, sand hills, and black gum and bay forests. Perhaps most surprising is the wide open vista of the swamp's many prairies or extended grasslands, 22 in all, which besides being stirring to the eye are also great places to see birds. So you see, not all of the Okefenokee is wet. There is water aplenty here, though, with over 60 named lakes and

120 miles of boating trails. And as you kayak or canoe on one of the water trails or on the old **Suwanee Canal** from the logging era, you'll notice the water is all very dark. This blackwater is not due to dirt or silt but to natural tannic acid released into the water from the decaying vegetation that gave the swamp its name. While I don't recommend that you drink the water, it's actually very clean despite its color.

As you'd expect on a national wildlife refuge, the Okefenokee hosts a huge variety of animal life: more than 400 species of vertebrates, including over 200 varieties of birds and more than 60 types of reptiles. Birders get a special treat in late November–early December when sandhill cranes come south to winter in the swamp. In January their colonies are at their peak, and the swamp echoes with their loud cries. Other common bird species you'll see are herons, egrets, and endangered wood storks and red-cockaded woodpeckers. The white ibis has seen a big spike in population in the refuge recently, as has the bald eagle. A great way to see the sandhill cranes and other birds of the Okefenokee is to hike the 0.75-mile boardwalk out to the 50-foot **Chesser Island Observation Tower** on the eastern end of the swamp. Get here by driving or biking the eight-mile round-trip **Wildlife Drive,** which also takes you by the old **Chesser Homestead,** the remnants of one of the oldest settlements in the swamp. You can also hike out to Chesser; indeed, there are many miles of hiking trails through the upland areas of the swamp near the East Entrance.

Probably the first creature one thinks of when one thinks of a swamp is the alligator. Certainly Okefenokee has plenty of them, and no one who has heard the roar of a male alligator break the quiet of the night will ever forget the experience. Most of the time, though, alligators are quite shy, and spotting them is an acquired skill. They often look like floating logs. Conversely, in warm weather you might see them out in the open sunning themselves. While no one can remember an incident of a gator attacking a human in the refuge, whatever you do, don't

alligator in the Okefenokee

feed alligators in the wild. As a Fish and Wildlife ranger in Okefenokee once told me: "If a gator attacks a human, at some point in the past someone has fed that gator. Gators get used to being fed. Unfortunately, they can't tell the difference between the person and the food." Believe it or not, the alligator is not even the top predator in the Okefenokee; that title belongs to the black bear. Biologists estimate that as many as 90 percent of alligator eggs laid in the refuge are eaten by the local black bear population. And as with the gators, don't feed the bears.

Recreation

For most visitors, the best way to enjoy the Okefenokee is to book a guided tour through **Okefenokee Adventures** (866/843-7926, www.okefenokeeadventures.com), the designated concessionaire of the refuge. They offer a 90-minute guided boat tour ($18 adults, $11 children) that leaves each hour, and a 2.5-hour reservation-only sunset tour ($25 adults, $17 children) that takes you to see the gorgeous sunset over Chesser Prairie. Extended or custom tours, including multiday wilderness excursions, are also available. They also rent bikes, canoes, and camping gear, and even run a decent little café where you can either sit down and have a meal or take it to go out on the trail.

Camping and Accommodations

If fire and water levels permit, it's possible to stay the night in the swamp, canoeing to one of the primitive camping "islands" in the middle of the refuge. You need to make reservations up to two months in advance, however, by calling **U.S. Fish and Wildlife** (912/496-3331, Mon.-Fri. 7am-10am). A nonrefundable fee ($10 pp, includes entrance fee) must be received 16 days before you arrive (mailing address: Okefenokee National Wildlife Refuge, Route 2, Box 3330, Folkston, GA 31537). Campfires are allowed only at Canal Run and Floyds Island. A camp stove is required for cooking at all other shelters. (Keep in mind that in times of extreme drought or fire threat, boat trips may not be allowed. Always check the website for the latest announcements.)

Privately owned canoes and boats with motors under 10 hp may put in with no launch fee, but you must sign in and out. No ATVs are allowed on the refuge, and bicycles are allowed only on designated bike trails. Keep in mind that some hunting goes on in the refuge at designated times. Pets must be leashed at all times.

At the **Stephen Foster State Park** (17515 Hwy. 177, 912/637-5274, fall-winter daily 7am-7pm, spring-summer daily 6:30am-8:30pm, tent sites $24, cottages $100), a.k.a. the **West Entrance,** near Fargo, Georgia, there are 66 tent sites and nine cottages.

Information and Services
At the main East entrance is the federally-run **Richard S. Bolt Visitor Center** (912/496-7836, www.fws.gov, July-Aug. and Dec.-Jan. Mon.-Fri. 9am-5pm, Feb.-June and Sept.-Nov. daily 9am-5pm), which has some cool nature exhibits and a surround-sound orientation video. At the West entrance is the new state-run **Suwanee River Visitor Center** (912/637-5274, www.gastateparks.org, Wed.-Sun. 9am-5pm), a "green" building featuring an orientation video and exhibits.

Getting There and Around
The best way to access the Okefenokee, and the one I recommend, is the **East Entrance** (912/496-7836, www.fws.gov, Mar.-Oct. daily dawn-7:30pm, Nov.-Feb. daily dawn-5:30pm, $5 per vehicle), otherwise known as the **Suwanee Canal Recreation Area.** This is the main U.S. Fish and Wildlife Service entrance and the most convenient way to hike, rent boating and camping gear, and observe nature. An easy way to get to the East Entrance is by taking the Kingsland exit off I-95 onto Highway 40 west. Go through Kingsland and into Folkston until it dead-ends. Take a right, then an immediate left onto Main Street. At the third light, make a left onto Okefenokee Drive (Hwy. 121) south.

Families with kids may want to drive a bit farther and hit the **North Entrance** at the privately run **Okefenokee Swamp Park** (U.S. 1, 912/283-0583, www.okeswamp.com, daily 9am-5:30pm, $12 adults, $11 ages 3-11) near Waycross. Here you will find a more touristy vibe, with a reconstructed pioneer village, serpentarium, and animals in captivity. From here you can take various guided tours for an additional fee. There's camping at the nearby but unaffiliated **Laura S. Walker State Park**

(5653 Laura Walker Rd., 800/864-7275, www.gastateparks.org). Be aware that the state park is not in the swamp and isn't very swampy. Get to the North Entrance by taking I-95 exit 29 and going west on U.S. 82 about 45 miles to Highway 177 (Laura Walker Rd.). Go south through Laura S. Walker State Park; the Swamp Park is several miles farther.

If you really want that cypress-festooned, classic swamp look, go around the Okefenokee to **Stephen Foster State Park** (17515 Hwy. 177, 912/637-5274, fall-winter daily 7am-7pm, spring-summer daily 6:30am-8:30pm), a.k.a. the **West Entrance,** near Fargo, Georgia. Guided tours are available.

FOLKSTON
The chief attraction in Folkston, the little town right outside the refuge's East Entrance, is the excellent ◖ **Inn at Folkston Bed and Breakfast** (509 W. Main St., 888/509-6246, www.innatfolkston.com, $120-170). There is nothing like coming back to its cozy Victorian charms after a long day out in the swamp. The four-room inn boasts an absolutely outstanding breakfast, an extensive reading library, and a whirlpool tub.

A five-minute drive from the Inn is another Folkston claim to fame, the viewing depot for the **Folkston Funnel** (912/496-2536, www.folkston.com), a veritable train watcher's paradise. This is the spot where the big CSX double-track rail line following the top of the ancient Trail Ridge hosts 60 or more trains a day. Railroad buffs from all over the South congregate here, anticipating the next train by listening to their scanners. The first Saturday each April brings buffs together for the all-day Folkston RailWatch.

WAYCROSS
Fans of the old *Pogo* will recall Waycross (www.waycrosstourism.com) from the comic strip; and yes, there's a real "Fort Mudge" nearby. Pogo was fictional, but real-life Waycross natives include musician Gram Parsons and actor Ossie Davis. Seat of Ware County, Waycross has a wide-open feel, a legacy of the fact that the city

literally grew around the railroad, its design based on the tracks coming into town. Today Waycross is still one of the South's busiest rail centers, and many of the trains that course through Folkston Funnel go through town.

So of course the centerpiece of Waycross's downtown renovation is the restored **Historic Passenger Rail Depot** (315 Plant Ave., 912/283-3744, Mon.-Fri. 10am-5pm), built in the early 1900s, complete with Spanish Revival touches. It currently houses the town visitors center and Chamber of Commerce; get walking tour information to enjoy downtown Waycross's interesting and somewhat unusual architectural styles, some with Mediterranean flair.

The museum of note in Waycross is the **Okefenokee Heritage Center** (1460 N. Augusta Ave., 912/285-4260, http://okefenokeeheritagecenter.com, Tues.-Sat. 10am-4:30pm, adults $7, children ages 6-18 $5, children 5 and under free). Set on 20 acres of land, it features a historic locomotive, a recreated Waycross courthouse, an 1830s home, and an African American history exhibit.

A few miles south of town is **Obediah's Okefenok** (5115 Swamp Rd., 912/287-0090, www.okefenokeeswamp.com, daily 10am-5pm, $6.50 adults, $5 children), restored homestead of one of the first settlers and swamp guides in the Okefenokee: Henry "Obediah" Barber. In addition to the home—the oldest remaining on the swamp and now on the National Register of Historic Places—there are plenty of wildlife viewing opportunities, including from a long boardwalk.

The best restaurant in town, indeed, in the entire area for many, many miles around, is **C Pond View Fine Dining** (311 Pendleton St., 912/283-9300, www.pondviewinn.com, Wed.-Sat. 6pm-10pm, $20), in an attractively restored downtown storefront. From a huge rib eye to crab cakes to smoked salmon *à la* vodka, they will set you up with a fine repast to recharge you after a long day in the nearby swamp. What's more, there's a four-room inn (rooms $100) upstairs, a nice break from the usual mediocre chain accommodations typical of the area.

THE GOLDEN ISLES

More than any other area in the region, the Georgia coast retains a timeless mystique evocative of a time before the coming of Europeans, even before humankind itself. They're called the Golden Isles because of the play of the afternoon sun on the vistas of marsh grass; another nickname, "the Debatable Land," is a nod to a centuries-long role as a constantly shifting battleground of European powers.

On the map it looks relatively short, but Georgia's coastline is the longest contiguous salt marsh environment in the world—a third of the country's remaining salt marsh. Abundant with wildlife, vibrant with exotic, earthy aromas, constantly refreshed by a steady, salty sea breeze, it's a place with no real match anywhere else. Filled with rich sediments from rivers upstream and replenished with nutrients from the twice-daily ocean tide, Georgia's marshes from the mainland to the barrier islands are an amazing engine of natural production. Producing more food energy than any estuary on the East Coast, each acre of marsh produces about 20 tons of biomass—four times more productive than an acre of corn.

Ancient Native Americans held the area in special regard, intoxicated not only by the easy sustenance it offered but its spiritual solace. Their shell middens, many still in existence, are not only a sign of well-fed people but those thankful for nature's bounty. Avaricious for gold as they were, the Spanish also admired the almost monastic enchantment of Georgia's coast, choosing it as the site of their first colony in North America. Their subsequent chain of Roman Catholic missions are now long gone

© JIM MOREKIS

HIGHLIGHTS

◖ Jekyll Island Historic District: Relax and soak in the salty breeze at this onetime playground of the country's richest people (page 362).

◖ The Village: The center of social life on St. Simons Island has shops, restaurants, a pier, and a beachside playground (page 370).

◖ Fort Frederica National Monument: This tabby fortress from the first days of English settlement in Georgia is excellently preserved (page 372).

◖ Harris Neck National Wildlife Refuge: This former wartime airfield is now one of the East Coast's best birding locations (page 379).

◖ Cumberland Island National Seashore: Wild horses—such as the ones that live here—might not be able to drag you off this evocative, undeveloped island paradise (page 388).

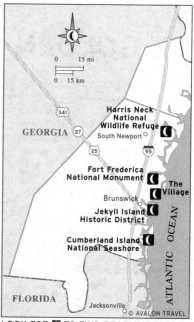

LOOK FOR ◖ TO FIND RECOMMENDED SIGHTS, ACTIVITIES, DINING, AND LODGING.

but certainly testified to their own quest here. While the American tycoons who used these barrier islands as personal playgrounds had avarice of their own, we must give credit where it's due: Their self-interest kept these places largely untouched by the kind of development that has plagued many of South Carolina's barrier islands to the north. Though isolated even today, the Golden Isles played an irreplaceable role in the defense of the young United States. It was here that massive live oaks were forested and used in the construction of the bulked-up superfast frigates of the fledgling U.S. Navy. The USS *Constitution* got its nickname, "Old Ironsides," from the strength of these pieces of Georgia oak, so resilient as to literally repel British cannonballs during the War of 1812. Although the South Carolina Sea Islands are generally seen as the center of Gullah culture, the African American communities of the Golden Isles, Georgia's Sea Islands, also boast a long and fascinating history of survival, resourcefulness, and proud cultural integrity carried on to this day.

HISTORY

For over 5,000 years, the Golden Isles of what would become Georgia were an abundant food and game source for Native Americans. In those days, long before erosion and channel dredging had taken their toll, each barrier island was an easy canoe ride away from the next one—a sort

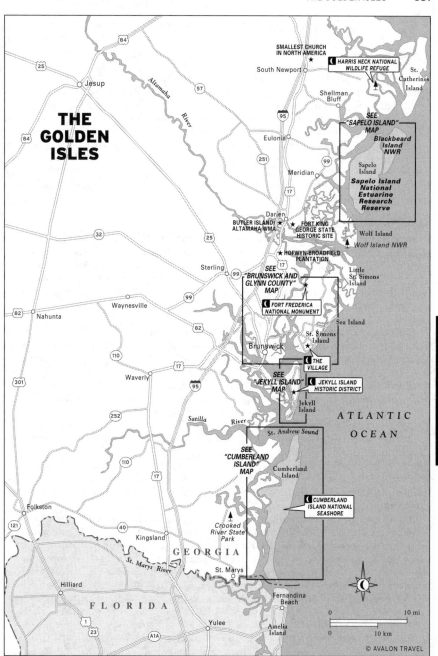

THE GOLDEN ISLES

of early Intracoastal Waterway—and there was bounty for everyone. But all that changed in 1526 when the Golden Isles became the site of the first European settlement in what is now the continental United States, the fabled San Miguel de Gualdape, founded nearly a century before the first English settlements in Virginia. Historians remain unsure where expedition leader Lucas de Ayllón actually set up camp with his 600 colonists and slaves, but recent research breakthroughs have put it somewhere around St. Catherine's Sound. San Miguel disintegrated within a couple of months, but it set the stage for a lengthy Spanish presence on the Georgia coast that culminated in the mission period (1580-1684). Working with the coastal chiefdoms of Guale and Mocama, almost all of Georgia's barrier islands and many interior spots hosted Catholic missions, each with an accompanying contingent of Spanish regulars. The missions began retreating with the English incursion into the American Southeast in the 1600s, and the coast was largely free of European presence until an early English outpost, Fort King George near modern-day Darien, Georgia, was established decades later in 1721. Isolated and hard to provision, the small fort was abandoned seven years later.

The next English project was Fort Frederica on St. Simons Island, commissioned by General James Edward Oglethorpe following his establishment of Savannah to the north. With the final vanquishing of the Spanish at the Battle of Bloody Marsh near Fort Frederica, the Georgia coast quickly emulated the profitable rice-based plantation culture of the South Carolina Lowcountry.

During the Civil War the southern reaches of Sherman's March to the Sea came down as far as Darien, a once-vital trading port that was burned to the ground by Union troops. With slavery gone and the plantation system in disarray, the coast's African American population was largely left to its own devices. Although the famous "40 acres and a mule" land and wealth redistribution plan for freed slaves was not to see fruition, the black population of Georgia's Sea Islands, like that of South Carolina's,

developed an inward-looking culture that persists to this day. The generic term for this culture is Gullah, but in Georgia you'll also hear it referred to as Geechee, local dialect for the nearby Ogeechee River.

As with much of the South after the Civil War, business carried on much as before, with the area becoming a center for lumber, the turpentine trade, and an increasing emphasis on fishing and shrimping. But by the start of the 20th century, the Golden Isles had become firmly established as a playground for the rich, who hunted and dined on the sumptuous grounds of exclusive retreats such as the Jekyll Island Club.

PLANNING YOUR TIME

Generally speaking, the peak season in this area is March-Labor Day. With the exception of some resort accommodations on St. Simons Island, Little St. Simons Island, and Sea Island, lodging is generally far more affordable than up the coast in either Savannah or Charleston.

Many travelers take I-95 south from Savannah to the Golden Isles, but U.S. 17 roughly parallels the interstate—in some cases so closely that drivers on both roads can see each other—and is a far more scenic and enriching drive for those with a little extra time to spend. Indeed, U.S. 17 is an intrinsic part of the life and lore of the region, and you are likely to spend a fair amount of time on it regardless.

Geographically, Brunswick is similar to Charleston in that it lies on a peninsula laid out roughly north-south. And like Charleston, it's separated from the Atlantic by barrier islands, in Brunswick's case St. Simons Island and Jekyll Island. Once you get within city limits, however, Brunswick has more in common with Savannah due to its Oglethorpe-designed grid layout. Brunswick itself can easily be fully experienced in a single afternoon. But really—as its nickname "Gateway to the Golden Isles" indicates—Brunswick's main role is as an economic and governmental center for Glynn County, to which Jekyll Island and St. Simons Island, the real attractions in this area, belong.

Both Jekyll Island and St. Simons Island are well worth visiting, and have their own separate pleasures—Jekyll more contemplative, St. Simons more upscale. Give an entire day to Jekyll so you can take full advantage of its relaxing, open feel. A half-day can suffice for St. Simons because most of its attractions are clustered in the Village area near the pier, and there's little beach recreation to speak of.

Getting to the undeveloped barrier islands, Sapelo and Cumberland, takes planning in advance because there is no bridge to either.

Both require a ferry booking and hence a more substantial commitment of time. There are no real stores and few facilities on these islands, so pack along whatever you think you'll need, including be food, water, medicine, suntan lotion, insect repellent, and so on. Sapelo Island is limited to day use unless you have prior reservations, with the town of Darien in McIntosh County as the gateway. The same is true for Cumberland Island National Seashore, with the town of St. Marys in Camden County as the gateway.

Brunswick and Glynn County

Consider Brunswick sort of a junior Savannah, sharing with that city twice its size to the north a heavily English flavor, great manners, a city plan with squares courtesy of General James Oglethorpe, a thriving but environmentally intrusive seaport, and a busy shrimping fleet. While Brunswick never became the dominant commercial center, à la Savannah, that it was envisioned to be, it has followed the Savannah model in modern times, both in terms of downtown revitalization and an increasing emphasis on port activity. Sadly, unlike Savannah, Brunswick has not seen fit to preserve the integrity of its six existing squares, all but one of which (Hanover Square) have been bisected by streets or built on.

The first real English-speaking settler in the area, Mark Carr, began cultivating land near Brunswick in 1738, but the city wasn't laid out until 1771, in a grid design similar to Savannah's. Originally comprising nearly 400 acres, Brunswick was named for Braunschweig, the seat of the House of Hanover in Germany and also for the Duke of Brunswick, a brother of King George III. When the Civil War started, most white citizens fled, and wharves and key buildings were burned to keep them out of Union hands. Brunswick saw a boom in population during World War II as a home of wartime industry such as the J. A. Jones Construction Company, which in a two-year span built 99 massive Liberty ships and at its peak employed 16,000 workers (they managed to build seven ships in a single month in 1944).

Since the war, the shrimping industry has played a big role in Brunswick's economy, but lately the local shrimping industry is in steep decline, both from depleted coastal stocks and increased competition from Asian shrimp farms. Hit hard by the recent economic downturn, Brunswick has seen better days. Despite an admirable effort at downtown revitalization centering on Newcastle Street, most visitors to the area seem content to employ Brunswick, as its nickname implies, as a "Gateway to the Golden Isles" rather than as a destination in itself.

SIGHTS
Brunswick Historic District
Technically, Brunswick has an "Old Town" district on the National Register of Historic Places as well as an adjacent district called "Historic Brunswick" centering on the storefronts of Newcastle Street. Since it's all pretty close together, we'll consider it all one nice package. Unlike Savannah, which renamed many of its streets in a fit of patriotism after the American Revolution, Brunswick's streets bear their original Anglophilic names, like Gloucester, Albemarle, and Norwich. You'd be forgiven for thinking that Brunswick's Union Street is a post–Civil War statement of national unity, but the name actually commemorates the union

THE GOLDEN ISLES

THE GOLDEN ISLES

BRUNSWICK AND GLYNN COUNTY

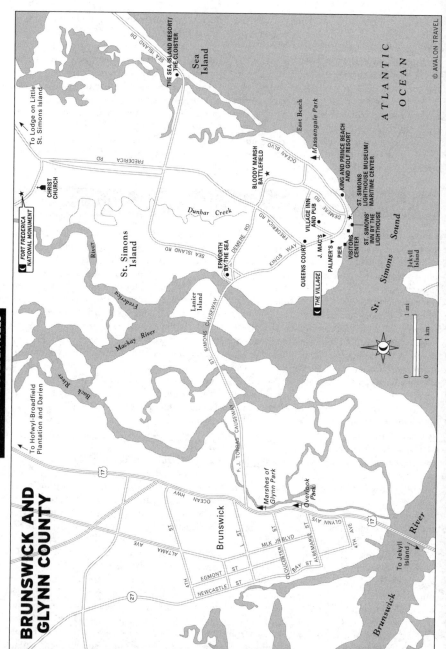

© AVALON TRAVEL

of Scotland and England in 1707. Most of the visitor-friendly activity centers on **Newcastle Street,** where you'll find the bulk of the galleries, shops, and restored buildings. Adjacent in the more historic areas are some nice residential homes.

The new pride of downtown is **Old City Hall** (1212 Newcastle St.), an amazing circa-1889 Richardsonian Romanesque edifice designed by noted regional architect Alfred Eichberg, who also planned many similarly imposing buildings in Savannah. City Hall reopened in 2004 after extensive renovations, bringing back to life its great vintage fireplaces and refitting its original gaslight fixtures.

Another active restored building is the charming **Ritz Theatre** (1530 Newcastle St., 912/262-6934, www.goldenislearts.org), built in 1898 to house the Grand Opera House and the offices of the Brunswick and Birmingham Railroad. This ornate three-story Victorian transitioned with the times, becoming a vaudeville venue, then a movie house. Under the management of the Golden Isles Arts and Humanities Association since 1989, the Ritz now hosts performances, studios, an art gallery, and classes.

Mary Ross Waterfront Park

This downtown gathering place at Bay and Gloucester Streets also has economic importance as a center of local economic activity—it's here where Brunswick's shrimp fleet is moored and the town's large port facilities begin. Unfortunately, nearby is a huge factory, dispensing its unpleasant odor over the waterfront 24-7. In 1989 the park was dedicated to Mary Ross, member of a longtime Brunswick shrimping family and author of the popular Georgia history book *The Debatable Land.* While the book is still a great read, sadly Ms. Ross was wrong when she wrote that the tabby ruins in the area were of Spanish origin. Devastated by the discovery that they actually dated from later and were of English construction, she vowed never to publish another word again.

At the entrance to the park is a well-done model of a Liberty ship, like the thousands that were built in Brunswick during World War II.

Lover's Oak

At the intersection of Prince and Albany Streets, you'll find the Lover's Oak, a nearly 1,000-year-old tree. Local lore tells us that it has been a secret meeting place for young lovers for centuries (though one does wonder how much of a secret it actually could have been). It's about 13 feet in diameter and has 10 sprawling limbs.

Marshes of Glynn

Amid the light industrial sprawl of this area of the Golden Isles Parkway is the interesting little **Overlook Park,** just south of the visitors center on U.S. 17—a good, if loud, place for a picnic. From the park's picnic grounds or overlook you can see the fabled Marshes of Glynn, which inspired Georgia poet Sidney Lanier to write his famous poem of the same title under the **Lanier Oak,** located a little farther up the road in the median.

Hofwyl-Broadfield Plantation

South Carolina doesn't own the patent on well-preserved old rice plantations, as the Hofwyl-Broadfield Plantation (5556 U.S. 17, 912/264-7333, www.gastateparks.org, Thurs.-Sat. 9am-5pm, last main house tour 4:45pm, $5), a short drive north of Brunswick, proves. With its old paddy fields along the gorgeous and relatively undeveloped Altamaha River estuary, the plantation's main home is an antebellum wonder, with an expansive porch and a nice house museum inside, with silver, a model of a rice plantation, and a slide show. There's also a nice nature trail.

William Brailsford of Charleston finished the plantation in 1807, which soon passed into the hands of the Troup family, who expanded the holdings to over 7,000 acres. Rice finally became financially unfeasible in the early 20th century, and the plantation turned to dairy farming, a pursuit that lasted until World War II. Ophelia Troup Dent would finally will the site to the state of Georgia in 1973.

© JIM MOREKIS

Lanier Oak, near the fabled Marshes of Glynn

The best way to get here is by taking U.S. 17 north of Brunswick until you see the signs; the plantation entrance is on the east side of the road.

ENTERTAINMENT AND EVENTS

The **Golden Isles Arts and Humanities Association** (1530 Newcastle St., 912/262-6934, www.goldenislesarts.org) is an umbrella organization for many arts activities in the Brunswick, Jekyll, and St. Simons area. They also manage the historic **Ritz Theatre** (1530 Newcastle St., 912/262-6934) in downtown Brunswick, which offers a yearly performance season that's worth checking out if you have a free weekend night.

Nightlife

Brunswick is a conservative place with little bar scene to speak of. But a few miles offshore is quite a different story when the **Emerald Princess Dinner and Casino Cruises** (Gisco Point, 912/265-3558, www.

emeraldprincesscasino.com, Mon.-Thurs. 7pm-midnight, Fri.-Sat. 11am-4pm and 7pm-1am, Sun. 1pm-6pm, $10) is operating. This is the classic gambling and party boat experience, with the action starting when the *Emerald Princess* slips into international waters and out of domestic gambling regulations. Ten bucks for the cruise gets you a light dinner. Drinks and chips, of course, are on you. No one under age 21 is allowed, and minimum and maximum bets vary by table. Reservations are required. To get to the dock, take U.S. 17 over the massive Sidney Lanier Bridge. Take a left onto the Jekyll Island Causeway and then an immediate left onto Gisco Point Drive. Follow signs into the parking lot.

Performing Arts

Based in St. Simons Island, the **Coastal Symphony of Georgia** (912/634-2006, www.coastalsymphonyofgeorgia.org), under the baton of Vernon Humbert, plays concerts in Brunswick during its season at different venues. Check the website for details. **Art Downtown**

IN THE FOOTSTEPS OF BARTRAM

The West has its stirring tale of Lewis and Clark, but the Southeast has its own fascinating—if somewhat less dramatic—tale of discovery, in the odyssey of William Bartram. In March 1733, the 36-year-old Bartram—son of royal botanist John Bartram and definitely a chip off the old block—arrived in Savannah to begin what would become a four-year journey through eight Southern states and colonies. As Lewis and Clark would do in the following century, Bartram not only exhaustively documented his encounters with nature and with Native Americans, he made discoveries whose impact has stayed with us to this day.

Young "Willie," born near Philadelphia in 1739, had a talent for drawing and for plants, which, of course, thrilled his father, who wrote to a friend that "Botany and drawing is his darling delight." A failure at business, Bartram was happy to settle on a traveling lifestyle that mixed both his loves: art and flora. After accompanying his father on several early trips, Bartram set out on his own at the request of an old friend of his father's in England, Dr. John Fothergill, who paid Bartram 50 pounds per year plus expenses to send back specimens and drawings.

Though Bartram's quest would eventually move farther inland and encompass much of the modern American South, most of the first year was spent in coastal Georgia. After arriving in Savannah he moved southward, roughly paralleling modern U.S. 17, to the now-dead town of Sunbury, through Midway, and on to Darien, where he stayed at the plantation of Lachlan McIntosh on the great Altamaha River, which inspired Bartram to pen some of his most beautiful writing. Bartram also journeyed to Sapelo Island, Brunswick, St. Marys, and even into the great Okefenokee Swamp. Using Savannah and Charleston as bases, Bartram mostly traveled alone, either by horse, by boat, or on foot. Word of his trip preceded him, and he was usually greeted warmly by local traders and Indian chiefs (except for one encounter with a hostile Native American near the St. Marys River). In many places, he was the first Euro-pean seen since De Soto and the Spanish. His epic journey ended in late 1776, when Bartram gazed on his beloved Altamaha for the last time. Heading north and crossing the Savannah River south of Ebenezer, he proceeded to Charleston and from there to his hometown of Philadelphia—where he would remain for the rest of his days.

At its publication, his 1791 chronicle, *Travels Through North and South Carolina, Georgia, East and West Florida,* was hailed as "the most astounding verbal artifact of the early republic." In that unassuming yet timeless work, Bartram cemented his reputation as the country's first native-born naturalist and practically invented the modern travelogue. Thanks to the establishment of the William Bartram Trail in 1976, you can walk in his footsteps—or close to them, anyway, since historians are not sure of his route. The trail uses a rather liberal interpretation, including memorials, trails, and gardens, but many specific "heritage sites" in coastal Georgia have their own markers, as follows:

- River and Barnard Streets in Savannah to mark his disembarkation and the beginning of his trek

- LeConte-Woodmanston Plantation in Liberty County (Barrington Ferry Rd. south of Sandy Run Rd. near Riceboro)

- 1.5 miles south of the South Newport River off U.S. 17

- St. Simon's Island on Frederica Road near the Fort Frederica entrance

- Off Highway 275 at Old Ebenezer Cemetery in Effingham County

Among the indigenous species Bartram was the first to record are:

- Fraser magnolia
- Gopher tortoise
- Florida sandhill crane
- Flame azalea
- Oakleaf hydrangea

THE GOLDEN ISLES

(209 Gloucester St., 912/262-0628, www.art-downtowngallery209.com) hosts locally written shows performed by the Brunswick Actors Theatre in its black box space and showcases local visual artists in its attached Gallery 209. The **Brunswick Community Concert Association** (912/638-5616, www.brunswickcommunityconcert.org, $25 adults, $10 students) brings an eclectic variety of high-quality national and regional vocal acts to various venues. The **C.A.P.E. Theater** (916 Albany St., 912/996-7740, www.capetheater.org), short for Craft, Appreciation, Performance, and Education, is a community group that performs a mix of classics and musicals at various venues. No reservations are necessary unless you're attending a dinner theater show, which is about $30 adults, $15 students. The town's main dance group is **Invisions Dance Company,** which performs out of **Studio South** (1307 Grant St., 912/265-3255, www.studio-southga.com).

Festivals

Each Mother's Day at noon, parishioners of the local St. Francis Xavier Church hold the **Our Lady of Fatima Processional and Blessing of the Fleet** (www.brunswick.net), begun in 1938 by the local Portuguese fishing community. After the procession, at about 3pm at Mary Ross Waterfront Park, comes the actual blessing of the shrimp-boat fleet.

Foodies will enjoy the **Brunswick Stewbilee** ($9 adults, $4 children), held on the second Saturday in October 11:30am-3pm Pro and amateur chefs match skills in creating the local signature dish and vying for the title of "Brunswick Stewmaster." There are also car shows, contests, displays, and much live music.

SHOPPING

Right in the heart of the bustle on Newcastle is a good indie bookstore, **Hattie's Books** (1531 Newcastle St., 912/554-8677, www.hatties-books.net, Mon.-Fri. 10am-5:30pm, Sat. 10am-4pm). Not only do they have a good selection of local and regional authors, you can also get a good cup of coffee.

the historic Ritz Theatre in downtown Brunswick

Like Beaufort, South Carolina, Brunswick has made the art gallery a central component of its downtown revitalization, with nearly all of them on Newcastle Street. Near Hattie's you'll find the eclectic **Kazuma Gallery** (1523 Newcastle St., 912/279-0023, Mon.-Fri. 10am-5:30pm, Sat. 10am-2pm) as well as the **Ritz Theatre** (1530 Newcastle St., 912/262-6934, Tues.-Fri. 9am-5pm, Sat. 10am-2pm), which has its own art gallery inside. Farther down is **The Gallery on Newcastle Street** (1626 Newcastle St., 912/554-0056, Thurs.-Sat. 11am-5pm), showcasing the original oils of owner Janet Powers.

SPORTS AND RECREATION
Hiking, Biking, and Bird-Watching

As one of the Colonial Coast Birding Trail sites, **Hofwyl-Broadfield Plantation** (5556 U.S. 17, 912/264-7333, www.gastateparks.org, Tues.-Sat. 9am-5pm, Sun. 2pm-5:30pm) offers a great nature trail along the marsh. Clapper rails, marsh wrens, and a wide variety of warblers come through the site regularly.

Birders and hikers will also enjoy the **Earth Day Nature Trail** (1 Conservation Way, 912/264-7218), a self-guided, fully accessible walk where you can see such comparative rarities as the magnificent wood stork and other indigenous and migratory waterfowl. There are observation towers and binoculars available for checkout. To get here, take U.S. 17 south through Brunswick. Just north of the big Sidney Lanier Bridge, turn left on Conservation Way; you'll see signage and come to a parking lot.

Just across the Brunswick River from town is **Blythe Island Regional Park** (6616 Blythe Island Hwy., 912/261-3805), a 1,100-acre public park with a campground, picnic area, and boat landing. The views are great, and it's big enough to do some decent biking and hiking. The best way to get here is to get back on I-95 and head south.

Another scenic park with a campground is **Altamaha Park of Glynn County** (1605 Altamaha Park Rd., 912/264-2342), northwest of Brunswick off U.S. 341, with 30 campsites and a boat ramp.

Kayaking and Boating

Most recreational adventurers in the area prefer to launch from St. Simons Island. The key public landing in Brunswick, however, is **Brunswick Landing Marina** (2429 Newcastle St., 912/262-9264). You can also put in at the public boat ramps at **Blythe Island Regional Park,** which is on the Brunswick River, or the **Altamaha Park of Glynn County** (1605 Altamaha Park Rd., 912/264-2342), on the Altamaha River slightly north.

For expert guided tours at a reasonable price, check out **South East Adventures** (1200 Glynn Ave./U.S. 17, 912/265-5292, www. southeastadventure.com), which has a dock right on the fabled "Marshes of Glynn."

ACCOMMODATIONS

In addition to the usual variety of chain hotels—most of which you should stay far away from—there are some nice places to stay in Brunswick, if you want to make it a base of operations, at very reasonable prices. In the heart of Old Town in a gorgeous Victorian is the **McKinnon House** (1001 Egmont St., 912/261-9100, www.mckinnonhousebandb. com, $125), which had a cameo role in the 1974 film *Conrack.* Today, this bed-and-breakfast is Jo Miller's labor of love, a three-suite affair with some plush interiors and an exterior that is one of Brunswick's most photographed spots. Surprisingly affordable for its elegance, the **WatersHill Bed & Breakfast** (728 Union St., 912/264-4262, www.watershill.com, $100) serves a full breakfast and offers a choice of five themed suites, such as the French country Elliot Wynell Room or the large Mariana Mahlaney room way up in the restored attic. Another good B&B is the **Brunswick Manor** (825 Egmont St., 912/265-6889, www.brunswickmanor.com, $130), offering four suites in a classic Victorian and a tasty meal each day.

The most unique lodging in the area is the **Hostel in the Forest** (Hwy. 82, 912/264-9738, www.foresthostel.com, $25, cash only), essentially a group of geodesic domes and whimsical tree houses a little way off the highway. Formed over 30 years ago as an International Youth Hostel, the place initially gives off a hippie vibe, with an evening communal meal (included in the rates) and a near-total ban on cell phones. But don't expect a wild time: No pets are allowed, the hostel discourages young children, and quiet time is strictly enforced at 11pm It's an adventurous, peaceful, and very inexpensive place to stay, but be warned that there is no heating or cooling. To reach the hostel, take I-95 exit 29 and go west for two miles. Make a U-turn at the intersection at mile marker 11. Continue east on Highway 82 for 0.5 miles. Look for a dirt road on the right with a gate and signage.

FOOD

Brunswick is notorious for its paucity of dining options, more so since the economic downturn claimed a few of the more notable names. The most famous restaurant in the Brunswick

BRUNSWICK STEW

Of course, Virginians being Virginians, they'll insist that the distinctive Southern dish known as Brunswick stew was named for Brunswick County, Virginia, in 1828, where a political rally featured stew made from squirrel meat. But all real Southern foodies know the dish is named for Brunswick, Georgia. Hey, there's a plaque to prove it in downtown Brunswick–although it says the first pot was cooked on July 2, 1898, on St. Simons Island, not in Brunswick at all. However, I think we can all agree that "Bruns-wick stew" rolls off the tongue much more eas-ily than "St. Simons stew."

In any case, it seems likely that what we now know as Brunswick Stew is based on an old co-lonial recipe, adapted from Native Americans, that relied on the meat of small game—origi-nally squirrel or rabbit but nowadays mostly chicken or pork—along with vegetables like corn, onions, and okra simmered over an open fire. Today, this tangy, thick, tomato-based delight is a typical accompaniment to barbecue along the Lowcountry and Georgia coasts, as well as a freestanding entrée on its own. Done tradi-tionally and correctly, a proper pot of Bruns-wick Stew is an involved kitchen project taking most of a day, but it's worth it. Here's a typical recipe from Glynn County, home of the famous Brunswick Stewbilee festival held the second Saturday of October:

SAUCE

Melt ¼ cup butter over low heat, then add:
1¾ cups ketchup
¼ cup yellow mustard
¼ cup white vinegar

Blend until smooth, then add:
½ tablespoon chopped garlic
1 teaspoon ground black pepper
½ teaspoon crushed red pepper
½ ounce Liquid Smoke
1 ounce Worcestershire sauce
1 ounce hot sauce
½ tablespoon fresh lemon juice

Blend until smooth, then add:
¼ cup dark brown sugar
Stir constantly and simmer for 10 minutes, being careful not to boil. Set aside.

STEW

Melt ¼ pound butter in a two-gallon pot, then add:
3 cups diced small potatoes
1 cup diced small onion
2 14½-ounce cans chicken broth
1 pound baked chicken
8-10 ounces smoked pork

Bring to a boil, stirring until potatoes are nearly done, then add:
1 8½-ounce can early peas
2 14½-ounce cans stewed tomatoes
1 16-ounce can baby lima beans
¼ cup Liquid Smoke
1 14½-ounce can creamed corn

Stir in sauce. Simmer slowly for two hours. Makes one gallon of Brunswick Stew.

The first Brunswick Stew was cooked in this pot.

area is at the humble but renowned **Georgia Pig** (2712 U.S. 17 S., 912/264-6664, Mon.-Thurs. 11am-7pm, Fri.-Sat. 11am-9pm, Sun. 11am-8pm, $6-10). Go over the South Brunswick River on I-95 and take exit 29 onto U.S. 17 to find this roadside classic. It serves a good pulled-pork sandwich in the tomato-based sauce common to the region.

INFORMATION AND SERVICES

The **Brunswick-Golden Isles Visitor Center** (2000 Glynn Ave., 912/264-5337, daily 9am-5pm) is at the intersection of U.S. 17 and the Torras Causeway to St. Simons Island. It features the famous pot in which the first batch of Brunswick stew was cooked over the bridge on St. Simons. A downtown **information station** is in the Ritz Theatre (1530 Newcastle St., 912/262-6934, Tues.-Fri. 9am-5pm, Sat. 10am-2pm).

The newspaper of record in town is the **Brunswick News** (www.thebrunswick-news.com). The main **post office** (805 Gloucester St., 912/280-1250) is in downtown Brunswick.

GETTING THERE AND AROUND

Brunswick is directly off I-95. Take exit 38 to the Golden Isles Parkway, and take a right on U.S. 17. The quickest way to the historic district is to make a right onto Gloucester Street. Plans and funding for a city-wide public transit system are pending, but currently Brunswick has no public transportation.

Jekyll Island

Few places in the United States have as paradoxical a story as Jekyll Island. Once the playground of the world's richest people—whose indulgence allowed it to escape the overdevelopment that plagues nearby St. Simons—Jekyll then became a dedicated vacation area for Georgians of modest means, by order of the state legislature. Today, it's somewhere in the middle—a great place for a relaxing nature-oriented vacation with some of the perks of luxury owing to its Gilded Age pedigree.

HISTORY

In prehistoric times, Jekyll was mainly a seasonal getaway for Native Americans. Indigenous people visited the area during the winter to enjoy its temperate weather and abundant shellfish. The Spanish also knew it well, calling it Isla de Las Ballenas (Island of the Whales) for the annual gathering of calving right whale families directly off the coast every winter—a mystical event that happens to this day. After securing safe access to the island from the Creeks in 1733, Georgia's founder, General James Oglethorpe, gave the island its modern name, after his friend Sir Joseph Jekyll.

The first English settler was Major William Horton in 1735, recipient of a land grant from the general, and the tabby ruins of one of Horton's homes remain today. A Frenchman, Christophe Du Bignon, purchased the island in 1800 and remained a leading figure. A mysterious event happened in 1858, when Jekyll Island was the final port of entry for the infamous voyage of *The Wanderer,* the last American slave ship. After intercepting the ship and its contraband manifest of 409 African slaves—the importation of slaves having been banned in 1807—its owners and crew were put on trial in Savannah.

As a home away from home for the country's richest industrialists—including J. P. Morgan, William Rockefeller, and William Vanderbilt—in the late 1800s and early 1900s, Jekyll Island was the unlikely seat of some of the most crucial events in modern American history. It was at the Jekyll Island Club that the Federal Reserve banking system was set up, in a secret convocation of investors and tycoons, in 1910. Five years later, AT&T President Theodore Vail, on the grounds of the club, would listen in on the first transcontinental phone call.

THE GOLDEN ISLES

Jekyll's unspoiled beauty prompted the state legislature in 1947 to purchase the island and—ironically, considering the island's former history—declare it a totally accessible "playground" for Georgians of low to middle income (a causeway wasn't completed until the mid-1950s). This stated public mission is why prices on the island—currently administered on behalf of the state by the Jekyll Island Authority—have stayed so low and development has been so well managed. Every so often a controversial redevelopment plan is proposed, with the potential to introduce high-dollar resort-style development to parts of Jekyll for the first time since the days of J. P. Morgan and company. Residents and conservationists alike continue to work together to protect this magical barrier island known as "Georgia's Jewel."

ORIENTATION

You'll have to stop at the entrance gate and pay a $6 "parking fee" to gain access to this state-owned island. A friendly attendant will give you a map and newsletter, and from there you're free to enjoy the whole island at your leisure.

As you dead-end into Beachview Drive, you're faced with a decision to turn either left or right. Most scenic and social activity is to the north, a left turn. For more peaceful beach-oriented activity with few services, turn right and head south. One historical reason for the lesser development at the south end is due to the fact that segregation laws were still in effect after the state's purchase of Jekyll in 1947. African American facilities were centered on the south end, while white activities were in the north.

SIGHTS
◖ Jekyll Island Historic District

A living link to one of the most glamorous eras of American history, the Jekyll Island Historic District is also one of the largest ongoing restoration projects in the southeastern United States. A visit to this 240-acre riverfront area is like stepping back in time to the Gilded Age, with croquet grounds, manicured gardens, and even ferry boats with names like the *Rockefeller*

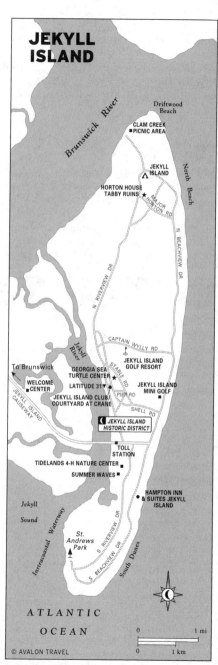

and the *J. P. Morgan.* The Historic District essentially comprises the buildings and grounds of the old **Jekyll Island Club,** not only a full-service resort complex—consisting of the main building and several amazing "cottages" that are mansions themselves—but a sort of living history exhibit chronicling that time when Jekyll was a gathering place for the world's richest and most influential people.

The Queen Anne-style main clubhouse, with its iconic turret, dates from 1886. Within a couple of years the club had already outgrown it, and the millionaires began building the ornate cottages on the grounds surrounding it. The Chicora cottage is gone, demolished after the supposedly accidental gunfire death of Edwin Gould in 1917, with only a hole in the ground remaining, but most of the others have been fully restored as lodgings. In 2000 a renovation took place for the most magnificent outbuilding, the 24-bedroom Crane Cottage, a Mediterranean villa that also hosts a fine restaurant. The most recent renovation was the 2010 reopening of the Indian Mound Cottage, once William Rockefeller's vacation getaway, to tours.

The **Jekyll Island Museum** (100 Stable Rd., 912/635-4036, www.jekyllisland.com, daily 9am-5pm, free), in the Historic District at the old club stables, houses some good history exhibits. The museum also provides a number of guided themed tours (daily 11am, 1pm, and 3pm, $16 adults, $8 ages 6-12) focusing on the Historic District, including the popular "Passport to the Century" (which includes entrance to two restored cottages) and "In the Service of Others" (focusing on the support staff of the golden age of the Jekyll Island Club). You can also purchase a guidebook for self-guided tours of the Historic District.

Georgia Sea Turtle Center

Within the grounds of the Historic District in a whimsically renovated historic 1903 building is the Georgia Sea Turtle Center (214 Stable Rd., 912/635-4444, www.georgiaseaturtlecenter. org, Mon. 10am-2pm, Tues.-Sun. 9am-5pm, $6 adults, $4 children), which features interactive exhibits on these important marine creatures, for whom Jekyll Island is a major nesting ground. Don't miss the attached rehabilitation building, where you can see the Center's turtles in various states of treatment and rehabilitation before being released into the wild. Children and adults alike will enjoy this unique opportunity to see these creatures up close and learn about the latest efforts to protect them.

Helping to raise awareness about the need to protect the nesting areas of the big loggerheads that lay eggs on Jekyll each summer, the Sea Turtle Center also guides nighttime tours (early June-Aug. daily 8:30pm and 9:30pm) on the beach in order to explain about the animals and their habitat and hopefully to see some loggerheads in action. These tours fill up fast, so make reservations in advance.

Driftwood Beach

Barrier islands like Jekyll are in a constant state of southward flux as currents erode the north end and push sand down the beach to the south end. Hence the creation of Driftwood Beach, as the soil erodes from under the large trees, causing them to fall and settle into the sand. In addition to a naturalist's wonderland, it's also a starkly beautiful and strangely romantic spot. The newsletter you get as you enter the island has a map with Driftwood Beach on it, but here's a tip: Drive north on Beachview Drive until you see a pullover on your right immediately after the Villas by the Sea (there's no signage). Park and take the short trail through the maritime forest, and you'll find yourself right there among the fallen trees and sand.

Horton House Tabby Ruins

Round the curve and go south on Riverview Drive, and you'll see the large frame of a two-story house on the left (east) side of the road. That is the ruins of the old Horton House, built by Jekyll's original English-speaking settler, William Horton. Horton's house has survived two wars, a couple of hurricanes, and a clumsy restoration in 1898 to its current state of preservation at the hands of the Jekyll Island Authority and various federal, state, and local

JEKYLL ISLAND'S MILLIONAIRE'S CLUB

After the Civil War, as the Industrial Revolution gathered momentum seemingly everywhere but Georgia's Golden Isles, a couple of men decided to do something to break the foggy miasma of Reconstruction that had settled into the area and make some money in the process. In the late 1870s, John Eugene DuBignon and his brother-in-law Newton Finney came up with a plan to combine DuBignon's long family ties to Jekyll with Finney's extensive Wall Street connections in order to turn Jekyll into an exclusive winter hunting club. Their targeted clientele was a no-brainer: the newly minted American mega-tycoons of the Industrial Age. Finney found 53 such elite millionaires willing to pony up to become charter members of the venture, dubbed the Jekyll Island Club. Among them were William Vanderbilt, J.P. Morgan, and Joseph Pulitzer. As part of the original business model, in 1886 Finney purchased the island from DuBignon for $125,000.

With the formal opening two years later began Jekyll Island's half-century as a premier playground for the country's richest citizens, centered on the Victorian winter homes, called "cottages," built by each member and preserved today in the Historic District. While it was formed as a hunt club, the Jekyll Island Club welcomed the millionaires' families. In the 1920s, the focus began shifting to golf, and you can still play a portion of the historic course at the club today. By 1900 the club's membership represented one-sixth of the world's wealth. And the word *exclusive* has never been more appropriate: Nonmembers were not allowed to enjoy the facilities, regardless of social stature. Winston Churchill and even President McKinley were refused admission.

As the mega-rich are wont to do even today, these influential men often mixed business with pleasure. In 1910, secret meetings of the so-called "First Name Club" led to the development of the Aldrich Plan, which laid the groundwork for the modern Federal Reserve System.

Under assumed names, Senator Nelson Aldrich, Assistant Treasury Secretary A. Piatt Andrew, Banker's Trust vice president Benjamin Strong, National City Bank president Frank Vanderlip, investment banker Paul Warburg, and J.P. Morgan partner Henry P. Davison came into the Club with the cover story of participating in a duck hunt. After they arrived by train at Brunswick, the stationmaster told them the cat was out of the bag and a gaggle of reporters had already gathered. But Davison took the stationmaster aside, saying, "Come out, old man, I will tell you a story." Returning a few minutes later, Davison told his colleagues, "That's all right. They won't give us away." What Davison's "story" was remains a mystery, but it must have been a pretty compelling one.

A few years later, AT&T president Theodore Vail, nursing a broken leg at his Mound Cottage on Jekyll, participated in the first transcontinental telephone call on January 25, 1915, among New York City, San Francisco, and the special line strung down the coast from New York and across Jekyll Sound to the club grounds. Also on the line were the telephone's inventor, Alexander Graham Bell, his assistant Thomas Watson, the mayors of New York and San Francisco, and President Woodrow Wilson.

The millionaires continued to frolic on Jekyll through the Great Depression, but worsening international economic conditions reduced membership, even though the cost of membership was lowered in 1933. The outbreak of World War II and the resulting drain of labor into the armed forces put a further cramp in the club's workings, and it finally closed for good in 1942. By the time prowling German U-boats began appearing off the Georgia coast, prompting island-wide blackouts, the Jekyll Island Club era already seemed like ancient history. The state would acquire the island after the war in 1947, turning the once-exclusive playground of millionaires into a playground for all the people.

Jekyll Island's Driftwood Beach

partners. His first house, also made of tabby, was burned by the Spanish during their retreat after losing the Battle of Bloody Marsh on nearby St. Simons Island. But the intrepid major rebuilt on the same spot in 1742, continuing to farm barley and indigo plants on the surrounding grounds as well as hosting Georgia's first brewery, the ruins of which are nearby.

Frenchman Christophe Poulain du Bignon would live in the Horton House for a while after purchasing the island in the 1790s. Across the street from the house is the poignant little **Du Bignon Cemetery,** around which winds a nicely done pedestrian and bike path overlooking one of the most beautiful areas of marsh you'll see in all the Golden Isles.

ENTERTAINMENT AND EVENTS

There's no real nightlife to speak of on Jekyll, it being intended for quiet, affordable daytime relaxation. The focus instead is on several annual events held at the **Jekyll Island Convention Center** (1 N. Beachview Dr., 912/635-3400, hwww.jekyllislandconventioncenter.com), which has undergone a massive restoration to bring it in line with modern convention standards.

In the beginning of the new year comes one of the area's most beloved and well-attended events, the **Jekyll Island Bluegrass Festival** (www.aandabluegrass.com). Many of the genre's biggest traditional names come to play at this casual multiday gathering. The focus here is on the music, not the trappings, so come prepared to enjoy wall-to-wall bluegrass played by the best in the business. Keep in mind that during this weekend the island is awash in RVs from all over the country, so if you're camping, you'd better make reservations.

In September as the harvest comes in off the boats, the **Wild Georgia Shrimp and Grits Festival** (www.jekyllisland.com, free admission), seeks to promote the value of the Georgia shrimping industry by focusing on how good the little critters taste in various regional recipes.

SPORTS AND RECREATION
Hiking and Biking

Quite simply, Jekyll Island is a paradise for bicyclists and walkers, with a very well-developed and very safe system of paths, totaling about 20 miles, running the entire circumference of the island, going by all major sights, including the Jekyll Island Club in the Historic District. In addition, walkers and bicyclists can enjoy much of the seven miles of beachfront at low tide.

Rent your bikes at **Jekyll Island Miniature Golf** (100 James Rd., 912/635-2648, daily 9am-8pm, $5.25 per hour, $11.50 per day). Take a left when you dead-end after the entrance gate, then another left.

Bird-Watching

The **Clam Creek Picnic Area** on the island's north end is on the Colonial Coast Birding Trail, and without even trying you will see a wide variety of wading birds and shorebirds. Shell collectors will also have a blast, as will those with a horticultural bent, who will marvel at the variety of species presented in the various ecosystems on the island, from beach to marsh hammock to maritime forest.

Golf and Tennis

True to Jekyll Island's intended role as a playground for Georgians of low to medium income, its golf and tennis facilities—all centrally located at the middle of the island—are quite reasonably priced. The **Jekyll Island Golf Resort** (322 Captain Wylly Rd., 912/635-2368, www.jekyllisland.com, green fees $40-60) comprises the largest public golf resort in Georgia. A total of 63 holes on four courses—Pine Lakes, Indian Mound, Oleander, and Ocean Dunes (nine holes)—await. Check the website for "golf passport" packages that include local lodging.

The adjacent **Jekyll Island Tennis Center** (400 Captain Wylly Rd., 912/635-3154, www.gate.net/~jitc, $25 per hour) boasts 13 courts, seven of them lighted, as well as a pro shop (daily 9am-6pm).

If a different kind of golf is your thing, try **Jekyll Island Miniature Golf** (100 James Rd.,

912/635-2648, Sun.-Thurs. 9am-8pm, Fri.-Sat. 9am-10pm, $6).

Fishing

Continuing north on Beachview Drive at the very top of the island is the well-done **Clam Creek Picnic Area** (daily dawn-dusk, free). This facility on the Colonial Coast Birding Trail has a spacious fishing pier over the Jekyll River and a trailhead through the woods and out onto the beach. About a 20-minute walk on the sand gets you to Driftwood Beach from the other side.

A good local fishing charter company is Captain Vernon Reynolds's **Coastal Expeditions** (3202 E. 3rd St., 912/265-0392, www.coastalcharterfishing.com), departing from the Jekyll Harbor Marina. Half-day and full-day trips are available; call for rates.

Kayaking and Boating

Most kayaking activity in the area centers on St. Simons across the sound. But **Tidelands 4-H Nature Center** (100 Riverview Dr., 912/635-5032, www.tidelands4h.org) offers a variety of Jekyll-oriented guided kayak tours and also rents kayaks and canoes March-October.

Water Parks

Summer Waves (210 S. Riverview Dr., 912/635-2074, www.jekyllisland.com, Memorial Day-Labor Day, $20 adults, $16 children under 48 inches tall) is just what the doctor ordered for kids with a surplus of energy. The 11-acre facility has a separate section for toddlers to splash around in, with the requisite more daring rides for hard-charging preteens. Hours vary, so call ahead.

Horseback Riding and Tours

Victoria's Carriages and Trail (100 Stable Rd., 912/635-9500, Mon.-Sat. 11am-4pm) offers numerous options, both on horseback as well as in a horse-drawn carriage, including carriage tours of the island (Mon.-Sat. every hour 11am-4pm, $15 adults, $7 children). There's a 6pm-8pm night ride ($38 per couple). Horseback rides include a one-hour beach ride ($55) that leaves at 11am, 1pm, and 3pm and a sunset ride (6:30pm, $65) that lasts a little over an hour. Victoria's is at the entrance to the Clam Creek Picnic Area on the north end of the island directly across the street from the Jekyll Island campground.

The **Tidelands 4-H Center** (912/635-5032) gives 1.5-2-hour Marsh Walks (Mon. 9am, $5 adults, $3 children) leaving from Clam Creek Picnic Area, and Beach Walks ($5 adults, $3 children) leaving Wednesdays at 9am from the St. Andrews Picnic area and Fridays at 9am from South Dunes Picnic Area.

Captain Vernon Reynolds's **Coastal Expeditions** (3202 E. 3rd St., 912/265-0392, www.coastalcharterfishing.com, $24 adults, $10 children) provides dolphin tours March-May Tuesday-Saturday at 1:30pm, and three trips daily June-August.

ACCOMMODATIONS
Under $150
The **Days Inn** (60 S. Beachview Dr., 912/635-9800, www.daysinnjekyll.com, $100) has seen a remodeling and is the best choice if budget is a concern (and you don't want to camp, that is). It has a good location on the south side of the island with nice ocean views.

$150-300
Any discussion of lodging on Jekyll Island begins with the legendary (**Jekyll Island Club** (371 Riverview Dr., 800/535-9547, www.jekyllclub.com, $199-490), which is reasonably priced considering its history, postcard-perfect setting, and delightful guest rooms. Some of its 157 guest rooms in the club and annex areas are available for under $200, and even the finest, the Presidential Suite, tops out at under $500 in high season (Mar.-Oct.). There are 60 guest rooms are in the main club building, and several outlying cottages, chief among them the Crane, Cherokee, and Sans Souci Cottages, are also available. All rates include use of the big outdoor pool overlooking the river, and a neat amenity is a choice of meal plans for an extra daily fee.

Despite its auspicious beginnings, the club has not been a total success story. The state tried to run it as a resort in the 1950s and 1960s but gave up in 1971. With Historic Landmark District status coming in 1978, restoration wasn't far behind, and the club was first run as a Radisson. Now operated by Landmark, the club is one of the "Historic Hotels of America" as ranked by the National Trust for Historic Preservation. Keep in mind that not all the fixtures are original and the present interior design scheme was done with an eye to current commercial taste (those crusty old millionaires would never have gone for pastels).

The first new hotel on the island in 35 years, (**Hampton Inn & Suites Jekyll Island** (200 S. Beachview Dr., 912/635-3733, www.hamptoninn.com, $180-210) was built according to an exacting set of conservation guidelines, conserving much of the original tree canopy and various low-impact design and building techniques. Quite simply, it's one of the best ecofriendly hotel designs I've experienced. An elevated wooden walkway to the beach preserves as much of the natural dune-scape as possible, though keep in mind that the trade-off is that you can't see the ocean from the hotel. The beach isn't far away, and the walk-in saltwater pool is particularly enjoyable and relaxing.

Camping
One of the niftiest campgrounds in the entire area is the **Jekyll Island Campground** (197 Riverview Dr., 912/635-3021, tent sites $25, RV sites $32). It's a friendly place with an excellent location at the north end of the island—a short drive or bike ride from just about anywhere and directly across the street from the Clam Creek Picnic Area, with easy beach access. There are more than 200 sites, from tent to full-service pull-through RV sites. There's a two-night minimum on weekends and a three-night minimum on holiday and special event weekends; reservations are recommended.

FOOD
Cuisine offerings are few and far between on Jekyll. I'd suggest you patronize one of the

Jekyll Island Campground is a great place to spend the night.

three dining facilities at the **Jekyll Island Club** (371 Riverview Dr.), which are all open to non-guests. They're not only delicious but pretty reasonable as well, considering the swank setting. My favorite is the **◖Courtyard at Crane** (912/635-2400, lunch Sun.-Fri. 11am-4pm, Sat. 11am-2pm, dinner Sun.-Thurs. 5:30pm-9pm, $27-38). In the circa-1917, beautifully restored Crane Cottage, one of the old tycoon villas, the Courtyard offers romantic evening dining (call for reservations) as well as tasty and stylish lunch dining in the alfresco courtyard area or inside. The lunch menu—a great deal for the quality—is Mediterranean heavy, with wraps, sandwiches, and soups. The dinner menu moves more toward wine-country casual chic, with a lot of pork, veal, and beef dishes to go with the requisite fresh seafood. As a plus, the coffee is great—not at all a given in Southern restaurants. Casual dress is OK.

For a real and figurative taste of history, make a reservation at the **Grand Dining Room** (912/635-2400, breakfast Mon.-Sat. 7-11am, Sun. 7-10am, lunch Mon.-Sat. 11:30am-2pm, brunch Sun. 10:45am-2pm, dinner daily 6-10pm, dinner $26-35), the club's full-service restaurant. Focusing on continental cuisine—ordered either à la carte or as a prix fixe "sunset dinner"—the Dining Room features a pianist each evening and for Sunday brunch. Jackets or collared shirts are required for men.

For a tasty breakfast, lunch, or dinner on the go or at odd hours, check out **Café Solterra** (912/635-2600, daily 7am-10pm), great for deli-type food and equipped with Starbucks coffee. There are two places for seaside dining and cocktails at the historic Jekyll Island Club Wharf. **Latitude 31** (1 Pier Rd., 912/635-3800, www.crossoverjekyll.com, Tues.-Sun. 5:30-10pm, $15-25, no reservations) is an upscale seafood-oriented fine-dining place, while the attached **Rah Bar** (Tues.-Sat. 11am-close, Sun. 1pm-close, depending on weather) serves up oysters and shellfish in a very casual setting; try the Lowcountry boil or the crab legs.

INFORMATION AND SERVICES

The **Jekyll Island Visitor Center** (901 Downing Musgrove Causeway, 912/635-3636, daily 9am-5pm) is on the long causeway along the marsh before you get to the island. Set in a charming little cottage it shares with the Georgia State Patrol, the Center has a nice gift shop and loads of brochures on the entire Golden Isles region. Don't hesitate to ask questions of the person taking your $5 entrance fee when you get to the island itself.

The **U.S. Postal Service** keeps an outpost at 18 South Beachview Drive (912/635-2625).

GETTING THERE AND AROUND

Jekyll Island is immediately south of Brunswick. Take I-95 exit 38 to the Golden Isles Parkway. Take a right onto U.S. 17 and keep going until you cross the huge Sidney Lanier Bridge over the Brunswick River. Take an immediate left at the foot of the bridge onto the Downing Musgrove Causeway (Jekyll Island Rd.). This long, scenic route over the beautiful marshes eventually takes you directly onto Jekyll, where you'll have to pay a $5 per vehicle fee to get onto the island. Once on the island, most sites are on the north end (a left as you reach the dead-end at Beachview Dr.). The main circuit route around the island is Beachview Drive, which suitably enough changes into Riverview Drive as it rounds the bend to landward at the north end.

Many visitors choose to bicycle around the island once they're here, which is certainly the best way to experience both the sights and the beach itself at low tide.

St. Simons Island

Despite a certain reputation for aloof affluence, the truth is that St. Simons Island is also very visitor-friendly, and there's more to do here than meets the eye. Think of St. Simons—with a year-round population of about 13,000—as a smaller, less-hurried Hilton Head and you've got the right idea. For those looking for island-style relaxation with no high-rise cookie-cutter development—but still all the modern amenities and luxuries—St. Simons fits the bill perfectly. A major difference from Hilton Head is that St. Simons respects much of its history, and a lot of it is still left to enjoy, particularly the expansive and archaeologically significant Fort Frederica National Monument.

HISTORY

St. Simons Island and its much smaller, symbiotic neighbor Sea Island (originally Long Island) were well known to Native Americans as a hunting and fishing ground. Eventually the Spanish would have two missions on St. Simons, one at the south end and one at the north end, as well as a town for nonconverted native peoples called San Simon, which would eventually give the island its modern name. A lasting European influence didn't come until 1736 with General James Oglethorpe's construction of Fort Frederica. The fort and surrounding town was a key base of operations for the British struggle to evict the Spanish from Georgia—which culminated in the decisive Battle of Bloody Marsh south of the fort—but fell into decline after the Spanish threat subsided.

In the years after American independence, St. Simons woke up from its slumber as acre after acre of virgin live oak was felled to make the massive timbers of new warships for the U.S. Navy, including the USS *Constitution*. In their place was planted a new crop—cotton. The island's antebellum plantations boomed to world-class heights of profit and prestige when the superior strain of the crop known as Sea Island Cotton came in the 1820s.

On St. Simons in 1803, one of the most poignant chapters in the dark history of American slavery was written. In one of the first documented slave uprisings in North America, a group of slaves from the Igbo region of West

Africa escaped custody and took over the ship that was transporting them to St. Simons from Savannah. But rather than do any further violence, immediately upon reaching shore on the west side of St. Simons, the slaves essentially committed mass suicide by walking into the swampy waters nearby, which forever after would be known as Ebo Landing (a corruption of the original Igbo).

The Civil War came to St. Simons in late 1861 with a Union blockade and invasion, leading Confederate troops to dynamite the lighthouse. Initially St. Simons was a sanctuary for freed slaves from the island's 14 plantations, and by late 1862 over 500 former slaves lived on St. Simons, including Susie King Taylor, who began a school for African American children. But in November of that year all former slaves were dispersed to Hilton Head and Fernandina, Florida. St. Simons was chosen as one of the implementation sites of General William Sherman's Special Field Order No. 15, the famous "40 acres and a mule" order giving the Sea Islands of South Carolina and Georgia to freed slaves. However, Sherman's order was quickly rescinded by President Andrew Johnson.

The next landmark development for St. Simons didn't come until the building of the first causeway in 1924, which led directly to the island's resort development by the mega-rich industrialist Howard Coffin of Hudson Motors fame, who also owned nearby Sapelo Island to the north. By 1928, Coffin had completed the Sea Island Golf Club on the grounds of the old Retreat Plantation on the south end of St. Simons Island. He would move on to develop the famous Cloisters resort on Long Island (later Sea Island) itself.

ORIENTATION

Because it's only a short drive from downtown Brunswick on the Torras Causeway, St. Simons has much less of a remote feel than most other Georgia barrier islands and is much more densely populated than any other Georgia island except for Tybee. Most visitor-oriented activity on this 12-mile-long, heavily residential island about the size of Manhattan is clustered at the south end, where St. Simons Sound meets the Atlantic. The main reasons to travel north on the island are to golf or visit the historic site of Fort Frederica on the landward side.

The main roads to remember are Kings Way, which turns into Ocean Boulevard as it nears the active south end of the island, called "The Village"; Demere ("DEM-er-ee") Road, which loops west to east around the little island airport and then south, joining up with Ocean Boulevard down near the lighthouse; Frederica Road, the dominant north-south artery; and Mallory Street, which runs north-south through the Village area and dead-ends at the pier on St. Simons Sound. (You'll notice that Mallory Street is sometimes spelled "Mallery," which is actually the correct spelling of the avenue's namesake: Mallery King, child of Thomas King, owner of the historic Retreat Plantation.)

SIGHTS
◖ The Village
Think of "The Village" at the extreme south end of St. Simons as a mix of Tybee's downscale accessibility and Hilton Head's upscale exclusivity. This compact, bustling area only a few blocks long offers not only boutique shops and stylish cafés but vintage stores and busking musicians. While visitors and residents here tend toward the affluent, they also tend not to be as flashy about it as in some other locales. You'll find the vast majority of quality eating spots here, along with most quality lodging. It's fun to meander down Mallory Drive, casually shopping or noshing, and then make your way out onto the short but fun **St. Simons Pier** to enjoy the breeze and occasional spray coming off the sound. The long, low, sprawling building immediately to the north overlooking the expanse of Massengale Park is the old Casino building, now used for local government offices and community meetings.

St. Simons Lighthouse Museum
Unlike many East Coast lighthouses, which tend to be in hard-to-reach places, anyone can walk right up to the St. Simons Lighthouse

GOLDEN ISLES ON THE PAGE

And now from the Vast of the Lord will the
*   waters of sleep*
Roll in on the souls of men,
But who will reveal to our waking ken
The forms that swim and the shapes that
*   creep*
Under the waters of sleep?
And I would I could know what swimmeth
*   below when the tide comes in*
On the length and the breath of the
*   marvelous marshes of Glynn.*
                                    –Sidney Lanier

Many authors have been inspired by their time in the Golden Isles, whether to pen flights of poetic fancy, page-turning novels, or politically oriented chronicles. Here are a few of the most notable names:

· **Sidney Lanier:** Born in Macon, Georgia, Lanier was a renowned linguist, mathematician, and legal scholar. Fighting as a Confederate during the Civil War, he was captured while commanding a blockade runner and taken to a POW camp in Maryland, where he came down with tuberculosis. After the war, he stayed at his brother-in-law's house in Brunswick to recuperate, and it was during that time that he took up poetry, writing the famous "Marshes of Glynn," quoted above.

· **Eugenia Price:** Although not originally from St. Simons, Price remains the best-known local cultural figure, setting her *St. Simons Trilogy* here. After relocating to the island in 1965, she stayed here until her death in 1996. She's buried in the Christ Church cemetery on Frederica Road.

· **Tina McElroy Ansa:** Probably the most notable literary figure currently living on St. Simons Island is award-winning African American author Tina McElroy Ansa. Few of her books deal with the Golden Isles region, but they all deal with life in the South, and Ansa is an ardent devotee of St. Simons and its relaxed, friendly ways.

· **Fanny Kemble:** In 1834, this renowned English actress married Georgia plantation heir Pierce Butler, who would become one of the largest slave owners in the United States. Horrified by the treatment of Butler's slaves at Butler Island, just south of Darien, Georgia, Kemble penned one of the earliest antislavery chronicles, *Journal of a Residence on a Georgian Plantation in 1838-1839.* Kemble's disagreement with her husband over slavery hastened their divorce in 1849.

Museum (101 12th St., 912/638-4666, www.saintsimonslighthouse.org, Mon.-Sat. 10am-5pm, Sun. 1:30pm-5pm, $6 adults, $3 children). Once inside, you can enjoy the museum's exhibit and take the 129 steps up to the top of the 104-foot beacon—which is, unusually, still active—for a gorgeous view of the island and the ocean beyond. The museum offers a "Family of Four" package admission ($25) for two adults and two children as well as a combo ticket to the nearby Maritime Center ($10 adults, $5 children.

The first lighthouse on the spot came about after planter John Couper sold this land, known as Couper's Point, to the government in 1804 for $1. This original beacon was destroyed by retreating Confederate troops in 1862 to hinder Union navigation on the coast. Traces of its foundations are near the current facility. The current lighthouse dates from 1872, built by Irishman Charles Cluskey, who was responsible for a lot of Greek Revival architecture up and down the Georgia coast. Attached to the lighthouse is the oldest brick structure in Glynn County, the 1872 lighthouse keeper's cottage, now the museum and gift shop run by the Coastal Georgia Historical Society.

Maritime Center
A short walk from the lighthouse and also administered by the Coastal Georgia Historical Society, the Maritime Center (4201 1st St.,

The Village is the center of activity on St. Simons Island.

912/638-4666, www.saintsimonslighthouse. org, Mon.-Sat. 10am-5pm, Sun. 1:30pm-5pm, $6 adults, $3 children) is at the historic East Beach Coast Guard Station. Authorized by President Franklin Roosevelt in 1933 and completed in 1937 by the Works Progress Administration, the East Beach Station took part in military action in World War II, an episode chronicled in exhibits at the Maritime Center. On April 8, 1942, the German U-boat U-123 torpedoed and sank two cargo ships off the coast of St. Simons Island. The Coast Guardsmen of East Beach station mounted a full rescue effort, saving many crewmen of the merchant ships, including one ship's canine mascot. The Coast Guard's tenure on East Beach ended after a 1993 fire burned down their boathouse. Two years later the station was decommissioned, and the Coasties moved to a new station in Brunswick.

The Maritime Center offers a "Family of Four" package admission ($25) for two adults and two children as well as a combo ticket

to the St. Simons Lighthouse ($10 adults, $5 children).

◖ Fort Frederica National Monument

The expansive and well-researched Fort Frederica National Monument (Frederica Rd., 912/638-3639, www.nps.gov/fofr, daily 9am-5pm, $3 adults, free under age 15) lies on the landward side of the island. Established by General James Oglethorpe in 1736 to protect Georgia's southern flank from the Spanish, the fort (as well as the village that sprang up around it, in which the Wesley brothers preached for a short time) was named for Frederick Louis, the Prince of Wales. The feminine suffix -*a* was added to distinguish it from the older Fort Frederick in South Carolina.

You don't just get to see a military fort here (actually the remains of the old powder magazine; most of the fort itself eroded into the river long ago); this is an entire colonial town site a mile in circumference, originally modeled after a typical English village. A self-guided walking

Fort Frederica on St. Simons Island

tour through the beautiful grounds—the oak trees here have the longest, most luxurious Spanish moss I've ever seen—shows foundations of building sites that have been uncovered, including taverns, shops, and the private homes of influential citizens. Closer to the river is the large tabby structure of the garrison barracks.

As for the actual fort itself, from its location astride a bend in the Frederica River you can instantly see why this was such a strategic location, guarding the approach to the great Altamaha River. The Frederica garrison took part in the unsuccessful attack on St. Augustine, Florida, in 1740 and was also the force that sallied out of the fort and southward to repulse the Spanish at Bloody Marsh two years later.

Take in the accompanying exhibits in the visitors center, including a 23-minute film shown every half-hour 9am-4pm, which is actually quite good. A park ranger also gives informative talks throughout the day, and there are occasional re-enactments by uniformed colonial "soldiers."

Bloody Marsh Battlefield

There's not a lot to see at the site of the Battle of Bloody Marsh (Frederica Rd., 912/638-3639, www.nps.gov/fofr, daily 8am-4pm, free), but—as with the similarly stirring site of Custer's Last Stand at the Little Bighorn—your imagination fills in the gaps, giving it perhaps more emotional impact than other, more substantial historic sites.

Essentially just a few interpretive signs overlooking a beautiful piece of salt marsh, the site is believed to be near the place where British soldiers from nearby Fort Frederica ambushed a force of Spanish regulars on their way to besiege the fort. Frederica's garrison, the 42nd Regiment of Foot, was augmented by a company of tough Scottish Highlanders from Darien, Georgia, who legend says attacked to the tune of bagpipes. The battle wasn't actually that bloody—some accounts say the Spanish lost only seven men—but the stout British presence convinced the Spanish to leave St. Simons a few days later, never again to project their once-potent military power that far north in the New World.

While the Battle of Bloody Marsh site is part of the National Park Service's Fort Frederica site, it's not at the same location. Get to the battlefield from the fort by taking Frederica Road south, and then a left (east) on Demere Road. The site is on your left as Demere Road veers right, in the 1800 block.

Christ Church

Just down the road from Fort Frederica is historic Christ Church (6329 Frederica Rd., 912/638-8683, www.christchurchfrederica.org, daily 2pm-5pm). The first sanctuary dates from 1820, but the original congregation at the now-defunct town of Frederica held services under the oaks at the site as early as 1736. The founder of Methodism, John Wesley, and his brother Charles both ministered to island residents during 1736-1737.

The original church was rendered unusable by Union occupation during the Civil War. A handsome new church, the one you see today, was funded and built in 1883 by a local mill owner, Anson Dodge, as a memorial to his first wife. But Christ Church's claim to fame in modern culture is as the setting of local novelist Eugenia Price's *The Beloved Invader*, the first work in her Georgia trilogy. The late Price, who died in 1996, is buried in the church cemetery.

Tours

St. Simons Island Trolley Tours (912/638-8954, www.stsimonstours.com, daily 11am, $22 adults, $10 age 4-12, free under age 4) offers just that, a ride around the island in comparative comfort, leaving from the pier.

ENTERTAINMENT AND EVENTS
Nightlife

St. Simons is far from Charleston's or Savannah's league when it comes to partying, but there is a fairly active nightlife scene, with a strong dose of island casual. Unlike some areas this far south on the Georgia coast, there's usually a sizeable contingent of young people out looking for a good time. The island's premier club, **Rafters Blues and Raw Bar** (315½

Mallory St., 912/634-9755, www.raftersblues.com, Mon.-Sat. 4:30pm-2am), known simply as "Rafters," brings in live music most every Thursday-Saturday night, focusing on the best acts on the regional rock circuit.

My favorite spot on St. Simons for a drink or an espresso—or a panini for that matter—is **Palm Coast Coffee, Cafe, and Pub** (316 Mallory St., 912/634-7517, www.palmcoastssi.com, daily 8am-10pm). This handy little spot, combining a hip, relaxing coffeehouse with a hearty menu of brunchy items, is in the heart of the village. The kicker, though, is the cute little bar the size of a large walk-in closet right off the side of the main room—a little bit of Key West on St Simons. Mondays are open mike nights.

Inside the Village Inn is the popular nightspot the **Village Pub** (500 Mallory St., 912/634-6056, www.villageinnandpub.com, Mon.-Sat. 5pm-midnight, Sun. 5-10pm). Slightly more upscale than most watering holes on the island, this is the best place for a quality martini or other premium cocktail.

Performing Arts

Because of its close proximity to Brunswick, a short drive over the bridge, St. Simons has a symbiotic relationship with that larger city in areas of art and culture. Each summer, beginning Memorial Day weekend and continuing into September, there are several Jazz in the Park concerts by regional artists. The shows are usually Sunday 7pm-9pm on the lawn of the St. Simons Lighthouse, and the beautiful setting and calming breeze is a delight. Admission is charged; bring a chair or blanket if you like.

Cinema

The island has its own multiplex, the **Island Cinemas 7** (44 Cinema Lane, 912/634-9100, www.georgiatheatrecompany.com).

SHOPPING

Most shopping on St. Simons is centered in the Village and is a typical beach town mix of hardware and tackle, casual clothing, and souvenir stores. A funky highlight is **Beachview Books** (215 Mallory St., 912/638-7282, Mon.-Sat.

10:30am-5:30pm, Sun. 11:30am-3pm), a rambling used bookstore with lots of regional and local goodies, including books by the late great local author Eugenia Price. Probably the best antiques shop in this part of town is **Village Mews** (504 Beachview Dr., 912/634-1235, Mon.-Sat. 10am-5pm).

The closest thing to a mall is farther north on St. Simons at **Redfern Village,** with some cute indie stores like **Beach Cottage Linens** (912/634-2000, Mon.-Fri. 10am-5:30pm, Sat. 10am-5pm), **Thomas P. Dent Clothiers** (912/638-3118, Mon.-Sat. 9:30am-6pm), and the craftsy **Rarebbits and Pieces** (912/638-2866, Mon.-Sat. 10am-5:30pm). Redfern Village is on Frederica Road, one traffic light past the corner of Frederica Road and Demere Road.

SPORTS AND RECREATION
Beaches
Keep going from the pier past the lighthouse to find **Massengale Park** (daily dawn-dusk), with a playground, picnic tables, and restrooms right off the beach on the Atlantic side. The beach itself on St. Simons is underwhelming compared to some in these parts, but nonetheless it's easily accessible from the pier area and good for a romantic stroll if it's not high tide. There's a great playground, Neptune Park, right next to the pier overlooking the waterfront.

Kayaking and Boating
With its relatively sheltered landward side nestled in the marsh and an abundance of wildlife, St. Simons Island is an outstanding kayaking site, attracting connoisseurs from all over. A good spot to put in on the Frederica River is the **Golden Isles Marina** (206 Marina Dr., 912/634-1128, www.gimarina.com), which is actually on little Lanier Island on the Torras Causeway right before you enter St. Simons proper. For a real adventure, put in at the ramp at the end of South Harrington Street off Frederica Road, which will take you out Village Creek on the seaward side of the island.

Undoubtedly the best kayaking outfitter and tour operator in this part of the Golden

Isles is **SouthEast Adventure Outfitters** (313 Mallory St., 912/638-6732, www.southeast-adventure.com, daily 10am-6pm), which also has a location in nearby Brunswick. Michael Gowen and company offer an extensive range of guided tours all over the St. Simons marsh and sound area as well as trips to undeveloped Little St. Simons Island to the north. Prices vary, so call or go to the website for information.

Hiking and Biking
Like Jekyll Island, St. Simons is a great place for bicyclists. Bike paths go all over the island, and a special kick is riding on the beach almost the whole length of the island (but only at high tide). There are plenty of bike rental spots, with rates generally $15-20 per day depending on the season. The best place to rent bikes is **Monkey Wrench Bicycles** (1700 Frederica Rd., 912/634-5551). You can rent another kind of pedal-power at **Wheel Fun Rentals** (532 Ocean Blvd., 912/634-0606), which deals in four-seat pedaled carts with steering wheels.

Golf and Tennis
A popular place for both sports is the **Sea Palms Golf and Tennis Resort** (5445 Frederica Rd., 800/841-6268, www.seapalms.com, green fees $70-80) in the middle of the island, with three nine-hole public courses and three clay courts. The **Sea Island Golf Club** (100 Retreat Rd., 800/732-4752, www.seaisland.com, green fees $185-260) on the old Retreat Plantation as you first come onto the island has two award-winning 18-hole courses, the Seaside and the Plantation. Another public course is the 18-hole **Hampton Club** (100 Tabbystone Rd., 912/634-0255, www.hamptonclub.com, green fees $95) on the north side of the island, part of the King and Prince Beach and Golf Resort.

ACCOMMODATIONS
Under $150
A charming and reasonable place a stone's throw from the Village is **⟨ Queens Court** (437 Kings Way, 912/638-8459, $85-135), a traditional roadside motel from the late 1940s,

with modern upgrades that include a nice outdoor pool in the central courtyard area. Despite its convenient location, you'll feel fairly secluded.

One of the most interesting lodgings in the Lowcountry and Georgia coast is **Epworth by the Sea** (100 Arthur J. Moore Dr., 912/638-8688, www.epworthbythesea.org, $90-100). This Methodist retreat in the center of the island boasts an entire complex of freestanding motels and lodges on its grounds, in various styles and configurations. Cafeteria-style meetings are the order of the day, and there are plenty of recreational activities on-site, including tennis, volleyball, baseball, football, soccer, and basketball. They also rent bikes, which is always a great way to get around St. Simons. Everyone loves the **Lovely Lane Chapel,** a picturesque sanctuary that is a favorite spot for weddings and holds services Sunday at 8:45am (casual dress OK). Researchers can utilize the resources of the **Arthur J. Moore Methodist Museum and Library** (Tues.-Sat. 9am-4pm).

You couldn't ask for a better location than the **St. Simons' Inn by the Lighthouse** (609 Beachview Dr., 912/638-1101, www.saintsimonsinn.com, $120-300), which is indeed in the shadow of the historic lighthouse and right next to the hopping Village area. A so-called "condo-hotel," each of the standard and deluxe suites at the Inn are individually owned by off-site owners—however, each guest gets full maid service and a complimentary breakfast.

$150-300

The best-known lodging on St. Simons Island is the ◖ **King and Prince Beach and Golf Resort** (201 Arnold Rd., 800/342-0212, $249-320). Originally opened as a dance club in 1935, the King and Prince brings a swank old-school glamour similar to the Jekyll Island Club (though less imposing). And like the Jekyll Island Club, the King and Prince is also designated as one of the Historic Hotels of America. Its nearly 200 guest rooms are spread over a complex that includes several buildings, including the historic main building, beach

villas, and freestanding guesthouses. Some standard rooms can go for under $200 even in the spring high season. Winter rates for all guest rooms are appreciably lower and represent a great bargain. For a dining spot overlooking the sea, try the **Blue Dolphin** (lunch daily 11am-4pm, dinner daily 5-10pm, $15-30). The Resort's Hampton Club provides golf for guests and the public.

An interesting B&B on the island that's also within walking distance of most of the action on the south end is the 28-room **Village Inn & Pub** (500 Mallory St., 912/634-6056, www.villageinnandpub.com, $160-245), nestled among shady palm trees and live oaks. The pub, a popular local hangout in a renovated 1930 cottage, is a nice plus.

Over $300

Affiliated with the Sea Island Resort, the **Lodge at Sea Island** (100 Retreat Ave., 912/638-3611, $650-2,500) is actually on the south end of St. Simons Island on the old Retreat Plantation. Its 40 grand guest rooms and suites all have great views of the Atlantic Ocean, the associated Plantation Course links, or both. Full butler service makes this an especially pampered and aristocratic stay.

FOOD

While the ambience at St. Simons has an upscale feel, don't feel like you have to dress up to get a bite to eat—the emphasis is on relaxation and having a good time.

Breakfast and Brunch

◖ **Palmer's Village Cafe** (223 Mallory St., 912/634-5515, www.palmersvillagecafe.com, Tues.-Sun. 7:30am-2pm, $10-15), formerly called Dressner's, is right in the middle of the Village's bustle. It's one of the island's most popular places but still with enough seats so you usually don't have to wait. Sandwiches and burgers are great, but breakfast all day is the real attraction and includes lovingly crafted omelets, hearty pancakes, and a "build your own biscuit" menu.

Named for the birthday that the original

three co-owners share, **Fourth of May Deli** (444 Ocean Blvd., 912/638-5444, breakfast daily 7am-1pm, lunch daily 11am-9pm, $8-20) is a popular breakfast and lunch place in the Village. Breakfast focuses on specialties like eggs benedict and huevos rancheros, along with some fantastic breakfast burritos, a comparative rarity in the South.

Seafood

Despite its somewhat unappetizing name, **Mullet Bay** (512 Ocean Blvd., 912/634-9977, daily 11:30am-10pm, $7-18) in the Village is a favorite good old-fashioned Southern seafood place, the kind where you get a big fried platter with two sides and hushpuppies. A popular seafood place right in the action in the Village is **Barbara Jean's** (214 Mallory St., 912/634-6500, www.barbarajeans.com, Sun.-Thurs. 11am-9pm, Fri.-Sat. 11am-10pm, $7-20), which also has a great variety of imaginative veggie dishes to go along with its formidable seafood menu, including some excellent she-crab soup and crab cakes. They also have plenty of good landlubber treats for those not inclined to the marine critters.

Fine Dining

◖ **J. Mac's Island Restaurant** (407 Mallory St., 912/634-0403, www.jmacsislandrestaurant.com, Tues.-Sat. 6pm-9pm, $20-30) is the Village's high-end restaurant, one that wouldn't be out of place in downtown Charleston or Savannah. Owner J. Mac Mason and head chef Connor Rankin conspire to bring a fresh take on Southern and seafood classics, with adventurous entrées like seared "Creamsicle" marlin with jumbo asparagus and sweet corn puree-seared filet with gorgonzola and herb gratin.

Inside the King and Prince Resort, you'll find the old-school glory of the **Blue Dolphin** (201 Arnold Rd., 800/342-0212, lunch daily 11am-4pm, dinner daily 5-10pm, $15-30), redolent of the *Great Gatsby* era. The Blue Dolphin claims to be the only oceanfront dining on the island, and the views are certainly magnificent.

INFORMATION AND SERVICES

The **St. Simons Visitors Center** (530-B Beachview Dr., 912/638-9014, www.bgivb.com, daily 9am-5pm) is in the St. Simons Casino Building near Neptune Park and the Village. The main newspaper in St. Simons is the *Brunswick News* (www.thebrunswicknews.com). The **U.S. Postal Service** (800/275-8777) has an office at 620 Beachview Drive.

GETTING THERE AND AROUND

Get to St. Simons through the gateway city of Brunswick. Take I-95 exit 38 for Golden Isles, which will take you to the Golden Isles Parkway. Take a right onto U.S. 17 and look for the intersection with the Torras Causeway, a toll-free road that takes you the short distance onto St. Simons.

Immediately as you cross the Frederica River onto the island, look for a quick right onto Kings Way to take you directly to the Village area. You can also take a quick left onto Demere Road to reach Frederica Road and the more northerly portion of the island, where you'll find Fort Frederica and Christ Church.

LITTLE ST. SIMONS ISLAND

This 10,000-acre privately owned island, accessible only by water, is almost totally undeveloped—thanks to its salt-stressed trees, which discouraged timbering—and boasts seven miles of beautiful beaches. All activity centers on the circa-1917 ◖ **Lodge on Little St. Simons Island** (1000 Hampton Point Dr., 888/733-5774, www.littlestsimonsisland.com, from $625), named by *Condé Nast Traveler* as the top U.S. mainland resort in 2007. Within it lies the famed Hunting Lodge, where meals and cocktails are served. With 15 ultra-plush guest rooms and suites in an assortment of historic buildings, all set amid gorgeous natural beauty—there are five full-time naturalists on staff—the Lodge is a reminder of what St. Simons proper used to look like. The guest count is limited to 30 people.

Getting There and Around

Unless you enlist the aid of a local kayaking charter company, you have to be a guest of the Lodge to have access to Little St. Simons. The ferry, a 15-minute ride, leaves from a landing at the northern end of St. Simons at the end of Lawrence Road. Guests have full use of bicycles once on the island and can also request shuttle transportation just about anywhere.

SEA ISLAND

The only way to enjoy Sea Island—basically a tiny appendage of St. Simons facing the Atlantic Ocean—is to be a guest at (**The Sea Island Resort** (888/732-4752, www. seaisland.com, from $700). And guests visiting now are truly lucky; the legendary facility, routinely ranked as one of the best resorts on the planet, completed extensive renovations in 2008. Unfortunately, the economic

downturn sent the institution into bankruptcy as of this writing; they do plan to stay in business, however. The rooms at the Resort's premier lodging institution, **The Cloister,** nearly defy description—enveloped in Old World luxury, they also boast 21st-century technology. And the service at The Cloister is equally world-class, featuring 24-hour butler service in the European tradition. There are hundreds of cottages for rental on Sea Island as well, all of which grant temporary membership in the Sea Island Club and full use of its many amenities and services.

Getting There and Around

Get to Sea Island by taking Torras Causeway onto the island and then making a left onto Sea Island Causeway, which takes you all the way to the gate marking the only land entrance to Sea Island.

Darien and McIntosh County

It doesn't get near the attention or the number of visitors as Savannah to the north or the St. Simons-Jekyll area to the south, but the small fishing and shrimping village of Darien in McIntosh County has an interesting historic pedigree of its own. It is centrally located near some of the best treasures the Georgia coast has to offer, including the Harris Neck National Wildlife Refuge, the beautiful Altamaha River, and the sea island of Sapelo, and it also boasts what many believe to be the best traditional seafood restaurants in the state.

HISTORY

Unlike Anglophilic Savannah to the north, the Darien area has had a distinctly Scottish flavor from the beginning. In 1736, Scottish Highlanders established a settlement at the mouth of the Altamaha River at the bequest of General James Oglethorpe, who wanted the tough Scots protecting his southern border against the Spanish. They called it Darien, honoring the failed 1697 settlement in Panama.

Leading them was John McIntosh Mohr, who would go on to father several sons who would become famous in their own right and eventually lend his surname to the county. The Scots brought a singularly populist sentiment to the New World. When Georgia planters lobbied to legalize slavery, which was outlawed by Oglethorpe, the Scots of Darien signed a petition against them in 1739—believed to be the first organized protest of slavery in America. The Darien settlers were also known for keeping more cordial relations with the Native Americans than the area's English settlements. Of course, they were a frugal bunch too.

Darien's heyday was unquestionably in that antebellum period, when for a brief time the town was the world's largest exporter of cotton, floated downriver on barges and shipped out through the port of Darien. The Bank of Darien was the largest bank south of Philadelphia in the early 1800s. A prosperous rice culture grew up around the Altamaha estuary as well, relying on the tidal flow of the area's acres and acres of marsh. Almost nothing from this period remains, however, because on June 11, 1863, a force of mostly African American Union troops under the command of Colonel Robert G. Shaw (portrayed in the movie *Glory*) burned Darien to the ground, with all its homes and warehouses going up in smoke.

After the Civil War, lumber became the new cash crop, and Darien once again became a thriving seaport and mill headquarters. The late 1800s saw a new reliance on shrimping and oystering, industries that survive to this day. A different kind of industry prospered in the years after World War II. In those pre-interstate highway days, U.S. 17 was the main route south to booming Florida. McIntosh County got a bad reputation for "clip joints," which would fleece gullible travelers with a variety of illegal schemes. This period is recounted in the best-seller *Praying for Sheetrock* by Melissa Fay Greene.

SIGHTS
Smallest Church in North America

While several other churches claim that title, in any case fans of the devout and of roadside kitsch alike will enjoy the tiny and charming little **Memory Park Christ Chapel** (U.S. 17, daily 24 hours). Built in 1949 by local grocer Agnes Harper, the church—which contains a pulpit and chairs for a dozen people—was intended as a round-the-clock travelers' sanctuary on what was then the main coastal road, U.S. 17. Upon her death, Harper simply willed the church to Jesus Christ. The stained-glass windows are imported from England, and there's a guestbook so you can leave any note of appreciation. Get there by taking I-95 exit 67 and going south a short way on U.S. 17; the church is on the east side of the road.

◖ Harris Neck National Wildlife Refuge

Literally a stone's throw away from the

Memory Park Christ Chapel, the "Smallest Church in North America"

© JIM MOREKIS

Harris Neck National Wildlife Refuge

"Smallest Church" is the turnoff east onto the seven-mile Harris Neck Road leading to the Harris Neck National Wildlife Refuge (912/832-4608, www.fws.gov/harrisneck, daily dawn-dusk, free). In addition to being one of the single best sites in the South from which to view wading birds and waterfowl in their natural habitat, Harris Neck also has something of a poignant backstory. For generations after the Civil War, an African American community descended from the area's original slaves quietly struggled to eke out a living by fishing and farming. But their land was taken by the federal government in World War II to build a U.S. Army Air Force base, primarily to train pilots on the P-40 Tomahawk fighter, the same plane used by the famed Flying Tigers. After the war, the base was decommissioned and given to McIntosh County as a municipal airport. But the notoriously corrupt local government so mismanaged the facility that the feds once again took it over, eventually transferring it to

the forerunner of the U.S. Fish and Wildlife Service.

Now a nearly 3,000-acre nationally protected refuge, Harris Neck gets about 50,000 visitors a year to experience its mix of marsh, woods, and grassland ecosystems and for its nearly matchless bird-watching. Its former life as a military base has the plus of leaving behind a decent system of roads, many of them based on old runways. Most visitors use the four-mile "wildlife drive" to travel through the refuge, stopping occasionally for hiking or bird-watching. In the summer, look for egrets, herons, and wood storks nesting in rookeries. In the winter, waterfowl like mallards and teal flock to the brackish and freshwater pools. You can see painted buntings late April-late September.

Kayaks and canoes can put in at the public boat ramp on the Barbour River. Near the landing is an old African American cemetery, publicly accessible, with some charming handmade tombstones that evoke the post-Civil War era of Harris Neck before the displacement of local citizens to build the airfield.

To get here, take I-95 exit 67 and go south on U.S. 17 about one mile, then east on Harris Neck Road (Hwy. 131) for seven miles to the entrance gate on the left.

Shellman Bluff

Just northeast of Darien is the old oystering community of Shellman Bluff. It's notable not only for the stunning views from the high bluff but for fresh seafood. Go to **Shellman's Fish Camp** (912/832-4331) to put in for a kayak or canoe ride. Save room for some food; there are some great seafood places here.

To get to Shellman Bluff, take I-95 exit 67 for South Newport and get on U.S. 17 south. There are two easy ways to get to Shellman Bluff from U.S. 17: East on Minton Road and then left onto Shellman Bluff Road, or east on Pine Harbor Road followed by an immediate left onto Shellman Bluff Road. In either case, take Shellman Bluff Road until it dead-ends, then a right onto Sutherland Bluff Drive.

Darien Waterfront Park

Right where U.S. 17 crosses the Darien River, find the **Darien Welcome Center** (U.S. 17 and Fort King George Dr., 912/437-6684, daily 9am-5pm). From there it's a short walk down some steps to the newly refurbished little Darien Waterfront Park. This small but charming area on a beautiful bend of the Darien River—a tributary of the mighty Altamaha River just to the south—features some old tabby warehouse ruins, some of the only remnants of Darien's glory days as a major seaport and old enough to have century-old live oaks growing around them. To the east are the picturesque docks where the town shrimp-boat fleet docks.

McIntosh Old Jail Art Center

Within Darien proper is the **McIntosh Old Jail Art Center and Welcome Center** (404 North Way, 912/437-7711, www.visitdarien.com, Tues.-Sat. 10am-4pm), which also hosts several small art galleries and the McIntosh County History Museum.

Vernon Square

Right around the corner from the Welcome Center on Washington Street is Vernon Square, a charming little nook of live oaks and Spanish moss that was the social center of Darien in the town's antebellum heyday. The **Darien Methodist Church** on the square was built in 1843, damaged during the Civil War, then rebuilt in 1884 using materials from the first church. The nearby **St. Andrews Episcopal Church,** built in 1878, was once the site of the powerful Bank of Darien. Nearby is the affiliated and equally historic **St. Cyprian's Episcopal Church** (Fort King George Rd. and Rittenouse St.) built by an African American congregation and one of the largest tabby structures still in use anywhere.

Fort King George State Historic Site

The oldest English settlement in what would become Georgia, Fort King George State Historic Site (1600 Wayne St., 912/437-4770, www.gastateparks.org/fortkinggeorge, Tues.-Sun. 9am-5pm, $5 adults, $2.50 children) for a short time protected the Carolinas from attack, with its establishment in 1721 to its abandonment in 1727. Walking onto the site, with its restored 40-foot-tall cypress blockhouse fort, instantly reveals why this place was so important: It guards a key bend in the wide Altamaha River, vital to any attempt to establish transportation and trade in the area. In addition to chronicling the ill-fated English occupation of the area—plagued by insects, sickness, danger, and boredom—the site also has exhibits about other aspects of local history, including the Guale Indians, the Spanish missionary presence, and the era of the great sawmills. Nature lovers will enjoy the site as well, as it offers gorgeous vistas of the marsh. Fort King George holds regular reenactments, living history demonstrations, and cannon firings; go to the website for details.

To get here, take U.S. 17 to the Darien River Bridge, and then go east on Fort King George Drive. There's a bike route to the fort if you want to park in town.

Butler Island

South of Darien is the Altamaha River, Georgia's largest and only undammed river as well as one of the country's great estuarine habitats, with the second-largest watershed on the East Coast. It's a paradise for outdoors enthusiasts, one that amazed and delighted famed naturalist William Bartram on his journey here in the late 1700s. Over 30,000 ducks visit each year mid-October-mid-April on this key stop on the Colonial Coast Birding Trail.

A great way to enjoy the river ecosystem is at the **Altamaha Waterfowl Management Area** (912/262-3173, http://georgiawildlife.dnr.state. ga.us, $3). This was the site of Butler Island Plantation, one of the largest and most successful tidewater plantations in the antebellum era. (The 75-foot brick chimney just off U.S. 17 is part of an old rice mill belonging to the plantation.) In 1834, planter Pierce Butler II married English actress Fanny Kemble, who would go on to write one of the earliest antislavery chronicles, *Journal of a Residence on a Georgian Plantation in 1838-39*, about what she saw during her short stay at Butler Island. Just past the chimney is a large plantation house, which now houses offices of the Nature Conservancy. There's a picnic ground nearby. The dominance of the plantation culture in this area is proved by the dikes and gates throughout the marsh, still plainly visible from the road. Many are still used by the Georgia Department of Natural Resources to maintain bird habitat. Birds you can see throughout the area include endangered wood storks, painted bunting, white ibis, all types of ducks, and even bald eagles.

Some of the best hiking and birding in the area is just south of the chimney on U.S. 17. Park on the east side of the road at an old dairy barn, and from there you'll find the trailhead for a four-mile round-trip hike on the Billy Cullen Memorial Trail, which offers great bird-watching opportunities and interpretive signage. On the other side of U.S. 17 is the entrance to the Ansley Hodges Memorial, where a 0.25-mile hike takes you to an observation tower. Be aware that hunting goes on near this area on some Saturdays during the year.

Kayaks and canoes can easily put in at the state-run landing at **Champney River Park** right where U.S. 17 crosses the Champney River. There are a variety of fish camps up and down this entire riverine system, providing fairly easy launching and recovery.

TOURS

Altamaha Coastal Tours (229 Ft. King George Rd., 912/437-6010, www.altamaha. com) is your best bet to take a guided kayak tour (from $50) or rent a kayak (from $20 per day) to explore the beautiful Altamaha River, Georgia's longest.

ACCOMMODATIONS

If you want to stay in McIntosh County, I strongly recommend booking one of the five charming guest rooms at **■ Open Gates Bed and Breakfast** (301 Franklin St., Darien, 912/437-6985, www.opengatesbnb.com, $125-140). This lovingly restored and reasonably priced inn is on historic and relaxing Vernon Square in downtown Darien. Owners Kelly and Jeff Spratt are not only attentive innkeepers who rustle up a mean breakfast, they're also biologists who can hook you up with the best nature-oriented experiences and tours on this part of the coast.

FOOD

McIntosh County is a powerhouse in the food department, and as you might expect, fresh and delicious seafood in a casual atmosphere is the order of the day here. A Shellman Bluff favorite is **■ Speed's Kitchen** (Shellman Bluff, 912/832-4763, Thurs.-Sat. 5pm-close, Sun. noon-close, $10-20), where people move anything but fast and the fried fish and crab-stuffed flounder are out of this world. Take a right off of Shellman Bluff Road onto Sutherland Bluff Drive. Take a right onto Speed's Kitchen Road.

One of my favorite restaurants—indeed, one of my favorite experiences, period—is ◖ **The Old School Diner** (1080 Jesse Grant Rd. NE, Townsend, 912/832-2136, http://oldschooldiner.com, Wed.-Fri. 5:30pm-9:30pm, Sat.-Sun. noon-9:30pm, $15-30, cash only), located in a whimsical semirural compound seven miles off U.S. 17 just off Harris Neck Road on the way to the wildlife refuge. Run by the gregarious comfort-food culinary genius Jerome Brown, the restaurant is a reflection of the man himself—warm, inviting, eccentric, and full of life. The interior almost defies description, but here goes: Imagine a series of rambling, dimly-lit rooms with no identifiable decor, every wall and surface covered with memorabilia, kitsch, and endless photographs of diners (yes, one of them will be you—the servers take your picture at the end of the meal). However, it's Chef Jerome's food that has people driving here from literally all over Georgia (last time I was here I met someone who had driven in from Augusta, about three hours away): succulent fresh seafood in the coastal Georgia tradition—delicately fried and imbued with the subtle, inviting flavors of soul food. Not a seafood fan? His ribs are also some of the best anywhere. Old School's prices aren't so old school, but keep in mind that the portions are huge, rich, and filling. And besides, no one comes all the way out here to scrimp and save—this is an experience you'll never forget. Reservations are recommended, and remember, it's cash only. They take no plastic of any kind, and there are no ATMs nearby.

Even farther off the main roads than the Old School Diner, the community of Shellman Bluff is also well worth the drive. Find ◖ **Hunter's Café** (Shellman Bluff, 912/832-5771, lunch Mon.-Fri. 11am-2pm, dinner Mon.-Fri. 5-10pm, Sat.-Sun. 7am-10pm, $10-20) and get anything that floats your boat—it's all fresh and local. Wild Georgia shrimp are a particular specialty, as is the hearty cream-based crab stew. Take a right off Shellman Bluff Road onto Sutherland Bluff Drive, then a left onto New Shellman Road. Take a right onto the unpaved River Road and you can't miss it.

On the Darien waterfront, you'll find **Skipper's Fish Camp** (85 Screven St., Darien, 912/437-3579, www.skippersfishcamp.com, daily 11am-9pm, $15-25), which, as is typical

People come from many miles away to eat at The Old School Diner.

for this area, also hosts a marina. Try the fried wild Georgia Shrimp, fresh from local waters. South of Darien just off U.S. 17 on the Altamaha River, try **Mudcat Charlie's** (250 Ricefield Way, 912/261-0055, daily 8am-2pm, $10-20), where fresh seafood is served in a friendly and very casual atmosphere, yes, right in the middle of a busy fish camp.

INFORMATION AND SERVICES

The **Darien Welcome Center** (1111 Magnolia Bluff Way, www.visitdarien.com, Mon.-Sat. 10am-8pm, Sun. 11am-6pm) is located within the Preferred Outlets mall just off I-95 at exit 49.

The closest hospital is the Brunswick campus of **Southeast Georgia Health System** (2415 Parkwood Dr., Brunswick, 912/466-7000, http://sghs.org).

GETTING THERE AND AROUND

U.S. 17 goes directly through Darien. The closest I-95 exit is exit 49. Once you get off U.S. 17, Darien is a pretty bike-friendly place; you can park the car downtown and ride your bike east on Fort King George Drive to visit Fort King George.

SAPELO ISLAND

Another of those amazing, undeveloped Georgia barrier islands that can only be reached by boat, Sapelo also shares with some of those islands a link to the Gilded Age.

History

The Spanish established a Franciscan mission on the north end of the island in the 1500s. Sapelo didn't become fully integrated into the Lowcountry plantation culture until its purchase by Thomas Spalding in the early 1800s. After the Civil War, many of the nearly 500 former slaves on the island remained, with a partnership of freedmen buying land as early as 1871.

Hudson Motors mogul Howard Coffin bought all of Sapelo, except for the African

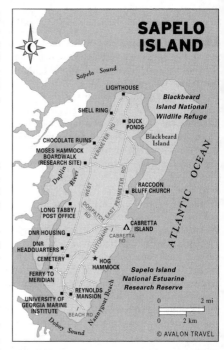

American communities, in 1912, building a palatial home and introducing a modern infrastructure. Among Coffin's visitors were two presidents, Calvin Coolidge and Herbert Hoover, and aviator Charles Lindbergh. Coffin hit hard times in the Great Depression and in 1934 sold Sapelo to tobacco heir R. J. Reynolds, who consolidated the island's African Americans into the single Hog Hammock community. By the mid-1970s the Reynolds family had sold the island to the state, again with the exception of the 430 acres of Hog Hammock, at the time with slightly more than 100 residents. Today most of the island is administered for marine research purposes under the designation of **Sapelo Island National Estuarine Research Reserve** (www.sapelonerr.org).

Sights

Once on the island, you can take guided tours under the auspices of the Georgia Department of Natural Resources. Wednesday 8:30am-12:30pm is a tour of the **R. J. Reynolds Mansion** (www.reynoldsonsapelo.com) on the south end along with the rest of the island, including Hog Hammock and the Long Tabby ruins. Saturday 9am-1pm is a tour of the historic **Sapelo Lighthouse** on the north end along with the rest of the island. June-Labor Day there's an extra lighthouse-island tour Friday 8:30am-12:30pm March-October on the last Tuesday of the month they do an extra-long day trip, 8:30am-3pm Tours cost $10 adults, $6 children, free under age 6. Call 912/437-3224 for reservations. You can also arrange private tours.

Another key sight on Sapelo is a 4,500-year-old **Native American shell ring** on the north end, one of the oldest and best preserved anywhere. Beach-lovers will especially enjoy the unspoiled strands on Sapelo, including the famous **Nannygoat Beach.**

Accommodations
While it's theoretically possible to stay overnight at the **R. J. Reynolds Mansion** (www.reynoldsonsapelo.com), it is limited to groups of at least 16 people. Realistically, to stay overnight on Sapelo you need a reservation with one of the locally owned guesthouses. One recommendation is Cornelia Bailey's six-room **The Wallow** (912/485-2206, call for rates) in historic Hog Hammock. The Baileys also run a small campground, **Comyam's Campground** (912/485-2206, $10 pp). Another option is **The Weekender** (912/485-2277, call for rates).

Getting There
Visitors to Sapelo must embark on the ferry at the **Sapelo Island Visitors Center** (912/437-3224, www.sapelonerr.org, Tues.-Fri. 7:30am-5:30pm, Sat. 8am-5:30pm, Sun. 1:30pm-5pm, $10 adults, $6 ages 6-18) in little Meridian, Georgia, on Highway 99 north of Darien. The visitors center actually has a nice nature hike of its own as well as an auditorium where you can see an informative video. From here it's a half-hour trip to Sapelo over the Doboy Sound. Keep in mind you must call in advance

for reservations before showing up at the visitors center. April-October it's recommended to call at least a week in advance.

ST. CATHERINE'S ISLAND
The interior of this beautiful island off the coast of Midway, Georgia, is off-limits to the public, but you can visit the beach up to the high-water mark by boat, enjoy its beautiful unspoiled beaches, and spy on local wildlife. While that's about all you can do, it's important to know a little of the interesting background of this island. Owned and administered by the St. Catherine's Island Foundation, it's unusual in that it has a 25-foot-high bluff on the northern end, an extraordinarily high geographic feature for a barrier island in this part of the world.

Once central to the Spanish missionary effort on the Georgia coast, St. Catherine's was found to be home to over 400 graves of Christianized Native Americans (a large shell ring also exists on the island). Declaration of Independence signer Button Gwinnett made a home here for a while until his death from a gunshot wound suffered in a duel in Savannah in 1777. After General Sherman's famous "40 acres and a mule" order, a freed slave named Tunis Campbell was governor of the island, living in Gwinnett's home. But when the order was rescinded, all former slaves had to leave for the mainland. In 1986, American Museum of Natural History archaeologist David Hurst Thomas began extensive research on Spanish artifacts left behind from the Santa Catalina de Guale mission, including foundations of living quarters, a kitchen, and a church—possibly the first church in what is now the United States. Today, however, the island, a National Historic Landmark, is better known as host to a New York Zoological Society project to recover injured or sick animals of endangered species and nurse them back to health for a possible return to the wild.

The closest marinas for the trip to the island's peaceful beaches are Shellman Fish Camp (1058 River Rd. NE, Townsend, 912/832-4331) in McIntosh County and Halfmoon Marina (171 Azalea Rd., Midway, 912/884-5819) in Liberty County.

BLACKBEARD ISLAND

While no one is positive if the namesake of Blackbeard Island actually landed here, the legends tell us he used it as a layover—even leaving some treasure here. Now federally administered as **Blackbeard Island National Wildlife Refuge** (912/652-4415, www.fws.gov/blackbeardisland), the island is accessible to the public by boat and gets about 10,000 visitors a year. Plenty of hiking trails exist, and the bird-watching is fantastic. It's also a major nesting ground for the endangered loggerhead turtle. Cycling is permitted, but overnight camping is not. For charters to Blackbeard, I recommend **SouthEast Adventures** (313 Mallory St., St. Simons, 912/638-6732) on St. Simons Island.

Cumberland Island and St. Marys

Actually two islands—Great Cumberland and Little Cumberland—Cumberland Island National Seashore is the largest and one of the oldest of Georgia's barrier islands, and also one of its most remote and least developed. Currently administered by the National Park Service, it's accessible only by ferry or private boat. Most visitors to Cumberland get here from the gateway town of St. Marys, Georgia, a nifty little fishing village that has so far managed to defy the increasing residential sprawl coming to the area.

ST. MARYS

Much like Brunswick to the north, the fishing town of St. Marys plays mostly a gateway role, in this case to the Cumberland Island National Seashore. That being said, it's a very friendly little waterfront community with undeniable charms of its own and a historic pedigree going back to the very beginnings of the nation.

History

As early as 1767, once the Spanish threat subsided, plans were made to establish a town, then known as Buttermilk Bluff, in the area near the Florida border. But it wasn't until 20 years later that a meeting was held on Cumberland Island to close the deal with Jacob Weed to purchase the tract—acquired by confiscation from two loyalist landowners—for the grand sum of $38. The first influx of immigration to the area came as French Canadian refugees from Acadia (who would become known as Cajuns in Louisiana) came to St. Marys after being deported by the British. Another group of French speakers came, fleeing Toussaint Louverture's slave rebellion in Haiti.

During the colonial period, St. Marys was the southernmost U.S. city and enjoyed not only importance as a seaport but was militarily important as well. Ironically, this strategic importance came into play more during the conflict with Great Britain than with anything to do with the Spanish. In 1812 a British force took over Cumberland Island and St. Marys, with a contingent embarking up the river to track down the customs collection. However, in a bloody skirmish they were ambushed by American troops firing from the riverbanks. They vowed to avenge their loss by burning every building between the St. Marys and the Altamaha Rivers, but the ensuing peace treaty ending the War of 1812 brought a ceasefire.

Unlike towns such as Darien, which was put to the torch by Union troops, St. Marys was saved from destruction in the Civil War. The lumber industry boomed after that conflict as well as the local fishing and shrimping industries. A hotel was built in 1916 (and hosted Marjorie Kinnan Rawlings, author of *The Yearlings*), but tourists didn't discover the area until the 1970s. It was also then that the U.S. Navy built the huge nuclear submarine base at Kings Bay, currently the area's largest employer with almost 10,000 employees. Development has increased in the area, with suburban sprawl beginning to cover the area like mushrooms after a heavy rain. Indeed, there's so much growth in the St. Marys-Camden County area that it's increasingly considered an outpost of

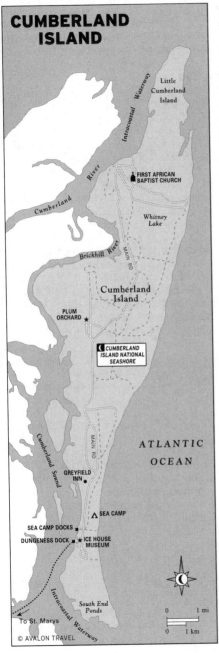

CUMBERLAND ISLAND

Little Cumberland Island

Intracoastal Waterway

River

Cumberland

FIRST AFRICAN BAPTIST CHURCH

Whitney Lake

Brickhill River

MAIN RD

Cumberland Island

PLUM ORCHARD

CUMBERLAND ISLAND NATIONAL SEASHORE

ATLANTIC OCEAN

Cumberland Sound

MAIN RD

GREYFIELD INN

SEA CAMP

SEA CAMP DOCKS
DUNGENESS DOCK   ICE HOUSE MUSEUM

Intracoastal Waterway

South End Ponds

To St. Marys

0   1 mi
0   1 km

© AVALON TRAVEL

the huge Jacksonville, Florida, metropolitan area to the south.

Orientation

As in Brunswick, the waterfront faces opposite the ocean and is instead oriented west, toward a river, in this case the St. Marys River. Most activity in downtown St. Marys happens up and down Osborne Street, which perhaps not coincidentally is also how you get to the **Cumberland Island Visitor Center** (113 St. Marys St., 912/882-4335, daily 8am-4:30pm) and from there board the *Cumberland Queen* for the trip to the island.

Sights

Tying the past to the present, it's only fitting that the home of the Kings Bay Submarine Base (which is not open to the public) has a museum dedicated to the "Silent Service." The **St. Marys Submarine Museum** (102 St. Marys St., 912/882-2782, www.stmaryssubmuseum. com, Tues.-Sat. 10am-4pm, Sun. 1pm-5pm, $5 adults, $3 children) on the riverfront has a variety of exhibits honoring the contribution of American submariners. There's a neat interactive exhibit where you can look through the genuine sub periscope that sticks out of the roof of the museum.

The most notable historic home in St. Marys is the **Orange Hall House Museum** (311 Osborne St., 912/576-3644, www.orange-hall.org, Tues.-Sat. 9am-4pm, Sun. 1pm-4pm, $3 adults, $1 children). This beautiful Greek Revival home, circa 1830, survived the Civil War and was the center of town social life during the Roaring '20s, when it was owned by a succession of socialites from up north. The home is gorgeous inside and out, particularly during the holidays when it gets the full decorative treatment.

Events and Recreation

As a nod to its Cajun history, St. Marys hosts a heck of a **Mardi Gras Festival** each February, closing down six blocks of the riverfront for a parade. There's also live entertainment, vendors, and a costume ball.

For outdoor recreation near St. Marys, go to **Crooked River State Park** (6222 Charlie Smith Sr. Hwy., 912/882-5256, www.gastateparks.org, office Fri.-Wed. 8am-10pm, Thurs. 8am-5pm), which is not only a great place to put in for kayaking trips, including jaunts to Cumberland Island, but also has a wide range of lodging options as well. A key stop on the Colonial Coast Birding Trail, Crooked River features its own nature center and is near a historic site just upriver, the tabby ruins of the McIntosh Sugar Works—actually a lumber mill from the early 1800s. The easiest way to get here is to take I-95 exit 3 and go about eight miles east. To rent kayaks or book kayak and ecotours, try **Up the Creek Xpeditions** (111 Osborne St., 912/882-0911, www.upthecreekx.com), which can take you all around the area, including out to Cumberland Island.

Accommodations

Don't even think about staying at a chain hotel when you're in St. Marys. Stay at one of these cute historic inns for a song. The most notable lodging for historic as well as economic value is the 18-room **Riverview Hotel** (105 Osborne St., 912/882-3242, www.riverviewhotelstmarys.com, under $100). The waterfront locale, like many old hotels in this area, has a great retro feel. It was built in the 1920s and has hosted such notables as author Marjorie Rawlings, John Rockefeller, poet Sidney Lanier, and Andrew Carnegie. **◖ Emma's Bed and Breakfast** (300 West Conyers St., 912/882-4199, www.emmasbedandbreakfast.com, under $200) is situated on four beautiful acres in downtown St. Marys in a grand Southern-style mansion with all the trappings and hospitality you'd expect. You can also hang out on the stunning veranda at the historic **◖ Goodbread House** (209 Osborne St., 912/882-7490, www.goodbreadhouse.com, under $200), which offers rates below $100 in the off-season. The 1870 house features sumptuous interiors, including a classic dining room in which awesome breakfasts are served.

More outdoorsy visitors can stay at cottage, tent, or RV sites at **Crooked River State Park**

(6222 Charlie Smith Sr. Hwy., 912/882-5256, www.gastateparks.org). There are 62 tent and RV sites (about $22) and 11 cottages ($85-110) as well as primitive camping ($25).

Food

St. Marys cannot compete in culinary sophistication with Charleston or Savannah, but it does have some of the freshest seafood around. One of the best places to eat seafood on the waterfront in St. Marys is at **Lang's Marina Restaurant** (307 W. St. Marys St., 912/882-4432, lunch Tues.-Fri. 11am-2pm, dinner Wed.-Sat. 5pm-9pm, $15-20). The other premier seafood place is **Trolley's** (109 W. St. Marys St., 912/882-1525, Sun.-Thurs. 11am-9pm, Fri.-Sat. 11am-10pm, $15-20).

Information and Services

The **St. Marys Convention and Visitors Bureau** (406 Osborne St., 912/882-4000, www.stmaryswelcome.com) is a good source of information not only for the town but for Cumberland Island, but keep in mind that this is not actually where you catch the ferry to the island.

Getting There and Around

Take I-95 exit 3 for Kingsland-St. Marys Road (Hwy. 40). This becomes Osborne Road, the main drag of St. Marys, as it gets closer to town. The road by the waterfront is St. Marys Street.

◖ CUMBERLAND ISLAND NATIONAL SEASHORE

Not only one of the richest estuarine environments in the world, Cumberland Island National Seashore (912/882-4335, www.nps.gov/cuis) is quite simply one of the most beautiful and romantic places on the planet, as everyone learned when the "it" couple of their day, John F. Kennedy Jr. and Carolyn Bessette, were wed on the island in 1996. With more than 16 miles of gorgeous beach and an area of over 17,000 acres, there's no shortage of beauty either, and the island's already remote feel is further enhanced by the efforts that have been taken to protect it from development.

Cumberland is far from pristine: It has been used for timbering and cotton, is dotted with evocative abandoned ruins, and hosts a band of beautiful but voracious wild horses. But it is still a remarkable island paradise in a world where those kinds of locations are getting harder and harder to find.

History

Like modern-day Americans, the Timucuan Indians also revered this site, visiting it often for shellfish and for sassafras, a medicinal herb common on the island. Cumberland's size and great natural harbor made it a perfect base for Spanish friars, who established the first missionary on the island, San Pedro Mocama, in 1587. In fact, the first Christian martyr in Georgia was created on Cumberland, when Father Pedro Martinez was killed by the Indians.

As part of his effort to push the Spanish back into Florida for good, General James Oglethorpe established Fort William at the south end of Cumberland—the remains of which are now underwater—and a hunting lodge named Dungeness, an island place-name that persists today. While land grants were made in the 1760s, they saw little follow-through, and by the time of naturalist William Bartram's visit in 1774, Cumberland Island was almost uninhabited. But inevitably, the Lowcountry planters' culture made its way down to Cumberland, which was soon the site of 15 thriving plantations and small farms. After the Revolution, the heirs of one of its heroes, General Nathanael Greene, established Dungeness Plantation in 1802, its central building a now-gone tabby structure right on top of an ancient shell mound.

Actual military action wouldn't come to Cumberland until the War of 1812, when the British came in force and occupied the island for two months, using Dungeness as their headquarters. In the process they freed 1,500 slaves, who would then emigrate to various British colonies. In 1818, Revolutionary War hero General "Light-Horse" Harry Lee—father of Robert E. Lee—arrived on Cumberland's

shore, in failing health and determined to see the home of his old friend General Greene one last time. He died a month later and was buried here, his son returning later to erect a gravestone. Light-Horse Harry remained on Cumberland until 1913, when his remains were taken to Lexington, Virginia, to be beside those of his son. His gravestone on Cumberland remains to this day.

The Civil War—and another freeing of slaves—came again in the 1860s, when Union troops occupied the island. At war's end Cumberland was set aside as a home for freed African Americans—part of the famous and ill-fated "40 acres and a mule" proposal—but politics intervened: Most of Cumberland's slaves were rounded up and taken to Amelia Island, Florida, although some settled at the north end (the "Settlement" area today).

As elsewhere on the Georgia coast, the Industrial Revolution came to Cumberland in the form of a vacation getaway for a mega-tycoon, in this case Thomas Carnegie, industrialist and brother of the better-known Andrew Carnegie of Carnegie Library fame. Carnegie built a new, even grander Dungeness, which suffered the same fate as its predecessor in a 1959 fire.

Cumberland Island narrowly avoided becoming the next Hilton Head—literally—in 1969 when Hilton Head developer Charles Fraser bought the northern tip of the island and began bulldozing a runway. The dwindling but still influential Carnegies joined with the Georgia Conservancy to broker an agreement that resulted in dubbing Cumberland a National Seashore in 1972, saving it from further development. A $7.5 million gift from the Mellon Foundation enabled the purchase of Fraser's tract and the eventual incorporation of the island within the National Park system.

Sights

The ferry typically stops at two docks a short distance from each other, the Sea Camp dock and the Dungeness dock. At 4pm, Rangers offer a "Dockside" interpretive program at the Sea Camp. A short way farther north at the

THE GOLDEN ISLES

WILD HORSES OF CUMBERLAND

© PAULA STEPHENS/123RF.COM

horses on the beach of Cumberland Island

Cumberland Island's famous wild horses are not actually direct descendants of the first horses brought to the island by Spanish and English settlers, although certainly feral horses have ranged the island for most of recorded history. The current population of 250 or so is actually descended from horses brought to the island by the Carnegie family in the 1920s.

Gorgeous and evocative though these magnificent animals are, they have a big appetite for vegetation and are frankly not the best thing for this sensitive barrier island ecosystem. But their beauty and visceral impact on the visitor is undeniable, which means the horses are likely to stay as long as nature will have them. And yes, these really are *wild* horses, meaning you shouldn't feed them even if they approach you for food, and you certainly won't be riding them.

Dungeness Dock, Rangers offer a "Dungeness Footsteps Tour" at 10am and 12:45pm, concentrating on the historic sites at the southern end of the island. Also at the Dungeness dock is the little **Ice House Museum** (912/882-4336, daily 9am-5pm, free) containing a range of exhibits on the island's history from Native American times to the present day.

Down near the docks are also where you'll find the stirring, almost spooky **Dungeness Ruins** and the nearby grave marker of Light-Horse Harry Lee. Controversy continues to this day as to the cause of the 1866 fire that destroyed the old Dungeness home. Some say it was those freed slaves on the north end who lit the blaze, but others say it was the plantation's final owner, Robert Stafford, who did it out of spite after his former slaves refused to work for him after the war.

Moving north on the Main Road (Grand Ave.) you come to **Greyfield Inn** (904/261-6408, www.greyfieldinn.com). Because it is a privately owned hotel, don't trespass through the grounds. A good way farther north, just off the main road, you'll find the restored, rambling 20-room mansion **Plum Orchard,** another Carnegie legacy. Guided tours of Plum Orchard are available on the second and fourth Sunday of the month ($6 plus ferry fare); reserve a space at 912/882-4335.

At the very north end of the island, accessible only by foot or by bicycle, is the former freedmen's community simply known as **The Settlement,** featuring a small cemetery and the now-famous **First African Baptist Church** (daily dawn-dusk)—a 1937 version of the 1893 original—a humble and rustic one-room church made of whitewashed logs in which the 1996 Kennedy-Bessette marriage took place.

Sports and Recreation

There are more than 50 miles of trails all over Cumberland, about 17 miles of nearly isolated beach to comb, and acres of maritime forest to explore—the latter an artifact of Cumberland's unusually old age for a barrier island. Upon arrival, you might want to rent a bicycle at the **Sea Camp docks** (no reservations, arrange rentals on the ferry, adult bikes $16 per day, youth bikes $10, $20 overnight).

Shell-and-sharks-teeth collectors might want to explore south of Dungeness Beach as well as between the docks. Unlike some parks, you are allowed to take shells and fossils off the island.

Wildlife enthusiasts will be in heaven. More than 300 species of birds have been recorded on the island, which is also a favorite nesting ground for female loggerhead turtles in the late summer. Of course, the most iconic image of Cumberland Island is its famous **wild horses,** a free-roaming band of feral equines who traverse the island year-round, grazing as they please.

Accommodations

The only "civilized" lodging on Cumberland is the 13-room **C Greyfield Inn** (Grand Ave., 904/261-6408, www.greyfieldinn.com, $475), ranked by the American Inn Association as one of the country's "Ten Most Romantic Inns." Opened in 1962 as a hotel, the Greyfield was originally built in 1900 as the home of the Carnegies. The room rates includes meals, transportation, tours, and bicycle usage.

Many visitors opt to camp on Cumberland (reservations 877/860-6787, limit of seven nights, $4) in one of three basic ways: at the **Sea Camp,** which has restrooms and shower facilities and allows fires; the remote **Stafford Beach,** a good hike from the docks and with no facilities; and pure wilderness camping farther north at **Hickory Hill, Yankee Paradise,** and **Brickman Bluff,** all of which are a several-mile hike away, do not permit fires, and have no facilities of any kind. Reservations are required for camping. All trash must be packed out on departure, as there are no refuse facilities on the island. Responsible alcohol consumption is limited to those 21 and over.

Getting There and Around

The most vital information about Cumberland is how to get ashore in the first place. Most visitors do this by purchasing a ticket on the *Cumberland Queen* at the **Cumberland Island Visitor Center** (113 St. Marys St., St. Marys, 912/882-4335, daily 8am-4:30pm, $20 adults, $18 seniors, $12 under age 13) on the waterfront at St. Marys. The ferry ride is 45 minutes each way. You can call for reservations Monday-Friday 10am-4pm The ferry does not transport pets, bicycles, kayaks, or cars. However, you can rent bicycles at the Sea Camp docks once you're there. Every visitor to Cumberland over age 16 must pay a $4 entry fee, including campers.

March 1-November 30, the ferry leaves St. Marys at 9am and 11:45am, returning from Cumberland at 10:15am and 4:45pm March 1-September 30 Wednesday-Saturday, there's an additional 2:45pm departure from Cumberland back to St. Marys. December 1-February 28 the ferry operates only Thursday-Monday.

One of the quirks of Cumberland, resulting from the unusual way in which it passed into federal hands, is the existence of some private property on which you mustn't trespass, except where trails specifically allow it. Also, unlike the general public, these private landowners are allowed to use vehicles. For these reasons, it's best to make sure you have a map of the island, which you can get before you board the ferry at St. Marys. There are no real stores and very few facilities on Cumberland. *Bring whatever you think you'll need,* whether it be food, water, medicine, suntan lotion, insect repellent, or otherwise.

BACKGROUND

The Land

From its highest point at Brasstown Bald overlooking the Tennessee border, to the sandy barrier islands of the coast, Georgia's geography and geology work together. Though it's hundreds of miles away, the Blue Ridge mountains of North Georgia have a major influence on the coast, and it's there that your overview of Georgia's natural landscape should begin.

GEOGRAPHY AND GEOLOGY
Regions

The **Blue Ridge,** southernmost part of the Appalachian Mountains and named for its distinctive haze, pushes 100 miles into the central and northeast section of North Georgia.

Formed from a collision about 300 million years ago between the North American and African continents, the Appalachians were originally at least as tall as the Himalayas are today. But erosion has taken its toll, and they are mere shadows of their former selves. The erosion has had the side effect of making the mountains' rich bounty of gold, copper, marble, and other minerals particularly accessible, the extraction of which has molded the economic and cultural character of all of North Georgia. The mountainous topography has also contributed to a more benign economic sector, with hikers, rafters, and other outdoor

© KEITH SPAULDING/123RF.COM

CONTINENTAL SHELF

SOUTH CAROLINA

NORTH CAROLINA

Tides ±3 feet

GEORGIA

Tides ±10 feet

Shelf

Continental Shelf

FLORIDA

ATLANTIC OCEAN

Tides ±3 feet

© AVALON TRAVEL

20 miles wide, so named because it's there where rivers make a drop toward the sea, generally becoming navigable. Georgia's key cities on the fall line are, from east to west, Augusta on the Savannah River, Milledgeville on the Oconee River, Macon on the Ocmulgee River, and Columbus on the Chattahoochee River.

The **Upper Coastal Plain** begins adjacent to the fall line zone. There you can sometimes spot sand hills, usually only a few feet in elevation, generally thought to be the vestigial remains of primordial sand dunes and offshore sandbars. The Ohoopee Natural Dunes area near Swainsboro is the most notable example. Well beyond the fall line is the **Lower Coastal Plain,** gradually built up over 150 million years by sedimentary runoff from the Appalachian Mountains. The entire Coastal Plain was sea bottom for much of the earth's history, and in some eroded areas you can see dramatic proof of this in prehistoric shells, sharks' teeth, and fossilized whalebones and oyster beds, often many miles inland.

Sea level has fluctuated wildly with climate and geological changes through the eons. At various times over the last 50 million years, the Coastal Plain has submerged, surfaced, and submerged again. Its particular soil types nurtured the enormous primordial Longleaf Pine forests of pre-European contact. A fire-activated habitat, the longleaf forests were perpetuated by the Native American habit of setting huge controlled burns.

Rivers

We know that it's in Appalachia where so much of the coast's freshwater (in the form of rain) comes together and flows southeast, in the form of alluvial, or sediment-bearing, rivers, to the Atlantic Ocean. But the specific origins of many of Georgia's mighty rivers are not always so obvious.

The headwaters of the great Savannah River, for example, are near deep Tallulah Gorge in extreme North Georgia. The Flint River, one of the South's most scenic, essentially begins as runoff drainage near Atlanta (the creek that eventually becomes the Flint actually runs

adventurers coming to see the hundreds of waterfalls all through the Blue Ridge region and its foothills.

Along the border with the Carolinas, the Blue Ridge crest in places is part of the **Eastern Continental Divide.** The Blue Ridge doesn't extend into the northwest portion of Georgia however, which is often called the **"Ridge and Valley"** country. There you will find smaller ranges like the Cohuttas, and the Cumberland Plateau. They are separated from the Blue Ridge by several geologic formations and faults, along the general route marked by Highway 5. The Blue Ridge's southern boundary and the beginning of the Piedmont region are generally considered to be along the Brevard Fault.

Georgia's most populous geological region, the **Piedmont** is a rocky, hilly area. This is where you will find stone outcroppings, such as the great granite features of Stone Mountain and Arabia Mountain, both outside Atlanta. The Piedmont is bordered on the east by the **fall line,** an ancient Mesozoic shoreline about through a culvert under a runway at the Atlanta airport). Some rivers form out of the confluence of smaller rivers, such as Georgia's mighty Altamaha, actually the child of the Ocmulgee and Oconee Rivers in the middle of the state.

While most Georgia rivers begin as mere trickles down from the Blue Ridge, visitors from drier climates are sometimes shocked to see how huge the rivers can get farther towards the coast of Georgia, how wide and voluminous as they saunter to the sea, their seemingly slow speed belying the massive power they contain. To be sure, damming and dredging have enlarged the sheer quantity of water in many of them.

The **blackwater river** is a particularly interesting Southern phenomenon, duplicated elsewhere only in South America and one example each in New York and Michigan. While alluvial rivers generally originate in highlands and carry with them a large amount of sediment, blackwater rivers originate in low-lying areas and move slowly toward the sea, carrying with them very little sediment.

Rather, their dark tea color comes from the tannic acid of decaying vegetation all along their banks, washed out by the slow, inexorable movement of the river toward the sea. While I don't necessarily recommend drinking it, "blackwater" is for the most part remarkably clean and hygienic despite its dirty color.

Blackwater courses featured prominently in this guide are Ebenezer Creek near Savannah and the Suwannee River, which originates in the Okefenokee Swamp and empties in the Gulf of Mexico. Georgia's Altamaha River is a hybrid of sorts because it is partially fed by the blackwater Ohoopee River.

With very few exceptions, Georgia's rivers have been heavily dammed, mostly for hydroelectric power. The Altamaha is the only major undammed river. The Flint River, while heavily impounded downstream, has a nearly 200-mile-long stretch of undammed course.

Where there are dams there are lakes, and Georgia has plenty of artificially-constructed reservoirs, most converted into recreational and fishing areas. During the big push for hydropower in the early 20th century, no beautiful natural feature was immune; even portions of scenic Tallulah Gorge were submerged in the craze to electrify metro areas, primarily Atlanta. Chief examples of manufactured, heavily-trafficked lakes today include Lake Lanier, Lake Seminole, Lake Burton, Lake Chatuge, Lake Rabun, Lake Sinclair, Lake Oconee, and the multiple Savannah River lakes: Hartwell, Russell, and Clark's Hill (Strom Thurmond).

FLINT RIVER

It's not the biggest or the most undeveloped river in Georgia, but the Flint takes its place among the most scenic and naturally vital in the state. It begins humbly, as ground seepage in a culvert south of Atlanta, its headwaters trickling under a runway at Hartsfield-Jackson International Airport.

Over the course of the next 220 miles, the Flint River runs free and undammed, a remarkable resource for wildlife and recreation alike. The large wetlands the Flint helps feed are the farthest inland swamps in the United States.

Though the Flint is eventually impounded near Albany and several points south, this long unfettered run is prized as prime habitat for shoal bass, the Halloween darter, freshwater mussels, crayfish, and the endangered shoals spider lily, first discovered by William Bartram in the 1770s.

Many of these species, some found only in this area, faced imminent threat in 1974, when a hydroelectric dam was proposed in the Sprewell Bluff area on the east side of Pine Mountain, one of the richest habitats on the Flint River. Then-Governor Jimmy Carter vetoed the project, a courageous move that helped establish the modern conservation movement. Sprewell Bluff Wildlife Management Area today is a popular spot for anglers, rafters, hunters, birders, and hikers.

Estuaries

The place where a river interfaces with the ocean is called an estuary, and it's perhaps the most interesting place of all. Estuaries are heavily tidal in nature (indeed, the word derives from *aestus,* Latin for tide) and feature brackish water and heavy silt content. The Georgia portion of the U.S. coast typically has about a 6-8-foot tidal range, and the coastal ecosystem depends on this steady ebb and flow for life itself. At high tide, shellfish open and feed. At low tide, they literally clam up, keeping saltwater inside their shells until the next tide comes. Waterbirds and small mammals feed on shellfish and other animals at low tide, when their prey is exposed. High tide brings an influx of fish and nutrients from the sea, in turn drawing predators like dolphins, who often come into tidal creeks to feed.

Salt Marsh

All this water action in both directions—freshwater coming from inland, saltwater encroaching from the Atlantic—results in the phenomenon of the salt marsh, the single most recognizable feature of the Georgia coast. (Freshwater marshes are more rare, Florida's Everglades being perhaps the premier example.)

Far more than just a transitional zone between land and water, marsh is also nature's nursery. Plant and animal life in marshes tends to be not only diverse, but encompassing multitudes. Though you may not see its denizens easily, on close inspection you'll find the marsh absolutely teeming with creatures. Visually, the main identifying feature of a salt marsh is its distinctive, reed-like marsh grasses, adapted to survive in brackish water. Like estuaries, marshes and all life in them are heavily influenced by the tides, which bring in nutrients.

Beaches and Barrier Islands

The often stunningly beautiful, broad beaches of Georgia are almost all situated on barrier islands, long islands parallel to the shoreline and separated from the mainland by a sheltered body of water. Because they are formed by the deposit of sediment by offshore currents, they change shape over the years, with the general pattern of deposit going from north to south (that is, the northern end will begin eroding first).

Most of the barrier islands are geologically quite young, only being formed within the last 25,000 years or so. Natural erosion, by current and by storm, combined with the accelerating effects of dredging for local port activity has quickened the decline of many barrier islands. As the name indicates, barrier islands are another of nature's safeguards against hurricane damage. Though ephemeral by nature, barrier islands have played an important role in the area's settlement. In fact, nearly every major settlement on the Georgia coast today, including Savannah, Darien, and Brunswick, is built on the vestiges of massive barrier islands that once guarded a primordial shoreline many miles inland from the present one.

By far the largest of these ancient barrier islands, now on dry land, is the Trail Ridge, which runs from Jesup, Georgia, alongside the Okefenokee Swamp down to Starke, Florida. The Trail Ridge's height along its distance made it a favorite route first for Native Americans and then for railroads, which still run along its crest today. The Trail Ridge is actually responsible for the formation of the Okefenokee Swamp. The Ridge effectively acts as a levee on the swamp's eastern side, preventing its drainage to the sea.

CLIMATE

One word comes to mind when one thinks about Southern climate: hot. That's the first word that occurs to Southerners as well, but virtually every survey of why residents are attracted to the area puts the climate at the top of the list. Go figure.

How hot is hot? The average July high in Savannah is about 92°F. In Dalton on the other end of the state near the mountains, it's only a couple of degrees less during the same month. The wettest months do vary. Inland, the wettest months are often January and July. But on the coast, August and September are the wettest months. Despite what you might think, the coast doesn't get the highest precipitation in the state; the Blue Ridge sees significantly higher rainfall on average and is indeed one of the rainiest areas in the U.S.; something to keep in mind when camping.

In North Georgia things can get pretty frigid during the winter, as you might expect. The average January low in Hiawassee in the Blue Ridge is about 28°F. Most North Georgia towns will see maybe a week's worth of snow in a normal year; elsewhere in the state snow is largely absent, and on the coast almost entirely unheard of. Winters on the coast are quite mild, but can seem much colder than they actually are because of the dampness in the air. The average January low in Savannah is a balmy 39°F.

Hurricanes

The major weather phenomenon for residents and visitors alike is the mighty hurricane. These massive storms, with counterclockwise-rotating bands of clouds and winds pushing 200 miles per hour, are an ever-present danger to the coast in June-November of each year.

Historically the Georgia coast has been relatively safe, if not immune, from major hurricane activity. In fact, as of this writing the last really major storm to directly hit the Georgia coast was in 1898. Meteorologists chalk this up to the Georgia coast's relatively sheltered, concave position relative to the rest of the Southeastern coastline, as well as prevailing pressure and wind patterns that tend to deflect the oncoming storms.

Local TV, websites, and print media can be counted on to give more than ample warning in the event a hurricane is approaching the area during your visit. Whatever you do, do not discount the warnings. It's not worth it. If the locals are preparing to leave, you should too.

ENVIRONMENTAL ISSUES

The Piedmont area of Georgia, primarily around the Atlanta area, continues to experience rampant development, both in the form of residential areas as well as the highway system that serves them. As Atlanta spreads outward, it pushes more and more environmental issues on the surrounding area, particularly air pollution caused by auto traffic and stress on drinking water resources.

The coast of Georgia is experiencing a double whammy: Not only is it also under enormous development pressure, its distinctive wetlands are extraordinarily sensitive to human interference. New and often-poorly planned subdivisions and resort communities continue to pop up, though the recent economic downturn slowed that trend somewhat. Vastly increased port activity, particularly in Savannah, is taking a devastating toll on the salt marsh and surrounding barrier islands.

Logging

Logging and the timber industry have had an enormous effect on Georgia from top to bottom. The sturdy live oaks of the Sea Islands served to defend a young country, forming the basis for the hulls of mighty warships for the fledgling American Navy, such as the U.S.S. *Constitution*. By the middle of the 19th century, Georgia was the country's leading lumber producer and the leading manufacturer of naval stores such as turpentine and rosin. Naval stores were mostly derived from the vast and ancient longleaf pine forests of the Upper Coastal Plain, a species virtually logged to extinction as a result.

By 1890, Georgia sawmills were cutting more than 1.6 million board feet per day. The "pristine" Okefenokee Swamp was by no means immune; most of its old-growth cypresses were logged extensively during that period.

The mountains of North Georgia weren't immune either, and huge environmental damage was caused there as a direct result of logging. The copper industry caused extensive clear-cutting, the timber being needed for the smelters. Gold mining caused entire mountainsides to be hosed or detonated away. Shipment methods for felled timber involved makeshift dams, which were then blown up to intentionally cause the cut trees to flood downstream so they could go to market.

The cumulative effect of this devastation and overharvesting caused the number of lumber mills in North Georgia to decline dramatically in the early 20th century, accompanied by a decline in population. Indeed, this calamity directly brought about the national forest movement in the United States.

One of the first acquisitions was a 30,000-acre tract bought by the federal government in 1911, which would form the basis for the later, and much more enormous, Chattahoochee National Forest, now comprising over 700,000 acres, including 30,000-acre Cohutta Wilderness Area, largest in the eastern United States. To be sure, the National Forests also serve the logging industry as well, and their tracts are culled extensively to this day.

A new way forward came in the 1930s when Charles Herty, a chemist at the University of Georgia, and incidentally their first football coach, came up with a process to make white paper out of young pines. Thus began the great conversion of much old agricultural land to truly vast pine farms, which you're almost certain to see driving anywhere around Georgia's Coastal Plain. Those sulfurous paper mills you often see, and mostly smell, are where those pines eventually end up.

Mining

You don't often hear about it, but Georgia is actually one of the most heavily mined states in the country, and has been for much of its history. The most obvious example is the great gold rush of the 1830s and 1840s, the first in the country. Centered on the large and easily accessed vein of high-quality gold in the Dahlonega area, the gold rush not only brought an enormous financial boon to the state, it encouraged speedy settlement in the form of "Land Lotteries." Sadly, in order to make room for the settlers and eliminate competing claims to the gold, it was decided that North

Georgia's original inhabitants, the Cherokee Indians, would have to go. Thus began the tragic Trail of Tears, in which the Cherokee were removed at gunpoint to march in desolation to new homes in the Oklahoma Territory far away.

The gold mining brought environmental destruction, especially after the more easily obtained nuggets were panned from creeks and streams. Eventually huge hoses were used to literally wash away entire mountainsides, the ore then crushed and sifted for gold. Then came the dynamite and even more destruction.

Iron ore was the preferred mining industry in the northwest portion of the state in the Ridge and Valley country, but the techniques were similarly invasive. Stone is also extensively quarried throughout Georgia, including "Elberton granite" in the northeast portion of the state and marble from Pickens County in North Georgia.

However, the leading mineral export of Georgia is kaolin, or clay, harvested in huge quantities from cities in the Upper Coastal Plain, chiefly around Sandersville.

Air Pollution

Despite growing awareness of the issue, air pollution is still a big problem in Georgia. Automobile traffic around metro Atlanta contributes to poor air quality and appreciable amounts of smog. Paper mills on the coast still operate, putting out their distinctive rotten-eggs odor, and auto emissions standards are notoriously lax in Georgia. The biggest culprits, though, are coal-powered electric plants, which are the norm throughout the region and which continue to pour large amounts of toxins into the atmosphere.

Flora and Fauna

FLORA

The most iconic plant life of the region is the **Southern live oak,** the official state tree of Georgia. Named because of its evergreen nature, a live oak is technically any one of a number of evergreens in the *Quercus* genus, many of which reside on the Georgia coast; but in local practice, it almost always refers to the Southern live oak. Capable of living over 1,000 years and possessing wood of legendary resilience, the Southern live oak is one of nature's most magnificent creations.

Fittingly, the iconic plant of the coast grows on the branches of the live oak. Contrary to popular opinion, **Spanish moss** is neither Spanish nor moss. It's an air plant, a wholly indigenous cousin to the pineapple. Also contrary to folklore, Spanish moss is not a parasite nor does it harbor parasites while living on an oak tree, though it can after it has already fallen to the ground. Also growing on the bark of a live oak, especially right after a rain shower, is the **resurrection fern,** which can stay dormant for amazingly long periods of time, only to spring back to life with the introduction of a little water.

Other types of oaks are common throughout Georgia, including white, scarlet, and red oaks. The live oak may be Georgia's state tree, but far and away its most important commercial tree is the pine, used for paper, lumber, and turpentine. Rarely seen in the wild today due to tree farming, which has covered most of southern Georgia, the dominant species is now the **slash pine,** often seen in long rows on either side of rural highways. Before the introduction of large-scale monoculture tree farming, however, a rich variety of native pines flourished in the upland forest inland from the maritime forest, including **longleaf** and **loblolly** pines.

Right up there with live oaks and Spanish moss in terms of instant recognition would have to be the colorful, ubiquitous **azalea,** a flowering shrub of the *Rhododendron* genus.

Over 10,000 varieties have been cultivated through the centuries, with quite a wide range of them on display during blooming season: March-April. The Masters golf tournament in Augusta, in particular, has been closely associated with the azalea from its inception due to the masterful groundskeeping at Augusta National Golf Club.

Another great floral display comes from the **camellia,** a cold-hardy evergreen with flowers that generally bloom in late winter (January-March). Other colorful ornamentals of the area include the ancient **Southern magnolia,** a native evergreen with distinctive large white flowers (evolved before the advent of bees in North America); and the **flowering dogwood,** which for its very hard wood—great for daggers, hence its original name "dagwood"—is actually quite fragile.

Up in the mountains, throngs of leaf-watchers come every autumn to enjoy the shifting colors of the Eastern cottonwood, the black walnut, the chalk maple, the white ash, and all kinds of hickory trees. Purely indigenous trees also on colorful display include the black tupelo, the red maple, the sycamore, and the sassafras. The evergreen Fraser fir of Christmas tree fame grows naturally only in Fannin County.

Moving into watery areas, you'll find the remarkable **bald cypress,** a flood-resistant conifer recognizable by its tufted top, its great height (up to 130 feet), and its distinctive "knees," parts of the root that project above the waterline and which are believed to help stabilize the tree in lowland areas. Much prized for its beautiful, pest-resistant wood, great stands of cypress once dominated the coast; sadly, overharvesting and destruction of wetlands has made the magnificent sight of this ancient, dignified species much less common. The acres of **smooth cordgrass** for which the Golden Isles are named are plants of the *Spartina alterniflora* species.

FAUNA
On the Land

Perhaps the most iconic land animal, or semi-land animal, anyway, of Georgia is the legendary **American alligator,** the only species of crocodile native to the area. Contrary to their fierce reputation, locals know these massive reptiles, 6-12 feet long as adults, to be quite shy. If you come in the colder months you won't see one at all, since alligators require warm temperatures to become active and feed. Often all you'll see is a couple of eyebrow ridges sticking out of the water, and a gator lying still in a shallow creek can easily be mistaken for a floating log. But should you see one or more gators basking in the sun—a favorite activity on warm days for these cold-blooded creatures—it's best to admire them from afar. A mother alligator, in particular, will destroy anything that comes near her nest. Despite the alligator's short, stubby legs, they run amazingly fast on land, faster than you, in fact.

If you're driving on a country road at night, be on the lookout for **white-tailed deer,** which, besides being quite beautiful, also pose a serious road hazard. Because development has dramatically reduced the habitat and therefore the numbers of their natural predators, deer are very plentiful throughout the area.

The coast hosts fairly large populations of playful **river otters.** Not to be confused with the larger sea otters off the West Coast, these fast-swimming members of the weasel family inhabit inland waterways and marshy areas, with dominant males sometimes ranging as much as 50 miles within a single waterway.

While you're unlikely to encounter an otter, if you're camping you might easily run into the **raccoon,** an exceedingly intelligent and crafty relative of the bear, sharing that larger animal's resourcefulness in stealing your food. Though nocturnal, raccoons will feed whenever food is available. Rabies is prevalent in the raccoon population and you should always, always keep your distance.

Another common campsite nuisance, the **opossum** is a shy, primitive creature that is much more easily discouraged. North America's only marsupial, an opossum's usual "defense" against predators is to play dead. That said, however, they have an immunity to snake venom and often feed on the reptiles, even the most poisonous ones.

Once fairly common in Georgia, the **black bear** has suffered from hunting and habitat destruction. There are about 5,000 left in the wild in Georgia, in three areas: The North Georgia mountains, the Ocmulgee River watershed in Middle Georgia, and the Okefenokee Swamp.

In the Water

Without a doubt the most magnificent denizen, if only part-time, of the Southeastern coast is the **North American right whale,** which can approach 60 feet in length. Each year from December to March the mothers give birth to their calves and nurse them in the warm waters off the Georgia coast in an eons-old ritual. (In the summers they like to hang around the rich fishing grounds off the New England coast, though biologists still can't account for their whereabouts at other times of the year.) Whaling and encounters with ship propellers have taken their toll, and numbers of this endangered species are dwindling fast now, with less than 500 estimated left in the world.

Another of humankind's aquatic cousins, the **Atlantic bottle-nosed dolphin,** is a frequent visitor to the coast, coming far upstream into creeks and rivers to feed. Don't be fooled by their cuteness, however. Dolphins live life with gusto and aren't scared of much. They're voracious eaters of fish, amorous and energetic lovers, and will take on an encroaching shark in a heartbeat.

Another beloved part-time marine creature of the barrier islands of the coast is the **loggerhead turtle.** Though the species prefers to stay well offshore the rest of the year, females weighing up to 300 pounds come out of the sea each May-July to dig a shallow hole in the dunes and lay over 100 leathery eggs, returning to the ocean and leaving the eggs to hatch on their own after two months.

The most abundant and sought-after recreational species in the coastal area is the **spotted**

sea trout followed by **red drum.** Local anglers also pursue many varieties of **bass, bream, sheepshead,** and **crappie.** It may sound strange to some accustomed to considering it a "trash" fish, but many types of **catfish** are not only plentiful here all throughout Georgia but are a common and well-regarded food source.

Recreational lakes, almost all constructed by people, are found throughout the state, and the chief fish on them is the largemouth bass. The biggest are typically caught on the western lakes such as Walter F. George and Seminole on the Alabama border (you can also catch shoal bass there as well). But the Savannah River lakes of Hartwell and Clark's Hill are great bass grounds as well, as are the adjacent lakes Sinclair and Oconee. Lake Lanier outside Atlanta is known for its striped and spotted bass.

Trout fishing, for three main species (rainbow, brown, and brook), is done on 4,000 miles of rivers and streams, though quirky soils in Georgia mean they aren't as productive as some states. There are extensive regulations on trout fishing in Georgia; go to www.georgiawildlife.com for full info. Popular spots include the Conasauga River, the Chattahoochee River, Hoods Creek, Jones Creek, Amicalola Creek, and Dukes Creek. Interestingly, trout fishing on Moccasin Creek off Lake Burton is limited to those 12 and under and senior citizens.

Crustaceans and shellfish have been a key food staple in the area for thousands of years, with the massive shell middens of the coast being testament to Native Americans' healthy appetite for them. The beds of the local variant, the **eastern oyster,** aren't what they used to be, due to over-harvesting, water pollution, and disruption of habitat. Oysters spawn May-August, hence the old folk wisdom about eating oysters only in months with the letter "r," so as not to disrupt the breeding cycle.

Each year in April-January, shrimp boats trawl for **shrimp,** the most popular seafood item in the United States. Another important commercial crop is the **blue crab,** the species used in such Lowcountry delicacies as crab cakes. You'll often see floating markers bobbing up and down in rivers throughout the region. These signal the presence directly below of a crab trap, often of an amateur crabber.

A true living link to primordial times, the alien-looking **horseshoe crab** is frequently found on coastal beaches during the spring mating season (it lives in deeper water the rest of the year). More closely related to scorpions and spiders than crabs, the horseshoe has evolved hardly a lick in hundreds of millions of years.

In the Air

Birds in Georgia come in four types: permanent residents like the **northern cardinal;** summer breeders like the **indigo bunting;** winter residents that return north to nest in the spring; and spring and fall migrants flying between summer nesting grounds in Northern states and Canada.

Up in the mountains at significant elevation is the only place you'll see **Canada warblers, winter wrens, veerys, yellow-bellied sapsuckers,** and **dark-eyed juncos.** Georgia is visited by 11 hummingbird species during the year, but only the tiny **ruby-throated hummingbird** is known to nest here.

Down in **wiregrass** country of Middle and South Georgia among the pines you'll find the most common area woodpecker, the huge **pileated woodpecker** with its huge crest. Less common is the smaller, more subtly marked **red-cockaded woodpecker.** Once common in the primordial inland longleaf pine forests, the species is now endangered, its last sanctuaries being the big tracts of relatively undisturbed land on military bases and on wildlife refuges.

When on the coast, consider yourself fortunate to see an endangered **wood stork,** though their numbers are on the increase. The only storks to breed in North America, they're usually seen on a low flight path across the marsh. Often confused with the wood stork is the gorgeous **white ibis,** distinguishable by its orange bill and black wingtips. Like the wood stork, the ibis is a communal bird that roosts in colonies.

Other similar-looking coastal denizens are

© MIKE2FOCUS/DREAMSTIME.COM

snowy egret

the white-feathered **great egret** and **snowy egret,** the former distinguishable by its yellow bill and the latter by its black bill and the tuft of plumes on the back of its head. Egrets are in the same family as herons. The most magnificent is the **great blue heron.** Despite their imposing height, up to four feet tall, these waders are shy. So how to tell the difference between all these wading birds at a glance? It's actually easiest when they're in flight. Egrets and herons fly with their necks tucked in, while storks and ibises fly with their necks extended.

Dozens of species of shorebirds comb the beaches, including **sandpipers, plovers,** and the wonderful and rare **American oystercatcher,** instantly recognizable for its prancing walk, dark brown back, stark white underside, and long, bright-orange bill. And don't forget the delightful, water-loving **painted bunting,** particularly drawn to the barrier islands of the coast and riverine areas near the marsh.

The **bald eagle,** which had no recorded nests anywhere in the state as recently as the late 1970s, has made quite a comeback thanks to aggressive conservation policies. The chief raptor of the salt marsh is the fish-eating **osprey.**

And of course don't forget the Georgia state bird, the oddly charming **brown thrasher,** typically found churning up dirt and leaves close to the ground in residential areas.

Insects

Down here they say that God invented bugs to keep the Yankees from completely taking over the South. And insects are probably the most unpleasant fact of life in the Southeastern coastal region.

The list of annoying indigenous insects must begin with the infamous **sand gnat.** This tiny and persistent nuisance, a member of the midge family, lacks the precision of the mosquito with its long proboscis. No, the sand gnat is more torture-master than surgeon, brutally gouging and digging away its victim's skin until it hits a source of blood. Most prevalent in the spring and fall, the sand gnat is drawn to its prey by the carbon dioxide trail of its breath.

While long sleeves and long pants are one way to keep gnats at bay, the only real antidote to the sand gnat's assault (other than never breathing) is the Avon skin care product Skin So Soft, which has taken on a new and wholly unplanned life as the South's favorite anti-gnat lotion. In calmer moments grow to appreciate the great contribution sand gnats make to the salt marsh ecosystem as food for birds and bats.

Running a close second to the sand gnat are the over three dozen species of highly aggressive **mosquito,** which breed anywhere a few drops of water lie stagnant. Not surprisingly, massive populations blossom in the rainiest months, in late spring and late summer, feeding in the morning and late afternoon. Like the gnat, the mosquito homes in on its victim by trailing the plume of carbon dioxide exhaled in the breath; the biters are always female.

But undoubtedly the most viscerally loathed of all pests on the Lowcountry and Georgia coasts is the so-called "palmetto bug," or **American cockroach.** These black, shiny, and sometimes grotesquely massive insects, up to two inches long, are living fossils, virtually unchanged over hundreds of millions of years. And perfectly adapted as they are to life in and among wet, decaying vegetation, they're unlikely to change a bit in 100 million more years.

Popular regional use of the term "palmetto bug" undoubtedly has its roots in a desire for polite Southern society to avoid using the ugly word "roach" and its connotations of filth and unclean environments. But the colloquialism actually has a basis in reality. Contrary to what anyone tells you, the natural habitat of the American cockroach—unlike its kitchen-dwelling, much-smaller cousin, the German cockroach—is outdoors, often up in trees. They only come inside human dwellings when it's especially hot, especially cold, or especially dry outside. Like you, the palmetto bug is easily driven indoors by extreme temperatures and by thirst.

Other than visiting the Southeast during the winter, when the roaches go dormant, there's no convenient antidote for their presence. The best way to keep them out of your life is to stay away from decaying vegetation and keep doors and windows closed on especially hot nights.

History

BEFORE THE EUROPEANS

Based on studies of artifacts found throughout the state, anthropologists know that the first humans arrived in Georgia at least 13,000 years ago, at the tail end of the Ice Age. During this **Paleoindian Period,** sea levels were over 200 feet lower than present levels, and large mammals such as wooly mammoths, horses, and camels were hunted for food and skins. However, rapidly increasing temperatures, rising sea levels, and efficient hunting techniques combined to quickly kill off these large mammals, relics of the Pleistocene Era, ushering in the **Archaic Period.** Still hunter-gatherers, Archaic Period Indians began turning to small game such as deer, bear, and turkey, supplemented with fruit and nuts.

The latter part of the Archaic era saw more habitation on the coasts, with an increasing reliance on fish and shellfish for sustenance. It's during this time that the great **shell middens** of the Georgia coast trace their origins. Basically serving as trash heaps for discarded oyster shells, the middens grew in size and as they did they took on a ceremonial status, often being used as sites for important rituals and meetings. Such sites are often called **shell rings,** and the largest yet found was over 9 feet high and 300 feet in diameter.

The introduction of agriculture and improved pottery techniques about 3,000 years ago led to the **Woodland Period** of Native American settlement. Extended clan groups were much less migratory, establishing year-round communities of up to 50 people, who began the practice of clearing land to grow crops. The ancient shell middens of their forefathers were not abandoned, however, and were continually added onto.

Native Americans had been cremating or burying their dead for years, a practice which eventually gave rise to the construction of the first **mounds** during the Woodland Period. Essentially built-up earthworks sometimes marked with spiritual symbols, often in the form of animal shapes, mounds not only contained the remains of the deceased, but items like pottery to accompany the deceased into the afterlife. The most notable Woodland sites in Georgia are the **Rock Eagle Effigy** outside Eatonton and the amazing **Kolomoki Mounds** site near Blakely, which at its peak was the most populous settlement north of Mexico.

Increased agriculture led to increased population, and with that population growth came competition over resources and a more formal notion of warfare. This period, from about 800AD-1600AD, is termed the **Mississippian Period** and is the apex of Native American culture north of Mexico.

It was the Mississippians who would be the first Native Americans in what's now the continental United States to encounter European explorers and settlers after Columbus. The Native Americans who would later be called **Creek Indians** were the direct descendants of the Mississippians in lineage, language, and lifestyle.

The Mississippians were not only prodigious mound builders, they also constructed elaborate wooden villages and evolved a top-down class system. Their cities, generally positioned along key trails and rivers, formed a sophisticated network of trade and interrelationships that spanned Florida up to Ohio.

Along with Kolomoki, which was begun a bit earlier and also was a Mississippian site, there are two notable Mississippian mound sites in Georgia: **Etowah Mounds** outside Cartersville and **Ocmulgee Mounds** in Macon, which also features the newer **Lamar Mound.**

By about 1400AD, however, change came to the Mississippian culture for reasons that are still not completely understood. In some areas, large chiefdoms began splintering into smaller subgroups, in an intriguing echo of the medieval feudal system going on concurrently in Europe. In either case, the result was the same: The landscape of the Southeast became less peopled, as many of the old villages, built around huge central mounds, were abandoned. As tensions and paranoia between the chiefdoms increased, the contested land between them became more and more dangerous for the poorly armed or poorly connected. Indeed, at the time of the Europeans' arrival much of the coastal area was more thinly inhabited than it had been for many decades, a situation only exacerbated by the diseases introduced by the explorers.

THE SPANISH ARRIVE

The first serious exploration of the coast came in 1526, when Spanish adventurer Lucas Vazquez de Ayllon and about 600 colonists made landfall at Winyah Bay in South Carolina, near present-day Georgetown. They didn't stay long, however, immediately moving down the coast and trying to set down roots in the St. Catherine's Sound area of modern-day Liberty County, Georgia.

That colony, called San Miguel de Gualdape, was the first European colony in America. (The continent's oldest continuously occupied settlement, St. Augustine, Florida, wasn't founded until 1565.) The colony also brought with it the seed of a future nation's dissolution: slaves from Africa. While San Miguel de Gualdape lasted only six weeks due to political tension and a slave uprising, conclusive artifacts from its brief life have been discovered in the area.

Of far greater impact was Hernando de Soto's infamous, ill-fated trek of 1539-1543 from Florida through southwest Georgia to Alabama, where the Spanish explorer died of a fever after four years of depredations against the indigenous population. Setting ashore near modern Tampa Bay, de Soto and his men crossed the Florida Panhandle into Georgia near modern Bainbridge on the Flint River. Traveling up the Flint, they passed near present-day Montezuma, then crossed to the east side of the river to the chiefdom of Toa.

They progressed until they came to the Ocmulgee River, where they found an island where meat had been abandoned still roasting on a wooden barbacoa frame over a wood fire—the first recorded instance of barbecue in Georgia. Shortly after they came to the Ichisi chiefdom near the Lamar mound site at Macon, where after a peaceful greeting with the chief de Soto ordered a cross set atop a mound. North from Macon they encountered several more chiefdoms, crossing the Savannah River a bit north of modern Augusta, beginning the portion of their trek through the Carolinas and east Tennessee before turning back into Georgia at the Indian town of Coosa, where Carters Lake now lies.

It was now August 1540. De Soto left Coosa and headed back south, crossing the Etowah River near the Etowah Mound site at present-day Cartersville, stopping at a chiefdom near modern Rome, Georgia. By September they had passed into Alabama, never to see Georgia again. He did not find the gold he anticipated, but de Soto's legacy was soon felt throughout the Southeast in the form of various diseases for which the Mississippian tribes had no immunity whatsoever: smallpox, typhus, influenza, measles, yellow fever, whooping cough, diphtheria, tuberculosis, and bubonic plague.

While the cruelties of the Spanish certainly took their toll, far more damaging were these deadly diseases to a population totally unprepared for them. Within a few years, the Mississippian people, already in a state of internal decline, were losing huge percentages of their population to disease, echoing what had already happened on a massive scale to the indigenous tribes of the Caribbean after Christopher Columbus's expeditions.

As the viruses they introduced ran rampant, the Europeans themselves stayed away for a couple of decades after the ignominious end of de Soto's fruitless quest. During that quarter-century, the once-proud Mississippian culture continued to disintegrate, dwindling into a shadow of its former greatness. In all, disease would claim the lives of at least 80 percent of all indigenous inhabitants of the western hemisphere.

The Mission Era

It's rarely mentioned as a key part of U.S. history, but the Spanish missionary presence on the Georgia coast was longer and more comprehensive than its much more widely known counterpart in California.

St. Augustine governor Pedro Menendez de Aviles, over "biscuits with honey" on the beach at St. Catherine's Island in Georgia with a local chief, negotiated for the right to establish a system of Jesuit missions in two coastal chiefdoms: the Mocama on and around Cumberland Island, and the Guale (pronounced "wallie") to the north. Those early missions, the first north of Mexico, were largely unsuccessful. But a renewed, organized effort by the Franciscan Order came to fruition during the 1580s. Missions were established all along the Georgia coast, from the mainland near St. Simons and Sapelo Islands, on the Altamaha.

Spanish power waned under the English threat, however. A devastating Indian raid in 1661 on a mission at the mouth of the Altamaha River, possibly aided by the English, persuaded the Spanish to pull the mission effort to the barrier islands. But even as late as 1667, right before the founding of Charleston, South Carolina, there were 70 missions still on the Georgia coast. Pirate raids and slave uprisings finished off the Georgia missions for good by 1684. In an interesting postscript, 89 Native Americans—the sole surviving descendants of Spain's Georgia missions—evacuated to Cuba with the final Spanish exodus from Florida in 1763.

OGLETHORPE'S VISION

In 1729, the colony of Carolina was divided into north and south. In 1731, a colony to be known as Georgia, after the new English king, was carved out of the southern part of the Carolina land grant. A young general, aristocrat, and humanitarian named James Edward Oglethorpe gathered together a group of trustees to take advantage of that grant.

While Oglethorpe would go on to found Georgia, his wasn't the first English presence. A garrison built Fort King George in modern-day Darien, Georgia, in 1721. A cypress block-house surrounded by palisaded earthworks, the fort defended the southern reaches of England's claim for seven years before being abandoned in 1728.

On February 12, 1733, after stops in Beaufort and Charleston, the ship *Anne* with its 114 passengers made its way to the high-est bluff on the Savannah River. The area was controlled by the peaceful Yamacraw tribe, who had been encouraged by the powers-that-be in Charleston to settle on this vacant land 12 miles up the river to serve as a buffer for the Spanish. Led by an elderly chief, or *mico*, named Tomochichi, the Yamacraw enjoyed the area's natural bounty of shellfish, fruit, nuts, and small game.

Ever the deft politician, Oglethorpe struck up a treaty and eventually a genuine friend-ship with Tomochichi. To the Yamacraw Oglethorpe was a rare bird, a white man who behaved with honor and was true to his word. The tribe reciprocated by helping the settlers and pledging fealty to the crown. Oglethorpe reported to the trustees that Tomochichi per-sonally requested "that we would Love and Protect their little Families."

In negotiations with local tribes the persua-sive Oglethorpe convinced the coastal Creek to cede to the crown all Georgia land to the Altamaha River "which our Nation hath not occasion for to use" in exchange for goods. The tribes also reserved the Georgia Sea Islands of Sapelo, Ossabaw, and St. Catherine's. Oglethorpe's impact was felt farther down the Georgia coast, as St. Simons Island, Jekyll Island, Darien, and Brunswick were settled in rapid succession, and with them the entrench-ment of the plantation system and slave labor.

While the trustees' utopian vision was largely economic in nature, like Carolina the Georgia colony also emphasized religious free-dom. While to modern ears Oglethorpe's orig-inal ban of Roman Catholics from Georgia might seem incompatible with this goal, the reason was a coldly pragmatic one for the time: England's two main global rivals, France and Spain, were both staunchly Catholic countries.

Spain Vanquished

Things heated up on the coast in 1739 with the so-called War of Jenkins' Ear, which despite its seemingly trivial beginnings over the humilia-tion of a British captain by Spanish privateers was actually a proxy struggle emblematic of changes in the European balance of power. A year later Oglethorpe cobbled together a force of settlers, Indian allies, and Carolinians to reduce the Spanish fortress at St. Augustine, Florida.

The siege failed, and Oglethorpe retreated to St. Simons Island to await the inevitable coun-terattack. In 1742, a massive Spanish force invaded the island but was eventually turned back for good with heavy casualties at the **Battle of Bloody Marsh.** That clash marked the end of Spanish overtures on England's colo-nies in America.

Though Oglethorpe returned to England a national hero, things fell apart in Savannah. The settlers became envious of the success of Charleston's slave-based rice economy and began wondering aloud why they couldn't also make use of free labor.

With Oglethorpe otherwise occupied in England, the Trustees of Georgia—distant in more ways than just geographically from the new colony—bowed to public pressure and re-laxed the restrictions on slavery and rum. By 1753 the trustees voted to return their char-ter to the crown, officially making Georgia the 13th and final colony of England in America.

With first the French and then the Spanish effectively shut off from the American East Coast, the stage was set for an internal battle between England and its burgeoning colonies across the Atlantic.

REVOLUTION AND INDEPENDENCE

It's a persistent but inaccurate myth that Georgia was reluctant to break ties with England. While the Lowcountry's cultural and economic ties to England were certainly strong, the **Stamp Act** and the **Townshend Acts** combined to turn public sentiment against the mother country there as elsewhere in the colonies. Planters in what would be called Liberty County, Georgia, also strongly agitated for the cause. War broke out between the colonists and the British in New England, and soon made its way southward. Three Georgians—Button Gwinnett, Lyman Hall, and George Walton—signed the Declaration of Independence on July 4, 1776.

The British took Savannah in 1778. Royal Governor Sir James Wright returned from exile to Georgia to reclaim it for the crown, the only one of the colonies to be subsumed again into the British Empire. A polyglot force of colonists, Haitians, and Hessians attacked the British fortifications on the west side of Savannah in 1779, but were repulsed with heavy losses.

Such a pitched battle was rare in Georgia; the bulk of the Revolutionary War in the Southern theater was a guerrilla war of colonists versus the British as well as a civil war between patriots and loyalists, or **Tories.** The main such engagement in Georgia was the Battle of Kettle Creek in February 1779. In which a Loyalist force specifically intended to gather support in the backcountry for the royal cause was defeated by a combined militia force under Colonel Andrew Pickens of South Carolina and Colonel John Dooly and Lieutenant Colonel Elijah Clarke of Georgia.

After independence, two Georgians, Abraham Baldwin and William Few Jr., signed the new U.S. Constitution in 1787. Georgia became the fourth state to enter the Union when it ratified the Constitution on January 2, 1788. It was during that decade that the University of Georgia, first university in the nation established by a state government, was granted its charter, opening its doors in Athens in 1801.

THE ANTEBELLUM ERA

In 1786, a new crop was introduced that would only enhance the financial clout of the coastal region: cotton. A former loyalist colonel, Roger Kelsal, sent some seed from the West Indies to his friend James Spaulding, owner of a plantation on St. Simons Island, Georgia. This crop, soon to be known as **Sea Island cotton** and considered the best in the world, would supplant rice as the crop of choice for coastal plantations. At the height of the Southern cotton boom in the early 1800s, a single Sea Island cotton harvest on a single plantation might go for $100,000 in 1820 money!

While Charleston was still by far the largest, most powerful, and most influential city on the Southeastern coast of the United States, at the peak of the cotton craze Savannah was actually doing more business. It's during this time that most of the grand homes of downtown Savannah's Historic District were built. This boom period, fueled largely by cotton exports, was perhaps most iconically represented by the historic sailing of the SS *Savannah* from Savannah to Liverpool in 29 days, the first transatlantic voyage by a steamship.

Another crucial agricultural breakthrough happened in Georgia: Eli Whitney's invention of the cotton gin while visiting the Mulberry Grove plantation of Catharine Greene, widow of General Nathanael Greene. The dramatic efficiencies introduced by the cotton gin not only increased the South's dependence on that staple crop, it also further reinforced the slave economy, already well established through the rice trade.

The Gold Rush

Cotton wasn't the only moneymaker in Georgia in the antebellum era. The North Georgia mountains were the site of America's first gold rush. By 1830 4,000 miners were panning for gold on one creek alone. The amount and quality of gold was so extravagant that the U.S. Mint opened a branch office in Dahlonega in 1838. Before closing at the outbreak of the Civil War it had produced 1.5 million gold coins.

Of course the original inhabitants of the Gold Rush land were Cherokee Indians. Writing in a tribal newspaper, one said of the rush, "Our neighbors who regard no law and pay no respects to the laws of humanity are now reaping a plentiful harvest.... We are an abused people." Those words were prophetic, and decades of government activity oriented toward removing Creek and Cherokee from Georgia came to a head when gold was used as an excuse to take final action.

The Trail of Tears

Even before the Gold Rush, the state of Georgia had held "Land Lotteries" to distribute land seized from Cherokees and Creeks through various treaties often of dubious provenance; the land seized totaled about three quarters of the state's land area. Around the time of the Gold Rush, a series of court decisions led to a potential Constitutional crisis involving the state of Georgia and the federal government under President Andrew Jackson, who, while fully supporting Indian removal, was also concerned with asserting federal power over the states.

As the extent of the gold deposits were realized and with the signing of the pivotal Treaty of New Echota in 1835, the U.S. Army found the legal justification to forcibly remove remaining Cherokees from Georgia into "Indian Territory" in present-day Oklahoma. Events came to a head during the unusually frigid winter of 1838-39, when thousands of Cherokee were forced onto what became known as the "Trail of Tears," about 4,000 dying on the miserable journey without proper food and clothes.

The Railroad

During the pivotal antebellum era of the 1830s to the 1850s, the construction of rail lines connecting Georgia's major cities of the time—Athens, Augusta, Macon, and Savannah—was another huge development in Georgia. Atlanta, originally named Terminus, was founded in 1837 as the end of the rail system's line. By the outbreak of Civil War, Georgia had more miles of rail lines than any other Southern state, a fact that at the end of that conflict would haunt the state.

Secession

Long-simmering tensions between Southern states, primarily South Carolina, and the federal government over the issue of the expansion of slavery reached a tipping point with the election of the nominally abolitionist president Abraham Lincoln in November 1860.

During the subsequent "Secession Winter" before Lincoln took office in January, seven states seceded from the union, first among them South Carolina, followed by Mississippi, Florida, Alabama, Georgia, Louisiana, and Texas. Georgia's Secession Convention in the state capital of Milledgeville was among the most divided of all, given that large portions of the state, particularly the north and the southeast, had little economic interest in slavery.

However, Georgians played key roles in the nascent Confederate government, with Alexander H. Stephens of Crawfordville acting as vice president, Robert Toombs of Washington its secretary of state, and Thomas R.R. Cobb of Athens as the author of the Confederate Constitution. Meanwhile, pugnacious Georgia Governor Joseph E. Brown frequently butted heads with Confederate President Jefferson Davis over issues of, ironically enough, state's rights.

CIVIL WAR

War finally began with the firing on Ft. Sumter in Charleston harbor by secessionist forces. Almost immediately the South Carolina and Georgia coasts were blockaded by the much-larger Union Navy. Union forces used newly developed rifled cannons in 1862 to quickly reduce Fort Pulaski at the mouth of the Savannah River—previously thought impregnable and the world's most secure fortress—garrisoning it and leaving Savannah itself in Confederate hands.

White Southerners evacuated the coastal cities and plantations for the hinterland, leaving slaves behind to fend for themselves. In some coastal areas, African Americans and Union garrison troops settled into an awkward coexistence. Many islands under Union control, such as Cockspur Island where Fort Pulaski sat, became endpoints in the Underground Railroad.

Georgian troops served the Confederacy in every theater of the war, but large-scale fighting

three cannons on top of Fort Pulaski

didn't hit the state until the Union pushed down into North Georgia from Chattanooga, Tennessee, which along with Atlanta was a major rail hub for the Confederacy. The last major Confederate victory of the war came at Chickamauga in September 1863, when Confederate General Braxton Bragg, with considerable assistance from General James Longstreet, a Georgia native, pushed Union troops under General William Rosecrans back into Tennessee after three days of brutal fighting. However, the Union Army still held Chattanooga and continued to consolidate their forces for General William Sherman's eventual push to capture the real prize, Atlanta, and deal a dual blow to the Confederacy by seizing a major transportation and commercial hub as well as likely guaranteeing Lincoln's re-election later in 1864.

The spring was a fateful one for the South, as Sherman's initial forays into the area north of Atlanta were successful. Unrest in the top Confederate ranks led to Jefferson Davis firing General Joseph Johnston and replacing him

with General John B. Hood, even as Sherman's army was gathering for the final assault only five miles from the city. Hood's attacks against the Union lines were too little, too late, and by the end of the summer of 1864 Hood had evacuated Atlanta and left it to its fate. Sherman telegraphed Lincoln, "Atlanta is ours and fairly won."

It was during roughly the same period that the notorious Camp Sumter POW camp operated near Andersonville, the name by which it's mostly known today. At its height of prisoner population, so many captured Union troops roasted in the sun within its unsheltered, stockaded space that it would have been the Confederacy's fifth largest city.

After three months of occupying Atlanta, Sherman was set to begin his fabled "March to the Sea" in an attempt to break the Southern will to fight for good, by destroying the means of supporting an army. On his way out of Atlanta in November, he gave the order to burn everything in the city that might be useful to the Southern war effort. The arson extended

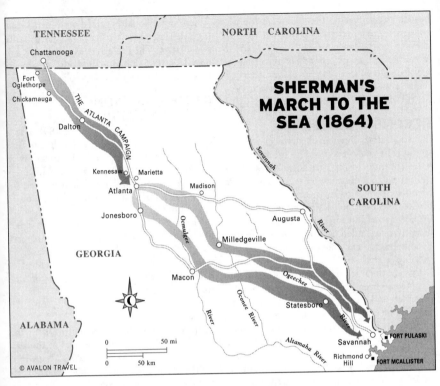

SHERMAN'S MARCH TO THE SEA (1864)

to private residences, and the entire downtown area burned in a massive and controversial conflagration.

The March to the Sea was made easier by Hood's removal of his forces to the west in an effort to draw Sherman towards Tennessee again. Sherman didn't take the bait, and with the way clear to the coast, he broke standard protocol not only by splitting his forces, but by operating without a supply line, instead wanting his army to forage off the land and whatever supplies they could take from the populace.

He divided his 60,000-man army into two equal wings: one would head towards Augusta and the other towards Macon. They both met at the state capital of Milledgeville, where the statehouse was ransacked and anything of remote military value was put to the torch. A Confederate cavalry force under General Joseph Wheeler harried Union forces the whole

way, but to little effect. Union "bummers" took what they wanted from local farms, and railroad-wrecking crews heated railroad tracks into twisted messes called "Sherman's neckties."

Newly-freed former slaves followed in the Union Army's wake virtually the entire way to the sea, their numbers growing each week. On December 9 at Ebenezer Creek outside Savannah, a Union commander, ironically named Jefferson Davis, ordered a pontoon bridge taken away before the entourage of the emancipated could cross. Many drowned in the attempt to cross the creek on their own. Scathing headlines in the North resulted, but Sherman backed Davis's decision as militarily sound. In Savannah, Sherman concluded his March to the Sea in December 1864, famously giving the city to Lincoln as a Christmas present, along with 25,000 bales of cotton.

But Georgia wasn't quite out of the war's

headlines yet. Fleeing the disintegrating war zone in Virginia, Jefferson Davis met with his cabinet for the last time on May 5, 1865, in Washington, Georgia, essentially dissolving the Confederate government. Five days later, still on the run, he was captured by Union cavalry near Irwinville in the center of the state.

RECONSTRUCTION

For a brief time, Sherman's benevolent dictatorship on the coast held promise for an orderly postwar future. In 1865, he issued his sweeping "40 acres and a mule" order seeking dramatic economic restitution for coastal Georgia's free blacks. However, politics reared its ugly head in the wake of Lincoln's assassination and the order was rescinded, ushering in the chaotic Reconstruction era, echoes of which linger to this day.

Even as the trade in cotton and naval stores resumed to even greater heights than before, urban life and racial tension became more and more problematic. It was at this time that the foundation for Jim Crow and its false promise of "separate but equal" was laid. Racial in origin, the Jim Crow laws also displayed a clear socioeconomic bias as well; it was during Reconstruction that in some areas the practice evolved of wealthy whites walking on one side of the streets and poor whites and all blacks walking on the other side.

Atlanta was gradually rebuilt and quickly regained its dominant transportation status. In an acknowledgement of the city's overriding importance to the state, the state capital was moved there from Milledgeville in 1868, a scant four years after it was burned to the ground. By 1880, Atlanta had surpassed Savannah as Georgia's largest city. The "New South" movement, spearheaded by *Atlanta Journal-Constitution* editor Henry W. Grady, posited a region less about agriculture than about industry and progressive thought.

Despite the upheaval of Reconstruction, the Victorian era in Georgia was remarkably robust, with fortunes being made and glittering downtowns and residential areas rebuilt all over the state. A number of newly-minted African American millionaires gained prominence during this time as well, most notably in Atlanta and Macon. The exclusive Jekyll Island Club opened in 1886, bringing the world's wealthiest people to the Georgia coast to play.

RECONCILIATION AND DEPRESSION

The Spanish-American War of 1898 was a major turning point for the South, the first time since the Civil War that Americans were joined in patriotic unity. President McKinley himself addressed troops bivouacked in Savannah's Daffin Park before being sent on to fight in Cuba.

For all that, agriculture remained a vital part of Georgia's economy. Cotton remained crucial, as did logging. Throughout the late 1800s Georgia was the world's leading producer of naval stores, derived from vast tracts of pine trees.

FDR

Beginning in 1915 the old cotton-growing states of the South saw the arrival of the tiny but devastating boll weevil, which all but wiped out the cotton trade. Sharecroppers, a large percentage of the population and never far from economic disaster in the best of times, were especially hit hard. Old-tensions flared as the Ku Klux Klan was revived on Stone Mountain.

During the 1920s, then-New York Governor Franklin D. Roosevelt began visiting the Warm Springs area of Georgia to seek relief from his worsening polio symptoms. He saw firsthand the struggle of rural Southerners, and these experiences would influence many domestic initiatives, such as the Rural Electrification program, after he was elected president in 1932.

The coming of the Great Depression in the early 1930s was for most Georgians just a worsening of an already bad economic situation. While FDR's New Deal programs had some positive effect, they were later in coming to the South and were less effective because of resistance on the part of state politicians such as Governor Eugene Talmadge of Georgia, who was a staunch segregationist to boot and sought to limit any benefits of Roosevelt's largesse to white citizens only.

The cities fared a good bit better due to their transportation and manufacturing importance. Atlanta in particular weathered the Depression well, at the same time seeing a robust growth in the black middle class, a background that nurtured a young Martin Luther King Jr. in the then-prosperous black neighborhood called "Sweet Auburn." The auto bug bit Atlanta hard (it's still felt there today) and the first car suburbs were built.

The chief legacy today of the Depression era in Georgia, other than FDR's Little White House at Warm Springs, is the work of the Civilian Conservation Corps (CCC), a 10-year jobs program which resulted in the construction of most of Georgia's state parks, many of which feature original structures built by "Roosevelt's Tree Army" that are still very much in use today. Parts of the great Appalachian Trail were also cleared by the CCC, with many of the shelters used by through-hikers today still in steady use.

Gone with the Wind

Another development in the 1930s, which would have far-reaching ramifications for Georgia, was the writing of *Gone with the Wind* by Margaret Mitchell over a 10-year span in Atlanta. Shortly after her dramatic tale of the waning days of the Confederacy was published in 1936, it became a global sensation. A short three years later, Atlanta became the toast of a nation as Hollywood's elite gathered there for the world premiere of the film version. The book and film remain some of America's most popular and enduring cultural motifs, and probably resulted in untold billions of dollars in ancillary benefits for Georgia tourism.

WORLD WAR II AND THE POSTWAR BOOM

With the attack on Pearl Harbor and the coming of World War II, military facilities of all kinds swarmed into Georgia, making the state absolutely indispensable to the war effort. Populations and long-depressed living standards rose as a result. In many outlying areas, such as the Sea Islands, electricity came for the first time.

The enormous Bell Bomber plant was built in Marietta near Atlanta, producing thousands of B-29 bombers for the final air offensive against the empire of Japan. Robins Air Force Base near Macon became one of America's largest and most important domestic air bases. Fort Benning in Columbus became the U.S. Army's main infantry, paratrooper, and Ranger training base. The "Mighty Eighth" Air Force was founded in Savannah, and enormous Fort Stewart was built in nearby Hinesville. In shipyards in Savannah and Brunswick, hundreds of Liberty ships were built to transport cargo to the citizens and allied armies of Europe.

America's postwar infatuation with the automobile—and its troublesome child, the suburb—brought exponential expansion of metro areas, especially Atlanta, along with a callous disregard for much of the historic fabric of the past. It was in response to the car-craze that several society matrons in Savannah got together and founded the Historic Savannah Foundation, which helped preserve many of the priceless structures that today form the basis of Savannah's thriving tourist economy.

CIVIL RIGHTS

Contrary to popular opinion, the civil rights era wasn't just a blip in the late 1960s. The gains of that decade were the fruits of efforts begun decades prior. Many of the efforts involved efforts to expand black suffrage. Though African Americans secured the nominal right to vote years before, primary contests in Georgia were not under the jurisdiction of federal law. As a result, Democratic Party primary elections, de facto general elections because of that party's total dominance in the South at the time, were effectively closed to African American voters.

Other efforts, such as the groundbreaking "Albany Movement" of the early 1960s, sought to equalize and integrate public facilities and common areas. The efforts in Albany were at first unsuccessful, but their methods of peaceful resistance to segregationist policies were deeply influential on civil rights leaders such as Martin Luther King Jr., who took part in them.

Atlanta public schools began integrating in 1961. In 1965 the city would elect its first black alderman, and 11 African Americans were elected to the state legislature. Julian Bond, Georgia's first black congressman, was sent to Washington in 1967. Atlanta's first African American mayor, Maynard Jackson, was elected in 1969.

The civil rights era would spawn another political career, when a peanut farmer in tiny Plains, Georgia, was inspired to fight for social justice and equality by running for the Georgia State Senate. Jimmy Carter would go on to be governor in 1971 and then U.S. president in 1976. In an intriguing and somewhat prophetic blend of the forces that would shape American politics into the Obama era, Carter was both the first statewide Southern officeholder to publicly embrace full civil rights as well as the first evangelical Christian president.

GEORGIA TODAY

Throughout the 1980s, Georgia, and especially Atlanta, underwent an enormous boom driven by many of the same factors contributing to similar success stories throughout the U.S. Sun Belt. When the economic boom of the 1990s came, Atlanta was firmly cemented as a major convention and corporate business center.

Down in Savannah, their big tourism boom, still going on today, began with the publication of John Berendt's *Midnight in the Garden of Good and Evil* in 1995. A year later, Atlanta would host the 1996 Summer Olympics, which though marred by a bombing in Centennial Olympic Park, was pulled off quite successfully and signaled Atlanta's emergence as a truly global city, not that there was ever really any doubt.

The economic downturn of 2008 and beyond brought a significant downscaling in government expenditures, which visitors most clearly see at some state parks and recreational facilities. However, as of this writing that situation has begun to stabilize.

The main focus in Georgia today is on grappling with the issues of development and, to a lesser extent, immigration. The so-called "Water Wars" between Atlanta and other claimants to the drinking water of the Chattahoochee River watershed have generally been settled in the courts in Atlanta's favor, though that city's continued rampant expansion means fighting over resources will be a constant feature moving forward.

Georgia's booming Hispanic population, largely in the form of those employed in the construction industry around Atlanta and the migrant farming communities of rural Georgia, was dealt a blow with recent strict legislation meant to curtail illegal immigration.

Government and Economy

GOVERNMENT

The capital of Georgia, of course, is Atlanta. The state legislature (technically called the General Assembly) meets 40 days a year "under the Gold Dome," or statehouse downtown. The upper house is the State Senate, which has 56 seats. The lower house is the House of Representatives, currently with 180 seats.

The governor of Georgia serves a four-year term and lives in the Governor's Mansion in Buckhead.

Georgia is unique among all states in the union for the extraordinary number of counties it has: 159. This is not just a product of the state's sheer physical size; Montana is a good bit larger physically and only has 56 counties. Georgia's huge number of fairly small-sized counties is a direct result of the old **county unit system,** a method of political organization begun in 1917 whereby votes in party primary elections were awarded by county: urban counties six votes each, town counties four votes, and rural counties two votes each. What the county unit system meant in practice was that

Georgia's capitol building in Atlanta

Georgia's rural counties could exert political control far outstripping their actual share of the population.

The county unit system wasn't removed until 1962 after a landmark court case which President Jimmy Carter would later call "one of the most momentous political decisions of the century in Georgia."

Political Parties

For many decades, the South was dominated by the Democratic Party. Originally the party of slavery, segregation, and Jim Crow, the Democratic Party began attracting Southern African American voters in the 1930s with the election of Franklin D. Roosevelt. The allegiance of black voters was further cemented in the Truman, Kennedy, and Johnson administrations.

The region would remain solidly Democratic until a backlash against the civil rights movement of the 1960s drove many white Southerners, ironically enough, into the party of Lincoln. This added racial element, so confounding to Americans from other parts of the country, remains just as potent today.

The default mode in the South today is that white voters are massively Republican, and black voters massively Democratic. Since Georgia is 63 percent white, doing the math translates to an overwhelming Republican dominance. Republicans gained control of the Georgia governorship in 2002, both houses of the General Assembly in 2004, and have only consolidated control since.

In the 2012 presidential election, Republican Mitt Romney received 53 percent of Georgia's popular vote to Democrat Barack Obama's 45.

ECONOMY

Thanks largely to Atlanta's economic importance, Georgia hosts over 25 Fortune 1,000 company headquarters, including Home Depot, UPS, Coca-Cola, Delta Airlines, Gulfstream Aerospace (in Savannah), and Aflac (in Columbus). Kia Motors recently opened its first U.S. assembly plant in West Point near Atlanta.

While the Peach State isn't actually the nation's largest producer of peaches anymore (that would be South Carolina), its agricultural output is truly impressive. Chicken processing and export are extremely important, with Gainesville claiming the title of "Poultry Capital of the World." Albany is the center of world pecan production. Georgia is also the biggest grower of peanuts in the country. Other major agricultural products are apples, soybeans, corn, and of course sweet Vidalia onions.

The extractive industries are also well represented. Georgia is the national leader in clay and kaolin production and export, and other mined products include granite, marble, and limestone.

While the textile industry isn't what it used to be, Dalton is still called the "Carpet Capital of the World."

The military is a huge economic driver in Georgia. The state hosts some of America's biggest and most vital bases, including Ft. Benning in Columbus, Ft. Stewart near Savannah, Robins Air Force Base near Macon, Moody Air Force Base near Valdosta, Ft. Gordon in Augusta, and the nuclear submarine Navy Base at Kings Bay.

Cargo shipping at the port of Savannah has increased dramatically over the past decade, with that port being the nation's fastest growing and fourth busiest.

People and Culture

Contrary to how the region is portrayed in the media, Georgia is hardly exclusive to natives with thick accents who still obsess over the Civil War and eat grits three meals a day. As you will quickly discover, in some areas, such as Atlanta, Savannah, and St. Simons Island, there are plenty of transplants from other parts of the country. You can spend a whole day in Atlanta and not hear a single drawl or twang.

In any case, don't make the common mistake of assuming you're coming to a place where footwear is optional and electricity is a recent development (though it's true that a few islands didn't get electricity until the 1950s and 1960s). Because so much new construction has gone on in the South in the last quarter-century or so, you might find some aspects of the infrastructure, specifically the roads and the electrical utilities, actually superior to where you came from.

As part of the much-maligned Appalachian region, North Georgia has perhaps faced the steepest climb to respectability. The popular and critically acclaimed film *Deliverance*, based on the James Dickey novel, did little to dispel traditional notions of North Georgia as an uneducated, dangerous backwater. However, beginning in the 1960s, a project of Rabun County High School led to the groundbreaking *Foxfire* magazine and series of books, chronicling the vanishing folkways and culture of the Blue Ridge mountains for future generations to appreciate.

POPULATION

Georgia is the ninth most populous state in the union, with nearly 10 million people. Atlanta of course is by far its biggest city, its metro area accounting for half of that total. The next largest cities in Georgia are Augusta, Columbus, Savannah, Athens, and Macon. The demographic breakdown shows that whites make up 63 percent of the population and African Americans 31 percent. While the Latino population is under 10 percent, it is the most rapidly growing demographic.

RELIGION

Of religious Georgians, the leading denomination by far is Baptist, followed by Methodist, Roman Catholic, and various other lesser-known denominations. Less than 1 percent of Georgia's population is Jewish and Islamic.

MANNERS

The prevalence and importance of good manners is the main thing to keep in mind about the South. While it's tempting for folks from more outwardly assertive parts of the world to take this as a sign of weakness, that would be a major mistake.

Southerners use manners, courtesy, and chivalry as a system of social interaction with one goal above all: to maintain the established order during times of stress. A relic from a time of extreme class stratification, etiquette and chivalry are ways to make sure that the elites are never threatened, and, on the other hand, that even those on the lowest rungs of society are afforded at least a basic amount of dignity.

But as a practical matter, it's also true that Southerners of all classes, races, and backgrounds rely on the observation of manners as a way to sum up people quickly. To any Southerner, regardless of class or race, your use or neglect of basic manners and proper respect indicates how seriously they should take you, not in a socioeconomic sense, but in the big picture overall.

The typical Southern sense of humor—equal parts irony, self-deprecation, and good-natured teasing—is part of the code. Southerners are loath to criticize another individual directly, so often they'll instead take the opportunity to make an ironic joke. Self-deprecating humor is also much more common in the South than in other areas of the country. Because of this, you're also expected to be able to take a joke yourself without being too sensitive.

Another key element in Southern manners is the discussion of money, or rather, the non-discussion. Unlike some parts of the United States, in the South it's considered the height of rudeness to ask someone what their salary is or how much they paid for their house. Not that the subject is entirely taboo, far from it. You just have to know the code.

For example, rather than brag about how much or how little they paid for their home, a Southern head of household will instead take you on a guided tour of the grounds. Along the way they'll make sure to detail: A) all the work that was done; B) how grueling and unexpected it all was; and C) how hard it was to get the contractors to show up.

Depending on the circumstances, in the first segment, A, you were just told either that the head of the house is made of money and has a lot more of it to spend on renovating than you do, or they're brilliant negotiators who got the house for a song. In part B you were told that you are not messing around with a lazy deadbeat here, but with someone who knows how to take care of themselves and can handle adversity with aplomb. And with part C you were told that the head of the house knows the best contractors in town and can pay enough for them to actually show up, and if you play your cards right they might pass on their phone numbers to you with a personal recommendation.

See? Breaking the code is easy once you get the hang of it.

ESSENTIALS

Getting There and Around

AIR

Hartsfield-Jackson Atlanta International Airport (6000 North Terminal Pkwy., 404/530-6600, www.atlanta-airport.com, airport code ATL) is the world's busiest, serving nearly 100 million passengers a year. Its flagship airline is Delta, comprising 60 percent of the airport's traffic. In all, about two dozen airlines fly in and out; domestic highlights include Southwest, AirTran, American, United, and US Airways, with international highlights including Air France, British Airways, KLM, Korean Air, and Lufthansa.

The state's second most comprehensive airport is **Savannah/Hilton Head International Airport** (400 Airways Ave., 912/964-0514, www.savannahairport.com, airport code SAV) directly off I-95 at exit 104, about 20 minutes from downtown Savannah. Airlines with routes into and out of SAV include AirTran (www.airtran.com), American Eagle (www.aa.com), Continental (www.continental.com), Delta (www.delta.com), Northwest Airlink (www.nwa.com), United Express (www.ual.com), and US Airways (www.airways.com).

The only other major airport in Georgia is **Augusta Regional Airport** (1501 Aviation Way, 706/798-3236, www.flyags.com, airport code AGS).

Another option for coastal and southeast

Georgia is **Jacksonville International Airport** (2400 Yankee Clipper Dr., 904/741-4902, www.jia.com, airport code JAX) about 20 miles north of Jacksonville, Florida. While it's a two-hour drive from Savannah, this airport's proximity to the attractions south of Savannah makes it attractive for some visitors.

CAR

The road-building lobby is politically very powerful in Georgia, and as a result the state and county highways here are appreciably better funded and maintained than in many other states. When possible I always choose the state highway over the Interstate, because they are comparatively less crowded and in many cases are of equal or better quality and get me where I want to go at least as quickly.

But if you prefer traveling on the Interstate highway system, Georgia is very well served. It includes north-south I-95, north-south I-75 and I-85 (which combine through Atlanta), the east-west I-20 across the northern half of the state, and the least-traveled example, east-west I-16 between Savannah and Macon.

Shorter connecting Interstate highways include the notorious I-285 around Atlanta, I-575 through North Georgia, I-185 from Columbus to I-85 proper, the small loop of I-516 in Savannah, and two "shortcut" segments, I-675 south of Atlanta and I-475 around Macon.

A common landmark road throughout the coastal region is U.S. 17, which used to be known as the Coastal Highway and which currently goes by a number of local incarnations as it winds its way down the coast, roughly paralleling I-95.

Rental Car

Unless you are staying in public transit-rich Atlanta or perhaps walkable Savannah, a vehicle is mandatory in order to enjoy your stay in Georgia. You need either a valid U.S. driver's license from any state or a valid International Driving License from your home country, and you must be at least 25 years old to rent a car.

If you do not either purchase insurance coverage from the rental company or already have insurance coverage through the credit card you rent the car with, you will be 100 percent responsible for any damage caused to the car during your rental period. While purchasing insurance at the time of rental is by no means mandatory, it might be worth the extra expense just to have that peace of mind.

Some rental car locations are in cities proper, but the vast majority of outlets are in airports, so plan accordingly. The airport locations have the bonus of generally holding longer hours than their in-town counterparts. Hartsfield-Jackson Atlanta International Airport (6000 North Terminal Pkwy., 404/530-6600, www.atlanta-airport.com, airport code ATL) has its own building for rental cars, with 10 agencies to choose from.

TRAIN

Two areas of Georgia, the southeast coastal portion and the northern portion, are served by two lines of the national rail system: **Amtrak** (www.amtrak.com). Amtrak stations on the northern route are: Atlanta (1688 Peachtree St. NE), Gainesville (116 Industrial Blvd.), and Toccoa (47 N. Alexander St.). Stations on the southeast route are: Savannah (2611 Seaboard Coastline Dr.) and Jesup (176 NW Broad St.).

Recreation

ON LAND
Camping

Georgia is a camper's paradise, with an extraordinary state park system that delivers in both quantity and quality. **Georgia State Parks** (www.gastateparks.org) charge a $5 per vehicle parking fee per day on top of whatever the camping fees are, generally around $25 per night. However if you plan on visiting multiple parks in one day—entirely possible in some areas with a high volume of parks, such as North Georgia—one day pass gets you into all parks for that day. There are plenty of private campgrounds as well, but if at all possible utilize the state parks system, not only because it's great, but because increased use will help ensure adequate future funding.

Camping is also possible at several Forest Service campgrounds within the massive **Chattahoochee National Forest** (www.fs.usda.gov). These sites are more geared to tent camping and are less expensive, around $15 a night, but with a lower level of amenities compared to the fairly deluxe standards of many Georgia state parks.

Unlike in the Western states, bears are a much less prevalent hazard in Georgia campgrounds. However, raccoons and opossums can and will get into your foodstuff; take precautions. In the lower portions of Georgia during the warmer months, gnats and mosquitoes are persistent pests, especially at dusk feeding time. Bring repellent.

Hiking, Biking, Climbing, and Caving

Georgia offers many hundreds of miles of excellent, multi-habitat hiking, and that's not even counting the nearly 100 miles of the Appalachian Trail. Nearly every state park offers its own trail system, from short-ish to quite extensive, and there are voluminous wilderness areas, mostly managed by the U.S. Forest Service.

North Georgia is far and away the hiking capital of the state, particularly the stretch from the Cohutta Wilderness east to Brasstown Bald,

the Appalachian Trail, and the Raven Cliffs Wilderness. But the Pine Mountain area around FDR State Park north of Columbus offers a particularly gratifying trail system as well.

Several areas of Georgia offer extensive climbing opportunities. The chief examples of environments conducive to good rock climbing and bouldering are Cloudland Canyon State Park and the entire Lookout-Pigeon Mountain area in northwest Georgia; Tallulah Gorge State Park in northeast Georgia; Mt. Yonah in north-central Georgia; Currahee Mountain at Toccoa; and Providence Canyon in southwest Georgia.

Spelunking is particularly popular in the northwest corner of the state, or "TAG Corner" (signifying the borders of Tennessee, Alabama, and Georgia). Cloudland Canyon is the premier starting place for your experience, which typically is done under the auspices of a guided tour unless you're already an experienced spelunker.

Plenty of Georgia municipalities are offering extensive greenway networks for urban walking and biking. Chief examples include Atlanta's BeltLine, the Columbus Riverwalk, the Augusta Riverwalk, the Ocmulgee Greenway in Macon, and the North Oconee River Greenway in Athens.

Mountain biking is popular everywhere in the Piedmont and North Georgia areas, but is particularly impressive on the Bear Creek Trail near Ellijay, the Bull Mountain run around Dahlonega, the Pinhoti North Trail near Dalton, the Pinhoti South Trail near Summerville, and the very popular trail network around Helen. Unicoi State Park has its own mountain bike trail network.

ON WATER
Fishing and Boating

In Georgia, a regular fishing license is $9, a one-day license $3.50. A separate license is required for trout fishing. Go to http://georgiawildlife.com for more information or to purchase a license online.

Georgia is full of recreational lakes with

full boat access. Chief among them are Clarks Hill, Lake Hartwell, and Lake Russell on the Savannah River; Lake Lanier, Lake George, and Lake Seminole on the Chattahoochee River; Lake Oconee and Lake Sinclair on the Oconee River; and Lake Rabun, Lake Burton, Lake Tallulah Falls, and Lake Tugalo on the Tallulah River.

Georgia's rivers also provide extensive trout and flyfishing opportunities, with the best examples being Dukes Creek near Helen, the Conasauga River in the Cohutta Wilderness, the Chattooga River in northeast Georgia, Dicks Creek near Cleveland, and the upper Flint River.

One of the coolest things about the Georgia coastal area is the prevalence of the Intracoastal Waterway, a combined artificially-constructed and natural sheltered seaway going from Miami to Maine. Many boaters enjoy touring the coast by simply meandering up or down the Intracoastal, putting in at marinas along the way. Dozier's operates a Waterway Cruising Guide to the Intracoastal Waterway at www. waterwayguide.com.

Beaches

By law, beaches in the United States are fully accessible to the public up to the high-tide mark during daylight hours, even if the beach fronts private property and even if the only means of public access is by boat. While certain seaside resorts have over the years attempted to make the dunes in front of their property exclusive to guests, this is actually illegal, though it can be hard to enforce.

On federally run National Wildlife Refuges, access is limited to daytime hours, from sunrise to sunset.

It is a misdemeanor to disturb the **sea oats,** those wispy, waving, wheat-like plants among the dunes. Their root system is vital to keeping the beach intact. Also never disturb a turtle nesting area, whether it is marked or not.

The main beach in Georgia is outside Savannah at **Tybee Island,** with full accessibility from end to end. The beach on the north end is smaller and quieter, while the south end is wider, windier, and more populated. There

are public parking lots, but you can park at metered spots near the beach as well.

Farther south, a very good beach is at **Jekyll Island,** a largely undeveloped barrier island owned by the state. There are three picnic areas with parking: **Clam Creek, South Dunes,** and **St. Andrew.**

Nearby **St. Simons Island** does have a beach area, but it is comparatively narrow and small. Adjacent **Sea Island** is accessible only if you're a guest of the Sea Island Club.

The rest of Georgia's barrier islands are only accessible by ferry, charter, or private boat. Many outfitters will take you on a tour to barrier islands such as Wassaw or Sapelo; don't be shy about inquiring. The most gorgeous beach of all is at **Cumberland Island National Seashore.**

Kayaking, Canoeing, and Rafting

Whitewater rafters will particularly enjoy Georgia, with excellent runs on the **Chattooga and Chattahoochee Rivers.** The Chattahoochee near Atlanta is already known for its various "Shooting the Hootch" activities, but the Hootch near Columbus is getting a boost from a city project to demolish some obsolete earthwork dams and construct a whitewater course there to encourage tourism. The **Flint River** also contains some whitewater sections near Thomaston.

Most every state park in Georgia, it seems, has some kind of lake on which you can do some canoeing. Most of them offer canoe rental for very reasonable rates.

The best pure kayaking areas are found on the Coastal Plain, especially in the vast Altamaha River basin. The **Altamaha River Canoe Trail** extends 140 miles from Lumber City to the Altamaha estuary near Darien.

The **Okefenokee Swamp** offers many miles of kayaking within its vast interior, with multiple canoe trails. Because it is federally run, however, there are some guidelines. Go to www. fws.gov/okefenokee/WildernessCanoeing.html for more info.

The Savannah area has rich kayaking and canoeing at **Tybee Island, Skidaway Island,** and the blackwater **Ebenezer Creek** west of town.

Tips for Travelers

WOMEN TRAVELING ALONE

Women should take the same precautions they would take anywhere else. Many women traveling to this region have to adjust to the prevalence of traditional chivalry. In the South, if a man opens a door for you, it's considered a sign of respect, not condescension.

Another adjustment is the possible assumption that two or three women who go to a bar or tavern together might be there to invite male companionship. This misunderstanding can happen anywhere, but in some parts of the South it might be slightly more prevalent. Being aware of it is the best defense; otherwise no other steps need to be taken.

ACCESS FOR TRAVELERS WITH DISABILITIES

While the vast majority of attractions and accommodations make every effort to comply with federal law regarding those with disabilities, as they're obliged to do, the very historic nature of many parts of this region means that some structures simply cannot be retrofitted for maximum accessibility. This is especially the case with various house museums. This is something to find out on a case-by-case basis, so call ahead.

The sites administered by the National Park Service in this book (MLK Jr. National Historic Site, Jimmy Carter NHS, Andersonville NHS, Ocmulgee Mounds, Chickamauga and Kennesaw Mountain battlefield sites, Fort Pulaski, Fort Frederica, and Cumberland Island National Seashore) all strive to be as wheelchair-accessible as possible.

Many Georgia state parks have ADA-accessible trails. See www.gastateparks.org for more info.

GAY AND LESBIAN TRAVELERS

Don't believe all the negative propaganda about the South. The truth is that the metropolitan areas are tolerant of homosexuality, and gay and lesbian travelers shouldn't expect anything untoward to happen. Atlanta in particular is extraordinarily gay-friendly, as is the university town of Athens and cosmopolitan Savannah.

Outside the metro areas, locals are less welcoming to gay men and lesbian women, although overt hostility is rare. The best approach is to simply observe dominant Southern mores for anyone here, gay or straight. In a nutshell, that means keep public displays of affection and politics to a minimum. Southerners in general have a low opinion of anyone who flagrantly espouses a viewpoint too obviously or loudly.

SENIOR TRAVELERS

Both because of the large proportion of retirees in the region and because of the South's traditional respect for the elderly, the area is quite friendly to senior citizens. Many accommodations and attractions offer a senior discount, which can add up over the course of a trip. Always inquire *before* making a reservation, however, as checkout time is too late.

TRAVELING WITH PETS

While the United States is very pet friendly, that friendliness rarely extends to restaurants and other indoor locations. More and more accommodations are allowing pet owners to bring pets, often for an added fee, but please inquire *before* you arrive. In any case, keep your dog on a leash at all times. As a general rule, keep dogs off of beaches unless you see signage saying otherwise; as of this writing Jekyll Island is the only Georgia beach that one could call dog friendly.

Health and Safety

CRIME

While crime rates are indeed above national averages in many of the areas covered in this book, especially in inner city areas, incidents of crime in the more heavily trafficked tourist areas are no more common than anywhere else. In fact, these areas might be safer because of the amount of foot traffic and police attention.

By far the most common crime against visitors here is simple theft, primarily from cars. (Pickpocketing, thankfully, is rare in the United States.) Always lock your car doors. Conversely, only leave them unlocked if you're absolutely comfortable living without whatever is inside at the time.

Should someone corner you and demand your wallet or purse, just give it to them. Unfortunately, the old advice to scream as loud as you can is no longer the deterrent it once was, and in fact may hasten aggressive action by the robber.

If you are the victim of a crime, *always call the police.* Law enforcement wants more information, not less, and the worst thing that can happen is you'll have an incident report in case you need to make an insurance claim for lost or stolen property.

Remember that in the United States as elsewhere, no good can come from a heated argument with a police officer. The place to prove a police officer wrong is in a court of law, perhaps with an attorney by your side, not at the scene.

For emergencies, always call 911.

AUTO ACCIDENTS

If you're in an auto accident, you're bound by law to wait for police to respond. Failure to do so can result in a "leaving the scene of an accident" charge, or worse.

In the old days, cars in accidents had to be left exactly where they came to rest until police gave permission to move or tow them. However, Georgia recently loosened regulations so that if a car is blocking traffic as a result of an accident, the driver is allowed to move it

enough to allow traffic to flow again. That is, if the car can be moved safely. If not, you're not required to move it out of the way.

Since it's illegal to drive in these states without auto insurance, I'll assume you have some. And because you're insured, the best course of action in a minor accident, where injuries are unlikely, is to patiently wait for the police and give them your side of the story. In my experience, police react negatively to people who are too quick to start making accusations against other people. After that, let the insurance companies deal with it. That's what they're there for.

If you suspect any injuries, call 911 immediately.

ILLEGAL DRUGS

Marijuana, heroin, methamphetamine, and cocaine and all its derivatives are illegal in the United States with only a very few, select exceptions, none of which apply to Georgia. The use of ecstasy and similar mood-elevators is also illegal. The penalties for illegal drug possession and use in Georgia are quite severe.

ALCOHOL

The drinking age in the United States is 21. Most restaurants that serve alcoholic beverages allow those under 21 inside. Generally speaking, if a venue only allows those over 21, someone asking to see identification will greet you at the door.

Drunk driving is a problem on the highways of America, and Georgia is no exception. Always drive defensively, especially late at night, and obey all posted speed limits and road signs, and never assume the other driver will do the same. You may *never* drive with an opened alcoholic beverage in the car, even if it belongs to a passenger.

Until recently Georgia had the most restrictive "blue laws" in the nation restricting the retail sale of alcoholic beverages. However, recent legislation has allowed cities to hold referenda on whether or not to allow alcohol package sales on Sunday; as a result, many cities now allow the practice.

GETTING SICK

Unlike most developed nations, as of this writing the United States has no comprehensive national health care system (there are programs for the elderly and the poor). Indeed, the mere proposal of it seems quite polarizing.

Visitors from other countries who need non-emergency medical attention are best served by going to freestanding medical clinics. The level of care is typically very good, but you'll be paying out of pocket for the service, unfortunately.

For emergencies, however, do not hesitate to go to the closest hospital emergency room, where generally the level of care is also quite good, especially for trauma. Worry about payment later. Emergency rooms in the United States are required to take true emergency cases whether or not the patient can pay for services.

Call 911 for ambulance service.

Pharmaceuticals

Unlike many European nations, antibiotics are available in the United States only on a prescription basis and are not available over the counter. Most cold, flu, and allergy remedies are available over the counter. While homeopathic remedies are gaining popularity in the United States, they are nowhere near as prevalent as in Europe.

Drugs with the active ingredient ephedrine are available in the United States without a prescription, but their purchase is often tightly regulated to cut down on the use of these products to make the illegal drug methamphetamine.

VACCINATIONS

As of this writing, there are no vaccination requirements to enter the United States. Contact your embassy before coming to confirm this before arrival, however.

In the autumn, at the beginning of flu season, preventive influenza vaccinations, simply called "flu shots," often become available at easily accessible locations like clinics, health departments, and even supermarkets.

HUMIDITY, HEAT, AND SUN

There is only one way to fight the South's high heat and humidity, and that's to drink lots of fluids. A surprising number of people each year refuse to take this advice and find themselves in various states of dehydration, some of which can land you in a hospital.

Remember: If you're thirsty, you're already suffering from dehydration. The thing to do is keep drinking fluids *before* you're thirsty, as a preventative action rather than a reaction.

Always use sunscreen, even on a cloudy day. If you do get a sunburn, get a pain relief product with aloe vera as an active ingredient. On extraordinarily sunny and hot summer days, don't even go outside between the hours of 10am and 2pm.

HAZARDS
Insects

There might be a lot more mosquitoes in Georgia than you're used to. Because of the recent increase in the mosquito-borne West Nile virus, the most important step to take in staying healthy in Georgia is to keep mosquito bites to a minimum. Do this with a combination of mosquito repellent and long sleeves and long pants, if possible. Not every mosquito bite will give you the virus; in fact, chances are quite slim that one will. But don't take the chance if you don't have to.

The second major step in avoiding insect nastiness is to steer clear of **fire ants,** whose large, gray or brown-dirt nests are quite common throughout the state. They attack instantly and in great numbers, with little or no provocation. They don't just bite, they inject you with poison from their stingers. In short, fire ants are not to be trifled with.

While the only real remedy is the preventative one of never coming in contact with them, should you find yourself being bitten by fire ants, the first thing is to stay calm. Take off your shoes and socks and get as many of the ants off you as you can. Unless you've had a truly large amount of bites—in which case you should seek medical help immediately—the best thing to do next is wash the area to get any venom off, and then disinfect with alcohol. Then a topical treatment such as calamine lotion or hydrocortisone is advised. A fire ant bite will leave a red pustule that lasts about a week. Try your best not to scratch it so that it won't get infected.

Outdoor activity, especially in woodsy, undeveloped areas, may bring you in contact with another unpleasant indigenous creature, the tiny but obnoxious **chigger,** sometimes called the redbug. The bite of a chigger can't be felt, but the enzymes it leaves behind can lead to a very itchy little red spot. Contrary to folklore, putting fingernail polish on the itchy bite will not "suffocate" the chigger, because by this point the chigger itself is long gone. All you can do is get some topical itch or pain relief and go on with your life. The itching will eventually subside.

Threats in the Water

While enjoying area beaches, a lot of visitors become inordinately worried about **shark attacks.** Every couple of summers there's a lot of hysteria about this, but the truth is that you're much more likely to slip and fall in a bathroom than you are to even come close to being bitten by a shark in shallow Atlantic waters.

A far more common fate for area swimmers is to get stung by a **jellyfish,** or sea nettle. They can sting you in the water, but most often beachcombers are stung by stepping on beached jellyfish stranded on the sand by the tide.

If you get stung, don't panic; wash the area with saltwater, not freshwater, and apply vinegar or baking soda.

Lightning

The southeastern United States is home to vicious, fast-moving thunderstorms, often with an amazing amount of electrical activity. Death by lightning strike occurs often in this region and is something that should be taken quite seriously. The general rule of thumb is if you're in the water, whether at the beach or in a swimming pool, and hear thunder, get out of the water immediately until the storm passes. If you're on dry land and see lightning flash a distance away, that's your cue to seek safety indoors. Whatever you do, do not play sports outside when lightning threatens.

Information and Services

MONEY

Automated Teller Machines (ATMs) are available in all urban areas covered in this book. Be aware that if the ATM is not owned by your bank, not only will that ATM likely charge you a service fee, but your bank may charge you one as well.

While ATMs have made travelers checks less essential, travelers checks do have the important advantage of accessibility, as some rural and less-developed areas have few-to-no ATMs. You can purchase travelers checks at just about any bank.

Establishments in the United States only accept the U.S. dollar. To exchange foreign money, go to any bank.

Generally, establishments that accept credit cards will feature stickers on the front entrance with the logo of the particular cards they accept, though this is not a legal requirement. The use of debit cards has dramatically increased in the United States. Most retail establishments and many fast-food chains are now accepting them. Make sure you get a receipt whenever you use a credit card or a debit card.

MEDIA AND COMMUNICATIONS
Newspapers and Websites

The closest thing to a national newspaper in the United States is *USA Today,* which you will find at diverse locations from airports to gas stations. The national paper of record is the

New York Times, which is available in larger urban areas but only rarely in outlying areas.

Georgia's two largest circulation papers are both in Atlanta, the mainstream *Atlanta Journal-Constitution* (www.ajc.com) and the alt-weekly *Creative Loafing* (www.clatl.com). Augusta's main paper is the *Chronicle* (www.chronicle.augusta.com). Macon's is the *Telegraph* (www.macon.com). The daily in Columbus is the *Ledger-Enquirer* (www.ledger-enquirer.com).

In Athens the mainstream paper is the *Banner-Herald* (www.onlineathens.com), while the longtime alt-weekly is *The Flagpole* (www.flagpole.com).

In Savannah, the daily newspaper of record is the *Morning News* (www.savannahnow.com). The alt-weekly is *Connect Savannah* (www.connectsavannah.com).

In South Georgia, key papers include the Albany *Herald* (www.albanyherald.com) and the Valdosta *Daily Times.*

The main paper in the much more sparsely populated Golden Isles region is the *Brunswick News* (www.thebrunswicknews.com), but many people read the newspaper of record of nearby Jacksonville, Florida, the *Florida Times-Union* (www.jacksonville.com).

Internet Access

Visitors from Europe and Asia are likely to be disappointed at the quality of Internet access in the United States, particularly the area covered in this book. Fiber optic lines are still a rarity, and while many hotels and B&Bs now offer in-room Internet access (some charge, some don't, make sure to ask ahead), the quality and speed of the connection might prove poor.

Wireless (Wi-Fi) networks also are less than impressive, though that situation continues to improve on a daily basis in coffeehouses, hotels, and airports. Unfortunately, many hot spots in private establishments are for rental only.

Phones

Generally speaking, the United States is behind Europe and much of Asia in terms of cell phone technology. Unlike Europe, where "pay-as-you-go" refills are easy to find, most American cell phone users pay for monthly plans through a handful of providers.

Still, you should have no problem with cell phone coverage in urban areas. Where it gets much less dependable is in rural areas and on beaches. Bottom line: don't depend on having cell service everywhere you go. There are areas of extreme South Georgia and in the mountains of North Georgia where cell service is spotty to nonexistent, though often better than you might expect given the isolation.

As with a regular landline, anytime you face an emergency call 911 on your cell phone.

All phone numbers in the United States are seven digits preceded by a three-digit area code. You may have to dial a "1" before a phone number if it's a long-distance call, even within the same area code.

RESOURCES

Suggested Reading

NONFICTION

Bryson, Bill. *A Walk in the Woods: Rediscovering America on the Appalachian Trail.* New York, NY: Anchor, 2006. Entertaining and affecting tales from the length of the Appalachian Trail.

Carter, Jimmy. *Keeping Faith: Memoirs of a President.* Fayetteville, AR: University of Arkansas Press, 1995. The 39th president's own account of his time in the White House from Plains, Georgia.

Gray, Marcus. *It Crawled From the South: An R.E.M. Companion.* Da Capo Press, 1997. The complete guide to the band R.E.M., from personal histories to lyrics.

Greene, Melissa Fay. *Praying for Sheetrock.* New York, NY: Ballantine, 1992. Greene explores the racism and corruption endemic in McIntosh County, Georgia, during the civil rights movement.

Greene, Melissa Fay. *Temple Bombing.* Da Capo Press, 1996. An account of the 1958 bombing of an Atlanta synagogue involved with civil rights by white supremacists.

Hannon, Lauretta. *The Cracker Queen: A Memoir of a Jagged, Joyful Life.* New York, NY: Gotham, 2010. A humorous recounting of the more dysfunctional aspects of the author's life in Middle Georgia and Savannah.

Jones, Bobby. *Down the Fairway.* Latham, NY: British American Publishing, 1995. Golf history, lore, and lessons from the great Atlantan who founded Augusta National Golf Club.

Kemble, Fanny. *Journal of a Residence on a Georgian Plantation in 1838-1839.* Athens, GA: University of Georgia Press, 1984. English actress's groundbreaking account of her stay on a rice plantation in McIntosh County, Georgia.

Morgan, Philip (ed.). *African American Life in the Georgia Lowcountry: The Atlantic World and the Gullah Geechee.* Athens, GA: University of Georgia Press, 2010. Readable work of scholarship on the history and folkways of Georgia's Gullah-Geechee people.

Pomerantz, Gary M. *Where Peachtree Meets Sweet Auburn: A Saga of Race and Family.* New York, NY: Penguin Books, 1997. The story of Atlanta's rise to prominence as told through the eyes of two influential families, one white and one black.

Ray, Janisse. *Ecology of a Cracker Childhood.* Minneapolis, MN: Milkweed Editions, 2000. Heartfelt memoir of growing up amid the last stands of the longleaf pine ecosystem in southeast Georgia.

Washington, James Melvin (ed.). *A Testament of Hope: The Essential Writings and Speeches of Martin Luther King, Jr.* New York, NY:

HarperOne, 1990. A collection of work by the Atlanta native and civil rights icon.

White, Bailey. *Mama Makes Up Her Mind: And Other Dangers of Southern Living.* Da Capo Press, 2009. Thomasville native recalls her eccentric mother in tales adapted from the author's popular NPR segments.

FICTION

Berendt, John. *Midnight in the Garden of Good and Evil.* New York, NY: Vintage, 1999. Not exactly fiction but far from completely true, this modern crime classic definitely reads like a novel while remaining one of the unique travelogues of recent times.

Caldwell, Erskine. *Tobacco Road.* Athens, GA: University of Georgia Press, 1932. Lurid and sensationalist, this portrayal of a shockingly dysfunctional rural Georgia family during the Depression paved the way for *Deliverance.*

Dickey, James. *Deliverance.* New York, NY: Delta, 1970. Gripping and socially important tale of a North Georgia rafting expedition gone horribly awry.

Harris, Joel Chandler. *The Complete Tales of Uncle Remus.* New York, NY: Houghton Mifflin, 2002. The Atlanta author broke new ground in oral history by compiling these African American folk stories.

Mitchell, Margaret. *Gone with the Wind.* New York, NY: MacMillan, 1936. Atlanta author's immortal tale of Scarlett O'Hara and Rhett Butler and one of the most popular books of all time.

O'Connor, Flannery. *Flannery O'Connor: Collected Works.* New York, NY: Library of America, 1988. A must-read volume for anyone wanting to understand the South and the Southern Gothic genre of literature.

Internet Resources

TOURISM AND RECREATION
EXPLORE GEORGIA
www.exploregeorgia.com
The state's official tourism website.

GEORGIA STATE PARKS
www.gastateparks.org
Vital historical and visitors' information for Georgia's underrated network of historical state park sites along the coast, including camping reservations.

NATURE
GEORGIA DEPTARTMENT OF NATURAL RESOURCES WILDLIFE RESOURCES DIVISION
www.georgiawildlife.com
Lots of specific information hunting, fishing, and outdoor recreation in Georgia's various regions.

OCEAN SCIENCE
http://oceanscience.wordpress.com
A blog by the staff of Savannah's Skidaway Institute of Oceanography, focusing on barrier island ecology and the maritime environment.

PADDLE GEORGIA
www.garivers.org
Georgia River Network site that clues you in on guided trips and tours of the state's rivers, creeks, and marshes.

FOOD
CREATIVE LOAFING'S OMNIVORE
http://clatl.com/blogs/omnivore
The dynamic food blogging of the critics of Atlanta's alt-weekly.

GEORGIA ORGANICS
www.georgiaorganics.org
Get the inside scoop on farm-to-table sustainable cuisine.

SAVANNAH FOODIE
www.savannahfoodie.com
An insider's look at the Savannah restaurant scene.

HISTORY AND CULTURE
CIVIL WAR IN GEORGIA
www.gacivilwar.org
Official site marking the sesquicentennial (150th anniversary) of the Civil War in Georgia, with statewide information on events, sites, reenactments, and more.

FOXFIRE
www.foxfire.org
Website of the longstanding nonprofit cultural organization based in Rabun, Georgia, which seeks to preserve Appalachian folkways.

LOSTWORLDS
www.lostworlds.org
Well-researched and readable exploration of Georgia's extensive pre-Columbian Native American history.

NEW GEORGIA ENCYCLOPEDIA
www.georgiaencyclopedia.org
A mother lode of concise, neutral, and well-written information on the natural and human history of Georgia from prehistory to the present.

Index

A

Aaron, Hank: 292
Abraham Baldwin Agricultural College: 333
accidents, car: 421
Administration Building, University of Georgia: 142
African American culture/history: general discussion 20; African American Monument 238, 240; APEX Museum 33; Augusta 164; Black Heritage Festival 280; Calvin Baber Museum and African-American Resource Center 162; civil rights 411; Cumberland Island 391; Dorchester Academy and Museum 310; First African Baptist Church 242; Harris, Joel Chandler 44; Harris Neck 380; historically black colleges/universities 46; Jack Hadley Black History Museum 336; Jarrell Plantation Historic Site 205; Lt. Henry O. Flipper Burial Site 337; Lucy Craft Laney Museum of Black History 169; Macon 188; Martin Luther King Jr. National Historic Site 30-32; Massie Heritage Center 259; Morgan County African American Museum 158; Morton Theatre 143; National Black Arts Festival 56; Negro Heritage Trail Tour 276; Pin Point 269, 270; Pleasant Hill Historic District 197; Ralph Mark Gilbert Civil Rights Museum 259; Savannah 237; Sea Island African Americans 310-311; Second African Baptist Church 245; Stone Mountain history 87; St. Simons Island 369; Tubman African American Museum 193; Tubman Pan African Festival 200
agriculture: 329, 333
A. H. Stephens Historic Park: 163
air pollution: 397
air travel: 80, 416-417
Albany: 20, 329-330
Albany Civil Rights Institute: 20, 329
Albany Museum of Art: 330
alcohol: 421
Alice Walker Driving Trail: 212
alligators: 345, 346, 399
Allman, Duane: 196, 197
Allman, Gregg: 197

Allman Brothers Band: 196, 198
Allman Brothers Band Museum: 13, 17, 185, 197
All Saints' Episcopal Church: 336
alpaca: 115
"Alpine" village of Helen: 105
Altamaha Coastal Tours: 16, 382
Altamaha Park of Glynn County: 359
Altamaha River Trail: 16, 419
Altamaha Waterfowl Management Area: 382
Alta Vista Cemetery: 90
Americus: 12, 320-321
Amicalola Falls State Park: 11, 93, 110-111
amusement parks: Callaway Gardens 217; Six Flags Over Georgia 44; Stone Mountain Park 86; Wild Adventures 341
Andalusia: 185, 208, 209
Anderson, Paul: 104
Andersonville: 12, 15, 324, 326
Andersonville National Cemetery: 324, 325
Andersonville Village: 325
Andrew Low House Museum: 255
Angelou, Maya: 240
animals: 399-402
Anna Ruby Falls: 109
Ansa, Tina McElroy: 371
antebellum era: 406
antiques: Atlanta 58; Madison 158; Savannah 285, 286
APEX Museum: 33
Appalachian Trail: general discussion 11, 15; Southern Terminus Approach Trail 111; through Georgia 112-114; Wildcat Creek access 102
aquariums: Atlanta 28; Flint RiverQuarium 329; Tybee Island Marine Science Center 275; University of Georgia Marine Educational Center and Aquarium 269
Arabia Mountain National Heritage Area: 90
Arch, University of Georgia: 141
Archaic Period: 402
architecture: Alpine 105; Andrew Low House Museum 255; Athens 146; Eatonton 212; Fitzgerald 334; Fox Theatre 39; Governor's Mansion 43; Grand Opera House 192-193; Green-Meldrim House 254; Hay House 190;

Hyatt Regency Savannah 240; Jekyll Island Historic District 363; Lapham-Patterson House Historic Site 337; Ledger-Enquirer Building 224; Lucas Theatre for the Arts 244; Madison 157; Milledgeville 206, 208; Norris, John 259; Old City Hall (Brunswick) 355; Olde Pink House 244; Owens-Thomas House 248; Penfield Historic District 162; prairie 263; Preston, William Gibbons 242; Robert Toombs House 178; Sacred Heart Cultural Center 169; Scarborough House 260; St. Joseph Catholic Church 191; Swan House 42-43; Tour of Homes and Gardens 280; Victorian District, Savannah 261; Washington 179; wrought iron 256
Armillary Sphere: 256
Armstrong House: 262
art galleries/crafts: Atlanta 58; Augusta 173; Brunswick 358; Clayton 97; Decatur 85; Folk Pottery Museum of Northeast Georgia 107; Genuine Georgia Artisan Marketplace 162; Lardworks Studio and Lasso The Moon Alpaca Farm 115; Mark of the Potter 110; McIntosh Old Jail Art Center 381; Savannah 251; Watkinsville 156
Ashford Manor: 156
Athens: 16, 139-155; Civil War sights 14; music sights 17, 138, 149; nightlife 138, 146; weather 9
Athens Human Rights Festival: 149
Athens Twilight Criterium: 148
AthFest: 148
AthHalf: 148
A3C Hip Hop Festival: 57
Atlanta: 21-81; accommodations 66-69; African American history 20; Civil War sights 14; culinary tour 18; entertainment/events 47-57; food 70-78; greater Atlanta 81-91; highlights 22; history 22; information/services 78-79; itineraries 11; lingo 78; maps 24-25, 29; music sights 16-17; neighborhoods 26-27; nightlife 47-51; planning tips 8, 26; recreation 62-65; shopping 58-62; sights 28-47; transportation 79-81
Atlanta BeltLine: 63
Atlanta Botanical Garden: 39
Atlanta Braves: 11, 64
Atlanta Cyclorama: 14, 34
Atlanta Falcons: 64

Atlanta Film Festival: 55
Atlanta Food & Wine Festival: 56
Atlanta-Fulton Public Library: 33, 37
Atlanta Greek Festival: 57
Atlanta Hawks: 64
Atlanta History Center: 11, 14, 22, 42
Atlanta Jazz Festival: 56
Atlanta Pride: 57
Atlanta Silverbacks: 64
Atlanta Streets Alive: 57
Atlanta Underground Film Festival: 56
Atlanta University Center: 20, 46, 47
Atlantic Station: 27
Augusta: 164-177; African American history 20; Civil War sights 14; music sights 17; weather 9
Augusta Canal Interpretive Center: 170
Augusta Canal National Heritage Area: 138, 170
Augusta Entertainment Complex: 172
Augusta GreenJackets: 174
Augusta Museum of History: 17, 20, 167
Augusta RiverHawks: 174
Augusta Riverwalk: 138, 166
Augusta Visitor Center: 167, 172
authors: general discussion 18; Angelou, Maya 240; Bartram, William 357; Berendt, John 237; Caldwell, Erskine 164; Carson McCullers Center for Writers and Musicians 225; Dickey, James 101; DuBois, W.E.B. 46; Golden Isles as inspiration for 371; Harris, Joel Chandler 44, 212; Kemble, Fanny 382; Lanier, Sidney 192, 355; McCullers, Carson 220; Mitchell, Margaret 35, 37, 411; O'Connor, Flannery 206, 208, 209, 211, 255; Ross, Mary 355; Savannah Book Festival 280; Walker, Alice 212
auto accidents: 421
Automatic for the People: 149
auto travel: 417
Averitt Center for the Arts: 229
aviation museums: 202, 338
Aviation Wing: 88
azalea: 217, 398

B
B-52s: 140, 149
Babyland General Hospital: 109
Bacchanalia: 18, 77
backpacking: Appalachian Trail 112-114; Cloudland Canyon State Park 133; Cohutta

Wilderness Area 123; Providence Canyon State Outdoor Recreation Area 327; Vogel State Park 117

Bainbridge: 339

bamboo: 283

banking: 423

Banks Lake National Wildlife Refuge: 342

barbecue: Athens 152; Atlanta 72; Augusta 175; and Brunswick stew 360; Columbus 227; first recorded 404; Fresh Air Barbecue 204; Macon 201; Old Clinton BBQ 205, 212; Pine Mountain 219; Savannah 299, 304; Tomlin's Barbecue (Clayton) 98; *see also specific place*

barrier islands: 313, 391, 395

Bartow History Museum: 124

Bartram, William: 357

baseball: 64, 292

basketball: 64

bats: 134

Battlefield Park: 261

Battlefield Park Complex: 260

Battle of Bloody Marsh: 405

Battle of Kettle Creek: 179

Bay Street: 240

beachcombing: 16, 391

beaches: 375, 385, 388, 395, 419

Beach Institute: 256

Beacon Range Light: 246

bears: 105, 346, 399

beer: 149

Bell Auditorium: 172

Berendt, John: 237

Berry, Martha: 129

Berry College: 129

best-of itinerary: 11-13

Big Chicken: 88

Big House: 13, 17, 185, 197

"Big Oak": 336

biking: general discussion 418; Athens 148, 150; Atlanta 63; Augusta Canal 171; Callaway Gardens 217; Jekyll Island 366; Ocmulgee River Heritage Trail 200; Savannah 290; Savannah tours 276; St. Simons Island 375

Billy Carter's Gas Station: 322

birds: 400

bird-watching: Altamaha Waterfowl Management Area 382; Blackbeard Island 386; Brunswick 359; Butler Island 382; Chesser Island Observation Tower 345;

George L. Smith State Park 230; Grand Bay 342; Harris Neck Wildlife Refuge 380; Hofwyl-Broadfield Plantation 358; Jekyll Island 366; Lamar Q. Ball Jr. Raptor Center 228; Oconee National Forest 161; Okefenokee National Wildlife Refuge 345; Ossabaw Island 314; Savannah 291; Silver Lake Wildlife Management Area 340; Wassaw Island National Wildlife Refuge 313; Youmans Pond 309

Blackbeard Island: 386

Blackbeard Island National Wildlife Refuge: 386

black bears: 346

Black Forest Bear Park: 105

Black Heritage Festival: 280

Black Rock Mountain State Park: 12, 101

Blackstock Winery's: 120

blackwater river: 394

Blairsville: 115-116

Bloody Marsh Battlefield: 373

Blue and Gray Museum: 333

Blue Hole: 117

Blue Ridge: 392

Blue Springs Marina: 161

Blue Willow Inn: 19, 163

Bly Gap: 114

Blythe Island Regional Park: 359

boating: general discussion 418; Brunswick 359; Chattahoochee River 63; Fort Yargo State Park 156; High Falls State Park 205; Jekyll Island 366; Lake Lanier 89; Lake Sinclair 211; Savannah River Lakes 180; Savannah water tours 276; St. Simons Island 375; Wassaw Island National Wildlife Refuge 313

Bobby Brown Outdoor State Recreation Area: 182

Bohemian Hotel: 13, 293

Bonaventure Cemetery: 13, 233, 265

Booker T. Washington Community Center: 199

bookstores: Athens 150; Atlanta 59; Brunswick 358; Clayton 98; Retro Cinema and Books 158; Savannah 286; St. Simons Island 374

Booth Western Art Museum: 124

Boxwood: 157

Brasstown Bald: 15, 93, 116-117

Breman, William: 40

Bridal Veil Falls: 103

Broad Street Historic District: 17, 167

Broadway Tackle & Canoe Rentals: 171
Broughton Street: 13, 246, 284
Brown, James: 17, 164, 167, 195
Brunswick: 353-361
Brunswick Historic District: 353
Brunswick stew: 360
Brunswick Stewbilee: 358
Bryan County: 312
Buckhead: general discussion 27; accommodations 67; food 75; historic changes 55; sights 42-44
Buckhead (Piedmont): 162
bugs: 401
Bull Sluice Falls: 99
Butler Island: 382
butterflies: 217
Butts-Mehre Heritage Hall Sports Museum: 144

C
Cabbage Patch dolls: 109
Cabbagetown: 27
Cairo: 340
Caldwell, Erskine: 18, 164
Caledonia Cascade: 103
Calhoun Square: 258
Callaway Gardens: 217
Callaway Plantation: 179
Calvin Baber Museum and African-American Resource Center: 162
camping: 418
Camp Lawton: 230
Camp Sumter: 324
Candler Oak: 263
Cannonball House: 192
canoeing/kayaking: general discussion 419; Brunswick 359; Champney River Park 382; Chattooga Wild and Scenic River 99; Crooked River State Park 388; Ebenezer Creek 313; Flint River 219, 339; George L. Smith State Park 230; Harris Neck Wildlife Refuge 380; itineraries 14-16; Jekyll Island 366; Ocmulgee River Heritage Trail 200; Okefenokee National Wildlife Refuge 346; Richard B. Russell State Park 181; Savannah 277, 288; Savannah Rapids Park 170; St. Simons Island 375
Canyon Climbers Club: 14, 133
Cape Fear: 281
Capitol Museum: 33
Capricorn Record: 198

Carboniferous Period: 342
Carnegie Branch Library: 263
carpeting: 126
carriage tours: 276
car shows: 122
Carson McCullers Center for Writers and Musicians: 225
Carter, Billy: 322
Carter, Jimmy: 12, 40, 320-328
Carter Center: 40
Carter Family Compound: 323
Cartersville: 124-129
car travel: 417
Cathedral of St. John the Baptist: 233, 254
caves: general discussion 418; Ellison's Cave 134; TAG Corner 132, 133; tours 14
Cecil B. Day Butterfly Center: 217
cell phone services: 424
Celtic Cross: 246
cemeteries: Alta Vista Cemetery 90; Andersonville National Cemetery 324, 325; Bonaventure Cemetery 265; Colonial Cemetery 252; Du Bignon Cemetery 365; Laurel Grove Cemetery 266-267; Linwood Cemetery 225; Lt. Henry O. Flipper Burial Site 337; Marietta Confederate Cemetery 88; Memory Hill Cemetery 209, 211; Myrtle Hill Cemetery 130; Oak City Cemetery (Bainbridge) 340; Oakland Cemetery 35; Riverside Cemetery 196; Rose Hill Cemetery 196
Centennial Olympic Park: 11, 28
Centers for Disease Control Museum: 42
Central State Hospital: 210
Chapel, University of Georgia: 142
Charlemagne's Kingdom: 105
Charles, Ray: 195, 329
Charles H. Morris Center: 246
Charles Oddingsells House: 245
Chastain Park: 62, 63
Chatham Artillery Guns: 241
Chattahoochee National Forest: 418
Chattahoochee River: 63, 419
Chattahoochee River Summer Splash: 56
Chattahoochee River Trail: 226
Chattooga Wild and Scenic River: 15, 93, 99-101, 419
Cherokee Nation: 125-126, 127
Cherry Blossom Festival: 200
Chesser Homestead: 345

Chesser Island Observation Tower: 345
Chestatee Wildlife Preserve: 122
Chickamauga & Chattanooga National Military Park: 14, 93, 127
Chief McIntosh House: 204
Chieftains Museum and Major Ridge Home: 130
Chief Vann House Historic Site: 126
chiggers: 423
children's activities: Babyland General Hospital 109; Black Forest Bear Park 105; Callaway Gardens 217; Chestatee Wildlife Preserve 122; Georgia Aquarium 28; Georgia Children's Museum 193; Helen Tubing and Water Park 106; Imagine It! The Children's Museum of Atlanta 30; LanierWorld 89; Six Flags Over Georgia 44; Splash in the 'Boro 229; Stone Mountain Park 86; Tellus Science Museum 124; Wild Adventures 341; Zoo Atlanta 33
Chili Cookoff: 158
Chippewa Square: 251
"Chitlin' Circuit": 195
Christ Church: 374
Christ Episcopal Church: 244
Christmas: 284, 338
Church-Waddel-Brumby House: 140
City Hall of Athens: 143
City Hall of Savannah: 241
City Market: 13, 242-243, 285
Civilian Conservation Corps (CCC): 411
civil rights: 259, 411
Civil War Museum: 312
Civil War sights: general discussion 14, 407-410; Andersonville 324, 326; Athens 140; Atlanta History Center 42; Augusta 165; Battle of Tunnel Hill 126; Camp Lawton 230; Cannonball House 192; Chickamauga & Chattanooga National Military Park 93, 127; Civil War Museum 312; Confederate Memorial 263; Confederate Powderworks 171; Crawfordville 180; Darien 379; double-barrel canon 143; Fort Pulaski National Monument 270-273; history at sea 222; Irwinville 333; Kennesaw Mountain National Battlefield Park 88; Lookout Mountain Battlefield 128, 132; Marietta 86, 88; Milledgeville 206; National Civil War Naval Museum 220; Reconstruction 410; Robert Toombs House 178; Sherman, General William T. 160; Stone Mountain 86, 87; St. Simons Island 370; see also specific place
Clark Atlanta University: 46
Clarkesville: 109
Clark's Hill Lake: 182
classical music: 52
Classic Car Show: 122
Classic City Brew Fest: 149
Claxton: 230
Claxton Bakery: 230
Clayton: 12, 15, 97-99
Cleveland: 109
climate: 9, 395
climbing: 418
Cline-O'Connor-Florencourt House: 209
Clisby-Austin house: 126
Clocktower Museum: 130
Cloudland Canyon State Park: 14, 93, 132
CNN Studio Tour: 32
Cobb, Thomas Reade Roots: 146
Cobb, Ty: 181
Coca-Cola: 30, 31, 45, 124
Coca-Cola Space Science Center: 223
Cochrans Falls: 111
Cockspur Beacon: 272
Cohutta Mountains: 122-123
Cohutta Wilderness Area: 123
Cold War: 274
college football: 65, 140, 142, 341
Colonial Cemetery: 252
colonial period: 193, 233
Colquitt, "Mural City": 317, 331-332
Columbia Square: 244
Columbia Theatre: 177
Columbus: 14, 220-228
Columbus Museum: 224
Columbus State University: 224
communications: 423
Compound: 17, 51
Confederate Memorial: 263
Confederate Monument: 168
Confederate Powderworks: 171
Consolidated Gold Mines: 118-119
The Conspirator: 281
Conyers: 163
Cotton Hall: 332
cotton trade: 188, 406
country stores: 107
courtesy: 415

Courtyard at Crane: 19, 368
covered bridges: 156, 164, 230
Covington: 163
crafts: see art galleries/crafts
Crawfordville: 14, 180
Creek Indians: 403
crime: 421
Crisson Gold Mine: 118
Crooked River State Park: 388
culinary tour: 18-19
culture, the: 414-415
Cumberland Island: 386-391
Cumberland Island National Seashore: 16, 350, 388-391, 419
Cunningham House: 245
Currahee Military Museum: 104
Cyclorama, Atlanta: 34, 37

D

Daedalus Gallery: 251
Daffin Park: 265
Dahlonega: 118-122
Dahlonega Gold Museum State Historic Site: 11, 118, 121
Dahlonega Literary Festival: 120
Dalton: 126
Dalton Depot: 127
Darien: 378-386
Darien Methodist Church: 381
Darien Waterfront Park: 381
Darien Welcome Center: 381
Dauset Trails Nature Center: 204
Davenport, Isaiah: 245
Davidson-Arabia Nature Preserve: 90
Davis, Jefferson: 333
Dean Rusk Hall: 142
Decatur: 22, 27, 81-85
Decatur County Historical and Genealogical Society Museum: 340
Declaration of Independence: 171, 244
Deen, Paula: 237, 241
Deliverance: 18, 99, 101
Demosthenes Hall: 141
Depression era: 410
design museum: 40
DeSoto Falls: 122
Desotorow Gallery: 251
Desposito's: 13, 19, 303
Dickey, James: 18, 101
Dick's Creek Falls: 99

Dicks Creek Gap: 114
Dillard: 98
Dillard House: 19, 98
disabilities, access for travelers with: 420
disease: 42
diving: 289
doctors: 422
Dogwood Festival: 55
dolphins: 399
Dolphin Tales: 28
dolphin tours: 367
Dorchester Academy and Museum: 310
Dorothy Chapman Fuqua Conservatory: 39
Douglass Theatre: 20, 195
Dowdell's Knob: 218
downtown Atlanta: 28-33, 66-67, 70
Downtown Macon Visitor Information Center: 199
Driftwood Beach: 363
drinking: 277, 278, 421
driving: 417
drugs: 421
Druid Hills: 27, 41-42, 76
Drummer Boy Museum: 325
Du Bignon Cemetery: 365
DuBois, W.E.B.: 46
Duke, Derek: 274
Duke's Creek: 108
Duke's Creek Falls: 108
dunes: 229
Dungeness Ruins: 16, 390

E

Eagle Tavern Museum & Welcome Center: 156
Earle May Boat Basin Park: 339
Eastern Continental Divide: 393
Eastside Savannah: 264-266
Eatonton: 212
Eatonton-Putnam Chamber of Commerce: 212
Ebenezer Creek: 288, 313, 419
economy: 413-414
Eddie's Attic: 17, 83
Egyptian artifacts: 41
1842 Inn: 12, 201
Einstein's: 11, 73
Elberton: 183
Elder Mill Covered Bridge: 156
Elijah Clark State Park: 182
Elizabeth on 37th: 13, 302
Eliza Thompson House: 13, 256, 295

Ellicott Rock Wilderness Area: 100
Ellijay: 122
Ellis Square: 13, 242, 243
emergencies: 422
Emmet Park: 246
Emory University: 45
Empire State South: 11, 73
Enota Mountain Retreat: 117
environmental issues: 396
environmental study: 225
estuaries: 394
Etowah Indian Mounds Historic Site: 93, 125, 403
explorers, European: 357, 403-404

F

Factor's Walk: 240
Fairlie-Poplar: 27
Fall Festival: 283
fall foliage: 101, 134
farms/farmer's markets: Atlanta 60; Decatur 85; Jimmy Carter Boyhood Farm 323; Koinonia Farms 320; Savannah 287; Tully Family Farm 43
fauna: 399-402
FDR Country: 214-219
FDR Historic Pools and Springs: 216
FDR Memorial Museum: 215
FDR's Little White House: 12, 185, 214
FDR State Park: 185, 218
Federal Reserve: 361, 364
Fed Museum: 38
Fernbank Museum of Natural History: 41
Fernbank Science Center: 41
Festhalle: 105
film festivals: Atlanta Underground Film Festival 56; Macon Film Festival 200; Savannah Film Festival 246, 283
Finster, Howard: 131
Fire Station Number 6: 30
First African Baptist Church: 20, 233, 242, 391
First Baptist Church: 252
fish: 400
fishing: general discussion 418; A. H. Stephens Historic Park 163; Black Rock Mountain State Park 101; Callaway Gardens 218; Flint River 219; Florence Marina State Park 328; Fort Yargo State Park 156; Grand Bay 342; High Falls State Park 205; Lake Marvin 134; Lake Seminole 340; Lake Sinclair 211; Lake

Walter F. George 331; Magnolia Springs State Park 230; Moccasin Creek State Park 101; Oconee National Forest 161; Savannah 289; Savannah River Lakes 180; Smithgall Woods State Park 108
Fitzgerald: 15, 333
536 Martin Luther King Jr. Blvd: 198
Five Points: 27
Flannery O'Connor Childhood Home: 255
Flannery O'Connor Room: 209
flea markets: 97
Flint River: 219, 339, 394, 419
Flint RiverQuarium: 329
Flood, Curt: 292
flora: 398
Florence Marina State Park: 328
Flovilla: 204
flowers: 398
Flying Biscuit Cafe: 16, 74
folk art/culture: Folk Pottery Museum of Northeast Georgia 107; Foxfire Museum & Heritage Center 98; Harris, Joel Chandler 44; Paradise Garden 131; Pasaquan 228; Ridge and Valley Country 129; Savannah Folk Music Festival 283; *Swamp Gravy* 332
Folk Pottery Museum of Northeast Georgia: 107
Folkston: 347
Folkston Funnel: 347
food: Atlanta Food & Wine Festival 56; Brunswick stew 358, 360; Chili Cookoff 158; culinary tour 18-19; Deen, Paula 241; Fried Green Tomato Festival 205; fruitcakes 230; Georgia Apple Festival 122; Mayhaw Festival 332; pecans 334; Savannah Foody Tour 276; Savannah Seafood Festival 283; Shellman Bluff 381; Sorghum Festival 115; Vidalia Onion Museum 230; Waffle House Museum 81; Wild Georgia Shrimp and Grits Festival 365; *see also* barbecue
football: 64
Forces of Nature: 281
Ford family: 312
Forrest, General Nathan Bedford: 130
Forrest Gump: 252, 281
Forsyth Fountain: 263
Forsyth Park: 13, 233, 262
Forsyth Park Café: 263
Fort Benning: 220
Fort Frederica National Monument: 13, 350, 372
Fort Hawkins: 193

Fort King George State Historic Site: 381
Fort McAllister State Historic Site: 14, 312
Fort Morris State Historic Site: 310
Fort Mountain State Park: 123
Fort Oglethorpe: 129
Fort Pulaski National Monument: 13, 15, 233, 270-273
Fort Stewart Museum: 311
40 Watt Club: 17, 146, 149
Fort Yargo State Park: 156
Fountain of Rings: 28
Fourth of July: 282
Foxfire Mountaineer Festival: 98
Foxfire Museum & Heritage Center: 98
Fox Theatre: 11, 22, 39
Fragrant Garden for the Blind: 263
Franklin Square: 242
Fraternity and Sorority Row: 146
Fred Hamilton Rhododendron Garden: 117
Freedom Park: 63
Fresh Air Barbecue: 19, 204
Fried Green Tomatoes: 204
Fried Green Tomato Festival: 205
Frogtown Cellars: 120
Fuqua Orchid Center: 39

G

Gainesville: 14, 90
Gallery Espresso: 251
gardens: Atlanta Botanical Garden 39; Callaway Gardens 217; Fall Festival 283; Fragrant Garden for the Blind 263; Fred Hamilton Rhododendron Garden 117; John A. Sibley Horticultural Center 217; LeConte-Woodmanston Botanical Garden 309; Lewis Vaughn Botanical Garden 163; Lockerley Arboretum 210; Meadow Garden 169; NOGS Tour of Hidden Gardens 282; Oak Hill & The Martha Berry Museum 130; Pebble Hill Plantation 337; Secret Garden Tour 200; State Botanical Garden of Georgia 143; Thomasville Rose Show & Festival 338; Tour of Homes and Gardens 280; Trustees Garden 245; Whimsical Botanical Gardens 204; Wormsloe State Historic Site 268
Gateway Park: 195
Gator: 281
Geechee Kunda: 310
General Nathan Bedford: 130

General's Daughter: 281
Genuine Georgia Artisan Marketplace: 162
geography: 392
geology: 392
George L. Smith State Park: 230
George T. Bagby State Park: 331
Georgia Apple Festival: 122
Georgia Aquarium: 11, 22, 28
Georgia Aviation Hall of Fame: 203
Georgia Children's Museum: 193
Georgia College & State University: 209, 211
Georgia College Museum: 211
Georgia Conservancy: 133
Georgia Girl Guides: 133
Georgia Guidestones: 183
Georgia International Horse Park: 164
Georgia Mountain Fair: 117
Georgia Mountain Fall Festival: 117
Georgia Museum of Agriculture & Historic Village: 333
Georgia Museum of Art: 143
Georgia Nature Center: 156
Georgia Rural Telephone Museum: 317, 321
Georgia Sea Turtle Center: 363
Georgia Southern Planetarium: 229
Georgia Southern University: 228
Georgia Southern University Museum: 229
Georgia Sports Hall of Fame: 193
Georgia State Panthers: 65
Georgia State Parks: 418
Georgia State University: 47
Georgia Tech: 44, 65
Georgia Theatre: 17, 142, 149
Gertrude Herbert Institute of Art: 171
ghost tours/haunted sights: general discussion 13; Central State Hospital 210; Haunted Pillar 168; Oakland Cemetery 36; Savannah 275
Gift, The: 281
Gilded Age: 361, 362, 364
Gilmer County Historical Society and Civil War Museum: 123
Gingerbread Man: 281
Girl Scout National Center: 248
Girl Scouts: 248, 249
Glory: 281
Glynn County: 353-361
Golden Isles: 349-391; Brunswick and Glynn County 353-361; culinary tour 19; Cumberland Island and St. Mary's 386-391; Darien and McIntosh County 378-386;

highlights 350; history 351, 352; Jekyll Island 361-369; maps 351; planning tips 9, 352; St. Simons Island 369-378
Golden Isles Arts and Humanities Association: 356
gold mining: general discussion 397; Consolidated Gold Mines 118-119; Crisson Gold Mine 118; Dahlonega Gold Museum State Historic Site 118; Duke's Creek Falls 108; history of 406; North Georgia history 121
Gold Rush Days: 120
golf: Athens 151; Atlanta 64; Augusta 174; Gordonia-Alatamaha State Park 231; Highland Walk 181; Jekyll Island 366; Lake Lanier 89; Lake Walter F. George 331; Masters golf tournament 172, 174; Mountain View Course 217; Richard B. Russell State Park 181; Ritz-Carlton Lodge, Reynolds Plantation 160; Savannah 290; St. Simons Island 375
Gone with the Wind: 35, 37, 411
Gone with the Wind Museum: Scarlett on the Square: 86
Gordon, William: 248
Gordonia-Alatamaha State Park: 231
government: 412-413
Governor's Mansion: 43
"Gracie": 265
Grand Bay: 342
Grand Bay Wetland Education Center: 342
Grand Opera House: 192-193
Grand Theater: 335
Grant, General Ulysses S.: 326
Grant Park: 27, 33-36, 62
Gray: 205
Great Depression: 410
Greek culture: 57, 283
Greene, Nathanael: 243
Greene County Historical Society Museum: 162
Greene Square: 245
Green-Meldrim House: 15, 253
Greensboro: 161
Greensboro Chamber of Commerce: 161
Greensboro Florist and Gift Shop: 162
Greyfield Inn: 390, 391
Grit, The: 17, 19, 153
Gutstein Gallery: 251
Gwinett Gladiators: 65

H

H&H Restaurant: 17, 198, 202
Habersham Winery: 106
Habitat for Humanity Global Village and Discovery Center: 320
Hadley, Jack: 336
Haitian monument: 243
Halloween: 57
Hamilton-Turner Inn: 256
Hampton Lillibridge House: 245
hang gliding: 132
Hard Labor Creek State Park: 163
Hardy, Oliver: 177
Harlem: 176
Harris, Joel Chandler: 18, 44, 212
Harris Neck Wildlife Refuge: 350, 379-381
Hart, Nancy: 182, 183
Hart Outdoor Recreation Area: 181
Hartsfield-Jackson International Airport: 10
Haunted Pillar: 168
Haygood House: 156
Hay House: 12, 185, 190
hazards: 422-423
health: Centers for Disease Control Museum 42; Roosevelt's work for 214, 216; and safety 421-423
heat: 395
heatstroke: 422
Helen: 12, 15, 93, 104-110
Helen Arts and Heritage Center: 106
Helen Tubing and Water Park: 106
Helton Creek Falls: 117
HemlockFest: 120
Henry W. Grady School of Journalism and Mass Communication: 142
Herb House: 246
Heritage Hall: 157
Herty Field: 142
Hiawassee: 117
High Falls State Park: 205
High Museum of Art: 11, 22, 36
High Shoals Falls: 117
Hiker, The: 263
hiking: general discussion 418; Altamaha Waterfowl Management Area 382; Amicalola Falls State Park 111; Arabia Mountain National Heritage Area 91; Blackbeard Island 386; Brasstown Bald 116; Brunswick 359; Cloudland Canyon State Park 133; Cohutta Wilderness Area 123; Duke's Creek

Falls 108; Ellicott Rock Wilderness Area 100-101; FDR State Park 218; Flint River 219; Fort Mountain State Park 123; Grand Bay 342; Hard Labor Creek State Park 163; itineraries14-16; Kennesaw Mountain National Battlefield Park 88; Lake Strom Thurmond 182; Oconee National Forest 161; Pigeon Mountain 134; Raven Cliff Falls 108; Savannah 290; Smithgall Woods State Park 108; Springer Mountain 112; St. Simons Island 375; Tallulah Gorge State Park 103; Unicoi State Park 109; Vogel State Park 117; Wassaw Island National Wildlife Refuge 313; Wildcat Creek 102
Hilton Savannah DeSoto: 254
hip hop: 57
Hispanic population: 412
Historic District of Savannah: 243-261
Historic Ebenezer Baptist Church: 30
Historic Passenger Rail Depot: 348
Historic Savannah Theatre: 252
Historic Trolley Tour: 172
Historic Western & Atlantic Railroad Tunnel: 126
history: 402-412
hockey: 65
Hodgson Hall: 263
Hofwyl-Broadfield Plantation: 355
Hogpen Gap: 114
Holiday Tour of Homes: 284
Hood, General John Bell: 126
horseback riding: A. H. Stephens Historic Park 163; Berry College 130; Dahlonega 120; Georgia International Horse Park 164; Hard Labor Creek State Park 163; Jekyll Island 366; Lake Lanier 89; Pine Mountain 218; Trackrock Stables 116
horses, wild: 390, 391
Horton House Tabby Ruins: 363
Hostel in the Forest: 16, 359
humidity: 395, 422
humor: 415
Hunter Holmes Academic Building,: 141
Hunter House: 157
hunting: Grand Bay 342; Oconee National Forest 161; Ossabaw Island 315; Smithgall Woods State Park 108
hurricanes: 9, 270, 396
Hyatt Regency Savannah: 295
hydrogen bomb, Tybee: 274

I
I-16: 228-231
I-20: 159, 162
Ice House Museum: 390
"I Have a Dream" speech: 87
Ila Dunlap Little Library: 142
Imagination Theater: 329
Imagine It! The Children's Museum of Atlanta: 30
IMAX theaters: 329
Imperial Theatre: 17, 168
Independent Presbyterian Church: 252
Indian Springs State Park: 12, 185, 203-204
Inman family: 42
Inman Park: 27, 74
Inman Park Festival: 55
insects: 401, 422-423
Internet access: 424
Intown Macon: 191
Irish culture: 246, 247, 280
Iron Horse: 162
Irwinville: 15, 333
Isaiah Davenport House Museum: 245
Isle of Hope: 269
itineraries: 11-20

J
Jack Hadley Black History Museum: 20, 336
Jackson, Andrew: 127
Jackson, Shoeless Joe: 292
Jackson Oak: 143
James Brown Arena: 172
Jane Hurt Yarn Interpretive Center: 102
Jarrell Plantation Historic Site: 205
Jay, William: 260
jazz: 56, 282
Jefferson County Courthouse: 177
Jefferson Davis Memorial Historical Site: 333
Jekyll Island: 361-369, 419
Jekyll Island Bluegrass Festival: 365
Jekyll Island Club: 13, 361, 363, 367
Jekyll Island Historic District: 13, 350, 362
Jekyll Island Museum: 363
jellyfish stings: 423
Jepson Center for the Arts: 250, 251
Jerusalem Evangelical Lutheran Church: 312
Jewish community: 258, 283
Jewish Heritage Museum: 40
Jimmy Carter Boyhood Farm: 317, 323
Jimmy Carter country: 320-328

Jimmy Carter Library and Museum: 40
Jimmy Carter National Historic Site: 20, 321
"Jingle Bells": 256, 257
John A. Sibley Horticultural Center: 217
John Marlor Art Center: 211
Johns Mountain: 134
Jones, Bobby: 164
Jones, Noble: 268
Jones Street: 256
Joshua Hill Home: 157
Juliette: 204-205
Juliette Gordon Low Birthplace: 248

K

kayaking: see canoeing/kayaking
Kehoe House: 245
Kelly, Emma: 229
Kemble, Fanny: 371, 382
Kennedy-Bessette marriage: 391
Kennesaw Mountain National Battlefield Park:
    14, 88
King Birth Home: 30
King Center for Nonviolent Social Change: 30
King Jr., Martin Luther: Albany Civil Rights
    Institute 329; Dorchester Academy and
    Museum 310; "I Have a Dream" speech 87;
    Martin Luther King Jr. Birthday Celebration
    54; Martin Luther King Jr. Day Parade 280;
    Martin Luther King Jr. National Historic Site
    30-32; sights 20
Kiser House: 328
kite boarding: 289
Koinonia Farms: 320
Kolomoki Mounds Historic Park: 317, 330, 403
Ku Klux Klan: 87, 130

L

Lady & Sons restaurant: 241
Lafayette Square: 254
Lake Hartwell: 180
Lake Lanier: 89-90
Lake Oconee: 159
Lake Oconee Welcome Center: 160
Lake Russell: 181
Lake Seminole: 340
Lake Sinclair: 211
Lake Strom Thurmond: 182
Lake View: 218
Lake Walter F. George: 331
Lamar Building: 168

Lamar Mound: 403
Lamar Q. Ball Jr. Raptor Center: 228
Laney-Walker Historic District: 168
Lanier, Sidney: 192, 355, 371
Lanier Oak: 355
Lapham-Patterson House Historic Site: 317,
    337
Lardworks Studio and Lasso The Moon Alpaca
    Farm: 115
The Last Song: 281
Laurel & Hardy Museum: 177
Laurel Grove Cemetery: 266-267
Laurel Grove North: 267
Laurel Grove South: 267
Lawrence Shoals Recreational Area: 161
leaf peeping: 101, 134
LeConte-Woodmanston Botanical Garden: 309
Ledger-Enquirer Building: 224
Legend of Bagger Vance: 281
Lenox Square: 11, 60
Lewis Vaughn Botanical Garden: 163
LGBT community: Atlanta Pride 57; Savannah
    Pride Festival 282; Savannah resources 306
LGBT travelers: 420
Liberty Bell Swimming Pool: 218
Liberty County: 308-312
Liberty Hall: 163
Liberty Theatre Cultural Center: 226
libraries: Athens 155; Atlanta 80; Atlanta-
    Fulton Public Library 33, 37; Carnegie
    Branch Library 263; Jen Library 246; Jimmy
    Carter Library and Museum 40; Robert W.
    Woodruff Library 46
lighthouses: Beacon Range Light 246;
    Cockspur Beacon 273; Sapelo Lighthouse
    385; St. Simons Lighthouse Museum 370;
    Tybee Lighthouse 273
lightning: 423
Lights on Macon: 13, 199
Linwood Cemetery: 225
Liquid Sands Glass Gallery: 251
Little Five Points: 27, 74
Little Five Points Halloween: 57
Little St. Simons Island: 377
Little Tybee Island: 288
live oaks: 336, 398
living history museums: Civil War Museum
    312; Foxfire Museum & Heritage Center 98;
    Westville 328; Wormsloe State Historic Site
    268

Lockerley Arboretum: 210
loggerhead turtles: 386, 399
logging: 396
Longstreet, General James: 128
Longstreet Society: 90
Lookout Mountain: 132
Lookout Mountain Battlefield: 128, 132
Lookout Mountain Flight Park and Training
    Center: 132
Louisville: 177
Lover's Oak: 355
Low, Juliette Gordon: 248, 249, 267
Low, William "Billow": 255
Lower Coastal Plain: 393
Lowndes County Historical Society & Museum:
    341
Lt. Henry O. Flipper Burial Site: 337
Lucas Theatre for the Arts: 244
Lucy Craft Laney Museum of Black History:
    20, 169
Lumpkin: 328
Lutherans: 314
Lyndon House Art Center: 146

M

Macon: 12, 188-203; African American history
    20; music sights 17
Macon Film Festival: 200
Madison: 14, 138, 157-164
Madison Morgan Cultural Center: 157
Madison Museum of Art: 157
Madison Presbyterian Church: 158
Madison Square: 253
Madison Visitors Center: 157
Magnolia Springs State Park: 14, 230
Main Street Gallery: 97
manners: 415
Mantle, Mickey: 292
Maranatha Baptist Church: 322
marathons: 63
"March to the Sea": 160
Mardi Gras: 387
Margaret Mitchell House and Museum: 37
Marietta: 86
Marietta/Cobb Museum of Art: 88
Marietta Confederate Cemetery: 88
Marietta Museum of History: 88
Marine Memorial: 262
marine studies: 269, 275
Maritime Center: 371

marshes: 14-16, 395
Marshes of Glynn: 355
MARTA public transit: 80
Martin, Eddie Owens: 228
Martin Luther King Jr. Birthday Celebration: 54
Martin Luther King Jr. Boulevard: 259
Martin Luther King Jr. Day Parade: 280
Martin Luther King Jr. National Historic Site: 11,
    20, 22, 30-32
Martus, Florence: 238
Mary Mac's Tea Room: 18, 72
Mary Ross Waterfront Park: 355
Mason, Lowell: 252
masonry fortification: 272
Massengale Park: 375
Massie Heritage Center: 259
Masters golf tournament: 172, 174
Mayhaw Festival: 332
McCullers, Carson: 18, 220
McIntosh, Chief: 204
McIntosh County: 378-386
McIntosh Old Jail Art Center: 381
Meadow Garden: 169
media: 423
medical care: 422
medications: 422
Memory Hill Cemetery: 209, 211
Memory Park Christ Chapel: 379
mental hospitals: 210
Mercer, John: 265
Mercer family: 257, 264
Mercer University: 162
Mercer-Williams House Museum: 256
Messenburg, Charles Reb: 196
Mexican-American War: 256
Michael C. Carlos Museum: 22, 41
Middle Georgia: 184-231; along I-16 228-231;
    Civil War sights 14; Columbus 220-228;
    culinary tour 19; FDR Country 214-219;
    highlights 185; Indian Springs State Park
    and Juliette 203-205; Macon 188-203; maps
    186; Milledgeville 206-213; planning tips 8,
    184
Midnight in the Garden of Good and Evil: 237,
    245, 257, 264, 281
Midtown Atlanta: 27, 36-41, 67, 72
Midway: 308-312
Midway Church: 309
Midway Museum: 309
Mighty Eighth Air Force Museum: 267

military museums: Currahee Military Museum 104; Mighty Eighth Air Force Museum 267; National Civil War Naval Museum 220; National Infantry Museum and Soldier Center 222; National Prisoner of War Museum 324; Signal Corps Museum 172

Milledgeville: 14, 206-213

Miller Theater: 168

millionaire's club: 362, 363, 364

mining: 108, 397; see also gold mining

Minnehaha Falls: 103

"Miss Fanny": 179

missionaries, European: 404

Mississippian Period: 403

Mistletoe State Park: 182

Misty Mountain Model Railroad: 115

Mitchell, Margaret: 18, 35, 37, 86, 411

Moccasin Creek State Park: 101

Monastery of the Holy Spirit: 138, 164

money: 38-39, 423

Montaluce Estates: 120

Monterey Square: 233, 256

Moon River: 269

Morehouse College: 46

Morgan County African American Museum: 158

Morgan County Courthouse: 157

Morris Brown College: 47

Morris Museum of Art: 167

Morton Theatre: 142

mountain biking: general discussion 418; Athens 150; Berry College 130; Georgia International Horse Park 164; Tallulah Gorge State Park 103; Unicoi State Park 109

Mountain Creek Lake: 218

Mountain Crossings at Walasi-yi: 113

mountaineers: 98

mountains: 14-16

Mountain View Course: 217

movie sets: Conyers 163; Savannah 252, 281

Mrs. Wilkes' Dining Room: 13, 19, 300

Mulberry Inn: 245, 293

murals: 177, 331-332

"Murmur" Railroad Trestle: 17, 149

Museum District: 193

Museum of Arts and Sciences: 193

Museum of Aviation: 185, 202

Museum of Design Atlanta: 40

Museum of Fine Arts: 211

music: A3C Hip Hop Festival 57; Allman Brothers Band 196, 198; Allman Brothers Band Museum 197; Athens 138, 139, 140, 146, 149; AthFest 148; Atlanta 47-49, 52; Brown, James 164, 167; Carson McCullers Center for Writers and Musicians 225; Charles, Ray 329; "Chitlin' Circuit" 195; Imperial Theatre 168; itinerary 16-18; jazz 56, 282; Jekyll Island Bluegrass Festival 365; "Jingle Bells" 257; Macon 199; Mason, Lowell 252; Mercer, John 264, 265; Oliver, King 259; Opry House Juliette 205; Rose Hill Cemetery 196; Savannah 279; Savannah Music Festival 282

Music Midtown: 56

music/record stores: Athens 150; Atlanta 62; Decatur 85; Wuxtry Records 149

Myrtle Hill Cemetery: 130

N

Nacoochee Mound: 107

Nancy Hart Cabin: 183

Nannygoat Beach: 385

Nantahala Outdoor Center: 100

Nathanael Greene Monument: 243

National Black Arts Festival: 56

National Civil War Naval Museum: 220, 222

National Infantry Museum and Soldier Center: 185, 222

National Prisoner of War Museum: 12, 317, 324, 325

Native American culture/history: general history 402-403; Booth Western Art Museum 124; Chief Vann House Historic Site 126; Columbus Museum 224; Creek 206; Dahlonega 118; Etowah Indian Mounds Historic Site 93, 125; Indian Removal Act 127; Indian Springs State Park 203-204; Kolomoki Mounds Historic Park 330; Macon 188; Nacoochee Mound 107; Native American shell ring 385; negotiations with Oglethorpe 405; New Echota Historical Site 125-126; Ocmulgee Indian Celebration 200; Ocmulgee National Monument 194; Okefenokee National Wildlife Refuge 343; Ossabaw Island 314; Rock Eagle Effigy 212; Stone Mountain 87; Tomochichi 248; Track Rock Petroglyphs 116; Trail of Tears 127, 130, 407

Natural History Museum and Planetarium: 211

natural history museums: 41

Neels Gap: 112-113

Newcastle Street: 355

New Ebenezer: 312, 314
New Ebenezer Retreat and Conference Center: 313
New Echota Historical Site: 125, 127
NOGS Tour of Hidden Gardens: 282
Norris, John: 259
Northeast Georgia History Center: 90
North Georgia: 92-134; Blairsville 115; Brasstown Bald 116-117; Cartersville area 124-129; Civil War sights 14; Cohutta Mountains 122-123; culinary tour 19; Dahlonega 118-122; Helen 104-110; highlights 93; maps 94, 95; planning tips 8, 93; Rabun County 96-104; Ridge and Valley Country 129-134; weather 396
North Georgia College and State University: 118, 119
North Oconee River Greenway: 150
nuclear bomb, Tybee: 274

O

Oak City Cemetery (Bainbridge): 340
Oak Hill & The Martha Berry Museum: 130
Oakland Cemetery: 35, 37
Oakley, Berry: 196
Oatland Island Wildlife Center: 264
Obediah's Okefenok: 348
oceanography: 269
Ocean Voyager: 28
Ocmulgee Indian Celebration: 200
Ocmulgee National Monument: 12, 185, 194, 403
Ocmulgee River Heritage Trail: 200
Oconee Forest Park: 150
Oconee Springs Park: 211
O'Connor, Flannery: 18, 206, 208, 209, 211, 255
Officer's Row: 274
Oglethorpe, General James Edward: 164, 236, 240, 314, 404
Oglethorpe Square: 248
Ohoopee Dunes Natural Area: 16, 229, 393
Okefenokee Adventures: 346
Okefenokee Heritage Center: 348
Okefenokee National Wildlife Refuge: 317, 343-347, 419
Okefenokee Swamp: 16, 342-348
Oktoberfest: 105
Oktoberfest on the River: 283
Old Capital Museum: 207
Old City Hall (Brunswick): 355

Old Clinton BBQ: 205, 212
Old College: 142
Olde Pink House: 244
Olde Town Conyers: 163
Old Fort: 245
Old Fort Jackson: 264
Old Fort Screven: 273
Old Fourth Ward: 27
Old Gaol: 161
Old Governor's Mansion: 208
Old Jail Museum: 163
Old Jefferson Hotel: 177
Old Market: 177
Old Salem Park Recreational Area: 161
Old Sautee Store: 107
Oliver, King: 259
Oliver Hardy Festival: 177
Olmstead Linear Park: 41
Olympics: 28, 45, 164
140 E. Washington Street: 149
onions, Vidalia: 230
opera: 52
Opry House: 205
Orange Hall House Museum: 387
orchids: 39, 156
Ordeal of Dr. Mudd: 281
Ossabaw Island: 313
Ossabaw Island Foundation: 314
Otis Redding Memorial Library: 199
Otis Redding Statue: 17, 195
Our Lady of Fatima Processional and Blessing of the Fleet: 358
Out on Film: 57
Overlook Park: 355
Owens-Thomas House: 13, 233, 248
Oxbow Meadows Environmental Learning Center: 225

P

Paleoindian Period: 402
Panola Mountain State Park: 90
Paradise Garden: 93, 131
Parks Ferry Recreational Area: 161
Parks on Chehaw: 329
Pasaquan: 12, 185, 228
Peachtree Road Race: 56, 63
Pebble Hill Plantation: 337
pecans: 334
Pei Ling Chan Gallery: 251
Pemberton, John: 31, 225

Penfield Chapel: 162
Penfield Historic District: 162
Penniman, Richard "Little Richard": 195
Penny Savings Bank: 169
performing arts: Atlanta 51-54; Averitt Center
    for the Arts 229; Brunswick 356; Columbus
    226; Fox Theatre 39; Georgia Theatre
    142; Grand Opera House 192-193; Historic
    Savannah Theatre 252; Ritz Theatre 355;
    Savannah 279; Springer Opera House 224;
    St. Simons Island 374; Thomasville 338
Performing Arts Center: 143
pets, traveling with: 420
pharmaceuticals: 422
Phi Kappa Hall: 141
Phipps Plaza: 11, 61
phones: 321
phone services: 424
physical therapy: 216
Picnic in the Park: 283
Piedmont: 135-183; Athens 139-155; Augusta
    164-177; Civil War sights 14; culinary tour
    19; geography 393; highlights 138; Madison
    157-164; maps 136-137; planning tips 8, 138;
    Savannah River Lakes 180-183; Washington
    177-180
Piedmont Hotel: 90
Piedmont National Wildlife Refuge: 205
Piedmont Park: 27, 62, 63
Pierpont, James L.: 256, 257, 267, 341
Pigeon Mountain: 133
Pine Mountain: 12, 217
Pine Mountain Trail: 218
Pinnacle Gallery: 251
Pin Point: 269
Pin Point Heritage Museum: 20, 269
placer mining: 121
Plains: 12, 320, 321-324
Plains Depot Museum and Presidential
    Campaign Headquarters: 321
Plains High School Visitors Center and
    Museum: 322
Plains Peanut Festival: 321
planetariums: Fernbank Science Center 41;
    Georgia Southern Planetarium 229; Natural
    History Museum and Planetarium 211;
    Thronateeska Heritage Center 329
planning tips: 8-10
plants: 398
Pleasant Hill Historic District: 17, 197

Plum Orchard: 390
Pocket, The: 134
pocosin bog: 342
Poetter Hall: 254
polio: 214, 216
politics: 412-413
pollution: 397
Poncey-Highland: 27
Pond View Fine Dining: 16, 348
Poor House and Hospital: 263
population: 414
POW camps: 324, 326
Power of the Past Museum: 338
Presidential Campaign Headquarters: 321
Preston, William Gibbons: 242
Price, Eugenia: 18, 371
Providence Canyon State Outdoor Recreation
    Area: 12, 317, 327
public transit: 10, 80
Pylons, the: 149

R

Rabun County: 96-104
Rabun County Historical Society: 97
Rabun County Welcome Center: 97
Radium Springs: 330
railroads: Augusta Museum of History 167;
    Conyers 163; Dalton Depot 127; Folkston
    Funnel 347; Historic Western & Atlantic
    Railroad Tunnel 126; history of 407; model
    105, 115; Roundhouse Railroad Museum:
    260; SAM Shortline 324; train travel 417;
    Washington 177; Waycross 347, 348
Ralph Mark Gilbert Civil Rights Museum: 20,
    259
raptors: 228
Raven Cliff Falls: 108
Raven Cliffs Wilderness Area: 15, 108
Ray Charles Plaza: 329
Reconstruction: 410
recreation: general discussion 418-419;
    itineraries 14-16; outfitters, Atlanta 62;
    outfitters, Savannah 285; see also specific
    place
Redding, Otis: 17, 195
Regency architecture: 248
religion: 414
R.E.M.: 17, 139, 149
rental cars: 417
Revolutionary War: general discussion 405;

Augusta 165; Greensboro 161; Haitian monument 243; Hart, Nancy 182; Midway 309; Savannah 261; Sunbury 310
Reynolds, John: 244
Reynolds Plantation: 160
Reynolds Square: 244
rhododendrons: 117
Rialto Center for the Arts: 47
rice plantations: 355
Richard, Little: 17, 195
Richard B. Russell State Park: 181
Richardson, Howard: 274
Richmond Hill: 312
Richmond Hill Historical Society and Museum: 312
Ridge, Major: 127
Ridge and Valley Country: 129-134, 393
Ritz Theatre: 355
RiverCenter for the Performing Arts: 226
rivers: 393
Riverside Cemetery: 196
Riverside Theatre: 226
River Street: 233, 238
Riverwalk, Columbus: 223
R. J. Reynolds Mansion: 385
Robert Toombs House: 178
Robert W. Woodruff Library: 46
Robin Lake: 218
Robinson, Jackie: 340
Rockdale County Covered Bridge: 164
Rock Eagle Effigy: 212, 403
Rocks on the Roof: 13, 277
Rocktown Trail: 134
Rogers House and Rose Cottage: 158
Rome: 129-130
Rome-Floyd County Visitors Center: 129
Roosevelt, First Lady Eleanor: 215
Roosevelt, Franklin Delano: 214, 410
Roosevelt Warm Springs Institute for Rehabilitation: 216
Roots: 281
Rose Garden: 338
Rose Hill Cemetery: 17, 196
Rose Lawn House Museum: 124
Ross, Mary: 355
Roundhouse Railroad Museum: 260
Rousakis Plaza: 238
Royston: 181
running/walking trails: Athens 150; AthHalf 148; Atlanta 63; Augusta Riverwalk 166;

Berry College 129; Callaway Gardens 217; Forsyth Park 262; Jekyll Island 366; Ocmulgee River Heritage Trail 200
Russell Dam & Lake Office & Visitor Center: 181
Ruth, Babe: 292

S

Sacred Heart Catholic Church: 209
Sacred Heart Cultural Center: 169, 172
Saig: 304
salt marsh: 395
Salzburgers: 314
SAM Shortline: 324
Sand Arts Festival: 282
sand dunes: 229, 267
Sanford Stadium,: 142
Sapelo Island: 20, 384-385
Sapelo Island National Estuarine Research Reserve: 384
Sapelo Lighthouse: 385
Sautee Nacoochee: 107
Sautee Nacoochee Vineyards: 107
Savannah: 13, 232-308; accommodations 293-296; African American history 20; city layout 237; Civil War sights 14; entertainment/events 277-284; food 19, 297-305; highlights 233; history 235-237; information/services 305-306; maps 234; planning tips: 8, 237; recreation: 288-293; shopping 284-287; sights 238-277; tours 275-277; transportation 307-308; weather 395
Savannah Book Festival: 280
Savannah Braves: 292
Savannah College of Art and Design (SCAD): 241, 246
Savannah Cotton Exchange: 242
Savannah Film Festival: 246, 283
Savannah Folk Music Festival: 283
Savannah Greek Festival: 283
Savannah History Museum: 260
Savannah Irish Festival: 280
Savannah Jazz Festival: 282
Savannah Music Festival: 282
Savannah National Wildlife Refuge: 288
Savannah-Ogeechee River Canal: 267
Savannah Pride Festival: 282
Savannah Rapids Park: 170
Savannah River: 166
Savannah River Lakes: 180-183

Savannah Sand Gnats: 291, 292
Savannah Seafood Festival: 283
SCAD Museum of Art: 251, 261
Scarbrough House: 260
Scarlett on the Square: 86, 88
science museums: Coca-Cola Space Science
    Center 223; Fernbank Science Center 41;
    Museum of Arts and Sciences 193; Telfair
    Academy of Arts and Sciences 250;
    Tellus Science Museum 124; Thronateeska
    Heritage Center 329; University of Georgia
    Marine Educational Center and Aquarium
    269
Scottish Highlanders: 378
Scottish Rite Temple: 254
Scull Shoals Mill Village: 162
sculpture: Atlanta Botanical Garden 39; Big
    Chicken 88; Brown, James 167; Camp
    Sumter 324, 325; "Gracie" 265; Hiker, The
    263; Iron Horse 162; Madison Museum of
    Art 157; Otis Redding Statue 195; Paradise
    Garden 131; Polio Hall of Fame 216; Rock
    Eagle Effigy 212; Romulus and Remus statue
    129; Sleepy Hollow Enterprises 115; State
    Capitol 33; Waving Girl statue 238
Seabrook Village: 309
seafood: 283
Sea Island: 378, 419
Sea Island African Americans: 311
sea turtles: 363
secession, Confederate: 178, 206, 407
Second African Baptist Church: 245
Secret Garden Tour: 200
Seminole State Park: 340
senior travelers: 420
Senoia: 91
Settlement, The: 391
Shakespeare performances: 54
Shalom House: 333
"Shalom Y'all" Jewish Food Festival: 283
shark attacks: 423
Shellman Bluff: 381
shell rings: 385, 402
Sherman, General William T.: Green-Meldrim
    House 254; Kennesaw Mountain National
    Battlefield Park 88; "March to the Sea" 160
Ships of the Sea Maritime Museum: 260
shrimping: 355, 365
Sidewalk Arts Festival: 282
Sidney Lanier Cottage: 192

Signal Corps Museum: 172
Signers Monument: 171
Silver Lake Wildlife Management Area: 340
6th Cavalry Museum: 129
Six Flags Over Georgia: 44
6th Street Railroad Bridge: 166
Skidaway Institute of Oceanography,: 269
Skidaway Island: 269, 419
Skidaway Island State Park: 269
Skidaway Narrows: 288
Sleepy Hollow Enterprises: 115
Smallest Church in North America: 379
Smithgall Woods State Park: 108
soccer: 64
Social Circle: 163
So-No: 27
Sorghum Festival: 115
Soul Bar: 17, 172
SouthEast Adventures: 386
South End: 274
Southern Terminus Approach Trail: 111
South Georgia: 316-348; Civil War sights
    15; highlights 317; Jimmy Carter country
    320-328; maps 318-319; Okefenokee Swamp
    342-348; planning tips 9; southwest Georgia
    329-335; Thomasville 335-342
Southside Savannah: 268-270
Spanish-American War: 263, 410
Spanish colonists: 403-404
Speed's Kitchen: 19, 382
Spelman College: 46
Spelman College Museum of Fine Art: 47
spelunking: 132, 133
Splash in the 'Boro: 229
sports: Athens 151; Atlanta 64; baseball 64,
    292; Butts-Mehre Heritage Hall Sports
    Museum 144; college football 65, 140,
    142, 341; Georgia Sports Hall of Fame
    193; Savannah 291; University of Georgia
    Homecoming 149
Sprewell Bluff Wildlife Management Area: 219
Springer Mountain: 11, 112
Springer Opera House: 224, 226
springs: FDR Historic Pools and Springs
    216; Indian Springs State Park 203-204;
    Magnolia Springs State Park 230; Radium
    Springs 330; Roosevelt Warm Springs
    Institute for Rehabilitation 216; Warm
    Springs 214
Stagecoach House: 157

St. Andrews Episcopal Church: 381
Star Community Bar: 17, 47
State Botanical Garden of Georgia: 138, 143
State Capitol: 33
Statesboro: 228
St. Catherine's Island: 385
St. Cyprian's Episcopal Church: 381
Steffen Thomas Museum of Art: 162
St. EOM: 228
Stephen Foster State Park: 16, 347
Stephens, Alexander H.: 163
Stephenson, M.F.: 121
Stetson-Sanford House: 207, 209
stew, Brunswick: 360
St. Joseph Catholic Church: 191
St. Mary's: 386-391
St. Mary's Steeple: 149
St. Marys Submarine Museum: 387
Stone Mountain: 14, 86, 87
Stone Mountain Fourth of July: 56
Stone Mountain Park: 86
St. Patrick's Day: 247, 280
St. Paul's Episcopal Church: 169
St. Simons Island: 13, 369-378, 419
St. Simons Island Village: 350, 370
St. Simons Lighthouse Museum: 370
St. Simons Pier: 370
Sugar Creek Marina: 161
summer: 9
Summer Waves: 366
Sunbury: 309, 310
sun stroke: 422
surfing: 289
Suwanee Canal: 345
Swamp Gravy: 332
Swan House: 11, 42
Sweet Auburn: 20, 27
Sweet Home Alabama: 163, 180
swimming: Athens 151; Atlanta 64; Blue Hole
    117; Bridal Veil Falls 103; Fort Mountain State
    Park 123; Fort Yargo State Park 156; Hard
    Labor Creek State Park 163; Savannah River
    Lakes 180
Swiss-style village: 105
synagogues: 258

T
Tabernacle Baptist Church: 169
Tabor House Tearoom: 123

TAG Corner: 132
Tallulah Gorge State Park: 12, 16, 93, 102
Tate Student Center: 143
Taylor-Grady House: 146
telephone museums: 321
telephone services: 424
Telfair, Mary: 249
Telfair Academy of Arts and Sciences: 250, 251
Telfair Art Fair: 283
Telfair Museums: 13, 233, 250
Telfair Square: 249
Tellus Science Museum: 124
temperatures: 9, 395
Temple Mickve Israel: 258
Tennessee border: 124
tennis: Atlanta 64; Jekyll Island 366; Savannah
    290; St. Simons Island 375
theft: 421
Thomas, Justice Clarence: 269, 270
Thomas, Steffen: 162
Thomas County Museum of History: 336
Thomasville: 20, 335-342
Thomasville Rose Show & Festival: 338
312 E. Broad Street: 149
Three Graces at the Lankford Manor: 333
Three Sisters Vineyards: 120
Thronateeska Heritage Center: 329
Thurmond Lake Office & Visitors Center: 182
Tic-Toc Room: 195, 199, 202
Tifton: 333
Tobacco Road: 164
Tobacco Road novel: 18, 164
Toccoa: 104
Toccoa Falls: 104
Tomochichi: 248
Toombs, Robert: 178
Tour of Homes and Gardens: 280
Tours of Homes: 179
Town Park: 158
Trackrock Campground: 116
Track Rock Petroglyphs: 116
Trackrock Stables: 116
Trahlyta Falls: 117
Trail of Tears: 127, 130, 407
train travel: 417
transportation: 10, 416-417
Travelers Rest State Historic Site: 104
Treaty of New Echota: 127
Tree That Owns Itself: 143
Trinity United Methodist Church: 251

trolley tours: Augusta 172; Milledgeville 213; Savannah 275; Stetson-Sanford House 208; St. Simons Island 374
Troup Square: 256
T.R.R. Cobb House: 146
Truck and Tractor Pulls: 333
Trustees Garden: 245
Trustees Theatre: 246
tubing: 120
Tubman African American Museum: 20, 193
Tubman Pan African Festival: 200
Tugaloo State Park: 180
Tully Family Farm: 43
Tunnel Hill: 14, 126
260 N. Jackson Street: 149
Tybee Beach Bum Parade: 282
Tybee Island: 270-275, 297, 419
Tybee Island Marine Science Center: 275
Tybee Island Museum: 273
Tybee Island Pirate Festival: 283
Tybee Lighthouse: 13, 273
Tybee Post Theater: 273
Tybrisa Pavilion II: 275
Tybrisa Street: 275
Ty Cobb Museum: 181

U

UGA Visitors Center: 143
Uncle Remus: His Songs and His Sayings: 44
Uncle Remus Museum: 212
Unicoi Gap: 114
Unicoi State Park: 109
Union County Courthouse: 115
Unitarian Universalist Church of Savannah: 256
University of Georgia: 138, 141
University of Georgia Homecoming: 149
University of Georgia Marine Educational Center and Aquarium: 269
Upper Coastal Plain: 393
Uptown Columbus: 224
U.S. Custom House: 241
USFS Park: 211

V

vacation sights, for 1900s industrialists: 361, 364
vaccinations: 422
Vail, Theodore: 364
Valdosta: 341
Vanna: 181
vegetation: 398
Vernon Square: 381
Victoria Bryant State Park: 181
Victorian District, Savannah: 261-264
Vidalia Onion Museum: 230
Vietnam War Memorial: 246
Village, the (St. Simons Island): 13, 350, 370
vineyards: see wine/wineries
violent crime: 421
Virginia Hand Callaway Discovery Center: 217
Virginia-Highland: 27, 76
Virginia-Highland Summer Fest: 56
Visitors Center Covington: 163
Visitors Center of Ellijay: 123
Visitors Center of Thomasville: 335
Vogel State Park: 15, 117

WXYZ

Waffle House Museum: 81
Walker, Alice: 18, 212
Walking Dead: 91
walking tours: Athens 141; Atlanta 63; Bainbridge 340; Chickamauga & Chattanooga National Military Park 128; CNN Studio Tour 32; Covington 163; Forsyth Park 262; Fort Frederica National Monument 373; Jimmy Carter Boyhood Farm 323; Macon 199; Memory Hill Cemetery 211; Piedmont Hotel 90; Riverside Cemetery 196; Savannah 275, 276; St. Paul's Episcopal Church 169; Thomasville 335
Wallace, Paula: 241
Warm Springs: 12, 214
war museums: 220-223
Warren Square: 245
Washington: 14, 177-180
Washington Historical Museum: 178
Washington Square: 245
Wassaw Island National Wildlife Refuge: 313
waterfalls: Amicalola Falls State Park 110-111; Anna Ruby Falls 109; Cloudland Canyon State Park 133; DeSoto Falls 122; Dick's Creek Falls 99; Duke's Creek Falls 108; FDR State Park 218; Hiawassee 117; Lake McIntosh: 204; Minnehaha Falls 103; Raven Cliff Falls 108; Tallulah Gorge State Park 102, 103; Toccoa Falls 104; Vogel State Park 117

waterfront Savannah: 238-242, 285
water parks: Helen Tubing and Water Park 106; Jekyll Island 366; LanierWorld 89; Splash in the 'Boro 229; Wild Adventures 341
Watkinsville: 156
Waving Girl statue: 238
Waycross: 16, 347
weather: 9, 395
Welcome Center of Fitzgerald: 334
Wesley Monumental United Methodist Church: 259
West Broad Street: 259
West End: 27, 44
Western art: 124
Westobou Festival: 172
Westside Atlanta: 27, 77
Westside Savannah: 266-268
Westville: 328
wetlands: 394
wheelchair access: 420
Whimsical Botanical Gardens: 204
Whistlestop Cafe: 204
Whitewater Project: 226
white-water rafting: general discussion 419; Chattahoochee River 63; Chattooga Wild and Scenic River 99-100; Columbus 226; Flint River 219; itineraries 14-16
Widespread Panic: 149
Wild Adventures: 341
Wildcat Creek: 102
Wild Chicken Festival: 335
Wilde, Oscar: 225, 252
Wilderness Southeast: 277
wildflowers: 91
Wild Georgia Shrimp and Grits Festival: 365
wild horses: 390, 391
wildlife: general discussion 399-402; Chestatee Wildlife Preserve 122; Cohutta Wilderness Area 123; Cumberland Island

wild horses 390, 391; Georgia Sea Turtle Center 363; Lamar Q. Ball Jr. Raptor Center 228; loggerhead turtles 386; Oatland Island Wildlife Center 264; Ohoopee Dunes Natural Area 229; Okefenokee National Wildlife Refuge 345; Parks on Chehaw 329; Wassaw Island National Wildlife Refuge 313
Wildlife Drive: 345
Wildwater Rafting: 100
William Breman Jewish Heritage Museum: 40
William Bull Sundial: 244
Williams, Jim: 257
Wilson, Ellen Axon: 130
Wilson, Woodrow: 165, 171
Windsor Hotel: 12, 321
wine/wineries: Atlanta Food & Wine Festival 56; Dahlonega 118, 119-120; Habersham Winery 106; Sautee Nacoochee Vineyards 107
Wingate's Lodge & Marina: 340
winter: 9
Wirz, Colonel Henry: 326
Wolf Mountain Vineyards: 119
women travelers: 420
Woodland Period: 402
Woodrow Wilson Boyhood Home: 171
Woody Gap: 112
World of Coca-Cola: 11, 30, 31
World War II: 411
World War II Memorial: 240
Wormsloe State Historic Site: 268
Wren's Nest: 44
Wright Square: 247
wrought iron: 256
Wuxtry Records: 17, 149, 150
Youmans Pond: 309
yurts: 205
Zeppelin's: 16, 97
zipline tours: 89, 217
Zoo Atlanta: 22, 33

List of Maps

Front Color Map
Georgia: 2-3

Discover Georgia
Chapter divisions map: 9

Atlanta
Atlanta: 24-25
Downtown Atlanta: 29
Greater Atlanta: 82

North Georgia
North Georgia: 94-95
Rabun County: 96
Chattooga Wild and Scenic River: 99
Appalachian Trail: 111
Appalachia Trail Through Georgia: 113

Piedmont
Piedmont: 136-137
Athens: 139
University of Georgia: 141
Augusta: 165

Middle Georgia
Middle Georgia: 186-187
Macon: 189
Downtown Macon: 190
Columbus: 221

Savannah
Savannah: 234
Downtown Savannah Sights: 239
Tybee Island: 271
Downtown Savannah Accommodations, Food
    and Entertainment: 294

South Georgia
South Georgia: 318-319
Okefenokee National Wildlife Refuge: 344

The Golden Isles
The Golden Isles: 351
Brunswick and Glynn County: 354
Jekyll Island: 362
Sapelo Island: 384
Cumberland Island: 387

Background
Continental Shelf: 393
Sherman's March to the Sea (1864): 409

www.moon.com

DESTINATIONS | ACTIVITIES | BLOGS | MAPS | BOOKS

MOON.COM is ready to help plan your next trip! Filled with fresh trip ideas and strategies, author interviews, informative travel blogs, a detailed map library, and descriptions of all the Moon guidebooks, Moon.com is all you need to get out and explore the world—or even places in your own backyard. While at Moon.com, sign up for our monthly e-newsletter for updates on new releases, travel tips, and expert advice from our on-the-go Moon authors. As always, when you travel with Moon, expect an experience that is uncommon and truly unique.

KEEP UP WITH MOON ON FACEBOOK AND TWITTER
JOIN THE MOON PHOTO GROUP ON FLICKR

MAP SYMBOLS

▦	Expressway	◖	Highlight	✗	Airfield	⚲	Golf Course
	Primary Road	○	City/Town	✈	Airport	P	Parking Area
	Secondary Road	◉	State Capital	▲	Mountain	⬢	Archaeological Site
-------	Unpaved Road	⊛	National Capital	✦	Unique Natural Feature	⬧	Church
- - - -	Trail	★	Point of Interest			⬛	Gas Station
··········	Ferry	•	Accommodation	🖑	Waterfall	◠	Glacier
▬▬▬	Railroad	▾	Restaurant/Bar	▲	Park		Mangrove
▬▬▬	Pedestrian Walkway	▪	Other Location	◨	Trailhead		Reef
▥	Stairs	∆	Campground	✗	Skiing Area		Swamp

CONVERSION TABLES

$°C = (°F - 32) / 1.8$
$°F = (°C \times 1.8) + 32$
1 inch = 2.54 centimeters (cm)
1 foot = 0.304 meters (m)
1 yard = 0.914 meters
1 mile = 1.6093 kilometers (km)
1 km = 0.6214 miles
1 fathom = 1.8288 m
1 chain = 20.1168 m
1 furlong = 201.168 m
1 acre = 0.4047 hectares
1 sq km = 100 hectares
1 sq mile = 2.59 square km
1 ounce = 28.35 grams
1 pound = 0.4536 kilograms
1 short ton = 0.90718 metric ton
1 short ton = 2,000 pounds
1 long ton = 1.016 metric tons
1 long ton = 2,240 pounds
1 metric ton = 1,000 kilograms
1 quart = 0.94635 liters
1 US gallon = 3.7854 liters
1 Imperial gallon = 4.5459 liters
1 nautical mile = 1.852 km

MOON GEORGIA

Avalon Travel
a member of the Perseus Books Group
1700 Fourth Street
Berkeley, CA 94710, USA
www.moon.com

Editor: Elizabeth Hollis Hansen
Series Manager: Kathryn Ettinger
Copy Editor: Naomi Adler Dancis
Graphics Coordinator: Elizabeth Jang
Production Coordinator: Elizabeth Jang
Cover Designer: Elizabeth Jang
Map Editor: Albert Angulo
Cartographers: Kaitlin Jaffe, Andy Butkovic,
   Heather Sparks
Proofreader: Nikki Ioakimedes
Indexer: Rachel Kuhn

ISBN-13: 978-1-61238-345-3
ISSN: 1078-7267

Printing History
1st Edition – 1995
7th Edition – September 2013
5 4 3 2 1

Text © 2013 by Jim Morekis.
Maps © 2013 by Avalon Travel.
All rights reserved.

Front cover photo: Callaway Gardens in
Georgia © Nancy Rotenberg / Jaynes Gallery /
DanitaDelimont.com

Title page photo: Savannah's beautiful Forsyth Park
© Jim Morekis

Interior color photos: p. 6 butterfly © Jim Morekis;
p. 7 Savannah riverfront © Americanspirit/
Dreamstime.com; p. 8 (inset) blooming azalea in
Savannah © dndavis/123rf.com, (bottom) dawn over
Lake Burton © Jim Morekis; p. 8 (top left) Amicalola
Ruby Falls © Jim Morekis, (top right) South Georgia
swamp and cypress tress © Sayran/Dreamstime.com,
(bottom left) wild horses on Cumberland Island ©
Paula Stephens/123rf.com, (bottom right) the "Alpine
Village" of Helen; p. 8 © Jim Morekis; p. 10 (top left)
© Rose Waddell/Dreamstime.com, (top right) ©
Jim Morekis, (bottom) © Jim Morekis; p. 11-16 © Jim
Morekis; p. 17 courtesy of The Big House; p. 18-19 ©
Jim Morekis; p. 20 © VisitSavannah.com

Printed in Canada by Friesens

KEEPING CURRENT

If you have a favorite gem you'd like to see included in the next edition, or see anything
that needs updating, clarification, or correction, please drop us a line. Send your com-
ments via email to feedback@moon.com, or use the address above.